D1345671

The Lands of St Peter

by the same author

THE PAPAL STATE UNDER MARTIN V
A SHORT POLITICAL GUIDE TO THE ARAB WORLD

The Lands of St Peter

THE PAPAL STATE
IN THE MIDDLE AGES
AND
THE EARLY RENAISSANCE

PETER PARTNER

EYRE METHUEN
LONDON

First published 1972
Eyre Methuen Ltd
11 New Fetter Lane, London EC4P 4EE
Copyright © 1972 by Peter Partner
Printed in Great Britain
by Willmer Brothers Ltd, Birkenhead

SBN 413 25790 8

I dedicate this book to my family,
who have so far tolerated my eccentricities
without complaint.

Von Sonn' und Welten weiss ich nichts zu sagen,
Ich sehe nur, wie sich die Menschen plagen.

Faust, Prolog im Himmel

Contents

Illustrations and Maps

A*

Preface

The subject of this book is the Papal State, the 'lands of St Peter', which was a recognisable dominion or principality from the middle of the eighth century until 1870, although it did not enjoy complete political autonomy until the thirteenth century.

I would define the Papal State as the rule of the Roman bishop in Rome and in the Italian regions which were politically subject to him. I have not dealt with his rule in the Comtat Venaissain in Provence, and I have touched rather lightly on his possession of the papal enclave of Benevento. My treatment of the provinces of the Papal State has tried to do some justice to their geographical and historical diversity.[1] I have attempted to supply some guidance to the reader who is not acquainted with the Italian topography, particularly in the form of maps, and also by means of the descriptive chapter on the Papal State at the end of the Middle Ages.

The topic of the Papal State raises the whole question of the distinction between 'spiritual' and 'temporal' power. This distinction is properly the concern of canon law, and I have not felt it my business to treat it at length. I have first noticed the term 'temporal power' used in contemporary documents to describe papal political supremacy in 1156,[2] but only much later was it employed to describe papal political rule generally. I have, after some hesitation, avoided the use of the term 'temporal power' to describe the subject of my book, because the exercise of this power clearly had manifestations – such as the feudal relationship in which the pope stood to some European rulers outside Italy – which did not concern the Papal State.

The constitutional and legal history of the Papal State has to deal

---

[1] The term 'States of the Church' is sometimes used in preference to 'Papal State', but it seems to me to have little to commend it. With the exceptions of Campagna and Sanabi none of the important papal provinces had a continuous existence throughout the Middle Ages.

[2] Below, p. 194.

quite extensively with the relations between Frankish kings, Frankish and later emperors, and popes, especially as these relate to the 'restitutions' claimed by the Holy See, the 'protection' afforded by kings and emperors to popes, and the 'donations' of territory to the popes. My intention has been to deal with them so that they do not swamp the political and social history, and so that the history of the Papal State is not made to appear a transition from one set of legal definitions to another. The Papal State was a country inhabited by people whose circumstances and aims were as mutable as those of any other human society. To treat the topic in this way has meant emphasising the local political difficulties and involvements of such 'world-historical' figures as Gregory VII and Innocent III; I do not wish to diminish their lofty stature, but my view is that a man may be as well known by his actions in his back yard as by those in the market place.

It seems to me that a history of the papacy which dwells unduly on the peak points of papal power and prestige runs the risk of subordinating political reality to the history of ideas. The most explicit and conscious attempt to avoid this danger is that made by Haller in his famous book,[1] whose title could be rendered in English: 'The Idea and the Reality of the Papacy'. Only a continuous history can bring out the local nature of many of the political objectives of the popes, though these co-existed with others of a more lofty sort.

No doubt there are ambiguities of method in what I have tried to do. The term 'Papal State' is a modern one, hardly used by contemporaries to refer to the papal patrimony in the long period with which this book is concerned.[2] This seems to me to be a question of terminology, and of only minor importance. Similar questions present themselves for any history which treats of the medieval antecedents of a modern state. The capital difficulty of the subject is another one: that the history of the Papal State is both that of a great religious institution and of several Italian regions. A tidy treatment of the topic is impossible.

A political history of the kind which follows is not fashionable at the moment. Historians of our day tend to find wars boring, unless they happen to be caught in one. I find boring neither wars nor the politics which produce them, and I make no apology for the way in which they

---

[1] J. Haller, *Das Papsttum: Idee und Wirklichkeit* (Urach-Stuttgart, 1950).
[2] Cf. S. Z. Ehler, 'On applying the modern term "state" to the Middle Ages', *Medieval Studies presented to Aubrey Gwynn, S.J.* (Dublin, 1961), pp. 492–501; E. Dupré-Theseider, 'Sur les origines de l'état de l'église', *L'Europe aux IXe-XIe siècles. Aux origines des États nationaux* (Warsaw, 1968), pp. 93–103.

dominate this book. Nor do I apologise for re-writing an oft-told tale. Though the history of the papal lands appears often enough in the general histories of the papacy, there seems to me to be little appreciation in many of these books of the continuity of the territorial factors in papal policy. Nor is there much acknowledgement of the feeling of direct personal responsibility to the saint which made the 'land of St Peter' into something approaching a battle-cry for Pope Gregory VII. It is hard in the twentieth century to understand how Cardinal Albornoz in the fourteenth could feel that he was fighting for 'the Patrimony of the Crucified One'. We may not approve of these feelings, and indeed there were many medieval men who did not approve them. But to make sense of the Middle Ages we must try to comprehend them.

Bibliographical Note

The list of books written in or translated into English on the subject of the medieval Papal State is a short one. F. Gregorovius, *History of the City of Rome in the Middle Ages* (1900–2) and L. Duchesne, *The Beginnings of the Temporal Sovereignty of the Popes* (1908) are both classics of historical writing, though in very different ways. T. Hodgkin, *Italy and her Invaders* (Oxford, 1880–99) is another nineteenth-century classic. D. Waley, *The Papal State in the Thirteenth Century* (1961) and P. Partner, *The Papal State under Martin V* (1958) are more specialised monographs. G. Mollat, *The Popes at Avignon 1305–78* (1963) contains a long and important section on 'The Papacy and Italy' which is almost entirely concerned with the Papal State. W. Ullmann, *The Growth of Papal Government in the Middle Ages,* 3rd ed. (1970) contains a discussion of the origins of the Papal State. P. Llewellyn, *Rome in the Dark Ages* (1971) is a detailed account of the early period. J. Larner, *Lords of Romagna* (1965) is concerned with the social history of the later period.

Two modern church histories are especially useful: H. Jedin and J. Dolan (ed.), *Handbook of Church History,* iii (1969) and iv (1970); A. Fliche, V. Martin (ed.) and others, *Histoire de l'Eglise depuis les origines jusqu'à nos jours,* vi (E. Amann, Paris, 1947), vii (Amann, 1948), viii (Fliche, 1946), ix (Fliche, R. Foreville, and J. Rousset, 1946–53), x (Fliche, C. Thouzellier and Y. Azais, 1950), xiv (E. Delaruelle, R. Labande, P. Ourliac, 1962–3).

Annual bibliographies of works on papal history emerge in *Archivum Historiae Pontificiae, Revue d'histoire ecclésiastique,* and *Rivista della storia della chiesa in Italia.* The last is especially useful for its sections on the church history of the Italian regions.

Political histories of Italy: C. G. Mor, *L'età feudale* (Milan, 1952–3); L. Simeoni, *Le Signorie* (Milan, 1950); N. Valeri (ed.), *Storia d'Italia,* i, 2nd ed. (Turin, 1967). The last is notably less detailed than the others, but contains valuable surveys by distinguished scholars.

NOTE ON SOURCES

To write a book of this sort is to experience sharply the contrast between the nature of the sources which are at the disposal of the historian of the early Middle Ages, and those for the latter Middle Ages and the early modern period. In the first case the historian uses a very small number of texts, almost all of which have been minutely examined by generations of historians. In the second case he confronts an immense variety of documents, tens of thousands of which are printed in full or in summary, but of which a vast number of others can be studied only in manuscript. In the case of the earlier history the historian has a reasonable chance of reading most of the more important primary sources for himself, but hardly any of reading the whole of the accretions of historical commentary. In the case of the later history he has perhaps a rather better chance, but not the smallest hope of mastering the manuscript sources. Professor Daniel Waley has remarked that in the march of Ancona alone 246 *archives* were recorded in a recent survey.[1] If one province of the Papal State can offer such a profusion of unprinted material, the historian thinks also of the great archive deposits of Perugia and Bologna and resigns himself to the admission that his knowledge can only be patchy and small.

The sources on the origins of the Papal State present special problems of interpretation, especially the series of papal biographies in the *Liber Pontificalis*. The main sources were collected in a small volume by J. Haller (1907), but there is a more recent collection of the same kind edited by H. Fuhrmann, *Quellen zur Entstehung des Kirchenstaates* (Göttingen, 1967). The best analysis of the papal life of Stephen II is in the article of L. Levillain.[2] The later papal lives are discussed by H. Löwe in the bibliographical handbook of Wattenbach-Levison.[3]

I have not succeeded in reading the whole series of the accounts of

---

[1] *The Papal State in the Thirteenth Century*, p. 90n.
[2] 'L'avénement de la dynastie carolingienne et les origines de l'état pontifical', *BEC*, xciv (1933), pp. 225–95.
[3] *Deutschlands Geschichtsquellen im Mittelalter, Vorzeit und Karolinger*, IV. Heft (Weimar, 1963), pp. 455 ff.

the papal provinces in the fourteenth century in the Vatican Archives
in the *Introitus et Exitus* and the *Collectoriae Camerae* series.[1] Much
of this material was looked at or published in summary by the Austrian
historian Schaefer and the Italian Antonelli, but a knowledge of the
whole is desirable. For the fifteenth century I have examined the main
series of papal registers in the Vatican Archives from John XXIII to
the end of the pontificate of Eugenius IV.[2]

[1] Cf. K. A. Fink, *Das Vatikanische Archiv* (Rome, 1951), pp. 49–50. There is a valuable
typescript list of the Fondo Camerale by Mons. Guidi, kept in the Vatican Archives. There
are approximately 150 volumes in these series which deal with the fourteenth-century Papal
State in one aspect or another. I have used *Introitus et Exitus*, vol. 21, and *Collectoriae*, vol.
203. Cf. K. H. Schaefer, *Deutsche Ritter und Edelknechte in Italien* (Paderborn, 1911); and the
articles by M. Antonelli in *ASR*, xxv–xxvii (1902–4), xxx (1907), xxxi (1908), xlvi (1923),
lviii (1935) which are also based on this series of documents.
[2] There is a brief note on these sources in my *Papal State under Martin V*, pp. 199–200.

Acknowledgements

I have received kindnesses from many men and women of learning while I have been preparing and writing this book. I feel particular gratitude towards Professor C. R. Cheney and Dr T. S. R. Boase (formerly President of Magdalen) both for their encouragement and for their generosity in lending me rare and valuable books. I also thank the teachers who, both twenty-odd years ago and subsequently, encouraged my interest in these studies. Dr Philip Jones, Professor Lionel Butler and Professor Ernest Jacob taught and helped me at one stage or another. I owe special debts to Mr Karl Leyser, who guided my faltering steps through Stubbs's *Charters* long ago, and who more recently read the earlier chapters of this book in manuscript, to Dr Anthony Luttrell, who read the later chapters, and to Professor Christopher Brooke, who read the whole manuscript. I have had friendly advice from continental scholars, especially from Dr Wolfgang Hagemann, the Deputy Director of the German Historical Institute in Rome. Dr Arnold Esch generously sent me his important book on Boniface IX as soon as it was published. The profit I have drawn from the work of Professor Waley will be evident. The responsibility for errors which remain in this book is naturally my own.

Both the British Academy and the British School at Rome gave me grants towards the carrying out of preliminary specialised studies, and the Warden and Fellows of Winchester College granted me a valuable grace term. I wish to express my gratitude for the unselfish help of those in charge of libraries and archives, especially those of the Vatican. The Library of Southampton University has kindly allowed me to use its facilities, and without the London Library, that great resource of the private scholar in this country, the book could not have been written.

Abbreviations

AMDR	*Atti e memorie della R. Deputazione di Storia Patria per le provincie di Romagna*
AMPMod	*Atti e memorie della R. Deputazione di Storia Patria per le provincie Modenesi*
AMSM	*Atti e memorie della R. Deputazione di Storia Patria per le Marche*
Arch. Frat. Praed.	*Archivum Fratrum Praedicatorum*
Arch. f. Urk.	*Archiv. für Urkundenforschung*
ASI	*Archivio Storico Italiano*
ASL	*Archivio Storico Lombardo*
ASPN	*Archivio Storico per le provincie Napoletane*
ASR	*Archivio della R. Società Romana di Storia Patria*
BEC	*Bibliothèque de l'École des Chartes*
BISI	*Bullettino dell'Istituto Storico Italiano per il Medio Evo*
BSU	*Bollettino della R. Deputazione di Storia Patria per l'Umbria*
DA	*Deutsches Archiv*
EHR	*English Historical Review*
Gött. Nachr.	*Nachrichten von der Königl. Gesellschaft der Wissenschaften zu Göttingen*
HZ	*Historische Zeitschrift*
JEccH	*Journal of Ecclesiastical History*
Mélanges	*Mélanges d'Archéologie et d'Histoire de l'École Française de Rome*
MIöG	*Mittheilungen des Instituts für österreichische Geschichtsforschung*
PBSR	*Papers of the British School at Rome*
Quellen	*Quellen und Forschungen aus italienischen Archiven und Bibliotheken*
Röm. Quart.	*Römische Quartalschrift für christliche Altertumskunde und für Kirchengeschichte*
RSCI	*Rivista della storia della chiesa in Italia*
SDSD	*Studi e Documenti di Storia e Diritto*
SG	*Studi Gregoriani* (edited by G. B. Borino)
Stud. Romagn.	*Studi Romagnoli*
VSWG	*Vierteljahrschrift für Sozial- und Wirtschaftsgeschichte*
ZfKG	*Zeitschrift für Kirchengeschichte*
ZSSRG. Kan.Abt.	*Zeitschrift der Savigny-Stiftung für Rechtsgeschichte, Kanonistische Abteilung*

OTHER WORKS

Cod. Car.   *Codex Carolinus* (in *Monumenta Germaniae Historica, Epistolae Karolini Aevi,* i)

Esch   A. Esch, *Bonifaz IX. und der Kirchenstaat* (Tübingen, 1969)

Fantuzzi   M. Fantuzzi, *Monumenti Ravennati de'secoli di mezzo* (Venice, 1801–4)

Finke, *AA*   H. Finke, *Acta Aragonensia* (Berlin-Leipzig, 1908–22)

I.P.   P. F. Kehr, *Italia Pontificia* (Berlin, 1906–35)

J.-E., J.-L.   P. Jaffé, *Regesta Pontificum Romanorum ab condita ecclesia ad annum post Christum natum MCXCVIII*, S. Loewenfeld and P. Ewald (ed.), 2nd ed. (Leipzig, 1885–8)

Mansi   J. D. Mansi, *Sacrorum conciliorum nova et amplissima collectio* (Florence-Venice, 1759–98)

MGH   *Monumenta Germaniae Historica. D* indicates the diplomas, *DO III* for the diplomas of Otto III, etc.

Migne, *P.L.*   J. P. Migne, *Patrologiae cursus completus. Series latina*

Partner, *Papal State* P. Partner, *The Papal State under Martin V* (1958)

Potthast   A. Potthast, *Regesta Pontificum Romanorum inde ab a. post Christum natum MCXCVIII ad a. MCCCIV* (Berlin, 1874–5)

Raynaldus   O. Raynaldus, *Annales ecclesiastici post Baronum* (Lucca, 1747–56)

Reg. Farf.   *Regesto di Farfa compilato da Gregorio da Catino*, I. Giorgi and U. Balzani (ed.) (Rome, 1879–1914)

RRIISS   L. A. Muratori, *Rerum Italicarum Scriptores*

R.S.   *Rolls Series, Rerum Britannicarum Medii Aevi Scriptores*

Theiner, *C.D.*   A. Theiner, *Codex Diplomaticus Dominii Temporalis Sanctae Sedis* (Rome, 1861–2)

Tomassetti, *C.R.* G. and F. Tomassetti, *La Campagna Romana* (Rome, 1910–26)

Waley, *P.S.*   D. Waley, *The Papal State in the Thirteenth Century* (1961)

The Lands of St Peter

Chapter 1

Rome, Byzantium and the Franks

I

On all the great feast days the eighth-century bishops of Rome conducted the holy liturgy in the church appointed as the 'station'. The procession assembled at the Lateran patriarchate, the great palace which was the seat of government. Clerical officers, the acolytes and 'guardians', preceded the papal procession on foot, while mounted lay-constables controlled the crowd. Other officers then came on horseback – the deacons, the *primicerius* or chief officer of the guardians, the regionary notaries, the regionary guardians, the regionary subdeacons. The cortège was splendidly dressed, some with their horses trapped in the white silk formerly worn by the Roman civil officers. Then came the 'apostolic one'. Then the great dignitaries and judges of the clerical administration, the major-domo, the treasurer and controller of the wardrobe, the almoner, the financial controller.[1] Petitioners would await the pope on foot; he would stop to hear them, and their cases would be presented to him by the controller or the almoner. The clergy had preceded the pope to the church, and the cardinal priests waited on his left hand, the bishops of the dioceses adjacent to Rome on his right. The Roman people waited also, the women apart from the men, the aristocrats roped off near the altar in the *senatorium*, the cross-bearers of the seven ecclesiastical regions of Rome in their places, the papal choristers ready to do their part. The pope dismounted, entered the sacristy, and was robed for the holy office. The liturgy which has come to serve as the model for the western Catholic world began.

'Papalism' is something which modern men think of primarily as a system of general ideas. But like much else in Christianity, it is more the product of local history than of abstract thought. The Roman liturgy of the eighth century arises from a connection between religion

[1] M. Andrieu, *Les Ordines Romani du haut Moyen Age* (Louvain, 1931–56), ii, pp. 67–92 The Latin titles of these officers were *vicedominus, vestararius, sacellarius, nomenclator*.

and society so tight and so organic that it is hard to grasp in present-day terms. And even if we can so grasp it, it remains difficult to bridge the gap between the small, poor, politically isolated Roman community of the early Middle Ages, and the doctrines which a century after 750 had knit the Roman rite and Roman jurisdiction into the social fabric of western Europe. That this ruined and reduced provincial city should so impose itself on the western world seems at first fortuitous. But it is at least partly explained by the persistence into the barbarian, post-classical world of the social coherence and unity of what was the most fundamental in the civilisation which had preceded it, the ancient city. In ancient Rome religion had been hardly distinguishable from civic patriotism; the Christian chief priest or *pontifex* who followed the pagan in Rome became up to a point the focus for the same patriotic tradition.

That the Bishop of Rome should develop a doctrine of the organic unity of Christian society, and of his own divinely appointed leadership of that society, was assisted also by the way the early Church understood the social content of the gospel it preached. Christianity is the religion of the people of God, or as the fathers of the Church claimed: 'We are the true people of Israel.' As the fathers read the Old Testament, Israel was a human society as well as a religious ideal; when God said that he would defend his people, he was talking politics. The city of God is not of this world, but the people of God are truly and corporeally a people, a social group, and not a metaphorical expression.

Even at the worst moments of the break-up of the ancient world, the political leadership of bishops was occasional and fitful, the effect of temporary abdication by the lay power. The adoption of Christianity by the empire of Constantine in the fourth century brought no access of political power to the Church. It brought wealth, and to the huge public buildings which the empire went on constructing as long as life was left in it, were now added churches: Constantine and his mother built great Christian basilicas from Jerusalem to Trier. Immense gifts of land and valuables were made to churches which possibly were already far from poor: the list of Constantine's largesse in the official chronicle of the popes is the first of its kind, and a very long one. The annual cost of the Church to the empire came to exceed the cost of the imperial civil service.[1]

Justinian's reconquest of Italy was launched in 536, to recover the Italian provinces from the Ostrogoth power which had ruled there since

[1] A. H. M. Jones, *The Later Roman Empire* (Oxford, 1964), ii, p. 934.

489. The devastation and depopulation of Italy during the wars of the Emperor Justinian were immense. The Roman people and the Roman aristocracy suffered terribly in this period; that the popes made common cause with the latter is probable from the *Pragmatic Sanction on the petition of (Pope) Vigilius* of 554, which was issued largely in aristocratic interests. As a great landowner and a great civil servant, the pope was bound to be one of the leaders of the Roman senatorial class. For Italy a new period began in which, though the institutions of the fifth century were to some extent restored, the political and social reality was the subjection of the peninsula to Greek interests. The papacy was not exempt from this. Though Justinian assigned them a certain function in Italian government, the Italian bishops were weak in the face of imperial power.

Justinian's re-establishment of Roman rule in Italy lasted less than a generation. In 568 northern Italy was overrun by the Lombards, and within a few years these new Germanic invaders had conquered a large part of Italy – approximately the Lombard plain, Liguria except part of the coast, much of Emilia, most of Tuscany, and a great deal of the mountainous area stretching south down the centre of Italy, including the 'duchies' of Spoleto and Benevento. To the 'Romans' remained Venetia, Istria, the exarchate of Ravenna, Picenum or Pentapolis in the east, the duchies of Rome and (at most periods) Perugia, much of southern Italy southwards from Campania, and Sicily. The most important strategic zone in Byzantine Italy became the mountain road (the Via Flaminia) which led from the lower Tiber into the hills of Umbria to descend again into the exarchate of Ravenna, the principal province of eastern Italy and the seat of the administration. This road, which connected Rome with Ravenna, was the lifeline of Byzantine Italy, and immense effort was devoted to its defence. Another connected and equally important area was the part of north Etruria which became known as 'Lombard Tuscany'.

Byzantium was not indifferent to the wresting away of half Italy by the Lombards. But Byzantine power was unequal to the immense strains thrown on it in this and other parts of the empire. Greek generals – many of whom were Germans – fought tenaciously against the Lombards. Important points such as Classis beside Ravenna, and Perugia in the vital communications line over the Appenines, were recaptured from the Lombards in the bitter fighting of many decades. But what was always evident was that Roman Italy was only one sector, and that not the most important, of the lines of defence of an empire whose interests went from Egypt to the Persian frontier, from the Black Sea up the Danube. When Pope Pelagius II wrote to the Emperor Tiberius II in 584 that the military needs of the empire in Italy were hardly supplied, and that Rome was practically undefended, he was making the kind of plea which Greek Italy was to carry to Constantinople for a century and a half. Byzantium was not utterly deaf to the complaints of the Italian provincials, but it needed to husband its resources for other issues which might mean life and death for the whole empire.

The government in Italy practised the policy that the empire had practised for centuries, that the best way to combat barbarians is with other barbarians. Divide and rule was the great Byzantine maxim, as it has been that of other colonial powers. But in Italy this policy was to find only a limited application. Pope Pelagius II, besides writing to the emperor, also wrote to the Frankish Bishop of Auxerre, that 'it is not a vain matter that your kings should share the same orthodox faith as that of the empire'. But although there was a limited Frankish intervention in Italy on behalf of the Greeks against the Lombards, it failed; after the unsuccessful expedition of 590 the Franks did not again seriously intervene. The only remaining expedient was to pit Lombard against Lombard, and the existence of semi-autonomous Lombard duchies of Benevento and Spoleto lent itself to some extent to this policy.

In 1590 the monk and *apocrisarius* Gregory, surnamed by later generations the Great, became Roman bishop. Almost simultaneously, Lombard pressure on the Roman duchy became more and more intense. Gregory had before entering the clergy been an important imperial official, the *praefectus urbi*. A man of his ability and prestige was bound to be important in the Lombard war, especially at a time when the frail line of communication between Rome and Ravenna was frequently cut by the enemy. Gregory on some occasions virtually assumed the direction of the war to secure the Via Cassia and the northern environs of Rome; he also on his own responsibility made a peace (which did not last long) with Ariulf, the Lombard Duke of Spoleto. The peace was made 'without cost to the empire', and so probably was made at the price of 'protection' money paid to Ariulf by the pope himself. Already the economic power of the Roman Church was of political importance. The provisioning of Rome; the re-settlement of refugees from areas invaded by Lombard forces; the defence of Naples: all these were matters which under the stress of war fell into Gregory's competence.

Nothing in Gregory's career declares him, nevertheless, as anything but the loyal subordinate of the empire.[1] His policies were often over-ruled both by the imperial officials in Italy and by the emperor in Byzantium; Gregory's peace with Ariulf was broken by the Byzantine exarch, who launched a vigorous counter-attack down the whole line of the Via Flaminia. Gregory had his own Lombard policy. Partly because of his hopes of a Lombard conversion to Catholicism through Queen Theodelinda, and partly because of his interest in peace as the greatest of the Roman landowners, this policy was more appeasing than official Byzantine policy; it is doubtful whether Gregory (or the other Romans) wanted to endorse the policy of total war in order to expel the Lombards from Italy. They knew that in practice this meant the withdrawal of troops from the defence of Rome, and their employment in offensive operations which brought the Romans no relief. But in practice the issues on which Gregory is known to have resisted imperial policy were not temporal but spiritual; he defended his peace with Ariulf to the emperor, but the most vigorous protest he made to Byzantium was against the imperial decree forbidding civil servants to enter the Church.

Gregory should certainly not be seen as a war leader. His thoughts on war are best shown in his sombre homilies on the prophet Ezekiel: 'Cities, castles, farms are destroyed; the land is laid waste. No peasants remain in the fields; the cities are almost empty; those who remain are pitilessly stricken; imprisoned, mutilated, slain. And Rome, the one-time mistress of the world, to what do we see her reduced? Assailed by every misfortune, her citizens ruined, assaulted by enemies, her build-ings in collapse; we see revealed in her what was prophesied by the Prophet Ezekiel of Samaria. . . .' Gregory's work of pastor and mentor, and intercessor and negotiator with the barbarians, is best summed up in the formula in the papal *Liber Diurnus* which probably refers to him: 'Only the power of God and of the prince of the apostles, trans-mitted through the medium of his vicar the Roman pontiff, modifies and tempers the ferocity of the neighbouring enemies . . . those whom armed force fails to make humble, bend before pontifical prayer and persua-sion.'[2]

Gregory's genius was practical: his pontificate makes no mark on the history of the papal ideology. His attitude to the emperors – even to the murderous Phocas, whose usurpation he recognised immediately – was

[1] Cf. E. H. Fischer, 'Gregor der Grosse und Byzanz', *ZSSRG*, lxvii, *Kan. Abt.* xxxvi (1950), pp. 15–144, especially at pp. 67–8, 77–97, 129–44.
[2] Th. von Sickel (ed.), *Liber diurnus Romanorum Pontificum* (Vienna, 1889), p. 53. In the edition of H. Foerster (Berne, 1958), pp. 116, 214, 323–4. Cf. O. Bertolini, 'I papi e le relazioni politiche di Roma con i ducati longobardi', etc., *RSCI*, vi (1952), p. 45.

never less than deferential. His status in the universal Church was not negligible, but it is unlikely that an emperor would have offered him, particularly when referring to matters outside Italy, the famous tribute paid in 445 to Pope Leo the Great by the Emperor Valentinian III: 'That [papal] verdict would have been valid throughout Gaul even without imperial enforcement. For what limits can there be to the authority in the Church of a bishop as great as he?' By contrast with his predecessor Leo, Gregory had to deal not only with a physically present empire, but with an empire inspired by a coherent theory of state control of the Church, and a long tradition of its practical application. With this Byzantine 'servitude' the popes had to contend for another century, but there is no evidence that they thought it such. The only alternative which seemed to present itself to Gregory was to become 'a Lombard bishop' and to exchange the rule of Byzantium for that of barbarians and heretics.

II

The huge landed estates of the Roman Church were among the largest concentrations of landed property in Byzantine Italy. The Roman bishop administered both the lands of the mother Church itself, and the lands of the Roman basilicas which were classified as *tituli*.[1] The piety of the early Middle Ages, which preserved the Registers of Gregory the Great, has enabled us to know where the great landed estates of the Roman See were, and how they were exploited. They had existed before Gregory's day, and probably more plentifully than when the peninsula had for over half a century been devastated by war. There is evidence in the official papal chronicle, the *Liber Pontificalis,* which was prepared in the Lateran offices from which the papal patrimony was administered. Pope Gelasius, for example, was rich enough to supply Rome in time of famine – an example to be followed by very many of his successors, including Gregory. Gelasius also had a list of the possessions of the Roman Church drawn up, which remained as the standard reference book in the papal financial offices.

The great papal accumulation of landed property which is revealed by Gregory's Registers must have been yet larger in the earlier period. The list of lost or partly lost papal estates under Gregory includes those in Africa, which appear at this time to have been in the hands of the

---

[1] Cf. S. Kuttner, 'Cardinalis: the history of a canonical concept', *Traditio,* iii (1945), pp. 129–214, at pp. 152 ff.

THE PAPAL STATE
┼AND ITS NEIGHBOURS┼
In the earlier Middle Ages

imperial exarch, in Gaul, and in Dalmatia, which was ravaged by Slavs and Avars. Other patrimonies in Liguria had been seized by the Lombards. In Corsica and Sardinia – where Popes Pontian and Callistus had once been condemned to hard labour in the mines – the see still held lands, though they were difficult to exploit. The great mass of the profitable estates of the Roman See was in southern Italy, especially in Sicily, but also in Calabria, and Apulia. Around Rome there was also a most valuable patrimony, extending south down the Via Appia, north-east into Sabina, north into southern Etruria. Other estates were in the south of Pentapolis (the area stretching down the Adriatic from Rimini to Ancona) and in the region of Ravenna, besides hundreds of smaller farms in other places.

The popes had an elaborate organisation of land management,

modelled more or less on that for the imperial domain. 'Rectors of the patrimony' were appointed for each major territory, drawn from a larger group of subordinate Roman officials – subdeacons or notaries and 'guardians' (*defensores*) many of whom were laymen. Papal supervision of the rectors was close; their relations with the government and tax collectors were supervised, their seizure of property in anticipation of legal process reprimanded, the abuses of extraordinary weights and measures and reckonings of money by which they squeezed the peasants, the *coloni*, rectified. The 'rectors' and 'defenders' were important men, quite likely to be employed as ambassadors or papal envoys. Between the rector and the masses of free and unfree peasants was a class of *conductores,* themselves either *coloni* or slaves, whose status was something between that of a reeve and of a small farmer.

These huge clerical estates had formed in a world where the great estate, the *latifundium,* was the ruling social as well as the ruling economic phenomenon. At the same time that the great senatorial families became once more Italian, instead of Byzantine and cosmopolitan, their control of the Italian countryside became yet closer from the Italianisation of the army, which they dominated. Endless war meant the decay of the civil authority outside the towns, the conscription of peasants and their permanent subjection to local military service and to burdens of carriage and service in kind for the army. When this occurred to papal settlements like Gallipoli or Squillace (both in Apulia), the Church seemed to be controlling military posts for the State and exercising public powers, but this is not so. The church lands remained in the sphere of private law.[1]

To what purpose were these huge church incomes directed? The most important was the provisioning of the city of Rome. At this period the Bishop of Rome undertook the responsibility, which his successors preserved until 1870, for feeding the Roman proletariat. Not only the born Romans, but the hordes of refugees from the Lombard war, were entered on Gregory's charity lists. On these, the names of three thousand nuns alone were to be found. The pope possessed something between an immense soup kitchen and a public ministry of supply. Huge quantities of corn (including those due to the State for taxes in kind) were shipped from the southern estates of the Church and stocked in her Roman granaries – not only corn but all manner of food. It is true that the population of Rome was immensely reduced. Even in Gregory's day, agriculture was going on within the walls of Rome, and a century later when the Tiber flooded, 'the fields, vineyards and olives were laid waste, and most of the Romans were unable to sow their land'.[2] But the papal responsibility was a heavy one. The diaconates of Rome were developed in this period in order to store and distribute the grain of the Church and to act as centres of social welfare.[3]

The Roman Church was on the way to replacing important parts of the public power, though it did not seek to do so. Not only were great quantities of imperial corn stored in the papal granaries, but because of the complete breakdown of the Roman banks (the last seems to have disappeared during Gregory's pontificate) the papacy was compelled to act as banker for the imperial army. This led to the confiscation of the

[1] Cf. E. Caspar, *Geschichte des Papsttums* (Tübingen, 1933), ii, p. 333. For the patrimonies, ibid. pp. 323–30.
[2] L. Duchesne (ed.), *Liber Pontificalis* (Paris, 1886), i, p. 399.
[3] O. Bertolini, 'Per la storia delle diaconie Romane nell'Alto Medio Evo sino alla fine del secolo VIII', *ASR*, lxx (3rd ser., i, 1947), pp. 1–145. Also in O. Bertolini, *Scritti Scelti di Storia Medioevale*, ed. O. Banti (Livorno, 1968), pp. 309–456.

B

treasure of the Roman Church by Isaac the Patrician and Maurice the
Cartulary in 640, on the pretext that it was due to the army for arrears
of pay.

The decay of the imperial administration in Rome itself placed more
on the shoulders of the bishop. The prefect of the city – the very office
which Gregory once occupied – ceased to exist; so also did the *cura
palatii,* and the great imperial Roman palaces began their long decline
into medieval ruin. As for the senate, Gregory himself lamented that it
was no more. As the seventh century progressed, other state services
became a papal responsibility. The aqueducts and walls of Rome, both
vital to the security of the city, became maintained by the popes. The
exarch, the head of the Byzantine administration in Italy, had his
headquarters in Ravenna and not in Rome, and the 'dukes' (*duces*) and
tribuni to be found in and near Rome at the head of defence, were
military and not civil officials. On the other hand, the popes themselves
stood at the head of an efficient and highly organised bureaucracy. The
papal notaries and *defensores,* the *arcarius* and *sacellarius,* the head and
second-in-command of the financial offices, the *nomenclator* who assisted
in dealing with petitions – all these constituted a civil service which by
the late seventh century was probably the most effective administration
in Western Europe. On the other hand Pope Agatho (678–81) was so
hard pressed for good officials that he had to do the work of the *arcarius*
himself, and sign his own receipts.

III

For the whole of the seventh and into the eighth century Byzantine
Italy remained in a state of intermittent emergency and war, stretched
to hold open the fragile line of communication across Lombard territory
from Ravenna to Rome, and fighting not on a single front but over a
vast area. Once the Arab invasions had begun in the fourth decade of
the seventh century, the empire was firmly engaged in a struggle for life
with the Muslims which would never allow it to consider Italy as more
than a side-show.

A great peace between the empire and the Lombards was signed
between 678 and 681. The frontiers established by this peace are unknown, but the agreement is of great importance as marking the
recognition by Byzantium, a century after they took place, of the
Lombard usurpations of imperial territory in Italy. The boundaries of

the 681 peace possibly re-appeared in the eighth century as the territorial limits of the claims made by the popes to the Franks.

The inability of the Byzantine Empire to defend its Italian subjects did not mean that its rule was tolerant or kind. The seventh century was, indeed, one of the most painful times of trial in papal history. The plundering of the treasure of the Roman Church in 640, after the death of the rich but doctrinally suspect Pope Honorius, preceded a period of theological differences between the eastern emperors and the Roman bishops. Like the earlier differences between Constantinople and Egypt in Justinian's time, the religious quarrels masked regionalist disputes between the capital and the provinces.

Pope Martin's consecration in 649 took place without seeking imperial confirmation of his election, and he also called a synod at Rome against the imperial definition in the Monothelite controversy. The Exarch Olympius, who then came to Rome to arrest Martin and proclaim the imperial definition, was unable to do so because of the unreliability of his own troops and the opposition of at least a part of the Roman army.[1] He therefore changed sides, made peace with the pope and, subsidised by papal funds, went to the south of Italy where he died fighting against the Muslims. It was on a charge of complicity in this 'rebellion' of Olympius that Pope Martin was arrested, taken to Constantinople, tried and condemned to death. The sentence was commuted to exile in the Crimea, where the broken man died after a few months. His martyrdom is primarily part of the history of Rome's claims to define the faith. But one cannot overlook the element of Italian regionalism which enters this story – when Martin's Greek adherent Maximus the Confessor was examined at Constantinople he was asked: 'Why do you love the Romans and hate the Greeks?'

In 680 Constantine IV summoned the Roman envoys to the Sixth Oecumenical Council at Constantinople and accepted the Roman theological definitions, abandoning those which his predecessors had vainly tried to impose. But conflict between Rome and Constantinople again broke out under Pope Sergius, who was elected in 687 in spite of an attempt by the exarch to exert illegal pressure on the electors. Sergius refused to accept the disciplinary canons of the Eastern Church after their issue by the 'Quinisext' Council[2] in 692 which the Emperor Justinian II ordered to be kept in the West. When the imperial official

[1] *Liber Pontificalis*, i, p. 339n.
[2] So called because held to complete the work of the Fifth and Sixth General Oecumenical Councils.

Zacharias came to arrest the pope and despatch him to Constantinople
for a fate like that of Popes Martin and Vigilius, Italian regionalism
again intervened, and this time more effectively. To oppose the arrest
of the pope the army of Ravenna marched on Rome against the government forces. It met with no opposition, but probably got the support
of the Roman militia, and with trumpets blowing entered Rome. The
terrified Zacharias took refuge under the pope's bed in the Lateran
patriarchate: the imperial attempt on the pope had miserably failed.
That the Italian soldiery should come to the pope's help against the
government suggests that there was no longer an imperial army of
peninsular Italy; what went under this name was an Italian militia
of uncertain loyalty. The Arabs continued to press hard in the western
Mediterranean: Byzantine Africa fell in 697 and Sicily was threatened.
By the beginning of the eighth century the hold of Byzantium on Italy
was extremely weak, and in a military sense scarcely existed.

It is tempting, knowing the outcome, to imagine the popes as plotting
and planning their future escape from what has been called their 'almost
self-imposed thraldom'[1] to Constantinople. But the existence of such a
plan is the conjecture of modern historians; and it may be questioned
whether we do well to attribute such a programme to men whose main
concerns were to preserve the faith and to survive. Greek sovereignty
was not 'self-imposed' but accepted because there was no political alternative. Menacing, semi-barbarous, and full of hate for Rome, the
Lombards could not be accepted as masters. The mere facts of political
geography made the unity and independence of the Byzantine provinces in Italy impossible. Immediately present to the minds of the popes
must have been the immense dangers of a complete break with the
empire. Even apart from the Lombard threat, such a break would
mean their material ruin. Nearly all the most valuable properties of
the Roman See were in southern Italy, which was unlikely to fall out
of imperial control. Equally, a break with the empire might mean the
loss of the spiritual allegiance of the bishops of south Italy, or Ravenna
(which was to some extent the spiritual rival of Rome), or of Venetia
and Istria. All this explains how extremely cautious and even reluctant
the popes were in cutting their ties with Byzantium. But the continued
bankruptcy of Byzantine military power meant that the ties were
bound to weaken, even if the Italian provincials were anxious to preserve
them.

[1] G. J. Talland, *The Church and the Papacy* (London, 1944), p. 364.

IV

In 710 the first move towards the breakaway of the Italian provinces occurred. The leaders and the militia of Ravenna were angered by a particularly savage proscription by the restored Emperor Justinian II against the archbishop and *curia* of the city. They elected their own leader in one George, the son of a proscribed official, and ruled Ravenna and northern Pentapolis in defiance of the empire. In this Pope Constantine had no part; his views may be deduced from the comment of the official papal biography on the blinding of the Archbishop of Ravenna, which it describes as a fitting punishment for his disobedience to the apostolic see. Pope Constantine in the same year was summoned to Constantinople, not ignominiously but with honour, to confer with the emperor. What agreement he made is unknown, as Justinian II was overpowered and murdered shortly after the pope's return to Rome in 711.

The Byzantine Empire was now moving towards the worst period of the Arab wars, the year-long siege of Constantinople in 717–18. All over the Byzantine world, the 'Roman' way of life faced its supreme crisis. The empire accepted as leader the great Leo 'the Isaurian', who shortly afterwards chose to rally the people by the religious programme of the destruction of the holy images. Whatever the true nature and motives of the iconoclast movement, nothing could have emphasised more brutally the cultural and religious split between the eastern and western parts of the empire. Even in Naples and southern Italy, hitherto and later the stronghold of Byzantine loyalism, the iconoclast decrees were rejected. The natural leader of western resistance to iconoclasm was, of course, the Roman See.

The clash between Leo the Isaurian and the papacy began not over the iconoclast decrees (although the iconoclast policy was probably already launched in the east when it occurred) but over the spoiling of church property. Pope Gregory II, a Roman, was one of three important popes in the eighth century to have been brought up from childhood by the papal bureaucracy in the Lateran patriarchate, where he made his career, and became *sacellarius* (financial controller) and librarian. His biography, a carefully written propagandist work, part of which was published in Europe (and read by Bede in Northumbria) while he was still alive, calls him 'a determined defender of the goods of the Church', a description which his career fully bears out. The first stage of the struggle with which the biography acquaints us, probably in 725 or 726, shows him already under sentence of arrest by the emperor on a capital charge. The attempt to arrest him (the biography says, murder him) was frustrated by the Romans, who killed one of the imperial officials responsible. A second attempt to seize him and replace him by another bishop was then made by Paul the exarch, the newly arrived head of the Byzantine government in Italy. This time the charges are given, that he 'hindered the collection of taxes in Italy, and the despoiling of the churches which had been carried out elsewhere'. The sense is that Leo's reforms had included the collection of a tax in Byzantine Italy and the mulcting of church property throughout the empire, including Italy. The arrest was again frustrated by the Romans, who on this occasion induced the Lombards of the duchy of Spoleto to close the passes across the Apennines to the exarch's troops.

Only then, with the Roman duchy in open rebellion, were the imperial decrees forbidding the images published in Italy (probably in 727). The effect of the decrees was to release all that hatred for the Greeks which had accumulated in Byzantine Italy north of the Neapolitan campagna. The Italians elected local leaders (*duces*) and wanted to elect an emperor, but the pope dissuaded them, 'hoping for a change of heart in the emperor'. This did not prevent him from leading the Italians in a bitter civil war, in the course of which it is evident that the local territorial aristocracy, and particularly the Roman aristocracy, were the backers of the popes. Eutychius, the next exarch, when he sent agents from Naples to Rome to accomplish what the Exarch Paul had failed to do, ordered that the pope be arrested 'together with the magnates of Rome'. The arrest was again frustrated, and the 'great and lesser men' of Rome took an oath to defend the pontiff. In Ravenna at least an imperialist faction appeared, and fought the revolutionaries. The Lombards, and particularly King Liutprand eagerly took the chances now offered to them. Sutri, thirty miles north of Rome, was seized for a short time by Liutprand in 727–8, but ransomed by the pope. Liutprand also marched on Rome against the pope on behalf of the Exarch Eutychius, but (doubtless again for a substantial bribe) was reconciled to Gregory. In spite of these hostilities the pope dissuaded the Italians from supporting a pretender to the empire who was put forward by troops in Byzantine Italy, and he caused the Roman army to arrest him and to send his head to Constantinople – telling the Italians 'not to waver in their loyalty to the Roman Empire'.

The papal exhortation just quoted, and the lack of reference to further fighting, suggest that even before Gregory II's death in 731 the civil war had petered out, perhaps leaving imperial officials in nominal control of provinces which were in fact independent. Certainly the government was not strong enough to try to punish the rebels, and the resistance of Italy to the iconoclast decrees continued. But in spite of the leadership by the popes of this resistance, as of the Italian revolution, they still clung to imperial sovereignty. The consummate insolence of Gregory II's letters to the emperor (if these texts are genuine, which is uncertain) did not prevent his appealing to that sovereignty as if it was in full force. The same recognition of imperial control appears to have been continued in the earlier part of his pontificate at least, by his successor Gregory II, who by paying a large sum to the Duke of Spoleto induced him to make peace and to restore the village of Gallese 'within the structure of the holy Empire and of the Roman army dear to the body of Christ'.[1] But the 'Roman army', which is the complement of the empire, shows how Byzantine sovereignty had been reduced by the political realities to a mere name. Political power seems to be shared between the 'Roman army', the militia which had reappeared in history only a century earlier, and the Bishop of Rome. The early Christian idea of the people of a city as the people of God, a social body which is also part of the body of Christ, was being grafted into the medieval alliance of the popes with the Roman landed aristocracy.

V

In these obscure years the slow transformation of the papacy from an occasional to a permanent political authority was taking place. The Roman clergy had for many years been slowly assuming duties, privileges and powers which properly belonged to imperial authority. Not only the powers, but the marks of power. The 'Lateran patriarchate' after the beginning of the eighth century became 'the Lateran palace'. The *ordines Romani* conferred a splendour and ostentation on the ceremonies of the Roman Church which was partly borrowed from the empire. The Roman clerics, like the imperial officials, claimed the processional adorning of their horses with white silk. Between the humble attire of Gregory the Great's pontifical procession in the plague of 590, and the solemn pomps of the Roman Church in the early eighth century, there is already a great gap. But the legal situation was unchanged. There is no sign that the popes exercised public powers, nor was imperial sovereignty over Rome and the Italian provinces even implicitly rejected by the Roman bishops. For changes in political status and public law to

[1] *Liber Pontificalis*, i, pp. 420–1 and note.

come about, a new and yet more revolutionary situation was needed.

The transitional stage in which the Italian provinces of the empire now found themselves must have seemed to most contemporaries a transition from Greek to Lombard rule – at the very best the prelude to something akin to the restoration of the Romano-German kingdom of Theodoric the Ostrogoth. Against this possibility the popes struggled desperately, though relying on diminished assets. In 733 all the patrimonies of the Church in south Italy, the financial backbone of the papacy, were confiscated by the emperor. Given the uses to which the income of the patrimony was put, it was a confiscation carried out as much against Rome as against its bishop. Ravenna itself had fallen to Liutprand for a period, probably 732–3. When he resumed his pressure against Rome in 739 there was so much the less money to buy him off. In this period, the darkest in the history of the Italian provinces, the alliance between the Roman duchy and the Lombards of Spoleto broke down, after Transamund of Spoleto had been heavily defeated by the Lombard king. The Roman frontier towns on the borders of Lombard Tuscany fell, (Amelia, Orte, Bomarzo, Bieda), and although Liutprand's main effort was not yet directed against Rome itself, his appearance before the city in 739 seemed to announce the final Lombard victory in central Italy and the end of independent Rome. In despair Pope Gregory sent an embassy to Charles Martel, the Frankish mayor of the palace, whom he addressed as 'sub-king', and to whom he referred as 'patrician'. The embassy, the first of its kind the Frankish kingdom had ever known, was honourably received, but failed in its purpose. Liutprand had helped Charles against the Arabs only two years earlier, and had 'adopted' his son Pippin. The pope's case was also weakened by the fact that Liutprand had acted primarily against the rebellious Transamund, and not against Rome. The time for Frankish intervention was not yet.

Much as the popes feared him, there is no indication that Liutprand had the intention of annexing Rome, at all events as an immediate political aim. What had troubled him had been the Roman alliance with Spoleto. In 741 the Syrian Pope Gregory III was succeeded by the Greek, Zacharias, who immediately and successfully launched a policy of conciliating Liutprand. In 742 the pope met Liutprand at Terni, and the Lombard king agreed to restore 'to blessed Peter prince of the Apostles' the four border villages taken two years earlier, together with the papal estates in central Italy seized by the Lombards in the course of the preceding wars. The pope returned to Rome, the biographer says, 'with the palm of victory'.

Liutprand doubtless intended the Romans to leave Ravenna to its fate, but when he attacked the latter in the following year, Zacharias scored a yet more notable success. 'Leaving Rome under the control of the patrician and duke' (a wording which seems intended to imply that the pope was now the effective ruler of the city) Zacharias travelled through the district of Ravenna to the Lombard kingdom. At Pavia he induced Liutprand to restore 'to the empire' the district around Ravenna, and two-thirds of the territory of Cesena. Either because he was grateful for this papal mediation, or in hope of bribing Zacharias, the Emperor Constantine V, at the pope's request, made him a gift of the large estates of Ninfa and Norma, at the foot of the Monti Lepini, presumably in partial compensation for the confiscated southern patrimonies. A stage seemed to have been reached at which the emperor tacitly and for the moment recognised the strong position now occupied by the pope in Byzantine Italy. Italy itself enjoyed a brief respite of peace, the first for twenty years.

Little as we know of him (although his portrait was found in S. Maria Antiqua), Zacharias was perhaps the most subtle and able of all the Roman pontiffs, in this dark corridor in which the Roman See hovered just inside the doors of the Byzantine world. This skilful diplomat, who secured benefits from the severe Constantine V, fended off Liutprand and his successor Ratchis, and 'amassed a great treasure' in Rome, was the last Greek Bishop of Rome.

The most eventful of all his political decisions was taken in 749, when Pippin the Short had for four years ruled the kingdom of the Franks after the re-establishment of the *fainéant* Merovingian king, Childeric. The political bankruptcy of the Meroving house which had ruled Francia for two and a half centuries was known to all, but the legal attributes of kingship had until then remained with the old dynasty. In that year Pippin sent an embassy to Pope Zacharias to know 'whether it was good or not' that the legitimate king of the Franks (the infant Childeric, on whose behalf he purported to rule) did not exercise royal power. Zacharias replied, that it was better that he should be king, who had royal power, than he who had not. By that reply he decided the fate of the papacy and, if indirectly, the fate of Europe. If he did not himself legitimise the new Frankish dynasty, he pointed the way to it. He could scarcely know that the new dynasty he thus approved would, by the end of the century, conquer the Western world from the Pyrenees

B*

to the Elbe, nor that it would be secured by firm bonds to the papacy when Charlemagne carried it to world power. Within a short time of Zacharias's answer, the Frankish magnates and bishops assembled at Soissons, hailed Pippin as king, and saw him anointed (probably by the Anglo-Saxon Bishop Boniface) to the kingship. The first Arnulfing king of the Franks had come to rule with the consent of the pope, and the sacramental oil was applied by a bishop who was also a papal agent.

Whether Zacharias was executing a long-meditated papal plan, or whether he merely tried to play off Franks against Lombards as a short-term expedient, we do not know. When Zacharias died in 752 he was succeeded by Stephen II, a Roman orphan who like Gregory III had been bred from early childhood in the Lateran patriarchate. Aistulf, who succeeded Ratchis as king of the Lombards, abandoned the hesitations of his predecessors and decided that the time was near to absorb Rome and the Roman duchy. In 752 he demanded a Lombard protectorate over Rome: the Romans were asked to pay annual tribute of one gold *solidus* a head, and were to acknowledge him as overlord. This time the desperate attempts of Pope Stephen to fend off the Lombards by negotiation and bribery failed. Neither he nor the Byzantine emissary who appeared on the scene at this point could wring concessions from Aistulf. Barefoot, and carrying a holy image on his own shoulders, the pope led his clergy to S. Maria Maggiore and placed ashes on the heads of the wailing people, while he nailed to the crucifix the treaty which Aistulf had broken. Having thus invoked God, Pope Stephen wrote to Pippin, and appealed for Frankish aid.

The envoy from Byzantium, John the Silentiary, made one more appearance in Italy, and ordered the pope to make a further personal approach to Aistulf, in the emperor's name. The pope obeyed, and asked for a safe conduct from the Lombards. But at the same time Pippin responded to Stephen's appeal, telling him to count on the Franks for support, and then agreeing that the pope should in person travel to Francia, escorted there by the Frankish envoys.

On 14 October 753 the pope left St Peter's for Pavia, accompanied by the two Frankish envoys and the imperial agent, John the Silentiary: the Roman magnates escorted him only as far as the Lombard border. In Pavia Aistulf still felt himself strong enough to refuse concessions; that the Franks would actually send an army against their Lombard allies was not at all certain, and he knew that the Greeks were powerless in Italy. When the pope asked him to restore Ravenna and the exarchate and the other territories of the empire[1] which he and his predecessors had taken, he refused, as he refused John the Silentiary. When Aistulf was told of the pope's wish to travel to Francia he 'ground his teeth like a lion', but dared not obstruct him. So on 15 November 753 Pope Stephen, together with the chief officers of the papal court, left Pavia for Francia. Having arrived at Pavia in company with the imperial agent he left it alone, in order to act independently. The papacy had made a decisive step. Perhaps it took it not because it had a 'plan' to free itself from Byzantine rule, but because the Bishop of Rome identified himself with the cause of the 'Italian Province', and read in Isaiah and the gospel his duty to protect 'God's flock', the 'peculiar people of God'. And even while Stephen negotiated in Pavia, his relation to the Byzantine emperor suffered a further change. Preparations were being made in Constantinople for the great iconoclast council which was to open on 10 February 754. Constantine V had not yet, in the papal view, absolutely committed himself to an anti-Roman policy: he was now to do so irrevocably.

Pippin met the papal cortège on 6 January 754, not on the border but at Ponthion in Champagne, where there was a royal estate. If the papal chronicle is truthful, the dismounted king met the pope at the approaches to the settlement, and Pippin acted as groom, leading the papal horse and its rider among the chanting clergy to the palace. The pope on his side (an action not reported in the papal chronicle) then fell before the king in sackcloth, with ashes on his head, with tears asking him 'that in accordance with the peace treaties (between Romans and Lombards) he would support the suit of St Peter and of the republic of the Romans'. The king replied by swearing to hold himself at the behest of the pope, and 'to restore the exarchate of Ravenna and the rights and territories of the republic'. It is unlikely that he intended the Byzantine Empire to be in any way the beneficiary of this promise. The nature of the engagements entered into by either side cannot be known except by a process of learned inference. That either side took a hold-oath to the other (as has been suggested) seems unlikely. But certainly

[1] At any rate as far as Ravenna was concerned, Pope Stephen seems to have acted as an imperial agent (cf. *Liber Pontificalis*, i, p. 446). W. Ullmann, *The Growth of Papal Government in the Middle Ages*, 3rd ed. (London, 1970), p. 61n., treats this opinion as a 'well-known' error, but for another view see O. Bertolini, 'Il problema delle origini del potere temporale dei papi', etc., in *Miscellanea Pio Paschini*, i (Rome, 1948), pp. 103–71, at pp. 124–6 (also in *Scritti Scelti*, pp. 487–547); and cf. also E. Caspar, *Pippin und die römische Kirche* (Berlin, 1914), pp. 92–4.

Pippin assumed a duty of protection towards the Roman bishop.[1]

Frankish diplomacy was thus put to work for the papal cause, and the first of three missions was despatched to Aistulf to ask him to honour the Roman-Lombard treaties as the pope demanded, but without effect. What now was to come to the proof, was whether or not the Franks were willing to go to war on behalf of their king's papal protégé. It was a delicate moment for the new dynasty, which having used the Roman Church in its attempt to secure legitimacy, now found itself asked to engage in a war which many of the Frankish magnates did not want to fight.

In April 754 the general assembly of the Franks met at Quierzy-sur-Oise where, in spite of the withdrawal of some magnates from the council, Pippin publicly renewed the promise he had made to Pope Stephen at Ponthion, apparently on this occasion naming the territories which he promised to 'restore' to the pope. Soon after Pippin had executed this promise in writing, the pope proceeded with the king to St Denis and solemnly anointed Pippin and his two sons as 'king and patrician of the Romans', blessing Queen Bertrada and the Frankish nobles. The pope's right to confer the title of 'patrician' is unclear, but his intention officially to bless the dynasty is evident. It is possible that the conferment of the title was intended to help disarm the opposition of some of the Frankish nobles to an Italian expedition.[2]

The Frankish embassies to Aistulf failed in their object. In the spring of 755 the Frankish host was summoned to Braisne-sur-Vesle, near Soissons, and set out for Italy. The reluctance of Pippin to come to open war is shown by the despatch of a further Frankish embassy to Aistulf offering him a large indemnity for the restoration of 'papal' territories to their owner. But this also failed to move the Lombard king, so the Frankish army moved over Mont Cénis, encountering and sharply defeating Aistulf almost immediately at Susa. Aistulf's camp was looted, while he fled and shut himself up in the capital, Pavia.

Pippin had not been over-anxious to fight the Lombards, and he showed himself pleased enough to make Aistulf promise under a 'terrible

---

[1] P. E. Schramm, 'Das Versprechen Pippins und Karls des Grossen für die römische Kirche', *ZSSRG*, lviii, *Kan. Abt.* xxvii (1938), pp. 180–217. Haller's thesis (cf. *Das Papsttum*, i, pp. 420–1, 554 ff.) that Pippin swore an oath of vassalage to Stephen has not won general acceptance. Cf. Schramm, pp. 184–5. For the chronology cf. L. Levillain, 'L'avènement de la dynastie carolingienne et les origines de l'état pontifical', *BEC*, xciv (1933), pp. 225–95. I do not agree with Levillain about the Donation of Constantine (Levillain, pp. 231–4).
[2] Cf. J. Deér, 'Zum Patricius-Romanorum-Titel Karls des Grossen', *Archivum Historiae Pontificiae*, iii (1965), pp. 32–86, at p. 49.

oath' to restore Ravenna and the other cities, and to acknowledge Frankish supremacy in some form. Pippin then left Italy. The extent of the political revolution is clear; the treaty was signed between 'Romans, Franks and Lombards', and of the Byzantine Empire and its rights not a word is said. The pope acted in these events on behalf of 'blessed Peter and the holy Church of God *of* the republic of the Romans'. If we do not press these rather cloudy phrases too hard for precise legal meanings, their political significance is clear enough. The *res publica Romanorum* was a term used then and later for the political entity of the Roman people. But it also in a sense belonged to the Roman Church, and in one text the pope actually refers to *nostrae Romanorum reipublicae*.[1] We can see how tightly the political interests of the Romans were associated with the religious authority of the pope.

Even after the Frankish intervention, the position of the Romans continued to be critical. Pippin having left Italy, Aistulf calmly disregarded the treaty and his oath, and save for one town in the Tiber valley, failed to return 'a foot of land' to the Roman power: moreover, on New Year's Day of 756 he appeared with two large armies at the gates of Rome, demanded that the pope (evidently the main culprit) be handed over, and conducted in a savage and ruthless manner a three months' siege of the city. The Lombard army plundered the valuable ornaments and offerings in the tombs of the martyrs outside the city – provoking the translation of many of the relics to churches within the walls. If any of the ecclesiastics who had gone to Francia with Pope Stephen had returned congratulating themselves on the successful emancipation of the Roman See from an heretical emperor, their joy must soon have turned into sorrow. In three months Frankish envoys were busy at Rome. The pope's appeals to the Franks grew more and more hysterical, culminating in a fancy piece of rhetoric by which he made St Peter himself take part in the correspondence.

By the time Pippin's army eventually moved again against the Lombards in April 756, Aistulf had already abandoned the siege of Rome and returned to Pavia. He was again defeated by the Franks, and again treated by them with remarkable gentleness, though to some profit to themselves. To the Franks Aistulf had to give hostages and a third of his treasure, and to promise a future yearly tribute of 12,000 *solidi*. For the pope he had to execute a document by which he promised in detail to return to him Ravenna and most of the exarchate, most (but

[1] I. Giorgi and U. Balzani, *Il regesto di Farfa* (Rome, 1879–1914), ii, no. 90, p. 83. Cf. Ullmann, 3rd ed., pp. 61–4, where a different view is taken.

not all) of the towns in Pentapolis, some towns in Emilia, Comacchio (at the mouth of the Po) and Narni. The list of towns, when added to the area known as the duchy of Rome, allows us to sketch the very rough outline of a zone in Italy which in effect was under neither Greek nor Lombard rule, and which fell under the influence of Rome and its bishop. Exactly what determined the frontiers of this area is far from clear, but the most probable explanation is that these were the limits of the landed estates owned by the bishops and the nobility of Rome and Ravenna.

The Byzantine power did not let this revolutionary derogation of its rights pass without protest. While Pippin's army was still on the march in 756, two Byzantine envoys arrived in Rome. Proceeding in some consternation to Marseilles, one of them eventually found Pippin near Pavia. His promises of a large bribe to the Frankish king were refused: Pippin firmly said that he had undertaken this expedition not for money but for love of blessed Peter and for the remission of his sins. The liberated cities were, he said, the property of St Peter and the Roman Church. Fulrad, the Abbot of St Denis, then collected the keys of the cities of Emilia, the exarchate and Pentapolis, and placed them on the tomb of St Peter in Rome, together with the documents recording the 'donation' of Pippin to the Church. In the following year, in the civil war which followed Aistulf's death, the Lombard magnate Desiderius promised further 'restitutions' to the papacy, in return for Frankish-papal support in his struggle for the Lombard crown. Most of the cities in Emilia and Pentapolis which were omitted from the list of towns made over in the preceding year, were now promised to the pope, thus restoring the frontier more or less to its position before Liutprand began his conquests earlier in the century. It is possible that the boundaries mentioned in the 'donation' of Pippin followed the boundaries in an earlier treaty between the Byzantine Empire and the Lombards. The Roman habitat in Italy was – in principle at least – protected against its Lombard neighbour.

VI

The revolutionary change in the political position of the Roman See called into existence new and speculative developments in the thought of the clerks in the Lateran patriarchate. The basic claims behind papal primacy and jurisdiction had all been stated long before the eighth

century, even if they had only been spasmodically and partially vindi-
cated. Now the thrusting of Byzantine sovereignty into the background
and the emergence of a new political relationship with the Frankish
kingdom, called for reconsideration of the position of the popes *vis-
à-vis* the empire. For the first time in its history the Roman See now
exercised something which might blossom into temporal sovereignty,
although it was not yet so. Thus the pope entered into close relations
with a Frankish monarchy, under circumstances which left him a good
deal of freedom in defining what those relations would be. Propagandist
documents were bound to emerge. One such document, which puts the
papal case with the utmost subtlety and skill (and which happens to be
our main historical source for most of these events), is the series of lives
of the popes which has already been mentioned, the *Liber Pontificalis*.
Another which may have been prepared at the time of Stephen II
or his immediate successors, is one of the most famous documents of
medieval history, the *Constitutum Constantini imperatoris* or so-called
Donation of Constantine.

The forged 'Donation' of Constantine is the conflation of a legend
concerning the fabulous conversion of Constantine by Pope Silvester
(the *Actus Sylvestri*) with a whole list of political, religious and protocol
ambitions of the Roman See of the eighth century. Constantine is made
to confer on Silvester not only the 'Lateran palace', a transformation
of the real Lateran patriarchate, and patrimonial estates all over the
empire but his crown and imperial *regalia,* besides giving the higher
Roman clergy the same protocol privileges and ornaments as patricians
and consuls. This subsuming of imperial to papal protocol is especially
significant, in a political context in which the pope was in fact trying to
usurp the place of the empire in Italy. But it is in 'Roman' Italy, alone,
and not elsewhere, that the forger of the *Constitutum Constantini* wants
to replace imperial by papal rule. The later Middles Ages understood
the 'Donation' as conferring rule on Pope Silvester by Constantine over
the whole West, and this seems at first confirmed by 'the city of Rome
and all provinces of Italy and the western regions', in which the pope
is given power and possession. But the forger either did not know, or
chose to disregard, that Constantine's empire included provinces north
and west of Emilia: by the 'western regions' he simply understood 'Italy
and the islands'. And by 'Italy' he understood not the peninsula but the
ancient Roman province. The territories to which the pope sought
to lay claim in the *Constitutum Constantini* corresponded approximately with the 'Donation' of lands in Italy, which Pippin was said to

have made in favour of Pope Stephen in 756. The *Constitutum Constantini* seems designed to support the assumption of public powers by the Roman bishop, at the head of an autonomous Roman 'province' of Italy. It is an important propagandist document. But to assume, as some scholars have done, that it was also a sort of political instrument, is to go far beyond the evidence. There is no proof that the Donation was shown by Stephen II to the Franks, or even that it was known to him at all. It has been argued that there is no textual quotation from the Donation in papal documents before the eleventh century.[1] The Donation seems to be better used as evidence of the political ideas current in Roman clerical circles in the late eighth century, than as a key to certain specific political events.

VII

Few things are more impressive in the history of the temporal power than the way in which its politics immediately formed certain patterns which were to recur for centuries. Stephen II died in 757. He was succeeded, after a short period of tumult in which an opposition party proclaimed the archdeacon Theophylact pope, by his brother Paul. Paul, yet another pope who had grown to manhood in the Lateran patriarchate, was like the others a bureaucrat, constantly employed by his brother and perhaps by his brother's predecessors on important diplomatic missions. Paul's secular government was not an entirely good omen for the future of papal rule, being marked by harshness and irregularities which the official biographer blames on 'unprincipled worldings'. Attempts to resist his financial demands by the notables of Ravenna seem to have been punished by death. His brother had named the officials in the exarchate, although it is doubtful if papal intervention was more than spasmodic, for the Archbishop Sergius of Ravenna was said to have ruled there, like the exarch.[2] But the failure of Stephen to make the archbishop accept Roman government in the exarchate was not really reversed. The inability of the pope to impose his rule there without opposition was to have permanent effects on the Papal

[1] H. Fuhrmann, 'Konstantinische Schenkung und abendländisches Kaisertum', *DA*, xxiv (1966), pp. 63–178, at pp. 120–1. Fuhrmann has also recently edited the text: *Das Constitutum Constantini (Konstantinische Schenkung)*, in *MGH, Fontes iuris Germani antiqui*, x. Cf. also Ullmann, *Papal Government*, 3rd ed., p. 478.

[2] Agnellus, *Liber pontificalis ecclesiae Ravennatis (MGH, Scriptores rerum Langobardorum)*, pp. 379–80.

State, which for centuries was to enjoy only a very restricted political position in the exarchate.[1]

The temporal power of the popes emerged largely because of Lombard threats, but also in response to the ambitions of the Roman nobles, those rich and greedy potentates who – in the eyes of the other Italians at least – habitually insisted on governing all things.[2] These magnates, whom Paul I associated with the clergy in a declaration of Roman loyalty to Pippin,[3] were inevitably jealous of the new power of their priests. It is a rivalry which is apparent in the forged Donation of Constantine, with its insistence on the equality of the Roman clergy with the senate. But before we are tempted to treat this jealousy as a secular struggle for power between the clerical bureaucracy and the Roman nobility, it is necessary to look at the social structure of the Roman Church. There was no sharp distinction in Roman society between lay nobles and clerical administrators; there was a military *ordo* and a sacerdotal *ordo*, but in effect the two merged into one another. A large number of the papal administrative offices had originally been held by laymen, but by the time of Gregory the Great or at all events by a century later the men holding these offices, though they married and usually belonged to the upper nobility, were in minor clerical orders. The *defensores,* whose leader or *primicerius* was one of the great officers of state, were tonsured lower clergy without a special *ordo*.[4] Such a one was Theodotus *consul et dux,* the uncle of the future Pope Hadrian I, who under Stephen II became *primicerius defensorum.* Moreover this practice rested on a broader social basis by which the nobility as a fairly general practice often caused their sons to enter the ranks of the lower clergy without their even leaving the parental home. For a child to become a *lector,* the lowest clerical grade recognised at Rome, all that was necessary was for the parents or guardians to

[1] Cf. O. Bertolini, 'Sergio arcivescovo di Ravenna (744–69) e i papi del suo tempo', *Stud. Romagn.,* i (1950), pp. 43–88; idem, 'Le prime manifestazioni concrete del potere temporale dei papi nell'esarcato di Ravenna, 756–7', *Atti dell'Istituto veneto di Scienze Lettere ed Arti. Classe scienze morali e lettere,* cvi, pt. 2 (1948), pp. 280–300. Both articles are also in *Scritti Scelti,* pp. 549–91, 593–612.

[2] 'sic omnia disponebat, ut soliti sunt modo Romani facere' (Agnellus, loc. cit.). Cf. Agnellus, p. 385, where an apocalyptic writing attributed to the Archbishop of Ravenna prophesies that the Roman nobles will be captured and exiled 'on account of their riches'. And cf. P. E. Schramm, *Kaiser, Rom und Renovatio,* 2nd ed. (Darmstadt, 1957), i, pp. 18–19.

[3] *Codex Carolinus,* apud *MGH, Epistolarum iii, Epistolae Merowingici et Karolini Aevi,* i, no.37, pp. 547–8.

[4] B. Fischer, 'Die Entwicklung des Instituts der Defensoren in der römischen Kirche', *Ephemerides Liturgicae,* xlviii (1934), pp. 443–54.

bring him to the personal attention of the pope, who would examine him by a public reading at one of the nocturnal vigils in church. If he satisfied the 'apostolic one', the pope, merely by pronouncing a short formula over the child, made him reader (*lector*). Alternatively a child could enter the papal household, where there were both lay and tonsured chamberlains (*cubicularii*); or he could go into the papal choir (*schola cantorum*).[1] Or finally he could be made a 'clerk', again without leaving his father's house, and again without belonging to a special *ordo*; such was the early career of Pope Nicholas I in the ninth century. When this wide diffusion of clerical orders is taken into account it becomes practically impossible to talk of a true clash of interests between the military and clerical *ordines*; the two were too closely intertwined. It would make more sense to speak of struggles between factions (which could contain both noble and clerical elements) for the control of the Lateran bureaucracy. At various periods the strictly clerical element predominated in these factional struggles, at others the noble. But this must not blind us to the social unity of Rome and its Church; only in the twelfth century when the Roman court began to become European in character did the situation fundamentally change.

VIII

The political situation of the Romans was uncertain so long as the Lombard kingdom continued to exist. Christopher, who succeeded Theodotus as *primicerius* under Paul I, was an able and ruthless politician, hated and feared by the Greeks and by a faction of the Roman nobles, although he was the trusted servant of the pope.[2] Around Christopher there gathered a feud which reveals the inevitable divisions in Roman society which the existence of two outside powers, Frank and Lombard, both intriguing in Rome, was bound to create. The interests of these two powers in Rome were conflicting, and an unhappy period followed in which the Romans were the pawns of one side or the other.

As Pope Paul lay dying in the Church of S. Paolo fuori le Mura in June 767, the 'Duke' Toto, one of the landed magnates, assembled his

---

[1] M. Andrieu, 'Les ordres mineurs dans l'ancien Rit Romain', *Revue de Sciences Religieuses*, v (1925), pp. 232–74.

[2] The Byzantines suggested to Pippin that Christopher was acting for the papacy without the knowledge of the pope; Pope Paul denied this (*Cod. Car.*, no. 36, p. 546, lines 25–35). For what follows see H. Zimmermann, *Papstabsetzungen des Mittelalters* (Graz–Vienna–Cologne, 1968), pp. 14–25.

dependants and tenants in Nepi, north of Rome, and marched on Rome down the Via Flaminia. In spite of the counter move of another 'duke', who marched from the south of Rome with his tenants and those of the Roman Church to oppose Toto; in spite also of an oath taken by the contending parties not to bring their forces into the city, Toto broke into Rome and as soon as the pope's death was announced proceeded to have his own brother, the layman Constantine, 'elected' as pope. The opposing 'duke' was executed and the *primicerius* Christopher, after taking asylum in St Peter's, was allowed with his son to retire to a monastery in Lombard territory. The illegally elected 'pope' remained undisturbed in office for over a year. But Christopher and his son Sergius travelled north to find Desiderius and enlist his help. With an armed force supplied by the Lombard Duke of Spoleto, Sergius marched from Rieti and appeared outside the walls of Rome in July 768. Toto was killed in the ensuing battle.

Christopher separated himself politically from his Lombard allies. A Lombard priest called Waldipart had procured the election of a Roman called Philip as pope; Christopher had this election annulled. The Forum was still the political centre of Rome; Christopher gathered the Romans near the arch of Septimius Severus and caused the people and clergy to elect as bishop a Sicilian called Stephen, a member of the Lateran clergy.

The revolution was not bloodless. The main supporters of the 'pseudo-Pope' Constantine were blinded and mutilated; Waldipart also was murdered. Constantine was led in mock procession seated on a woman's side-saddle; he also was blinded, though some time after the *coup*. In the following New Year Constantine was brought before a synod of bishops; when he presumed to defend himself the holy fathers cuffed and kicked him from the council chamber. The victory of the Lateran clergy was at the same council perpetuated by a decision that the pope must henceforth be elected by the upper clergy of Rome, the cardinal priests and the deacons. The Roman nobles and people were allowed only to approve the election after the clergy had effected it. This decision governed papal elections for the following half-century, and marks the highest point of the power of the Roman clergy in the early Middle Ages.

The revolution of the *primicerius* Christopher was quickly overtaken by events. The death of Pippin in 768 led to changes in Frankish policy. The Queen Mother Bertrada, seeking to reconcile her sons Carloman and Charles, and to reconcile Franks and Bavarians, went to Italy to the

Lombard King Desiderius to arrange marriages between the Lombard and Frankish royal houses. She then went to Rome (where the pope's first reaction to her diplomacy had been to make a violent protest against this alliance with the 'perfidious and stinking' Lombards) to make Stephen III accept the new direction she had given to Frankish policy.

Christopher and Sergius had always been the enemies of the Lombards, and they had finally damned themselves with Desiderius when, after accepting his help to get rid of 'Pope' Constantine, they had at once thrown the alliance over and had the Lombard agent Waldipart executed. Pope Stephen III was a weak and vacillating man, and not one to stand up for his former patron Christopher (whose domination he in any case resented) against such a man as Desiderius. At hand to encourage him to throw Christopher to the Lombard wolves were his own brother, the 'Duke' John, and a papal chamberlain named Paul Afiarta.

The papacy was now in effect the victim of the quarrels in the Frankish royal family. Charles was the son-in-law of Desiderius; and Rome was the object of the political jealousies of the two brothers and of Charles's nominal ally, the Lombard king.[1] Late in 771 Desiderius appeared at the gates of Rome, with the connivance of Afiarta and the Lombard party. Christopher and Sergius prepared the city for defence, and confronted Pope Stephen in the Lateran, hoping to seize Afiarta. They failed, and Pope Stephen fled outside the city walls to St Peter's, where he entered into correspondence with the enemy. Carloman's envoy in the city encouraged Christopher and Sergius to hold out, but their troops melted away, and under safe conduct from the pope they gave themselves up in St Peter's. Stephen did not protect them from the vengeance of Desiderius and Afiarta (nor perhaps from that of other persons whose friends suffered in the bloody *coup* of 768). At dusk the two men were taken from St Peter's and their eyes put out: the father died three days later. The blind son lived a little longer, until Afiarta's agents had him removed from prison and horribly done to death. Christopher had been a loyal servant of the papal idea, for which he now suffered at the hands of the pope himself. Pope Stephen III only outlived him by a short time.

---

[1] Cf. M. Lintzel, 'Karl der Grosse und Karlmann', *HZ*, cxi (1929), pp. 1–22 (also in *Ausgewählte Schriften* (Berlin, 1961), pp. 10–26); I cannot entirely accept his chronology.

IX

Stephen was succeeded by a Roman aristocrat, Hadrian I, the nephew of one *consul et dux* and the uncle of another, the donor of rich family estates to the Roman See. He was an able and determined politician, no man of straw as Stephen III had been. But until the Lombard problem was solved there could be no peace in Rome. Its solution depended, eventually, on the evolution of Frankish politics.

In December 771 Carloman, the co-ruler of Francia, died. The Lombard King Desiderius in 773 opened an attack on the Roman duchy which quickly brought him to Viterbo, with the intention of assaulting Rome. At the time of the attack Carloman's widow was sheltering in the Lombard kingdom with Duke Autchar and her two infant sons. No doubt Desiderius thought that he was strong enough to take a foretaste of revenge against Charles, who two years earlier had repudiated his wife, the daughter of the Lombard king. But Desiderius's estimate of his own strength was mistaken. The Franks stayed united under Charles, and showed no sign of supporting Carloman's heirs. In consequence the Roman enterprise became too dangerous for Desiderius, and when he and his Frankish ally Autchar were threatened by Pope Hadrian with anathema, they tamely complied and retreated from Viterbo back into Lombard territory.

The abortive attack on the Romans in 773 was hardly more than the death rattle of the old Lombard kingdom. Although Charles hesitated to attack Desiderius, he finally did so a few months later, in the autumn of 773. As had always happened before, the Lombards were beaten in the open, and shut themselves up in Pavia. Charles after besieging the city for six months left a holding force, and himself marched south to Rome. Pavia was to fall in June, and after its capture the Lombard kingdom was absorbed in the Frankish Empire.

The ceremonial, pious nature of Charles's Roman journey is evident from its date – Charles arrived outside Rome on Easter Saturday (2 April 774). Pope Hadrian nevertheless received the news of his arrival 'in an ecstasy of astonishment'. The pope, certainly, had been up to some political doings which would not please his guest; most notably he had taken hold-oaths from the nobles of the Lombard duchy of Spoleto, and was trying to place this large and important area under Roman control.

The protocol of the royal visit, whether improvised or planned, went through without hitch. The king was met a league outside the city by a military guild and choirs with palm and olive branches, showing crosses for reverence 'as the custom is for the exarch or patrician'. The pope received and embraced him in the atrium of St Peter's. The godson of the popes, anointed and proclaimed by them as a child, now hero and victor, had come home to his mother Church, or so the papal biographer is at pains to suggest. Charles asked permission to enter the city to make his further devotions, and oaths were taken by the Romans and Frankish magnates not to attack one another – the need for such oaths makes one wonder if the political realities behind the protocol were quite as friendly and trustful as appeared. The pope's 'ecstasy of astonishment' at Charles's approach may well have amounted to fear that Rome would be stormed and looted. However, he was satisfied of Charles's intentions, and pope and king crossed the Tiber into the city.

On Easter Wednesday the pope got down to diplomatic business, and asked the king to fulfil the 'promise' made by Pippin to Pope Stephen II at Quierzy in 754, a document which he had read to Charles on the spot. The king agreed to do so, and a new document was drawn up, so far as we know in the same terms as the old, subscribed by the king himself and the magnates and sworn to with solemn oaths. One copy was laid on the altar and then in the confession of St Peter and another conserved in the papal archives.

The papal biographer says that the donations specified certain named territories which were to be handed over to the pope or confirmed in his possession, and that these territories occupied a vast area – some two-thirds of Italy. According to his account they were the island of Corsica and the Lombard kingdom south of Luni on the Ligurian coast and of a line drawn through Monte Bardone across the Apennines, through Emilia to Mantua and so north to Monselice. The account also claims that Charles promised not only the exarchate of Ravenna but the provinces of Venetia and Istria. The 'grant' included Pentapolis (the Roman duchy is not mentioned, being already in papal control) and also the Lombard duchies of Spoleto and Benevento i.e. the whole south of Italy save for Sicily and the Greek coastal areas. This claim resembles that of the forged Donation of Constantine, that is: 'the provinces of Italy' and 'the islands'. That these places and boundaries were actually named by Pippin in 754 and Charles in 774 is well established. What we do not know is what they meant by them. It is very likely that the boundaries were those named in earlier treaties made at the beginning of the century or earlier between the Lombards and the empire. Now that imperial authority had vanished they could no longer be a frontier in the full political sense, but they continued to mark the line between Lombards and 'Romans' which Pippin in effect guaranteed. That only frontiers, and not towns, were named in the treaty, seems unlikely; if this was so it was quite different in form from the ninth-century treaties between emperors and popes, which named specific places and regions, as had the promise deposited on the altar of St Peter in 756.

When Charles was in Rome in Easter 774 the political effect of a similar guarantee was different, because the Lombard kingdom, instead of being a continuing menace, was about to be swallowed up by the Franks. When Charles named these frontiers he was in effect guaranteeing that he, as ruler of the Lombard kingdom, was not going to overstep them. On the other hand he was not guaranteeing not to exert political authority outside them – he was creating a 'papal state' perhaps, but not a fully independent one. Imperialists establishing themselves in new territory often begin by guaranteeing to the subject peoples that their separate identity and (especially in the Middle Ages) their law will be respected. This was what Charles was doing, besides implying that in view of the peculiar relationship between popes and the Frankish kingdom he would see that papal estates would be restored to the Holy See. Beyond this he was granting the 'Romans' a sort of autonomy under the popes. But how limited and trammelled that autonomy was stands out in practically every line of Hadrian's correspondence with Charles, with its insistence on the unfulfilled restitutions due to the Holy See.[1]

Up to the beginning of Hadrian's pontificate the popes had gone on granting a measure of recognition to the emperor in Constantinople. The papal chancery last dated its documents by the year of the Byzantine emperor in 772. The election of the popes was formally communicated to the emperors probably until Hadrian.[2] As late as the first year of Hadrian's pontificate, the pope sent malefactors to Constantinople for judgement.[3] The Greek cultural presence in Rome continued on a modest scale in seven or eight Greek monasteries and as many churches; Pope Paul had put Greek monks into his new foundation of San Silvestro (which was also dedicated to St Stephen and St Dionysos), and there were papal foundations for Greek monks in Rome even

---

[1] The 774 settlement is still best dealt with by E. Caspar, *Pippin und die römische Kirche* (Berlin, 1914), pp. 99–145. Cf. also P. Kehr, 'Die sogennante karolingische Schenkung von 774', *HZ*, lxxx (1893), pp. 385–441.

[2] This is the conjecture of O. Bertolini, 'I rapporti di Zaccaria con Constantino V e con Anasvado', etc., *ASR*, lxxviii (3rd ser., ix, 1955), pp. 1–21 (*Scritti Scelti*, pp. 463–84).

[3] *Liber Pontificalis*, i, p. 490.

as late as the following, the ninth century, such as that founded by
Leo IV on the Via Tiburtina. The way in which the Roman Church
took account of the Greeks was attested not only by the mixed Greek and
Roman inscriptions in the deaconry of S. Maria Antiqua, but by the
Greek and Latin tablets of the creed which Hadrian's successor Leo III
placed in St Peter's. But these were the evidences of a dying connection; and though a 'Greek party' may have existed in Rome at the end
of the eighth century, and occasionally is spoken of in the next, its political weight was not great.[1]

But in Italy, while the Lombard thrust had been destroyed forever,
the distant Frankish protector had become an adjacent overlord. The
defeat of Desiderius had opened up, it is true, the possibility of extending
Roman influence over the neighbouring Lombard duchies of Spoleto
and Benevento. But this local advantage was of little account beside the
great issue of the relations of the papacy with Charles. Charles was
already a conqueror in 774: at the head of his undivided kingdom
he had defeated not only the Lombards but also the Saxons. Although
the immense conquests which he was to make could not be predicted, it
was already clear that the pope must be in some sense his dependant.
The question was, how dependent? This was an issue more important
than the territorial position of the pope and the Romans in Italy, an
issue which in the end was that of the papal claim to exercise a 'principate' over the Church. The Byzantine domination, so long as it lasted, had
made the practical vindication of this claim impossible. Now Pope
Hadrian had to ask himself whether the Frankish domination would
have a different result. The relationship which from 800 onwards takes
the name of 'the papacy and the empire' was in effect already in existence. Hadrian's policy in this crucial matter would only be to lean as
heavily as possible on the friendship and protection which Pippin, the
founder of the new Frankish dynasty, had given to the popes, and by
implication at least to emphasise that the legitimacy of the Frankish
kings was based on the Petrine powers. In 774 Charles's great victories
over the Pagans were only beginning. Pope Hadrian constantly suggested
that these victories – over the Saxons, the Muslims, the Frisians, the
Avars – were due to the intercession of St Peter. To Hadrian's good
fortune Charles was a great politician, who recognised that the papacy

---

[1] A. Michel, 'Die griechischen Klostersiedlungen zu Rom bis zur Mitte des 11. Jahrhunderts'.
Ostkirchliche Studien, i (Würzburg, 1952), pp. 32–45; B. Hamilton, 'The City of Rome and
the Eastern Churches in the Tenth Century', *Orientalis Christiana Periodica*, xxvii (1961),
pp. 5–26.

had an important place in the Frankish political system; and eventually he gave it a yet more important one. Had he been a mere war-leader seeking after loot, the subsequent history both of the popes and of Europe would have been very different.

X

Within the limits imposed by King Charles, Pope Hadrian obtained a territorial settlement in Italy which, while it fell far short of what he asked, still amounted to favoured treatment. The three main areas in which he asked for restitution were the exarchate of Ravenna, over which the archbishop exercised political power in defiance of the 754 settlement, and the lands in the duchy of Spoleto and on the Tyrrhenian coast, where Roman claims encroached on the areas controlled by the Lombard Duke of Spoleto and the Greek Duke of Naples. With the last-mentioned claim was connected the papal demand for the restoration of the papal patrimonial estates in the Neapolitan duchy.

To ask whether a papal state was yet in existence is to ask a question without an answer. Many governments existed in the Middle Ages to which one would hesitate to apply the description 'states'. The territorial unit over which the pope rather tentatively presided was not only ill-defined but lacked even a name. The 'rights' or 'property' of the Church (*iura, dicio, ecclesiae*) or the 'restitutions' due to the Church, are as near, at this period, as we can get. It was not yet called, as it later came to be, the 'patrimony' or 'land' of the Church (*patrimonium, terra, ecclesiae*). But Hadrian was not afraid to tell the legitimate sovereign of Italy, the Emperor Constantine VI, that Charles had 'restored by force of arms to the apostle of God, to whom they rightly belonged, provinces, cities, villages and other territories, and also patrimonial possessions, which had been detained by the perfidious Lombard race'. The implied claim of independence from Byzantine sovereignty is clear; and it is not surprising that the same letter includes a quotation from the *Actus Sylvestri*, the source of the forged Constantinian Donation.[1]

With the fall of Pavia and the assumption by Charles of the title of king of the Lombards in the summer of 774, Frankish rule or overlord-

---

[1] J. D. Mansi, *Sacrorum Conciliorum nova et amplissima collectio* (Florence, 1766), xii, cols. 1075–6; P. Jaffé, *Regesta Pontificum Romanorum*, 2nd ed. (Leipzig, 1885), ed. by Ewald, usque ad annum 882, and by Loewenfeld for subsequent years, no. 2442. See also Mansi, xii, cols. 1057–60, and W. Levison, 'Konstantinische Schenkung und Silvester-Legende', *Miscellanea Francesco Ehrle*, ii (Vatican City, 1924), pp. 159–247, at p. 212 (also in Levison, *Aus Rheinischer und Fränkischer Frühzeit* (Düsseldorf, 1948), at p. 434); Fuhrmann, in *DA*, xxii (1966), p. 121.

ship of Italy, save for the Greek areas, became definite. The pope soon
protested violently to Charles that Leo, the Archbishop of Ravenna,
denied him the just exercise of his political rights in the exarchate. In
775 he was alarmed by the complete failure of Charles to recognise
Roman claims over the Lombard duchies of Spoleto and Benevento. He
protested also at the action of the Frankish envoy in travelling there
without even calling at Rome, and in consorting with elements who
planned a *coup d'état* to take over Rome and imprison the pope.

To secure the return of the papal patrimonies in Neopolitan territory
the pope for a time seized the coastal town of Terracina as a pledge. In
alliance with the Lombards of Spoleto the Romans attacked the Neapolitans – the first military campaign in the history of the Papal State –
and Hadrian asked Charles (who did not satisfy him) to attack Gaeta
and Naples on his behalf. In 781 Charles at last re-appeared in Italy,
and visited Rome at Easter. He gave Hadrian only partial satisfaction.
The government of Ravenna and Pentapolis was secured to him – an
easier operation now that Archbishop Leo was dead – and Charles
restored to him the papal estates in Sabina, adjoining the Roman district,
which had been confiscated by the Lombard rulers. A confusion between
Roman landlordship and Roman political rule intruded into the negotiations. In the very document in which Hadrian in 778 addresses Charles
as the 'new Constantine', the pope goes on to use language which makes
it clear that his claims referred to landed estates and not to political rule.[1]
Though the papal claims were basically political they were also
patrimonial, as can be seen from the references to patrimonies in the
texts of the ninth-century pacts between emperors and popes.

The great grievance of Pope Hadrian in these years was the failure
of Charles to intervene against the 'iniquitous' Arichis, the Lombard
'prince' of Benevento. Charles was too cautious for a long time to act
against this powerful magnate, who gave him no overt trouble, and in
any case he was not anxious to encourage Roman claims over the
two Lombard duchies. After Charles's victories over the heathen Saxons
of 786, for which Pope Hadrian ordered thanksgiving throughout the
western Christian world, the Frankish king was again free to visit Italy.
Arichis was now pressed extremely hard. He sent his younger son

[1] *Cod. Car.*, no. 60, p. 587, referring to land in those areas which had been given to the popes
by various 'emperors, patricians and other godfearing persons'. No reference to political
rule seems meant here, as 'patricians and other godfearing persons' had no right to convey it.
That rights in private law were intended is also indicated by the reference to Sabina, which
Hadrian claimed as part of the papal estates. Cf. *Cod. Car.*, no. 69, p. 599. I cannot agree
with Ullmann, *Papal Government*, 3rd ed., pp. 92–3.

Grimoald as a hostage to Charles and promised a heavy tribute for the duchy. At this point both Arichis and his elder son died (August 787). His heir was in Frankish hands, and the moment seemed ripe for a Frankish subjugation of the Beneventan duchy, by which the pope would be a main beneficiary. Once more Hadrian was disappointed. In spite of the pope's urgent plea that a Frankish host fall on the duchy in the coming spring of 788 – not, as he disingenuously explained, because of any territorial greed on his part[1] – Grimoald was returned from Francia to his inheritance, there to become an independent prince.

The pope had, it is true, extracted some important concessions from Charles while the king was in Italy in 787. The most important, or at all events the most permanent in effect, was an extensive grant of towns in Lombard Tuscany, from Città di Castello in the north-east to Orte, Viterbo, Tuscania and the volcanic rock country of south-west Etruria. These towns were to remain for centuries the heart of the papal province called the 'Patrimony of St Peter in Tuscany'. More debatable was the grant to the pope of towns which the Lombard Beneventan dukes had carved from Roman-Byzantine territory in more recent times. On the one hand there were the Beneventan towns on the left of the river Liris (Sora, Arpino, Circe). On the other, the towns commanding the main road from Rome to Capua, and Capua itself. This was a grant, in effect, of a vital military road and a vital military junction, made presumably in order that the Romans might hold the main road into southern Italy on behalf of the Franks; but it was too ambitious a programme for the modest resources of eighth-century Rome. Within a few months the pope was complaining that the authorities of Benevento had handed him over the keys of the cities in question, but had insisted that the population remain Beneventan subjects. 'And of what use are cities', he enquired, 'without their inhabitants?' The transfer of the cities had in fact been a mere show; they remained in Beneventan control.

XI

Rome and its bishops were richer, more powerful, and more secure under Hadrian than any other time in the eighth century.[2] The list of churches, palaces, monasteries, rebuilt or extensively adorned by

---

[1] *Cod. Car.*, no. 80, p. 613, lines 27–32.

[2] Gregory II was hard hit by his payments to Liutprand, and so was Gregory III (731–41), who also had to buy off the Lombards of Spoleto. Gregory III was rich enough to rebuild some Roman churches, and to replace the bronze on the cupola of the Pantheon. Zacharias (741–52) is said by the *Liber Pontificalis* (i, p. 434) to have amassed great treasure, and to

Hadrian, both in Rome and in the Roman district, is by far the longest and most impressive of that of any of the early medieval popes. Charles gave rich gifts to the Roman Church. The English king Offa undertook to make a substantial annual payment to Rome – the origin of the tribute later called 'Peter's pence'. The Holy See began to acquire estates in the Frankish lands. The walls, towers and aqueducts of Rome were not neglected. Hadrian continued and expanded the policy of consolidating the papal estates in the Roman district, and re-grouping the peasants who worked them in larger administrative units termed *domus cultae*, in which the population was more easily available for military and labour service. The most notable of these new *domus cultae* was the huge estate of Capracorum near Veii, which was based on an extensive dona-tion from Hadrian's own family lands. With its own new church built by Hadrian and its own *militia*, Capracorum is an example of a new social and military structure given to the countryside by means of the seigniorial power of the Roman Church. The return to the Church of the Sabine estates, the increased security which the papal estates in Campagna and Pentapolis must have also enjoyed, all contributed to the material power and resources of the Roman See. These had, in spite of the confiscation of the south Italian estates and the tribute paid to the Lombard kings, never fallen below a certain level during the century but they now reached a new stability.

However improved the political position of the popes was, it was always within the limits of Frankish overlordship. In 783 judges from Ravenna who had been guilty of oppression and exporting Christian slaves to Muslim countries fled to the Frankish court and appealed to Charles. It is doubtful if Charles sent them to Rome for judgement,

have begun the policy of consolidating papal estates on a new administrative basis as *domus cultae*. He established these as far away as Anzio and Mola di Gaetà—the last are possibly connected with the exploitation of the nearby estates of Norma and Ninfa, given him by Constantine V. See O. Bertolini, 'La ricomparsa della sede episcopale di "Tres Tabernae" nella seconda metà del sec. VII e l'istituzione delle "domus cultae" ', *ASR*, lxxv (3rd ser., vol. vi, 1952), pp. 102–9; idem, 'Per la storia delle diaconie Romane', ibid. lxx (1947), pp. 122–7; idem, article 'Patrimonio di San Pietro' in *Enciclopedia Cattolica*. Further, E. Sjöqvist, 'Studi archeologici e topografici intorna alla Piazza del Collegio Romano', *Opuscula Archaeo-logica vol. iv edidit Institutum Romanum Regni Sueciae* (Lund, 1946), pp. 47–156; J. Lestocquoy 'Administration de Rome et Diaconies du VIIe au IXe siècle', *Rivista di archaeologia cristiana*, vii (1930), pp. 261–98. But there seems to have been a decline in public works and their endowment under Stephen II (752–7) and his brother Paul (757–67). There is little or no building or economic activity recorded in the troubled pontificate of Stephen III (768–72). An exception, which may have some connection with the forged Constantinian Donation, is Paul's foundation of the Greek monastery of S. Silvestro in Capite. (G. Ferrari, *Early Roman Monasteries* (Rome, 1957), pp. 302–12.)

for in 790–1 the pope is still complaining of men in Ravenna and Pentapolis who deny the sovereignty (*dicio*) of the pope, and flee to Francia
to appeal to Charles. The pope asks that as no Frank is allowed to go to
Rome without permission, so no papal subjects should be allowed without the pope's leave to go to Charles, either on courtesy visits or to seek
justice.[1] But there is no sign that Charles satisfied Hadrian on this point.
Within the judicial and administrative system of the Frankish dominions
the Papal State was a privileged area, but it was within the system
nonetheless.

It was not only on Charles that the stability of the Papal State rested,
but on the balance which Hadrian had achieved between the clerical
and aristocratic elements in Rome. Hadrian can probably be counted
as the first great magnate pope of the Middle Ages. Backed by his family
wealth and lands, he was served in diplomacy and administration by his
lay nephew the *consul et dux* Theodore, and his clerical nephew the
primicerius Pascal. Both he and his dead uncle, the earlier *primicerius,*
had served in the Lateran bureaucracy while retaining their connection
with the aristocracy. Hadrian is a type, and a successful type, who is
repeated on many occasions until the end of the Middle Ages and indeed
for the whole period of the *ancien régime*. As was the case for many such
popes, the papacy was fortunate in his pontificate, but unfortunate in
the reaction which followed his death.

XII

Under Hadrian the new political system of Rome and the Roman
state was not subjected to any real strain. A weak pope would reveal the
true nature of the system, and show how dependent it was on Frankish
power. This revelation was delayed no longer than the next pontificate.
Leo III, who was elected after Hadrian's death in 795, like several of his
predecessors was brought up in the Lateran patriarchate, and was soaked
in the traditions of the Roman clergy. He was not an aristocrat, a fact
which almost proved fatal to him. From the very beginning his attitude
to the Frankish monarchy implied a closer connection and a greater
degree of dependence than that of any previous pope. His first act was
to despatch to Charles the protocol of the election (as had been the use
with the Byzantine emperor), together with a declaration of loyalty,
and the keys and banner of the city of Rome.

Charles expressed himself willing to carry out for Leo the agreement

[1] *Cod. Car.*, nos. 75, 94, and see also no. 86 (787–91).

he had made with Hadrian, and claimed for himself the duty of defending the Church by force of arms against the infidels and pagans without, and of increasing the faith within. To Leo he attributed the duty of prayer for the victory of Christian arms, and of the following and enforcing the holy canons, particularly those relating to simony.[1] His determination to regulate church matters did not exclude Rome: in 797–8 there was a determined attempt by the Frankish court to rebuild and reform the important Roman monastery of S. Paolo fuori le Mura.[2] On the other hand the passive resistance of Leo III seems to have frustrated the idea.

For Leo the issues were precipitated in 799 by a revolution in Rome which almost cost him his life. The aristocratic elements in Rome, particularly the nephew of Hadrian I and some others who had held high office in the former pontificate, seized Leo in the course of a ceremony and attempted to blind and mutilate him. He managed to secure the protection of the Frankish troops in Spoleto, and then in the late summer of 799 he travelled over the Alps to seek Charles, who was campaigning in Saxony, and to ask him for justice.

There is no indication that Charles seized this papal appeal for aid as something for which his policy had been waiting. Leo had to find him in distant Paderborn in Saxony, and though it is probable that negotiations which contemplated Charles's assumption of the imperial dignity took place in Paderborn, they were evidently exploratory and not conclusive.[3] The pope was honourably received, and consecrated churches in Germany; the serious accusations of misconduct and simony which his enemies made against him did not affect this. In the autumn he returned honourably to Rome, with a commission of bishops and officials appointed to enquire into the case. The evidence of royal favour was enough to secure a good reception for Leo III at Rome in November, and his restoral to his normal position – but there the matter rested, with the pope continuing under the grave suspicion which had been cast on him, until a whole year later, in November 800, when the king found time to visit Italy.

---

[1] Alcuin, apud *MGH, Epistolarum*, tom. iv (*Epistolae karolini aevi*, ii) nos. 92–4.
[2] Cf. Ferrari, op. cit., pp. 254–64.
[3] Cf. P. Classen, 'Karl der Grosse, das Papsttum und Byzanz', *Karl der Grosse. Lebenswerk und Nachleben*, W. Braufels (ed.), i (Düsseldorf, 1965), pp. 537–608; H. Beumann, 'Die Kaiserfrage bei den Paderborner Verhandlungen von 799', *Das erste Jahrtausend. Kultur und Kunst im werdenden Abendland an Rhein und Ruhr*, W. H. Elbern (ed.), i (1962), pp. 296–317. Cf. also Beumann, 'Nomen imperatoris. Studien zur Kaiseridee Karls d. Gr.', *HZ*, clxxxv (1958), pp. 515–49.

From the point of view of his Byzantine policy, and from the point of view of the Anglo-Saxon ideas of hegemonial Christian kingship which Alcuin, the Anglo-Saxon scholar in his court, had been urging on him, Charles was interested in assuming the imperial name. Leo's visit to Paderborn had brought these matters to a head, but it is probable that Leo and Charles had failed to reach complete agreement – which is scarcely surprising when the complexity of the issues is considered. Leo's particular interest was that he should be cleared of the accusations against him, and that his accusers should be punished, but for neither of these purposes was it necessary for Charles to assume the imperial title.[1] On 23 December the pope, before a council of Frankish and Italian bishops, declared under oath his innocence of the accusations of his Roman enemies.[2]

The next step was the prosecution of the former revolutionary leaders who had been kept in Frankish custody for over a year. But on Christmas Day, before this had taken place, another and more dramatic event had occurred. Charles went to mass in the basilica of St Peter, perhaps dressed in the *chlamys* of the Roman patrician. When he rose from prayer the pope placed a crown on his head, and the Roman people in the basilica, 'considering how he favoured and defended the Roman Church and its vicar', acclaimed him as emperor, greeting him with the *laudes* or ceremonial acclamatory hymns, with which they had honoured him on former visits to Rome, as king. The pope 'worshipped' him, in the Byzantine fashion of prostration. Finally, the pope proceeded to anoint and crown the king's son, Charles.

Charles had not added new legal powers to his existing rule – even in Rome, his powers as *patricius* were quite sufficient for his political needs. His reasons for assuming the imperial name were complex, and involved many spheres of policy; the politics of Rome and its bishops were only one factor among many. Indeed Charles's motives in submitting to the ceremony of 800 are far less clear than the motives of Pope Leo in imposing it on him. Pope Leo stood to gain by something which enabled the legal condemnation of his assailants. His wish for a

---

[1] Cf. P. E. Schramm, 'Die Anerkennung Karls des Grossen als Kaiser', *HZ*, clxxii (1951), pp. 449–515. H. Fichtenau, 'Karl der Grosse und das Kaisertum', *MIöG*, lxi (1953), pp. 257–334, and W. Mohr, 'Karl der Grosse, Leo. III.' etc., *Bulletin du Cange*, xxx (1960), pp. 39–98, are more sceptical in approach. Much of the immense literature is quoted by Classen in the article cited above, and there is a learned and helpful bibliographical discussion in D. A. Bullough, *'Europae Pater*. Charlemagne and his achievement in the light of modern scholarship', *EHR*, lxxx (1970), pp. 59–105.

[2] Cf. Zimmermann, *Papstabsetzungen* (1968), pp. 26–37, 231.

tight association of the Frankish monarchy with the papacy had already been made plain. When Charles entered the city in 800 Leo had arranged for the banners of Rome to be presented to him, and the *laudes* to be sung, in token of sovereignty. He needed Frankish protection in order to support the integrity of the 'restitutions' made to the Roman See, and also to protect him against the aristocratic faction. How much he was prepared to pay for this protection is something we can never with certainty know. He knew that Hadrian, who enjoyed Charles's personal esteem and friendship and was in a strong position in Rome, had had to pay quite a heavy price in the loss of independence for Frankish support; as one in a weaker position than Hadrian he was presumably prepared to pay a heavier price – though always with the reservation of his loyalty to the tradition of the Roman See.

Leo III survived the events of 800 by sixteen years, Charlemagne by fourteen. During that period Leo III appears as only a secondary figure both in the political history of the West and in the life of the Church. His political standing in Italy was that of the leader of the 'cities of the Romans' – more or less autonomous, but experiencing a great deal of friction with Pippin, the sub-king of Italy and the royal *missi,* with whom the pope had to co-operate, and about whom he frequently complained to the emperor.[1] He also remonstrated with Charles that the royal *missi* in Roman territory had imposed taxes, so that the papal officials were unable to collect the sums due to Leo as ruler.[2]

The long list of donations and restorations in the Roman churches show Leo as a splendid patron and builder. The works of art lavished on the churches, the great halls built in the palaces of the Lateran and of St Peter's, the restoration of Sant'Apollinare in Classe at Ravenna, the reconstruction of S. Paolo fuori le Mura after an earthquake – these things bespeak a rich and proud ruler. The Frankish royal house and the Frankish bishoprics sent rich gifts; Cenwulf of Mercia sent him money, as his predecessor Offa had to Hadrian. Money from Saxon and Frankish pilgrims flowed freely to Rome. But other things show Leo as less secure. His position *vis-à-vis* the rival see of Ravenna was delicate.[3] Already the political and economic problems posed by Arab sea-borne raids on Italy and the Islands were becoming urgent.

---

[1] Caspar, *Das Papsttum unter fränkischer Herrschaft* (Darmstadt, 1956), pp. 147 ff. For the papal *missi* holding court with the imperial *missi* in Tuscany, see C. Manaresi, *I placiti del 'Regnum Italiae'* (Rome, 1955), i, no. 25, p. 77.

[2] *MGH, Epistolarum,* v (*Epistolae karolini aevi,* iii), p. 89.

[3] Ibid. pp. 91, 101.

Leo assured Charles that he had provided for the defence of the coast, but said he was anxious for the security of the Corsican patrimonies of the Church – of the papal claim to rule in Corsica which is contained in the Caroline donation and the *Constitutum Constantini* he breathed no word.[1]

Charles did not reappear in Italy after 800; his business there was done. Leo went once more over the Alps in 804–5 to give Charles information on a doctrinal question, but there was no more political consultation of any great importance. In the important negotiations between Charles and Byzantium over the relations of the two great powers and the two empires, the pope played but a modest part.[2] The See of Rome is named in Charlemagne's will as the first metropolitan of the empire – perhaps it was with conscious irony that Charles in the will left a silver table inscribed with a plan of Constantinople to the basilica of St Peter at Rome, and another with a plan of Rome to the hated rival, the Archbishop of Ravenna. It is extremely hard to see Leo, who described himself as 'the most pusillanimous', as the proud representative of a triumphant papal principle. It is easier to see him as the dignified head of a great bishopric of whose past the Franks were proud – the chief bishopric of the Frankish Empire.

[1] Ibid. pp. 96 ff.
[2] He ratified the treaty with the Byzantines of 812, *Annales Regni Francorum*, Pertz-Kurze (ed.) (Hanover, 1895), p. 136. I am unable to follow all the arguments of W. Ohnsorge, *Das Zweikaiserproblem im früheren Mittelalter* (Hildesheim, 1947), pp. 20–31, or the same author's remarks in his *Abendland und Byzanz* (Darmstadt, 1958), pp. 79–110, 184 ff.

Chapter 2

The successors of Charlemagne

I

In the 'division of the kingdom' between his three sons, which Charlemagne drew up in 806, he states simply what bound him to the Church of Rome. The obligation to defend the Roman Church and its rightful possessions had been handed to him by his father and grandfather, and he now transmitted it to his sons. This obligation, he had said elsewhere,[1] was defined in the treaty between the Frankish kingdom and the Roman Church – the first treaty being that between Pippin and Stephen, which was renewed and modified on many subsequent occasions by later rulers. We know too little about these agreements: the earliest evidence we have is the text of the treaty between Louis the Pious and Paschal I in 817.[2] The texts of Charlemagne's treaties with the Holy See are lost, though the pact of 817 must at least reflect their contents. The papal account in the *Liber Pontificalis* of Hadrian's agreement with Charlemagne is fairly evidently one-sided and incomplete. The letters which Hadrian wrote to Charles about the unfulfilled legal claims of his see – the 'restitutions' or *'iustitiae'* for which it asked – were with important earlier papal letters preserved by Charles's orders. The Frankish side of the correspondence is almost entirely missing. There seems however no reason to believe that Charles thought that the events of 800 had radically altered his relations with the Holy See.

The hub of the Roman problem had been, and continued to be, the party struggles inside the Roman nobility and the Lateran bureaucracy. Political and economic power rested essentially with the Church. But the nobles, who just as much as the Church owed the recovery of their patrimonial lands to the Frankish overlords, were bound to continue to be the main factor in Roman politics. To describe the conflict as one

---

[1] *MGH, Epistolae*, v (*Karolini Aevi*, ii), p. 137.
[2] Cf. E. E. Stengel, 'Die Entwicklung des Kaiserprivilegs für die römische Kirche 817–962', *HZ*, cxxxiv (1926), pp. 216–41 (reprinted with some important additions in his *Abhandlungen und Untersuchungen zur mittelalterlichen Geschichte* (Köln-Graz, 1960), pp. 218–48).

between the nobility and clergy is to over-simplify and distort it, since (as has been said above) the chief magnates were themselves virtually a part of the clergy. The quarrel which emerged at the beginning of the ninth century was rather about the degree to which the administration of the papal estates should be centralised. Since the decay of imperial administration in the seventh century the Church had virtually taken over the responsibility of the central power for the provisioning of Rome. The papal estates which provided the necessary food and money had from their inception been run by a centralised clerical bureaucracy. The withdrawal of imperial power and the triumph of the pro-Frankish clerical bureaucracy meant, on the one hand, the tightening of clerical control of the economic apparatus. But it also opened the way to increased magnate pressure on the administration and to the gradual breaking-down of some (but not all) of the central clerical organisation. Of this two of the most important parts were the diaconates and the *domus cultae*.

By the death of Hadrian I there were eighteen diaconates, which took the place of the old administration of the *annona* or the government corn supply, and the *frumentationes* or corn dole. They were staffed partly by clerks and partly by laymen. Sometimes their titular head (the *pater* or *dispensator*) would be a person of great distinction, such as Theodotus, the *primicerius* under Zacharias (probaby the uncle of Pope Hadrian I), or Eustace the *dux Romae* under Stephen II.[1] By contrast with the outlying or peripheral churches of the cardinal priests, which dated from the time when Christians were not much found in the smart quarters, the diaconates were placed in the most populous areas of the centre of the city. The oldest is possibly S. Maria Antiqua, in the former library of Augustus in the palace facing the Forum, at the foot of the Palatine hill. Six or seven of the diaconates were placed actually in the old imperial offices connected with the corn supply. On the other side of the Palatine hill, S. Teodoro was in the old public granaries, the *horrea Agrippiana*. Nearby at the foot of the Aventine, S. Maria in Cosmedin was built under the ruins of the temple of Ceres, Liber, and Libera, in the former corn supply offices, the *statio annonae*. There was a whole group of diaconates in the Forum: SS. Cosma and Damiano, in the Temple of the Penates by the *Tres Fates*; S. Adriano, in the *Curia Hostilia*; SS. Sergio and Bacco, in the *Rostra*; S. Maria Nuova (later S. Francesca Romana) in the columns before the

---

[1] Cf. O. Bertolini, 'Per la storia delle diaconie romane', etc., *ASR*, lxx (1947), pp. 1–145 (*Scritti Scelti*, pp. 309–456).

temples of Venus and Roma. These churches, on whose steps Gibbon pondered the *Decline and Fall,* were the active heart of early medieval Rome.[1] There was far to go before the Forum became the *Campo Vaccino,* the cowpatch, as it was when Gibbon knew it in the eighteenth century.

The life of the diaconates was both practical and liturgical. When the poor came for the *lusma,* they went in procession, sang hymns, received a ritual washing from the diaconate staff, and only then took their dole. Besides the diaconates there were *xenodochia* or hostels for pilgrims, orphanages, old peoples' homes, hostels for official papal guests, buildings to receive and entertain the *scholae* of foreign pilgrims.

The work of the popes in building, repairing and decorating the city, and assuring its public services, reached a point which it probably did not attain again until the late Renaissance. An important part of this was simply in making safe the old buildings which, already two centuries earlier under Gregory the Great, had begun to collapse through neglect. The diaconate of S. Maria in Cosmedin was threatened by the ruinous state of the overhanging temple of Ceres, Liber, and Libera; Pope Hadrian I set a large labour force to work for a year to demolish the temple by burning its wooden beams, before he reconstructed the church. The unfortunate diaconate of SS. Sergio and Bacco in the Forum was destroyed by the collapse of the temple of Concordia, and had to be rebuilt. The twelve miles circuit of the walls of Rome, and its host of watch-towers, were still kept in repair in the ninth century. The huge system of aqueducts, built to supply a city of two million people with upwards of a hundred million gallons of water a day, could not be maintained; but some were nonetheless kept in use. One branch of the Aqua Marcia – probably the one which had supplied the Baths of Caracalla – was diverted down to the river. It was repaired both by Hadrian I and by Nicholas I (858–67), and under Nicholas was said to supply almost the whole needs of Rome. Several popes, the last of whom was again Nicholas, repaired the branch of the Aqua Traiana which supplied St Peter's and the Janiculum. The Aqua Claudia was another important source, which supplied the Lateran. Hadrian I carried out important works on it with the help of labour gangs from the peasantry in the Campagna, and so did Paschal I.[2]

The economic basis for this intense activity had to be a broad one.

[1] R. Valentini and G. Zucchetti, *Codice topografico della città di Roma* (Rome, 1942), ii.
[2] Ibid. and also I. A. Richmond, *The City Wall of Imperial Rome* (Oxford, 1930); T. Ashby, *The Aqueducts of Ancient Rome,* I. A. Richmond (ed.), (Oxford, 1935).

An important part of it was the new organisation of papal estates in *domus cultae,* which had been begun by Zacharias and extended and strengthened by Hadrian and Leo III. The *domus cultae* were virtually new settlements up to twenty miles in diameter, with sometimes (as in the case of Hadrian's foundation of Capracorum) their own considerable churches. Their organisation was novel, because more centralised, though they probably in most cases represented new administrative groupings and not new land settlements; the lands within a *domus culta* continued to be attributed to individual Roman churches, except when the popes who set them up added new estates. The building activity of the Holy See outside Rome was not great, and Leo III's major works at Ravenna are exceptional. So also was the papal villa which Gregory IV (824–44) constructed near his new town at Ostia. But the general effect of the *domus cultae* was to increase not only the economic power of the Roman clergy, but also their social and even military power. The produce of Capracorum was by Hadrian's orders distributed separately at the Lateran, through what seems to be a separate charity organisation. The organised peasantry of the papal estates, sometimes under the name of the *familia sancti Petri,* had been a force in the turbulent politics of the last three decades of the eighth century and continued to be so into the ninth. In times of political crisis they could act as a counterbalance to the 'Roman army' and frustrate noble influence.

II

The Roman council of 769 had said that the pope should be elected by the senior clergy of Rome, disregarding the part which tradition gave to the Roman people – and so to the Roman nobles. Certainly this gave the cardinal priests and suburbicarian bishops a constitutional position superior to that of the nobles, and also in a sense to that of the six main bureaucratic officers, the *iudices ordinarii* or *iudices de clero* who, until the tenth century at any rate, were normally only in minor orders. On the other hand, this body of officials, which is sometimes taken to be exclusively clerical, was itself composed, very often if not usually, of members of the highest aristocracy. The history of the papal officials disgraced by John VIII[1] makes it quite clear that even if the *primicerius,* the *secundicerius,* the *nomenclator* and *vestararius* and others were in minor orders, they were in fact married noblemen, who in this case used their official positions ruthlessly for their own profit. The balance be-

[1] For John VIII see p. 67 below.

tween lay and clerical elements in the government was thus very delicately adjusted. The *iudices de clero* were often laymen, and their influence combined with that of the *iudices dativi* or lay judges was formidable.[1] But papal authority lay over all proceedings, and many of the state trials of the period were conducted as church synods. Papal rule was not soft; it was rather harsh. From Hadrian's time onwards there are frequent references to exiles and refugees from papal justice; the question of whether they should be given asylum in Frankish territory was one of the standard ones to agitate Frankish-papal relations. There were also confiscations of land and property from those exiled or condemned.

It is not surprising, then, that the troubles of the early years of Leo III's pontificate were repeated in the last. In 815 there was said to have been a plot by Roman nobles against the pope's life, as a result of which the supposed instigators were executed at Leo's orders. The new emperor, Louis, took the executions ill, although he professed himself satisfied with the explanations of a papal mission. Before things could develop further, Leo died. His death caused serious riots and disturbances; the re-organised papal estates in the countryside (the *domus cultae*) were burned by the Romans, and property said to have been confiscated by his government was violently taken back by its supposed owners. The Anglo-Saxon scholar in the Frankish court, Alcuin, had frequently referred to the ungovernable temper of these Romans, whom he called the 'disgraceful people' (*iniquus populus*). For the next few years they repeatedly showed their temper, in defiance of the government and of the Frankish *missus*.

Elected in these delicate political conditions, the next pope, Stephen IV, hurried to Francia to get royal support. This he obtained; he also obtained from Louis the confirmations of the Frankish guarantees of the papal political position in Italy, probably with additions designed to strengthen the pope's position in Rome against the turbulent nobles. It may have been a good moment for the pope to exert pressure of this sort on Louis, because the Franks who had ruled Italy in the preceding decades and had tended to take a firm line against papal claims, were now in disgrace or eclipse. Wala, a member of the Frankish royal house, who had had great power in Italy until Charlemagne's death, had been with his brother Adalard thrust from office at the beginning of

---

[1] T. Hirschfeld, 'Gerichtswesen der Stadt Rom vom 8. bis 12. Jahrh.', *Arch. f. Urk.*, iv (1912), pp. 419–562, at pp. 449–62. J.E.3366 was accepted by Hirschfeld, but has been shown by S. Kuttner to be an eleventh-century forgery. 'Cardinalis: the history of a canonical concept', *Traditio*, iii (1945), pp. 129–214, at pp. 193–6. Cf. C. G. Fürst, *Cardinalis. Prolegomena zu einer Rechtsgeschichte des römischen Kardinalskollegiums* (Munich, 1967), p. 72.

Louis's reign in 814. The emperor's nephew Bernard, the King of Italy, was probably already alienated from his uncle, and beginning to drift towards the rebellion which he undertook in 818. Under these circumstances Stephen IV was able to get favourable terms, which were defined or repeated in the treaty which was sent to Paschal I who succeeded Stephen early in 817.

The 817 treaty is the first well-authenticated document to define the temporal power of the popes and their relations with the Frankish monarchy.[1] Although it lists places and areas, and does not try to mark off a frontier for the Papal State, we know from the 'division of the kingdom' of 806 that a frontier was considered to exist.[2]

The frontier of 817 reflects the cutting down by Charlemagne of Hadrian I's original ambitious claims. It ran from the Tyrrhenian coast at Massa Marittima (Populonia) and Rosella north of Lake Orbetello and inland south of Lake Trasimene, thus including a large part of Lombard Tuscany, but running far south of the early Roman claims. It included the Via Amerina, which skirted the important castle of Gallese, and went through Amelia to Perugia to rejoin the Via Flaminia by way of Gubbio, at Scheggia. This was a 'Roman' corridor across the Apennines through Fossombrone and Urbino in order to communicate with the exarchate of Ravenna, which with Pentapolis is again assigned to papal jurisdiction. The pact says explicitly that this jurisdiction is to be the same as that exercised by the pope in Rome and its duchy. Near Rome, the grant of the small mountain area of Sabina and Rieti was maintained: this was the only part of Charlemagne's grant of the duchy of Spoleto actually assigned to the popes. Apart from this they ruled 'Campagna' as far south as the river Garigliano. The papal patrimonies in the duchy of Naples are also mentioned in the guarantee.[3] A section of the grant which corresponded less well with the political facts was the renewal of the grant of Capua and the road leading to it, which in fact remained firmly in the control of Sicon of Benevento.

Louis the Pious made far-reaching concessions to Pope Paschal. He expressly promised not to encroach on the powers of jurisdiction and administration (*dispondendi vel iudicandi*) in the area assigned to the pope, except at the pope's request. He also promised to grant extradition

---

[1] T. Sickel, *Das Privilegium Ottos I. für die römische Kirche* (Innsbruck, 1882).

[2] *MGH, Capitularia*, i, p. 126.

[3] Cf. J. Gay, 'L'Etat pontifical, les Byzantins et les Lombards sur le littoral campanien', *Mélanges*, xxi (1908), pp. 487–508.

of political refugees and fugitives from justice from the Papal State.[1] And finally, in a clause which in effect was directed against the Roman nobility, he guaranteed not to intervene in papal elections, which under the terms of the Council of 769 thus remained reserved to the higher Roman clergy. The election having been made, the new pope was not obliged to notify the Frankish ruler of his election until after his consecration.

The agreement of 817 was an extremely liberal definition of the terms of the Frankish protectorate. Louis the Pious had loyally carried out the instructions of Charlemagne to his sons in the division of 806 to protect the Roman Church and its rights in so far as was reasonable. The essence of the political position of the popes was their protected status. As an inevitable consequence, the papacy could not hope to avoid interference from the protecting power from the moment that its own internal leadership was in question. This was the lesson of 799, to be repeated endlessly throughout the Middle Ages. Paschal I, no less than Leo III, came into conflict with the Roman nobility and acquired, deservedly or not, a reputation for harshness and injustice. The opposition in Rome gained friends in the papal bureaucracy, and won over two of its most distinguished figures, Theodore the *primicerius* and his son-in-law Leo. Theodore had carried out several important diplomatic missions to the Frankish court, where he enjoyed the reputation of being firmly pro-Frankish.

Early in 824 Paschal carried out a *coup d'état* against Theodore and Leo; calling in the rural militia, the *familia sancti petri,* from the papal estates he had the two men blinded and executed.[2] But the Frankish political climate was no longer favourable to this sort of independent papal action. Louis had sent his eldest son Lothar to Italy and Lothar, at Paschal's invitation, had come to Rome in the spring of 823 to be

---

[1] An important exception was that men were allowed to appeal to the Frankish government against the oppression of over-powerful magnates (*potentiores*) in Roman territory. It is evident that the public powers granted to the popes were limited. Extradition had always been a thorny question: cf. *MGH, Capitularia,* i, p. 201, and *Cod. Car.,* no. 51, p. 573, lines 3–24; nos. 75, 94, pp. 605, 632.

[2] W. Ullmann, 'The origins of the Ottonianum', *Cambridge Historical Journal,* xi (1953–5), pp. 114–28, at pp. 124–5 dismisses these events as 'a disturbance which on no account can be taken as constituting an oppression carried out against the Roman populace'. But cf. K. Hampe, 'Die Berufung Ottos des Grossen nach Rom durch Papst Johann XII.', *Historische Aufsätze, Karl Zeumer zum 60. Geburtstage* (Weimar, 1910), pp. 153–67, at pp. 161–2. The *Annales Regni Francorum,* Pertz-Kurze (ed.), (1895), ad a.824, p. 166, have: 'statum populi Romani iam dudum quorundam praesulum perversitate depravatum . . . ut omnes, qui rerum suarum direptione graviter fuerant desolati . . . '; and the Ottonianum attributes 'inrationales asperitates' to the popes (Sickel, p. 181).

crowned emperor. Wala, who in the past had been associated with an active policy in Italy, was now re-instated in favour after his earlier disgrace, and accompanied Lothar. A policy of the assertion of Frankish rights in Italy now became probable. In 823 Lothar heard a case between Paschal and the great Sabine monastery of Farfa, in which the young emperor virtually quashed the submission which Farfa had made to the Holy See in 817, and asserted its status as a royal protected monastery in a manner far from careful of Paschal's dignity. This new Frankish government in Italy was not likely to look kindly on the execution of the pro-Frankish Theodore, and it did not. Nevertheless, it reluctantly accepted Paschal's *fait accompli,* after he had purged himself of the murders by an oath before a great number of bishops, to whom he defiantly announced that the murdered men were guilty of treason and deserved their death.

Very shortly afterwards Paschal died, and his death was the signal for a strong reaction, first on the part of the Roman opposition and then on that of the Frankish protectorate. Paschal's successor Eugenius II, who seems to have been elected at the instance of the Frankish magnate Wala, was also the candidate of the Roman nobility. The Roman notables who had been in exile in Francia returned, and the Lateran patriarchate was compelled to restore their confiscated property. Finally the Frankish government issued and persuaded Eugenius to accept the so-called *constitutio Romana,* which represented a complete reversal of the policy towards the Holy See expressed in the treaty of 817. The new law, which is said by the Frankish chronicles to have been occasioned by papal mis-government, was an energetic assertion of Frankish rights of administration and justice in Rome. It first stipulates that persons under the special protection of the pope or the emperor are inviolable – this presumably to avoid further judicial murders of Frankish partisans like Theodore. The Romans are to choose which law they prefer among Roman, Frankish or Lombard, thus giving the Roman nobles the opportunity to escape from the harsh administration of Roman law by papal officials. The Roman magistrates are to present themselves to the emperor so that he may identify and admonish them. Two permanent *missi,* one imperial and one papal, are to be set up in Rome, so that Roman cases may in the last resort be referred back to the emperor. Finally and perhaps most important, the election of the pope is to be made by the Romans, both nobles as well as clergy – thus in effect annulling the provision of the council of 769 which reserved the election to the upper clergy. When the pope acceded, the Romans had to

C*

take an oath of loyalty to the Frankish government, and the pope had to swear to rule with equity in Rome (*pro conservatione omnium*).[1]

The *constitutio Romana* is a vigorous assertion of Frankish sovereignty. It also affected the relations between the popes and the Roman nobility, which in almost every clause it influenced in favour of the latter. The two permanent *missi* were in fact kept in Rome in the ninth century though they were sometimes chosen from among local notables. Sitting in the imperial palace which adjoined St Peter's, the imperial *missus* was a permanent reminder of Frankish power, even when he found it hard to uphold it. But the Roman nobility were always present, always pressing their demands, always anxious to overturn the unpopular papal *domus cultae* and to make the Lateran patriarchate grant them church lands for low rents. How the constitution of 824 worked against the pope and encouraged the independence of the great landowners and the great landowning corporations, was shown when five years later the two *missi* in Rome heard another case between the pope and the abbey of Farfa about some disputed lands. The decision again went against the pope, and although Gregory IV announced his intention of appealing to the emperor, the *missi* put the abbey in possession.[2]

III

The collapse of Byzantine naval power in the western Mediterranean exposed the coasts of Italy, France and Spain to attack from a number of Arab centres.[3] The early years of the ninth century had seen the growth of a number of new Muslim powers in North Africa, with strong maritime interests and aggressive instincts. The Aglabid dynasty in Tunisia

---

[1] The text, *MGH, Capitularia*, i, no. 161, pp. 322–4. Bertolini, 'Osservazioni sulle "Constitutio Romana" e sul "Sacramentum" ' etc., *Studi A. de Stefano* (Palermo, 1956), pp. 43–78, and in *Scritti Scelti*, pp. 705–38, has argued against the thesis maintained by Ullmann, in the article cited in note above, that the papal oath of 824 was falsified in 963. Bertolini's refutation of Ullmann has been generally accepted. Cf. Stengel, *Abhandlungen und Untersuchungen*, p. 223n.; H. Zimmermann, 'Das Privilegium Ottonianum von 962 und seine Problemgeschichte', *MIöG*, Ergbd. xx (1962), pp. 147–90, at p. 188; L. Santifaller, *Zur Geschichte des Ottonischen-Salischen Reichskirchensystems*, 2nd ed. (Vienna, 1964), p. 158; F. Kempf, in *Handbuch der Kirchengeschichte*, iii, pt. 1 (1966), p. 238n.

[2] C. Manaresi, *I Placiti del 'Regnum Italiae'*, i (1955), no. 38, p. 118; for Leo the imperial *missus* see Bullough in *Le Moyen Age* (1961), pp. 219–45, at p. 225.

[3] W. Ohnsorge, *Abendland und Byzanz* (Weimar, 1958), pp. 148–82; A. A. Vasiliev, *Byzance et les Arabes* (Brussels, 1935–50), i, pp. 127–37, 143–4; F. Dölger, *Byzanz und die europäische Staatenwelt* (Speyer, 1953), pp. 330 ff. G. Lokys, *Die Kämpfe der Araber mit den Karolingern bis zum Tode Ludwigs II.* (Heidelberg, 1906) is still useful, and M. Amari, *Storia dei Musulmani di Sicilia*, C. A. Nallino (ed.) (Catania, 1933–9) remains fundamental.

and the Idrisi in Morocco were particularly dangerous for Sicily and southern Italy. These were not the 'pirates' which European history books frequently name the Arab raiders of this period, but highly organised powers.

The history of Arab attack on Sicily is hardly less old than that of the Arab conquest of North Africa; the first major attack was the fleet sent by Musa ibn Nusayr in 704–5, and attacks across the narrow straits of Bizerta had been intermittent throughout the eighth century. Soon after the beginning of the ninth century the continuing weakness of Byzantium and the beginnings of weakness in the empire of Charlemagne encouraged a more intense pressure, which affected Frankish Italy. From 805 onwards attacks on Sardinia, Corsica and the islands mounted in violence. Small Frankish fleets were sent out, with limited success, and in 812 Wala had been sent to Italy in order to co-ordinate military action throughout Frankish Italy against the Arab raids. Leo III was involved both in the defence of the Latin coasts, and in acting as an intermediary in reporting to the emperor the Muslim policies of the Byzantine Duke of Naples.[1]

Eight hundred and twenty-seven was a disastrous year for the Christians in the Mediterranean. Crete fell to the Andalusians who had just been expelled by the Abassid government from Alexandria. In Frankish Spain Cerdaña was ravaged and Barcelona besieged. And in Tunis a *jehad* or holy war was preached against Sicily by the talented Persian *qadi* of Kairouan, Abu Abdullah Asad ibn al-Furat ibn Sinan. No major town was taken by the Arab forces in Sicily for over four years after the great attack of 827 – not until the fall of Palermo in 831. But enough bricks were dislodged for the wall of the Christian coastal defences to begin to collapse. After the initial stages of the Sicilian campaign the Aglabid forces in Sicily began to accept help from Muslims all over the Mediterranean – in particular from the Balearic Islands and Spain, and from Crete. Asad, who had executed his men when they proposed to leave Sicily and to treat the expedition as an ordinary raid, had not lived to see his venture become one of the last major territorial gains of Islam from 'Rome'.

The multiplication of coastal raids was at once felt. Nothing encouraged the Arabs so much as Christian disunity – it was indeed the Byzantine pretender Euphemios who had called them into Sicily in 827. Now in 835 Naples called in the 'Saracens' (the 'sons of Hagar') to help them against the Lombard duchy of Benevento. Neapolitan galleys,

[1] *MGH, Epistolae*, v (*Karolini Aevi*, iii), p. 585.

within a few years, were helping the Arabs in the siege of Byzantine
Messina. Even more serious was the civil war in the Lombard duchy
itself, which led to both Radelchis and his opponent Siconulf calling on
different Arab forces for help. As a result, between 838 and 842 practically the whole of southern Italy was invested by Arab forces. Radelchis
in 839–40 allowed the Berber Khalfun to take Bari, which thereupon
became the most important of the mainland Arab bases. Siconulf in
reply called in the Arabs from Crete, and allowed them to occupy
Taranto; and finally another Arab force under 'Massar' took Benevento,
and invested the whole of the Garigliano area.

Both the coasts and the hinterland, particularly where it could be
attacked from bases like Bari and Benevento, were pitilessly plundered.
The Arabs operating in the upper Liris devastated the lands of the
great monasteries – the environs of Monte Cassino and San Vincenzo al
Volturno, and in 846 Subiaco. The Adriatic coast and the marches of
Fermo and Camerino received the same treatment. Three Frankish
monks of Farfa went to the Abruzzi to preach to the Muslims; one of
them was placed in charge of the government of the area by the
emperor. But these witnesses of the common faith of Franks and Romans
fared badly; the Arab raiders butchered them. The coastal area round
Rome was raided: Civitavecchia (Centumcellae) had been destroyed
early in the century and now it was the turn of the other coastal towns.

The economic effects of these attacks have to be measured over the
long term of a century and more of intermittent Arab piracy and war.
Certainly the Roman people, both lay and clergy, lost very heavily, but
it is far from certain that we should place more than a part of the blame
on these Arab raids for the economic decline of southern Italy which
was so apparent in the later Middle Ages. The location of many of the
patrimonial estates of the Roman Church in the Campagna makes it
almost certain that in the eighth and early ninth centuries the ancient
drainage and irrigation systems of Latium were still substantially in use.
Areas like Ninfa, 'Tres Tabernae', and Formia and the hinterland of
Terracina would not have been reckoned important and valuable possessions at this time if this was not so. Malaria was certainly not yet the
scourge that it later became, because the malarial swamps of the Roman
District did not yet exist. It is true that over much of south Italy grazing
had already since the sixth century displaced cultivation, and goats
probably did quite as much damage to farming as the Saracens. The
Arabs brought commerce to Naples and the southern cities, as well as
devastation to the countryside. The long-term economic effects of their

raids were less drastic than was once thought. In the longer perspective the political collapse of the Carolingian world and the feudalisation of its society were probably more important factors in economic decline than these external ones.

Not until three-quarters of the way through the ninth century – that is to say when papal and Frankish rule in Italy were facing their final collapse – was the economic strain really seriously felt in Rome. At the beginning of the century the city was the religious centre of a great empire, and the object of pilgrimage from as far away as Britain and Ireland. Paschal I (817–24) increased the number of pilgrims by his policy of bringing in the relics of the martyrs from outlying churches and catacombs, and displaying them in churches in the centre of the city. Paschal, like Hadrian I and Leo III, was a builder, and his face may still be seen in the mosaics of his three churches of S. Cecilia, S. Prassede and S. Maria in Domnica; while in the luxurious 'chapel of Paradise', which he built in honour of his mother Theodora in the Church of S. Prassede, the mosaics include a portrait of his mother, and a representation of his episcopal throne, the see of Peter. His successors also built – Gregory IV (827–44) reconstructed the great basilica of S. Maria in Trastevere; Sergius II (844–7) reconstructed S. Silvestro and S. Martino dei Monti. The last great builder was Leo IV (847–55), the constructor of the Leonine city, whose most important religious building was the Church of the SS. Quattro Incoronati, the last great church of the ninth century.[1] It is significant that this church also, in which Leo IV's basilica can still be seen under the reconstructions after the Normans burned it in 1084, was a centre of devotion to St Silvester, who might after the fabrication of the Constantinian Donation be considered the special patron of the theocratic pretensions of the Holy See.

The 'new' building of eighth- and ninth-century Rome was reconstruction. Hadrian I's work at Capracorum was the re-handling of an ancient villa; Leo III at Ravenna, Paschal I at S. Prassede and Gregory IV at S. Maria in Trastevere at Rome – these popes merely re-built the old churches. There was pictorial art in plenty – much of it called into being by the Roman reaction to Greek iconoclasm. While sometimes rather wooden in execution, it was in detail of great magnificence and splendour. The frescoes of the time of Pope Zacharias in S. Maria Antiqua, the great mosaics of Paschal I in the apses of S. Maria in

---

[1] G. Matthias, *Le Chiese di Roma dal IV al X secolo* (Rocca San Casciano, 1962), pp. 228 ff. He conjectures an increase in population in the eighth century, with a consequent increase in building on the periphery of the city (p. 249).

Domnica and S. Prassede, all have the spaciousness and grandeur of the Roman view of life. Placed beside its humanistic sixth-century model at SS. Cosma and Damiano the S. Prassede mosaic is stationary and stiff, but it does not lack dignity or force.

The smaller things are better realised and more satisfying: the reliquaries of jewelled silver, the processional crosses, the golden and jewel-encrusted icons.[1] Here again, what survives of the work of Paschal I's time is the most impressive. The dazzling little mosaics in Paschal's own 'chapel of Paradise' in S. Prassede are more beautiful than the great mosaic composition in the apse. The enamelled cross of the same date from the Lateran *sancta sanctorum,* with its tenderly rounded scenes of the nativity and childhood of Christ, is one of the most beautiful works of art of the Middle Ages.

There are also still in existence from Paschal's time fragments of Persian and other oriental fabrics which testify to eastern importation into ninth-century Rome of luxury materials – less utilitarian than the imported Egyptian papyrus on which the popes wrote their correspondence. But the few wretched fragments which have survived in corners for twelve centuries can give us hardly a remote glimpse of the decorative splendours described in the *Liber Pontificalis.* Page after page lists the gifts of the pontiffs to the Roman churches, and describes a splendour which could only have been provided by a rich and flourishing society with the power to purchase widely abroad: the huge figured curtains which decorated the doors of the churches and hung between the columns of the nave; the gold-embroidered altar-cloths of silk with the Biblical 'histories' worked on them; the sumptuously worked and jewelled liturgical vestments. The *Liber Pontificalis* records only the gifts of the popes, and makes little mention of the gifts of the Frankish emperors and magnates, none of those of the pilgrims who came from all over the Frankish and Anglo-Saxon world; the glories of the Roman churches at this time must have been a wonder which compared with, if they did not rival, those of Byzantium. Until the mid-ninth century the flood of gifts continued: Leo IV made 'splendid gifts to the holy places'; then in a few years, as the Arab pressure rose, the river contracted to a miserable trickle.

If its economic effects have been exaggerated, there is no doubt of the political importance of the Arab threat. In Italy it was divided and sporadic – had it been better concentrated and organised it is hard to see how south Italy could have failed to share the fate of Sicily. Not

[1] C. Cecchelli, *La Vita di Roma nel Medio Evo* (Rome, 1960), i.

only the Carolingians but the Byzantines were too weak to react in an adequate way to the Arab pressure in the west. In Asia Minor things went badly, and in 838 Amorium, the home of the Byzantine dynasty, fell to the Abassid armies. The Emperor Theophilus looked for help where he could find it. In 839 he sent embassies both to Louis the Pious and to the Umayyad caliph at Cordova.[1] The marriage of the Frankish Louis II with a Byzantine princess was suggested, and combined Frankish-Byzantine operations were contemplated, probably in North Africa. The Byzantine *patricius* Theodosius Babutzikos was in Venice in the new year of 840 for further negotiations with the Franks, and was probably at the Frankish court yet again in the summer of 842 at Trier. A papyrus fragment of a Frankish letter to the Greeks about these negotiations has survived. But they were doomed to run into sand; the Frankish civil wars and the succession question had reached a crisis, and the peril of barbarian raids in the north of the empire was quite as serious if not more so than the Arab threat in the south. Neither Louis the Pious nor Lothar was in a position to undertake grandiose military plans in the Mediterranean. Messina fell in 842, thus putting the whole of western Sicily into Muslim hands. Frankish power in Italy continued to decline.

IV

Gregory IV died in 844; his last years were overshadowed by the Arab threat, which he tried to fend off by the fortification of Ostia. His successor Sergius II was a Roman noble, of the same family as Stephen IV, and as the later ninth-century Pope Hadrian II. The election of Sergius was disputed, but he prevailed over the counter-election of the deacon John through the support of the Roman nobility. What followed repeated, with minor variations, the events of twenty years earlier. Lothar refused to be satisfied with the protocol announcement of the election, which had taken place in the absence of his *missi*, and sent his son Louis II and his bastard Bishop Drogo of Metz, to investigate it. The Frankish army invaded the Papal State; from its entry into papal territory near Bologna it burned and plundered as far as the environs of Rome. Louis was at first refused entry into the city, and the pope refused also to allow the Roman nobles to take an oath of allegiance to Louis. As the pope interpreted the constitution of 824, the Romans were

[1] E. Levi Provençal, 'Un échange d'ambassades entre Cordoue et Byzance au IX siècle', *Byzantion*, xii (1937), pp. 1–24.

obliged to swear fealty to the conqueror but not to his son (this in spite of the fact that Louis had been exercising royal powers in Italy for three or four years). So the pope and the bishops swore fealty to Lothar, the papal election was confirmed, and the pope crowned Louis as king of the Lombards – though by what right he did this is unclear.

Before Louis left Rome, a visitor arrived whose presence was of some significance for Frankish policy. Siconulf of Benevento appeared and offered Louis a large bribe for Frankish investiture with the duchy. There were no immediate consequences, but the incident pointed to the increasing Frankish interest in the Italian south.

The brief pontificate of Sergius (844–7) was an unhappy one. After a short time the pope was completely incapacitated by gout, and the real ruler of Rome was his unpopular brother Benedict. It is hard to tell from the biased account in the papal chronicle just what Benedict's crimes amounted to. His power rested on the combination of Frankish with papal authority; he seems to have managed to persuade the emperor to appoint him to the offices of both imperial and papal *missus* in Rome; to this cumulation of secular offices he added the bishopric of Albano. He is said to have ruled absolutely and despotically, allowing no appeal either to the pope or the emperor. If we can believe the papal chronicler he plundered the monasteries and pious foundations – though it may be that he simply neglected Rome in favour of the papal estates in the Campagna.[1]

But by far the worst failure of Benedict's government was its omission to act on the warning of the Frankish count in Sardinia, in the summer of 846, that a major Arab raid on Rome was imminent. About seventy-three ships landed a force estimated at 11,000 men including 500 horse, which on 23 August overpowered the newly built defences and captured Ostia. Both the Romans and the Franks were taken completely by surprise. The Romans somewhat unfairly sent the foreign *scholae* of Frisian, Frankish and Saxon pilgrims into the front line at Porto. They then retreated to the city, and left the unfortunate foreigners to be cut to pieces. The Arab force then pressed down the right bank of the Tiber down the Via Aurelia, where traces of the battles remained in the local place names for the rest of the Middle Ages. On 27 August they sacked St Peter's, which lay undefended without the walls. The great treasures of the church, which we know from the papal records to have been beyond description magnificent, were looted, as was the Confession of St Peter itself, the greatest and holiest shrine in Christendom. It was

[1] Cf. *Liber Pontificalis*, ii, p. 97.

cupidity which above all inspired the sack; but although it was not at this time usual for Muslims to desecrate Christian churches for the sake of desecrating them, excavation has revealed that the tomb of the apostle was wantonly smashed.[1] This was not a casual raid, but the operation of a large army which must have been carefully planned by the Aglabid government. No doubt it arranged the expedition with full consciousness of the moral shock which it would give to Christendom, and took care that the great Christian shrine should be desecrated as well as robbed.

After the sack of St Peter's, the Roman army under a few Frankish leaders was badly mauled in Prati (the *campus Neronis*), and the rest of Rome outside the Aurelian walls was pillaged, including the great basilica of St Paul. An attempt was made to storm the city which failed. What happened after this is obscure. It seems that a Frankish force appeared and pursued some of the Arabs deep into the Campagna, only perhaps to meet afterwards with a check. Another part of the invading force, which had re-embarked and landed at Gaeta, was also dislodged. The Frankish army, perhaps led by Louis himself, had at least reacted to the attack, even if it failed to avenge it. At all events the Christians had the satisfaction that the returning Arab fleet was overwhelmed by a storm and sunk in the straits of Messina.

Christendom had been hurt at its head, and although the political unity of the Christian empire was now weak, its sense of religious unity was strong. The far-off memory of the struggle with the Saracens in 846 survived in the *chansons de gestes* down to the later Middle Ages. The immediate political effect of the sack of St Peter's was also considerable. The Romans, who had hitherto been resentful of the Franks, had to turn to them again for protection. The Frankish monarchy, which was also having to deal with the Arabs in Provence and elsewhere, had to treat southern Italy from now on as a major centre of war. Lothar, in the following year,[2] said that the sack was on account of his sins and particularly because of his allowing the desecration of churches – perhaps he was thinking of the invasion of the Papal State by his son Louis in 844. He also said that if the Saracens were allowed to hold

---

[1] P. Lauer, 'Le poème de la destruction de Rome et les origines de la cité Léonine', *Mélanges.* xix (1899), pp. 307–61. Damage to the tomb of the Apostle, J. Toynbee and J. Ward Perkins. *The Shrine of St Peter* (London, 1956), pp. 227–9; E. Kirschbaum, *The Tombs of St Peter and St Paul* (1959), pp. 162–3.

[2] *MGH, Capitularia*, ii, pp. 65–7. Cf. R. Poupardin, in *Le Moyen Age*, 2nd ser., x (1906), pp. 1–26, 245–74, ibid. xi (1907), pp. 1–25, in appendix; L. Dupraz, *Zeitschrift f. Schweiz. Geschichte* (1936), xvi, pp. 241–93.

Benevento they would then spread into the Papal State ('Romania') and thence into the rest of Italy. He therefore organised a major expedition against the Arabs under Louis, to start operations in the early spring of 848. He also ordered a general tax to be imposed throughout his lands towards the construction of fortifications round St Peter's.

By the time this capitulary was issued, Pope Sergius was dead. His successor Leo IV was elected in a single day and consecrated in haste, because of the still imminent Arab threat. Pope Leo proved to be a strong and rich ruler. His churches have already been mentioned. The great wall round St Peter's to which all Frankish Christendom contributed, was completed in six years; the area within the new enceinte has been known ever since as the Leonine city. The huge tufa blocks of the Leonine wall remain as evidence that Rome could still build; the contribution of the papal estates in the Campagna to the wall is still vouched for by a couple of surviving inscriptions. Leo restored the walls of the city also, and built or re-built some fifteen towers. Porto was re-fortified. Near Centumcellae on the coast he built a new fortified enclosure to re-house the long displaced population – the walls can still be seen among the Maccarese vineyards. But the rehoused citizens preferred their old site, and after a time they left 'Leopolis' again for the 'Civita vecchia'.

In 848 the Frankish expedition to south Italy planned in the preceding year took place. It was a considerable affair, with naval support supplied on the Adriatic coast by the Venetians and the papal ships in Pentapolis, and on the Tyrrhenian side by the Neapolitans. It was successful, the Arab leader 'Massar' was captured and executed by Louis. Through Frankish mediation the two contestants for the duchy of Benevento at last came to terms, and Siconulf and Radelchis divided the duchy into the principalities of Benevento and Capua – a frontier which remained in one form or another for most of the Middle Ages.

In 849 a fresh Arab attack followed from Sardinia. No Frankish forces were available, and the only allies to present themselves were the Neapolitans, who as the rivals of Rome in Campagna and as the allies of the Arabs in most of the campaigns since 845 did not inspire much confidence. However, the Roman and Neapolitan ships attacked the new Arab invasion fleet; God sent them a Christian wind, and they destroyed it. Those Arabs who were not crucified or imprisoned were sent to work on the new fortifications of St Peter's, on the Leonine wall.

In spite of the success of this independent Italian defence, the Frankish protectorate was something which Pope Leo could not treat lightly.

But he was a dignified and respected figure, well able to press his own case at the Frankish court. He had to deal both with a Roman opposition and with the recalcitrant Archbishop of Ravenna, who with his brother Gregory, the Duke of Emilia, had pretty well excluded papal government from the exarchate. The Franks listened to the discontented elements and made it difficult for the pope to deal with them. When the pope condemned three men to death for the murder of a papal envoy the emperor intervened on their behalf; when the pope on the other hand interceded for his men against imperial justice, he was rebuffed.[1] But the pope's diplomacy was not unsuccessful; when he crowned Louis II as emperor in 850 the treaties between the Frankish Empire and the Roman Church were renewed.[2]

The continued Arab pressure from Bari brought appeals to the Franks from the great protected monasteries of Monte Cassino and San Vincenzo al Volturno, whose huge estates were exposed to attack. But although the Arabs in Bari were quite isolated from those on the other coasts[3] they were too hard a nut for Louis to crack, and the expedition of Louis against Bari in 852 was a failure. In the following year the pope is encouraging the emperor to new exertions against the Arabs; this time the exhortation is in the tones of one proclaiming a holy war, and paradise is promised to those of the Frankish army who fall in battle. At the same time Pope Leo is personally in charge of the defences of the Roman littoral.[4] This warrior and builder pope, was his lavish gifts of jewels and stuffs to the Roman churches, and splendid presents to the Roman nobles[5] is a proud, worldly but very impressive figure. He also, by his construction of the Leonine city, became the main architect of medieval Rome. From Leo's time, Ponte Elio (the present Ponte Sant'Angelo) became the main bridge of Rome, leading from St Peter's to the Via Lata, the main street of the medieval city, and the quarter where most of the great nobles lived. Dominating the bridge was the Mausoleum of Hadrian (Castel Sant'Angelo), still retaining some of the marbled splendour of its origins, but the main fortification of Rome as it had been since the Gothic war of 545. The Via Papalis led from the bridge to the Capitol or Campidoglio, the seat of civil government. The

---

[1] *MGH, Epistolae*, v, pp. 587, 592, 608. See however Leo's apologetic letter offering to revise his own judgements in the presence of imperial *missi*, ibid. p. 607.

[2] P. Kehr, *Gött. Gelehrte Anzeigen* (1896); Stengel, *HZ* (1926), p. 225.

[3] Abu-Mufarraq the ruler of Bari applied to the Caliph of Bagdad for investiture. Amari, i, p. 499.

[4] *MGH, Epistolae*, v, pp. 585, 601.

[5] *Liber Pontificalis*, ii, pp. 114, 125.

main markets became Campo dei Fiori and the Circo Agonale (the present Piazza Navona), both of them off the Via Papalis. The Lateran palace, which was far from the new axis of the city, now shared its position as centre of government with the buildings round St Peter's.

The friction between the Franks and the popes went on. It was extremely irritating to Leo that Louis insisted on supporting the imperial *missus,* the rebellious Arsenius, Bishop of Orte, and his talented but unboundedly ambitious son (just possibly nephew) Anastasius, whom Leo made cardinal priest of San Marcello, but then having repented of his act, placed under anathema. This affair probably lies behind the fortification of Orte and Amelia at this period. Rebellion was already rife in Ravenna, where the pope went in person to reduce the archbishop and his brother to obedience in 853. Other rebellious figures had been causing people to take hold-oaths to them[1] and there was talk of a Byzantine-inspired conspiracy in Rome.

When Pope Leo IV died in 855 neither the emperor nor his *missi* were in Rome. Arsenius, the father of the anathematised Anastasius, was at Gubbio with the other Roman exiles – evidently this high plateau in the Umbrian Apennines, near the frontiers of Ravenna and Pentapolis was outside the area of direct papal control.[2] A new pope, Benedict III, was elected by the nobles and people. The Roman delegation which went to announce the election to the Franks met the exiles at Gubbio. Here Arsenius made it clear to them that his nephew enjoyed Frankish support, and the loyalty of the delegation to Benedict was shaken. Then the Frankish *missi* and their troops appeared at Orte, and accompanied Anastasius and Arsenius to Rome, with the intention of compelling the Romans to proceed to a new election. Clearly at this new election they wanted Anastasius to be chosen pope. Anastasius entered Rome with the Franks in triumph, and he had the satisfaction of tearing down and hacking to pieces the sacred images containing Leo IV's declaration of anathema against him, which the dead pope had caused to be set up on the doors of St Peter's. But he then met with a check. The Roman clergy refused to proceed to a new election, and protested that Anastasius, as a priest who had been anathematised, could not be elected to another office. So a compromise was reached. The

---

[1] Ibid. p. 127.

[2] The boundaries of Roman control are unclear. Urbino seems to have been under papal control: cf. *I.P.,* iv, p. 221, no. 2. San Marino was not: cf. P. Aebischer, 'Le placitum feretranum de 885 et les origines de Saint-Marin', *Le Moyen Age,* lxvi (1960), pp. 1–36; idem, in *Bulletin du Cange* (1960), xxx, pp. 1–13; C. Manaresi, 'Il placito feretrano', *Stud. Romagn.,* viii (1957), pp. 497–509.

election of Benedict was confirmed by the Franks. Anastasius was not restored to his own church, but was sent to the monastery of S. Maria in Trastevere. From this time on Anastasius, whose profound Greek scholarship made him remarkable in ninth-century Rome, was one of the main influences in shaping the policy of the Roman See.

The most important figure in Benedict III's short pontificate, however, was not Anastasius but the deacon Nicholas. The papal chronicle remarks in surprise that Benedict gave the main share in government to Nicholas 'whom he actually preferred to his own kinsmen'. It is useful to remind oneself that in the Middle Ages nepotism was not an abuse, but a method of government. Nicholas evidently got himself on very good terms with the Frankish administration, so that when Benedict died in 858, the Emperor Louis himself came to Rome to supervise the election, and obtained the choice of the deacon Nicholas as pope. Nicholas, the successful Frankish candidate at one election, then as pope proceeded to consult and depend on Anastasius, the failed Frankish candidate at another. It is not without irony that these two men proved to be two of the most formidable exponents of the papal theocratic idea in the history of the Middle Ages, and that the Frankish Empire came the nearest it had ever come to dependence on the Roman See, as the result of their efforts.

V

The first test of strength for the government of Pope Nicholas was with the old rival, the archbishopric of Ravenna, and indirectly also with the imperial government. The power and privileges of the Metropolitan Church of Ravenna were based on imperial grants which began in the fifth century, and had been strengthened under the Byzantine exarchs. Ravenna had been one of the great centres of government and culture of Byzantine Italy, as its great churches bear witness. The emergence of the Papal State had been extremely unwelcome to the archbishops of Ravenna, who had resisted and often defied papal authority from the very beginnings of the papal temporal power. Hadrian I had quarrelled bitterly and frequently with Ravenna, and so had his successors. There had been occasional understandings between the two sees, notably in the great papal privilege for Ravenna issued by Paschal I in 819. But it is doubtful how far Rome actually governed the exarchate. The officials in Ravenna were appointed on some occasions at least by the pope; a lawsuit involving Ravenna was judged by the *missi* of the pope and emperor sitting together.[1] The Frankish kingdom inevitably tended to take Ravenna under its wing; the archbishops of Ravenna played their own hand in Frankish politics, and one of them, Archbishop George, was unwise enough to go to Francia at the height of the quarrels between the Carolingian brothers, and was in Lothar's camp in the battles of 841. The exarchate was geographically remote from Rome, particularly because the duchy of Spoleto formed a wedge down the central mountain chain between the two areas. When Leo IV quarrelled with John, the Archbishop of Ravenna, and his brother, the Duke of Emilia, in 850, the point at issue was not whether the pope should rule in Ravenna, but whether he could protect his own subjects and his own patrimonial estates from the aggression of the archbishop and his brother.

Leo IV had travelled to Ravenna in person in 853 to settle his quarrel with Archbishop John. But John and his brother were not easily disposed of; the archbishop was on extremely good terms with the Emperor Lothar, and he continued to act as he pleased in the exarchate until a fresh quarrel with Rome broke out in 860. This time Pope Nicholas chose his ground better than his predecessors; he took issue with the Archbishop of Ravenna not only on the old score of civil misgovernment, but on the issue of the relations of the see of Ravenna with its suffragan bishops. Here the papacy was on far stronger canonical ground. According to Nicholas the dozen or more bishoprics subject to Ravenna had had their elections illegally interfered with by the metropolitan, and had been prevented either from appealing or even from travelling to Rome. To prevent a bishop from travelling *ad limina apostolorum* was certainly a serious matter, and Nicholas secured the support of the Italian bishops against John of Ravenna. At a Roman synod which probably took place in February 861,[2] fifty-five bishops excommunicated the Archbishop of Ravenna. The Emperor Louis sent his *missi* to intervene on Archbishop John's behalf, but Nicholas politely repulsed them. John himself appeared in Rome for a short time, but fled when things went against him. Nicholas, reputedly at the urgent request of the notables of Ravenna, himself went there and restored to their owners the lands and goods confiscated by John and his brother – in Ravenna as in Rome, most of the political struggles seem to have centred in the end

[1] C. Manaresi, *I placiti del 'Regnum Italiae'* (1955), i, p. 139.
[2] H. Fuhrmann, 'Papst Nikolaus I. und die Absetzung des Erzbischofs Johanns von Ravenna', *ZSSRG, Kan. Abt.*, lxxv (1958), pp. 353–8. For the quarrel under Leo IV, *MGH, Epistolae*, v (*Karolini Aevi*, iii), pp. 587, 592, 607.

around confiscations of property. John in the meantime had again gone to Pavia to appeal to the emperor, but this time Louis refused to help him. He was compelled to appear at another synod at Rome in November, consisting mainly of bishops from the Papal State, and to make a full submission. The synod marks one of the most important stages in the subjection of Ravenna to Rome.[1] John's metropolitan jurisdiction was limited; he promised not to interfere in the elections of his suffragan bishops, not to impose illegal taxes on them, and to allow them to appeal and to travel to Rome. He promised to leave judgements in civil suits to the papal officials in Ravenna, and to return the papal patrimonies he had usurped. Finally he had to guarantee to appear in Rome every two years to account for himself. To place a great archbishop on probation like this was a striking victory for the forward policy of Nicholas and Anastasius. It had considerable significance for the temporal power, and more for the relations of Nicholas with the Frankish government, which had failed to protect John of Ravenna.

Nicholas I had by this time become deeply involved in Frankish politics. The wish of the childless Lothar II, King of mid-Francia, to repudiate his childless wife Theutberga, brought the pope in his capacity as arbiter of canon law into the centre of the conflicts of the Frankish kings. The Emperor Louis, who was in the same camp as his brother Lothar, had countenanced placing the affair in the hands of a pope whom he thought would do his wishes. When Nicholas refused to authorise the divorce, Louis came in 864 with an army to Rome; Louis II's hostile invasion as King of Italy of twenty years earlier was thus repeated. With him came all the exiles and the enemies of the pope – the deposed German bishops, John of Ravenna and his brother Gregory, the disgraced Bishop Radoald of Porto – all confidently expecting to see Nicholas humiliated and overcome.

The fidelity of the Romans, both lay and clergy, was suspect, and Nicholas might have been forgiven for making the sort of compromise with Frankish power which other popes had made in similar circumstances – particularly in 824 and 844. But Nicholas was a strong man, whose belief in the spiritual power of his office enabled him not only to stand up to violence which was offered him, but to keep the loyalty of his people. The Roman people, nobles and clergy, went in procession to the *memoria Petri* at St Peter's. Frankish troops broke up the demonstration, and in the course of the repression the cross of St Helena was smashed to pieces by a Frankish soldier (it was retrieved by an English-

[1] K. Brandi, 'Ravenna und Rom', *Arch. f. Urk.*, ix (1924), pp. 1–38.

man). The brother of the Bishop of Köln forced his way into the church, killed the sacristan, and deposited his brother's protest on the Confession of St Peter by force.

But the pope's passive resistance triumphed. Making his way to St Peter's he spent two days and nights there in fasting and prayer. The emperor at the same time fell ill, and lost the battle of wills in which he had engaged with the pope; he abandoned the attempt to force Nicholas to submit and withdrew from Rome, whence he retreated to Ravenna. The Romans were left once again to contemplate the devastation which the Frankish army had carried out, against both religious and layfolk. But Nicholas's diplomatic aims were achieved, and although his policy for the divorce was not yet accepted by the Frankish kings, the way was opening for its success.

Nicholas, who was one of the greatest executants of the papal idea, seems to have treated temporal rule as a secondary matter. The chief objects of his policy were the royal divorce of Lothar II, the schism of the Byzantine Patriarch Photius, and the conversion of the Moravians and Bulgars. All these pertained to spiritual authority alone. Unlike some other great popes of his century, he took little direct part in meeting the Arab threat, although this continued as serious as ever. In the great Frankish expedition against Bari of 867, the Papal State played only a subordinate part. The pope refused to pay more than a part of treasure sent him by the newly-converted Bulgarian khan, towards its expenses. He also protested to the emperor and to King Charles the Bald that the Frankish bishops had no business to be guarding the coast against Arab pirates – the soldiers of Christ were to serve *him* alone, and leave war to laymen.[1] This is a long way from the warlike actions of Pope Leo IV and of the later Pope John VIII.

Nicholas certainly was not indifferent to the fate of the patrimonies of the Roman See. One of the functions of the Roman delegation to the synod in Constantinople in 861 was to raise the old question of the papal patrimonies in the Byzantine areas of south Italy; and in the synod which judged John of Ravenna it is plain that the questions of the papal patrimonies and of Roman political power in Ravenna were not foreign to the pope. But the sublime intransigence which characterised Nicholas in spiritual matters was much less evident in temporal ones. In the very letter in which he asked for payment of the revenues of the east Frankish patrimonies for the Holy See, Nicholas remarked that Louis could send the money to somewhere 'inside Frankish territory,

[1] *MGH, Epistolae*, vi, p. 309.

such as Bologna or Ravenna', then the pope would have it collected.[1]
These cities had from the beginning formed an important part of papal
claims. It was true that the exarchate of Ravenna was becoming a political appendage of the kingdom of Italy, but it is surprising to find the
pope apparently recognising the fact.

Rome was still rich enough. Nicholas fed the poor in the old imperial
manner, handing out food tickets marked with his name, to be honoured
on a day marked by knots on a string. The forts at Ostia were restored,
and so were some of the Roman aqueducts. The pope did not build
much, but his diplomacy was probably expensive: missions to Bulgaria
and Constantinople were costly. It was becoming hard for a spiritual
head to rule Rome.

By the middle of the ninth century the grip of the Roman nobility
on the machinery of clerical government was embarrassingly tight. The
popes themselves were most of them noble; Nicholas's successor Hadrian
II (867–72) was of the same family as Sergius II and Stephen IV. The
main officers – not only the *duces* and the *magistri militum* but the
great clerical officers – were noble. A whole generation of these officials
was disgraced under John VIII (872–82), and the pope's condemnation gives some startling information on the way Rome was governed.[2]
A ruined noble named George of Aventino, son of the *primicerius*
Gregory, had re-made his fortune by marrying the niece of Pope
Benedict III (855–8). He not only betrayed her for the daughter of the
nomenclator Gregory, but is said to have murdered his wife 'more or
less publicly' with the connivance of his future father-in-law Gregory.
The latter was the son of Theophylact the *nomenclator* and the brother
of Stephen the *secundicerius*. He served as *nomenclator* or chief financial
officer under Hadrian II and also under John VIII, who remarked that
his rule had been nothing but plunder and robbery. Gregory's daughter
Constantina had first married the son of 'the most powerful Pippin the
vestiarius', and had left him for another noble, whom she in turn deserted
for the assassin George of Aventino.

Under Hadrian II these scandals penetrated the papal palace at the
Lateran itself. Pope Hadrian like many clerics of the time had been
previously married, and both his wife and daughter lived in the papal
palace. The pretender to his daughter's hand was one Eleutherius, who
was a brother of no less a person than the learned and subtle Anastasius.
Repulsed, Eleutherius kidnapped the girl, and then murdered both his

[1] Ibid. p. 338.
[2] *MGH, Epistolae*, vii, p. 326.

prospective bride and her mother, the daughter and wife of the pope. Anastasius was suspected of encouraging the murder, and was for a short time in deep disgrace, but he was too powerful and well-connected (particularly with the imperial family, where he was perhaps influential with the emperor's daughter Irmingard),[1] for Hadrian to deal with; within a year or two he was fully restored to favour. His father Arsenius at the same time died under circumstances which seemed to the monks of Monte Cassino to be those of divine justice. But Arsenius had continued to occupy the most important posts until the end; his mission to Francia at the end of the pontificate of Nicholas had been the final successful stroke in papal policy against the divorce of Lothar. The scandal of Eleutherius ended with the arrest and execution of the principal offender, but his close clerical relations went untouched.

In spite of his family's misfortunes, Hadrian II was a great and dignified nobleman, who as a churchman defended all the essential traditions of Nicholas I.[2] But his prestige was undermined, not only by the scandals round the Lateran palace, but because from the day of his consecration to that of his death, the emperor stayed continuously in Italy, and spent his main energies on Italian issues. The pope lived rather in the emperor's shadow, and Hadrian's position was the weaker in that Lambert, the Frankish Duke of Spoleto, had his own numerous hangers-on in Rome, and when he entered the city behaved as its master. The Italians thought of Louis II as a great and pious ruler, and certainly whatever the practical limits to his power in the west were, he was a potentate considerable enough for his alliance to be sought by the Byzantines. In terms of Italian politics, Hadrian was a subordinate; and although the tone of letters coming from the papal chancery remained firm and conservative, their draughtsman may often have been Anastasius, who was a go-between for the pope with Louis, and the author of much of both papal and imperial policy.

The great aim of Louis II was the extirpation of the Muslim bases on the Italian mainland; it was this which made him appreciated and sought after by the Byzantines. But it was a hard task which he set himself. The Arabs of southern Italy were discordant and divided – but so, equally, were the Christians. After 875, the bloody and intelligently directed power of Ibrahim II, the Emir of Kairouan, lay behind

[1] Cf. E. Perels, *Papst Nikolaus II. und Anastasius Bibliothecarius* (Berlin, 1920), pp. 234–5, There is some doubt about this connection.

[2] Lapôtre, pp. 219, 221; Ullmann, *Growth of Papal Government*, pp. 211–12. L. Halphen, *Charlemagne et l'Empire Carolingien* (Paris, 1949), p. 401 takes another view ('sans grand prestige, accueillant et serviable') and cf. Perels, p. 239.

Arab rule in Sicily. Ibrahim was to die fighting the Christians at Cosenza, in 902. The resurgence of the Byzantine navy under the Macedonian dynasty of Basil I was beginning to bode ill for the Muslims, but the way was not clear for the relief of Christian south Italy until after the overthrow of the Aglabid dynasty, to which Ibrahim had belonged, by the Fatimid revolution of 909.[1] Louis II depended on Byzantine sea-power, and on the help of the petty Christian states of south Italy – Benevento, Spoleto, Capua, Salerno, Naples and others. Because these states feared that the overthrow of the Arabs would mean their own subordination to the victor, and also because they wanted to trade with infidels and get a share of their loot, they would not unite against the Muslim except for very short periods. Naples and the states in the Gulf of Salerno were particularly vexatious in their alliance with the Muslims, but almost all these petty Christian powers did the same at one time or another.

After several false starts, Louis II captured Bari in 871. But the triumph was short. A few months later the emperor was humiliatingly taken prisoner by his own vassals in a revolt at Benevento. The captivity was brief, but having failed to capture Taranto, and having quarrelled violently with his Byzantine allies, he died at Brescia in August 875.

VI

Hadrian II had predeceased his imperial master by some two and a half years. He had been succeeded in the Holy See by the venerable Roman deacon John. John VIII was a stern, able, and profoundly political figure, who found Rome in the gravest difficulties, and faced his responsibilities with desperate determination and energy. Even before the death of Louis II the Muslims were (as the pope put it) 'making themselves perfectly at home' in the Roman Campagna, as far away as Terracina and as close as the walls of the city. The pope raised his own fleet, and led his troops both on land and sea against the Saracens. Like his predecessor he found the house of Spoleto a grave peril to Rome. He also found a difficult situation in the city itself. The governing noble clique – the corrupt Gregory the *nomenclator* and his dissipated and bloodstained relatives – was a threat to someone who wanted to be a

---

[1] Cf. G Marçais, *La Berbérie Musulmane et l'orient au Moyen Age* (Paris, 1946), pp. 56–101; J. Gay, *L'Italie méridionale et l'empire byzantin depuis l'avènement de Basil I jusqu'à la prise de Bari par les Normands (867–1070)* (Paris, 1904), pp. 77 ff.

strong ruler. With Gregory's powerful faction was associated the distinguished and dissatisfied prelate, Formosus, who had played an important part in the conversion of the Bulgarians, but had not been allowed to become their primate.

John VIII is often represented as a worldly, even an imperialistic figure, but this seems unjust to a man on whom the whole burden fell, in a Rome whose position seemed no less desperate than when Aistulf camped outside the city a century earlier. Pope John found that the Carolingian Empire was just as powerless now to help the Romans, as the Byzantine Empire had eventually been in the earlier period. But it was some time before this hard truth was learned, and before the Italians realised that Louis II had been the last emperor powerful enough to be of decisive importance in the solution of their problems.

Immediately after the death of Louis II, John turned to Charles the Bald of west Francia. The pope called his candidate to Rome for coronation, and had the satisfaction of crowning him on Christmas Day, 875, the anniversary of 800. Anastasius and the higher clerks of Rome gave the new emperor, who was vain of his own learning, an academic commentary on the 'Feast of St Cyprian', a sort of learned religious pantomime which Charles had brought with him. It was the last time for over a century that the Roman court disposed of the cultural resources to offer such an entertainment.

But this appearance in Rome of the imperial protector was in fact unique. By February 876 Charles was in Pavia to obtain the Lombard crown. While he was there the papal legates brought accusations against Gregory the *nomenclator* and Bishop Formosus.[1] A month later, Gregory and his party fled from Rome; and Pope John claimed that the fugitives had led a dangerous conspiracy. Certainly if John's statements can be believed, Gregory led an unsavoury crew – though when it is considered that most of them had served the Holy See in high office for many years, one wonders whether, in ninth-century Roman noble circles, their character and behaviour were quite as exceptional as the pope made out. In addition to Gregory and his son-in-law, George of Aventino, the other *magister militum* involved was Sergius, the son of an earlier *magister militum*, who had married a niece of Pope Nicholas I. He is said to have stolen the treasure of the church while Nicholas lay dying, and then to have abandoned his wife for a whore named Walvisindula.

---

[1] *MGH, Epistolae,* vii, pp 25, 326 ff.; cf. Lapôtre, pp. 36 ff.; Zimmermann, *Papstabsetzungen,* pp. 49 ff. I follow Caspar's dates for the letters concerned.

Such were the associates, John claimed, of the learned and pious Formosus, Bishop of Porto. In a Roman synod held in the Pantheon in April, the pope charged them, that having been earlier in the year accused of defalcations, Gregory had one night seized the papal treasure and fled the city with Formosus and his other associates through Porta San Pancrazio on the Janiculum, leaving the city gates open behind them for the Muslims to enter if they wished. According to the Formosan party, their leaders had been so terrified by the threats uttered against them that they had not dared face trial. It was a crisis which in many ways resembled the earlier Roman crises of 799, 824 or 855. It is likely that on this as on earlier occasions the parties in Rome which favoured or opposed the Frankish protectorate (in this case, perhaps east-Frankish and west-Frankish parties) were important; and perhaps even more important was the influence in Rome of the Marquis of Spoleto. Fifty years earlier, when such matters had been reported to the emperor, he would have sent *missi* to look into the matter, and perhaps would have come later himself. But Charles the Bald was too weak to do either. Instead, at the Synod of Ponthion in the same year he made concessions to the papal legates which registered his own powerlessness. The imperial *missus* at Rome, the symbol and to some extent the instrument of the Frankish protectorate, was to be withdrawn. The old claims of the Holy See to rights of overlordship in Capua and perhaps also in Benevento, were recognised by the emperor; even imperial fiscal rights over the protected monasteries of Farfa, Rieti and Mount Soracte were ceded to the pope.[1] Had these concessions been made at a time of imperial strength they would have been of great importance; as things were, they deserve mention only as evidence of the Carolingian collapse.

A more realistic picture of the plight of the Church in Italy emerges from the acts of the synod which the pope held in Ravenna in July 877. The Council discussed the inability of the Church to prevent the wholesale seizure of its property by the magnates, or to enforce its discipline against the prevalent lawlessness: against abduction, rape,

---

[1] *MGH, Epistolae*, vii, p. 3; *Libellus de imperatoria potestate in urbe Roma* (G. Zuchetti (ed.), in *Fonti per la storia d'Italia*, 55, (Rome, 1920), pp. 191–210). Cf. A. Lapôtre, *L'Europe et le Saint-Siége a l'époque Carolingienne*, pt. 1, *Le pape Jean VIII* (Paris, 1895), pp. 308 ff.; Kehr, *Gött. Gelehrte Anzeigen*, (1899), pp. 377–84; Stengel, *HZ*, cxxxiv (1926), pp. 234–8; J. Haller, *Nikolaus I. und Pseudo-Isidor* (Stuttgart, 1936), pp. 193–8. The character of the *libellus* makes it very unlikely that its report of these concessions is exact. Kehr's proposed emendation of *patrimonia* for *patrias* seems doubtful, since the papal *patrimonia* in Benevento and Naples are not mentioned in the decree of the Synod of Ravenna in the following year. See immediately below.

murder, robbery and the other results of the anarchy. The excommunication which these offences entailed was to be promulgated in the other
dioceses, so that offenders should not go unremarked. The alienation or
feudal grant of the properties of the Roman Church – or in other words,
the dismembering of the Papal State – was forbidden, and the patrimonies and revenues so protected were mentioned by name. But as in
many documents of this kind, the exceptions are in some respects more
interesting than the prohibitions. Popes were left free to make feudal
grants either to their 'familiars', or to people especially useful or service-
able to the Roman Church. Such grants were John VIII's concession
of the patrimonies of Traetto and Fondi to the *dux* of Gaeta, and
Stephen V's enfeoffment to Bishop John of Pavia of the duchy of
Comacchio in 885. Louis II himself had made feudal grants in the
Papal State, in spite of the protests of John VIII who asked in vain that
offices in the patrimony should be conferred only for a year.[1]

Charles the Bald could not entirely stop his ears to the appeals of
the pope, who told him how the cruel fleets and armies of the Muslims
and the 'wicked Christians' were destroying the social and religious
order which the Roman pontiffs had laboriously built up and defended
over the past century. Conditions in Italy were anarchic – though the
same could be said for the Seine valley, for southern France, and for
many other parts of the empire. The watchword was plunder; when
the Christian seaports and rulers allied with the Muslims, what could
be called anxiety to trade with the Muslims was also from a different
point of view simply desire to share in the loot. Much of what was
plundered in the Roman Campagna must have ended in the hands of
Neapolitan 'merchants'.[2]

The political confusion in Italy was complete, and necessarily involved the clergy. The immense efforts of the pope to construct a coalition against the Muslims, in the furtherance of which he travelled
constantly in southern Italy, seemed on a couple of occasions (876–7) to
be near success, but the divisions of the Christians doomed them to
eventual failure. Capua, which the Holy See was particularly concerned
to make into a papal vassal state, proved as unreliable as the others.
The states would sometimes listen to the arguments of bribery; Amalfi
was promised 10,000 silver *mancusi* a year by the pope to defend his

---

[1] *MGH, Epistolae*, vii, p. 304. For the Synod of Ravenna, Mansi, *Concilia*, xvii, p. 337. For
the grant of Comacchio cf. Hartmann, *Geschichte Italiens im Mittelalter*, iii, pt. 2, pp. 100–1.
[2] F. A. Engreen, 'Pope John the Eighth and the Arabs', *Speculum*, xx (1945), pp. 318–30.
Cf. *MGH, Epistolae*, vii, p. 246.

coasts against Muslim naval attack. But the men of Amalfi were as greedy as all pirates; as soon as given 10,000, they asked for 12,000 and then returned to their Arab friends. Even so, a year or so later the pope was promising them the old bribe, and a bonus besides. It was perhaps better to pay a tribute to the Muslims direct; when Pope John fled to Francia in 878 he paid 25,000 *mancusi* to buy off the Arabs.[1] Guaifer of Salerno may have been bribed by the abandonment of papal claims on his principate. But the Muslims only gained in strength. In 878 Syracuse fell, and the Arab conquest of Sicily was completed. In 881–2 Muslim bands set up a great new base at the mouth of the river Garigliano, which offset the loss of Bari and Taranto on other coasts, and served to intensify the plunder and terrorization of south Italy, including the papal territory.

In several years of John's pontificate, particularly the last, the Romans could not venture outside the walls to harvest. To bribe the south Italian cities, the pope alienated the rich patrimonies of Fondi and Traetto, running from the vicinity of Terracina south as far as the river Garigliano. The Roman Campagna was partially depopulated, and the Roman See and the Roman churches and monasteries got little from their lands. The pope still had the customs revenue of Rome and its ports, the profits of coinage, the monies from the salt-pans at Ostia and elsewhere. But the fragile economy of Rome, and the perhaps even more fragile social arrangements which kept that economy largely in the hands of a clerical bureaucracy, were gradually collapsing.

The only strong, orderly, civilised power in south Italy was the Byzantine, now that under Basil the Macedonian was rebuilding its fleets in order to try to regain naval supremacy and to oust the Muslims from Italy. Soon after the Greek capture of Bari in 876, the pope was asking for naval aid from the Greek authorities in Italy.[2] In 878–9 he concluded his *rapprochement* with the Byzantines by recognising the rehabilitated Patriarch Photius – thus renouncing much of the policy of Nicholas I and Anastasius. He did not do this only in the interests of the temporal power; the hope of regaining Roman jurisdiction over the Bulgarian Church also influenced him. But the struggle with the Muslims weighed the heaviest. The disgruntled western emperor referred to the 'oppressions' of the Greeks in south Italy, but the pope in 880 disclaimed knowledge of them, and instead hastened to inform the western rulers

[1] Ibid. p. 85. For John and the s. Italian states, ibid. pp. 75, 81, 194, 218 and cf. epist. nos. 245, 246, 249.
[2] Ibid. p. 45 and cf. Gay, p. 110.

of Byzantine naval successes against the Arabs. By this time Byzantine ships had been lent to the pope for the defence of his coasts.[1]

A return by the popes to the acceptance of Byzantine domination was out of the question; the whole political and clerical system which had developed in the west in the preceding century forbade it. Rome's lot lay with the Franks. Even in Italian political terms, while Benevento and the southern states tended to fall back into the Byzantine orbit, Rome and Spoleto remained anchored to the north. But it was these adjacent minor powers, and especially Spoleto, which were the sharpest thorn in Roman flesh. 'What can we say of the infidels, when the Christians act in no better way, particularly those neighbours of ours who are termed "marquises"?'[2] Lambert of Spoleto and his brother-in-law Adalbert of Tuscany were the 'marquises' in question. The main offender was Lambert, the patron of the Formosan party in Rome, who looked covetously down from the Apennine border to the Roman territory.

From the spring of 876, when the Formosan exiles fled to Lambert, tension was acute. In October 877 Charles the Bald, who turned aside to meet the invasion of Italy by his cousin Carloman, ruler of Bavaria, died at Maurienne. Even the distant protector of the papacy had now left the scene. Lambert demanded hostages from the Romans, and then, alleging a command from Carloman, proclaimed his coming to Rome to restore the goods and property of the Formosan exiles. The pope announced to Lambert that he was going to travel north to get the help of Charles the Bald's son, Louis the Stammerer, in west Francia. But before he could leave, Lambert at the beginning of March appeared before Rome with his army and with the Roman exiles. The gates were opened to him by his party, and he occupied the city, while for a month the pope was blockaded in St Peter's. The Romans were prevented from coming in religious processions, or otherwise demonstrating in the pope's favour. Having endured humiliations 'which no vicar of blessed Peter had ever to suffer from king or emperor', the pope slipped down the Tiber in a Neapolitan galley on his way to Genoa and thence to Francia. But he got small satisfaction there from Louis the Stammerer or from any of the other Frankish kings, and when he returned to Rome at the end of the year his political problems were unsolved.[3]

Count Boso of Provence, on whom both Pope John and the Byzan-

[1] Ibid. pp. 141, 142, 148, 214, 225, 228.
[2] Ibid. p. 20.
[3] Ibid. pp. 56, 67, 74, and cf. epist. nos. 82, 83, 84, 87, 88. Cf. also Hartmann, iii, pt. 2, pp. 62–3.

1   Enamelled cross of the period of Paschal I (see p. 54)

tines at one time built some hopes, proved as defective in power as the rest of the Frankish magnates. The next Carolingian to intervene actively in Italian affairs came not from west Francia but from east. Charles III of Swabia ('the Fat'), brother of Louis the German, descended into Italy in the autumn of 879. But although the pope travelled to Ravenna at the behest of the king, the king would not come south to Rome at the behest of the pope. Charles was treated by Pope John with well-deserved mistrust. What other treatment could be accorded to a king who appointed as 'protectors' of the lands of St Peter none other than the feared and hated marquises of Spoleto and Tuscany?[1] When Charles finally marched towards Rome in the new year of 881 for coronation as emperor the pope forbade him to cross the papal frontier until agreement was reached on the terms of his coming. But Charles disregarded the order, just as he had disregarded earlier requests that he should ratify one of the pacts and privileges which his predecessors had accorded to the Roman Church.[2] Charles came to Rome, was crowned, and went straight back to north Italy; he had what he wanted, and he left the pope to the mercies of Lambert's 'rabid' successor as Marquis of Spoleto, Guy.

A year later, in February 882, John VIII again took part in an imperial meeting at Ravenna. The defence of church property in this part of Italy concerned him closely. Romanus, the Archbishop of Ravenna, had like his predecessors resisted papal authority in various ways, which in his case included hostility to the papal *duces* in Ravenna, John and Deusdedit, and the admission to Ravenna of Frankish agents from Spoleto. The archbishop had been condemned in a Roman synod in 881, it is not clear how decisively. Berengar of Friuli and the Doge John of Venice had both made attempts on the papal duchy of Comacchio; the marquises of Spoleto had encroached violently on the papal patrimonies in Pentapolis.[3] In the presence of the emperor in Ravenna the marquises promised to restore what they had seized in Pentapolis. But when Pope John afterwards went in person with the imperial *missus* to Fano to receive the promised restitutions, he met the customary disappointment, and came back with empty hands. Charles III was in no position to protect the lands of St Peter; the

---

[1] *MGH, Epistolae*, vii, p. 219. Cf. epist. no. 266.

[2] Ibid. pp. 199, 235.

[3] Ibid. pp. 89, 112, 116, 132, 140, 231, 248–51, 253, 258 and cf. epist. nos. 226, 311–14. For the marquises see p. 263 and cf. epist. no. 297. For the quarrels with Ravenna, pp. 291, 309, 312. For Comacchio see also P. Kehr, *Quellen und Forschungen aus italienischen Archiven und Bibliotheken* (1927), xix, pp. 68–9.

Opposite: 2 The legend of Pope Silvester and Constantine, in the fresco of the Quattro Incoronati Church at Rome

pope's cry of 'Where is their emperor?' went unheard. In his last letter to Francia he wrote in despair that not two armies but three and four were come against him; and that once more he could not issue out from the walls of Rome.[1] The endless civil wars of Capua, the wars of Gaeta, of Benevento, of Naples, of Amalfi, and of the Muslim mercenaries who helped first one of these and then another, mocked every papal attempt to find reliable allies. From Agropolis south of Paestum, and from the mouth of the Garigliano in the ruins of the ancient city of Minturnae, the Muslims continued to raid and plunder. Pope John's position in his own court did not survive his political failure. In December 882 the pope was poisoned by his 'familiars', and when this did not work fast enough, the head of Western Christendom was beaten to death with a hammer.

Nominally at least, the authority of Charles the Fat survived until his deposition at Tribur in 887. Charles even managed to imprison Guy of Spoleto for a short time during his Italian campaign of 883, but he made no lasting impression on the politics of central Italy. He made a last brief appearance in north Italy in the spring of 886, but his power there was null.

Among the immediate successors of John VIII, Hadrian III died in 885 after setting out to join Charles the Fat in Francia, but Stephen V in April 887 refused even to send legates to the emperor.[2] Church property in Italy was the helpless victim of the great magnates on the one hand, and of the Muslims on the other. By 883 the two greatest and best defended monasteries of south Italy, San Vincenzo al Volturno and Monte Cassino, had both been looted and destroyed by Muslims. Driving into Roman territory through the hills round Rieti, they plundered the hill country of Sabina as well as the plains. They penetrated north of Rome and down the Via Cassia; and on the Via Aurelia the bishopric and estates of Silva Candida were ravaged. In 898 after seven years of stubborn resistance the great imperial monastery of Farfa, whose possessions stretched across Italy to the Adriatic, and north as far as Ravenna, was sacked and abandoned. In 885 Stephen V at his accession made an official inspection of the main papal treasury at the Lateran and found it utterly bare. The immense heaps of ancient treasure, much of which (such as the Cross of Belisarius) had survived Byzantine and Lombard cupidity, had disappeared in a few years of disorder. Without imperial support the prosperity of Rome was at an

---

[1] *MGH, Epistolae*, vii, pp. 245, 267; cf. Ps. 78: 10, Ezek. 21: 1
[2] *MGH, Epistolae*, vii, p. 340.

end – though how far this was a crisis of church property and how far a true economic collapse, is still not entirely clear. It is noticeable that the noble Stephen V was still rich enough from his family estates to meet many of his economic responsibilities as pope.[1]

For thirty or forty years the great question of Roman politics, which split both aristocracy and clergy, was the party attached to Bishop Formosus of Porto. The faction proscribed by John VIII in 876 was not that of a few bandits; it was led by one of the most distinguished bishops of his generation, and by some of the richest and most powerful Roman families. Pope Marinus, who immediately succeeded John VIII in 882, recalled Formosus and re-instated him in his bishopric of Porto. Hadrian III, who succeeded Marinus in 884, had the main leader of the Formosan party, George of Aventino, blinded. He also caused a noble-woman, Maria the widow of the *superista* Gregory, to be whipped naked through the streets. But what she or her husband – who had been murdered in the atrium of St Peter's in the preceding pontificate – had done to deserve their treatment, we do not know.

Stephen V (885–91) had once again to accept the protectorate of Spoleto. Guy III of Spoleto's victory over Berengar on the river Trebia in February 889, and his understanding with his nephew Adalbert of Tuscany, made the pressure on Rome impossible to resist – though the pope still sent an appeal for help to Arnulf of Carinthia, Carloman's son. In 891 Pope Stephen crowned Guy and his ambitious wife Ageltrude, emperor and empress. The first non-Carolingian had taken the diadem and orb of empire.

The Formosan party triumphed with the election of Formosus himself as pope in 891. There was a doubt about the regularity of his election, both because his orders had once been removed, and because as ex-Bishop of Porto he followed the dubious precedent of Marinus, in exchanging one bishop's see for another. The domination of the house of Spoleto over Rome went on; in April 892 the pope crowned Guy's son Lambert as emperor, in a ceremony at Ravenna. The ancient pacts of the empire with the Roman See were again confirmed.

But in spite of the long connection of his party with the house of Spoleto, Formosus was not happy with Guy and Ageltrude. Like Stephen V, he appealed to Arnulf of Carinthia to come to Rome. Guy died in 894, and the way seemed clear for Arnulf. When he appeared before Rome at the end of 895 Ageltrude had thrown herself into the city with a small force, determined to hold it for her son Lambert. The

[1] *Liber Pontificalis*, ii, p. 192. For what follows see also Zimmermann, pp. 52 ff.

German forces had little trouble in storming the city, and the vigorous Ageltrude withdrew. After this modest victory, Arnulf was crowned emperor by the pope. But in a short time the new emperor suffered a stroke; the sick man was taken north to Germany and to obscurity. The last feeble attempt to restore the empire to a Carolingian had petered out, and Rome was abandoned to the play of local political forces. There was no longer anyone left to execute the treaties by which the Frankish rulers had promised to protect the Church of Rome.

Chapter 3

The House of Theophylact[1]

I

'Until the last day comes,' wrote the rhetor Auxilius at the end of the ninth century, 'holy church waxes and wanes like the moon, now resplendent with the sound life and doctrine of holy bishops, now like the moon obscured by the reprobate life and improper conduct of carnal priests.'[2] Or as another contemporary poet more shortly put it : 'Roman morals are as ruined as Roman walls.'

In 896 or early in 897 Pope Stephen VI had the nine-months-old corpse of Pope Formosus taken from the grave to be 'judged' by a synod of bishops. The dead man was condemned, and his tenure of the Roman See and consequently his ordinations as pope were pronounced invalid; the fingers which had pronounced benediction were torn from the body, and it was thrown into the Tiber. A few months later Stephen himself was imprisoned by his enemies and strangled.

The interests and influence of Ageltrude of Spoleto and her son Lambert were closely involved with all these Roman struggles. These interests were not absolutely identified with those of one Roman party or another. When Sergius, the single-minded enemy of the Formosans, failed to make good his claim to the papacy at the double election of 898, the house of Spoleto accepted the successful candidate John IX, and supported him in his attempt to quiet the Formosan controversy and to recognise Formosan orders. In return, John IX was willing to recognise Lambert as emperor, and to disclaim the coronation by Formosus of the 'barbarian' Arnulf. At the Council of Ravenna in 898 the close dependence of the Holy See on Lambert became evident.[3] The memory

---

[1] Many of the bulls of the tenth-century popes are discussed in the summaries newly edited by H. Zimmermann for the new edition of J. V. Böhmer, *Regesta Imperii*, ii, *Sächsische Zeit*, Fünfte Abt., *Papstregister 911–984* (Wien-Köln-Graz, 1969). This book appeared too late to be utilised for the present work.

[2] A. Dummler, *Auxilius und Vulgarius* (Leipzig, 1866), p. 86.

[3] Cf. Zimmermann, *Papstabsetzungen* (1968), pp. 60–3.

of Formosus was cleared and the validity of his ordinations confirmed; the clergy also laid down that henceforward the consecration of an elected pope should take place in the presence of the imperial *missi*. The Carolingian pacts with the Church and that of Guy III of Spoleto with Pope Stephen V were confirmed. The protectorate of Spoleto over the Papal State was emphasised by clauses which allowed Romans to appeal freely to the emperor, and which made Lambert fully responsible for putting down disorder in the territories of St Peter.

The 898 Council of Ravenna repeats in most essentials the complaints of the council which took place there in 877 about the feudalisation of church property and the running down of the papal patrimonies. The poverty of the Holy See had become more acute by the growth of the custom of plundering the Lateran palace and also the residences of the suburbicarian bishops, every time a pope died. We know that this had happened as early as the death of Nicholas I; but the abuse was now intolerable. The lack of police was such that the one great Roman building operation of the time, the reconstruction of the Lateran basilica after its collapse in an earthquake in 897, was unable to proceed because papal agents could not get the necessary wooden beams safely back from the papal woods to Rome. The pope complained that not only estates but towns had been taken from his see by the Franks of Spoleto.[1]

The protectorate of Spoleto over the Holy See did not end with Lambert's premature death in October 898, nor with the coronation of Louis of Provence by Pope Benedict IV in 901, during the few weeks which that unhappy prince spent in Rome. A new combination between the princes of Spoleto and the Roman factions was coming into being, which was to leave its own characteristic mark on the politics of the tenth century. The Roman priest Sergius, who with his faction spent seven years in exile after his failure in the papal election of 898, had his chance in the confusion after the death of Benedict IV in 903. Benedict's successor Leo was unseated after a few months by one Christopher. With the help of the Franks of Spoleto and possibly also of Tuscany, Sergius entered Rome in 904, threw Christopher to join Leo in prison and secured his own possession of the papal dignity. A reign of terror against the Formosan party began; the dissident clergy were thrown into prison, or exiled, or threatened with expulsion to Naples

---

[1] *MGH, Capitularia*, ii, p. 125.

for sale as slaves to the Muslims.[1] Sentences against the dead Formosus were again pronounced, and his ordinations condemned.

It is likely that the *coup d'état* of Sergius III in 904 was carried out with the help of two important men, who make their appearance on the political scene at this time.[2] Alberic of Spoleto was a Frankish noble who at the end of the ninth century, having probably secured interests in the county of Camerino, murdered Guy IV of Spoleto and took his duchy. At the same time there emerges in Rome a great noble house – whose earlier members are perhaps recorded without the connection being known to us – which plays a dominant part in Roman politics down to the eleventh century. Theophylact, head of a noble family whose palace was in the Via Lata (known to modern Rome as the Corso), and probably adjoining the Church of the Holy Apostles, is first known through a document of 901. In 904 he is referred to as *magister militum et vestararius,* that it is to say as head of the army and as one of the most important papal officials. In 906 he was addressed by Archbishop John of Ravenna, the future John X, as *gloriosissimus dux,* and in 915 he was 'senator' and head of the Roman diplomatic mission which sought support against the Muslims.

Judgement of the history of the house of Theophylact is almost from its beginnings made difficult by the nature of the evidence offered against it by the tenth-century writer Liutprand of Cremona, the bishop and client of Otto I. When Liutprand wrote in the seventh decade of the century it was in the imperial interest that the family of Theophylact should be presented in the blackest light possible. It is not surprising that while the piety of Theodora, wife of Theophylact, was extolled by a contemporary, Liutprand accused her of being the mistress of Pope John X.

It is however possible that Liutprand was on firmer ground in blackening the name of Theophylact's daughter Marozia, who is unhappy in being second to Lucrezia Borgia among the bad women of papal history. This able, ambitious and unscrupulous woman was said by Liutprand to have become the mistress of Pope Sergius III, and the mother by him of the future Pope John XI. There may be some truth

---

[1] *Auxilius und Vulgarius,* p. 60.

[2] L. Prosdocimi, 'Alberico di Spoleto', in *Dizionario Biografico degli Italiani;* G. Bossi, *Alberico I Duca di Spoleto* (Rome, 1918); P. Fedele, 'Ricerche per la storia di Roma e del papato nel secolo X', *ASR,* xxx (1910), pp. 177–247; ibid. xxxi (1911), pp. 75–115; R. L. Poole, *Studies in Chronology and History* (Oxford, 1934), pp. 215–22; E. Hlawitschka, *Franken, Alemannen, Bayern und Burgunder in Ober-Italien (774–962)* (Freiburg i.B., 1960), pp. 77, 115.

in the story, although to believe it true we must imagine that Marozia became involved in an intrigue with this elderly cleric when she was still a young girl.[1] What we know of the character of Sergius is anything but frivolous, and if there was an association between them it was probably as much political as romantic.

What we know of Marozia is that she made three marital connections, all of them political. The first was with Alberic of Spoleto, with whom she co-habited 'not as a wife, but according to the evil custom of the time',[2] and by whom she had a celebrated son, Alberic of Rome. The second was with Guy of Tuscany, by whom she had a daughter, another *femme fatale*, Bertha. The third marriage, whose political result was a Roman revolution led by her son Alberic, was with Hugh of Provence.

In political terms the rule of the house of Theophylact, and its alliance with the Prince of Spoleto, meant the restoration of order in Rome. Marozia's marriage or quasi-marriage with Alberic meant the attainment of a political balance between the Roman aristocracy and the Frankish magnates of Spoleto. A price had to be paid for this in the domination of the Church of Rome by the greatest of the noble families; the battle which the Roman clergy had been fighting for two centuries had been lost, and what had been lost could not be recovered until after the tremendous upheavals of the Reform movement of the eleventh century. In the narrower context of Roman political stability there was a gain; and there was possibly also a certain gain in the struggle to preserve church property; though in this case of no more than a limited nature. But in capitulating before the local nobility, the Roman bishopric was only doing what the Church was doing all over Europe.

Little is known of the rule of Sergius in Rome, save that he successfully rebuilt the Lateran basilica, and made a few dispositions in favour of dispossessed churches. John X, equally a protégé of the family of Theophylact, succeeded him in 911. John was a distinguished and able man, who before his accession to the pontificate had been Archbishop

---

[1] For Liutprand, who is a well-informed but highly tendentious writer, see Becker's introduction to his works, 3rd ed. (Hanover-Leipzig, 1915), pp. xix–xx; M. Lintzel, *Studien über Liutprand von Cremona* (Berlin, 1933) reprinted in *Ausgewählte Schriften*, ii, pp. 351–98. L. Duchesne accepted Liutprand's view of Marozia, 'Serge III et Jean XI', *Mélanges*, xxxiii (1913), pp. 25–64; but see I. Giorgi, 'Biografie farfensi di papi del X e del XI secolo', *ASR*, xxxix (1916), pp. 513–37. Kempf, *Handbuch der Kirchengeschichte*, iii, pt. i, p. 226, rejects Liutprand's account.

[2] G. Zucchetti (ed.), *Chronicon di Benedetto di S. Andrea* (Rome, 1920), pp. 158–9. For the sense of 'in consuetudinem malignam', ibid. p. 171.

of Ravenna. His greatest achievement was the part he played in the final expulsion of the Muslims from central Italy, for which the ground had been prepared by the series of successes scored against the Muslims by Byzantine forces, and by the opportune Fatimid revolution in Tunisia in 909, which removed the powerful Aglabid dynasty. So a Muslim heresy helped the cause of Latin orthodoxy.

The pivot of John's policy was his understanding with Alberic of Spoleto. When this had been assured local troops defeated the Muslims both north of Rome on the Via Cassia, and north-east in Sabina. The Muslim bands fell back from Narni and Orte and the remaining strong-points in Sabina, far south into the main base on the river Garigliano, where all the Muslims of central Italy were now collected. If they were to be finally overcome, this could be done only by a great Christian alliance of a sort which the popes had been trying in vain to achieve for the past fifty years and more.[1]

The Byzantine authorities were probably more important than Pope John and Alberic of Spoleto in the formation of the great Christian league, to which Byzantine diplomacy had also been tending since the winning over of the Prince of Capua and Benevento in 911 to the Greek clientèle. After Capua had come Naples, and then finally the unstable rulers of Gaeta, who were particularly important as the immediate neighbours of the Muslim army. In the early spring of 915 the *strategos* of the Greek province of Longobardia, Nicholas Picingli, arrived at Naples with a Greek army. The southern princes, including Capua-Benevento, Salerno, and Naples were gradually brought over. The nego-tiations were hard; the long history of betrayal behind most of the parties did not point to a trustful agreement. The southern petty states had to be bullied and bribed; the rulers of Naples and Gaeta were given the title of *patricius* by the Greeks. Theophylact and John, the senators of Rome, with an impressive array of Roman notables, promised on behalf of John X that the whole Roman patrimony, papal and private, of Traetto and Fondi, should be given to Gaeta, in furtherance of the expulsion of the Muslims from Benevento and the Papal State, and eventually from 'all Italy'. A war indemnity for Gaeta of a thousand *mancusi* a year was added as a bait. Finally the Christian army marched

---

[1] P. Fedele, 'La battaglia del Garigliano dell'anno 915 ed i monumenti che la ricordano', *ASR*, xxii (1899), pp. 181–211; O. Vehse, 'Das Bündnis gegen die Sarazenen vom Jahre 915', *Quellen*, xix (1927), pp. 181–204; G. Arnaldi, 'La fase preparatoria della battaglia del Garigliano del 915', *Annali della facoltà di lettere e filosofia*, iv (Naples, 1954), pp. 123–44; P. Egidi, 'Per l'iscrizione di Gaeta che ricorda la battaglia del Garigliano del 915', *ASR*, xlii (1919), pp. 306–10.

D*

to the Garigliano, and stood for three months, from June to August 915, outside the Saracen defences. The Muslim forces, enclosed in Minturnae and Monte d'Argento, were barred from help from the sea by the Greek fleet blockading the channel. In August the final assault was made, in which not only Alberic but Pope John took part in the hand-to-hand fighting. The issue was the desired one of the utter annihilation of the Muslims; the Arabs burned their forts and fled into the hills, where they were butchered in detail. The Arab peril in central Italy was past.

An even closer alliance of Alberic with the house of Theophylact followed; the advent of Berengar of Friuli in Rome in the following year for his coronation as emperor did very little to disturb the political balance of this part of Italy. At the coronation of Berengar the emperor was met by the pope's brother, Peter, and by a son of Theophylact. Of the last no more is heard, but Peter emerges a few years later in conflict with the party of Marozia in Rome. Alberic of Spoleto is last mentioned in 917.

Pope John continued to co-operate with Marozia, now married to Guy of Tuscany, until 925, and he took a leading part in the invitation issued by the Italian magnates to Guy's half-brother Hugh of Provence, going even to Mantua in 926 to meet and greet Hugh. But the hostility between the house of Theophylact and the pope's brother, the 'Marquis' Peter, led to one of the bloody clashes which were so familiar in Roman politics. In 928 the faction of Peter was no longer able to hold out in Rome, and he withdrew north up the Tiber to Orte. According to one source he called in the Hungarians to help him; whether this is true or not, on Peter's return to Rome he was surprised in the Lateran by a *coup d'état,* and murdered before the eyes of his brother the pope. Marozia and Guy then had the pope imprisoned (probably in Veroli), and, most probably, put to death. After two other short pontificates, in 931 Marozia's own son became pope as John XI.

Guy of Tuscany was dead by 931; on his death Marozia offered her somewhat bloodstained hand to Guy's half-brother, Hugh of Provence. In this iron age of politics the obstacles of canon law did not stand in the way of the happy couple. In the summer of 932 Hugh entered Rome with a small escort for the wedding celebrations; according to a chronicler his arrival was presaged by the appearance of a dragon in the Roman sky, stretching from the Esquiline to Porta Salaria.[1] But when Hugh with his Burgundian troops joined Marozia in the great castle of the Mausoleum of Hadrian (Castel Sant'Angelo), the Romans

---

[1] *Chron. di Benedetto di S. Andrea,* p. 165.

did not resign themselves humbly to a foreign yoke. Marozia's son by Alberic of Spoleto, Alberic of Rome, knew well that Hugh had already blinded his own half-brother Lambert of Tuscany, and he feared a like fate from his new father-in-law. The Romans swore oaths to the young Alberic and rose in rebellion. Hugh had not enough troops to resist, and fled the city, leaving his bride to fall captive to her own son, who cast her with his brother the pope into prison. Of Marozia no more is heard. In her place Alberic ruled alone, the 'senator of all the Romans', and the absolute ruler of Rome and the Papal State.

The temptation to treat Alberic as a sort of Cesare Borgia of the tenth century is strong. Much of what we know of Alberic and his mother is dramatic, but it comes from the fluent pen of Liutprand of Cremona. In essence Alberic's regime did not differ from what had gone before; long before 932 the dominance of his family over the papacy was an accomplished fact, and while he maintained the strong hold which the Roman nobility now had over the Roman clerical bureaucracy, the latter was by no means abolished – in fact it was in some respects strengthened. He certainly did not seek to secularise the papacy; his association with Odo of Cluny and the monastic reformers is – from whatever political motives – one of the most characteristic features of his policy. To ability Alberic added good luck. The attacks on Rome by Hugh of Provence came to an end in 942; from that time until Alberic's death in 954 no outside power seriously interfered with the Romans. In the tenth century such security came near enough to a miracle; no wonder his descendants referred to their *aurea progenies,* their golden lineage.

The need for a powerful ally in south Italy prompted Alberic, like earlier members of his family, to seek the favours of the Byzantines. The Emperor Romanus Lecapenus had been about to marry a daughter of Marozia to a son of his own, before the *coup* of 932 removed the *senatrix* from power; Alberic then unsuccessfully pursued the aim of marrying a Byzantine princess himself. The eunuch Theophylact, the son of Romanus Lecapenus, was in spite of his uncanonical election recognised as Patriarch of Constantinople by Alberic's brother, Pope John XI. It may be that jealousies connected with these abortive Byzantine marriages lay behind the revolt which the sisters of Alberic combined with the Roman opposition to foment, and which the prince suppressed. The search for points of Roman influence in south Italy also extended to Naples, whose ruler John III married Alberic's cousin Theodora.

The most striking thing about Alberic's rule is the way in which he associated himself with papal power in favour of the Cluniac monastic reform. Odo of Cluny, the most idealistic and distinguished churchman of the first half of the tenth century, was a close adviser of Alberic. He came on several occasions to Rome, and several times negotiated with the hostile Hugh of Provence on Alberic's behalf, including the crucial occasion of the siege of Rome. Alberic made Odo the 'archimandrite' or chief reformer of the monasteries of Rome and the district. The assistance of Odo and of the other monastic reformer John of Vendière (later Abbot of Gorze) was particularly valuable to Alberic. John of Gorze, whose activities ended at Gorze in Lorraine, originally planned to found a new monastery in the duchy of Benevento. The reform of Monte Cassino itself, which meant weaning its monks away from Capua and from the hostile Prince of Capua, Landulf, was a political victory for Alberic.[1]

By 935 Pope Leo VII had called Odo of Cluny to Rome. S. Paolo fuori le Mura, which Charlemagne had vainly tried to reform, was taken in hand by Odo and his monks, and subsequently by those of John of Gorze. The heart of the Roman reform was the new foundation of S. Maria on the Aventine, in the house of the family of Theophylact where Alberic had himself been born. To S. Silvestro in Capite (well known to English Catholics in Rome), in their native Via Lata quarter, Alberic and his family made important gifts of land, as he did to SS. Andrea and Gregorio on the Coelian hill. Other important Roman monasteries – S. Lorenzo and S. Agnese fuori le Mura – were reformed and re-endowed. Baldwin one of the monks placed by Odo in S. Maria on the Aventine, was sent by the pope to become the reforming Abbot of Monte Cassino, and at the great mother monastery was eventually succeeded by his pupil Aligernus.[2]

North of Rome the Benedictine houses were reformed and reinforced. Mount Soracte, the highest point in the gaunt tufa country which overlooks the Flaminia on one side and the Cassia on the other, was also the seat of the venerable monastery of S. Silvestro. After its recovery from the Arabs this house was still decayed and disordered, and its lands were said to have been granted out to Alberic's vassals. The family

---

[1] Mabillon, *Acta Sanctorum Ordinis Sancti Benedicti Saec. V* (Paris, 1685), p. 373; cf. B. Hamilton, 'Monastic Revival in tenth-century Rome', *Studia Monastica*, iv (1962), pp. 35–68; G. Antonelli, 'L'opera di Odone di Cluny in Italia', *Benedictina*, iv (1950), pp. 19–40; G. Arnaldi, 'Il biografo "romano" di Oddone di Cluny', *BISI*, lxxi (1959), pp. 19–37.

[2] Cf. Ferrari, *Early Roman Monasteries*, pp. 303–6, 257, 265; G. Arnaldi, *Dizionario Biografico degli Italiani*, ii, pp. 647 ff.; Partner, 'Notes on the lands of the Roman Church in the early Middle Ages', *PBSR*, xxxiv (n.s., xxi, 1966), pp. 68–78.

of Theophylact was powerful in this country, and Alberic's own brother was bishop of the adjoining town of Nepi. Alberic called Leo, a priest from the Church of the Holy Apostles adjoining his palace in the Via Lata, to reform the monastery; to trace and restore the monastery's lands he appointed Leo 'the chamberlain'. To the south-west of Soracte he sent Saint Odo's monks to reform the monastery of S. Elia, which overhangs the romantic ravine near his brother's town of Nepi.

Alberic and Leo VII restored and reformed Subiaco, the home of Western monasticism; they also made the monastery into one of the greatest landholders of the Roman District. Campagna may have been ruled for Alberic by a certain Count Benedict, who founded the important monastery of SS. Cosma and Damiano in Trastevere, and also played an important part in Alberic's diplomacy. With the great monastery of Farfa in Sabina Alberic's reform was only partly successful, at the best. This was virtually an episode in his struggle with Hugh of Provence, whose relative Ratfred was abbot of the monastery. In 936 Ratfred is said to have been poisoned by the supposedly dissolute monk Campo, who was shortly afterwards made Abbot by Hugh of Provence and supported there by Hugh's soldiers. The presence of Hugh's forces in this strongpoint on the Tiber must have added to the threat against Rome in these years; but Hugh's control of the duchy of Spoleto made a Roman riposte difficult. Campo's position was apparently at times neutral; in 940 the 'Duke and Rector' of Sabina, Ingebald, who had been given this office newly by Alberic, actually handed over to Campo the important fortress of Bocchignano. Cluniac monks were sent from Rome to try to reform the monastery, but they were threatened with murder, and fled back to the city.

Probably not until after the death of Hugh of Provence in April 947 did Alberic seriously try to unseat Campo and to replace him by Dagobert, a Roman nominee. But however unscrupulous and thieving Campo was, he was hard to deal with, and his acts as abbot were assented to by a papal delegate as late as a year before Alberic's death.[1] Roman control extended only to the Sabine lands of the monastery; its great possessions in Fermo and Camerino, centred round the holy relics of S. Vittoria on Monte Materano, were held first by the Burgundian Marquis Sarlio and then by Hildebrand the former accomplice of Campo. But the 'rectors' whom Alberic appointed annually in Sabina continued to be appointed by the popes after his death, and were of the first importance in establishing Roman government in the area. The

[1] *Reg. Farf.*, ii, no. 358, p. 61.

rectors were laymen, but the bishops of Sabina were employed as their auxiliaries; the Bishop of Sabina was given an immunity which exempted him and his clerks from lay jurisdiction and from being called to account in 'the palace'. This hardly looks like the creation of a ruler anxious to suppress clerical power.[1]

Alberic's yoke was nevertheless heavy on the Holy See, and not only his brother but Popes Marinus and Agapitus dared do nothing except under his orders. The politics of both the beginning and the end of his reign turned on oaths sworn by the Roman magnates: the first, before the *coup d'état* of 932, and the second just before his death in 953, when the magnates swore an oath – which they duly performed – to elect Alberic's bastard son Octavian as pope, on the death of Pope Agapitus II. Whatever the realities of power were, Alberic was careful to keep within the conservative legal formalities. Odo of Cluny and John of Gorze were called to Rome by the popes, and not by the prince; although Alberic held law pleas in his own palace by the Church of the Holy Apostles, the judges and the procedure were as accustomed. The titles he used – '*vestararius* and first senator, and duke of all the Romans' or 'prince and senator' – did not differ substantially from those employed by his grandfather Theophylact. Perhaps his most provocative moves, so far as papal temporal sovereignty was concerned, were to do with the inscriptions placed by him on the coinage; but in spite of the audacious 'Prince Alberic caused this to be struck' on some coins, the general pattern of the coins remained more or less what it had been. What gave Alberic his extraordinary power was the talisman of almost all power in the tenth century-victory in war. He repelled the formidable Hugh of Provence on at least three occasions, and the Hungarians once and finally; what distinguished him in the eyes of contemporaries was that 'no king of Lombard or transalpine parts managed to invade the Roman frontiers'.[2]

II

Alberic's son Octavian, who was duly elected pope when Agapitus died in 955 and took the name of John XII, was ill-cast for the role of priest-king. A young man in his early twenties, his chief pleasures were said by his enemies to have been women and hunting; even at a time when

---

[1] Kehr, *I.P.*, ii, p. 34, no. 54.
[2] *Chron. di Benedetto di S. Andrea*, p. 170. The remark is exaggerated; Hugh ravaged the environs of Rome several times.

some clerks knew little more Latin than anyone else, his ignorance was startling. Such was the type of many prince-bishops of his time, and long after it. But his fate eventually depended less on his morals than on his skill in diplomacy and war, in which his father had excelled. He was as hostile to the princes of Capua as his father had been, and he led a campaign against them with the help of the Marquis Theobald of Spoleto. The hostility of the Prince of Salerno caused the failure of the war, and Pope John had to sign a humiliating treaty obliging him to withdraw. This reverse then called down another; Berengar of Ivrea, observing that Theobald and John XII were in straits, sent an army against them under his son Guy. By 960 the situation of the Romans was so critical that Pope John resorted to the ancient expedient; he sent the Cardinal Deacon John and the *scriniarius* Azzo to ask the help of Otto the Saxon king.[1]

To call on the aid of northern and transalpine kings was no novelty for John XII's family. With the consent of his great-grandfather Theophylact, Berengar of Friuli had been crowned emperor in Rome by John X in 916; his grandmother Marozia had called on Hugh of Provence as her protector and bridegroom in 932. But his father Alberic had rejected this policy in favour of southern alliances and Roman independence; when Otto of Saxony had first entered Italy in 951 he had sent ambassadors to Rome, with a view to his coronation as emperor. Prompted by Alberic, Pope Agapitus had refused to receive him. Now in 960 Otto was not only a far different political proposition than had been Berengar or Hugh of Provence, but also a far stronger one than he himself had been ten years earlier. The rebellion of Otto's son, Liudolf, which had precipitated the greatest of the German civil wars, had been tamed; the great victory over the Hungarians on the Lechfield had been won; the pagan Slavs were being pushed back in the German east by victorious Christian armies. Now Otto stood at the head of the Christian west, anxious to raise his dignity and prestige in the eyes of the Byzantine Empire; anxious also to be sure of the direct help of the papacy in his great schemes for new bishoprics to help his colonial projects on the eastern frontier. His achievements were beginning to be comparable to those of Charlemagne; his idea of the part the Roman See could play in his empire was not unlike that of Charlemagne. In calling on Otto, John XII released the most powerful political force in Western Europe.

[1] Ibid. p. 174. Liutprand, *Opera,* J. Becker (ed.) (1915), p. 159. For what follows cf. Zimmermann, *Papstabsetzungen* (1968), pp. 77 ff.

In the late summer of 961 a great German army moved into north Italy. Berengar and his allies fled. Having assured himself of Lombardy, Otto sent his envoy ahead, and marched on Rome at the end of January 962. Outside the city on Monte Mario the emperor halted his troops, and his agents took oaths of non-aggression, and promised to restore the territory of the Roman Church. On Candlemas Day (2 February) he entered the Leonine city, acclaimed by the *scholae* and the clergy in the traditional way. He heard mass in St Peter's, offered rich gifts to the pope, and was crowned and anointed by him; while he took the traditional oaths to protect and defend the Roman Church. The pope and the Roman nobles swore on the Confession of St Peter not to comfort or receive the traitorous Berengar and his son Adalbert. The pope did his duty by approving the imperial proposals for the German Church. Finally on 13 February the emperor and the German nobles and bishops executed a treaty which confirmed the former agreements made by Frankish kings in protection of the Holy See and – in a confused and rather contradictory way – recited parts of them. The next day Otto left Rome for Pavia, to finish off Berengar's party.

The proliferation of oaths and guarantees boded ill for their execution. As had always happened under the Frankish emperors, the Romans quickly split into parties favouring and opposing the Germans. The weak papal government soon became restive under the imperial yoke, which could not fail to cut across the local and factional interests which had ruled in Rome undisturbed for so long. Within a few weeks the young pope had broken his oaths, and was in correspondence with the enemy – not only with Berengar but also with the Byzantines, to whom he sent envoys whom his rival, Pandulf of Capua, already set on playing the jackal, intercepted. While the emperor besieged Berengar and his wife Willa in Montefeltro, within papal territory, the pope sent ambassadors who protested that in spite of the imperial guarantee to return papal lands, papal vassals were being made to take oaths to the emperor. The imperial envoys to the pope (one of whom was the chronicler Liutprand of Cremona) were ill-used; the final act of defiance was to receive Berengar's son Adalbert when he landed on the Roman coast from his sojourn with the Muslims at Garde-Freinet (near Saint-Tropez), and to give him refuge in Rome.

It took Otto five years to break the Roman opposition. His first intervention was at the invitation of the imperialist group among the Roman nobles; in the autumn of 963 they seized the papal castle at S. Paolo fuori le Mura and invited the German army to enter Rome.

Otto duly arrived; he and his army glimpsed Pope John in his armour – a feudal prince at war – on the opposite bank of the Tiber, before he fled to the Campagna. The Romans took an oath not to elect another pope without imperial consent, then three days later a synod met under imperial leadership to decide canonically the fate of John XII. That Liutprand of Cremona was the official interpreter and guiding spirit of the synod shows that it was the tool of Otto's policy; Pope John was not only deposed by the synod from the papacy for his immorality, but taunted for the bad grammar of his correspondence. How delighted Liutprand would have been, to know that he was destined not only to destroy Pope John, but also to make it extremely difficult for historians a thousand years later to find out the truth about the house of Theophylact! Liutprand's stories about John – that he ordained a deacon in a stable;[1] that he 'invoked Jove and Venus' on the dice he played with – are too good to miss; but it is impossible not to feel that he is twisting the truth.

The Romans obediently elected the *protoscrinarius* Leo, one of the main curial officials, as pope. The first anti-German rebellion followed in January 964, before Otto had even left Rome. In February after the emperor and his army had left for the war on the Adriatic coast there was a successful counter-revolution. Pope Leo fled to Otto; Pope John held a counter-synod which was attended by many Italian bishops who had condemned him two months before; two cardinal bishops renounced their part in the election of Leo, which was naturally declared invalid. The Cardinal Deacon John and the *scriniarius* Azzo were punished by mutilation, and Azzo's hand, which had drawn up many papal letters, was chopped off. So were John's fingers which had drawn up a copy of the Donation of Constantine to impress the emperor. The acts of the synod, which were drawn up in proper canonical form and show the senior clergy of Rome protesting, with their bishop, against lay interference, show how tendentious Liutprand's narrative is.

Otto's power was not to be so lightly thrown off. In June the imperial army returned and laid siege to Rome in earnest; refugees from the city were mutilated and it was reduced by hunger. When Otto entered the city Pope John was already dead; the learned Benedict whom the Romans had elected to replace him renounced the papacy.[2] The Romans learned who was master; but the factions were still not

---

[1] Liutprand, p. 167. Cf. for Liutprand's credibility Zimmermann, pp. 86–7, 256–7; Lintzel, *Ausgewählte Schriften*, ii, pp. 368–9.

[2] Zimmermann, pp. 90 ff.

quieted. The plague of 964 and the famine which followed only increased discontent. On Pope Leo VIII's death in 965 the Romans elected under the eye of the imperial *missi* the Roman aristocrat John of Narni, who was acceptable to Otto, and as a member of the powerful family of the Crescenzi was also acceptable to the Roman aristocrats. John XIII was unable to control the city; in December 965 the prefect of the city Peter, whom Otto had appointed especially to keep order, led the Romans in rebellion. He was abetted by members of the clerical bureaucracy, and by some at least of the nobility of the Campagna. For almost a year Rome again enjoyed the independence of the days of Alberic, while the imperialist pope fled first to Pandulf Iron-Cap in Capua, and then to his native territory in Sabina. The day of reckoning came after December 965, when Otto marched south from Germany to restore order. There was no resistance from the Romans, but this helped them but little. In 966 twelve relatively humble popular officials (*decarcones*) were hanged; many nobles were blinded or exiled. The prefect of the city was hung by his hair from the 'horse of Constantine' (the equestrian statue of Marcus Aurelius which stood then in front of the Lateran basilica, and stands now on the Capitol), and then flogged round the city on a donkey with a 'tail' of wineskins filled with feathers. In appearance at least, the days of Roman independence were over. The old institution of a permanent imperial judge (*missus*) in Rome was not reintroduced, but from now on imperial officials would from time to time appear in Rome and sit in judgement alongside the papal ones.[1] No historian has yet satisfactorily related what is known of Otto's administration in Rome to the treaty and other engagements he entered into with the Roman Church in 962; it may indeed be that the treaty was only a mechanical compilation of more ancient documents, made without too precise thought of its political results.[2]

The century following the coronation of Otto as emperor in 962 is often referred to by historians as one of 'imperial hegemony' for the

---

[1] Otto's oath before he entered Rome in 962, not to hold judicial proceedings there, or concerning Romans, without papal advice, may have restricted the use of such officials. *MGH, Constitutiones et acta publica*, i, p. 21; Fuhrmann, *DA* (1966), pp. 124–5.

[2] There is a very carefully worked-out analysis of the development of the text of the Ottonianum in Stengel, *Abhandlungen und Untersuchungen zur mittelalterlichen Geschichte* (1960), pp. 218–48. Cf. also H. Zimmermann, 'Das Privilegium Ottonianum von 962 und seine Problemgeschichte', *MIÖG*, Ergbd. xx (1962), pp. 147–90. For Ullmann's thesis (in *Cambridge Historical Journal*, xi (1953–5), pp. 114–28) about the Ottonianum, see pp. 48–50 above, in notes. The article of H. Beumann, 'Das Kaisertum Ottos d. Gr. nach tausend Jahren', *HZ*, cxcv (1962), pp. 529–73, is helpful. For what follows see also Zimmermann, *Papstabsetzungen* (1968), pp. 98–9, 250–1.

papacy. It is indeed true that the churches in imperial Italy, and the Church of Rome with them, were firmly kept in this period within the general church policy, the *Reichskirchensystem*, of Otto and his successors. But the Roman bishopric was inextricably linked with the local aristocracy, as were many bishoprics in Europe at that time. In terms of practical politics imperial control of the Roman Church frequently broke down against the opposition of the Romans; Italy was in fact no exception to the successful resistance of regionalism to central government which was common to most of early medieval Europe. The very John XIII whom Otto restored to the papacy in 966 was probably the cousin of Alberic, although the branch of the family to which he is thought to have belonged – the Crescenzi – was becoming hostile to the main line of the house of Theophylact. Far from eschewing nepotism, Pope John made some remarkable and important alienations of papal lands for the benefit of his family. In 970 he granted the town of Palestrina for life to his sister the *senatrix* Stefania. To his nephew by his sister Stefania, Benedict, he gave the rectorate of Sabina, thus establishing this branch of his family in the middle Tiber area in positions from which they were not to be budged for three-quarters of a century.[1]

In 972 John XIII died, and was succeeded by Benedict VI. This was a choice displeasing to the Crescenzi, the family of the dead pope. Otto I died in 973; in the following year John XIII's brother Crescentius de Theodora had Pope Benedict unseated and murdered, and replaced by his own nominee Boniface VII. This did not last long; imperial agents dealt with the Roman revolt, turned out the intruder, and placed on the papal throne the former Bishop of Sutri, Benedict VII. Yet again, in fact, German power had only displaced one set of Roman nobles for another. Benedict VII was probably a member of the house of Theophylact; at all events he was an aristocrat, and his nephew is found as Count of Ariccia in 981.[2] So long as Otto II was in Italy the Roman factions were kept in order; but both he and Benedict VII died in 983, and as a result the next pope, John XIV, was overthrown and murdered by the Crescenzi, and replaced by the exiled anti-pope Boniface VII. After a short and violent pontificate of a year, Boniface also died.

---

[1] G. Bossi, *I Crescenzi. Contributo alla storia di Roma e dintorni* (Rome, 1915). Palestrina, *I.P.*, i, p. 185, no. 1. Bossi calls the Stefaniani of Sabina 'Crescenzi', although on the male side they were descendants of Benedict husband of Stefania *senatrix*, and Benedict was not from the Crescenzi. See however for the social importance of maternal kinship in Roman society H. Schwarzmaier, 'Zur Familie Viktors IV.', *Quellen*, xlviii (1968), pp. 74–7.

[2] L. M. Hartmann, *Tabularium Sanctae Mariae in Via Lata* (Vienna, 1895–1901), i, p.14. For these events cf. Zimmermann, *Papstabsetzungen* (1968), pp. 99–102.

His successor John XV could do nothing but bow before Crescenzi power; probably by his authority John Crescentius described himself in 986 as 'patrician of Rome'. Two years later another Crescentius, called 'de Nomentana' was 'senator of all the Romans', and by papal grant the ruler of the important port of Terracina. The visit of the Empress Theophanu, ruler in the minority of her son Otto III, in 989, did little or nothing to curb his power; he 'held all Rome' and Rome was said to have been in his day 'orderly under the law of the Apostle'. By this his supporters probably intended to mean that Rome was governed by him under papal sovereignty. Frankish clerical observers with different prejudices said at the Council of Rheims in 991 that no justice was to be had in Rome without bribing him.[1]

III

By the time Otto I crossed the Alps in 961 the decay of good order and security in Italy was already a century old. Profound social and governmental changes had taken place in the Roman territory. They may be described, although far from exactly, as 'feudal'. Feudal grants of the Frankish type were in fact unknown in tenth-century Rome, and there is no recorded use of the word 'feudum' in the Roman District before the early twelfth century. Grants were made either to the third generation (which was a common Roman form), or 'per libellum', or in emphyteusis. The granting of a 'benefice' was not practised as such. But though the name was lacking, we may wonder if the thing was not there. One or two tenth-century examples begin to point to a regime in the Roman District in which vassals were granted lands with a consequent obligation to make war at the behest of their lords.[2]

The regime of seigniorial property, military organisation, and personal dependence which did exist round Rome was not strictly in the legal sense 'feudal' but (as in Anglo-Saxon England) it was a closely compar-

---

[1] *Acta Concilii Causeiensis*, in *MGH, Scriptores*, iii, p. 691.

[2] *Statuti della provincia romana*, ii (Rome, 1929), p. 3; cf. also E. Stevenson, 'Documenti dell'archivio della cattedrale di Velletri', *ASR*, xii (1889), at p. 75; R. Morghen, 'Le relazioni del monastero Sublacense col papato, la feudalità e il comune nell'alto medio evo', *ASR*, li (1928), pp. 182–253 and especially at pp. 209–10; C. Calisse, 'Le condizioni della proprietà territoriale studiate sui documenti della provincia romana dei sec. VIII, IX, X', *ASR*, vii (1884), pp. 309–52, ibid. viii (1885), pp. 60–100; K. Jordan, 'Das Eindringen des Lehnwesens in das Rechtsleben der römischen Kurie', *Archiv für Urkundenforschung*, xii (1932), pp. 13–110; G. Falco, 'L'amministrazione papale nella Campagna e nella Marittima', *ASR*, xxxviii (1915), pp. 677–707; W. Kölmel, *Rom und der Kirchenstaat im 10. und 11. Jahrhundert bis in die Anfänge der Reform* (Berlin, 1931).

able phenomenon. Between the Arab invasions of the mid-ninth century and the end of the tenth, both the castle (*castellum*) and the fortified village (*castrum*) had become common if not universal in the Roman countryside. The rural population had been largely re-assembled in new centres – what surprise can this give our own generation, which has seen millions of peasants 'regrouped' in the wars of Vietnam, Malaya and Algeria? The papal *domus cultae,* very large handholding units under a strong central direction, could not survive in these altered conditions; they broke up and allowed the peasants to drift or be shepherded into new centres of habitation. The great *domus culta* of Capracorum, for example, fragmented into a number of smaller units, some of which at a rather later date became the centres of new seigniorial estates.[1]

As elsewhere in Europe the 'castles' of this early period of feudalism were simple enough. That at Paterno, near Mount Soracte, where the Emperor Otto III died in 1002, was a simple curtain wall with a raised walk for the defenders; others were probably of wood.[2] As elsewhere in Europe, the castles were often compact economic units, with local pasturage rights and other agricultural dues assigned for their support, and sometimes with rights over the military service of the neighbourhood.[3] Such grants were made by the popes, but monasteries and bishops would also grant castles to laymen, with the obligation to provide for their defence. Neither the Roman army nor the militia formerly raised from the papal estates was enough to meet the stringent military needs of the ninth and tenth centuries, and the Roman government was compelled, like other public authorities in Western Europe at the same time, to try to organise the local landlords and their levies into a coherent defensive system.

[1] See my article in *PBSR* (1966), quoted above, and also Mallett and Whitehouse, ibid. xxxv (1967). There is little evidence of how the *domus cultae* broke up, and it is noticeable that no occupation of Castel Porciano is proved before 1100 (ibid.).

[2] A. W. Lawrence, 'Early Medieval Fortifications near Rome', ibid, xxxii (1964), pp. 89–122.

[3] e.g. the castle of Subiaco, which was first granted to the monastery at the instance of Alberic, *I.P.,* ii, pp. 88–9, nos. 11, 18. The latter document of 958 lists with reference to the castle of Subiaco various lands 'cum glandaticis, herbaticis, vel quilibet alia datione, quae ad castelli jus pertinet, et ad nostrae sanctae Romanae ecclesiae soliti sunt persolvere'. Cf. Morghen, in *ASR,* li (1928), pp. 210, 226–8, whose comments do not really suffice. See also the important document for Farfa's castle of Bocchignano, *Reg. Farf.,* iii, no. 513. The grant made in 977 to Crescenzio de Theodora by the abbey of S. Andrea in Silice (also in the Velletri area) is comparable. The lay grantee promises military service, and the abbey continues to receive the rents of the tenements. Judicial rights are attributed to the 'consuls or viscounts', but some rights of private justice are reserved to the lay grantee, none to the grantor. Cf. Tomassetti, 'Feudalesimo romano', *Rivista internazionale di scienze sociali e discipline ausiliarie,* anno ii, vol. vi (1894), pp. 37–58.

The monasteries had played a central part in the military reforms of Alberic of Rome. Between the Via Flaminia and the Via Cassia, and in the valley of the river Aniene, Alberic had made the Benedictines supreme. The economic basis of this re-organisation was the historic patrimony of the Roman Church, which was in effect decentralised, and administered by individual Roman churches and monasteries and monasteries outside Rome, instead of by the old central administration for the papal estates. The *actionarii* or papal estate agents continued to exist, but their function was much reduced. The great *domus cultae* which ringed Rome passed largely into the possession of the Roman monasteries, particularly of S. Paolo fuori le Mura.

On the other hand we know both from the complaints of church councils and from the distribution of land ownership in the later period, that very many church estates found their way into the hands of Roman nobles. The chronicler of the monastery of St Andrew by Mount Soracte remarks that after the confusion of the Arab attacks most of the lands of the monastery had been granted to vassals of Alberic. As one of the magnates of Sabina pointed out in the course of the quarrels over the estates of the monastery of Farfa, in Roman law thirty years' prescription (forty years in privileged cases) conferred ownership, and if a layman held church property for that period and evaded payment of rent or recognition, his title became absolute. Most of the lands 'granted' by Alberic and his relatives to Roman churches had probably been church lands. It is moreover hard to determine whether church estates remained in the hands of the churches which owned the legal title, because instead of farming them in demesne they might grant them 'to the third generation' to laymen – thus the estate of the monastery of S. Cornelio, the ancient centre of Hadrian I's *domus culta* of Capracorum, which on paper belonged continuously to the monasteries of St Peter's, is known from another source to have been in the possession of a Roman nobleman. But such grants were not always entirely unfavourable to the Church. The grant by the Bishop of Velletri to a nobleman for the construction of a castle contains the obligation to cultivate and populate the area, and reserves a share in the agricultural profits for the bishop.[1]

Various emperors from Louis the Pious onwards passed laws applicable to Italy in order to revoke the alienations of church property to laymen. But although imperial protection was of some effect in defending the properties of the Church of Ravenna, it was hardly effectual

[1] Stevenson, *ASR* (1889), xii, pp. 73–80.

in the Roman District. Only the imperial monastery of Farfa managed to appeal with much result to imperial judges. Most of the estates of Farfa had been in fact in the first place carved out of the Sabine patrimony of the Holy See. This is clear in the grant of Stephen IV of 817, but it is also evident from the very compressed references in the papal privilege of 1049 that in the intervening centuries the memory of the early origins of the lands of the monastery had grown dim.[1]

The three key fortresses in the area were Arci to the south of the monastery, Tribuco to the west, and Bocchignano, overhanging it to the north. At the end of the tenth century and the beginning of the eleventh there was a bitter struggle between the so-called Crescenzi family of Sabina (who for most of the time held the office of papal rector) and the monastery, for the control of these castles. One of the castles, Bocchignano, had belonged to the papal *massa* of Salla, in the Sabine patrimony. It had been granted by the popes to a Roman magnate, possibly one Gratianus, whose daughter married the first-known papal rector of Sabina, the Frank Ingebald. Ingebald and his wife, following Alberic's policy of placing key castles in the hands of monasteries, granted Bocchignano to Farfa in 939. Over all three castles there was continuous conflict from the rise of the Crescenzi family to power in Sabina under John XIII to the breaking of their hegemony over the monastery by the emperors Henry II and Conrad II.

It must not be thought, because of the political confusion of the times, that the great landed estates were poorly cultivated and valueless. With the expulsion of the Muslims from central Italy in 915 the greatest single cause of destruction in the countryside was removed; the Hungarians never attained the destructive capacity of the Arabs in this part of Italy. The tenth century, particularly the latter part of the century, was a period of recovery and expansion in Italian agriculture. Vines and olives were being planted widely all over central Italy in this period, both by the *coloni* on the demesne lands of the church estates and – probably far more – by the *libellarii* who accepted church lands for small rents, with the obligation of improving, planting and populating them.[2] It was an era of re-population and rural activity, and although the rents charged by clerical landowners were low, they were appreci-

---

[1] *I.P.*, ii, pp. 60, 64, nos. 7, 28. For attempts to stop the alienation of church property see M. Uhlirz, 'Die italienische Kirchenpolitik der Ottonen', *MIöG*, xlviii (1934), pp. 201–321, at pp. 224–34, 288 ff.

[2] Cf. P. J. Jones, 'Per la storia agraria italiana nel medio evo', *Rivista Storica Italiana*, lxxvi (1964), pp. 287–348; Gino Luzzatto, *Per una storia economica italiana* (Bari, 1957), pp. 27–46.

able. When the castle of Bocchignano was recovered by the abbey of Farfa in 1014, the two-thirds of the land attached to it which were not in demesne were at once re-leased to smallholders with the duty to cultivate and improve them.

Some areas in the Roman District, far from expanding in the tenth and eleventh centuries, suffered decline and depopulation. One obvious reason for the decay of places on the coast like Corneto, Civita Vecchia, Cervetri, is failure to recover from the effects of earlier Arab raids; but there are other factors much harder to account for, such as alluvial deposits which changed the levels and courses of streams and rivers, and blocked ancient drainage systems. Some ancient centres such as Orchia, a city on the frontier of Lombard Tuscany, completely decayed, while new towns like Viterbo grew up and attracted their inhabitants. South of Rome the bishopric of Tres Tabernae on the Via Appia disappears from history in this period. But on the whole the country south of Rome seems to have been less liable to decay than certain areas to the north. While Ninfa and Norma, Anzio, Nettuno, Astura remained relatively flourishing centres for a long time, some places north and north-west of Rome, such as the bishoprics of Silva Candida and Porto, were still to decay during the wars of the Investiture Contest at the end of the eleventh century.[1]

IV

In 996 began five of the strangest and most remarkable years in the history of medieval Rome. A year earlier the Emperor Otto III, son of the Byzantine Princess Theophanu and pupil of the Greek Philagathos and the Frankish philosopher Gerbert, had come of age. He was an antiquarian imperialist, anxious to impose on the German and Latin worlds a 'renewed' empire. When Pope John XV appealed to him against the overmighty Crescentius, he responded readily; he was anxious to come to Italy to repeat the coronation ceremonies of his father and grandfather. By the time he was in Pavia, John XV had died. The Romans sent to Otto to know his will; to them he sent his relative Brun of Carinthia, a member of the Saxon royal family, to be elected in Rome as the first German pope. Perhaps this first of his acts towards the Roman See was the most revolutionary of all; he had treated the chair of Peter as any other imperial bishopric, to be placed at the disposal of the

[1] Cf. *PBSR*, xxxiv (n.s., xxi, 1966), pp. 77-8.

royal house. Gregory V is more important for who he was than for what he did.

In 996 Crescentius rebelled against the German pope and drove him from Rome; in the following year he had had the Greek Philagathos, Otto's former teacher and diplomat, elected pope in his stead. Byzantine policy had some part in this choice of pope. Otto was over the Alps, but at the end of the year he returned to Rome with an army to re-impose order after the traditions of his house. The Romans offered little resistance, and some of them were glad to see Crescentius overthrown. In so far as the revolution had been an attempt to re-introduce Greek influence instead of German, it failed as miserably as all earlier similar efforts. The headless body of Crescentius and those of a dozen of his followers were dragged to Monte Mario for exposure. Philagathos was taken and, in spite of the protests of Saint Nilus, shamefully mutilated; his living remains were judged and condemned by a synod. In April 998 the Frank Gerbert was made Archbishop of Ravenna, thus placing the two great sees under ultramontane heads. Three counties of Bobbio (Sarsina), Forlì and Forlimpopoli were at once donated to Archbishop Gerbert, underlining the fact that his appointment was intended to facilitate imperial government in Italy. Like many imperial bishops he did duty as a soldier as well as an administrator.[1]

On the Aventine, close to Adalbert's monastery of SS. Bonifacio and Alessio, the emperor built a new palace, far from the old imperial offices near St Peter's. He ate alone on a dais after the Byzantine style, not sitting with his sword companions in the hall like a German prince. In 999 Gregory V died, although a young man. Otto had him succeeded in the papacy by Gerbert, the Archbishop of Ravenna, who took the title of Silvester II, in itself reminiscent of the hierocratic pretensions of the Roman See, but related also to the 'new Constantine'.

In the Aventine palace Otto surrounded himself by officials whose titles bespoke the 'renewal of the empire of the Romans'. A *magister militiae*, a 'naval prefect', a 'master of the imperial palace', a *protospatharius* or sword bearer, a *'logotheta'* or chancellor – all these were new names for the German royal household, even if not always new offices. The office holders themselves are also not without interest. Some were ultramontane. But Otto clearly could not do without the Roman aristocracy. The Crescenzi were disgraced, but not reduced to

---

[1] *MGH, DO III*, no. 341, p. 770; cf. Schramm, *Kaiser, Rom und Renovatio*, i, p. 104; M. Uhlirz, 'Die Restitution des Exarchates Ravenna durch die Ottonen', *MIöG*, 1 (1936), pp. 1–34; for Gerbert as soldier see Uhlirz, ibid. (1934), pp. 255n., 285.

beggary or surrender. When Benedict the ruler of Sabina was called on to fulfil his undertaking in court to restore Cere (Cervetri) to the abbey of Farfa, he refused. Only when the emperor had his son Crescentius hanged before his eyes, did Benedict condescend to carry out the bargain – but this still failed to break his power in Sabina.

The eclipse of the Crescenzi meant the admission to favour of the house of Tuscolo, the main branch of the house of Theophylact. Gregory of Tuscolo, the 'naval prefect', was also lord of Anzio, and his son Alberic was 'master of the imperial palace'. Denounced as a 'tyrant' by S. Nilus, he nonetheless had the ear of emperor and pope, and when the Roman factions began to threaten revolution in 1001, it was he who warned the rulers.

Otto never possessed the overwhelming material power which would have been necessary to execute his ideas. He was ineffective in southern Italy, which was so important for the control of Rome. His attempt to replace the Prince of Capua by his own German nominee in 999 was defeated by a revolution there in the following year. When he was so angry with Benevento for foisting other relics on him than the body of St Bartholomew which had been promised, he sent an army against the town. It failed to force the walls, and returned without accomplishing anything. Otto had tried to get the help of the Duke of Gaeta, who was a relative of the house of Theophylact; but the effect of these military failures of the Roman nobles was that which failure in war always had in the tenth century – defeat meant desertion.

At the same time the emperor's nominee Pope Silvester was trying to impose order on the Roman magnates, and meeting with resistance. In order to subtract the port of Terracina from the rule of the Crescenzi he granted it in fee to Daifer of Traetto, with the obligation of military service – the first strictly feudal grant by a pope.[1] He became involved in conflicts with the nobles of Sabina which he was unable to settle on his own, and he therefore asked Otto to send an imperial *missus* to sit beside the papal judge and settle the case.

In July of 1000 Otto returned from his last sojourn north of the Alps to Italy. The whole of non-Byzantine southern Italy was in opposition or revolt against his regime, and unrest was widespread elsewhere. The envoys of Silvester and the Roman nobles met him at Como; they had much to discuss. The pope was asking for the 'restitution' of papal lands in the exarchate of Ravenna, which Gregory V had requested in 996,

---

[1] *I.P.*, ii, pp. 120–1; cf. Kölmel, *Rom und Kirchenstaat*, p. 40; Jordan, *Arch. f. Urk.*, xii (1932) pp. 38–40.

only to be put off by Otto with a temporary settlement which 'out of love for the pope' placed eight counties in Pentapolis south of Ravenna under the protection of the marquises of Spoleto and Camerino. It is possible that the papal requests for the 'restitution' of these lands had someting to do with Otto's failure in 996 to re-issue the 'donation' of Otto I to the papacy. At Ravenna the two main political questions, closely inter-related, were the 'restitution' of the lands of the Roman Church, and the recovery of those lands which the church of Ravenna had allowed to fall into the hands of feudal magnates. Ravenna and Comacchio, although formally 'restored' to the pope by Otto I in 967, had in fact been administered by the Empress Theophanu. Otto III in 996 failed to restore these places, and the third county of Ferrara, to Pope Gregory V. Finally in 999 Otto III created another faithful churchman, Leo of Vercelli, Archbishop of Ravenna, and made to his see an important donation which included Ravenna, the county of Ferrara, and the lands taken from the condemned Count Lambert.[1] Yet a further imperial grant was made to the Archbishop in 1001, which mentioned his rule in the whole area between the mountains and the sea, between the rivers Reno and Foglia.

In January 1001 Otto settled the fate of the eight counties in Pentapolis in a famous and remarkable document. He made over the counties to the pope, but he prefaced the donation by an account of the circumstances which made it necessary, and a biting criticism of the authenticity of the documents alleged by the popes for the 'restitutions' which they claimed. First of all Otto refers to the negligence of the popes, who have alienated church property both inside and outside Rome in order to raise money, and despoiled the very altars of Peter and Paul. The reference to the feudalisation of church property is clear; Gerbert had protested bitterly about this as Abbot of Bobbio, and again both he (as Archbishop of Ravenna) and the emperor had forbidden such alienations at the Council of Pavia in September 998.[2] Otto went on in the donation of 1001 to complain bitterly that having once vainly frittered

---

[1] *MGH, DO III*, no. 330, p. 758. This arrangement was accepted by Silvester (*I.P.*, v, p. 52, no. 166), and was to some extent a confirmation of privileges to Ravenna by Gregory V. Cf. also Uhlirz, article in *MIöG* (1936), cited above, and in *MIöG* (1934), pp. 264 ff.; idem, *Jahrbücher des deutschen Reiches unter Otto III.* (Berlin, 1954), pp. 353–60; W. Kölmel, 'Die kaiserliche Herrschaft im Gebiet von Ravenna (Exarchat und Pentapolis) vor dem Investiturstreit', *Hist. Jahrb.*, lxxxviii (1968), pp. 257–99, especially at pp. 274 ff.

[2] *MGH, Constitutiones et acta publica*, i, no. 23, p. 49. The argument is the same as that of *DO III*, no. 389 (see below); that an emperor cannot make valid grants of public property to corporations in mortmain.

away their possessions, certain popes had virtually claimed for themselves a substantial part of the empire. In order to make good this claim
the papal court had fabricated the Donation of Constantine, of which
Cardinal Deacon John 'of the mutilated fingers' had drawn up a copy
in gold script.[1] Charles (probably Charles the Bald) had drawn up a
document making over public imperial property (*nostra publica*) to the
papacy. But in attempting to convey public rights in this manner,
Charles was granting what was not his to give. Fabricated evidence
having been thus set aside (Otto concluded), he the emperor gave to the
pope (whom he himself had made pope) what was the emperor's to give,
and what was not already papal property. In other words, he made the
gift of the counties as a free gift, and not as a part-satisfaction of the
'restitutions' which the popes continually claimed.[2]

The inadequacies of Otto's power were fully revealed a few weeks
later in 1001. The rebellion of Tivoli after the murder of an imperial
official was put down by Otto without trouble. But this disturbance
precipitated the revolt of Rome itself and the siege of the emperor in his
palace on the Aventine. Escaping with scant dignity with the help of
Hugh of Tuscany, he had to leave the city, and to retire to Ravenna. In
the summer he was again near Rome, with his headquarters at the
castle of Paterno in the Benedictine-controlled area round Mount
Soracte. The 'servant of the apostles' had reached his term; on
24 January 1002 Otto died in the castle of Paterno, twenty-two years
old, of some unknown infection. He died under the shadow of Mount
Soracte, on the site of the legend of Constantine and Silvester which so
much offended him: when he died the gates of Rome were still closed
against him. His Italian policy had miserably failed.

V

Otto III's end did not mark the finish of German rule in Italy. On the
contrary, although the uncertainties of the succession to the throne
and of German politics in general meant that for long periods Italy
went its own way, imperial rule was renewed, and was no less brutal for
being so spasmodic. The emperor in Germany still needed papal help.
In central Europe papal approval was important in such matters as

---

[1] See p. 89 above.
[2] *MGH, DO III*, no. 389, p. 819; Schramm, *Kaiser, Rom und Renovatio*, ii, pp. 66–7; Ullmann,
Papal Government, 3rd ed., p. 240–6. Cf. Schramm, i, pp. 161–76; Kölmel (against Schramm),
Hist. Jahrb. (1968), loc. cit.

the foundation of the bishopric of Bamberg. On the Roman side Henry II's action against heresy, German missionary work in the Slav lands, even the possibility of imperial action against the fanatical Caliph Hakim of Egypt, were present in the papal mind. Whenever the emperor came to Italy he used his German soldiers ruthlessly, and insisted on his rights in Roman lands, both in the name of bishops and the execution of justice. Just as Otto III had made his cousin Brun, Bishop of Rome, so Henry II on his first Italian trip in 1014 made his half-brother Arnulf, Archbishop of Ravenna. The resistance of Italian magnates was feeble. In 1015 Arduin, the last indigenous 'king of Italy' before Victor Emmanuel II, died a disappointed and defeated man.

Germany hegemony in Italy was not shifted, and the Ottonian yoke remained. But other factors in the Mediterranean balance of power changed. In 1009 Melo, a citizen of Bari, led a revolt which badly shook Greek rule in southern Italy. He looked for and found support from all the anti-Greek elements in Italy: from the Lombard princes, and from the pope, who after the initial defeat of Melo gave his brother-in-law Datto control of a papal fortress on the banks of the lower Garigliano.[1] Melo also looked outside Italy, both to the emperor, to whom he went twice in Germany before 1020, and to a sea-going people who now interfered in Italian politics for the first time. With the encouragement of Guaimar of Salerno, messengers were sent to Normandy. Here the disorder of political and social life and the lack of portions for younger sons meant that young fighting men were only too willing to try their luck for land and loot in Italy. In or near 1017 a Norman force made its way to the war in south Italy, stopping at Rome on the way, and apparently getting some encouragement from Pope Benedict VIII. In the next year the Greek Catapan Bojoannes inflicted a defeat on Melo's forces which virtually crushed the rebellion, so the Norman reinforcement failed in its ostensible purpose. But although Bojoannes in his ten-year rule re-imposed Greek government in subject Italy, the Normans remained. They were used as mercenaries by the southern princes; once attached they were not to be shaken off.

On the surface at least, Rome after the death of Otto III continued in the old ways. Pope Silvester lived only untill 1003, and with his death the ties with Ottonian policy were broken. Once he also was out of

---

[1] This suggests that in spite of earlier concessions of the papal patrimony of Traetto to the rulers of Gaeta, the popes retained rights there. For what follows see J. Gay, *L'Italie meridionale et l'empire byzantin* (Paris, 1904), pp. 399–449; F. Chalandon, *Histoire de la domination normande en Italie et en Sicile* (Paris, 1907), i, pp. 1–111.

the way, the instigators of the anti-German revolt of 1001 seized power. Until 1012 the rulers of Rome were the Crescenzi family, with John the Patrician of Rome at their head, while another member of the family was 'prefect'.[1] Like his father John 'de Nomentana', John the patrician was accused of tyrannical behaviour and also of being 'so rapacious that he seized the offerings made to the altar of the apostles'. His death in 1012 altered the composition but not the method of Roman government. The Pope Gregory who was elected at the instigation of the Crescenzi was ousted by a member of the family of Theophylact, Pope Benedict VIII. With his accession to the papal throne, the Tusculan family entered their last tenure of supreme power in Rome. With their centre at Tuscolo above Frascati, protected by the adjacent fortress of Borghetto, patrons of the monasteries of Grotta-ferrata and Subiaco and of very many churches and religious houses in and round Rome, the Tusculan family held most of the traditional levers of power. Once again they had a member of the house as pope. Alberic, the brother of Pope Benedict, was *consul et dux*; another brother Romulus was 'senator of all the Romans' – this brother in 1024 himself succeeded to the papacy as John XIX.

How far the Tusculans initially owed their return to German support is unclear. Their father, Gregory 'the naval prefect' had been a figure in the court of Otto III, and Alberic the brother of Benedict VIII had been Otto's 'master of the imperial palace'. The old law of Roman politics had been that one party always looked to the foreigner. The new Tusculan pope called on Henry II to come to Italy. Henry came in the last days of 1013,[2] and held a synod at Ravenna to examine the question of the opposition to the archbishop. He deposed him, caused his own half-brother Arnulf to be elected to the archbishopric, and went on with Arnulf to Rome, where he and his queen were crowned on 14 February 1014. The opposition faction of the Crescenzi took the predictable step of siding with the anti-imperial faction in Italy. The coronation was therefore followed by a rising in Rome, led by the Crescenzi, in favour of Arduin's supporters, the sons of the Marquis Otbert II. The rising was swiftly put down.

Like other feudal bishops of his time, the pope had his own soldiery.

---

[1] G. Bossi, *I Crescenzi*, pp. 66–84; idem, 'I Crescenzi di Sabina Stefaniani e Ottaviani dal 1012 at 1106', *ASR*, xli (1918), pp. 111–70; Kölmel, *Rom und Kirchenstaat*, p. 158; Zimmermann, *Papstabsetzungen* (1968), pp. 115 ff.; G. B. Borino, 'L'elezione e la deposizione di Gregorio VI', *ASR*, xxxix (1916), pp. 161–256, 295–410, especially at p. 363.

[2] Cf. M. Fornasari, 'Enrico II e Benedetto VIII e i canoni del presunto concilio di Ravenna del 1014', *Rivista di Storia della Chiesa in Italia*, xviii (1964), pp. 46–55.

When Henry II sat with Benedict VIII to hear the plea of the abbey of Farfa against the Crescenzi, the emperor said in the pleadings: 'Lord pope, give me your troops, so that they can go with mine to take the castles belonging to my monastery.'[1] The revolution in Rome then intervened, and the German troops were employed for other purposes. But when it was over the pope with his forces marched into Sabina, and duly reduced the Crescenzi fortresses. There is no evidence whether these troops were Roman militia, or Tusculan feudal levies, or both. They were said to have been assisted in the siege by a miraculous drought.

The renewed rule of the Tusculan family after 1012 was not absolute in Rome or elsewhere. The Tusculans had to share their power with the other Roman families which were far too strongly entrenched in Rome and the District to expel – families which like the Tusculans themselves had long since passed from being senatorial landowners to being feudal barons. The Stefaniani relatives of the Crescenzi retained the prefecture of Rome under Benedict VIII, and the Ottaviani branch retained the rectorate of Sabina.[2] Benedict VIII, like the other feudal rulers of his day, had to play off one aristocratic faction against another; having in 1014–15 tried with some success to break the power of the Stefaniani in Sabina to give back to Farfa the castles they had usurped, after four or five years the pope reversed his alliances, and in alliance with his own family and the 'sons of Raynier' and the footmen swore to the Stefaniani that he would make the monastery restore the castles.[3] No one has managed to explain the identity of the 'sons of Raynier', though they may have been connected with the counts of Galeria. But the mention of the 'footmen' suggests elements of social conflict in this quarrel; in the towns round Rome the strife between 'knights' and 'footmen' was just beginning to be a major disturbing influence.

In the Campagna other families, or other branches of the same families, had to be reckoned with. Amatus of Ceccano, a relative of the Crescenzi, held the office of 'Count of Campagna' which in Alberic's day had been given to the ally of the Tusculans, Benedict. At Piperno,

---

[1] *Chron. Farf.*, i, pp. 68–9.

[2] Kölmel, pp. 60 ff.; Bossi, article quoted in *ASR*, xli (1918); Vehse, in *Quellen*, xxi (1929–30), pp. 144–9.

[3] *Hugonis Querimonium (Fonti per la Storia d'Italia*, xxxiii), p. 95. For the sons of Raynier, Bossi, pp. 128–9; Borino, *ASR*, xxxix (1916), pp. 193–201; Kölmel, pp. 159–60. No one seems to have commented on the significance of the *pedones* here; for their significance in Campagna, G. Falco, 'I comuni della Campagna e della Marittima nel medio evo', *ASR*, xlii (1919), p. 557.

Anagni and probably in other towns south of Rome, noblemen bore the title of 'duke'. Other nobles were entrenched in the valley of the Aniene, in conflict with the monastery of Subiaco.[1]

What made German help practically essential to the Tusculans was the old problem of the south. The papal alliance with the anti-Byzantine forces in southern Italy was in its earlier stages a failure. There may also have been a connection between Benedict's calling in the Normans and the military operations against the Arabs, which led in 1016 to the great sea victory over the Arab fleet by Pisans, Genoese, and other Christian 'defenders' who were inspired if not sent by the pope. But in 1018 Melo, the leader of the rebellion against the Greeks, was heavily defeated. The German Bishop Pilgrim, whom Henry II had sent as *missus* and 'chancellor' to Italy, was unable to do much to help the deteriorating situation of the emperor's friends there. In 1020 Pope Benedict celebrated Easter with the emperor at Bamberg. The meeting gave the pope at least part of what he wanted. Henry re-issued to the pope a new 'donation', a version of Otto I's solemn document of 962, which Otto III had refrained from re-issuing. The venerable and from a territorial point of view almost politically meaningless text was repeated almost as Otto's chancery had prepared it, with only one or two minor variants – the omission of Salerno, the ally of the Tusculans, from the southern possessions of the papacy; a minor grant of territory in Umbria made by the emperor in exchange for some papal lands in Germany.[2] The imperial guarantee of protection had been repeated, and in 1022 the emperor honoured the bond, and marched to Italy with a large army, one of whose most important duties was to redress the balance of power in the south. From the papal point of view it was high time; Datto had been driven from his papal fortress on the Garigliano and executed, and the hostile Pandulf of Capua had set his own brother in charge of Monte Cassino.

While the German campaign in southern Italy in 1022 was not an unqualified success – it did not secure the effective submission of Troia,

---

[1] Falco, 'L'amministrazione papale nella Campagna e nella Marittima dalla caduta della dominazione bisantina al sorgere dei comuni', ibid. xxxviii (1915), pp. 677–707; Jordan, *Arch. f. Urk.*, xii (1932), pp. 35–44. For Subiaco, see Morghen's article in *ASR*, li (1928), quoted above.

[2] Cf. J. Ficker, *Forschungen zur Reichs- und Rechtsgeschichte Italiens*, ii, pp. 332 ff.; Ullmann, *Papal Government*, 248–9. For the papal patrimonies in Germany, E. Perels, 'Päpstliche Patrimonien in Deutschland zur Karolinger- und Sachsenzeit', *Zeumer Festschrift* (Weimar, 1910), pp. 483–92. Documents on the exchange, *DH II*, nos. 382–4 and cf. the donation itself, *DH II*, no. 427. These are the lands round Cesi later known as the terra Arnulphorum.

3   Pippin's Donation to Pope Stephen

4   The Septizonium in the sixteenth century (see p. 135)

the key to northern Apulia – it had the usual effect of coercing the Lombard princes for a time, and it gave the Romans valuable breathing space. The pope accompanied the emperor to Capua and to Monte Cassino, where the abbot was replaced. The emperor's political aims were not accomplished by the time of his death (and that of the pope) in 1024. Benedict was succeeded without any apparent contradiction by his brother Romanus, the 'senator of all the Romans', who took the title of John XIX. But in the north the German palaces after the death of the emperor went up in flames. In 1026 the German troops marched back over the Alps under the new Emperor Conrad II. Conrad was crowned in Rome in 1027, and his relations with the Tusculans continued to be close in spite of the friendly reception which Pope John had given to the Byzantine envoys after his succession.[1] Ravenna and Rome shared the anti-German feeling of the north of Italy, notwithstanding the policies of the pope, and there were serious riots during Conrad's stay in both cities (that in Rome was seen by the Danish King of England, Cnut). But Conrad's attention was now politically reserved for the north rather than the south of Italy. The redoubtable Pandulf of Capua was allowed out of captivity to resume his power; the death of Guaimar of Salerno in 1027 and his succession by a minor robbed the papal-imperial party in the south of another valuable ally.

Even from Conrad, whose policy in Italy was stern to the point of savagery, the Tusculan popes could still extract valuable concessions. In 1032 John XIX died and was succeeded by his nephew Theophylact who took the name of Benedict IX – a grown man and not a child at his accession, contrary to what the old scholarship thought, but nevertheless an undistinguished and negligent man, whose retention of the papacy for twelve years seems a tribute to the entrenched power of his family rather than his own ability.[2] In 1038 nevertheless, while Benedict IX was with the emperor at Spello, Conrad issued a constitution which categorically stopped the application of the Lombard law system in Rome and the District, even in cases involving men who lived by Lombard law.[3] This was a considerable victory for the Roman nobility

---

[1] John XIX consented to the reorganisation of the bishoprics of Capitanata carried out by the catapan Bojoannes; he gained by Greek recognition of a new Latin metropolitan of Bari. Cf. H.-W. Klewitz, 'Zur Geschichte der Bistumsorganisation Campaniens und Apuliens im 10. und 11. Jahrhundert', *Quellen*, xxiv (1932–3), pp. 1–61, as corrected by H. Holtzmann, 'Der Katepan Boioannes und die kirchliche Organisation der Capitanata', *Nachrichten der Akademie der Wissenschaften in Göttingen, Phil.-hist. Klasse* (1960), no. 2, especially pp. 31–3.

[2] See the article by O. Capitani in *Dizionario Biografico degli Italiani*.

[3] *MGH, Const. et acta publica*, i, no. 37; cf. Schramm, *Kaiser, Rom und Renovatio*, i, pp. 275 ff.

Opposite: 5 The Tomb of Cecilia Metella (see p. 142)
6 A tower in the Roman Campagna

and their government; it is not surprising that in a document of the preceding year the pope had coupled imperial officials indifferently with papal ones in demanding obedience and forbidding the exaction of taxes by local noblemen or their officials.[1] Imperial jurisdiction in the Roman District was now accepted as a matter of course.

But the end of the Tusculan dynasty was now in sight. It was too paradoxical a situation to continue indefinitely, that in an empire where rational church government was in some degree linked with royal power, the person responsible for the government of the whole Western Church should be one of the most anachronistic and backward of the feudal bishops. And it was in the very nature of the papacy and of the complex but sternly held system of ideas on which it depended, to react, eventually, against what was only too evidently a corruption of its own ideals.

---

[1] Kehr, *I.P.*, ii, p. 26, no. 5. 'Ita ut si imperator aut marchio sive missi eorum aut nos aut successores nostri illuc venerimus nullo modo in jam dictis personis per publicos ministeriales colligatur nec eis injuria irrogetur.' The prohibition in this document against 'servitium vel ad angariam ducere vel ad districtum sive ad placitum protrahere' is more or less like that in the more frequently quoted bull to the Bishop of Porto, *I.P.*, ii, p. 20, no. 10 (1 August 1018).

Chapter 4

The break with the Empire

I

At the end of 1044 the Tusculan dynasty was shaken by a rising in Rome. The Romans united to depose the pope.[1] But in January of the following year the former government got the support of Trastevere in the city, and of the descendants of Count Octavian of Sabina without, and returned after some street fighting. The quarrel involved the two comital families of Sabina, the descendants of Count Octavian and of Stefania, who were opposed to one another as they had been in the earlier crisis of 1014. Though defeated in Rome, the Stefaniani had John, Bishop of Sabina elected as anti-pope (not without money changing hands) with the name of Silvester III. But by March 1045 the Tusculans and their ally and collateral relative, Count Gerard of Galeria, had re-imposed the rule of Benedict IX in Rome; John of Sabina returned excommunicate to his see, where he met with further violence.

But the troubles in Rome continued, and Benedict was unable to resume his peaceful enjoyment of the papacy. The esteemed Abbot of Grottaferrata (the protected abbey of the Tusculan family) offered himself as 'mediator', and the pope decided to resign. How he effected this is not clear. There was no set procedure for abdication; but it is hard to believe that the election of his successor did not have at least the semblance of the usual legal forms. It is clear that a large sum of money changed hands in connection with the election, although it is possible that the payment was a form of indemnity (*carta refutationis*) given by the incoming pope or his friends to his predecessor. Whether it is proper to speak actually of a sale of the papacy we do not know, but the taint

[1] For what follows see G. B. Borino's article in *ASR*, xli (1918) quoted above; idem, ' "Invitus ultra montes cum domno papa Gregorio abii" ', *Studi Gregoriani*, i (Rome, 1947), pp. 3–46; R. L. Poole, *Studies in Chronology and History* (1934), pp. 185–222; Zimmermann, *Papstabsetzungen* (1968), pp. 119 ff.

of money attached to the election, even if simony in the strict sense was avoided.[1]

The new pope had been a high official of the papal court, the former chancellor and librarian of the Holy See. By name John the Archcanon, surnamed Gratian, he took the papal name of Gregory VI. He had for long enjoyed the confidence of the Tusculan family, whose kinsman he probably was; he was the godfather of his predecessor Benedict IX. He was certainly a far more upright man than Benedict. His election was welcomed by the Romagnol hermit Peter Damian, and one of his clerical following was the able and idealistic young clerk, Hildebrand. Hildebrand had grown up in the Lateran bureau, and had had plenty of opportunity to know the former archcanon, whom after the debacle of the following year he was to accompany 'unwillingly' into exile in Germany.

Pope Benedict had transferred the papacy to Gregory VI in May 1045. For over a year there was little resistance to the new pope either in Italy or in Europe. His political future depended to a great extent on the new German king. The young and powerful Henry III had succeeded his father Conrad in 1039. Of his relations with Pope Gregory's predecessor, Benedict, little is known, though there may have been some tension over the affairs of southern Italy and over policy in the patriarchate of Aquileja in the north.[2] Gregory VI was a Tusculan nominee and in German eyes the continuator of Tusculan policies. It is possible that some of the Roman clergy had already drawn Henry's attention to the sad state of the Roman Church. It was certainly in royal interests that when he came to Italy he should be crowned by an undisputed pope who was free from the taints of simony or schism.

In September 1046 Henry III crossed the Brenner on his way south to Italy, and at Piacenza in November he is said to have received Pope Gregory honourably. The king then moved slowly through central Italy, settling church affairs as he went. By the time he reached Sutri, the last pilgrim stage before Rome on the Via Cassia, he had made up his mind about his attitude to Pope Gregory VI, and reached a decision critical for the future of the papacy and of his own dynasty. At Sutri he summoned the pope and held him as prisoner, and caused him to appear

---

[1] *De ordinando pontifice* in *MGH, Libelli de lite imperatorum et pontificum saeculis XI et XII*, i, pp. 8–14, at pp. 10–11. Cf. Zimmermann, p. 124n.; for the tract see Ullmann, *Papal Government*, pp. 263–5.

[2] Borino, *ASR*, xxxix (1916), pp. 166–9, and see also ibid. pp. 329–82; Zimmermann, pp. 125 ff; Kölmel, *Rom u. Kirchenstaat*, pp. 84–5, and C. Violante, *La pataria milanese e la riforma ecclesiastica*, i (Rome, 1955), pp. 47–58 take different viewpoints to that of Borino.

before one of the most famous synods of the Middle Ages, which was popularly, if wrongly, supposed to have deposed three popes.

How far Henry was actuated by political considerations and how far by religious repugnance to the circumstances of Gregory's election, it is now virtually impossible to decide – it is hard enough to disentangle motives which we would call religious from others which we would call imperialist, even when the evidence is clearer than in this case it is. Certainly Henry's position was extremely strong. By 1046 he had sub-dued the Hungarian monarchy – sending the Holy Lance as a trophy to Rome – quelled the dangerous Godfrey of Lorraine, and acquired a deserved reputation as the friend of holy men and the reformer of bishops. He had already replaced the two other great clerical figures of Italy, the archbishops of Milan and Ravenna.

Pope Gregory was faced at Sutri by the disapproval of the bishops and by charges of simony. Succumbing to the moral and political pressure brought on him, he renounced the papacy – not in the strict sense voluntarily, though perhaps there was a show of voluntary abdica-tion. John of Sabina (Silvester III) appeared before the council and was condemned by it. The Tusculan Theophylact (Benedict IX) was possibly cited to appear, but he fled to Monte Cavo in the Alban Hills, under the protection of his own family.

A day or so before Christmas 1046 the king held a further synod at Rome, the continuation of that of a few days earlier at Sutri. The former Gregory VI was sent in captivity over the Alps to end his days in Germany; this appears to have been the execution of a judgement under which he had been sentenced. Benedict IX was condemned. The king and the synod then turned to find a new pope. One German bishop having refused the task, another, Suidger of Bamberg, was on Christmas Eve elected pope under the name of Clement II. He was consecrated on Christmas Day, and immediately crowned Henry and Agnes as emperor and empress. At the same time the Romans elected Henry III as patrician, an office which might on historical precedent be claimed to give him a voice in deciding papal elections, besides the right of confirmation he possessed as emperor.[1]

The nomination of a German pope was in the tradition of Otto III, and was indeed the application to the Roman See of principles long since applied to other bishoprics and abbeys in imperial Italy. The Archbishop of Ravenna, the abbots of Farfa and S. Vincenzo al Volturno, the Bishop of Piacenza, were all at this time replaced by imperial nominees,

[1] Cf. Schramm, *Kaiser, Rom und Renovatio*, i, pp. 228–38; Ullmann, *Papal Government*, p. 251.

and one of the first acts of the new pope was to call a synod to regulate
the relations of the see of Ravenna with those of Aquileja and Milan.
For the eleven years following 1046 a series of German popes was
to bring papal and imperial policy closer than since the time of Silvester
II and Otto III.

In one form or another, Tusculan opposition to the changes made
in 1046 continued for forty years and more. At almost every papal
vacancy the Tusculans came out to press their own claimant on the
Holy See. Benedict IX himself left his fortress in the Alban Hills to
claim the papacy when Clement II died in 1047, and a coalition of
Roman nobles ruled for him in Rome from November of that year until
the summer of 1048. Benedict's brothers Peter and Gregory, and his
allies the counts of Galeria and Sabina, united with the people of Tivoli
to terrorise Rome and the District.[1] The town of Tivoli's aggression
against Rome foreshadows the 'communal' warfare of the twelfth
century. But at this stage probably the most important card in the
hands of the Tusculans was the support given them by the Marquis
Boniface of Tuscany.

A further German bishop was despatched as an imperial nominee
to Rome, and was elected pope as Damasus II, but he died after a few
weeks in office. Henry III then chose a man who was to prove very
important in papal history, Bishop Bruno of Toul, who came to Rome
and was elected with the name of Leo IX. The Romans accepted him
on his arrival as 'a most strong pope, whom the lord sent to free us
entirely from our enemies'.[2] They had not mistaken their man. Leo
protested that he was not elected to kill and destroy, and that to seek
peace with the Tusculans he would convene a synod at Rome (April
1049). But when Theophylact and his allies failed to appear at the
synod, war was declared: the Roman army laid waste the Tusculan
lands, destroyed their vines in the Alban hills, and besieged Tuscolo.
The Tusculans were not entirely crushed and they remained unreconciled at the end of the pontificate,[3] but their power was now held in
check.

---

[1] A. Poncelet, 'Vie et miracles du pape S. Léon IX', *Analecta Bollandiana*, xxv (1906), pp.
258–97, at p. 278; cf. *Liber Pontificalis*, ii, pp. 273, 331.

[2] Ibid. p. 277.

[3] He died praying for their conversion, 'Vie et miracles', p. 292. See also H. Tritz, 'Die
hagiographischen Quellen zur Geschichte Papst Leo IX.', *SG*, iv, pp. 191–364, at pp. 300–6.

II

The Swabian aristocrat, cousin of the emperor, the sworn enemy of all simony, as willing to fight his enemies in battle as to pray for them, Bruno of Toul was as a German bishop remarkable only for his dislike of corruption. But transferred to Rome and placed at the head of the ancient bureaucracy, as Leo IX he became a disturbing and disrupting force. His hatred of simony led to an influx of Lotharingian and Frankish prelates into the upper Roman clergy, which for the first time since its origins came under the leadership of elements foreign to the city aristocracy. Within a short time three able foreigners of this sort had replaced Romans; many others were to follow.[1]

A biographer of Leo IX (who may well have been Humbert of Moyenmoutier, the greatest of the early Reform cardinals), says that when Leo IX came to Rome in February 1049 he found himself desperately short of money, and that he was helped out by an embassy from the city fo Benevento, which brought him rich gifts.[2] This embassy led the pope into new directions in south Italy – directions which were in some senses decisive for the future course of the papacy. The south Italian policy of the Tusculan popes was obsolete for the new papacy, anchored as it was to dynastic alliances which now belonged to the anti-papal opposition. The growing power of the Normans in south Italy was evidently also going to lead to the revision of papal and imperial policy towards these robber bands which were now turning into governments; the decision had to be made whether to try to crush them completely, or to recognise them and to play them off against the other south Italian princes. The Emperor Henry III had already shown some flexibility about this; in 1047 he had deprived the Tusculan ally, Guaimar of Salerno, of the principate of Capua, and reinstated the dynasty of the Pandulf whom his father Conrad II had deprived. At the same time the emperor had 'invested' the Normans Rudolf of Aversa and Drogo of Apulia with the lands they held. This did not represent an irrevocable imperial decision to support the new Norman

---

[1] The Cardinal Bishops Hugh Candidus, Humbert of Moyenmoutier, Azelin of Compiègne. Leo later made a cardinal priest of Frederick of Lorraine, the brother of Duke Godfrey, and the later Pope Stephen IX. Cf. H.-W. Klewitz, 'Die Entstehung des Kardinalkollegiums', reprinted from *ZSSRG, Kan. Abt.*, xxv (1936), in *Reformpapsttum und Kardinalkolleg* (Darmstadt, 1957).

[2] O.Vehse, 'Benevent als Territorium des Kirchenstaates bis zum Beginn der Avignonesischen Epoche', *Quellen*, xxii (1930–1), pp. 87–160. For the authorship of the so-called Wibert biography, see Tritz's article cited in note 3 above, at pp. 229–86.

states, especially as the great abbey of Monte Cassino, now vigorously
directed by the imperial nominee Richer of Niederaltaich, continued
to suffer from Norman aggression. It rather reflected the hesitation of
imperial policy in the face of growing Norman power.[1]

After the original Beneventan embassy to Rome in early 1049, Leo IX
sent an archbishop (probably Humbert of Moyenmoutier)[2] to the city
to report. As a result, when Benevento shook off the dominion of
Pandulf of Capua in 1050, the Beneventans offered the city to the
pope – thus fulfilling one of the ancient eighth-century claims of the
Roman See. A further mission by Cardinal Humbert and the visit to
the city of Leo IX himself meant the acceptance of the transfer of power,
which was later legalised by the emperor at Worms in 1052, by the
grant of some form of imperial 'vicariate' to Pope Leo in Benevento.[3]

Leo IX's actions in Benevento, besides his wholehearted support of the
right and welfare of the monastery of Monte Cassino,[4] brought him
deeply into conflict with the Normans. Negotiations with them while
the pope was in Melfi in Norman territory before the church Council
of Siponto in 1050 led to no result. From the papal point of view the
solution of the Norman question was urgent, because until it was resolved
the immensely important Latinisation of the former Greek church
provinces of south Italy[5] could only be provisional. The Normans were
too politically important to be left out of such vital decisions. Drogo of
Apulia was being overtaken by his brother Robert Guiscard in the race
to plunder and digest southern Italy. Robert's prey was not only towns
like Cosenza but the southern lands of the Roman Church. It is not clear
whether these southern patrimonies were lands which had continuously
been in the possession of the Roman See, or whether they represented the
claims which the popes had always preferred against the Byzantine

---

[1] Cf. G. B. Borino, 'Per la storia della riforma della chiesa nel sec. XI', *ASR*, xxxviii (1915),
pp. 453–513, especially pp. 463 ff.; W. Wühr, 'Die Wiedergeburt Montecassinos unter seinem
ersten Reformabt Richer von Niederaltaich (+ 1055)', *SG*, iii, pp. 369–450, especially
pp. 411–23.

[2] 'Vie et miracles du pape S. Léon IX', p. 280 and n. For the tentative identification with
Humbert 'archbishop of all Sicily' cf. A. Michel in *SG*, i, pp. 66, 70–1, and idem, *Papstwahl
und Kirchenreform*, p. 133n. If Tritz's theory that Humbert is the author of the Wibert *Vita* is
correct, and the identification also correct, it is strange that Humbert does not mention this
legation in the *Vita*.

[3] Cf. Vehse's article cited in note 2 above, at p. iii. Papal rights in Bamberg and Fulda were
made over to the emperor as part of this agreement.

[4] Wühr, 'Die Wiedergeburt Montecassinos' at pp. 423–9.

[5] Cf. H.-W. Klewitz, 'Studien über die Wiederherstellung der römischen Kirche im Süditalien
durch das Reformpapsttum', *Quellen*, xxv (1934–5), reproduced in *Reformpapsttum und Kardinalkolleg*, pp. 135–205.

emperors. Leo's one concrete gain of Benevento was precarious; the Beneventans reproached him, saying that things were even worse for them now than before the transfer of power – 'then at least we managed to exist, but now we have been handed over to be devoured utterly'.[1]

The logical thing for Leo to do was to get the help of the empire, but like the popes of the eighth and ninth centuries he wanted a more aggressive south Italian policy than the emperor was anxious to execute. Leo himself obtained nothing at his meeting with the emperor in January 1051, nor did Cardinal Frederick of Lorraine, the papal chancellor, who was sent to Germany in the following year. The idea of a purely Italian resistance to the Normans collapsed in the same year, first because of the hostility of Guaimar of Salerno, and then because of his murder, which tilted the southern balance even further on the Norman side.

In the autumn of 1052 the pope himself crossed the Alps once more and met Henry III at Worms. He obtained the investiture of Benevento, and it seemed as though military support was going to be made available – an imperial army had actually been assembled to move against the Normans, but at the last moment the opposition of one of the German bishops led to the demobilisation of the army and the abandonment of a Norman war. What arguments Bishop Gebehard of Eichstädt (the future Pope Victor II) used against Leo IX we do not know, but they must have been effective, as the German magnates recalled contingents which were actually on the march.[2]

Leo IX was not entirely beaten by the reluctance of the German bishops and magnates: he assembled his own small army in Germany – largely of Swabians, but including freebooters from other regions – and marched it back to Italy. He reached Rome at Easter, and in late May set off with the army for the south. Early in June local forces from Rome and the District, Capua, the march of Fermo and the duchy of Spoleto, assembled at Monte Cassino. The pope had come to an understanding also with Argyrus the Greek catapan in Italy (Argyrus was, as it happened, the son of Melo, the leader of the earlier anti-Greek revolt), by which Argyrus was to co-ordinate Byzantine military action against the Normans with that of the pope. The major political game, played to get the full support of Henry III, had failed, but Leo had done all he could to secure a military and diplomatic make-weight. In the words

---

[1] S. Borgia (ed.), 'Vita Leonis' in *Memorie istoriche della pontificia città di Benevento*, ii (Rome, 1764), pp. 315–17. Cf. Kölmel, *Rom und Kirchenstaat*, p. 101.

[2] E. Steindorff, *Jahrbücher des Deutschen Reiches unter Heinrich III.* (Leipzig, 1881), ii, pp. 214–17.

E*

of one of his biographers, 'those who did not fear spiritual sanctions, he ordered to be smitten by a human sword'.[1]

Pope Leo was not a carnal-minded Roman noble of the sort that had for the most part filled the papal office for 175 years before him, but a saint, the convener of holy synods against simony and concubinage and all the evils of the Church, the acknowledged spiritual leader of most of Western Europe, to be revered for his holiness and his miracles as soon as he was dead. When such a man preached against the Normans (currently called 'Saracens') he was in effect preaching a holy war like those led against the Muslims by such ninth-century popes as John VIII. Leo was not merely a feudal bishop at the head of his troops: behind his words and actions stood the influence of the *treuga dei* (the truce of God), which had authorised bishops to lead armies against bandits and perjurers.[2] When such a man led an army, and was prepared (as afterwards happened) to preach over his war-dead and to proclaim them saints, an imprint was being given to the policies of the Reform popes which was never to be lost. It was acknowledged that the clergy themselves did not possess the right to use the sword (*ius gladii*), and largely on this ground Peter Damian reproached Leo IX for his military policy.[3] But it was also soon to be said by canonists and curial politicians that the Church possesses a judicial right as a part of its spiritual powers to call on the help of the secular sword.

It is one thing to appeal to arms, another to exercise them. The two armies neared one another at Civitate near Torremaggiore on the river Fortore in Capitanata. The Norman envoys came to the pope with the banner given them by the emperor at their investiture, but they refused the papal demand for the return of all the lands of St Peter. Both armies were badly supplied – the Normans lacked food and the papal troops water – and this made it the more difficult to postpone the conflict. The pope prayed and spoke with his troops and promised forgiveness of their sins; he then retired to the castle of Civitate to await the result of the battle, which took place on 18 June 1053. The result was the overwhelming defeat of the papal army; the Italian troops hardly

---

[1] 'Vita Leonis' in Borgia, *Memorie istoriche*, ii, p. 317: 'qui divino non timebant percuti gladio, illos mucrone percutere decrevit humano'.

[2] For this and for what follows see C. Erdmann, *Die Entstehung des Kreuzzugsgedankens* (Stuttgart, 1935).

[3] Cf. Erdmann, pp. 131–2. A. Stickler, 'Il potere coattivo materiale della chiesa nella Riforma Gregoriana secondo Anselmo di Lucca', *SG*, ii, pp. 235–85; idem, 'Il "gladius" nel registro di Gregorio VII', ibid, iii, pp. 89–103; idem, 'Il gladius negli atti dei concili e dei Romani pontefici sino a Graziano e Bernardo di Clairvaux', *Salesianum*, xiii (1951), pp. 414–45.

resisted the Norman attack, and the German centre which bore its full weight was annihilated.

The Norman victors met the defeated pope outside the town and begged his forgiveness; they led him as an honoured captive back to their camp. Before he finally left the battlefield Leo prayed for two days over the bodies of the slain, and when he was escorted back to Benevento, where he remained a virtual prisoner for eight months, he ordered a war memorial church to be built outside the gates of the city in honour of the fallen 'martyrs' on the papal side. Possibly the Normans made the pope an offer of military service, but if they did so it was not accepted.[1] Within a short time of his return to Rome, Leo died, already honoured as a saint (19 April 1054).

The pontificate of Leo IX's political opponent and successor, Gebehard of Eichstädt, as Pope Victor II (1054–7) marks probably the high water mark of the common action of empire and papacy in the period following the Synod of Sutri. The pope appears to have exercised for the emperor the offices of Duke of Spoleto and Marquis of Fermo, though the circumstances are unclear. Victor II is found investing the Bishop of Teramo with a castle in the duchy of Spoleto, by means of a banner which he confers 'on his own behalf and on that of the emperor'. It may be that this act was viewed by the pope as primarily his own, as Teramo was included in the Ottonian donation of 962. Though he may have acted on behalf of the emperor, the feudal concession is typical of a period in which feudal ideas were quickly gaining ground among the Roman bureaucracy.[2]

Henry III died at the age of thirty-nine on 5 October 1056, leaving an infant son whose regency was in the hands of the Empress Agnes and the pope, who was at this time in Germany. But on his return to Italy in 1057 the pope himself died (28 July 1057, at Arezzo).

The political state of the empire was now transformed. Godfrey of

---

[1] Cf. Dione Clementi, 'The relations between the papacy, the western Roman Empire and the emergent kingdom of Sicily and south Italy, 1050–1156', *BISI*, lxxx (1968), pp. 191–212, at pp. 198–206. See also the Escorial *Vita* printed by Tritz, *SG*, iv. pp. 358–63. Addressing the Roman clergy as he lay dying Leo IX referred to the papal dead at Civitate as 'martyrs' (Wibert, *Vita*).

[2] *I.P.*, iv, p. 312, no. 7. Cf. Ficker, *Forschungen*, ii, p. 322 and Kölmel, *Rom und Kirchenstaat*, pp. 115–16. For Roman feudalism see Jordan in *Arch. f. Urk.*, xii (1932), quoted above. For Victor II and Henry III see P. Kehr, 'Vier Kapitel aus der Geschichte Kaiser Heinrichs III.', *Abhandlungen der preussischen Akademie der Wissenschaften, Philosophisch-Historische Klasse*, Jahrg. 1930 (Berlin, 1931), pp. 49–61. For Teramo see Kehr, 'Die Belehnungen der süditalienischen Normannenfürsten durch die Päpste (1059–1192)', ibid. Jahrg. 1934 (1935), pp. 19–20. Cf. also C. Manaresi, *I placiti del 'Regnum Italiae'*, iii, (1960), nos. 403, 404, 417, 446.

Lorraine, the husband of Beatrice of Tuscany, had been disciplined by Henry III in 1055, but was by far the most powerful man in Italy. His brother Frederick, the Cardinal Priest and former Chancellor of the Roman Church, and subsequently the Abbot of Monte Cassino, was elected pope (2 August 1057) by the Roman clergy without the consultation with the imperial court which had been observed in papal elections in the preceding ten years. It is true that Frederick was a suitable candidate in that he had for some time been one of the most powerful members of the Roman bureaucracy, and was on the whole acceptable to that body; but the fact remains that his election as Stephen IX was a remarkable instance of the power of the house of Lorraine. The imperial court was too weak to insist on its rights, and his election as pope was recognised.

It was the initial intention of Stephen IX to return to the aggressive anti-Norman policy of Leo IX, and for this reason he caused the treasure of Monte Cassino to be transported to Rome to help finance the contemplated war.[1] The Romans, like the inhabitants of other Italian cities, had the habit of plundering the goods of their bishop as soon as he died, so Stephen IX probably began his pontificate as impecuniously as had Leo. He could on the other hand get the help of his brother Godfrey, now not only Marquis of Tuscany but in control of the duchy of Spoleto and the march of Fermo. No doubt, if Stephen had lived long in office, a new sort of dynastic imprint would have been given to the papacy by the house of Lorraine. But he did not live long enough for any possible inconsistencies between his reform ideas and his dynastic methods to come to the surface. On 29 March 1058 Stephen IX died in Florence.

All the forces of the Tusculan opposition at once came into action. Gregory of Tuscolo and Gerard of Galeria and their friends and relatives on 4–5 April had the Bishop of Velletri elected as Pope Benedict X – the election took place amid riots, and involved some sort of tax concessions to the Romans.[2] The political weight of a big section of the Roman nobility was involved – the Lords of Tuscolo, Palestrina, Nomentana and Galeria; the Tusculan dynasty of Monticelli, which had since the beginning of the century occupied much of the property of the monaster-

---

[1] He is said to have also led (before his pontificate) an army against Count Trasmund of Chieti, and to have deprived the violent nobleman Berardo of the bishopric of Penne, though he then invested him with the castles of the see. *Breve Chronicon ecclesiae Pennensis (Archiv der Gesellschaft f. ältere deutsche Geschichtskunde*, iv (1822), pp. 128–35).

[2] Peter Damian, apud Migne, *P.L.*, cxliv, col. 291. Cf. G. Meyer von Knonau, *Jahrbücher des Deutschen Reiches unter Heinrich IV. und Heinrich V.* (Leipzig, 1890), i, pp. 85 ff.; Poole, *Studies in Chronology and History*, pp. 152–3; Zimmermann, *Papstabsetzungen* (1968), pp. 140–4.

ies of Subiaco and S. Paolo fuori le Mura; Humbert, the Frankish Abbot of Subiaco, followed them. The feudal power of these gentry extended across the Apennines to the diocese of Osimo, where Benedict X made important feudal concessions of church lands to the local nobility.[1] It is not surprising that the Reform propagandists called the Tusculan regime 'the tyranny of the captains'.[2]

But against these local forces the reformers could call on those of the empire and of the Marquis of Tuscany. Hildebrand and his party carried out the revolutionary move of electing a new pope outside Rome; at Siena at the end of 1058 Gerard, Bishop of Florence was elected pope as Nicholas II. Like Leo IX he began his pontificate by summoning a synod against the Tusculan intruder; to this synod at Sutri came Godfrey of Lorraine as well as the Italian bishops. The Tusculans had taken power by a Roman *coup d'état* and could only be expelled by another. The armed force for such a *coup* was now available from Godfrey of Lorraine. Inside Rome the population of Trastevere was ready to rise against the Tusculans, and new elements, notably the converted Jew, Leo di Benedetto, were willing to join them. The presence of an armed force a few miles north of the city was enough to turn the scale inside Rome; Benedict X fled to his Tusculan allies at the castle of Passarano near Tivoli. How much part the Lotharingian troops took in the fighting in Rome is unclear, but on 24 January 1059 Nicholas II was enthroned in the Lateran. There are not many clear lines of demarcation in papal history, but this is perhaps one of them.

III

It is not often remarked how desperate the question of internal security was for the Reform papacy from its very beginnings. The papal regime of 1059 represented only a small number of foreign or foreign-trained clergy. The movement for church reform from which they came had only partially gained the support of the central Italian clergy, and in many places it was being ferociously resisted. If the reformers were not willing – and they were not – to pay the traditional price of a Roman papal dynasty, then they had to give the highest attention to security questions, and to foreign alliances which would uphold them against entrenched feudal power. It is not surprising that Hildebrand, the soul

[1] *I.P.*, iv, p. 209, no. 1. Laymen had taken church property in Osimo under Leo IX, ibid. no. 1. Cf. Peter Damian, *P.L.*, cxliv, cols. 207–8, 1022; Kölmel, pp. 88n., 120–1.
[2] Bonizo, *liber ad amicum*, MGH, *Libelli de lite*, i, p. 593; cf. Damian, ibid. pp. 90–3.

of the Reform party, should in spite of the military incapacity which he later demonstrated as pope have acquired the reputation as arch-deacon – perhaps earlier – of a tireless organiser of troops and campaigns;[1] not surprising also that as soon as Nicholas II had gained Rome he hurried over the Appenines to the march of Fermo to put down the opposition, and laid the population of Ancona under interdict because of their refusal to submit to Godfrey of Lorraine.[2]

When Nicholas II returned to Rome he proceeded to hold the great synod of April 1059 which decided on the new procedure for papal election by the cardinal bishops with the consent of the rest of the clergy.[3] At this vital meeting the question of security for the papal elections must again have been in the front of the minds of the reforming clergy. They were making the first major change in procedure for a papal election since the Roman constitution of Lothar in 824 – the first clerical change since the council of 769. But without political security such a change could be no more than a mockery, as everyone at the synod must have known. Whether the alliance with Godfrey of Lorraine could indefinitely provide such security was an open question. The emperor was a child (he was born on 11 November 1050), and the German government was unlikely to act in Italy except with Godfrey.

There was only one other power to which the Roman clergy could turn. Byzantium had been approached on a couple of occasions in the past few years, but the difficulties of co-operation with the Greeks were only too well known in Rome, and the Eastern Empire was in any case suffering from a series of severe political crises. The only practical alternative was the policy now offered by the Abbot Desiderius of Monte Cassino – an understanding with the Normans. The men of the Reform papacy saw that they possessed a bargaining counter for which the lawless Norman princes would pay very heavily – the legitimisation of Norman rule.[4] Such an act was probably only possible during a vacancy or minority in the empire.

Desiderius and other south Italian clerics were present at the Roman

---

[1] Wido of Ferrara, *de scismate Hildebrandi*, apud *MGH, Libelli de lite*, i, pp. 534, 554 (the second passage probably from Wibert's decree against Hildebrand); cf. also the much quoted passage from the *Liber de unitate ecclesiae conservanda*, R. Schwenkenbecher (ed.) (Hanover, 1883), p. 42.

[2] Peter Damian, ep. I, 7 (Migne, *P.L.*, cxliv, col. 211); cf. Dressler, *Petrus Damiani*, pp. 122–3; Borino, *SG*, iii, pp. 501–2.

[3] *MGH, Const. et acta publica*, i, no. 382, p. 538. Cf. Ullmann, *Papal Government*, pp. 323–5.

[4] Cf. Kehr, 'Die Belehnungen', etc., quoted in note 2 above, p. 115.

synod of April–May 1059. In June the pope left for southern Italy, on his way to a further great church council at Melfi, where a hundred bishops were to take part in the reform of the south Italian Church and its more secure attachment to Rome. On the way, probably in Capua, he invested Richard the Norman with the 'principate' of Capua. At Melfi he invested Robert Guiscard as 'Duke' of Apulia and Calabria, promising him the future investiture of Sicily if he took it from the Muslims; he also confirmed him in possession of those 'lands of St Peter' which he held, with the exception of Benevento. Guiscard agreed to a special payment of *census* of twelve pence of Pavia for each pair of oxen, in these 'lands of St Peter'.

These political and legal proceedings, of deciding importance for the future of the papacy and also of southern Italy, were arranged by the papal court with the greatest care.[1] The feudal lord, the pope, came into his subject's lands and received from him first the oath of fealty. He swore fidelity to the pope personally and to the Church, to do no harm and to abstain from acts personally or politically directed against him. He guaranteed that he would defend the rights and possessions of St Peter against all men, and that he would assist the pope to hold the Roman papacy securely. All the churches in his dominions he placed in the power of the pope, guaranteeing their fidelity to the Roman Church – a vital clause, this, which assured ultimate papal control of many churches in south Italy which in 1059 were still under Greek rule. Finally, in pursuance of the decrees of the Roman synod of 1059, he said that he would protect the 'best' of the Roman cardinals, clerks and laymen at the election of the pope's successor. He then on his knees before the pope swore homage, and received investiture, probably under the symbolic form of a banner which accompanied the investing words.

At this moment when the Western Empire was ruled by a child, and the Eastern Empire tottering towards partial dissolution, the Roman Church made good the claims to spiritual and temporal power in southern Italy which it had failed to establish during the crisis of the eighth century; it thus bound southern Italy to itself in a political system which lasted in one form or another until 1860. That this political system was feudal in form was significant of the degree to which eleventh-century Rome had been penetrated by feudal influences. The mere exacting of feudal oaths did not of itself effect a social or legal transformation in the feudal lord. Alexis Comnenus in 1098 obtained

[1] Kehr, pp. 6–24.

similar feudal oaths from the Normans, without thereby feudalising the Byzantine Empire. Roman law continued after 1059 to be the law of Romans and Roman clerks. But the willingness of the Roman papacy after 1059 to use feudal policies and feudal forms to obtain its political objectives was important for its political future both in Italy and in Europe. What mattered most was the will to exercise political power, irrespective of the juristic means by which power was exercised.[1] Yet the use of feudal means affected subsequent political ends.

The legal grounds on which Nicholas II claimed to invest the Norman princes in 1059 were never specifically stated. Essentially they derived from the imperial donations. Capua and the surrounding cities were among the oldest claims of the Holy See, and the promise to hand over Sicily 'if God gives it into our hands' had figured (probably) in the donation of 876 and certainly in that of 962. Marsia and Teramo and some other lands in the Abruzzi were to be found in the donation of 962. Other papal claims existed in Gaeta and Fondi and other parts of Campania, and Benevento had been established by Henry III as belonging in some degree to the popes. But the right to bestow either the rest of Apulia, or any of Calabria, can be found nowhere in the donations;[2] and can be explained only by reliance on the forged Constantinian donation, mixed with reminiscences of the patrimonies of the Roman Church which had existed in these areas before the eighth century, and been fruitlessly reclaimed from the Byzantine emperors.

In the same summer the first fruits of the Norman alliance were reaped by the papacy. A Norman force of 300 troops was sent north to join with the Romans in besieging the anti-pope Benedict and Count Gerard in the fortress of Galeria. This first attack failed, but later in the summer the pope himself returned with other Norman troops. This time 'all the fortified villages (*castra*) of Count Gerard from Galeria to Sutri were devastated', which shows how widespread was the territorial power of only a single one of the Tusculan nobles. Finally the castle of Galeria had to yield, and to deliver up the anti-pope to Nicholas II.[3]

[1] This is not the view of Ullmann, *Papal Government*, pp. 331–43. His discussion, although learned, is at times curiously divorced from political reality, e.g. in the comment (p. 334) that 'the pope was at least in theory the strongest European feudal monarch'.

[2] Cf. Kehr, pp. 14–22. Miss Clementi, in her article in *BISI* quoted above, does not mention that Marsia and Teramo are named in the donations.

[3] Peter Damian (pp. 90–3) and Bonizo (p. 593) in *MGH, Libelli de lite*, i; *Annales Romani* in *Liber Pontificalis*, i, p. 335. See also Borino in *ASR*, xxxviii (1915), pp. 197–200, 482, and idem in *SG*, iii, 488–9, 509–10; Zimmermann, *Papstabsetzungen*, pp. 143–4. Whether Hildebrand was instrumental in calling on the Norman force (as the *Annales Romani* say) is likely to remain in doubt. Cf. A. Fliche, *La réforme Grégorienne et la reconquête chrétienne* (Paris, 1946), p. 21n.

The victory was only the first move in a campaign to recover control of the Roman District. When the abbey of Farfa appealed to Nicholas II in Florence at the beginning of 1060 about the occupation of their castle of Tribuco by the Ottaviani counts of Sabina, the pope was strong enough to act against the Ottaviani so powerfully as not only to make them restore the castle, but also to make them give up the rectorship of Sabina. Though they retained a certain influence, partly through the later election of their kinsman John as Abbot of Subiaco in 1067, the Ottaviani sank to the rank of lesser nobility, pledged to the support of the Reform party.[1] Finally the pope returned to the attack against Count Gerard of Galeria, prompted by a piece of banditry carried out by the latter against the English Archbishop of York, who was despoiled of some of the large sums of money he carried in order to obtain the goodwill of the Roman See.[2]

The struggle with the Roman nobles was not settled by Nicholas II, and the power of the 'captains' was not broken by him in the decisive way his propagandist Bonizo afterwards suggested. When Nicholas died in July 1061 the whole grim business had to be gone through again. Gerard of Galeria was one of the nobles who, after the election by the Reform party of Anselm of Lucca as Alexander II, took part in the election of Cadalus of Parma an anti-pope, in Basle in October 1061.[3] Anselm of Lucca's election had duly been protected and pushed through at Rome by Richard of Capua and his Norman troops; the bargain of Melfi had already begun to operate to the advantage of the Reform party.

Cadalus of Parma, calling himself Honorius II, arrived at Rome in the spring of 1062 with a strong Lombard army, and with the diplomatic support of the imperial court. How strong his following was inside Rome itself is unclear, but he certainly had the support of the Tusculan nobles of the Roman Campagna, both the counts of Galeria and Tuscolo, and

---

[1] Vehse, *Quellen*, xxi (1929–30), pp. 150–2. He overlooks their later connection with Subiaco, for which see P. Egidi and others, *I monasteri di Subiaco* (Rome, 1904), i, pp. 91–6, and cf. also G. Bossi, in *ASR*, xli (1918), pp. 136–40; D. B. Zema, 'Economic reorganisation of the Roman See during the Gregorian Reform', *SG*, i, pp. 137–68, at p. 157. Zema's essay is, disappointingly, rather less than thorough in its exploration of the materials.

[2] William of Malmesbury, *De gestis pontificum* (Rolls Series, 1870), pp. 251–2; Peter Damian, *Libelli de lite* (*MGH*), i p. 91. Cf. *Historians of the Church of York* (*R.S.*, 1886) ii, pp. 346–7.

[3] Cf. F. Herberhold, 'Die Angriffe des Cadalus von Parma (Gegenpapst Honorius II.) auf Rom in den Jahren 1062 und 1063', *SG*, ii, pp. 447–503; G. B. Borino, 'Cencio del prefetto Stefano l'attentatore di Gregorio VII', *SG*, iv, pp. 373–440; Zimmermann, op. cit., pp. 148–51; Gerard of Galeria was accompanied at Basle by the abbot of the Tusculan-patronised monastery of St Gregory on the Coelian.

the Stefaniani Cencius *de praefecto,* who controlled Castel Sant'Angelo (the so-called 'tower of the Crescenzi'), and other important forts controlling the Tiber bridges.[1] Fighting went on at intervals for over two years. Initially the Roman army assembled by the supporters of Alexander II was bloodily defeated in the field of Nero, under Monte Mario. But Cadalus was still unable to cross the river and enter the city. By a long circuit he withdrew and marched round Rome to Tuscolo, where the poetasting Bishop Benzo of Alba (the political adviser and chronicler of the expedition) delighted in the spring flowers of the Alban hills.

After a somewhat mysterious intervention by Godfrey of Lorraine, Cadalus and his army marched north again to Lombardy – the lack of money to pay the troops also began to embarrass him. But in the following year he returned. As before, his partisans occupied many of the Roman fortresses, including the fort outside S. Paolo fuori le Mura. Once more he returned and stationed himself in Castel Sant'Angelo. But this time he found a force of Normans already in the city in the service of Alexander II. There were two battles with the Normans inside the city, both won by the forces of Cadalus. Hildebrand made a supreme effort, supported by Godfrey of Lorraine, to raise and pay more troops, and after the first defeated force of Normans had left the city on terms, they were replaced by a second force which entered the city from the Appian Way and also stormed the fort at S. Paolo fuori le Mura. The strongpoint of Cadalus in Castel Sant'Angelo now became his prison – the less agreeable because he was unable to pay the money which Cencius *de praefecto* and his former protectors demanded for their help. Late in 1063 or more probably in 1064 Cadalus left Rome for the last time, now abandoned by the Tusculans as by the imperial court. Much of the responsibility for his defeat rests with Godfrey of Lorraine, but perhaps even more with the Normans, who were now emerging as the irreplaceable stipendiaries of the Reform papacy.

The reformers in Rome can have had few illusions about the motives of the Norman leaders. The enfeoffment of the Normans was a marriage of convenience, which the old contrasting interests of the Romans with those of any strong southern power were bound to disrupt. In particular the Romans were anxious that the Normans should not eat up the 'principate' of Salerno (a guarantee of Norman non-aggression against the principates was included in the oaths of fealty of 1059 and 1062) or

---

[1] See the articles just quoted, and also C. Cecchelli, 'Castel S. Angelo al tempo di Gregorio VII', *SG*, ii, pp. 103–23.

Naples and the maritime cities of the Sorrento peninsula.[1] There was little hope that this oath would be kept, and the pope himself, to protect his southern interests, acted in a manner which the Normans found hostile. Thus Alexander II extended his patronage to a certain William of Montreuil who had broken his allegiance to his father-in-law Richard of Capua, and bound himself to the counts of Aquino and the dukes of Gaeta. After William had been accepted as a vassal of St Peter with the duty to defend papal Campagna, Richard of Capua retaliated in 1066 by seizing the papal border town of Ceprano, and ravaging the Campagna as far as Rome. In alarm Alexander II in 1067 appealed to the emperor for help, but the idea of an imperial expedition to Italy was unwelcome to Godfrey of Lorraine, who in the end settled the question by himself leading a large force to Aquino and compelling Richard's submission.

Many important changes in papal organisation began in the time of the Tusculan popes of the first half of the eleventh century. On the other hand, the fundamental administrative transformation of the Roman bureaucracy which emerges into the light in the twelfth century was a product of the later rather than the earlier Reform papacy.[2] By the pontificate of Alexander II the temporal position of the Roman See in Italy was probably rather stronger than it had been earlier in the century, but the policies of the early Reform popes in this respect rather continued than contradicted those of their predecessors.

The basis of papal temporal power remained the ancient patrimonies and the imperial donations of 962 and 1020. How much these meant in practice depended on the political conditions of the time. One of the most critical matters was the ability of Rome to stand up to her rival, Ravenna, whose archbishops were now feudal vassals of the emperor. Otto III had promised the Roman Church the restoration of the eight counties in Pentapolis, but he had also promised the Church of Ravenna control of the whole area between the Apennines and the sea, from the river Reno to the river Foglia (i.e. the later 'Romagna'). This promise was maintained and even extended by later emperors in a way which appears to have compromised the promises made by Otto III to Rome

---

[1] Kehr, 'Die Belehnungen', especially pp. 18–19. For what follows see also Meyer von Knonau *Jahrbücher*, i, pp. 542–57; Chalandon, *Histoire de la domination normande*, i, pp. 221–5.

[2] Out of the large literature on this subject I cite only the articles of K. Jordan, 'Die päpstliche Verwaltung im Zeitalter Gregors VII.', *SG*, i, pp. 111–35, and J. Sydow, 'Untersuchungen zur kurialen Verwaltungsgeschichte im Zeitalter des Reformpapsttums', *Deutsches Archiv*, xi (1955), pp. 18–73. Most of the conclusions of Zema, 'Economic reorganisation of the Roman See', *SG*, i, pp. 137–68, seem to me disproved by these authors.

about the eight counties in Pentapolis. Conrad II and later Henry IV confirmed the rights of Ravenna in the whole march of Camerino, including the counties of Osimo, Ancona, Senigallia and Fano, which clearly clashes with the Ottonian privilege.[1] On the whole it seems unlikely that the popes had any substantial temporal influence in this area, except perhaps in the county of Rimini, which was closely related to the Roman See, and which with Pesaro was the subject of feudal grants by eleventh-century popes.[2] It is significant that the only really important manifestations of papal power are in fact alienations of that power to the feudal nobility.[3] In geographically remote areas it was practically impossible for the popes to do anything else; papal lands in Grosseto and Soana had been conceded in this way, as had the lands of the monastery of S. Paolo fuori le Mura in and round Orbetello.[4] The excommunication launched by Nicholas II against Ancona seems to have been more a tribute to the power of Godfrey of Lorraine than to that of the pope. Nor, in spite of some attempts by the popes to exercise effective temporal power in Ferrara and Comacchio to the north and east of Ravenna, did they succeed in doing so.[5]

---

[1] *D H IV* no. 102, p. 133, (24 June 1063). Cf. *D H IV* nos. 418, 330. Conrad's privilege is lost.

[2] By the time of Benedict IX (1032–45) Rome was able to grant Rimini and Pesaro to a count – though this is not necessarily to be taken as a sign of strength. A further grant was made by Leo IX to Everard of Ancona, *I.P.*, iv, p. 174. Cf. Kölmel, *Rom u. Kirchenstaat*, pp. 72–3, where he seems to me to over-emphasise Roman rule and to overlook much evidence, and p. 88; I accept Kehr's dating of *I.P.*, iv, pp. 174, no. 6, pp. 182, no. 2 to Benedict IX and not to Benedict VIII. Cf. also *I.P.*, v, p. 131, no. 1. Nicholas II grants the monastery of S. Maria in Monte near Cesena various rights including an estate which he himself had given to the Roman Church, and the right to hold the market. It is uncertain if the frequently quoted reference by Peter Damian to Stephen, a Roman judge exercising jurisdiction at Osimo in about 1059 (*P.L.*, cxliv, col. 1022) proves Roman domination there. Victor II had only three years earlier been exercising jurisdiction as imperial marquis of Fermo (see p. 115 above) and a Stephen, Roman judge, took part in his *placitum* for Teramo. This may have been the same Stephen continuing in office. Cf. P. Compagnoni, *Memorie istoriche-critiche della chiesa e de' vescovi di Osimo* (Rome, 1782), i, pp. 391 ff.

[3] Clement II's withdrawal of the lands feudally held from the papacy by the grandsons of Count Alberic in the county of Pesaro (*I.P.*, iv, p. 183, no. 1 (24 September 1047), is an important exception. He withdrew them on the grounds that no *pensio* had been paid, and no feudal allegiance offered when he came to Pesaro. The lands were re-granted to the monastery of S. Tommaso in Foglia, where the pope lay dying.

[4] *I.P.*, iii, p. 255, no. 2; p. 262, nos. 1, 2. There is little trace of papal supremacy in Corneto, either at this period or later in the century. Cf. G. Dilcher, *Quellen*, xlii–xliii (1963), pp. 1–12; idem, 'Die Gräfin Mathilde und die Burg von Corneto', *Dep. di S.P. per le antiche Provincie Modenesi, Atti e Mem.*, 9th ser., iii (1963), pp. 432–43; P. Supino, 'Corneto precomunale e comunale', *BISI*, lxxix (1968), pp. 115–47.

[5] O. Vehse, 'Die Ferrareser Fälschungen', *Quellen*, xxvii (1936–7), pp. 1–108, especially at pp. 50 ff. Cf. A. Vasina, 'La giurisdizione temporale della chiesa ravennate nel Ferrarese verso la fine del secolo X', *Felix Ravenna*, 3rd ser., fasc. 25, lxxvi (1958), pp. 32–55.

In the cities of the Umbrian Apennine, most of which were mentioned in the donations, and round some of which there were certainly very ancient patrimonial possessions of the Roman Church, the popes had political influence and a certain number of judicial and fiscal rights. The rights of the Holy See in Urbino were extremely ancient. In Borgo San Sepolcro, Stephen IX granted the market rights of the burg.[1] In Città di Castello at the beginning of the eleventh century grants had been made of papal lands which still involved the collection of rents by the agents of the Holy See.[2] In Perugia, which was again an ancient possession in which church lands were very numerous, the influence of Rome was for the whole eleventh century very considerable. The important monastery of S. Pietro and its possessions were protected most effectively by the Holy See against the bishop;[3] imperial support was given to papal action here as it was elsewhere in the temporal power.[4]

In the adjacent mountain area of the duchy of Spoleto the popes had no substantial claim beyond the small region near Cesi transferred by Henry II in the donation of 1020. But hopes of getting some hold on the duchy had always existed in the papal palace. Victor II, at the height of papal-imperial amity, exercised some temporal influence on behalf of the emperor in the duchy of Spoleto. Not until the early twelfth century did the popes claim rights in the duchy, and then it was

---

[1] *I.P.*, iv, p. 109, nos. 3, 4.

[2] Ibid. no. 1 (December 1013). Città di Castello had been Roman in the eighth century, and is mentioned in Hadrian I's correspondence as well as in the imperial donations. Cf. also Schneider, *Die Reichsverwaltung in Toscana*, pp. 99–101.

[3] Papal *massae* in Perugia and its vicinity are listed in the *Liber censuum*, i, p. 349. They include Lake Trasimene and the islands in the lake, a claim which comes from the imperial donations. For papal protection of S. Pietro di Perugia, see T. Leccisotti and C. Tabarelli, *Le carte dell'archivio di S. Pietro di Perugia* (Milan, 1956), i, nos. 1–4.

[4] Cf. W. Hagemann, 'I diplomi imperiali per l'Abbazia di S. Pietro in Perugia', *BSU*, lxiv (1968), pp. 20–45, at pp. 25–7; the diploma is *D H III*, no. 179, pp. 221–3. The emperor on this occasion released the abbey of S. Pietro from the hospitality dues known as the *fodrum de castellis*. Cf. Carlrichard Brühl, *Fodrum, Gistum, Servitium Regis* (Köln-Graz, 1968), i, pp. 554n., 561, 738–9, in polemic with A. Haverkamp, 'De Regalien-, Schutz- und Steuerpolitik in Italien unter Friedrich Barbarossa bis zur Entstehung des Lombardenbundes', *Zeitschr. f. bayer. Landesgesch.* xxix (1966), pp. 69–70. I agree with Brühl that papal privileges exempting religious houses from the exaction of *fodrum* tended to follow prior imperial privileges of a similar sort. Cf. Stephen IX for S. Pietro di Perugia, *I.P.*, iv, p. 69, no. 16 (Leccisotti-Tabarelli, no. 8), and also Leo IX's privilege for Pomposa, *I.P.*, v, p. 181, no. 3, which had already been privileged by Otto III and Henry III (for the imperial diplomas see Brühl, i, p. 539n.). There is however no trace of an imperial privilege for the monastery of Val di Ponte, near Perugia, for which there is a privilege of Leo IX which forbids anyone to take *fodrum* there except the pope. *I.P.* iv, p. 77, no. 3, now edited by V. de Donato, *Le più antiche carte dell' abbazia di S. Maria Val di Ponte (Montelabbate)*, i (969–1170) (Rome, 1962), no. 6, p. 12.

on the pretext of succeeding to the ducal rights of the house of Canossa.[1]

There is not much evidence of a systematic reorganisation of the temporal power under the early Reform popes, though a certain amount may have grown naturally out of the political circumstances. Thus the quarrel between the Bishop of Silva Candida and the Bishop of Porto about the Church of St Adalbert (that founded by Otto III on the island in the Tiber) led in 1049 to the unseating of Crescentius of Silva Candida and his replacement by Humbert of Moyenmoutier. Between 1049 and 1053 (the last bulls were issued on Leo's return from his last visit to Germany), new bulls were issued to define the lands held by the bishopric of Porto, and also those held by St Peter's, for which the Bishop of Silva Candida had the main administrative responsibility.[2] No doubt this procedure led to increased vigilance about papal lands in lay hands round Rome.

New forms of social organisation were beginning to give the Roman government new opportunities. In Sabina after its pacification by Nicholas II he began to concede villages to what were in effect small rural communes, for a money rent and with the obligation of suit of court and accommodation tax (*fodrum*). In this area which had now for long been administered on a feudal basis by the monastery of Farfa and the counts, the old obligations towards the ancient Lateran palace court had for long been superseded by feudal forms.[3] In 1065 a grant of exemption for the canons of Velletri reveals the existence in the Maritime province of the feudal obligations of military service.[4] The picture which seems to emerge is that of a papacy steadily asserting its traditional rights, rather than seeking revolutionary changes.

---

[1] For Victor II see p. 115 above. Paschal II's grant to Terni (29 April 1109) relies on the powers exerted in the duchy by Matilda's mother, Beatrice. *I.P.*, iv, p. 20, no. 2. Kehr's version of the address to 'omnibus per Valeriam' (loc. cit.) cannot be right for a town on the Via Flaminia. Existing editions of the bull have 'pervalituram'. They are however all of them poor editions: *ASI*, 3rd ser., xxii (1875), pp. 384–5 ('schlecht genug' said Kehr, *Gött. Nachr.* (1898), p. 360); F. Angeloni, *Storia di Terni* (Pisa, 1878), pp. 560–1; E. Rossi-Passavanti, *Interamna dei Narti* (Rome-Orvieto, 1933), ii, pp. 86–7. Ficker, *Forschungen*, ii, pp. 322–3, did not refer to this important grant.

[2] *I.P.*, ii, pp. 20–1, nos. 12, 13; ibid. i, p. 139, no. 21, p. 146, no. 4, p. 147, no. 6. Cf. *PBSR*, xxxiv (n.s., xxi, 1966), pp. 68–70.

[3] See the grants to Rocca Antica (*I.P.*, ii, p. 72, no. 1) and Montasola (*Quellen*, xxi (1929–30), p. 172 and cf. pp. 153–7, ibid.). Brühl, *Fodrum, Gistum, Servitium Regis*, i, p. 560n., thinks that the second of these grants was a papal usurpation of imperial rights, so far as *fodrum* was concerned, but he has not proved his point.

[4] *I.P.*, ii, p. 103, no. 1. For the older forms of obligation to the sacred palace, current earlier in the century for Grottaferrata, see *I.P.*, ii, p. 42, no. 4 (May, 1037).

IV

On 22 April 1073, the day following the death of Alexander II, the Archdeacon Hildebrand was elected pope by acclamation of the people; he took the name of Gregory VII. Relations with Henry IV were already extremely strained; the election of the 'holy Satan' of the Reform party was likely to place the political security of the Reform papacy on test, as it was to test all the other institutions of the papacy. The political line taken by the new pope was clear, and consistent in most ways with his policies before his election. In Rome he had his own party centred round the rich Trastevere notable, Pietro di Leone.[1] His fear and dislike of Robert Guiscard, and his distaste for the progressive elimination of the great Lombard families of southern Italy, led him to patronise Gisulf, the last ruler of Salerno, who attended the Lenten synod at Rome in the following year, 1074, and afterwards followed him to the military operations north of Rome. In the summer of 1073 Gregory invested the Lombard prince Landulf VI with Benevento, receiving the oath in the 'sacred palace' of Benevento.[2] In September he invested Richard of Capua with the principate, with the significant clause in the oath of fealty, that Richard would swear fealty to the German king only when he was authorised to do so by the pope. Both then and in February of the following year, Gregory was fairly certain that he could control Guiscard, either by military means or by diplomacy.[3]

But even at this early stage of his pontificate, long before German forces threatened to appear in Italy, Gregory's armies, with the assembling of which his enemies so bitterly reproached him, were curiously ineffective in practice. At the Lent synod of 1074 Robert Guiscard was excommunicated, and it was arranged that an army supplied by Beatrice and Matilda of Tuscany should join the armies of Gregory, of the Archbishop of Ravenna, and of Gisulf of Salerno, in an operation which was first of all to open north of Rome against the 'counts of Bagnorea', and then was to be diverted to the south against the Normans. Who the counts of Bagnorea were is uncertain, but the expedition planned against them was in the event a fiasco, and that against the

---

[1] See (with some reservations) P. Fedele, 'Le famiglie di Anacleto II e di Gelasio II', *ASR*, xxvii (1904), pp. 399–440.

[2] Amato di Montecassino, *Storia de' Normanni*, V. de Bartholomaeis (ed.) (Rome, 1935), p. 299. For the *palatium* of Benevento see Brühl, *Fodrum, Gistum, Servitium Regis*, i, pp. 356, 370; and cf. *Das Register Gregors VII.*, E. Caspar (ed.), 2nd ed. (Berlin, 1955), i, no. 18a, p. 30 (cited as *Reg.*).

[3] Cf. *Reg.*, i, no. 25, p. 41, no. 46, p. 70; and also Chalandon, i, pp. 230–7.

Normans never even began. The army went north over Monte Cimino
to S. Fiano near Montefiascone in June, and broke up ignominiously
after quarrels among the leaders.[1]

Gregory's temperament, convictions and personal history tended to
make him sweep up all the clashes and divergencies of policy which had
plagued papal-imperial relations for years into a single burning issue.
Papal patronage of the Patarene religious faction in Milan had for long
frustrated imperial policy, and so had the recalcitrance of the popes
in other things affecting imperial bishoprics from Aquileja to Bremen.
Papal feudal lordship over the Norman princes was an implied rejec-
tion of the ancient treaties between popes and emperors, and so, it
could be argued, was the papal election decree of 1059. On the side of
the Roman reformers (although they were originally without any specific
intention to defy the emperor) the conviction was growing that only
root-and-branch extirpation of the feudal relationship between kings
and bishops could eliminate the sin of simony which was the greatest
single evil of the Church. On Henry IV's side the king and his advisers
felt that the veto of a few Italian bishops over important issues of policy
could no longer be tolerated. The conflict between the royal office and
the priesthood which has taken the historical name of 'Investiture
Contest' could no longer be averted.

The approach of this great quarrel with Henry IV made Gregory's
position in the city of Rome critically important. Initially it stood the
test well. The illness which seized on Gregory when he returned from
his abortive campaign (possibly malaria contracted at the papal coastal
estate of Lauretum)[2] led some of his Roman enemies into indiscretions.
Cencius *de praefecto,* the patron of Cadalus during the insurrection of
ten years earlier, seized some lands which his relative, the Count of
Galeria, had bequeathed to the Church. But on Gregory's recovery he
had Cencius tried and condemned, and took the opportunity to demolish
the tower at Ponte Sant'Angelo from which the agents of Cencius had
imposed tolls on Roman traffic.[3]

The papal decree against lay investiture of clerical offices was passed
in February 1075; as the year advanced the continuing quarrel over

---

[1] *Libelli de lite,* i, pp. 602, 604; cf. the dates in *Reg.,* no. 84, p. 119, no. 85, p. 121. Schneider,
Die Reichsverwaltung, p. 112n., knows nothing of a 'county' of Bagnorea. That the army
camped as near to Bagnorea as S. Fiano, Montefiascone (not Fiano Romano, as is often
said), may mean that this aim of the army was achieved.

[2] Cf. *ASR,* xlvii (1924), p. 20; *Reg.,* ii, no. 1, p. 124.

[3] For what follows see Borino, 'Cencio del prefetto Stefano', *SG,* iv, pp. 411–40. It is noticeable
that Cencius had lost control of Castel Sant'Angelo.

Milan, and the offensive imperial nominations to the sees of Fermo and Spoleto, made a sharper break imminent. Whether Cencius was approached by the royal ambassadors who spent most of the last four months of 1075 in Rome, or whether he was incited by other enemies of Gregory (they were numerous enough) is unknown, but on Christmas Eve of 1075, while the pope was celebrating mass in the basilica of S. Maria Maggiore, Cencius launched one of those sudden armed *coups* which had so often changed papal history. Outside the church there was torrential rain; while the pope stood at the altar, armed men broke in, seized him, and carried him off to a tower belonging to Cencius, which stood on the other side of the city. Had Gregory's popularity in the city been low, he might have been held until Henry's judges intervened, and the history of Europe might have been very different. But Gregory's partisans in Rome were in fact extremely strong. In the morning the tower of Cencius was surrounded by hostile troops. Gregory was rescued; the party of Cencius in the city – men and women – were massacred; the tower was destroyed. Cencius escaped into the Campagna, and thence to Henry's court, but his usefulness to the royal cause was practically at an end. When Henry's envoys from the Synod of Worms arrived at Rome at the Lent synod of 1076 to ask the Romans to eject Gregory from his see, they scarcely escaped with their lives.

The material security of Pope Gregory was guaranteed above all by the power of Countess Matilda of the house of Canossa; and from the formal break with Henry in 1076 until the falling away of the Matildine vassals in 1081 the actual physical safety of the pope was not seriously threatened. Gregory was inclined to be a little boastful about the forces which Matilda placed at his disposal, and he might well think with satisfaction of the splendid expectations which the Roman Church had after Matilda's testamentary disposition of all her allodial lands in Italy and Lorraine to St Peter.[1]

But though he enjoyed this powerful support in northern Italy Gregory's position farther south was far from strong. By the autumn of 1076 the final downfall of Gisulf of Salerno was evidently near, and the Norman princes, Robert Guiscard and Richard of Capua, were raiding the Roman Campagna as far as the Sabine hills. Other Normans were beginning the conquest of the Abruzzi (considered part of the march of Fermo) and of the south of the duchy of Spoleto.

---

[1] For 'boasting' of Tuscan support see his letter to the Corsicans, *Reg.*, v, 4, p. 351. The date of Matilda's donation (probably 1077–80) is discussed by A. Overmann, *Gräfin Mathilde von Tuscien* (Innsbruck, 1895), pp. 143–4.

As early as 1074 the lands of the great abbey of S. Clemente a Casauria were under attack, and the Norman lords were condemned on this account in the Lent synods of 1074 and 1075. It was an area of particular concern to the pope, because containing several towns which had been included in the Ottonian donation to the papacy in 962.[1] Gregory's attempt to use the native comital families to resist Norman pressure failed; he made the son of the Count of Marsia into the Abbot of Casauria and Bishop of Valva (an interesting divergence from 'Gregorian' principles), but this merely intensified Norman aggression against church lands. The defeat of Count Trasmund of Chieti at Ortona in 1076 meant the supremacy of Guiscard's nephew Robert of Loritello in the western Abruzzi.[2]

In other parts of southern Italy papal interests fared no better. In 1077 Salerno fell, and at the end of the year the Normans laid siege to the papal dependence of Benevento, which was only saved by the accident of the death of Richard of Capua and the succession of the less hostile Jordan. Near Rome the powerful monastery Farfa was disobedient to the pope, and the abbot was threatened with excommunication in the March synod of 1078. The abbey of Subiaco was faithful, but involved in a long and bitter struggle with the local feudatories. Wibert, Archbishop of Ravenna, was by the beginning of 1078 openly in rebellion, carrying with him the area traditionally subject to his see. Ravenna and Pentapolis as far south as the march of Fermo were thus lost to Gregory's obedience.[3]

In temporal terms the results of the second deposition of the king in March 1080 were to make the position of Gregory in Italy dangerous in the extreme, and to throw him into the hands of the Normans. The election of Wibert of Ravenna as anti-pope on 25 June 1080 was not a

---

[1] Ficker, *Forschungen z. Reichs- u. Rechtsgeschichte Italiens*, ii, pp. 363–4, says that there was never any question of papal authority in these areas (Rieti, Terni, Aquila, Norcia, Sulmona, Marsia) but I think he was not entirely correct. For the historical geography see *Liber censuum*, i, pp. 44–5, in notes; C. Rivera, 'Le conquiste dei primi normanni in Teate, Penne, Apruzzo e Valva', *Bull. della Reg. Dep. Abruzzese di Stor. Patr.*, 3rd ser., anno xvi (1925), pp. 1–94. For Casauria, *Chron. Casaurien.* (*RRIISS*, ii, pt. 2), cols. 864–5; cf. Amato di Montecassino, p. 325. Cf. also H. Müller, *Topographische und genealogische Untersuchungen* (1930), pp. 39–40.

[2] *Reg.*, i, 85a, p. 123; ii, 9, p. 138; ii, 52a, p. 197; v, 14a, p. 481. Cf. Rivera's article quoted above. For the defeat of Trasmund see Amato, p. 329, and the 'Breve Chronicon ecclesiae Pennensis', in *Archiv der Gesellschaft f. ältere deutsche Geschichtskunde*, iv, pp. 128–35, where the renunciation of the brothers of Bishop Berardo should be dated 1076 instead of 1073. For the question of Gregory VII's divergences from his own principles see P. E. Schramm, *Gött. Gel. Anzeigen* (1953), pp. 71–2.

[3] Cf. K. Jordan, 'Ravenna und Rom im Zeitalter Gregors VII.', *Atti del 11° Congresso internazionale di studi sull'alto medio evo* (1953), pp. 193–8.

small matter; both in Italy and Europe Clement III enjoyed very powerful support. In the summer of 1080 the pope announced a campaign in which the whole Papal State was supposed to send an army against Wibert, but this summons was without military effect.[1]

The hold of Gregory VII over the Roman people is one of the most remarkable things in the history of a city which had never been remarkable for loyalty and fidelity, and never was to be. Whether Gregory's own origins were Roman or not (and the question seems never likely to be settled), he had been one of the most vigorous leaders of the Roman government for over twenty years before he became pope. His greatest collaborators among the cardinals – Humbert of Moyenmoutier and St Peter Damian – were now dead. Hugh Candidus, who was probably the ablest of the remaining cardinals, had gone over to Henry IV in the early stages of the quarrel, leaving Gregory the greatest man in Rome in moral stature as well as in office. Perhaps the Romans, penetrated though they were by faction and jealousy, seized on Gregory's concern, above and beyond almost all other aims, with the dignity of Peter and the power of Rome. Only this could explain his capacity to sway the Roman people and clergy at times when loyalty to him could mean nothing but spoliation and the threat of massacre.[2]

The tortuous negotiations between Gregory and Robert Guiscard had come to an end in June of 1080, when Gregory was faced by the new situation in Germany after his deposition of the Salian king, and by the possibility of an alliance between Guiscard and the anti-King Rudolph which would make the pope into a junior partner in the anti-Salian combination. At Ceprano on the southern boundary of the papal lands Gregory met his old adversary Robert, who swore homage and fealty to him and was invested by him with 'the territory conceded to you by my predecessors Nicholas and Alexander'. That there was a failure to reach agreement about the boundaries of Robert's state is shown by the vagueness of this formula, and also by the further reservation that the pope merely tolerated his possession of 'the territory which you now hold unjustly, such as Salerno and Amalfi and part of the march of Fermo'. That there was an equal distrust on Robert's side appears in Robert's

---

[1] *Reg.*, viii, 7, p. 524. Cf. P. Kehr, 'Zur Geschichte Wiberts von Ravenna (Clemens III.)', *Sitzungsberichte der Preussischen Akademie der Wissenschaften* (1921, pt. 2), pp. 355–68, 973–88.
[2] For what follows, Meyer von Knonau, *Jahrbücher des Deutschen Reiches*, iii, pp. 391 ff., 432–54, 472–501, 521–60.

oath of fealty, which guarantees the lands of St Peter only 'after I have ascertained that you own them'.[1]

Early in 1081 Gregory was promising himself that Robert would either defend Rome if Henry came, or undertake an expedition to terrorise and subdue rebellion in papal territories if he did not.[2] But this hope was disappointed; Guiscard's ambitions now reached beyond Italy, and in May 1081, while Henry IV was approaching Rome, Robert Guiscard was embarking across the Adriatic for Corfu and Durazzo. On 21 May 1081, while the new champion of the Roman Church was thus otherwise engaged, the Emperor Henry arrived with a small army outside Rome and encamped on the north bank of the Tiber in Prati (the 'field of Nero'), where the anti-Pope Cadalus of Parma had first led his forces in 1062. His force was too small to lay siege to the city, and he must have counted on the existence of an anti-Gregorian party in Rome. But in this he was disappointed. In 1081 Rome was solidly loyal to the pope.[3] In June Henry retired to Tuscany.

But the Romans were only experiencing the first alarms of a war of attrition. In the summer of 1081 north and central Italy began to rally to Henry IV. The Matildine vassals fell away from their allegiance, and the powerful Tuscan shield which had protected Gregory VII suddenly crumbled. By the autumn Gregory was urgently writing to Robert of Guiscard across the Adriatic, congratulating him on the battle won near Durazzo, but appealing for help. Communications were precarious, and the pope refrained from affixing his leaden seal (*bulla*) to the letter, in case it should fall into the hands of the enemy and be used for their own purposes.[4] Henry marched through Tuscany and Romagna, burning and devastating the country in the manner of his ancestors. Early in 1082 he returned to Rome, with an army reinforced by Swabian and Lombard troops. Henrician propaganda was launched even more vigorously at the Romans than before.[5] Henry claimed he was willing to submit to the verdict of a Roman synod about the legitimacy of Gregory (of 'Clement III' whom he had brought with him in his army he tactfully said nothing). God had said not of one, but of two swords, that they were enough (Luke 22:38). When Gregory had

[1] Postquam scivero tue esse potestatis, *Reg.*, viii, 1a (p. 515). Cf. Kehr, 'Die Belehnungen', p. 26; Clementi, 'The relations', *BISI*, lxxx (1968), p. 34.
[2] *Reg.*, ix, 4 (p. 577).
[3] Ibid. ix, 11 (p. 589). Romani et qui circa nos sunt fido et prompto animo Dei et nostro servitio parati per omnia existunt.
[4] *Reg.*, ix, 17 (p. 597).
[5] Jaffé (ed.), *Bibliotheca rerum Germanicarum*, v (*Monumenta Bamburgensia*), p. 500.

purported to deprive Henry of his kingdom, he had acted as though there was only one sword, and as though the distinction between temporal and spiritual did not exist. The king now appealed to the Romans who had served his father and grandfather to support the rights of his family. But the city did not waver. In spite of the use of siege engines, of the collapse of part of the Leonine walls, and of a fire in the immediate neighbourhood of St Peter's, Henry was unable to enter the city from the north. He took the army north to Mount Soracte and after some difficulty forded the Tiber, but he was still unable to make much progress when he renewed the siege from the south. When summer approached, he again withdrew with his army to northern Italy, leaving Wibert in Tivoli to conduct the work of propaganda and subversion.

The strain of war was telling on every section of Roman society – both on the poorer, who could neither trade nor get out of the city to the fields, and on the aristocracy. But curiously it was the clergy who protested first. In May 1082 a meeting of the highest clergy, including some of the cardinal bishops who remained faithful to Gregory to the last, condemned the mortgaging of church property in order to raise money for the war against Henry.[1] The meeting resolved that church revenues could be used for the poor, for the maintenance of divine service, and for the redemption of captives, but under no circumstances to pay troops. Had this doctrine been accepted by the medieval papacy, its later history would have been very different! But what is revealed about the financial situation of the Roman Church by this document is quite as interesting as the moral views it contains. It is evident that the finances of the papacy were at this time quite inadequate to support a great war. In the following year Robert Guiscard contributed 30,000 *solidi* to Gregory VII's war chest – such contributions from lay allies were evidently common; as early as 1075 Gisulf of Salerno had contributed to the expenses of Gregory's army.[2] At the same period, although Matilda was defending her Apennine fortresses only with great difficulty, she had the treasure of the church of Canossa melted down and sent to Gregory for the same purpose.[3]

---

[1] Mansi, *Sacrorum conciliorum nova et amplissima collectio*, xx, cols. 577–8; cf. Z. Zafarana, 'Sul "conventus" del clero romano nel maggio 1082', *Studi medievali*, 3rd ser., vii (1966), pp. 399–403. There is a corrected list of the clerics at this meeting in Klewitz, *Reformpapsttum und Kardinalkolleg*, pp. 38–9, in note.

[2] *Storia de' Normanni di Amato di Montecassino* (Rome, 1935), p. 305. The contribution was of equipment, and was disappointing.

[3] Overmann, p. 150. A bizarre casualty of the financial stringency of the war was the ancient pagan fertility rite of the *cornomania*, celebrated on the Saturday before Low Sunday. The

In the spring of 1083 Henry and his forces returned to Rome, opening the attack this time from the south on the fortress of S. Paolo fuori
le Mura. Evidently the king now commanded both banks of the river,
as he spent Easter (9 April) at Santa Rufina, the seat of the bishopric
of Silva Candida. The Roman population was now hungry and
thoroughly sick of the war; Gregory's admonitions to battle and his
references to those soldiers who were willing to face death for secular
lords 'for a miserable wage', now fell short of their mark.[1] In June a
handful of German skirmishers found during the afternoon siesta that
part of the Leonine wall was unmanned. Within a short time the Leonine
city and most of the city across the river fell to Henry's troops; Gregory
VII was penned into Castel Sant'Angelo, and only the Lateran and
Coelian quarters were held by his troops. Henry built and garrisoned
a fort between St Peter's and the river to consolidate his gains, and
withdrew the main army.

Henry now made ready to carry out the programme he had enun-
ciated in his manifesto of the previous year. Hostages were taken from
the Romans, and oaths exchanged, with a view to holding a synod in
November which would finally decide the question of Gregory's
legitimacy. But the plan for a managed synod failed this time to materialise; in the course of the summer the German garrison in Rome was
almost wiped out by an infection picked up in the summer heat. The
Romans captured and destroyed Henry's new fort, and Rome returned
to papal control. When the synod met on 20 November it was presided
over by Gregory VII; it is extraordinary that as late as this date, when
Henry IV returned to Rome the Romans once more refused to admit
him.

But the end of the long struggle now approached. Henry IV now
disposed not only of his own army but of the funds supplied him by
the Greek emperor, Alexis Comnenus, to work against the common
Norman enemy. By 'corruption, terror and force' Henry achieved his
ends; when his troops finally forced their way into the city on 21 March
the Roman clergy and aristocracy at last, and finally, deserted Gregory's
cause. Thirteen cardinals and practically the whole Roman aristocracy

---

people came in procession to the pope at the Lateran, headed by a dancing clerk with a
crown of flowers, holding the *phinobolus*. The gifts offered to the pope included a cock, an
unbound young fox, and a fallow deer; the pope gave gifts of money. The ceremony was
abandoned not because of its pagan character but because of the expense. 'Hoc fuit usque
ad tempus pape Gregorii VII, sed postquam expendium guerre crevit, renuntiavit hoc.'
Liber censuum, ii, pp. 171–4.

[1] *Reg.* ix, 21 (p. 602); ix, 35 (pp. 627–8).

– the regional officials, the judges, virtually the entire military, civil and clerical bureaucracy – went over to Henry and to Wibert. Nor was this a temporary desertion; for almost twenty years most of the Roman bureaucracy remained in Wibert's obedience.[1]

On 24 March Wibert was enthroned as Clement III, and a week later he crowned Henry and his queen Bertha as emperor and empress. Gregory VII after some hesitation remained in Castel Sant'Angelo, while his partisans defended the Capitol and Palatine hills until they were overcome; his nephew Rusticus made a final desperate resistance in the ancient palace known as the Septizonium, until Henry's siege machines practically demolished it. But Robert Guiscard now understood that his own position was threatened by the imperial success; with a powerful army (which one hesitates to describe as a 'relief force') he approached Rome from the south. Henry made no attempt to wait and to offer battle; on 21 May he left Rome with Wibert. Three days later the Norman army arrived, to find the city held only by a German garrison quartered in the Lateran area. Guiscard waited three days, and then assaulted the city through the Flaminian gate. The German garrison engaged the Normans in central Rome, in the Via Lata quarter; in the street-fighting, and because the Normans fired the houses to clear the way to Castel Sant'Angelo, much of this quarter, the richest of Rome and the seat of the main Roman families, was demolished. Guiscard's troops then 'liberated' Gregory VII in Castel Sant'Angelo. When the Romans opposed the pillaging carried out by the liberating army, further street-fighting broke out, and the quarters of the Lateran and the Colosseum were 'destroyed' by fire and malice.

How great the destruction was in the Roman war of 1081–4 remains something of a puzzle. That the three main administrative centres – St Peter's, the Capitol, the Lateran – were all affected, is itself important. So also is the fact that the Via Lata quarter was inhabited by the richest aristocrats. Of particular churches, we know that between the Colosseum and the Lateran the two important churches of S. Clemente and of the SS. Quattro Incoronati were destroyed or so badly damaged that they had to be rebuilt; when the second of these churches was rebuilt in 1116 the area round it was said to have become uninhabited.[2] We know also that S. Lorenzo in Lucina and S. Silvestro were burned down, in the Via Lata quarter; although the nearby monuments of the Ara Pacis and

---

[1] Kehr, 'Zur Geschichte Wiberts von Ravenna', especially pp. 978–9. I accept Kehr's conjecture about the date of the defections.

[2] *I.P.*, i, pp. 41–2, no. 5.

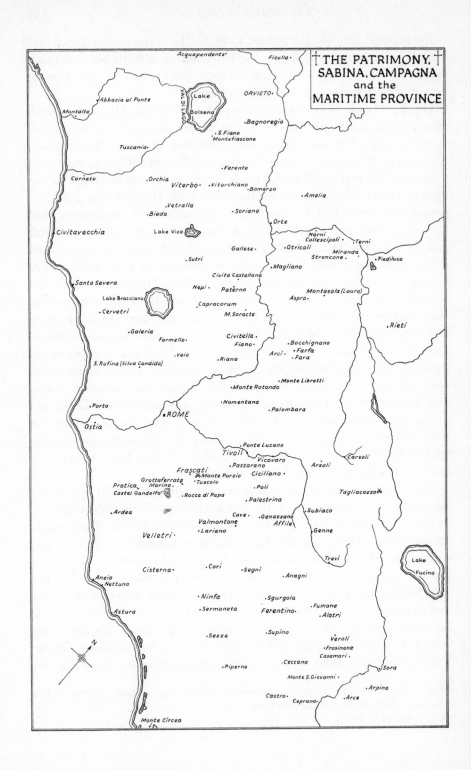

† THE PATRIMONY, †
SABINA, CAMPAGNA
and the
MARITIME PROVINCE

Acquapendente·

Ficulle·

·Abbazia al Ponte

Lake
Bolsena

ORVIETO·

Montalto·

·Bagnoregio

·S.Fiano
Montefiascone

Tuscania·

·Ferento

Corneto·

·Orchia

Viterbo·

·Vitorchiano

·Bomarzo

·Amelia

·Vetralla

·Soriano

·Bieda

Civitavecchia

Lake Vico

·Orte

Narni
Collescipoli·

·Terni

Gallese·

·Otricoli

Miranda
Stroncone·

·Magliano

·Piediluco

·Sutri

Civita Castellana

Santa Severa·

Nepi·

Paterno·

Montasola (Lauro)

Lake Bracciano·

Capracorum·

Aspra·

·Cervetri

M.Soracte·

·Galeria

Formello·

Civitella·
Fiano

·Bocchignano
·Farfa
·Fara

·Veio

·Riano

Arci·

·Rieti

S.Rufina (Silva Candida)·

·Monte Libretti

·Monte Rotondo

·Porto

·Nomentana

·Palombara

Ostia

·ROME

Ponte Lucano·

Tivoli·

Vicovaro·

Carsoli·

Frascati·

Passarano·

Ciciliano·

Arsoli·

Grottaferrata·
Marino·

Monte Porzio·
·Tuscolo

Pratica·
Castel Gandolfo·

·Rocca di Papa

·Poli

Tagliacozzo·

·Ardea

·Palestrina

Cave·

·Genazzano

Subiaco·

Valmontone·

Affile·

·Lariano

Genne·

Velletri·

Lake
Fucino

Trevi·

Cisterna·

·Cori

·Segni

Anzio·
Nettuno·

·Anagni

·Ninfa

·Sgurgola

·Fumone

Astura·

·Sermoneta

Ferentino·

·Alatri

·Sezze

·Supino

Veroli·

·Frosinone

·Piperno

·Ceccano

Casamari·

Monte S.Giovanni·

·Sora

Castro·

Ceprano·

·Arce

·Arpino

Monte Circeo·

obelisk of Augustus were unharmed, as was also an ancient triumphal arch over the Via Lata, which survived until the seventeenth century.[1] We know that the Septizonium on the Palatine was very badly damaged by Henry IV's war machines; on the other hand the Capitol was not so reduced as to be unusable, as the king dated documents from it shortly after its capture. Houses were cleared in the Borgo so that Henry's new fort (the 'palatiolum') could be built; on the other hand though there were fires near St Peter's, they were extinguished.

To count the cost of the war merely in terms of the destruction of ancient monuments and churches would in any case be absurd; moreover if we are to think mainly of the destruction of ancient Rome, then building and fortification carried out by the Roman nobility were probably many times more destructive of the ancient fabrics than the inefficient operation of eleventh-century siege engines. Many of the most splendid ancient decorations – for example the exterior marble statues and reliefs of Hadrian's mausoleum (Castel Sant'Angelo) – remained until the Renaissance. However, for the people who lived in Rome under Gregory VII the looting and destruction were not negligible But in social and economic effect the repeated devastation of the Roman countryside was probably far more important. Eleventh-century Rome was primarily an agricultural community; and what was decisive for its population and prosperity was the fate of the Roman Campagna.

For Gregory the sack of Rome by the Normans was the final collapse of his temporal power policy, which ensured that the desertion of his cause by the Roman bureaucracy would now be permanent. Thirty-five years of passionate and ably conducted political life had ended in apparent chaos. It was impossible for Gregory to remain in Rome after what had happened; he had the additional humiliation of having to accompany the Normans back to that Salerno which they had violently seized from his ally Gisulf, and against whose seizure he had protested as late as 1080. Gregory was not spiritually broken; he did not die in hate and chagrin as his successor Boniface VIII was to die after the outrage of Anagni in 1303, and Gregory's last great encyclical is as full of breadth and nobility as anything he ever wrote. But in Roman political terms he had lost the game. By 4 November 1084 – but probably much earlier than this – Clement III had returned to Rome as its undisputed bishop, and so he remained when Gregory VII died in Salerno on 25 May 1085.

[1] Cf. Emile Mâle, *The Early Churches of Rome* (London, 1960), pp. 123–9.

F

V

From Gregory VII's death to the turn of the eleventh century the temporal power of the Gregorian line of popes was concentrated in the south of Italy, and based on Norman assistance. Gregory's successor, though elected only in 1086, was Desiderius, the Abbot of Monte Cassino (Victor III), who throughout the war had maintained virtual neutrality for his monastery. His election was carried out under the influence of Jordan of Capua, who was dominant in the south of the Papal State both in this and in the beginning of the following pontificate. As far as the southern boundary of the Papal State and as far north as Sutri, Wibert was in control – his nephew Otto was 'Count' of Sutri.[1] Sabina and Tivoli were in the hands of Wibert's followers; imperial influence assisted the former Archbishop of Ravenna (who was also a member of a powerful Ravenna magnate family) to maintain a strong position on the Adriatic coast as far south as the Potenza and as far north as the Po.[2]

In March 1088 Victor III had a strong and able successor in the Cluniac Bishop of Ostia, Odo of Chatillon.[3] Norman influence and support continued to be very important for the papacy, and Urban II spent a great deal of time and effort in improving his position in the churches of southern Italy; the threat of an absolute Norman preponderance was much relieved by the death of Robert Guiscard (17 July 1085) and the rivalries of his successors and the death of Jordan of Capua (November 1090) gave Urban room for political manoeuvre in southern Italy which he was expert in utilising. Although Urban spent almost four years of the eleven of his pontificate in Rome, his position there improved only slowly. Early in the pontificate a Gregorian party re-appeared in the city under the leadership of the Pierleoni and Frangipani families, and of the prefect Benedict. But Urban's first visit to Rome in 1088 was a precarious interlude in a city commanded by the enemy obedience. Urban was anxious to be freely received by the Romans without Norman pressure,[4] and it was some time before this was

---

[1] A rising in Sutri displaced its Gregorian bishop, Bonizo, who was also the historian of the Reform papacy. For Wibertians in Velletri see *ASR*, xii (1889) (Stevenson); and in Veroli, S. Mottironi, *Carte di Sant'Erasmo di Veroli (937–1199)* (Rome, 1958). However in July 1085 the Gregorian Bishop of Ostia, the future Urban II, consecrated a church in Velletri. As pope in 1088 Urban II legislated for the church of Anagni while in Anagni in August 1088. *I.P.*, ii, p. 137, no. 7.

[2] *I.P.*, iv, p. 126, no. 1, the grant of half of the castle of Ariano, near Macerata, to an abbot.

[3] For what follows, Becker, *Papst Urban II.*, pp. 91–139.

[4] *ASR*, xxiii (1900), p. 278.

practical. On 28 June his troops from the Roman Campagna won a victory over those of Wibert in Rome which sent the latter out of the city to take refuge in Tivoli.[1] Wibert was brought back in 1091 by a Roman *coup d'état* at the time of Henry IV's victories in Italy, but the revolt of Henry's son and the resurgence of Matilda's power in northern Italy cancelled this advantage, and in early 1092 Wibert left Rome for ever. Even then the city remained the seat of some of his strongest supporters. Some of the bandits in Rome were executed, but when the crusading troops from north-west France entered Rome on their way to the Holy Land late in 1096, they still found rioters and robbers in St Peter's. Finally when Urban II, after the triumph of his European and crusading policies, entered Rome in 1097 with Matilda's troops, most of the city was won over to him, and the nobles bound by oaths. The last stronghold of Wibert in the city was Castel Sant'Angelo, which fell on 23 August 1098, a fortnight after the last Wibertian synod in Rome. And even so the English Archbishop Anselm was in 1099, in the last months of Urban's life, threatened with kidnapping by partisans of Wibert while on his way from the Lateran to St Peter's. Wibert was still able to continue in Albano, where he was when Urban II died on 29 July 1099, a fortnight after the crusading army took Jerusalem. Retreating to his last strongholds north of Rome, Wibert died on 8 September 1100 in Città Castellana. The attempts to create further anti-popes failed (although one was enthroned in the Lateran), and his obedience melted away.

Urban's southern policy was not in all ways successful – or perhaps it would be more accurate to say that it was successful if account is taken of his relatively weak point of departure. Though his church councils from the beginning of his pontificate onwards were held mostly in the south, and tended to concern themselves with the reorganisation and Latinisation of the south Italian Church, he registered some political setbacks. His failure to secure the feudal overlordship of Capua after the death of Jordan of Capua in 1090 was a major loss for the feudal policy of the popes in the Norman territories. He also failed to strengthen the papal hold on the important city of Benevento, which towards the end of the pontificate seemed about to slip out of papal control.[2]

Urban's successor, Paschal II (elected 13 August 1099), found a very different situation in southern Italy. Roger of Sicily lived long enough to present Paschal, at his accession, with a thousand ounces of gold,

---

[1] Kehr, 'Zur Geschichte Wiberts', pp. 984–6.
[2] Vehse, *Quellen*, xxii (1930–1), pp. 111–15.

which were used to pay mercenaries to chase Wibert to his last refuge in Città Castellana. But in 1101 Roger died, and the death of Guiscard's brother removed the last of the great eleventh-century Norman conquerors. The anarchy in Norman Italy for the following twenty years was in some respects an opportunity for the popes. Duke Roger of Apulia (who accepted investiture from Paschal II, as did his son William in 1114) was a weak man. He assisted Paschal with the recovery of Benevento, and offered no opposition to the policy by which the pope expelled the remnants of the old Lombard families from the city, and sent cardinal-legates and governors to build up papal rule there into something strong enough to resist both local and Norman pressure. When Paschal deprived Archbishop Landulf of Benevento at the Council of Ceprano in 1114 and re-imposed the rule of the papal governor, he marked an important step in the development of the temporal power.[1]

The terrorisation and looting of the Roman Campagna by the Normans went on as they had done for the past thirty years. On at least three occasions between 1108 and 1113 Robert of Capua spoiled and burned the towns in the south of the Papal State.[2] In Abruzzi the Norman occupation continued to be oppressive for the churches. Paschal II went on using the methods of his predecessors to combat this spoliation, and managed to exert some influence in the Abruzzi, but in 1111 he was still complaining that the possessions of St Peter in the march of Fermo and the duchy of Spoleto had not been restored.[3]

But Norman weakness and anarchy were in the end more harmful to the papacy than Norman aggression. As a military counterbalance to imperial power the Normans were now negligible. When the advance of Henry V into Italy was anticipated in 1110 Paschal went to southern Italy and appealed to the Norman princes for help, and took oaths from them that they would support him against Henry. But when the clash with Henry came he secured no effective Norman help. Norman armed assistance to the popes in this period was restricted to the despatch of small forces into the Campagna.

---

[1] Vehse, pp. 116–24.

[2] *Annales Ceccanenses* (*MGH, Scriptores*, xix), p. 282.

[3] Jaffé (ed.), *Mon. Bamberg.*, p. 281. Cf. Chalandon, *Domination Normande*, i, pp. 308–9. Papal authority was recognised in Teramo in 1108; F. Savini, *Il cartulario della chiesa Teramana* (Rome, 1910), no. ix, p. 16. If the pope controlled the lands of the bishopric he in effect controlled the town; cf. Savini, 'Sul dominio vescovile in Teramo e sulla condizione municipale della città sotto il medesimo', *Arch. Stor. Prov. Nap.*, xv (1890), pp. 805–25. Paschal continued the Gregorian policy of appointing members of the local comital families to bishoprics in the Abruzzi, e.g. the monk of Monte Cassino, Berardus, a member of the family of the counts of Marsi, who was Cardinal Deacon of S. Angelo in 1107 and Bishop of Marsi in 1110.

The schism of Wibert was the last round in the ancient contest of Rome and Ravenna. The comment of the papal biographer on the death of Wibert in 1100 is that 'Ravenna's insolence was overthrown, and the Roman Church breathed once more.' Ravenna had been the headquarters of the anti-Gregorian movement in Italy; at Ravenna some of the most notable imperialist propaganda had been compiled, including a forged document by which Leo VIII purported to return the whole Papal State to Otto the Great.[1] But the period in which an Italian archbishopric possessed the political and material power to be the seat of a great secular movement was now passing. Long before Wibert the feudality of Romagna and Pentapolis had become independent powers which at least rivalled those of the archbishopric. And soon both feudatories and bishops were to be rivalled by the new force of the commune. In the twelfth century the archbishops and clergy of Ravenna had to struggle hard to defend their lands and privileges.[2]

In the south of Pentapolis and in the north of the former march of Fermo a new 'march of Ancona' emerged under the Marquis Werner, the successor of Henry IV's supporter Raynier. This area had always been a hotbed of Wibertianism,[3] and in November 1105 Werner entered Rome with Maginulf, the last of the Wibertian anti-popes. He found plenty of supporters, both noble and popular ('horsemen and footmen'). The leader of the Roman conspiracy was Stefano de' Normanni, of the family of the Corsi; in the Pantheon Maginulf was 'elected' pope and transported thence to the Lateran. Fierce fighting followed on the Coelian hill, and the intruders were beaten by the loyalists. Maginulf was escorted by the defeated Werner back to Osimo in the march of Ancona, where he stayed in obscurity until called on by the Emperor Henry V in 1111. And so the last of the Wibertian anti-popes was rejected.

There was a Roman sequel to this episode, after Paschal had taken his revenge on the Wibertian faction in Rome by destroying all the houses of the Corsi. The head of the family, Stefano de' Normanni, rose again in rebellion and seized the fortress at S. Paolo fuori le Mura. He was expelled from the fortress by the Pierleoni faction (who made

---

[1] K. Jordan, 'Der Kaisergedanke in Ravenna zur Zeit Heinrichs IV.', *Deutsches Archiv*, ii (1938), pp. 85–128; idem, 'Ravennater Fälschungen aus den Anfängen des Investiturstreites', *Arch. f. Urk.*, xv (1938), pp. 426–48.

[2] Cf. A. Vasina, 'Lineamenti di vita comune del clero presso la cattedrale ravennate nei secoli XI e XII', in *La Vita Comune del Clero nei secoli XI e XII, Atti della Settimana di Studio*, ii (Milan, 1962), pp. 214–18.

[3] Cf. R. Sassi, *Le carte del monastero di S. Vittore delle Chiuse sul Sentino* (Milan, 1962), nos. 75, 79. *I.P.*, iv, p. 126, no. 1, Wibert's own concession of half the castle of Ariano, near Macerata.

keys to the fort from wax impressions), and made a feigned 'conversion to religion', but his submission did not last long.

Of all the feudal dynasties, the most powerful continued to be that of the counts of Tuscolo, the representatives of the ancient house of Theophylact. Gregory of Tuscolo had been one of the great figures of the earlier stages of the Investiture Contest; his son Ptolemy with Pietro della Colonna and his other brothers continued to lord it in the whole Maritime province as far south as Terracina. His family dominated most of the great roads to the south, beginning with the Via Appia, which they controlled at the fourth mile outside Rome by the great fort in the tomb of Cecilia Metella. Their control of the Appia was at least partly responsible for its decadence as a great thoroughfare in the Middle Ages. But even the Via Latina which partly replaced the Appia as the medieval route to the south was dominated by the dynasty. The fortress at Borghetto and the town of Tuscolo, and farther south the fortress which commanded the pass at Lariano, meant that the Latina could not be used without their consent. Farther south the counts of Tuscolo controlled the ports of Nettuno, Astura and Monte Circeo, where their fleet was based. Gregory and Ptolemy of Tuscolo maintained their own maritime foreign policy, on occasion co-operating with Gaeta in sending a fleet to Sardinia, on others fighting a commercial war against the same city.[1] At least one occasion in the eleventh century, other important towns such as Terracina and Velletri were under the control of the counts.[2]

When Paschal returned to Rome after the councils of 1106 and 1107 and his voyage to France, he found that Stefano de' Normanni had led a new rebellion in northern Latium, seizing Montalto and the strongpoints near Corneto in the very north of the Papal State.[3] Paschal attempted to deal with this situation by balancing the Roman factions against one another; when he left for the south in the summer of 1108 he left Pierleoni and Leone Frangipani in charge of the city and its environs, the Bishop of Tuscolo (Lavicum) in charge of the churches, and Ptolemy of Tuscolo in charge of the 'external patrimonies of St Peter' (i.e. the Campagna). This balance of power was a failure. Pietro della Colonna, Ptolemy's brother, had already had a brush with

[1] *Codex Diplomaticus Caietanus*, ii (Monte Cassino, 1891), no. 278, p. 169.
[2] Paschal II's bull for Velletri (*I.P.*, ii, p. 104, no. 2) appears to refer to the domination of the Tusculans over the city. Cf. Falco, *ASR*, xlii (1919), p. 567n.
[3] Jaffé (ed.), *Mon. Bamberg.*, p. 194, the strength of Wibertian feeling in northern Lazio appears in a letter from the Wibertian Bishop of Città Castellana, referring to miracles at the tomb of Wibert, and claiming that the Paschalian Bishop of Tuscania had been deposed.

Paschal over the village of Cave. Now he joined Stefano de' Normanni with the abbey of Farfa in rebellion, and the country north and south of Rome, from Sabina to Tivoli, Palestrina and Anagni, entered the area of dissidence. Ptolemy supported the revolt and tried to bar Paschal's return to Rome from the south, which was accomplished only with the help of Richard of Aquila's Norman troops. Albano was relieved, and after the pope's troops had been paid they assisted him to recover Rome and Tivoli, 'with much labour and bloodshed'. The claim was made by Paschal's biographer Pandulf that an effective 'peace' was imposed by Pope Paschal upon the Papal State from the failure of Maginulf as anti-pope in 1106 until 1116,[1] but it is a claim hard to believe in the light of the facts Peter himself relates. Perhaps Pandulf's vanity as an associate of the papal mercenaries lies behind his assertion. The Wibertians had earlier in the pontificate accused Paschal of alienating various church lands (including Ninfa and Ariccia) to the Tusculans, and the charge was probably not without foundation.[2]

If the counts of Tuscolo were the most formidable of the feudal nobility, they were also only its beginning. The lesser lords shared with the great their greed for church property, and their frequent rule in spite of the rights of St Peter. The counts of Ceccano were known in the Maritime province for their rule over Sezze and Segni; the lords of Pofi and Civitella for their aggression against the lands of the monastery of Subiaco and the adjoining bishoprics; the counts of Galeria in northern Latium were old enemies of the reformers, known in this period for the attempt of S. Maria Nuova and S. Paolo fuori le Mura to recover the centre of their dominions for the Church.[3] The heirs of Teobaldo di Cencio detained the property of S. Paolo fuori at Fiano and Civitella, in the region of Capena, at the important ford of the Tiber frequently used by imperialist armies.[4] On the other side of the Tiber the Ottaviani counts of Sabina and the counts of Todi and Otricoli pursued their interminable quest for the lands of the great monastery of Farfa.

---

[1] *Liber Pontificalis*, ii, p. 301. He says the peace would be 'almost incredible to posterity' (posteris vix credenda), and we do not know when he wrote this part of the biography—if after 1130 then the statement is understandable.

[2] *MGH, Scriptores*, vi, pp. 368–9; cf. *Liber Pontificalis*, ii, p. 303, for Paschal's concession of Ariccia to Ptolemy in 1116, and p. 153 below. In this context Waley, *P.S.*, p. 9n., confuses Paschal II with 'an imperialist anti-pope'.

[3] *I.P.*, ii, p. 28, nos. 3–5; cf. Tomassetti, *C.R.*, iii, pp. 36–7.

[4] *I.P.*, i, p. 169, nos. 17, 18. Cf. Tomassetti, iii, pp. 305 ff.

Farther into the Umbrian Apennines the nobility were scarcely conscious of papal temporal power; the family of the former Marquis Raynier of Spoleto were part of a world which had little to do with Pope Paschal.[1] Only at Terni, in the duchy of Spoleto bordering on the papal section of the Via Flaminia, was the pope able to secure recognition.[2]

The structure of society in the Roman Campagna and Sabina was deeply feudalised by 1100. When the men of Ninfa submitted to Pope Paschal – possibly in 1116 – they agreed to swear fealty, to come to the feudal host and to parliament, to attend the feudal court and observe the ban, to give hospitality dues (*fodrum*), tolls, and the tax for fealty (*fidantia*), and to do cartage and pannage services.[3] Some of the services are primarily patrimonial, but the feudal duties are the same essentially as those due from the men of Velletri. The tenurial relationships which the insecure conditions of the period produced can be seen in a Veroli document in which the lords of Monte San Giovanni concede land by charter on the same terms as those of the other freemen of the village, allowing the tenant in the event of war or famine to sell a part of the land without penalty.[4]

The bishops and abbots, while only exceptionally themselves feudatories, controlled feudal armies. The abbeys of Subiaco and Farfa were always full of armed men – the monks of Farfa with its twenty-seven castles complained that they were less well provided for than the abbey's mercenaries. The abbots themselves were very frequently sons of local comital families; at Subiaco the well-known reformer and Roman cardinal, Abbot Giovanni, was a member of the Ottaviani of Sabina, and his successor Peter was a connection of the Tuscolani. Peter's praises, sung by the chronicler after his death in 1145, were that he left the monastery 'in great prosperity, and full of well-equipped troops'.[5]

---

[1] Cf. the documents in favour of the cathedral of Gubbio in P. Cenci, 'Codice diplomatico di Gubbio dal 900 al 1200', *Archivio per la storia ecclesiastica dell'Umbria* (1915), pp. 125–502, no. 67 at p. 212 and no. 82 at p. 223. The second of these is 'tempore pape Paschalis'. The Gubbio documents are dated without reference to the popes from 1087 to 1107, and thenceforth with reference until 1117.

[2] P. 126 above, n. 1.

[3] Velletri, *I.P.*, ii, p. 103, no. 1; pp. 104–5, nos. 2, 3. Ninfa, *Liber censuum*, i, p. 407. For the word *curia* used in the Velletri document, see K. Jordan, 'Die Entstehung der römischen Kurie', *ZSSRG*, lix, Kan. Abt., xxviii (1939), pp. 96–152, at pp. 127 ff.

[4] Dated October 1099, C. Scaccia-Scarafoni, *Le Carte dell'Archivio Capitolare della Cattedrale di Veroli* (Rome, 1960), no. 85, p. 111.

[5] *Chron. Sublacen.* (*RRIISS*, xxiv, pt. 6), p. 21. For Abbot John of Subiaco (who was a soldier

In 1109, after the rebellion of the Tuscolani in the preceding year, Hildemund of Civitella (the hilltop town now known as Bellegra) had seized the two Subiaco castles of Affile and Ponza, near the monastery. Unable to re-take them with his own troops, the abbot called on Paschal II, who arrived with a force of Romans and levies from Campagna. The castles, which were held by Hildemund himself with his family, capitulated; the pope then granted them to the abbot for a payment of 100 pounds[1] passing the property by the transmission of a wand (*per ferulam*). The pope was said to have carried out this investiture 'as he had bestowed the other lands of Campagna', that is so that the monastery's ownership of the land was protected, and that the papal rights remained.[2] The castles had been included in earlier papal grants to the monastery,[3] and probably formed part of the great papal *massae* from which most of the monastery's property came. The transaction seems to be a translation into feudal terms of the earlier relations between the Roman See and the monastery. But this did not exhaust the matter. Having been granted the castles by the pope the abbot subsequently re-infeudated them to Hildemund from whom they had been taken. Hildemund swore fealty to the abbot for the castles, referring to another village which he held in fee (*in fegum*).[4] The irony of the affair was completed in 1121, when on the death of Abbot Giovanni, he was succeeded as Abbot of Subiaco by Pietro, Hildemund's brother. But the re-granting of such castles to feudal lords, once they had been made to recognise that the land was church property, was common practice. The same was done for Fiano and the castles in Capena, which the heirs of Teobaldo di Cencio had seized from S. Paolo fuori le Mura.[5]

---

as well as a reformer), see H. Schwarzmaier, 'Der Liber Vitae von Subiaco', *Quellen*, xlviii (1968), pp. 80–147, at pp. 97–103; K. Ganzer, *Die Entwicklung des auswärtigen Kardinalats im hohen Mittelalter* (Tübingen, 1963), pp. 29–31.

[1] Pounds of silver, which were naturally accounting and not coinage units. The sources frequently (as here) do not specify the variety of silver pence used, but I have indicated it where it is known. Pounds of Lucca and of Provins were both used as accounting units in the Roman area. See V. Pfaff, 'Die Einnahmen der römischen Kurie am Ende des 12. Jahrhunderts', *VSWG*, xl (1953), pp. 97–188.

[2] *Liber censuum*, i, p. 407, 'sicut commiserat alias terras Campanie; ita ut hereditas monasterii Sublacensis que ibidem est monasterio salva permaneret; cetera custodirentur ad jus beati petri. Et per ferulam investivit eum . . .' Cf. *Cronaca Sublacense del P.D. Cherubino Mirzio* (Rome, 1885), pp. 208–28; *Chron. Sublacen. (RRIISS)*, p. 17; P. Egidi et al., *I monasteri di Subiaco* (Rome, 1904), i, pp. 96–9.

[3] *I.P.*, ii, p. 89, no. 18, John XII's grant.

[4] *Il Regesto Sublacense del secolo XI*, Allodi and Levi (ed.) (Rome, 1885), no. 206, p. 246; Mirzio, pp. 226–7; cf. Jordan, *Arch. f. Urk.*, xii (1932), p. 49. Jordan seems to me to have misunderstood the circumstances in which the castles were captured.

[5] See note 4 above, p. 143.

F*

In Campagna and the Maritime province the bishops were important because of their demesne lands, but except in the case of a single bishop-count at Terracina in the mid-eleventh century, they were not the single or direct instruments of papal rule. In the towns the collections of notables who were later to form themselves into the commune were already to some extent treated by the popes as separate and distinct political groups. They were referred to by the popes as 'the men of Velletri, of Terracina, of Trevi' (*Velletranae urbis civibus, omnibus Vellitrensibus, Terracinensibus, Trevensibus*). The dukes and counts of the tenth century had disappeared, but the legally constituted commune had not yet emerged. The importance of bishops was as much feudal and dynastic as because of their office. When Crescentius, Bishop of Alatri, created a political crisis in 1113 by transferring the castle of Genne, which had been given in fee to him by the Abbot of Subiaco, to the men of Trevi, the most important facts in the case were his feudal relationship to the abbey, and the fact that both the Bishop of Alatri and the Abbot of Subiaco were members of the Ottaviani family of Sabina.[1]

It is too early to speak of recognition of the commune by the popes, but some pointers in this direction are to be found in the confusion of the wars of the Investiture Contest, and in privileges for fidelity to the papal cause – the privileges of Urban II and Paschal II for Velletri are examples, as is that granted by Paschal to Albano in 1107.[2] In both these cases the pope was in effect supporting the citizens against the lordship of the Tusculans. But though the popes acted against some feudal lords because of their attacks on church property or their support of schismatics, a general attack on feudal property was inconceivable; the pope was sometimes ready to confirm feudal privilege.[3]

The pope continued to depend, as he always had done, on the civil and military bureaucracy of Rome, which meant the factions among the Roman nobility. Roman nobles witnessed papal privileges, such as

---

[1] Cf. F. Carafa, 'Trevi dalle origini del comune al tramonto della signoria dei Caetani', *Bollettino della Sezione di Anagni della Società Romana di Storia Patria*, iii (1957).

[2] Velletri, *I.P.*, ii, pp. 104–5, nos. 2 and 3; there were earlier privileges from Gregory VII for the city and from Alexander II for the clergy. Albano, *Liber Pontificalis*, ii, p. 299, text in Tomassetti, *C.R.*, ii, p. 222. Both cities are given tax privileges. Paschal's bull for Velletri appears to recognise a certain right of the Tusculans in the city, while forbidding them to impose punitive impositions: ut videlicet loci vestri potentiores, quibus et vos suum jus non negetis, imponere vobis graviora non audeant. Cf. p. 142 above, n. 2.

[3] e.g. in the privilege for Lando of Veroli, *I.P.*, ii, p. 164. This confirmation is however not a bull, but is drawn up in the form of a private document. It was granted at a moment of great papal weakness, in October 1111.

that issued by Urban II for Velletri.[1] Not only did the traditional
Roman lay judiciary continue to give judgements in major cases involving church lands,[2] but Roman laymen took part in the Roman clerical
synods which gradually were turning into what later became the papal
consistory.[3] The leaders of the anti-Wibertian nobility, the Pierleoni and
Frangipani, accompanied the popes to the most important synods not
only in Italy but in France.[4] In the hands of these powerful and rich
magnates, with their fortified strongholds in the ruins of the great
public monuments of ancient Rome, the control of the city usually lay.
Outside the city they were hard pressed to compete with the power of
the Tusculans and the other comital families of the Campagna. Even
within Rome, a great military effort had been needed to break the hold
of the Wibertian aristocracy, and the fragility of the balance of power
between the Roman factions continued to be, as it had been since the
earlier Middle Ages, one of the most vulnerable points in the power
of the Roman See; no other medieval monarchy was exposed quite
to this degree of hazard. As the papal administrative machine extended
and strengthened itself in Christian Europe the paradox of Roman power
and Roman insecurity became even more evident. The Roman nobility
were by no means the only political problem which the popes faced in
Rome; the dissensions between the orders and generations of cardinals
were shortly to become a new element of political instability. And the
unsolved quarrel with the empire remained, menacing because of
imperial sovereignty in Italy, of imperial military power, and of the
permanent threat which it represented for the unity and order of the
Western Church. By 1111 there may have seemed some hope of negotiating a settlement. Agreements had been reached about investiture with
the Kings of France and England. Nevertheless, at the end of 1110 the
news that the German army was marching under Henry V into northern
Italy seemed more like a threat than a promise.

[1] *I.P.*, ii, p. 105, no. 3: auctoritate apostolica et corroboratione episcoporum ac nobilium
Romanorum.
[2] e.g. the case of the usurpations of the heirs of Teobaldo di Cencio, p. 143, n. 4. Lay
judges also took part in the lawsuit of the Bishop of Veroli with the Abbot of Monte Cassino,
I.P., ii, p. 157, no. 7.
[3] e.g. in the case between the Archbishop of Benevento and the Bishop of Troia, which is
important for this stage of the development of consistory. *I.P.*, ix, p. 207, no. 19, (*Gött, Nachr.*
(1898), p. 66). Non parva caterva episcoporum cardinaliumque et ceterorum ordinum
collecta fuisset, congregatis simul tam clericis quam laicis.
[4] Becker, *Urban II.*, i, pp. 105 ff.; Jordan, *ZSSRG, Kan. Abt.*, xxviii (1939), pp. 136–7. I do
not know why Jordan represents this participation of the Roman nobility in the administrative
working of the clerical administration as a novelty, (pp. 133–9).

When his army reached the south of Tuscany Henry V wrote to the Romans in the same vein as his father had used, magnifying the dignity of the city and its intimate connection with the empire. On 4 February 1111 the imperial ambassadors began the main negotiations with the papal representatives, headed by Pierleoni, in the little church of S. Maria in Turri, under the campanile of St Peter's. By some irony the doors of the church contained an inscription of the imperial donation with the names of the cities subject to the Holy See. The issue of this conference was unexpected and dramatic. The papal ambassadors conceded, as the price of the king's abandoning his claim to investiture, the abandonment of all claim by the Church to the *regalia* held by the bishops and abbots from the empire. It was a bold attempt by the pope to solve his greatest problem, by cutting straight through the living tissue of local, territorial and family rights which made up the flesh of the Medieval Church. As such it was doomed to failure from the opposition of the German bishops, and the king must have known it. Nevertheless, when it was communicated to him at Sutri, he ratified it subject to the consent of his bishops, and swore the oaths of protection and guarantee which the treaty required. The royal oath included a specific guarantee of the patrimony and possessions of St Peter.[1] On the papal side the preliminary treaty was sworn by Pierleoni alone – it seems at first incredible that this document, which involved the whole fate of the Church, should have been executed by a single Roman nobleman, but the explanation is no doubt to be found in the guarantees, which were basically for the king's safe entry into Rome. Hostages were to be exchanged on either side, to guarantee the pope's acceptance of the treaty and his coronation of the king. On 11 February the royal army encamped under Monte Mario, and on 12 February the Roman clergy greeted the king with the traditional ritual outside the Leonine city. For the first time for over half a century the German king entered Rome to be received by the Bishop of Rome as emperor-elect. Within St Peter's the pope awaited Henry with his cardinals and the Roman notables. The king entered the church, kissed and was kissed by the pope, and sat by him. Paschal, at the king's request, executed the treaty first, and read his renunciation of the *regalia* on behalf of the Church, and the reasons – the military service of the bishops and their lay functions – which had brought him to make this decision.

It was now the turn of the king to ratify his part of the treaty. But the treaty-making was no longer taking place in the discreet presence

[1] *MGH, Constitutiones et acta publica*, i, no. 83, p. 137.

of a few envoys, but publicly among the German bishops and princes who were going to be virtually stripped of their possessions if it was carried out. Medieval ceremonial easily degenerated into a riot, and this was what now happened. Uncertain what he should do, the king retired with the German bishops near the sacristy. While he deliberated the tumult increased, and both his execution of the treaty, and the continuation of his coronation by the pope, became impossible. The pope said mass at the high altar under the close watch of the German soldiers; only with difficulty could the holy elements be fetched for the sacrament. Paschal with his immediate following then sat under guard in the Confessional of St Peter. But elsewhere in the great church and its huge atrium, and outside in the Borgo down to the Tiber, there was chaos, fighting, bloodshed. The German soldiers saw and took the chance of ransom and plunder, and the higher Roman clergy and nobility were robbed and taken captive. When night fell the pope was a prisoner, and the great reconciliation between the priesthood and the empire had degenerated into an act of brigandage.

On the next day there was a sharp clash with the Romans in front of St Peter's, in which the king was knocked from his horse and came near to being killed, if a Lombard nobleman had not saved him. On 15 February the imperial force withdrew from Rome with its prisoners, crossed the Tiber near Mount Soracte, and camped on the left bank in the plain below Tivoli while the pope and his cardinals were imprisoned. Paschal was confined in the Sabine hill fort of Tribuco, belonging to the abbey of Farfa, and others in the small village of Corcolle near the army. A small force of Normans from Jordan of Capua had meanwhile advanced into the Campagna, and found the countryside strongly held by Tusculan troops on behalf of the emperor. There was no Norman help for the pope in his hour of peril. And the pope's disaster was also that of the Romans; very many of the magnates and their children had gone into captivity, and shivered half-naked in the February cold. The emperor naturally attracted the Roman opposition; and among the demands he made on the pope were that he should pardon Stefano de' Normanni, the banned head of the Corsi family. Maginulf, the anti-pope expelled from Rome in 1106, was brought from Osimo to the imperial camp, to be held there as a threat to Paschal.

After two months of captivity Paschal was brought from Tribuco to Ponte Mammolo, where the Via Tiburtina cuts the Tiber, and a treaty was signed there on 11 April. There the pope conceded investiture by cross and ring to Henry, and promised coronation. The king again

guaranteed the patrimony and possessions of the Roman Church.
These were events which concerned all the Latin world; English clerks
were informed by a letter from the imperial clerk Burkhard, who had
accompanied Henry I's daughter Matilda to her future husband
Henry V, in the preceding year.[1] On the following day the accords
were ratified, and on 13 April pope and king entered the Leonine city,
which was locked to exclude the Romans, and the coronation took place.
Without having entered Rome proper, Henry and his army marched
north to Tuscany. On the way farther north he met the elderly Countess
Matilda, whom he treated with careful respect. From Paschal he received
letters which rely on the promises made by Henry before he entered
Rome; the pope complained to him of the disobedience of a number
of towns – some of them former Wibertian strongholds – in the Papal
State, and referred to the orders the emperor had given for these places
to be restored to St Peter. Property of the Roman Church ('possessions of St Peter') was also being withheld in many areas of central
Italy.[2]

The humiliation and submission of the pope in 1111 was followed
by the reaction of the Gregorians; fifty years of church history could
not be put aside by an act of brute force, and there could not be a
concordat with the empire which was rejected by the clergy who had to
operate it. In 1112 the Treaty of Ponte Mammolo was cancelled by a
council held in the Lateran. The emperor had left no force behind in
central Italy, and Rome and the District subject to it returned to the
regime which had preceded Henry V's expedition. The monastery of
Farfa continued to defy the Roman regime and to correspond with
the emperor, but this was no change of the situation before 1111. Pope
Paschal made a great effort, not without success, to improve his position

---

[1] W. Holtzmann, 'England, Unteritalien und der Vertrag von Ponte Mammolo', in his
Beiträge zur Reichs- und Papstgeschichte des hohen Mittelalters (Bonn, 1957); cf. K. Leyser, 'England
and the Empire in the early twelfth century', *Trans. Royal Hist. Soc.*, 5th ser., x (1960), pp.
61–83.

[2] The disobedient towns: Città Castellana, Corcolle (where the cardinals had been
imprisoned), Montalto (the stronghold of Stefano de' Normanni), Monte Acuto and
Narni. Jaffé (ed.), *Mon. Bamberg.*, v, no. 154, p. 281 (3 May 1111). 'Nos tamen ea et comitatus
Perusinum, Eugubinum, Tudertinum, Urbeuetum, Balneum regis, Castellum Felicitatis,
ducatum Spoletanum, marchiam Fermanam, et alias beati petri possessiones per mandati
vestri praeceptionem confidimus obtinere.' This refers to Perugia, Gubbio, Todi, Orvieto,
Bagnorea, Città di Castello, the duchy of Spoleto and the march of Fermo (ibid). It is
inconceivable that at this moment of weakness the pope would claim political rule of the
duchy of Spoleto and the march of Fermo, and the claim must be for church property there.
If the claim was for political rule the exarchate of Ravenna would not be omitted. Cf. Gregory
VII, *Registrum*, vii, 14a, p. 481.

in southern Italy, and in the Papal State. According to the papal bio-grapher, after Henry's withdrawal Paschal recovered 'all the possessions of St Peter which Henry had taken'. In February 1113 Paschal held a synod in Benevento whose main object was to proceed against the pro-Norman element in the city under Landulf Burrellus, and to impose as ruler of Benevento, with the title of 'constable', a Beneventan noble called Landulf de Graeca. This energetic soldier fought the Normans outside the city and the pro-Norman party within. When Archbishop Landulf tried to expel Landulf de Graeca, the pope eventually at a further synod at Ceprano in 1114 deprived the archbishop and re-instated the constable. The use of church synods, and the frequent despatch of cardinals for these temporal ends were characteristic of the time. Certain cardinals such as Peter of Porto (the *doyen* of the cardinal bishops) and Hugh of Alatri seem to have been particularly used for temporal power missions, and the practice of making such feudal abbots and bishops as John of Subiaco and Crescentius of Alatri into cardinals was further feudalising the Roman clergy.

On 24 July 1115 the Countess Matilda died. Of the great donation of all her allodial lands to the Roman Church not a word was said by the pope, or none that has reached us. It is possible that in 1111 Henry V had made over new royal rights in northern Italy to her, and possible also that at the same time, in spite of the donation, she had bequeathed to her relative Henry V the allods earlier left to the Church, so that at her death he would acquire both imperial lands she had held of him, and the allods which she had not.[1] The death was a double danger for Paschal, in that it removed a powerful moderating influence on Henry, and made a fresh imperial descent on Italy almost inevitable. There was little that the pope could do in north Italy. In the south he tried to conciliate the warring Norman families, and in August 1115 established the truce of God among them in a council at Troia.[2] In the same summer he was in Benevento, consolidating his rule there and setting up a papal rector over the constable Landulf de Graeca.

In the period after the first withdrawal of Henry V, the delicate balance among the Roman factions on which the papal power depended began to crumble. The hostages still held by the emperor may have been a factor, but we have no certain knowledge of this. The Frangipani

[1] Overmann, *Gräfin Mathilde von Tuscien*, pp. 41–7; cf. L. Simeoni, 'Bologna e la politica italiana di Enrico V', *AMDR*, n.s., ii (1937), pp. 148–66. For the donation see p. 129 above.
[2] Chalandon, *Domination Normande*, i, pp. 317–18; Vehse, *Quellen*, xxii (1930–1), p. 124. For the truce of God observed by papal troops in Rome in 1105, see Jaffé (ed.), *Mon. Bamberg.*, p. 236.

and the Pierleoni, the two main families to have supported the Gregorian papacy, had worked in apparent harmony as late as 1108.[1] In 1113 and 1114 the Frangipani had still been in attendance at papal synods.[2] At the Roman Council of 1116, at which Paschal renewed his determination to resist Henry, it seemed as though not the Frangipani but Pierleoni, together with Peter the Prefect and Cardinal John of Gaeta (the future Gelasius II) and possibly also Pons, the Abbot of Cluny, were acting as the party of moderation in the *curia* which wanted to stop the breach with Henry V from being made even wider.[3]

Three weeks after the end of the council of 1116, Peter the Prefect died. He was the nephew of Ptolemy of Tuscolo, and his powerful family sought to have his young son succeed him in the office. Paschal's refusal, and his decision to grant the prefecture to one of the sons of Pierleoni, unleashed a Roman revolution. The faction of the Tuscolani rioted, while the pope as a precautionary measure made over the duties of the prefectorial office to the constable Landulf de Graeca, his military officer from Benevento.[4] Security measures taken in Rome by the small force of papal soldiers were ineffective; the regionary troops were won over by the opposition. In the solemn ceremonies of Holy Week and Easter Week the pope was roughly importuned in St Peter's, then his retinue (*familia*) were stoned as they followed him in the processions in the city. Finally the revolutionary faction took complete control of the city, and began to demolish the houses of the Pierleoni party; the pope fled from the Lateran palace to the papal fort in the monastery of Andrew and Gregory on the Coelian, and then left Rome for Albano and the Campagna. The new Roman regime wrote to Henry V, who had already entered Italy.

At this stage the usual bidding for the support of the Roman magnates

---

[1] P. 142 above.

[2] Jordan, *ZSSRG, Kan. Abt.*, xxviii (1939), p. 137. Cf. H.-W. Klewitz, 'Das Ende des Reform-papsttums', in his *Reformpapsttum und Kardinalkolleg*, pp. 209–59.

[3] Ekkehard of Aura, *Chronicon universale* (*MGH, Scriptores*, vi), pp. 250–1. Cf. Meyer von Knonau, vi, pp. 350–6.

[4] I interpret the passage in *Liber Pontificalis*, ii, 302, 'Vade P., et tu Const.' as referring to Pandulf the *guarzifer* (squire) in minor orders who was the author of the papal biography, and to the Constable of Benevento, Landulf de Graeca. J. M. March, *Liber pontificalis prout extat in codice manuscripto Dertusensi* (Barcelona, 1925), pp. 58–9, conjectures that 'Const.' means constable, but does not make this identification. So far as we know, there was no constable of the papal court in 1117; cf. Jordan's article quoted above. But the pope *had* a constable, Landulf de Graeca, who is referred to by Falco of Benevento as taking part on the papal side in the fighting in Campagna which followed the revolution of 1117. The cardinal deacon who witnessed the tradition of the prefecture to Landulf is not named (*Liber Pontificalis*, loc. cit.).

took place; the pope distributed 'gold, silver and precious things' to them, and attempted to bribe Ptolemy of Tuscolo by granting him the little town of Ariccia on the great Roman viaduct of the Via Appia, near Albano. But when Landulf the constable captured the young Tusculan 'prefect', the subject of the quarrel, in an ambush, and tried to take him down the Via Latina to imprisonment in the papal fortress of Fumone, Ptolemy laid a counter-ambush in the pass at Algido, and recovered his nephew.[1] The Maritime province was ablaze; Cardinal Hugh of Alatri held Terracina for Paschal, but most of the hills from Sabina to the foot of the Monti Lepini were in the hands of the Tusculans. In Rome the Pierleoni were besieged in their fortress of the Theatre of Marcellus and were bombarded by war machines installed on the Capitol. The pope returned to Castel Sant'Angelo in May, and after a further sojourn in the south in the summer he succeeded by the end of the year in quieting Rome.

Early in the New Year of 1117 Paschal left Rome, warned of the approach of imperial troops. In March Henry appeared in Rome, encouraged by his supporters the Abbot of Farfa, the Tusculan John of Monticelli,[2] and Ptolemy of Tuscolo, to whom he married his illegitimate daughter Bertha. He was also accompanied by his young English wife Matilda, whom after his own 'coronation' at the hands of the Portuguese bishop, Maurice of Braga, he had also 'crowned' as empress at Whitsun on 13 May. In the meantime Paschal had gone to Capua and Benevento, which had become his headquarters in the south, and where he could now be protected by his own troops instead of relying entirely on Norman support. He had, however, to make the concession of re-instating Landulf the deposed Archbishop of Benevento. Though Paschal had himself left Rome, the emperor found not a single Roman cleric of importance who would abandon the papal cause. Ralph the Archbishop of Canterbury spent a week in the imperial camp, and found the general opinion that Paschal would return to Rome as soon as Henry withdrew.[3] In spite of the failure of a Norman raid made into

[1] *Liber Pontificalis*, ii, 303 and n. Falco of Benevento (Migne (ed.), *P.L.*, clxxiii, col. 1168) does not identify the 'constable' as Landulf, but since he himself was of Benevento, where the constable's office was, the identification seems natural. For Algido see Tomassetti, *C.R.*, iv, pp. 542-3, 548-9.

[2] P. F. Kehr, 'Zur Geschichte Viktors IV. (Octavian von Monticelli)', *Neues Archiv*, xlvi (1926), pp. 53-85, at p. 80; cf. Klewitz, *Reformpapsttum*, pp. 230-5, and also Leyser, *Trans. Royal. Hist. Soc.*, x (1960), pp. 68-9.

[3] William of Malmesbury, *De Gestis Pontificum* (Rolls Series, 1870), pp. 129-31; Eadmer, *Historia Novorum* (R.S., 1884), pp. 242-3.

Campagna on Paschal's behalf while Henry was retreating to Sutri, Paschal did in fact return to Rome at the beginning of 1118, having passed the autumn in reducing the rebels in Campagna.

With pertinacity almost incredible in a sick old man who could scarcely sit upright, Paschal on his return to Rome immediately mounted war engines in the Castel Sant'Angelo to bombard the rebels in St Peter's. But a week after his return, on 21 January 1118, he died. It may be asked, whether this grimly determined pope, who spent so much of his pontificate in going from one siege to another, can be rightly accused, as he often is, of weakness in the big political issues. Perhaps a part of this so-called weakness was religious scruple (such as that which deterred him from excommunicating Henry after 1111), and perhaps another part – notably his acceptance of a premature and impractical solution of the question of investitures, in the first Roman negotiation – might be called rashness. He died leaving the problems of investiture and of Roman security both unsolved, and it is not surprising that his successor's pontificate, although brief, was one of the most tormented of the Middle Ages.

The allegiance of the Roman factions in this turbulent time must have been an obscure business even to contemporaries. The cardinals placed the election of Paschal's successor in the Church of S. Maria in Pallara, which was in the middle of the Frangipani fortresses in the Forum. They did not expect that, immediately after they had elected the Cardinal Deacon, John of Gaeta as pope (he took the title of Gelasius II), Cencio Frangipani would suddenly descend 'like a wild beast' onto the gathering, and drag poor John by his hair into a Frangipani gaol. This happened in the presence not only of the cardinals and the papal *familia,* but of the assembled Roman magnates. The first movement of the nobility was favourable to the new pope, and the Frangipani were compelled to release their prisoner. The 'counts and barons' (the first time that the Norman term 'baron' was applied to Roman nobles) appeared to accept the pope-elect. But after a short time the Frangipani mobilised their forces, and the first German soldiers made their appearance.[1] Intelligence of this new aggression reached the papal *familia* in time for the pope to be hurried by night from the Leonine city to a refuge by the Tiber, from which the papal party embarked in two galleys the next morning. When they reached Porto the storm was so considerable that

---

[1] Duchesne (ed.), *Liber Pontificalis,* ii, p. 314; March (ed.), pp. 170–1. Pandulf speaks of Germans actually in place on the banks of the Tiber; it is not clear if this was an advance guard or a garrison.

they could neither land nor put to sea, while the Germans on the north bank threw spears and threatened them with fire arrows dipped in pitch if they would not come in and submit. In the night the pope was landed on the south bank, and taken to the Benedictine castle (belonging to S. Paolo fuori le Mura) at Ardea – Pandulf the biographer with a fine reminiscence of Aeneas and Anchises makes his uncle the Cardinal Hugh of Alatri carry the venerable pope on his shoulders from Porto to Ardea. At Ardea Gelasius embarked in galleys which took him to safety in his own native town of Gaeta; here the Norman princes and clerics found him, did homage, and assisted in his consecration.

How fundamental the split was in the Roman nobility is unclear; the most important source to tell us about it was written by a partisan of Anaclete after the schism of 1130, and tends to make everything hinge on the treason of Cencio Frangipani.[1] There are indications that the nobles themselves regretted what had happened. The Corsi who rebelled in 1108 and young Peter the Prefect, the origin of the 1117 troubles, in 1118 took the papal side. But while he was engaged in hand to hand fighting to protect Gelasius in the fresh *coup* of the following year Stefano de' Normanni shouted to his opponents that the pope had got away, and added: 'What are you trying to kill us for? We are Romans like you, and your relations to boot. Get out! We're all tired of fighting and we want to go home.'[2] If one takes account of this sort of war weariness, and also of the fact that most if not all of the big Roman families had members who were Roman clerks if not cardinals, the suggestion that the Roman nobles coldly manipulated the papacy without thought or understanding of what their actions mean for the Church, is not really acceptable.[3]

On 2 March Henry arrived in Rome. As John of Gaeta, Gelasius had less than two years earlier at the Roman Council had been counted

---

[1] See March's introduction to his edition of the codex Dertusensis of the *Liber Pontificalis*, pp. 41–95. Pandulf is silent on the part played in this critical time by the Pierleoni, known to have been almost all-powerful both before and after 1118. Eadmer the Englishman calls Pierleoni in 1121 'praeclarissimi ac potentissimi principis Romanorum', (*Hist. Novorum*, p. 295), and cf. William of Malmesbury, *De Gestis Pontificum*, p. 128, 'summi Romanorum principis'. For the Anacletan Schism, see p. 168 below.

[2] Duchesne (ed.), *Liber Pontificalis*, ii, p. 316; March (ed.), p. 175. 'Quid, inquiens, facitis? quo ruitis? Papa quem queritis iam fuga elapsus est. Numquid et nos perdere cupitis? Et quidem romani sumus, similes uobis et si dici liceat consanguinei uestri. Recedite rogo, recedite ut et nos fessi pariter recedamus.'

[3] Cf. C. Erdmann, 'Mauritius Burdinus (Gregor VIII.)', *Quellen*, xix (1927), p. 229, quoting Schneider. This position was abandoned by Klewitz, nor is it maintained by F.-J. Schmale *Studien zum Schisma des Jahres 1130* (Köln-Graz, 1961), p. 15–28.

as of the pro-imperial party; he now despatched to Henry as an ambassador likely to be acceptable to the imperial court the Portuguese Bishop Maurice of Braga, who had been instrumental in crowning Henry in Rome during the crisis of 1117. But Henry's patience had run short with Roman bishops and factions. On 8 or 9 March he had Maurice of Braga consecrated pope as 'Gregory VIII' with the help of two Wibertinist cardinals of the earlier schism. The Roman factions, among whom the old Wibertinist sympathies were evidently not entirely dead, may have encouraged Henry to enthrone Maurice. The pope, shortly after the rumour of Maurice's election reached him, continued to refer to the emperor as 'my friend'. But within a month Gelasius proceeded to the step that Paschal, remembering his promises to Henry of 1111, had never taken; on 7 April Henry was excommunicated. The pope nevertheless continued to take a conciliatory attitude, and proposed a council in north Italy to settle the papal-imperial quarrel.

Norman help was valuable to Gelasius, although it did not give him the decisive control of Rome which he wanted. For a short time the imperial army took the offensive south of Rome, and besieged the castle of Torrice near Frosinone, in order to bar the route of the expected Norman march from Capua north to Rome. The siege had to be lifted without effect. The Norman princes and even the lesser barons had sworn fealty to Gelasius in Gaeta, and afterwards he had been received and comforted in Capua by its prince, Robert. Henry V left Rome for the north at the beginning of June, leaving a small German garrison behind, and leaving Maurice of Braga as 'pope' in possession of St Peter's. The attempt of a small Norman force sent by Robert of Capua to clear the Germans and their supporters from Rome was unsuccessful; the anti-pope remained where he was, and the other dissidents fortified themselves in Trastevere. The Norman princes and barons returned home, and when Gelasius returned to Rome from the south early in July his party travelled 'more like pilgrims than princes'.[1] The Bishop of Rome was no longer accustomed to such modes of travel.

But it is unkind to taunt poor Gelasius, of all popes, with having lost the habits of austerity. Before his pontificate he had been a hagiographer, and his trials in office must have come at least close to those of earlier saints. After the return of Gelasius to Rome under the protection of the Corsi he was still unable to budge the anti-pope from St Peter's. On 21 July Gelasius was persuaded to attend the holy offices in Santa

[1] Magis peregrini quam domini. *Liber Pontificalis*, ii, p. 315.

Prassede, which was situated among Frangipani strongpoints. In the middle of the ceremonies Frangipani troops stormed into the church, and hand to hand combat broke out for the custody of Gelasius. The pope was somehow smuggled out of the church, after being in the midst of the fighting. Still wearing some of the liturgical vestments, he was hurried onto horseback, and reached safety.

The unfortunate old gentleman could bear no more. If Pandulf the biographer is to be trusted he complained to his cardinals and familiars that he could no longer tolerate the Roman factions – he would prefer one emperor (even if a wicked one) to many. On 2 September 1118 Gelasius left Rome by sea for Pisa, on his way to exile in France. He left the senior cardinal bishop, Peter of Porto, in charge of Rome, and associated with him Hugh of Alatri in charge of Benevento.[1] The Tusculan Peter was confirmed as prefect, and general authority in temporal affairs at Rome remained with Stefano de' Normanni, the head of the Corsi. Of the Pierleoni, so powerful shortly before Gelasius and shortly after, there is no word. The town of Terracina was given the custody of Monte Circeo, which perhaps indicates that aggression on the part of Ptolemy of Tuscolo from his port at Monte Circeo was no longer feared.

On 29 January 1119, not much more than a year after he became pope, Gelasius II died in Cluny. It had been a dark hour for the papacy, and if it only just preceded the dawn, this was hidden to Gelasius. The unscrupulous Abbot Pons of Cluny did not succeed him, as Pons had hoped. The two cardinals with Gelasius in France named the aristocratic Guy of Vienne to follow him, the descendant of the counts of Burgundy, and the kinsman of the kings of England, France and Germany. Guy, who took the name of Calixtus II, was perhaps the most noble pope to sit on the papal throne since Otto III had made his relative Brun into Gregory V. By temperament and connections he was particularly well qualified to carry out the policy of appeasement with the empire which Gelasius had cautiously inaugurated – the policy which perhaps Paschal would have carried out before them if his errors and misfortunes in 1111 had not made this impossible. On the German side Henry was now more disposed to compromise than he had ever been. His anti-pope had been a ludicrous failure, recognised only in the few miles between Rome and Sutri (the old Wibertian stronghold), and in the dissident parts of the Apennines and central Italy which had

---

[1] *Liber Pontificalis*, ii, pp. 316–17. Cf. Vehse, *Quellen*, xxii (1930–1), pp. 128–9.

never been reconciled after the Wibertian schism.[1] In the rest of Europe, including Germany, he was ignored.

On 3 June 1120 Calixtus II entered Rome in triumph. He had already carried out important negotiations with Henry, already held major church councils; the Roman nobles submitted to him meekly. He had no immediate need of Norman help. Within two years the treaty with the emperor would be signed; within a further three the Salian dynasty which had struggled with the popes for fifty years would no longer rule Germany. For a long time the heroic conflict of the popes with the secular powers was to die down, while the institutional manifestations of the ideals of the Reform popes were to put down their roots in Europe. These new institutions, and their economic and social effects on Roman life, were to provide a new context for Roman rule in central Italy. The growing pains of the new administration, in particular those of the College of Cardinals, modified and to some extent transformed the old struggles of the Roman factions. The Roman court, which was itself a new appellation, was developing new methods of government, new resources, and recruiting a new personnel.[2] Even the conservative terminology of the Roman bureaucracy was quickly changing, and revealing that the struggle of the past fifty years to restore traditional clerical rights had been, in fact, a revolution.

[1] e.g. the document of November 1118, 'tempore domni Gregorii summi pontificis, regnante Henrico imperatore', dated Osimo. *Le carte della Abbazia di Chiaravalle di Fiastra*, i (Ancona, 1908), no. 16, p. 26.
[2] See Ullmann's chapter, *Growth of Papal Government*, pp. 310 ff; and cf. F. Kempf, 'Kanonistik und kuriale Politik im 12. Jahrhundert', *Archivum historiae pontificiae*, i (1963), pp. 11–52.

Chapter 5

Successors not to Peter but to Constantine

I

The renewal of the religious life of the European clergy remained the aim of the Roman bishops, and the approach of a settlement of the great quarrel with the empire brought hopes of progress in religious feeling and discipline. St Bernard at Clairvaux and St Norbert at Prémontré were setting patterns for the religious communities which were to renew and revitalise much of clerical life; both Norbert and other leaders such as Walter of Ravenna were feeling their way towards reforms which would affect the cathedral clergy as well as the religious of the monasteries. These spiritual impulses were closely connected with those that had brought the Reform papacy into existence, and its machinery of jurisdiction and power was used to support them. But in Rome the old problems remained, though changed policies had given them new forms. The relations of the Roman aristocracy with the Roman clergy had been altered by the permanent importation of foreign clerks into the highest bureaucratic positions. The non-Roman cardinals and officials were fundamental to the success of Reform policies, and they could not be driven out. But they drove a wedge between the clerical and the military orders, and were a permanent source of political instability and tension. Moreover, although under Calixtus and his successor there was no sign yet to reveal it, Rome was no exception to the rising numbers and importance of the non-noble urban classes which can be observed everywhere in Italy at this time, and which lay behind the communal movement. The uncontradicted pre-eminence of the 'captains', the Roman nobles with their great feudal possessions in the countryside, was soon to be challenged by other social groups. This challenge was to lead eventually, by an obscure gestatory process, to the birth of the Roman commune. But the old order died hard, and indeed with its solid basis of landed power and clerical influence was never fully overturned. In the Lateran Council of 1123 Calixtus II complained that oblations from the altar of St Peter's were still going to laymen, and that laymen were fortifying Roman churches for their own purposes.[1] The offerings made to the apostle himself were not immune from the old, quiet feudal corruption.

A few days after Calixtus had entered Rome, envoys from the city of Genoa signed a treaty with the higher Roman clergy and nobility which shows in a clear and harsh light how Rome was governed.[2] The right claimed by the Archbishop of Pisa to consecrate the bishops of Corsica was the immediate point at issue, but beyond this was the rivalry of the two maritime powers of Genoa and Pisa, who were constantly at war; and the maritime interests of the Romans (clearly referred to in treaties later in the century) must also have been a factor. The treaty was concluded between the Genoese and the main Roman magnates – Peter the prefect, Stefano de' Normanni, Leo Pierleoni, and Cencio Frangipani – in the presence of the former vicar of Rome, Peter the Bishop of Porto, and of other cardinals among whom was Peter Pierleoni. It was said to have been made with the pope's assent, and in view of what it said this must have been so. The Romans promised that for a large money consideration (1,200 silver marks to the pope and 300 to the Roman *curia,* besides large payments to single clerks and nobles) they would cause the pope to issue a privilege declaring the Corsican bishops subject to the Roman Church alone. The treaty was not merely the bribery of certain Roman nobles and clerks, but a treaty of alliance between Genoa and Rome, which specifically contemplated war between the Roman Church and Pisa as a result of its being made. The way it was made demonstrates what seems to have become in the course of the Investiture wars the historic right of the Roman nobility and clergy to share in the economic benefits of papal government: a right which later appeared in the guise of the money demands of the Roman commune against the popes, and those of the cardinals to share in some of the revenues of the Holy See. The claims of the Roman nobles may have arisen in part at least from the bribes which popes had offered to get their military support through the whole course of the wars of the Investiture Contest; the most recent of such bribes in 1120 had been that paid by Calixtus in the recovery of Rome. The share which the clerical *curia* obtained in gifts to obtain papal goodwill was also a usual one; contemporary with

[1] Mansi, xxi, col. 285. Cf. *I.P.,* i, p. 141, no. 28.
[2] *Annali Genovesi di Caffaro e de' suoi continuatori* (L. T. Belgrano (ed.)), *Fonti per la storia d'Italia,* xi, (Genoa and Rome, 1890), pp. 19–21. Belgrano prints the main document (dated 16 June 1120) in a note, but the text is equally important. Cf. also *I.P.,* iii, pp. 312–25, and for the later treaties I. Giorgi, 'Il trattato di pace e d'alleanza del 1165–6 fra Roma e Genova', *ASR,* xxv (1902), pp. 397–459.

the Genoese negotiation was that to obtain a papal privilege for Compostella, which also involved the payment of substantial sums to the *curia*.[1]

The Genoese treaty reveals something, though not overmuch, about contemporary Roman politics. That the Frangipani were included in the treaty as principal signatories suggests that in 1120 Calixtus was anxious to get the support, not only of the Corsi family and of the other late supporters of his predecessor Gelasius, but also of the former Roman opposition. Some of the fortifications in Rome belonging to the Frangipani were destroyed at this time by the pope's order; on the other hand, at some time in the pontificate Leo Frangipani was placed in charge of the pope's private guard of mercenaries, a position which was very useful to him during the election of Calixtus's successor. The situation of the Pierleoni in 1120 was evidently strong; the Genoese treaty was signed nearby the former titular church of Cardinal Peter Pierleoni, and the monetary share of the Pierleoni in the treaty was bigger than that of any other laymen (though not as large as the payment to Peter, Bishop of Porto, the former vicar of Rome). Probably the main idea of Calixtus was to balance one Roman family against another.[2]

The Norman states of the south were the most important of all the feudal dependencies which the papacy had acquired, or sought to acquire. Gregory VII's claims to feudal jurisdiction over Spain, Poland, England and other countries[3] had been of no practical importance for the Papal State; but effective exercise of feudal overlordship over the Normans south of the river Garigliano was vital to the temporal independence of the popes. The security of the papal enclave of Benevento, and the protection of the lands of Monte Cassino and the great southern monasteries were important but secondary; the prior question was that of the control of Norman military power. Since the death of Roger I of Sicily in 1101 conditions in Norman Italy had been favourable for the popes – that is to say, rather anarchic. But in 1112 the majority of Roger II had brought a man to power who wished to unite the inheritance of his uncle Robert Guiscard with that of his father, and whose ability and steadiness of purpose were equal to the business. Nothing could have contrasted more with papal interests than Roger's aim of uniting all the Normans of southern Italy under one ruler.

---

[1] K. Jordan, 'Zur päpstlichen Finanzgeschichte im 11. und 12. Jahrhundert', *Quellen*, xxv (1933–4), pp. 61–104, at pp. 84–7.

[2] Cf. Schmale, *Studien*, p. 23.

[3] Cf. Ullmann, *Papal Government*, pp. 333–4.

After Calixtus II had established himself in Rome in the summer of 1120 he proceeded in October to Benevento, where he received the liege homage of Duke William of Apulia, and invested him with the lands and honours his father and grandfather had had from the popes.[1] As a consequence of William's vassalage Calixtus undertook to place his territories under the protection of the Holy See while William went to Byzantium to seek a Greek bride in 1121. Roger of Sicily promptly took the opportunity to invade his cousin's possessions, and besieged Niceforo (Rocca Faluca), near Catanzaro in Calabria. But he found himself immediately faced by the diplomatic opposition of Calixtus, who had been in southern Italy since the end of July 1121, and who in November went south to Taranto and Catanzaro to attempt to make peace. The papal attempt at mediation failed, partly because the papal camp was overtaken by some kind of epidemic, and Calixtus was forced to give in to Roger. The renewal of the war between Roger and William led in 1125 to the momentous concession by the childless William, to make Roger his heir in the duchy.

The quarrels of the Norman nobles affected papal policy in the south of the Papal State. The Norman barons were an impediment to order in papal Campagna; when in 1123, following the murder of the papal count of Campagna, Calixtus led a punitive expedition to the south, Rainulf of Alife intervened to prevent him from punishing the papal counts of Ceccano, and only a minor baron was executed.[2] Rainulf of Alife (or of Avellino) was one of the most powerful Norman magnates, and he was to be important to papal policy for many years.

In the wider business of the schism and the empire, Calixtus was most successful. The anti-pope, Maurice of Braga, in his last refuge in Sutri, was attacked by a small force under the able Cardinal John of Crema, and on 23 April 1121 was led captive to Rome, where he was exhibited, to ridicule him, mounted backwards on a camel, before being taken off to end his days in various papal fortresses in Campagna. The formal end to the Investiture struggle came with the agreement negotia-

---

[1] Kehr, 'Die Belehnungen', pp. 33–6; cf. for what follows E. Caspar, *Roger II. (1101–54) und die Gründung der Normannisch-Sicilischen Monarchie* (Innsbruck, 1904), pp. 54–60; Vehse, 'Benevent als Territorium des Kirchenstaates', pp. 129–32; Chalandon, *Domination Normande*, i, pp. 321–3; *Liber Pontificalis* (codex Dertusensis), March (ed.), pp. 193–4.

[2] *Annales Ceccanenses* (*MGH, Scriptores*, xix), p. 282; *Lib. Pontificalis*, March (ed.), p. 195. For the identification of 'Ranulfi comitis de Airola' in the *Liber Pontificalis* with Rainulf of Avellino, or of Alife, see Garufi's note in the index to the *Chronicon* of Romualdo of Salerno (*RRIISS*, vii, pt. 1), p. 387. I have not identified the 'Crescentium comitem domni papae' who was murdered at Piperno in 1123, but he must have been papal count of Campagna. He is overlooked by Falco, *ASR*, xlii (1919), pp. 572–3.

ted at Worms on 23 September 1122. The sections of the agreement
which refer to the patrimonies of St Peter are not absolutely explicit, but
when the Emperor Henry V promised to 'restore to the holy Roman
Church the possessions and *regalia* of blessed Peter which have been
taken from her from the beginning of the quarrel until the present
time', it seems that the reference is to the political possessions of the
Roman Church in Italy.[1]

The end of the conflict with the empire meant also the end, for a
long period, of imperial intervention in the monasteries and bishoprics
of central Italy. Walter of Ravenna, the reforming canon of Porto who
had been consecrated Archbishop of Ravenna by Gelasius II, had in
the confused conditions of Gelasius's pontificate been kidnapped and
imprisoned. Under Calixtus he was able to return to his see and to
inaugurate a period of disciplined submission to Rome never before
known in the history of his bishopric. The depredations and irregularities
of his predecessors were solemnly condemned in 1123 at the Lateran
Council, and again in 1125 by the Ravennese clergy before Honorius II.[2]
In 1127 Walter made concessions of church property 'by our authority
on behalf of the church of Ravenna and by the authority of the lord
pope on the part of the holy Roman Church'.[3] It is most unlikely that
any of his predecessors would have used such a formula. Calixtus supported Walter in the claims of the see of Ravenna over the other bishoprics of Emilia,[4] but Walter was acting here rather as a reformer for the
Holy See. He was sharply called to order by Honorius II for excommunicating a noble of Ravenna who had appealed to the pope.[5]
Ravenna had been for practical purposes outside the orbit of Roman
rule from 1073 until 1120. That it should have found in Archbishop
Walter one of the most faithful defenders of papal supremacy of his time
was bound to have important consequences for papal temporal rule.

---

[1] The promise was closely parallel to that made by Henry V to Paschal II in 1111. Cf. E.
Bernheim, *Das Wormser Konkordat und seine Vorurkunden* (Breslau, 1906), pp. 13, 35–6. Calixtus
referred to this part of the promise in his letter to Henry of 13 December, 1122. I. Ott, 'Der
Regalienbegriff im 12 Jahrh.', *ZSSRG*, lxvi, *Kan. Abt.*, (1948), pp. 234–304, at p. 236, has
little to say on papal usage. Cf. pp. 210–11 below.

[2] Mansi, xxi, col. 286; A. Vasina, 'Lineamenti di vita comune del clero presso la cattedrale
ravennate nei secoli XI e XII', in *La vita comune del clero nei secoli XI e XII. Atti della settimana
di studio*, ii (Milan, 1962), p. 205.

[3] Fantuzzi, *Monumenti Ravennati*, iii, no. 22, p. 37 (2 August 1127). Cf. the same formula
on p. 38, in a document of 7 January 1129. The 'duchy of Ravenna' had been conferred by
Gelasius II on Walter as archbishop, *I.P.*, v, p. 57, no. 189. Cf. also Schmale, *Studien*, pp.
210–12.

[4] Ibid. p. 58, nos. 191, 192, 193 (Ferrara); cf. p. 250, no. 20 (Bologna).

[5] Ibid. p. 59, no. 195.

Though less vital than Ravenna, the renewal of papal supremacy over the great Sabine monastery of Farfa was to be important for the temporal power in the Roman area. Of the two contending abbots who had disputed the abbey since the death of Berardo III in 1119, the aristocratic Berardo IV, the imperial candidate who was also supported by Marquis Werner of the march of Ancona, had to give up his claim after the concordat of Worms and the Lateran Council, to the candidate with papal support. When this abbot, Guy, proved unworthy, Honorius II accepted his resignation and sent two cardinals to appoint a member of the family of the counts of Sabina as abbot.[1] From this point Farfa ceased to be a centre of resistance to Roman ideas and jurisdiction; territorially this had consequences not only for the province of Sabina, but also for the wide lands possessed by the abbey on the other side of the mountains in the march of Ancona. The gradual acceptance of papal power east of the Apennine watershed owed something to this, as well as to increased papal control in Ravenna. But whether in Campagna or Sabina, the papal rectors or counts continued to be drawn from the territorial nobility.

Calixtus died on 14 December 1124. The election that followed was as bedevilled by faction as that of Gelasius in 1118. 'The people' were said to have wanted the nobleman, Cardinal Sasso of Anagni, but he evidently failed to find powerful backers. When the cardinals assembled in the Lateran on 16 December they elected a Roman cardinal, Teobaldo dei Boccapecorini. But Teobaldo was unacceptable both to the Frangipani family and to the powerful Cardinal Aimeric, Chancellor of the Roman Church under Calixtus. While the clerks were singing the 'Te Deum' for Teobaldo, laymen under Roberto Frangipani, the commander of the pope's mercenary guard, broke into the church and acclaimed as pope a Bolognese cardinal, Lambert Bishop of Ostia. He was of humble stock; the snobbish Abbot of Monte Cassino later said of him that he had 'no idea who his parents were', but that he was 'full of learning from head to foot'. Without much apparent difficulty support was found for him among the nobles; Pierleoni's son flung the papal mantle over him. The next day Teobaldo was induced to renounce the papal office which had been offered him. Peter Bishop of Porto, the senior cardinal bishop, advised Lambert that he should withdraw. But on the third night Pierleoni and Peter the Prefect were corrupted by Leo Frangipani and Cardinal Aimeric as agents of Lambert, who 'as

[1] Cf. Vehse, *Quellen*, xxi (1929–30), pp. 164–5; Schuster, *L'imperiale abbazia di Farfa*, pp. 263 ff.

a learned man, understood the profound avarice of the Romans'. Pierleoni was promised (though the promise was not subsequently honoured) the important city of Terracina, and Peter the *castrum* of Formello just north of Rome.[1] The result was the approbation 'by all' of Lambert's election and his acclamation as Honorius II. According to the papal biographer Pandulf, the bitterness and political tension aroused by the election, and by the conduct of Honorius after it, led to the schism of 1130.

The first years of Honorius were full of warlike operations to restore order in the Papal State; perhaps he wished to show that he could lead a feudal army with no less vigour than his aristocratic predecessor. In the spring of 1125 he led an army into the Campagna, burning and terrorising villages, and obtained the submission of the counts of Ceccano. Some of their lands he gave to the Frangipani, though they did not keep them for long.[2] In the summer and early autumn he was at Monte Cassino and Benevento; in 1126 and 1127 he carried out further campaigns in the south of the Papal State. But on 26 June 1127, while Honorius was still in Campagna, Duke William of Apulia died, leaving Roger of Sicily his heir. The unification of the south of the peninsula under one ruler, so dangerous for Roman interests, had become practical politics.

Roger tried hard to persuade Honorius to invest him with the duchy of Apulia. Two days after the pope arrived in Benevento, Roger appeared outside the walls; money was offered, and the important Apulian city of Troia, besides the castle of Montefusco which had played a part in Beneventan politics in recent years, were offered to the pope. But Honorius took a strong line; the approaches were rebuffed, and the pope set about the organisation of the great feudal coalition in southern Italy against the Sicilian ruler. While the nobles of papal Benevento were flung into prison by Roger's vassals, Honorius at Troia pronounced his excommunication. Troia was conceded an important privilege by Honorius which virtually incorporated the town in the

---

[1] Pandulf says that Terracina had been recovered by Calixtus from a Count Monaldo, from whom he also brought the fort of 'Saxa'. For Formello see *Papers of the British School at Rome*, xxxiv (London, 1966), p. 76. There is something odd about these bribes: Terracina was one of the most important cities of the Papal State, and Formello an unimportant village.

[2] *Annales Ceccanenses*, p. 282; Dertusen (ed.), *Liber Pontificalis*, p. 207. Falco, *ASR*, xlii (1919), pp. 571–2 lays emphasis on the role of Calixtus II and Honorius II in Campagna, and certainly they tried to improve matters there after the disturbances of the Investiture Contest wars. For some qualifications about Honorius, see below.

Papal State.[1] In the last days of 1127 and the New Year of 1128 Hanorius was at Capua, attended by Rainulf of Alife and the young Prince Robert of Capua; the pope stated his case against Roger of Sicily and proclaimed plenary absolution from their sins (as Leo IX had before his troops fought at Civitate in 1053) for those who fell in the fight against him.

In June 1128 the Roman force under Honorius arrived at Benevento to join the armies of Robert of Caua and Rainulf of Alife. Other barons from Bari and Taranto joined them, and the great host marched south to find its enemy. But Roger was too clever to offer combat to this great army; he took up a position on the Brandano in Basilicata where he could not be brought to battle. In the murderous heat of July and August, without adequate provisions, the papal army waited until it rattled to pieces, and the barons broke away. Honorius could not politically afford, as the barons could, to fight another day. The Chancellor Aimeric and Cencio Frangipani were sent to Roger's camp to offer terms. Both Honorius and Roger marched north to Benevento, and at the bridge over the Calore (Roger feared to enter the city), the treaty was made. Honorius invested Roger with the duchy of Apulia, and Roger promised to refrain from aggression against Benevento, and not to absorb the principality of Capua. Of Troia there was no word, and the city submitted to Roger in the following year. The pope had suffered a humiliating defeat of the greatest importance, and it may well be that the Roman nobles were embittered against the Chancellor Aimeric and Cencio Frangipani, who negotiated the agreement.

The defeat of 1128 probably weakened the temporal power of Honorius during the last two years of his pontificate; the counts of Ceccano were able to recover the lands they had lost two years earlier. There is certainly no sign that in the struggle to preserve order and protect church lands in the Papal State Honorius obtained anything like a decisive success. Like other popes he had to pay dear, sometimes too dear, for noble support. To get the help of the Tuscolani (and according to Pandulf the biographer to marry his niece into their family) he handed over the town of Palestrina, which had revolted against the Tusculan magnate Pietro Colonna, back to its former owner; and although the Bishop of Palestrina had guaranteed the inhabitants against reprisals, Pietro Colonna took a savage revenge on them.[2] In the quarrels

---

[1] *I.P.*, ix, p. 213, no. 3; L. Zdekauer, 'Le franchigie concesse da Onorio II alla città di Troia (1127)', *Rivista italiana per le scienze giuridiche*, xxv (1898), pp. 242–57. Zdekauer does not mention the political implications of the grant.

[2] March (ed.), *Liber Pontificalis*, p. 206.

between the abbey of Subiaco and the town of Tivoli, Honorius unlike his predecessor was unable to prevent the Tivolese from attacking the monastery's villages. The abbey was most concerned to prevent Tivolese exploitation of new lands and to stop the building and habitation of a settlement in the fertile place of Casa Pompoli. In October 1128 Abbot Peter (who was a member of the Tuscolani) broke the peace he had sworn with Tivoli and destroyed Casa Pompoli, and built a new fort which dominated the disputed area of Gerano.[1] Rome and the pope had made no contribution to the maintenance of peace in the Aniene valley. Not far off, another branch of the Tusculan family had been restrained by Calixtus II in 1124 from aggression against monastic property on the Via Tiberina;[2] in the folowing year the same monastery of SS. Ciriaco and Nicola was trying to defend its possession of Cave near Palestrina.[3] North of Rome the counts of Galeria still held the centre of the old *massa Careia,* in spite of clerical prohibition.[4]

It is doubtful how serious was the economic damage done to the Roman District by the wars of the Investiture Conquest. Some centres were certainly abandoned, perhaps because of war conditions, but possibly also because of changes in the drainage system, and of the return of the rural population to areas which in the tenth and eleventh centuries had been deserted. The centre of the diocese of Santa Rufina or Silva Candida north of Rome disappeared so completely that it has only been identified again in the past few years by modern archaeologists, and the adjoining village of Porto was also depopulated.[5] On the other hand, in the Aniene valley villages were being re-populated in the early twelfth century which had been previously abandoned; the village of Casa Pompoli (Poggio), whose exploitation by the Tivolese was so objectionable to the abbey of Subiaco, was protected by 'ancient walls' and was surrounded by terraces which probably were already in existence before the twelfth century. North of Lake Bracciano some ancient centres of habitation such as Orchia and Bieda were going into decline, and towns such as Viterbo and Orvieto which had previously

---

[1] The original quarrel with Tivoli was over Sant'Angelo and Appollonio. See P. Egidi, *I monasteri di Subiaco,* i, 101–5; C. Mirzio, *Cronaca Sublacense* (Rome, 1885), pp. 231–46; *Chron. Sublacen. (RRIISS,* xxiv, pt. 6), p. 20; L. Bruzza, 'Regesto della chiesa di Tivoli', *Biblioteca dell'Accademia storico-giuridica,* vi, docs. 14–16 (in doc. 15 'R. abbas' is surely a slip for 'P. abbas').
[2] *I.P.,* i, p. 80, no. 4.
[3] Ibid. no. 5. For another similar case, ibid. p. 78, no. 2, and cf. F. Bartoloni, *Codice Diplomatico del Senato Romano (Fonti per la Storia d'Italia* (Rome 1942), p. 13, no. 12.
[4] *I.P.,* i, p. 67, no. 7.
[5] *I.P.,* i, p. 21, no. 14. The excavations carried out at the Santa Rufina site by the British School at Rome have not yet been fully reported.

been of secondary importance were becoming rich and populous.[1] It seems reasonable to suppose that the popes after the Investiture Contest ruled a more prosperous patrimony, in spite of political disorders past and to come.

II

Early in February 1130 Honorius was dying; he was taken to the Church of SS. Andrea e Gregorio on the Coelian hill, with motives that can only have been political. He died on 13 February. Aimeric the Chancellor procured that in spite of custom and although only a limited number of cardinals was present, the election should take place on the very same night of the pope's death. By this *coup d'état,* undertaken by Aimeric and his supporters to frustrate the power of Pietro Pierleoni 'at whose nod all Rome spoke or was silent', Gregory the Cardinal Deacon of S. Angelo was elected pope with the name of Innocent II, and enthroned in the Lateran (his consecration followed in S. Maria Nova in the Forum). No compromise between the two parties in the *curia* was possible after this act; on the following morning Cardinal Bishop Peter of Porto and the majority of the cardinals met with many laymen in the Church of S. Marco. The gathering elected Cardinal Peter Pierleoni, who was then enthroned and consecrated in St Peter's, and took the title of Anaclete II.

The predominance of the Pierleoni faction in Rome took only a few days to assert itself. There were disorders, and churches (including St Peter's) were looted, but political weight in the city was overwhelmingly for Anaclete, and the money distributed by his family only made his victory more certain. Rapidly the fortresses of the Frangipani and the Corsi became the only refuge of Innocent in Rome. In May he took a ship for Pisa, and travelled thence to Genoa and to France. In Rome the Frangipani abandoned their candidate and prudently submitted to Anaclete (just as the Pierleoni had submitted to Honorius in 1124). A major schism had come into being, to be settled only after several years of conflict and the intervention of many European states.

That the schism was not merely an incident in the struggle for power between Frangipani and Pierleoni is clear. The presence of the French

---

[1] L. Rossi and P. Egidi, 'Orchia nel Patrimonio', *ASR*, xxxi (1908), pp. 447–77. Cf. also *PBSR*, xxxiv (1966), pp. 77–8.

Cluniac Bishop Giles of Tuscolo among Anaclete's electors, and the fact that the learned and reputable Cardinal Pandulph of Pisa protested against Innocent's election and the next morning voted for Anaclete, show that the election of Pierleoni was not just an aristocratic plot. But it seems equally unconvincing to treat the schism as primarily occasioned by a split among the clergy about policies in the universal Church.

With the exception of a short resistance offered by the abbey of Farfa the Roman patrimony submitted almost solidly to Anaclete; and the Innocentian Abbot of Farfa was shortly sent into exile.[1] From Sutri to the very south of the Papal State, to Veroli and Ceccano, Anaclete was recognised and obeyed. However, if the Via Francigena, the pilgrim road, was for Anaclete, the Via Flaminia was not. In Umbria, where the influence of S. Ubaldo, the Bishop of Gualdo, was important, Innocent was recognised; Walter of Ravenna carried his suffragan bishops in Emilia and Romagna (with one or two exceptions) for Innocent. But that Anaclete's acceptance was so complete in a solid block of Roman territory was of some importance for the temporal power, since it avoided the weakening effects of a civil war. To be the pope of the Roman nobility had always meant political stability, in a limited sense, for the papal patrimony.

Norman support was quite as valuable to Anaclete as Roman. His family had long ago been in friendly relation with Roger of Sicily. In September 1130 he went south with the main members of the Pierleoni to Benevento, and on 27 September, having already received Roger's homage, he issued the bull of investiture which brought the kingdom of Sicily into existence, and gave a political form which lasted until 1860 to the relationship which had begun at Melfi in 1059. Roger and his heirs were invested with the crown of the kingdom of Sicily, Calabria and Apulia, with the right to be crowned by an archbishop of their kingdom, and for a tribute of 600 *scifati*. The chief region of the new kingdom, the *caput regni*, was to be Sicily. Roger also received an ill-defined right of domination over Naples, and the right to take hold-oaths from the men of papal Benevento. The privilege was witnessed by Anaclete's Pierleoni relations; the indication that Roger was making a treaty with a family as well as with a bishop was later confirmed by the solemn privilege made out by Roger to the Pierleoni family (on 28 January 1134).

It is doubtful whether this investiture can be made out as a surrender

[1] Cf. Vehse, pp. 166–7; Schuster, pp. 275–9; Schmale, p. 205.

G

of papal power for which Anaclete can be personally blamed. The pressure on the papacy to make such a concession had already made even the stiff-necked Honorius bend considerably in the same direction, and in the end Anaclete's rival, Innocent, was – after defeat in battle – to concede something substantially identical. But the particularly close concern of Anaclete's own family with the investiture suggests that he was acting as much as a member of the Roman aristocracy as its bishop. Certainly he needed Norman armed support, in spite of the power of his family; very quickly he summoned Norman soldiers to stage a *coup* against the popular leaders in Benevento, and in 1131 Roger's vassals Robert of Capua and Rainulph of Alife were called to Rome with their troops to protect Anaclete.

By 1132 the position of Anaclete and Roger was seriously threatened. In Europe Innocent had virtually won the struggle; French and German churches and governments gave him recognition; only in Italy and Scotland was Anaclete's cause widely supported. St Bernard, St Norbert of Magdeburg, Walter of Ravenna and those who supported new reforms in the monasteries, the cathedral churches and the *curia,* stood behind Innocent. Anaclete's party in the *curia* had tended to be the conservatives of the Gregorian movement; events now revealed how isolated they were in the Church as a whole. In the spring of 1132 the German King Lothar brought Innocent to Italy, at the same moment as Anaclete's ally Roger faced a serious rebellion by Robert of Capua and Rainulph of Alife. A revolution in Benevento placed the popular regime there on the side of the Apulian rebels against Roger and shortly afterwards on the side of Innocent II. In July Roger was sharply defeated by the rebels on the river Sarno.

If Lothar had brought a powerful army with him from Germany both Anaclete and Roger might have been brought down. But the rebellion of the Hohenstaufen had made Lothar unwilling to withdraw many troops from Germany, and he came relying (as the historian Otto of Freising remarked) more on morale than on military effect. In the spring of 1133, while Lothar came south down the Via Cassia, Innocent marched down the Via Aurelia, relying on Pisan and Genoese seapower to clear the coast road. Civitavecchia (probably handed over to Innocent's supporters the Corsi) and the towers along the shore north of Rome were stormed from the sea; the junction between the pope and the emperor was effected at Viterbo in early April. At the end of the month, after some negotiations with the Anacletan party in Rome had failed, Lothar was outside the city. The party in Rome and the

District favourable to Innocent in 1130 had come out for him once more, breaking their oath to Anaclete. But the material weakness of Innocent and Lothar meant that there could not be a decision save on the symbolic plane of the coronation of Lothar as emperor, which took place in the Lateran basilica on 6 June, while Anaclete remained in St Peter's and his troops continued to hold a good part of Rome. The divided control of the city, typical of the earlier wars of the Investiture Contest, was not resolved.

Two days later pope and emperor made an agreement for the government of the Matildine lands, the allods which the Countess Matilda had willed to the Holy See on her death in 1115. No pope had been in a position to enter into possession of the lands since then, but Honorius had made Count Albert of Verona into their papal vicar, probably without very much practical result. Now Innocent invested Lothar with these lands against an annual *census* of 100 pounds, and with the provision that the Matildine castellans and rectors should take an oath of fealty to the pope. The concession was extended to Lothar's son-in-law, Henry of Bavaria and his wife, on condition that they took oaths of homage and fealty to Innocent. The money given by Lothar to Innocent was specially mentioned in the clause justifying the grant – that both Lothar and Innocent were very short of money we know from St Bernard's letters, and from loans made by the Corsi to the pope. But the concession of the Matildine lands (not perhaps strictly a feudal investiture, since the emperor is not known to have sworn homage and fealty for them) was not entirely unfavourable to the papacy. Even if Lothar did not pay the *census,* the principle of papal right to the lands had been recognised by the empire. Lothar had taken an oath (accepted for the pope by Cencio and Oddo Frangipani) to defend and recover the *regalia* of St Peter, by which the Papal State may be directly understood.[1]

On the day of Lothar's coronation fresh riots broke out in Rome. It was clear that his military force was unequal to the task, and in the early summer he left Rome for Germany, followed on the voyage north after a few weeks by Pope Innocent. Rome and the Campagna reverted to Anacletan control. While Innocent stayed in Pisa, the main political and military struggle south of Rome became not that of the schism, but that of the resistance to Roger's attempt to unite the Norman states and the coastal cities under his rule. So far as possession of the Papal

---

[1] *MGH, Const. et acta publica,* i, nos. 115, 117, pp. 168–9. The oath is parallel with those taken by Henry V in 1111 and 1122.

State was concerned, both popes were dependent on the Norman contestants, Innocent on the rebellious magnates Robert of Capua and Rainulf of Alife, as was Anaclete on Roger.

In 1135 the two Hohenstaufen brothers submitted at last to Lothar, and the German war was over. The emperor and his son-in-law, Henry the Proud of Bavaria, were now ready for an Italian campaign; in the summer of 1136 they crossed the Alps with a large army, very different from the small force of 1133. Bologna, hostile to the emperor as in 1133 because of its quarrel with Walter of Ravenna, was taken. In the New Year of 1137 the German army split: a corps under Henry of Bavaria marched over the Alps to Tuscany to meet Innocent and conduct him to Rome, while the larger part of the army under Lothar marched south through Romagna and the march of Ancona on its way to Apulia, to seek the Norman usurper. Werner, the Marquis of the march, soon submitted, and those cities which closed their gates were taken.

In March of 1137 Innocent and St Bernard were at Viterbo, supported by the German troops of Henry of Bavaria. Innocent's actions suggest that he thought the military and political issue would be decided in the south in the war against Roger, and not by local fighting against Anaclete in Rome. Leaving Anaclete still entrenched in his strongplaces in Trastevere and St Peter's, Innocent travelled south. St Bernard remained in the Roman District, and small forces of German troops began to reduce the Anacletan centres in the Campagna. But Innocent and Duke Henry marched down the Via Latina to Monte Cassino.

After Lothar had swept through Apulia as far south as Bari, Roger offered him money, and asked for Apulia to be given to one of his sons as an imperial fief. Lothar refused, whether because of papal pressure or because he required a more decisive submission. It is possible that the Byzantine emperor was formally allied with Lothar against Roger by this time, and this may have also been a factor in determining Lothar's refusal. There was certainly friction between Innocent and Lothar about their respective legal positions in southern Italy. Lothar's troops were resentful that they were being used to pull clerical chestnuts from the fire, and there was at one stage a mutiny in the German army directed specifically against pope and cardinals. But Lothar's reluctance to bully the pope (a reluctance almost unique in the long history of papal-imperial relations) emerged in the somewhat absurd scene in which, because Innocent and Lothar could not agree which of them had the right of feudal investiture, they jointly invested Rainulf of Alife with the duchy of Apulia, with the pope holding one end of the banner which they gave to Rainulf, and the emperor the other! Innocent was clear that the war was conducted entirely for his benefit, since it was not only to free the papal patrimony proper but also the papal fiefs of Norman Italy. He referred to the subjection to St Peter of the whole area between Rome and Bari. Though both at Viterbo and at Benevento Henry the Proud of Bavaria was loth to give up the ransoms and booty which he thought belonged to the army, German behaviour was on the whole respectful of papal rights.

It is questionable whether Lothar's impressive campaign in south Italy was in the end more than an episode in the history of papal-Norman relations.[1] From a military point of view it was not decisive; after a long siege by Pisans and Germans and the surrender of the town, the citadel of Salerno still held out under the English Chancellor of the Norman kingdom, Robert of Saleby.[2] And in Sicily Roger's main forces (including the evacuated garrison of Salerno) remained intact. As Roger in October 1137 moved to the relief of Salerno, Lothar marched north from Rome on his way home to Germany – only to die as he reached the German side of the Alps (3 December 1137). Roger was able, in the absence of any substantial German garrisons there, to re-occupy the whole of south Italy. Bari, Troia, Capua, papal Benevento, all capitulated with little resistance; the imperial Abbot of Monte Cassino fled to Germany. Rainulf of Alife alone still resisted.

Anaclete died on 25 January 1138. A few weeks earlier, at the conference with St Bernard, Roger had after a formal re-examination of the claims of the two popes re-affirmed his allegiance to Anaclete. Although he allowed the Anacletan cardinals after their pope's death to proceed to the election of one of their number as 'Victor IV', Roger's clerical party was no longer of much use to him. After a few weeks Innocent gained possession of most of Rome. At the end of May Victor IV submitted to Innocent. Innocent had bribed the Roman magnates as was normal; even Anaclete's brothers the Pierleoni (and this prompt submission after so many years of hostility gives some idea of Roman venality) showed themselves ready to change sides. Small wonder that St Bernard, who had lived through most of the turbulent Italian years of the schism with Pope Innocent, referred contemptuously to the 'bottomless avarice of the Romans'.

---

[1] Cf. Kehr, 'Die Belehnungen', p. 41.
[2] Cf. A. Morey and C. N. L. Brooke (ed.), *Letters and Charters of Gilbert Foliot* (Cambridge, 1967), p. 29n.

The end of Innocent's duel with Roger was not yet in sight. So long as the indefatigable Rainulf of Alife lived, the papal party and the exiles perhaps had some chance of keeping at least a part of southern Italy out of Roger's direct control. In April 1139 Innocent excommunicated Roger at the great Lateran Council which re-established the unity and authority of the Western Church. Anaclete's bishops, including many of Roger's bishops, had their orders declared invalid. But in the same month Rainulf of Alife died at Troia. Innocent in June assembled the remaining exiles, joined them with a Roman army, and marched south into Roger's territory. It seems that Innocent still hoped by negotiating from strength to save the autonomy of the principate of Capua, at least. At San Germano near Monte Cassino Innocent treated with Roger's envoys without result. Then very imprudently the pope with his army crossed the river Gari and marched south in the direction of Capua. Roger let him pass, and then sent his son to ambush the papal forces near Galluccio. The manoeuvre was a complete success, and the papal army was routed. Like Leo IX in 1059 – and from a far worse position than that of Honorius II in 1128 – Innocent now had to negotiate as a prisoner.

Clever as papal diplomacy was, little could be saved from this wreck; the papal confirmation of Roger's status as king was inevitable. In order to give Roger the essential legitimisation of his kingdom from 1130, and yet to avoid confirming the anti-pope Anaclete's grant, the papal officials casuistically declared in the new concession (22 July 1139) that Sicily had always been a kingdom, and that its rule had been conceded to Roger by Honorius II.[1] The principate of Capua, which rightfully belonged to Robert of Capua who had fought with Pope Innocent at Galluccio, was now formally concerned with all its dependent claims (*integre*) to Roger. This was not only the betrayal of an ally but the justification for fresh aggression on Roger's part, since the principate of Capua carried with it claims to many counties of the Abruzzi which Roger had not yet attacked, and also to Naples which was about to submit to him. The fact that Innocent avoided investing King Roger with Sicily, Apulia and Capua as a single fief, but instead gave one banner to Roger for Sicily, one to his son Roger for Apulia and one to the other son for Capua, was cold comfort for the papal legists. Benevento was not mentioned in the treaty, but Roger accompanied Innocent to the city after its signature and allowed the pope to assume full powers there. The Normans were willing to respect the Church so

[1] Kehr, p. 42.

far as it was politically easy to do so, but would trample over it when their fierce appetite for power was denied.

The condition of the Papal State during the schism was certainly not flourishing. Innocent II recovered it by the force of German arms, with all the violence and destruction which this implied. When Innocent and Henry of Bavaria arrived at Viterbo in 1137 the hostility of the Innocentian and Anacletan parties had already resulted in the destruction of part of the suburbs.[1] Henry forced the town to pay a large indemnity of 3,000 'talents' (either marks or pounds), which the pope tried to claim from him because he owned the city. Lothar is said to have devastated the environs of Albano,[2] and on his return from the south to have destroyed a village near Palestrina which was claimed to have harboured robbers who preyed on the pilgrim routes. As he set out to return to Germany he destroyed Fara and Tribuco, places in the patrimony of the abbey of Farfa which had held out for Anaclete,[3] and further on his road north he subdued Narni and severely punished Amelia.

When Innocent returned as undisputed pope he found that church property had suffered widely in the schism. A biographer of St Bernard claimed that Rome was quickly restored to prosperity, that Innocent rebuilt churches, brought the exiles back and restored their property, and gave the churches back their lands. As the city had during the schism escaped the full horrors of civil war this statement is quite credible. Even so, the pope had to distribute a lot of money to the Roman nobles to make his regime acceptable; he also made an annual grant of 100 pounds to the 'judges and advocates' of the city which suggests an attempt to get the support of the middle section of the community.[4]

The list of church lands which had fallen to aristocratic cupidity during the schism is long and important. At the Lateran Council of 1139 cases were heard which involved the renewed seizure of Galeria by the counts of Galeria, the continued usurpation of a number of important villages in the area of Capena by Stefano di Tebaldo and his nephews, aggression by the town of Tivoli against monastic property in

---

[1] Annalista Saxo, *MGH, Scriptores*, vi, p. 773. Cf. *I.P.*, ii, p. 209, no. 1.

[2] Otto of Freising, *Chronica*, Hofmeister (ed.); p. 337. For Anacletan supporters in Albano, *I.P.*, i, p. 177, no. 3.

[3] Schuster, *L'imperiale abbazia*, p. 279.

[4] *Vita Prima Bernardi*, lib. 2, ch. vii, *P.L.*, clxxxv, pt. 1, col. 296. 'Innocentius ruinas restaurat, recolligit exsules, ecclesiis antiqua servitia, depopulatas colonias expulsis restituit, insuper et congrua dona largitur.' Cf. also *I.P.*, i, p. 180, no. 6. The oath of judges and advocates to pope, *Liber Pontificalis*, ii, p. 383.

S. Polo and elsewhere, the taking of Pratica on the Tyrrhenian coast by the Baronzini, and the taking of the castle of Nomentana by the Ottaviani of Sabina.[1] Most of this property was owned by the big monastery of S. Paolo fuori le Mura, which under abbot Anastasius had been one of the main Roman supporters of Anaclete; probably this was the excuse for the seizures. Also at the Lateran Council the Roman monastery of SS. Andrea and Gregorio on the Coelian complained that Oddo Count of Poli had occupied Poli and two other castles belonging to the monastery.[2] The Tuscolani family, which had probably held aloof from Anaclete in the schism, and had done homage to Lothar in 1137, had also taken the chance to feather its nest. In 1140 the monastery of Grottaferrata, which traditionally had been the protected house of the Tusculan family, complained that a lot of properties including the fortified villages of Nettuno, on the coast, had been taken by Ptolemy of Tuscolo; in the same year the Roman abbey of Sant' Alessio complained that Ptolemy had seized the island of Astura, near Nettuno.[3]

No doubt the most compelling argument for allowing Roman families to hold onto church lands which they had taken, was the sacrifices they claimed to have made on Innocent's behalf during the schism. Pietro Latrone of the Corsi, who was said to have risked death and danger in the service of the Roman Church, and who had also lent Innocent money, was granted Civitavecchia and the villages nearby in pledge during the schism.[4] Evidence of concessions made by Innocent to the Frangipani has not survived, but it would be very surprising if their services were not rewarded by some fairly important grant.[5] Innocent made even the erring Pierleoni papal rectors (*praesides*) of Sutri.[6]

Innocent II had made the settlement with Roger under coercion, and

---

[1] *I.P.*, i, p. 169, no. 20. Cf. Fedele, *ASR*, xxxv (1912), pp. 606–8. Trifone's texts (ibid. xxxi (1908), pp. 288 ff.) are less good than those in the old edition of Galletti, *Capena* (Rome, 1756), pp. 65–9. Lothar while he was in Italy had ordered Fiano Romano to return to the allegiance of S. Paolo fuori le Mura, and to renounce the *alieno dominio* (which must be of Stefano di Tebaldo). Cf. *DLIII*, no. 123, p. 209.

[2] *I.P.*, i, p. 106, no. 8. Cf. Fedele, *ASR*, xxxv (1912), pp. 586–7.

[3] *I.P.*, ii, p. 44, no. 10; ibid. i, p. 116, no. 4. Interesting details on the fisheries and agriculture of Anzio and Nettuno in the twelfth century in *C.R.*, ii, pp. 320–1.

[4] *I.P.*, i, pp. 190–1. He was also in possession of Cervetri, castrum Chere (ibid.). Cf. *I.P.*, i, p. 113, no. 1.

[5] Possibly in or concerning Terracina. Lucius II granted them Monte Circeo and also the revenues of Terracina (*I.P.*, ii, p. 119, no. 8; ibid. i, p. 191, no. 1; and cf. Contatore, *De Historia Terracinensi*, p. 53). Monte Circeo had in 1134 been held by a certain Marino of Terracina; cf. *I.P.*, ii, document quoted by Kehr on p. 122.

[6] *I.P.*, i, p. 190, no. 1.

Norman aggression in the Abruzzi meant that his hostility to Roger was renewed almost immediately. Far from being able to call on Norman armed help, as so many of his predecessors had done, Innocent was placed by the continuing Norman pressure in a very weak political position. The geography of Roger of Sicily's penetration into the Abruzzi (which few historians dealing with the Roman situation have examined) was dangerous in the extreme for the Roman frontiers.[1] As Roger's troops broke into 'Marsia' and the still vast unconquered mountain area between Lake Fucino and the Gran Sasso, they exposed the passes which led to the upper Aniene and the Roman duchy. All the fears which Gregory VII had experienced in the 1070s were now renewed.

The strategic key to the defences of Rome from the direction of the Abruzzi was Tivoli.[2] Tivoli's bishop, Guy, was a cardinal who had been appointed by Calixtus II, and who had followed Innocent II into exile, carrying out important missions in Milan and returning with the rest in 1137. As a curialist Guy owed his loyalty to the pope, but events were to show that in the twelfth century a suburbicarian cardinal bishop could still prefer his own to the Roman See. Tivoli was a prosperous town, with its own elected 'rector', and with communal development advanced enough for the 'populus' effectively to rule the town. The traditional rivals of Tivoli were the Romans and the abbey of Subiaco; they had fought both of these at once as recently as 1123.[3]

In the summer of 1140 the peril from the advance of Roger's troops into Marsia was felt to be acute. Oddo Frangipani, who was a relative of the counts of Marsi, fought with them against Roger's sons. In July Roger moved his troops up to the border of the Papal State as far as Ceprano, occupying the strongpoints of Arce and Sora on his side of the frontier. He was also said to have occupied 'lands of the Church in the Maritime province and Campagna', though which lands were concerned is unclear. At the beginning of August Tivoli, which commands the Via Valeria as it descends from the mountains into the Tiber valley, set about fortifying its environs against Roger. The inhabitants (*populus*) of the town and their rector 'donated' the Church of S. Angelo in

[1] For what follows, C. Rivera, 'L'annessione delle terre d'Abruzzo al regno di Sicilia', *ASI*, 1926, pt. 2, pp. 199–309; A Frugoni, 'Sulla "renovatio senatus" del 1143 e l'"ordo equestris" ', *BISI*, no. 62 (1950), pp. 159–74; P. Fedele, 'L'era del senato', *ASR*, xxxv (1912), pp. 583–610. Only the first deals with the military factors.

[2] Cf. V. Pacifici, 'Tivoli nel Medio Evo', *'Atti e memorie della società tiburtina di storia e d'arte'*, v–vi (1925–6), at pp. 277–90; G. Gascioli, 'Nuova serie dei vescovi di Tivoli', ibid. iii (1923), at pp. 108–22 Schmale, *Studien*, p. 50.

[3] For the quarrel with Subiaco see p. 167 above.

Valle Arcese, which commanded the river valley and the pass of Colle dello Stonio from the south, so that the Abbot of S. Angelo could fortify it. No doubt this 'donation' was largely a means of getting the church to pay for the fortification, and the abbot returned to Tivoli to ask for confirmation of the gift. The confirmation was given in public parliament, and again confirmed by the vicars of the cardinal bishop.[1]

III

Rome and its bishops could not be unaffected by the social and political forces which worked on other Italian cities, nor could they entirely conform to them. In Italy in general the possessing classes in the towns were organising themselves under 'rectors' and 'consuls' under what was already known in many places as the commune. In few places was this tendency specifically anti-feudal, and in Rome and its District it was certainly not so, as the spread of the commune virtually co-incided with that of feudalism; the 'knights' were often in fact one of the constitutive elements of the commune.[2] But the commune was nevertheless bound to modify the positions both of the great feudal nobility, the 'captains', and of the bishops. In the Roman area the bishops were the greatest of the feudal landlords and the automatic leaders of city life. In the Latian cities as in Rome itself, the bishops and the most important clerks disposed of a financial power which made them essential to the lay notables.[3] The absence of the bishop-count, and the impotence of the papal-appointed counts of Campagna,[4] meant that

---

[1] The relevant inscriptions are transcribed by Pacifici, loc. cit. For the topography see *Forma Italiae, Regio I*, vol. 3, *Tibur, pars altera*, Cairoli (ed.) (Rome, 1966), pp. 171–92.

[2] As, probably, at Nepi. Cf. P. Rajna, 'Un iscrizione Nepesina del 1131', *ASI*, 4th ser., xviii (1886), pp. 329–54, ibid. xix (1887), pp. 23–54. The best discussion of the early commune in the Roman area is still that of Falco, *ASR*, xlii (1919), pp. 555–92. For other manifestations of the commune within reach of Rome, see N. Kamp, *Istituzioni comunali in Viterbo nel Medioevo* (Viterbo, 1963), pp. 7–8; D. Waley, *Mediaeval Orvieto* (Cambridge, 1952), pp. 1–4; O. Vehse, 'Benevent als Territorium des Kirchenstaates', *Quellen*, xxii (1930–1), pp. 125–51; and for Rieti cf. the reference to a consul in *Chron. Farf.*, ii, p. 317. For Ravenna see A. Vasina, 'Ravenna e Forlì nel secolo XII. Una fase della storia delle leghe intercomunali', *AMDR*, n.s., x (1963), pp. 93–112.

[3] Cf. Falco, pp. 592–7.

[4] Who still existed in the early twelfth century; Falco missed the reference to a papal count in 1123 (above, p. 162, note 2); and also missed the office of papal count in Campagna held under Paschal II by the subdeacon Berardus, later bishop of Marsi and cardinal. Cf. Ganzer,

though the communes of Latium exercised the *regalia* of taxation and jurisdiction which belonged properly to St Peter, they were not taking them from the local bishop as happened often elsewhere in Italy.[1]

Alone among the Latian cities, Rome was ruled and the *regalia* held by priests. The prefect was appointed and controlled by the pope, and clerical control was such that a decree abolishing the custom which allowed the prefect to seize the goods of intestates dying in the Leonine city was published not only by the *curia* but also subsequently in the general Lateran Council of 1123.[2] It is true that aristocratic participation in the *curia* gave the laity a voice in policy, but the decline of the ancient offices – *arcarius, saccellarius, nomenclator* and others – into simple judicial posts meant that the military order, and also the laymen in minor clerical orders, were ceasing to play such an important part in Roman administration. And even if the magnates, some of whom held the judicial dignity of *consul Romanorum,* still had a substantial say in policy and perhaps a share in papal monies, there was now a substantial non-noble possessing class in Rome which was excluded from political life, and which would not have been so in other Latian cities. The constant quarrels of the cities one with another, especially about areas where landowners were drawn from more than one town, sharpened the discontent of those with property but without political power. Innocent's government had supplanted the much more Roman administration of Anaclete by a regime which leaned heavily on foreign clerks, and this again was likely to make the Romans restive. St Bernard always spoke of the Romans with contempt; it may be that his feelings were returned.

Innocent's hostility to Roger of Sicily continued unabated. In 1142 he negotiated with Conrad of Germany and with the Greek emperor to get support against Roger, but still without effect. In 1143 he succeeded in negotiating a settlement with recalcitrant Tivoli.[3] The pope accepted

---

Entwicklung des auswärtigen Kardinalats, p. 67.

[1] See for example the concession of toll dues in Osimo in 1126 by the bishop to the *minores et majores* of Osimo: L. Colini-Baldeschi, *Il libro rosso del comune di Osimo* (Macerata, 1909), p. 79. Osimo was a papal possession: *I.P.,* iv, p. 208. It is named in the donations.

[2] *I.P.,* i, p. 184, nos. 3, 4.

[3] I follow the order of events in Otto of Freising, who gives the only continuous account, *Chronica,* pp. 352–3. It seems to me to make better sense to place the submission of the Tivolesi before the subsequent revolution and the battle of 7 July, otherwise we have to explain how a cardinal bishop (Guy of Tivoli) led the Tivolese army against the pope. It also assists in solving the frequently noted difficulty in following the other details in Otto of Freising's account, that there is not much time for the revolution to take place between the battle of

the submission of the town and the county, reserving the right to appoint the rector, and getting control of the main strategic points on the route to the Abruzzi – Ponte Lucano, Vicovaro, S. Polo – besides other forts such as Ciciliano to the south-east of Tivoli. Hostages were given, and the Tivolese swore fealty to the pope.

The submission of Tivoli did not satisfy the Romans. Not only did the papal treaty with Tivoli cheat them of revenge for last year's defeat, but it checked them in pursuing the aim of most of the communal feuds of the time, to impoverish and enfeeble the enemy. They demanded the razing of the walls of Tivoli, and a humiliating surrender. It was not in the pope's interest either to permit the stripping of Tivoli, or to allow the Romans to dictate policy to him. He therefore refused. On his refusal the Romans stormed the Capitol, the seat of the prefect and the judges, and 'wishing to restore the ancient dignity of the City, set up the order of senators, which had lapsed for a long space of time, and renewed the war with Tivoli'. At Quintilolio, the site of an ancient villa on the road north-east from Tivoli to S. Antonio, the Tivolese and their Cardinal Bishop Guy were defeated and routed, though without provoking the fall of the town.

The communal revolution against the Roman bishop had occurred. It is possible that the senators who were set up in 1143 were appointed to direct the war against Tivoli and not to constitute a new form of government; the later commune dated the 'renovation' of the senate from 1144 and not from 1143. But 'due to the growing power of the people' the pope was unable either by bribes or threats to dissuade the revolutionaries; he took to his bed in despair, and on 24 September 1143 died.

The main lines of the new division of power between Rome and its bishop were not yet defined. The popes were weak because they could neither persuade the emperor to undertake an Italian expedition in their favour, nor conclude a satisfactory peace with the Norman regime in Sicily. They could rely on at least an important faction of the Roman magnates. Among the nobles loyal to the popes, the Frangipani were politically influential throughout central Italy, from the Abruzzi to Ravenna.[1] But this was not enough to turn the balance against the

---

7 July and Innocent's death on 24 September. By my reckoning the papal pact with Tivoli occurred at an unknown date before 7 July.

[1] *I.P.*, v, p. 136, no. 1 (29 December 1143). The tutor of the sons of Rainier Cavalcaconti and Boltruda Frangipani is granted papal lands in the county of Bertinoro. Witnessed by the Pierleoni and most of the important Roman families. The Frangipani were also relatives of the counts of Marsia, with whom they fought the Normans in the Abruzzi until late 1143.

new Roman commune. Neither of Innocent's short-lived successors, Celestine II and Lucius II, could stop the constitutional development of the new regime in Rome. Its leader was the nobleman Giordano di Pierleoni, who took the title of 'patrician', and was backed by the lesser people. The regalian rights of the Holy See fell into his hand, and the church revenues were confiscated. The houses and towers of cardinals and nobles hostile to the regime were looted or demolished.

In June 1144 Lucius II met Roger of Sicily on the border of the two states of Ceprano, for a political colloquy which lasted a fortnight. But these talks broke down, possibly over the question of papal sovereignty over the principate of Capua. War began again in the Roman Campagna; Roger laid siege to Veroli and to the Frangipani-protected seaport of Terracina, while his armies plundered and burned the countryside in the old way. There was a truce in the autumn of 1144, which left the question of the legitimacy of Roger's rule open. The Roman revolutionary government was strong enough now to make some constitutional act, whose precise date and content are unknown, and whose effect was to fix the commencing date of the 'era of the senate' at some time in the autumn of 1144. Lucius had appealed in vain to the German king. Early in 1145 he made a last desperate attempt to suppress the Roman regime by force, bringing troops into the city to attack the Capitol, the republican seat of government. But he failed, and died shortly afterwards – possibly from a wound received in the battle.

Neither Celestine nor Lucius were particularly original or able men. The cardinals, after the death of Lucius II, seem to have set out to elect a pope who should by character and training be closer to the changing times. They immediately settled on the Pisan pupil of St Bernard, the Cistercian Abbot of SS. Vincenzo e Anastasio alle Tre Fontane outside Rome, who, as Eugenius III became the first Cistercian pope (15 February 1145). The selection of this Cistercian abbot of a Roman monastery was a political gesture of the first order, even if Eugenius never quite as pope attained the stature to which the circumstances of his election seemed to point. St Bernard referred to his pope-pupil as 'a rustic, a poor thing in rags'.[1] This was probably a literary device to emphasise that God had chosen the humble, but its uses nevertheless announced a new era. The political process began during the Anacletan

---

Cf. Rivera, in *ASI* (1926), pp. 252–3.

[1] Ep. 237. Cf. H. Gleber, *Papst Eugen III. (1145–53)* (Jena, 1936).

Schism, by which the papacy became a European rather than a purely imperial affair, was to continue.

Eugenius was consecrated in Farfa, the abbey which had originally wanted him to bring his Cistercians into one of her own mountain dependencies, instead of going down into the Roman plain. Rome held out against him as it had against Lucius, but the Romans had many enemies. Not only the old magnate families but the new communes outside Rome were happy to oppose what was for them the Roman menace. Viterbo, the growing agrarian centre north of Lake Bracciano, acted as host to Eugenius; Tivoli was happy to take papal money to fight her old Roman enemies.

Faced by this hostility, the Romans made their first agreement with the pope. Reversing two of their more aggressive acts, they abolished the 'patriciate', and agreed to recognise the papal office of prefect. On his side the pope agreed that the senators (annually appointed) should hold office by his authority. The Romans had conceded substantial but not vital points; the pope had conceded the essential, the recognition of the communal regime. The pattern of Roman government had been decided in essence for over two centuries, even if its details were to be fought over for many years yet.

The ceremonial papal entry into Rome shortly before Christmas of 1145, the welcome of the regionary standard bearers and the rest of the traditional pomp, meant little. The hostility of the two governments remained. In a few weeks the pope moved to Trastevere, outside Roman jurisdiction. By the early spring of 1146 he had again abandoned the city for Sutri, Vetralla and Viterbo. The Romans renewed the war against Tivoli and Viterbo,[1] and revived the leadership of Giordano di Pierleoni. The rest of the year passed without any further settlement with the Romans, while the papal court busied itself with the preliminaries of the second crusade. In the New Year of 1147 Eugenius started north from Viterbo on his way to France, to unite the two great monarchies of the west in the service of the Church and the crusade.

Rome had in the meantime accepted a notable guest, the north Italian church reformer Arnold of Brescia, who after a supposedly heretical past had been absolved by the pope in Viterbo in 1145 or 1146.[2] Arnold's ideals for the clergy were of apostolic life, of ascetic rigour, and of the renunciation of all worldly goods. Level-headed and

[1] They did not destroy Tivoli, as is stated in Gleber, *Eugen III*, p. 23n. Nor is there evidence that Eugenius took part in a coalition against Tivoli (ibid.).
[2] For the disputed question of the date see Gleber, pp. 27–33 and A. Frugoni, *Arnaldo de Brescia nelle fonti del sec. XII* (Rome, 1954), pp. 129–30.

well-informed writers such as John of Salisbury and Gerhoh of Reichersberg were careful to avoid indiscriminate abuse of Arnold; St Bernard, whom Arnold had criticised as self-interested, denounced him violently as a heretic. After the departure of Eugenius, Arnold was welcomed by the Roman regime as a preacher who offered some moral justification for its anti-clericalism. That he had any important role in directing Roman politics is unlikely, but he brought to Rome a heterodox evangelicalism which went well with the social unrest of the communal movement, and was typical of north Italy from which he came. On 15 July 1148 Eugenius condemned Arnold as a 'schismatic', and complained that he had subverted church discipline in Rome. For the Romans Arnold's doctrines could be only a passing phase; their interests were in the long run too much involved with those of the papal bureaucracy. Heterodox and 'patarine' opinions failed to take permanent hold in Rome proper; they were received later in communes like Viterbo and Orvieto.

In the last days of 1148 the pope returned to Viterbo from his long stay over the Alps and in north Italy. In April 1149 he concluded a four-years truce with Roger of Sicily. Though the big question of the Sicilian investiture remained open, the truce was bound to be resented by the German king. In July 1149 Louis VII of France landed in Calabria from the crusade, and travelled north through the friendly Norman kingdom to visit Eugenius in October, before returning to France. The Romans choked with fury, and wrote to warn Conrad of this new anti-German trend in papal policy; they assured Conrad that they had rebuilt Ponte Milvio so that when he came to Rome his troops could enter the city without being harassed by the Pierleoni garrison in Castel Sant'Angelo. But though his presence was solicited by both sides, Conrad made no move to come to Italy.

The pope enjoyed the support of Ptolemy of Tuscolo as well as of Tivoli and of the Frangipani; he possibly also used Norman troops. But the attacks which the cardinal of Tivoli, nicknamed 'Guy the Maiden', launched on Rome in 1149, were a failure. Negotiations with the Romans for some time stuck over Roman reluctance to expel Arnold of Brescia, to whom they had promised support under oath. In October or November an agreement was made.[1] The senators and

---

[1] Wibald, ep. 437 (in Jaffé (ed.), *Bibliotheca Rerum Germanicarum*, i), seems to me more likely to be the text of a peace proposed at this time than one made when Wibald was later in Italy (as Gleber, p. 143, suggests). Gleber reads the document carelessly, e.g. he says the Romans 'agreed to pay the pope 50 pounds in tax', instead of the pope promising to pay them 500 pounds, as the text says. Cf. also F. Bartoloni, *Codice Diplomatico del Senato Romano dal MCXLIV al MCCCXLVII*, i (Rome, 1942), no. 8, p. 9.

the regions were to receive an annual *douceur* from the pope of 500 pounds according to custom. The revenues and patrimonies (*regalia*) of the Church, and its fortresses, were to be restored, except that the pope promised not to fortify the strongpoints of Riano and Magliano on the Via Flaminia.[1] The pope also promised to include Viterbo in the peace as soon as possible.

Eugenius's aims in the temporal power went further than the negative ones of defeating Roman independence. He had to compensate the Roman magnates for the help they were giving him against Rome, but he also in these last years of his pontificate started the policy of purchasing and consolidating castles which was taken over and developed by his successors. He bought a half-share in the town and fortress of Tuscolo – an important development which marks the beginning of the decline of the ancient Tusculan family. He bought a half-share in the strategic castle of Radicofani on the Via Cassia, on the frontier between Roman territory and Tuscany proper. He bought land at the fortified strongpoint of Ponte Lucano, on the Aniene near Tivoli.[2] Eugenius seems to have been able to expel the turbulent Filippo de Marano from the castles belonging to the abbey of Subiaco.[3] Whether the popes now had more money for paying soldiers and buying fortresses is not certain, but the strictures of St Bernard suggest that this was perhaps so. There are signs that the papal officials were carefully examining their records to see that no dues escaped them. It is also known that Eugenius re-organised the apportionment of one of the great traditional sources of revenue of the popes, the offerings at the altar of St Peter.[4]

Gerhoh of Reichersberg, who was well-informed about the papal *curia,* suggested that many of its moral and administrative troubles

---

[1] Both were in the zone dominated by S. Paolo fuori le Mura. Riano was acquired for the Holy See a few years later by Pope Hadrian IV (p. 194 below). Magliano was near Fiano Romano, the strongpoint which had been a subject of dispute with the Romans at the time of Lothar (p. 176 above, n. 1).

[2] Tuscolo, *Lib. cens.,* i, p. 382: Theiner, *C.D.,* i, no. 18, p. 14. Radicofani, *Lib. cens.,* i, p. 380 (*I.P.,* iii, p. 241, no. 14). Cf. also the pledge of castles to the pope by the counts of Vetralla, in the north of papal Tuscany. *Lib. cens.,* i, p. 384. Eugenius also acquired the fortress of Tintinanno north of Radicofani (*I.P.,* iii, pp. 250–1, where Hadrian IV is a slip for Eugenius III). Ponte Lucano, *I.P.,* ii, p. 79, no. 4. There is mention of the papal fort here in the oath of the men of Tivoli, *Lib. cens.,* i, p. 415; Theiner, *C.D.,* i, no. 21.

[3] *Cronaca Sublacense del P.D. Cherubino Mirzio,* document printed in the note, pp. 242–4.

[4] *I.P.,* i, p. 241, nos. 31, 32. Cf. P. Fabre, 'Les offrandes dans la basilique Vaticane en 1285', *Mélanges,* xiv (1894), pp. 225–40. For the enquiry into the sums owed to the pope by the Bishop of Rimini, 21 May 114, *Lib. cens.,* i, p. 88.

sprang from the need, which dated from the wars of Gregory VII, to raise ever larger sums of money to pay troops and to bribe the Romans and the feudal nobles. He accused the Romans in particular of accepting huge sums from the pope (11,000 pounds of Lucca from Hadrian IV, he claimed), and then of involving the Roman Church in their quarrels with the surrounding towns in the Campagna.[1] Gerhoh was probably right about this, and he touches on one of the great administrative and moral problems of the Roman Church, which was to bedevil it (and the verb is perhaps not ill-chosen) until the Renaissance. The Roman synod of 1082 which had condemned the mortgaging of church property to pay for the war of the Investiture Contest had said that church revenues should be used for the poor, for the maintenance of divine service and for the redemption of captives, but not for the payment of troops. It was a sobering thought for contemporaries that a century of reforming effort in the papal *curia* had done nothing to solve this great moral problem.

In the latter part of Eugenius's pontificate St Bernard wrote for his old pupil the *De consideratione,* the final words of the great abbot on the moral and spiritual problems of the Roman Church, with which he had been intimately concerned since the schism of 1130. The *De consideratione* deserves to be read with attentive regard to the political activity of its author. It is a treatise on the moral dilemma of spiritual power which reflects the experience of a lifetime of clerical diplomacy. St Bernard was down to the last years of Eugenius III concerned with the pope's political affairs, including those of the Roman commune. The saint was certainly involved in the attempts made to persuade Conrad III to lead a new German expedition to Italy.[2] The often-quoted passage in the *De consideratione* about the avarice and disobedience of the Romans has to be read in the light of this political situation.[3] Though in appearance rhetorical, it is closely related to fact. 'They (the Romans) take part in all papal business. Who can you quote to

---

[1] *Libelli de lite (MGH)*, iii, pp. 329, 356, 515.

[2] After 1149 Bernard turned his attention to a reconciliation between Conrad III and Roger of Sicily in the interests of a further crusade: ep. 256, and cf. Wibald's ep. 252, 273.

[3] Book IV, ch. 3. Cf. ep. 244, to Conrad. In general, J. Lecler, 'L'argument des deux glaives (Luc 22: 38) dans les controverses politiques du moyen age', *Recherches de Science Religieuse*, xxi (1931), pp. 299–339; W. Levison, 'Die mittelalterlichen Lehre von den beiden Schwerten', *DA*, ix (1952), pp. 14–42; W. Ullmann, *Papal Government*, 3rd ed., pp. 426–37 et passim. And further: E. Kennan, 'The "De Consideratione" of St Bernard of Clairvaux and the Papacy in the mid-twelfth century: a review of scholarship', *Traditio*, xxiii (1967), pp. 73–115; H. Hoffman, 'Die beiden Schwerter im Hochmittelalter', *DA*, xx (1964), pp. 78–114. The biblical citations concerned are Luke 22: 35–8, 49–51; Matthew 26: 51; John 18: 10.

me in the city who acknowledged your position as pope without a bribe or the hope of a bribe?' The pope is decked in gold, mounted on a white horse, surrounded by troops and officers. 'In this you have succeeded not to Peter but to Constantine. I advise you to tolerate this position for the time being, not to assert it as your right.'

The Romans are wolves rather than sheep: nevertheless it is the pope's duty to care for them and preach the gospel to them. If he is to attack them he is to do so with words and not with steel (a clear criticism of the papal war against the Roman commune). 'What! do you again seek to usurp the sword which you were twice ordered to replace in its sheath?' It is at this point that Bernard begins his argument about the pope's control of both the swords, the spiritual (i.e. the proclamation of the gospel) and the material. 'So this (the material sword) is certainly yours: even if it should not be drawn by your hand, it should probably (*forsitan*) be drawn with your consent.' Insisting (without any justification that modern men can ascertain) on the word *tuum* in the text of St Luke, St Bernard says that if the sword did not belong to Peter, the Lord would not have said 'it is enough', but 'it is little'. Both swords belong to the Church, but one is drawn by the priest, the other by the soldier, at the priest's behest, and at the emperor's command. The pope must draw his spiritual sword to 'evangelise' the Romans, no matter what their scepticism and their villainy.[1]

Eugenius could not find a final solution to his Italian problems; his existence depended on a delicate political balance which excluded final solutions. He concluded a fresh truce and an ecclesiastical concordat with Roger of Sicily in a meeting at Ceprano in 1150, but Roger's subsequent illegal coronation of his son (without an enfeoffment by the pope to either) showed how hollow the agreement was. Moreover Eugenius could not persuade his protector Conrad to work with Roger. The Byzantine emperor continued to be the ally of the German king.[2] Their understanding was dangerous to the pope in the religious field above all; but it also allowed the landing of Byzantine forces in the important Adriatic port of Ancona, primarily to threaten Roger of Sicily but with

---

[1] Gerhoh of Reichersberg also criticises the use of the material sword by the Church, *Libelli de lite*, iii, pp. 295, 343–6, 440–1, 462–3; idem, *P.L.*, cxciii, cols. 568–9. Cf. John of Salisbury, *Historia pontificalis*, M. Chibnall (ed.), p. 60, for the campaign of Guy the Maiden (who may have been the Cardinal Bishop of Tivoli). And further, P. Classen, *Gerhoh von Reichersberg* (Wiesbaden, 1960), pp. 130, 146, 228, 236 ff. Harsh criticism of the papal wars under Innocent II by a Byzantine monk, in Peter of Monte Cassino, *MGH*, vii, p. 833 (quoted by Norden, *Das Papsttum und Byzanz*, p. 100).

[2] Cf. P. Lamma, *Comneni e Staufer. Ricerche sui rapporti fra Bisanzio e l'Occidente nel secolo XII* (Rome, 1955), i.

the secondary result of planting Byzantine influence in an area where there was much church property.

The pope's relations with the Roman commune continued to be hostile. From the spring of 1150 until the autumn of 1152 Eugenius wandered in the Roman countryside. He built himself a palace at Segni, and recovered the papal fortress of Fumone.[1] His allies were still the Roman teritorial nobility, the Frangipani above all. Though Eugenius allowed it to be recorded in an inscription at Terracina that he 'restored many estates in the Roman Church', he tolerated a Frangipani hegemony over the city, and pledged to the Frangipani the village of Ninfa, which commands the Via Appia on the route of Terracina.[2] The pope, the Frangipani, and Pietro Latrone together endowed the Cistercian monastery of S. Maria di Falleri north of Nepi.[3] At the very end of the pontificate the Frangipani and Pierleoni and most of the important Roman families are found with the pope to witness the important papal acquisition of Radicofani.[4] In September 1152 Eugenius spoke of large-scale conspiracies of the 'rustic populace' in Rome, but he entered the city shortly afterwards and stayed there from December 1152 until shortly before his death. As so often before, he won over the Romans by bribery.

IV

On 15 February 1152 Conrad III had died. The succession of his Hohenstaufen nephew, Frederick Barbarossa, was the most important shift in imperial politics for the papacy since the death of the Emperor Henry V in 1126. Partisans of the Roman commune wrote to the new king condemning the 'heretical lie' of the Donation of Constantine. Though not dear to St Bernard, the Donation had been urged by many

---

[1] *I.P.*, ii, p. 158, no. 13, now printed in full in C. Scaccia Scarafoni, *Le carte dell'Archivio Capitolare della Cattedrale di Veroli* (Rome, 1960), no. 147, p. 191. For Eugenius's intervention between Ferentino and Silva Molle, *I.P.*, ii, no. 147, no. 4.

[2] Contatore, *De historia Terracinensi*, pp. 52–3; cf. *I.P.*, ii, p. 119, no. 7, and also *Annales Ceccanen.* (*MGH*, xix), p. 283. For Ninfa see *I.P.*, i, p. 192, no. 3. The *Liber Pontificalis* also records his 'recovery' of the village of Norma, on the hill overlooking Ninfa.

[3] *I.P.*, ii, p. 189, no. 5. For Eugenius's care of the Cistercian houses at Fossanova and Casamari, ibid. p. 169, no. 5 and cf. i, pp. 173–4.

[4] *I.P.*, iii, p. 241, no. 14. The place where this document was executed is not recorded, and it is not, as Gregorovius claims (Engl. trs. iv, pt. 2, p. 522), proof that the banished nobility had returned to Rome.

from the beginning of the century onwards as the foundation of papal temporal rule.[1]

In the New Year of 1153 papal diplomacy scored a notable success. The imperial and papal envoys concluded the Treaty of Constance, which defined the obligations of both powers in Italy almost entirely to the advantage of the Roman Church. Frederick agreed not to make peace with Roger of Sicily or the Romans without papal consent, and to try to make the Romans accept the same constitutional relationship with the Church which they had had in the century preceding the revolution of 1143. He also guaranteed (and one of the papal clerks who copied the treaty attached such importance to this clause that he adopted it as the marginal heading) to restore the *regalia* of St Peter, that is to restore the temporal power.[2] He finally agreed not to allow the Greek Empire to renew its old territorial power in Italy; the landing of Byzantine troops in Ancona had alarmed the papal court.[3] A similar undertaking to use papal troops to expel the Greeks was given by Eugenius.

Before a German expedition could materialise Eugenius died in Tivoli, Rome's old enemy, on 8 July 1153. His aged successor Anastasius IV carried out no major stroke of policy, and lived in office only a few months. He belonged to the Roman family of Subura and his election may point to a wish on the part of the cardinals to reach an understanding with the Romans.[4] But with the election of the Englishman Nicholas Breakspear as Pope Hadrian IV on 5 December 1154 the papacy was once more in able and energetic hands.

In the early spring of 1155 the Treaty of Constance was renewed between Pope Hadrian and Frederick Barbarossa. The German expedition under Frederick had entered north Italy in the autumn of 1154. Its march south to Rome was now therefore to be made under conditions not unfavourable to the papacy. German aid was particularly necessary to Hadrian because his relations with the new king of Sicily, William I, were already strained to the verge of war. Hadrian, from shortly after his accession, acted bluntly and brutally with the Romans, who in

---

[1] Cf. Wibald, ep. 403. Gerhoh of Reichersberg defended the Donation, *Libelli de lite*, iii, pp. 447–9. For its citation in a lawsuit between the abbey of Farfa and the Ottaviani under Paschal II, *Chron. Farfen.*, ii, pp. 229–50. Cf. G. Laehr, *Die Konstantinische Schenkung in der abendländischen Literatur des Mittelalters* (Berlin, 1926), pp. 54 ff.

[2] Cf. M. Maccarrone, *Papato e Impero dalla elezione di Federico I alla morte di Adriano IV (1152–9)* (Rome, 1959), pp. 50–1, 79–80; P. Munz, *Frederick Barbarossa* (1969), pp. 64 ff.

[3] Cf. Lamma, i, pp. 149–242.

[4] That he continued to rule with the aid of the Frangipani and Pierleoni appears from the witnesses to *I.P.*, i, p. 51, no. 9 (29 August, 1153). Cf. P. Classen, 'Zur Geschichte Papst Anastasius IV', *Quellen*, xlviii (1968), pp. 36–63, where his Roman origins are emphasised.

spite of the usual papal bribe at the beginning of the pontificate had allowed extremists to manhandle a cardinal. Hadrian placed the city under ecclesiastical interdict, which was not yet the wearisomely familiar sanction it later became, but a strange and frightening business. On 23 March the interdict was lifted on the condition of the banishment of Arnold of Brescia and his followers. Arnold escaped north of Rome, but the approaching German army arrested him, and handed him over to the prefect for execution.[1]

In early June Hadrian met the young king near Sutri. The nervousness of the clerks and the touchy susceptibilities of the German laymen were revealed by Frederick's refusal to perform the traditional household duty of marshal, to hold the pope's stirrup. The imperial coronation nevertheless took place on 18 June in St Peter's. In fulfilment of the treaty with Hadrian, Frederick showed himself stiff towards the Romans; he indignantly refused to pay them the bribe for which they asked, and contrary to custom closed Ponte Sant'Angelo and the Leonine city for the coronation ceremony, which the Romans were not allowed to attend. In consequence the Romans rioted outside Castel Sant'Angelo and in Trastevere. The riot was put down with the usual brutality, but Frederick never entered Rome proper. On the day after the coronation the German army marched north up the Via Flaminia, accompanied by Hadrian and the cardinals. Frederick crossed the Tiber and encamped near Tivoli, before returning through Spoleto to the north. The first Hohenstaufen intervention in Roman politics was virtually over.

For Pope Hadrian, Frederick had brought disappointment and disillusion. The German king did nothing to solve the two great papal problems of the Normans and the Romans. As the Germans had marched south towards Rome, the Normans had marched north into the Campagna. Crossing the frontier at Ceprano on 30 May, they plundered and burned as far as Frosinone and Ferentino. Earlier, they had besieged the papal enclave of Benevento. Only the rebellion of the feudal barons against William of Sicily in the early summer saved the Papal State from far worse. At the same time the Byzantine hold on Ancona tightened.

The presence of Frederick in the Roman District led to political clashes. The Roman commune had successfully asserted its authority in Sabina under Eugenius, and had fined the monastery of Farfa for

---

[1] *MGH, Libelli de lite*, iii, p. 347, and cf. pp. 440–1. For the criminal jurisdiction of the prefect see Hirschfeld, 'Gerichtswesen der Stadt Rom', *Arch. f. Urk.*, iv (1912), pp. 473–8. Cf. *Acta Sanctorum* (June), vii, pp. 49–50.

alleged offences, in spite of the presence of a papal official in the area.[1] Frederick sent his chaplain Heribert to the monastery, to collect the imperial hospitality tax (*fodrum*) in accordance with the policy of enforcing the collection of imperial *regalia* in Italy.[2] This produced an awkward clash with the papal authorities, who in spite of the precedents for imperial gathering of this exaction in the patrimony, were anxious to obstruct its collection.[3] When Frederick went on to take a feudal oath from Tivoli, Hadrian successfully protested and the Tivolese were released from the oath.[4]

Byzantine troops helped the rebels against William of Sicily, and with success. Bari and Trani fell, and Palaeologus the Byzantine general sent to Rome to offer Hadrian subsidies if he would enter the war. Although until this point Hadrian had stood out against the Greeks, this chance, offered after the fiasco of Frederick's departure, to hit at the Norman oppressor, was too tempting for him. Tearing up (in effect) the Treaty of Constance, he accepted an alliance with the Greeks and prepared an army to march south against the Norman king – as though the unhappy experiences of at least three popes had taught the papacy nothing. At the end of September Hadrian crossed the border with an army composed of nobles from Rome and the Campagna, and marched to Benevento. Here the Prince of Capua (fulfilling the old papal claim) did him homage. William of Sicily was sick; the Greeks made fresh conquests; new revolts broke out in Sicily. The outlook for the Norman kingdom was dark, and William's government offered large concessions to Pope Hadrian in Benevento to buy his withdrawal.

The majority of the cardinals with Hadrian were opposed to bargaining with the Normans, and the offers were refused. This turned out

---

[1] *I.P.*, ii, p. 70, no. 1 (22 February 1154). Ibid. p. 72, no. 2 (28 February 1154), a bull addressed to 'Sergio vicedomino Sabinensi'. The vicedominus was a financial official (cf. Jordan, *Stud. Greg.*, i, pp. 118, 119n.). It does not seem to me at all evident that Sabina was not under Roman control at this period (as is thought by Waley, *P.S.*, pp. 10–13). Under Innocent II the Abbot of Farfa was a cardinal (cf. Ganzer, *Entwicklung des auswärtigen Kardinalats*, pp. 81–3) and there is no sign that Farfa fell away from Eugenius III, who was consecrated there. Cf. also Schuster, *Imperiale Abbazia*, pp. 286–91, and for what follows see Kehr, 'Urkunden zur Geschichte von Farfa im XII Jahrhundert', *Quellen*, ix (1906), pp. 170–84.

[2] Cf. A. Haverkamp, 'Die Regalien-, Schutz-, und Steuerpolitik in Italien unter Friedrich Barbarossa bis zur Entstehung des Lombardenbundes', *Zeitschrift f. bayerische Landesgeschichte*, xxix (1966), pp. 3–156, especially at pp. 70 ff.; C. Brühl, *Fodrum, Gistum, Servitium Regis* (Köln-Graz, 1968), i, pp. 673–4, 787–9.

[3] Brühl, loc. cit.

[4] Theiner, *C.D.*, i, no. 21; *Lib. Pont.*, ii, p. 393; *MGH, Const. et acta publica*, i, p. 215. Cf. Maccarrone, p. 130.

to be a mistake. William of Sicily recovered, defeated the Greeks at Brindisi and Bari, and suppressed the feudal rebellion. When the Norman army closed in on Benevento in June 1156 it found the pope still there, and virtually defenceless. His only course was to bend before Norman military power as earlier popes had done, and to make the best settlement he could.

Unlike previous grants by the popes to the Norman kings, the 1156 agreement was bilateral in form. Both the ecclesiastical and the territorial questions between the two powers were settled in detail. King William, his son and heirs were conceded the kingdom by the pope; it was defined as the *regnum Siciliae*, the duchy of Apulia and principate of Capua, Naples, Salerno, Amalfi, and the territory of Marsia. Thus all the disputed territories (notably Capua and the Abruzzi) were now freely granted by the pope. The king was to pledge homage and liegance, and to pay 600 *scifati* annually for Apulia and Calabria, and a further 400 for Marsia. Whether this large tribute was actually and regularly paid, we have no means of knowing. William's heirs received a guarantee of papal approval for the inheritance. There was also an agreement, not included in the main document, that William would give the pope military and financial help against the Romans.

Having made this agreement Pope Hadrian returned to Rome. In Italian terms his position was stronger than that of any pope since the Roman revolution of 1143. But the agreement with William of Sicily had broken the Treaty of Constance, and was inescapably anti-German in intention. It contributed to the tension between the papal and German courts which came to a head in 1157, in the quarrel over the terms of the letter brought to Frederick in Besançon by the cardinal-legates. Within a short time imperial displeasure with Hadrian was bound to be translated into practical, even into military terms. In the pause between the conclusion of the Norman agreement and the execution of German counter-measures, Hadrian had an opportunity to assert his power in Rome and the patrimony which he did not miss. He has a probably well-deserved reputation as one of the founders of the late medieval temporal power. But the concordat of Benevento was the political basis on which the rest of his temporal administration was built.

Under Hadrian's practical rule the finances, the nerve of temporal power, received a great deal of attention. The pragmatism and fiscal realism of Anglo-Norman government, and its insistence on good financial records, perhaps made some impression on papal administration through Hadrian. He was not the only Englishman to make his mark on Italian government; Robert of Saleby had been chancellor of the Norman kingdom under Roger. Hadrian was an able administrator who used able agents. His chamberlain, the Cardinal Boso, was an experienced clerk and diplomatist whose tenure of the chamberlain's office seems to have been particularly important.[1] Boso's records of the financial and property transactions of the Holy See were full and careful; he also interested himself in the preservation of earlier rent-books and titles, besides working as a compiler and author of papal biographies. He distinguished himself by diligence rather than originality but this is no great fault in a civil servant. He appears to have been head of the papal household,[2] a function which was perhaps connected with his control of the papal soldiery. That this fiscal official was in effect at the head of temporal power policy was not accidental. Though the feudal barons of the Roman Campagna did possess some money resources (as we know from the loans they made to the Church), the pope alone could lay hands on large sums of money. With these he bribed the Roman commune and the territorial nobles, and bought or bought back the most important castles in the Campagna. The policy was that of Eugenius III, and was only a logical development of the policies pursued by the Reform popes.

A great deal of Hadrian's reorganisation of the Roman patrimony was carried out under feudal law. It has been remarked that his use of feudal forms would have come naturally to an Englishman of his period. While this is so, it must not be imagined that he introduced feudalism to the Roman countryside. The first instance of the use of the word *feudum* in the Roman region seems to be in the year 1126, but the institution of feudalism as a common legal and social practice antedates this by many years.[3] The first reference to subinfeudation to 'knights'

---

[1] F. Geisthardt, *Der Kämmerer Boso* (Berlin, 1936). There is no conclusive evidence that Boso was English, nor that he was Hadrian's nephew, as is sometimes stated. But see *Letters of John of Salisbury*, W. J. Millor (ed.), et al., i, p. 18n. Professor Brooke kindly helped me about this point.

[2] Geisthardt, pp. 55–6.

[3] The 1126 document, *I.P.*, i, p. 169, no. 20. The best text is in *ASR*, xxxi (1908), p. 289. Ferrucius vero iudex propter feudum quod habebat a monasterio illis concordari noluit. This part of the document was overlooked by Tomassetti; see his 'Documenti feudali delle provincie di Roma nel medio evo', *SDSD*, xix (1898), p. 293. For the infeudation by Paschal II to the Abbot of Subiaco see p. 145 above. The oath of the barons of the abbey of Casauria for the castles they held from the abbey (1111), *Chron. Casaur.* (*RRIISS*, ii, 2), col. 878.

is of 1140.[1] In Campagna the obligation to attend the papal host meant the provision of a mounted knight or knights.[2]

Hadrian's reorganisation of the papal patrimonies was probably more important for its administrative methods than for its practical results. There were only three years (1156–9) in which he had freedom of action in the patrimony, and when church property in the Roman area as a whole is considered, it may be doubted whether his success was more than partial. His main objective was the same as that of his predecessor, to restrict the revolutionary autonomy of the Roman commune. Papal allies against Rome remained the same, the Roman nobles and the emergent communes of the Roman region. Rome continued to hope for imperial support, during this last part of Hadrian's pontificate not without effect. The pope executed his policy by feudal means, but he had to pay heavily for the help he got. To the family of the prefect he acknowledged for their assistance against Rome the large debt of 2,000 marks, half of which he paid in cash, and for the rest pledged the important town and county of Cività Castellana, besides the village of Montalto.[3]

The distant commune of Orvieto, in the very north of the papal patrimony, was paid a 'benefice' of 300 pounds by the pope to help with the security of the Via Cassia from Sutri to the northern papal border fortress of Tintinanno (Rocca d'Orcia). The oath taken by the men of Orvieto was 'like that sworn by the other feudal tenants (*fideles*) for the *regalia* of St Peter'.[4] Closely connected with the feudal submission of the commune was that of the neighbouring counts of Calmaniare, who guaranteed the security of the pilgrim roads, and agreed to have Rocca San Stefano (dominating the Via Cassia near Sutri) manned by troops named by the pope.[5] No doubt this concern for the safety of pilgrims

---

[1] *I.P.*, ii, p. 44, no. 10; cf. Tomassetti, *SDSD*, vii (1886), p. 111. In the early twelfth century the Subiaco chronicle (Morghen's edition, p. 20) refers to the knight's equipment: 'In Sublaco dedit ei (Gregory of Anticoli) feudum unum et omnem unius militis apparatum.' For the knights of the Bishop of Teramo, in the Abruzzi, in 1121, see Savini, *Il comune Teramano* (Rome, 1895), pp. 93–4.

[2] *I.P.*, ii, p. 159, no. 19 (18 January 1159), 'et remiserunt, ut ita dicam, senioriam, videlicet servitium unius militis pro hoste facienda, quod curia domini pape exigere solebat.'

[3] Theiner, *C.D.*, i, no. 25. Cf. *Lib. cens.*, ii, pp. 431–9. Compare the pledges of villages by Innocent II to Pietro Latrone, in the same area (p. 176 above).

[4] Theiner, *C.D.*, i, no. 23. The pope's offer to mediate between Orvieto and Aquapendente (ibid.) is typical of subsequent papal policy.

[5] *Lib. cens.*, i, pp. 388–90. Waley, *Mediaeval Orvieto* (Cambridge, 1952), pp. 3–4, calls these documents records of purchases of land by the pope, but this is not quite exact. One records a purchase of two mills, but another is a 'donation' by the two counts of all their lands to the pope and the third a re-grant of the same lands to the same owners, except for special

was what had inspired Hadrian's predecessors, Anastasius and Eugenius, to acquire the border castle of Radicofani, which Hadrian himself fortified.[1] The free access of pilgrims to Rome was both a religious duty for the pope, and a matter of concern for the economies of the city and the *curia*.

We can have some idea of how Hadrian's court viewed his temporal power policy from the pope's biography by Cardinal Boso, the official most directly interested. Boso saw the submission of Orvieto as Hadrian's main achievement in this field; he says that Oriveto (which is mentioned in the imperial donations) had for a very long time withdrawn itself from papal jurisdiction, and that Hadrian was the first pope to enter the city (in the autumn of 1156) 'or to have any temporal power there'. This appears to be the first instance in which the expression 'temporal power' is used of the pope's political rule in the Tuscan patrimony. But when he comes to recording the rest of Hadrian's activity in the temporal power, Boso's touch is much less certain. Hadrian, Boso says, added great possessions and buildings to the patrimony of St Peter. He bought (the biographer begins) the castle of Corchiano from the Roman family of Boccaleone. Boso continues: 'He bought two excellent mills at Santa Cristina (Bolsena) from the counts of Calmaniare.' Nothing could illustrate better than this juxtaposition – which is not that of a humble clerk but of a high political official – the confusion of political objectives with patrimonial matters which is typical of feudal society.

Like most popes in the feudal period Hadrian was more concerned to get the ownership of church lands recognised than to compel their corporal restitution. The minor baron Adenulph of Aquapuzza (lying in the plain beneath the Monti Lepini, near Sermoneta) was besieged and forced to submit by a papal force. When he had displayed the flag of St Peter on the tower he went to the papal army, which was led by two cardinals (one of them the Chamberlain Boso), Oddo Frangipani, and the important local baron, Geoffrey of Ceccano. On the second day he waited barefoot and in a halter on the pope at Albano, handed over a wand to consign the castle, and 800 pounds bail. He then swore homage to the pope and was feudally invested with Aquapuzza, promising to serve with his knights and dependants, in full performance

conditions named for Rocca San Stefano. *Lib. cens.*, i, p. 394, a later pledge of Rocca San Stefano and half of two other fortresses by the counts to the pope, in return for a money payment.

[1] *Lib. Pont.*, ii, p. 396. He also acquired in this area the fortress of Montichiello, *Lib. cens.*, i, p. 408. On the Via Flaminia he acquired Corchiano and Riano (ibid. pp. 385, 396).

of his feudal duty (*per totam regaliam*).[1] How effective this comedy
was in maintaining order in Campagna is uncertain; one suspects that
the political price which had to be paid to Geoffrey of Ceccano for his
support was at least as important as the submission of the minor figure
or Adenulph.[2] A similar restoration to that of Adenulph was made to the
feudatory of the castle of Sgurgola, on the other side of the Monti
Lepini,[3] and another to the much more important Baron Oddo of Poli.
The popes were, Oddo's agreement states, to have no power of declaring
his fief forfeit unless he was declared to have acted against the pope
'by the judgement of his peers'.[4]

Like most feudal rulers, Hadrian did not mind if his vassals were strong,
provided they were obedient. In order to increase the number of papal
castles in Sabina, he allowed the counts of Aquino to take over the
whole of the fertile and strategically important hill of Monte San
Giovanni, to which there were many claimants, among them the Bishop
of Veroli. The price for this was the cession by the counts of the village
of Monte Libretti in Sabina, and it is to be doubted whether the
pope made a good bargain.[5] Connected in turn with this were the
pope's grants of local autonomy to the little rural communities of
Bocchignano and Lauro (Monte Asola) in Sabina; both these specifically
mention the *fodrum* due to the pope and the cardinals, probably in
reply to Frederick Barbarossa's claim to collect *fodrum* in Sabina in
1155.[6]

There are signs by Hadrian's time of a rather more professional
organisation of papal mercenary forces than the simple band (*masnada*)
led by a nobleman which had been responsible for papal security earlier
in the century. The pope now had the same entourage as other feudal

---

[1] *Lib. cens.*, i, p. 427.

[2] For the important family of Ceccano, who dominated Sezze, see Falco, in *ASR*, xlii (1919),
p. 600. He does not mention Hadrian IV's grant to Gregory of Ceccano of the castle of
Carpineto, *I.P.*, i, p. 29, no. 23.

[3] *Lib. cens.*, i, p. 400.

[4] Ibid. pp. 387–8, 'juste et juditio tuorum bonorum parium amittere debeatis qui in te
inimicitiam non habeant'.

[5] *Lib. cens.*, i, pp. 391–4; ii, p. 127 (8 April 1157). The witnesses include important nobles.
The counter-claims of the Bishop of Veroli, 18 January 1159, *I.P.*, ii, p. 159, no. 19. For
the pope's own house in Monte San Giovanni, which he leased from the bishop, ibid. and
no. 18 (also in Scaccia Scarafoni, *Le Carte*, no. 151, p. 198).

[6] *I.P.*, ii, p. 70, no. 2 (Bocchignano); Vehse, *Quellen*, xxi (1929–30), pp. 174–5 (Lauro). This
is one of the first indications that cardinals participated in the *regalia sancti Petri*, the temporal
revenues. The historical origin of the *fodrum* at Bocchignano and Monte Asola was probably
not that of the *fodrum regale* but of the *fodrum de castellis*. See Brühl, *Fodrum, Gistum, Servitium
Regis*, i, pp. 553, 560n.

rulers; this included several marshals. A papal chaplain in charge of the fort at Monte Libretti swore the oath 'of those who man the papal fortresses'. There was a 'constable' in charge of the troops guarding the fort at Corchiano; another papal castellan is recorded at Valmontone and a papal garrison was placed in Rocca San Stefano.[1] A papal fort was built in the deserted town of Orchia, near Viterbo and not far from Vetralla which had been acquired by Hadrian's predecessors. These fortresses, directly controlled by the pope, were only a proportion of those owned by the Church. Monasteries such as S. Paolo fuori le Mura,[2] Subiaco or Farfa controlled many others. It was to be a long time before the feudal power of the great monasteries was to be seriously eroded, and for the time being this power was firmly in the hands of the popes.

The submission of the Roman commune to Hadrian was far from complete. The commune negotiated independently with the emperor, and sent a detachment of troops to help in his siege of Milan in 1158. The Romans continued to encroach on church property.[3] The submissiveness of the Roman nobles to the pope was undoubtedly due more than anything to fear of the commune. The tide was turning against the tyranny of the aristocratic 'captains' who had terrorised Rome a century earlier; now the Roman levies devastated the lands of the magnates. Though harmful to papal interests in the short term, the growth of the Roman commune – and indeed the growth of other communes – eventually served papal interests by creating a new balance of power.

One of the first magnate families to feel the squeeze was the oldest of all, that of the counts of Tuscolo. The Colonna branch of the family had transferred half its rights in Tuscolo already to Eugenius III. With the death of the head of the main branch, Ptolemy II, in 1153, the family position weakened further.[4] Jonathan, one of Ptolemy's three sons, sumbitted to Hadrian in 1155. Jonathan temporarily transferred to the pope the forts of Montefortino and Faiola, in the Alban hills, but

---

[1] *I.P.*, i, p. 51, no. 9 (Anastasius IV) and *Lib. cens.*, i, p. 389 (Hadrian IV); both name Johannes Bonus marescallus. Two other marshals in *Lib. cens.*, i, p. 400. The chaplain of Monte Libretti, ibid. ii, p. 127; the constable of Corchiano, ibid. i, p. 400 (Malavolta; the comma after his name is otiose). The castellan of Valmontone, ibid. i, p. 128; Orchia, ibid. i, p. 395. Valmontone belonged to St John Lateran (*I.P.*, i, p. 28, no. 20), but under Eugenius III had been granted to a local baron (ibid. no. 18).

[2] Cf. G. Silvestrelli, 'Lo stato feudale dell 'abbazia di san Paolo', *Roma*, i (1923), pp. 221–31, 419–31.

[3] Cf. *I.P.*, i, p. 48, no. 3.

[4] G. Digard, 'La fin de la seigneurie de Tusculum', *Mélanges Paul Fabre* (Paris, 1914), pp. 292–302; Tomassetti *CR*, iv, pp. 394–5; *Lib. cens.*, i, pp. 382, 399.

continued to hold the more important fort in the pass of Lariano. The special consideration the Tusculan family felt it still enjoyed with the emperor made Jonathan except the emperor in the feudal oath he swore to Hadrian.

V

Hadrian's final quarrel with Frederick I was the product of a number of disturbing factors, which included the friction of the political questions of prestige, Hadrian's relations with Normans and Greeks, and (probably at first a minor matter) the imperial claims to exercise the regalian rights in the papal patrimony. The last was exacerbated when Frederick descended into Italy for the second time in 1158, and despatched envoys to collect imperial hospitality tax (*fodrum*) in Campagna and the Maritime province. But there was also the important question of eastern Italy. When Frederick's envoys went south down the Adriatic coast early in 1158 they found that Ravenna and Ancona had both made agreements with the Byzantine forces in Ancona.[1] The lukewarmness of eastern Italy in Frederick's cause was shown by the failure of most of the Romagnol bishops to attend the great imperial diet of Roncaglia (November 1158). Frederick wanted to suppress such disloyal deviations, but he was even more anxious for money.

At such a time the see of Ravenna was going to be of the utmost political importance. It had been occupied by the distinguished German cleric Anselm of Havelberg. After Anselm's death Frederick, in the autumn of 1158, nominated the north Italian nobleman Guy of Biandrata, who also happened to be a clerk in the Roman *curia*. The election, though possibly agreed to by Hadrian's legates, was not confirmed by the pope. The threat of a return by the see of Ravenna to eleventh-century conditions of direct dependence on the empire was quite unacceptable to Rome, at a time when imperial activity threatened Roman control of church possessions in the whole eastern area between the Po and the Norman frontier. Archbishop Anselm though a German in imperial service, had been an experienced man of marked

[1] H. Sudendorf, *Registrum oder merkwürdige Urkunden für die deutsche Geschichte*, pt. 2 (Berlin, 1851) pp. 131–3.

ability, independence and loyalty to Roman policies. But the threat to place a young clerk in the see of Ravenna, whose only real qualification was the emperor's favour, produced a crisis in the affairs of Ravenna which could be seen as the most important since the schism of Wibert in 1080. The reality of the menace to Roman control in eastern Italy was emphasised by Frederick's intervention in the affairs of the Romagnol bishopric of Faenza.[1]

For the popes it was their authority over the archbishopric of Ravenna and its suffragans which really counted. Their power had been vigorously exercised there on several occasions in the century. The metropolitan jurisdiction of Ravenna over its suffragans had on the whole been maintained by the popes since the time of Gelasius II.[2] The exception to this was Ferrara, which among the bishoprics of the exarchate had anciently been claimed as an area of papal regalian jurisdiction.[3] Ferrara had been exempted from the jurisdiction of Ravenna in 1139. Eugenius III had also intervened in the wars of Bologna, Faenza and Imola, in order to support the temporal power of the Bishop of Imola against the commune.[4] There were numerous papal interventions (particularly by Eugenius III) in the long-lived dispute between the sees of Ferrara and Ravenna over the estate called *massa Firminiana*. Possibly the most important papal act in Ravenna's temporal affairs was Celestine II's investiture of the Cavalcaconti heir with the papal lands in the county of Bertinoro.[5] Papal rights over other places in Romagna which were claimed as immediately subject to the Rome See, such as Rimini, had also been asserted during the first half of the twelfth century.

These important papal interests determined a vigorous reaction to Frederick's governmental measures in Romagna, and to his nomination of Guy to the see of Ravenna. At first politely, and then more vigorously Hadrian refused to accept Guy of Biandrata as Archbishop. Finally in the summer of 1159 the pope despatched a strong protest against the

---

[1] Stumpf, *Die Reichskanzler* (Innsbruck, 1865), no. 3824. Cf. Maccarrone, p. 274. For the special relation of the cathedral church of Faenza to the papacy, see *I.P.* v, pp. 150–1, nos. 4, 5 (Innocent II and Lucius II).

[2] See the documents listed in *I.P.*, v, pp. 57–64.

[3] O. Vehse, 'Ferrareser Fälschungen', *Quellen*, xxvii (1936–7), pp. 1–108. For the Roman cardinal given as bishop to Ferrara in 1139 see also Ganzer, *Auswärtigen Kardinalat*, pp. 92–3.

[4] *I.P.*, v, p. 272, no. 7; cf. A. Hessel, *Geschichte der Stadt Bologna* (Berlin, 1910), pp. 82–3.

[5] *I.P.* v, p. 136, no. 1 (quoted above, note 50). The *castrum* of Bertinoro had in 1130 been granted by the Archbishop of Ravenna to Cavalcaconte, Count of Bertinoro, with the feudal obligation of military service and attendance on the archbishop when he visited Rome. Fantuzzi, iv, p. 249.

whole trend of Frederick's policy in Italy.[1] The emperor was asked to send no more envoys to Rome without papal knowledge, as the 'magistrature and *regalia*' of Rome were fully subject to St Peter. The collection of imperial hospitality tax (*fodrum*) was to stop in the papal patrimonies, except on the occasion of the emperor's coronation. Italian bishops were to swear fealty to the emperor but not homage – a clause of great importance, intended to prevent church lands from coming under the full feudal control of the empire. Finally certain possessions of the Roman Church were to be restored by the emperor: Tivoli, Ferrara and two dependent estates (Massa and Ficarolo), the Matildine lands, 'all the lands from Acquapendente to Rome', the duchy of Spoleto, and the islands of Sardinia and Corsica. This last clause is understood by some scholars to be a comprehensive definition of papal territorial claims, but this is not certain.[2] As on previous occasions, the pope in 1159 was protesting against specific infractions of church rights.[3] The burden of the whole accusation was, as Hadrian's successor Alexander III wrote to Bishop Arnulf of Lisieux, that Frederick had 'violently invaded the patrimony of St Peter'.[4]

However, perhaps Frederick had good reason to be annoyed with the pope.[5] The Treaty of Benevento with William of Sicily was a violation of the agreement of Constance; and Hadrian's subsequent appeals to the Treaty of Constance therefore failed to carry weight. Frederick reasonably objected that Hadrian could not call on him to fulfil a treaty which the pope himself had already broken. Hadrian's dealings with the Sicilian and Byzantine governments could (more questionably) be interpreted as preparatory to a future anti-German alliance. Frederick's dealings with

---

[1] Rahewin, *Gesta Frederici*, Waitz-Simpson (ed.) (1912), pp. 276–7.

[2] Waley, *P.S.*, pp. 4–5 seems to me on uncertain ground in treating Hadrian's protest as 'a full statement of papal territorial claims', and probably mistaken in suggesting (ibid.) that the headings under which bishoprics were listed in a report of the Council of Pisa (1135) gives us any idea of papal territorial claims at that time. The bishoprics listed there as 'de civitatibus beati petri' are surely the bishops who ecclesiastically were immediately subject to the Roman See. E. Bernheim, 'Ein bisher unbekannter Bericht vom Council zu Pisa im Jahr 1135', *Zeitschrift f. Kirchenrecht*, xvi (1881), pp. 147–54, and cf. *Liber Censuum*, i, p. 243.

[3] It is arguable that in restricting the imperial right to take *fodrum* to the occasion of the emperor's coming for his coronation Hadrian was misrepresenting the existing custom; see Brühl, *Fodrum, Gistum, Servitium Regis*, i, pp. 672–3. But the case does not seem to me as clear on the side of the emperor as Brühl makes it.

[4] J.-L. 10627.

[5] Monsignor Maccarrone's defence of Hadrian's good faith towards Frederick (*Papato e impero*, p. 248) seems to me unconvincing. Cf. Lamma, i, p. 259; Chalandon, ii, pp. 258 ff.; Munz, *Frederick Barbarossa*, pp. 196 ff. Miss D. Clementi in *BISI*, lxxx (1968), pp. 196–7, does not mention the Treaty of Constance (see immediately below).

the Roman commune, which were so objectionable to the pope, were not directly in contradiction with the Constance agreement, which spoke of not making peace with the Roman regime, but not of abstaining from negotiation.

Frederick's reaction was to give his ambassadors instructions to reach an agreement with the pope if they could, and if not, to sign peace with the Roman commune. Most damaging of all for papal-imperial relations, in the summer of 1159 Hadrian received delegations from the north Italian cities. The intervention by the pope in the quarrel between the emperor and the Lombard towns was perhaps inevitable, but it was to be one of the most explosive issues of the age.

The extension of the papal-imperial struggle to northern Italy was, however, only one aspect of the widening of the horizons of the Roman Church at this period. The spiritual, political, jurisdictional activity of the Roman bishop and clergy was nearing its height in medieval Christian society. The Roman mission had in principle always been universal in scope, or as universal as the cultural consciousness of its bishops extended. It had failed to impose itself on Eastern Christendom, and in spite of many efforts was to fail again in the same endeavour. But in Western Christendom, though resisted to some extent by lay rulers and obstructed to some extent by heretical movements, papal leadership had experienced a success which can only astonish anyone who is aware of the fragmented nature of the societies with which it dealt.

How did the patrimony of the Church fit into this new picture, in which the social function of the Roman Church had been, as it were, projected from its own diocese over a huge area? When the primary duties of the Roman bishop ceased to be those of the custodian of the holy places of the martyrs, and came to be those of the head of a great administrative machine, was there a parallel change in his responsibilities for the lands of his Church? St Bernard clearly thought not, and his advice to Eugenius on dealing with the Romans is that of a conservative who wishes to preserve the spiritual function of the bishop intact; when the pope is unable to settle the political questions with which Roman politics present him, he is to call on the emperor to wield the material sword on his behalf.

There was little conscious effort by popes or emperors in the earlier twelfth century to change the traditional responsibilities which each had for the lands of the Roman Church; not until the 1180s were great innovations in this field even discussed. All emperors in this century except for Conrad took oaths or executed engagements to restore the

Opposite: 7 Henry VI's entry into Rome and his coronation by
          Celestine III

ROMA

Henri

Henri   celestini'

pimo manu ungit   secido brachia   tero henrig mp

Crisma

Quarto virga   Quinto anulu   Ultimo vga

cano capidas

Bellum rome o'Thib. eps lecd. abbas Wifhgen. p. de Sauoy

8 The battle for Rome, 1312

9 Henry VII crowned Emperor

Coronat a tribus cardinalibz in Jmpatore.

patrimonies of the Holy See, besides taking the oath of fidelity to the Roman Church which formed part of the coronation rite. The amount of compromise about specific contested points concerning the temporal power which proved possible between emperors and popes – for example about the Matildine lands, or about the *fodrum* due to the emperor – is impressive. The fiercest objections to the patrimonies of the Church came not from lay rulers but from heretical laity and clergy, who based their criticism on moral grounds. The emperors took no part in these attacks on orthodoxy, and Arnold of Brescia was executed not by the pope but by Frederick I.

Why, then, was the Papal State from the middle of the century onwards an increasingly serious subject of friction between popes and emperors? Probably the most important single reason was the relations of the two powers with the Norman kingdom of Sicily – a relationship complicated by papal feudal claims. But the very nature of twelfth-century government was perhaps to press jurisdictional rights in a more systematic way. Especially after Boso had given the relatively new papal office of chamberlain a new stamp of energy and administrative thoroughness, the will to rule the Papal State, which in the past had been so often languid, and subordinate to other political aims, became more vigorous. When confronted with an imperial administration which was also attempting to assert itself more aggressively, papal government in the temporal power was bound to run into difficulties. The popes supported the opposition to the empire in Lombardy; the emperors supported the opposition to the popes in Rome and the Papal State.

The greater the success the Roman bishops had in imposing their spiritual hegemony on Europe, the more they were likely to become involved in attempts to improve and extend their rule in the Papal State. This was true in a material sense, in that the economic benefits of spiritual rule – such as profits of jurisdiction, and payments from protected monasteries – flowed into Rome and were from an economic point of view part of the resources of the city. The Romans wanted direct control of these revenues if possible – hence the quarrels about payments by popes of gifts *presbyterium, beneficium*), war indemnities and similar extortions, and the question of control of the Roman mint. In order to protect its traditional liberties against the pressure of the Roman commune, the papacy had to react and to impose a form of rule on the Romans which would protect clerical privilege. This was an important stimulus to the development of papal temporal power, although there were moments when Roman pressure was so intense that it looked as

H

though things were going in the same way as elsewhere in the Italian cities, and the Roman clergy seemed in danger of expropriation and of being made to submit to lay control.

But there was also a sense in which the development of the spiritual power brought with it prestige, political and diplomatic opportunity, and the temptation to engage in temporal politics on a wider scale than had ever been possible for the Roman bishop before. The money profits of the spiritual power added to these opportunities, enabling the popes to engage soldiers and direct armies. In the mid-twelfth century this expansion of the temporal function was hardly if at all visible; as late as the last decade of that century the popes were still militarily and politically weak. Only the very end of the century saw the development of a more ambitious temporal programme, which began to push the popes from a stage in which they ruled over the greatest of the ancient Carolingian clerical 'immunities' to one in which they ruled something which could be called a 'state'. The renewal of imperial power in Italy during the second half of the twelfth century was then revealed to have been in many ways superficial. But this superficiality is more apparent to historians writing eight hundred years after the event, than it was to contemporaries. Though we can now see many weaknesses in the position of Frederick Barbarossa and his son Henry VI, to contemporaries they seemed strong and aggressive kings, to be feared and propitiated.

Chapter 6

The renewal of imperial authority

I

On 1 September 1159 Hadrian IV died. At the moment of his death imperial pressure on the papacy was stronger than it had been since the time of the Emperor Henry V, and it is not surprising that the cardinals were unable to agree about his successor. One group refused to accept the Sienese Cardinal Rolando Bandinelli, the former Chancellor, who was likely to continue the anti-German policies of his predecessor. They therefore tried to impose Octavian of Monticelli, a cardinal of the so-called Ottaviani family of the Campagna, with strong imperialist connections.[1] When Bandinelli accepted the papal mantle, Octavian tore it from his back. Octavian was acclaimed in St Peter's as Victor IV: Bandinelli after being held in Castel Sant'Angelo under the threat of Roman aggression was taken to Trastevere and thence outside Rome to the distant Frangipani fortress of Ninfa, on the road to Terracina, for consecration. At Terracina Alexander III (as Bandinelli called himself) met the envoys and received the first subsidies of William of Sicily.

There was no real question (as there had seemed to be in 1130) of the Romans deciding which of the two men should be their bishop. The papal schism was clearly a question of international politics, which would eventually be decided by the European princes. After the Council of Pavia in 1160 Victor IV became Frederick Barbarossa's pope, and the instrument of his policy. However, only in Germany, the imperial-dominated parts of Italy, Denmark and parts of the kingdom of Arles was Victor recognised.

The political situation was back to the days of Urban II and Paschal

---

[1] Cf. Kehr, 'Zur Geschichte Viktors IV. (Oktavian von Monticelli)', *Neues Archiv*, xlvi (1926), pp. 53–85; H. Schwarzmaier, 'Zur Familie Viktors IV. in der Sabina', *Quellen*, xlviii (1968), pp. 64–79. For Frederick's concession of Terni to Octavian's brothers in May 1159, see K. Zeillinger, 'Zwei Diplome Barbarossas für seine römischen Parteigänger (1159)', *DA*, xx (1964), pp. 568–81; Munz, *Frederick Barbarossa*, pp. 202–3, in note.

II, with one great change. At the turn of the eleventh century active opposition to the empire in Italy was virtually confined to the Normans of the south. But for Alexander there were the Lombard towns, whose economic and military capacity for resistance was in 1160 hardly known. A new pattern of papal-imperial conflict was beginning, which in appearance extended over the north and centre of the Italian peninsula as a vast struggle of conflicting ideas and loyalties, but in reality was a confused manifestation of the power of Italian towns and regions to assert their own particularist interests against central government of any kind.

Alexander's situation in the papal patrimony was not favourable for long, if it ever was so. The support of the Frangipani and the proximity of the Norman kingdom meant that for a time at least he was safe in Campagna and the Maritime province. Victor enjoyed the support of Peter the Prefect and Stefano di Tebaldo, whose lands were north of Rome, and of monasteries with important forts in the same area or in Sabina, notably S. Paolo fuori le Mura, Subiaco (for a few months) and Farfa. But neither pope was uncontested north or south of Rome; in Civitavecchia, Pietro Latro held out for Alexander, and in Sezze and the south of Campagna the important counts of Ceccano seem to have taken the imperial side. But the situation of Alexander deteriorated quickly; in the summer of 1161 he came secretly into Rome and stayed for a few days in the Frangipani forts near the Colosseum, but he was unable to stay in the city, and shortly afterwards found difficulty in finding any secure place in the Campagna. At the end of the year he embarked from Monte Circeo for Genoa, and thence for France, going the way of Innocent II, Gelasius and Urban.

The papal biographer describes a complete collapse of Alexander's authority in the patrimony at this time, so that the Germans and schismatics occupied 'the whole patrimony of Peter from Acquapendente to Ceprano, save for Orvieto, Terracina and Anagni, and the fortress of Castro' dei Volsci, Radicofani, the key to Roman Tuscany, fell in mid-1163, and the pope's brother and nephews were captured. The worst point for Alexander's party in the Papal State came during the winter campaign of the Chancellor Christian of Mainz in

---

[1] *Ann. Ceccan.*(*MGH, Scriptores*, xix), p. 284, says of Alexander: Hic venit Anagniam et acquisivit totam Campaniam, et misit in suo iure. This is a rather puzzling statement, as Victor IV was at Segni, only a few miles away, while Alexander III was at Anagni. Possibly Norman troops helped Alexander to hold Anagni and also to control the fortress of Fumone. *Liber censuum*, ii, p. 401, may refer to this, but B. Marchetti-Longhi, 'Pervetusta Fumonis Arx', *ASR*, xlvii (1924), pp. 190–320, at pp. 208 ff., denies this and attributes the document to Honorius II.

1164–5. Christian ravaged Campagna and the environs of Rome, and took Anagni, Castro dei Volsci and other strongpoints. But he did not possess the forces either to compel Rome to submit or to garrison what he had taken. Victor IV had died in 1164, and his successor Guy of Crema (Paschal III) whom Christian brought with him to Viterbo, could not command the support enjoyed by his Roman predecessor. When Christian marched north to Tuscany in the early spring of 1165 few places seem to have held out for Paschal III except Viterbo. A Norman army crossed the border, and the Romans were happy to join the Normans and burn the villages of Campagna with them. Rome (sweetened by bribery as was normal) made a formal submission to Alexander's vicar, the Bishop of Palestrina, and promised the submission of Sabina. In November 1165 Alexander, having travelled from France to Sicily and then to Rome, was able to enter his see in peace.

II

These were years of uncertainty and confusion in Italy, and of political claims which bore little relation to reality. Alexander's need for money made his political situation even weaker. Frederick Barbarossa taunted Alexander about his indebtedness, and although our information about the pope's finances is scanty,[1] the taunt probably had some substance. On returning to Rome the pope renewed Hadrian's policy of pledging papal villages.[2] His position in Rome was weak. But the Romans themselves claimed much that they did not possess. In their treaties with Genoa in 1165–6 (treaties which in spite of the so-called submission of the Roman commune to Alexander, quite fail to mention the pope's name) the Romans speak of the 'viscounts and bailiffs' in the seaports of Terracina, Astura, Ostia, Porto, Santa Severa and Civitavecchia as though these ports were firmly in Roman hands. But Terracina was controlled by the Frangipani, Astura by the counts of Tuscolo,[3] and Santa Severa and Civitavecchia by Pietro Latro. The most the Romans could have claimed was that these nobles were prepared to co-operate with them, and even this was untrue of the counts of Tuscolo.

Frederick Barbarossa was faced by problems which his material resources were inadequate to solve. In Italy he was at grips not only with the Italian communes and Alexander III, but with the Norman

---

[1] Cf. F. Schneider, 'Zur älteren päpstlichen Finanzgeschichte', *Quellen*, ix (1906), pp. 1–37.
[2] e.g., Ariccia near Albano, *I.P.*, i, p. 196; Schneider, p. 8.
[3] Cf. *ASR*, xxvii (1904), p. 389.

kingdom, and, less definitely, with the hazy ambitions of the Greek Emperor Manuel Comnenus. Manuel at this time made to Alexander the startling proposition that the Eastern and Western Churches should be united, and the undivided empire of east and west 'granted' to Manuel Alexander III.[1] That Frederick took the Greek threat seriously is shown by the military dispositions he made in the Italian expedition of 1166–7. Aiming eventually at the Norman kingdom, he halted his main army to besiege Ancona, the seaport on the Adriatic coast which had for some years been in close relations with the Byzantines.

Like all the other important communes, the Romans were engaged in a desperate struggle to subdue the points of economic or strategic importance in what they considered to be their territory. Tivoli had long ago become one of Rome's main objectives; now with the decline of the family of the counts of Tuscolo, Tuscolo and the Alban hills came under attack. Control of this area meant control of the Via Latina and the Via Appia, besides enjoyment of the tolls (*dominium guidonaticum*) and of the wool from the sheep-runs in the Abruzzi.[2] When Albano and Tuscolo refused to pay Roman taxation, the Romans attacked and destroyed Albano, and then against papal wishes attacked Tuscolo in the spring of 1167. Raino of Tuscolo persuaded his cousin Oddo Colonna to appeal to the emperor, then at the siege of Ancona. Rainald of Dassel had just arrived in the Roman area with a small German force; seeing the importance of the issue he persuaded another military bishop, Christian of Mainz, the imperial chancellor, to bring a force of Brabançon mercenaries to assist him and the Tusculans. The battle took place in the plain between the heights of Tuscolo and the hill of Monte Porzio. Though more numerous, the Romans were out-fought by the experienced German troops; they fled, and at the end of the day their bodies were scattered on the roads between Rome and Tuscolo 'like sheep' (29 May 1167).

The importance of the defeat of Monte Porzio was immediately

---

[1] J. Parker, 'The attempted Byzantine alliance with the Sicilian Norman Kingdom (1166–7)', *PBSR*, xxiv (n.s. xi, 1956), pp. 86–93; Lamma, ii, pp. 126–43.

[2] That control of wool was one of the most important disputed issues is clear from the passage (not hitherto cited in this connection) on the destruction of Tuscolo in Boncompagno, *Amicitia di maestro Boncompagno da Signa*, S. Nathan (ed.), *Miscellanea di letteratura del medio evo* (Società Filologica Romana, (Rome, 1909), vol. iii), pp. 83–4. 'unde vere diceris Tusculanum, inmo, ut verius fatear, Fusculanum, quia fuscum es factum et sine vellere iaces et lana'. For the 'dominium guidonaticum' see *Lib. cens.*, i, p. 382, Theiner, *C.D.*, i, no. 18 (Duchesne has 'dominio *et* guidonatico'). Tomassetti's view of Tuscolo as a barbarous threat to civilised life in the Roman Campagna ('La Pace di Roma', *Rivista Internazionale di Scienze Sociali*, xi, p. 19 of offprint) disregards these clashes of economic interest.

appreciated by Frederick, who hastily accepted some kind of compromise submission from Ancona and came with his main army over the Apennines to Rome, where Paschal III joined him. The attack on Rome was by land and sea; while Frederick arrived with his army, his allies, the Pisans attacked Astura and Civitavecchia. In order to give Paschal III access to the basilica the German troops stormed St Peter's, burning the little church of S. Maria in Turri beside the main church, and destroying its ancient doors which were inscribed with the imperial donations. The attack on St Peter's was less shocking than it may seem; the church had been fortified for most of the century. On 1 August, while Alexander III remained closeted in the Frangipani fortresses near the Colosseum, Frederick and Beatrice were crowned by Paschal III in St Peter's.

The Sicilian king managed to send money by galleys up the Tiber to Alexander, but not men. The pope slipped out of Rome in disguise, as he had done six years earlier, and three days later was at Monte Circeo, the Frangipani fortress on the coast. The papal biographer pictures him at the foot of the hill, picnicking with a few cardinals beside a spring; perhaps even the austere tastes of the twelfth century saw something idyllic in the fugitive rest in the August heat, above the rocks of Circe's cave.

The Roman commune was willing to submit to its conqueror and sovereign, but Frederick's victory was illusory. Within a week of the coronation there was heavy rain, which in the summer heat provoked a most violent outbreak of disease (possibly malaria) in the German army. Men died in hundreds within a day or so of the appearance of the pestilence. On 6 August, within days of his apparent triumph, Frederick broke camp and marched his decimated army north.

A mere scoreboard of the successes and failures of Alexander III and Frederick I in obtaining 'recognition' from Italian communes and bishops is not very informative. Alexander III had no permanent officials in Italy except a count of Campagna to whom no one paid much attention; Frederick sent officials and appointed dukes and marquises, but the authority exercised by all these was fitful and dependent on local conditions. In the wars of Frederick and Alexander the particularist interests of each city and region were the determining factors of political and religious allegiance, and this was to remain the case for the rest of the Middle Ages. The financial and political importance of the Italian bishops was far from exhausted, but it was declining while the strength of the communes increased. One of the most striking examples was

Ravenna; after 1167 the commune went over to Alexander while Archbishop Guy remained until his death in 1169 an ineffectual imperialist.
The policies of Venice affected the alignment of cities in Romagna; the
hostility of Faenza to Bologna and Ancona helped to keep her on the
whole loyal to the empire.[1] For both Bologna and Ferrara the freedom
of navigation of the Po and commercial relations with the Lombard
cities were very important factors; both these cities began the schism
period in the power of the emperor, and both after 1167 joined the
Lombard League and Alexandrine party.[2]

In the Roman area imperial officials continued to dominate Viterbo
and probably the area north of Viterbo even after the catastrophe of
1167; under the auspices of an imperialist 'count' Viterbo extended its
territory to Vetralla and the county of Bagnorea, and northwards to the
sea at Montalto, while the recalcitrant village of Ferento was destroyed.[3]
Here again, local interests seem to have predominated under an
imperialist cover. In Rome itself the priority of local interests was
brought painfully home to Pope Alexander. Continuing his normal policy
of exploiting the weakness of the Tusculan family by means of the
alliance of the Frangipani, Alexander in the summer of 1170 arranged
a treaty by which the Frangipani transferred some of their rights at
Terracina and Monte Circeo to Raino of Tuscolo (promising also to obtain
Segni and some adjacent villages for him from the pope), and in return
obtained from the Tusculan lord and the Holy See the town of Tuscolo
and the fort of Monte Cavo.[4] It may have seemed for a short time as
though Rome was going to swallow its hate for Tuscolo and submit.
In August 1170 a Roman citizen had a vision of the Lord speaking to
Peter about Roman crimes. There was a brief movement of piety in
the city: the Tusculan prisoners were released, and the fortress by St

[1] Cf. F. Güterbock, 'Zum Schisma unter Alexander III. Die Uberlieferung des Tolosanus und
die Stellungnahme der Romagna und Emilia', *Papsttum und Kaisertum* (Munich, 1926), pp.
376–97.
[2] Cf. Vehse, *Quellen*, xxvii (1936–7), pp. 10–13; Hessel, *Geschichte der Stadt Bologna*, pp. 100–15.
Hadrian IV had protested to Frederick about the latter's occupation of Ferrara (p. 199 above).
[3] The most recent book on Viterbo is that of N. Kamp, *Istituzioni Comunali in Viterbo nel
Medioevo*, i (Viterbo, 1963). Cf. also D. Hägermann, 'Beiträge zur Reichslegation Christians
von Mainz in Italien', *Quellen*, xlix (1969), pp. 211–18. Ferento was destroyed in 1172.
[4] It is usually said that the Frangipani ceded Terracina under this agreement, but the only
property which was actually to pass was the fortress of Traversa, besides the fort of Monte
Circeo and the holding of S. Felice, *SDSD*, vii (1886), p. 324. For the correction of date of
this document to 1170, see Digard, in *Mélanges Fabre*, quoted above. Before this agreement
Raino had tried to transfer Tuscolo to the prefect, Johannes Maledictus, in exchange for
Montefiascone.

Peter's destroyed.[1] But it did not last. The pope stayed for two years in the fortress of Tuscolo, but that he should peacefully take over the hated city was quite against Roman ideas. They obtained a concession from Alexander that he would allow them to demolish the walls of Tuscolo to a given level; when the Romans began this agreeable task, either from political calculation or from inability to stop themselves, they demolished both the buildings of the town and its walls, and left only the walls of the fortress intact. This breach of faith renewed the quarrel, and the pope returned to his wanderings in the southern Campagna. The Frangipani, for whom a marriage was arranged by the pope between Oddo Frangipani and Eudoxia, the niece of the Byzantine emperor, remained indispensable however to the pope. The frequent loans of the Frangipani family to the pope were secured on papal temporal possessions such as the income of the southern city of Benevento.[2] The Frangipani became the undisputed lords of the important port of Terracina, and the only recorded reaction of Alexander to their despotic rule there is an instruction to refrain from bringing clerks to secular judgement which implicitly recognises their usurpation of papal temporal rights in the city.[3]

In Romagna the acceptance of an Alexandrine archbishop of Ravenna in 1170 had confirmed the swing towards the Roman obedience. Fresh German efforts were made to redress the unfavourable balance. In 1173 an imperialist army with Venetian aid entered the march of Ancona and besieged Ancona. All the forces of resistance to the empire in the march and Romagna were assembled at Ancona under Boltruda Frangipani, Countess of Bertinoro, and they enabled the city to resist with success.[4] But in other parts of central Italy, even if imperial rule was intermittent, it was present. The imperial chancellor, Christian of Mainz, had been recognised not only in the northern patrimony and the march of Ancona but in the duchy of Spoleto and in places as near to Rome as Tivoli.[5] In the early spring of 1175 Christian renewed his alliances

---

[1] A. Wilmart, 'Nouvelles de Rome au temps d'Alexandre III', *Revue Bénédictine*, xlv (1933), pp. 62–78.

[2] *I.P.*, i, pp. 192–3.

[3] Cf. *Quellen*, xxxvii (1957), p. 76. For the *signoria* of the Frangipani in Terracina see Falco, *ASR*, xlii (1919), pp. 600–4. The highest point of their dominion there is the act of 1169 (Contatore, pp. 166–7).

[4] Cf. Boncompagni, *Liber de obsidione Ancone* (*RRIISS*, vi, pt. 3). This is a rhetorical work written about thirty years later, but is nevertheless valuable. For Boltruda see above, p. 180n. and cf. Lamma, ii, pp. 244–52.

[5] Cf. W. Lenel, 'Der Konstanzer Frieden von 1183 und die italienische Politik Friedrichs I., *Historische Zeitschrift*, cxxviii (1923), pp. 189–261, esp. pp. 225 ff. See especially Scheffer-

H*

with Faenza, and with numerous local troops assaulted and destroyed
S. Cassiano, the strongplace held by the Alexandrine Bishop of Imola.
This may in one sense be counted a victory for the empire, but in
another it was yet one more concession to local interests, in that it
settled the old quarrel between the citizens of Imola and their bishop
in favour of the commune.

III

In November 1176 the imperial envoys were received in consistory by
the pope at Anagni, to begin the critical peace negotiations. In the
preceding year the short-lived peace of Montebello between Frederick
and the Lombard League had been broken, and the Lombards had on
29 May 1176 inflicted on the emperor a momentous reverse at Legano.
Imperial policy was naturally directed to splitting Frederick's opponents:
pope, Lombards, and Sicilian kingdom, and, in the event, had some
success. At Anagni the preliminary articles of peace conceded to
Alexander what might be regarded as the minimum papal territorial
demands. The emperor was to restore and conserve 'all the *regalia* and
possessions of St Peter' as they had been since the time of Innocent II.
This phrase, or a very similar one, had been employed in all the negotiations between the Church and the empire since those of 1111; it had
last been used in the text of the Treaty of Constance in 1153[1] But the
phrase (see above, page 163) makes no distinction between the patrimonial possessions of the Church and their political control. The emperor
provisionally renounced possession of the claim to appoint the Roman
prefect, and promised the return of the allodial Matildine lands. The
vassals of the Church who had done homage to the emperor during
the schism were to be released and to return to their papal allegiance.

In 1177 the splendidly dressed papal galleys were rowed into Venice,
and the pope was received with a magnificence which concealed great
political uncertainties. From Venice he went (as the papal biographer put
it) to 'his Ferrara', to meet his rather distrustful Lombard allies. There
was much difficulty in agreeing where the conference with the emperor
should take place, and when the final negotiations took place in Venice

Boichorst, *Zur Geschichte des XII. und XIII. Jahrhunderts. Diplomatische Forschungen* (Berlin, 1897),
pp. 399–400; J. F. Böhmer and C. Will, *Regesta archiepiscoporum Maguntinensium* (Innsbruck,
1886). For the earlier submission of Gubbio, in this area, *MGH, Const. et acta publica*, i, p. 309,
no. 218 (8 November 1163).
[1] The deliberate conservative repetition by the imperial chancery of formulae used in the
1111 and 1122 treaties is suggested by the passage in Wibald, ep. 374, p. 502 (ed. Jaffé).

they reflected the distrust of the negotiators for one another. Frederick was unwilling to make all the concessions which his envoys had conceded to the Church in the preceding year at Anagni. When Alexander faced his antagonist of the past eighteen years in direct colloquy, the main difference was the territorial question. The emperor was willing to fulfil the treaty of Anagni in so far as it concerned the 'regalia and other possessions of the Roman Church'.[1] He made an exception only for the allodial lands of the Countess Matilda, and for the county of Bertinoro (which the Count of Bertinoro had bequeathed to the papacy a few days earlier). Both these Frederick argued, with at least some colour of justice, belonged to the empire, and he proposed to submit the questions to arbitration. Since the lands of the Countess Matilda had drifted into the possession of the Emilian communes and not that of the pope,[2] their exclusion from the settlement was no real political loss to Alexander. Only the county of Bertinoro, which Frederick seized forcibly from the papal garrison shortly after the peace of Venice was agreed, represented a real territorial loss for the papacy as compared with the treaty signed at Anagni. On the other hand the agreement that the Italian bishoprics should remain in the jurisdiction of the pope (in his 'disposition and judgement'), while it referred primarily to the schismatic bishops, meant also that the pope retained some power over the temporal possessions of these bishoprics.

The restoration of temporal possessions to the Holy See promised in the treaty was at least partly carried out. Christian of Mainz and Cardinal Rainier went together into Romagna for the transfer, which was executed with the exception of the castle of Bertinoro.[3] Alexander protested to Frederick about the appointment of Conrad of Lützelhard, Frederick's former commissioner in the march of Ancona, as Marquis of the march of Ancona, on account of the latter's attacks on bishops and church property in the area. The pope referred to the march of Ancona as 'partly belonging to the empire but largely to the Church'. Frederick's own perambulation of Romagna, the march, and the duchy of Spoleto,

---

[1] *Liber Pontificalis*, ii, p. 443. The report of this discussion seems to be overlooked by Waley, *P.S.*, pp. 17–18, who here appears to over-stress the advantage gained by Frederick at Venice. My divergence from Waley in some other matters will be apparent in what follows.

[2] Cf. Overmann, *Gräfin Mathilde von Tuscien*, pp. 67–71. Munz's statement that Frederick had *de facto* possessions of the lands (p. 330n.) seems doubtful.

[3] Rom. Sal., p. 294. I think 'Romania' here means Romagna and not the country round Rome, because the same cardinal was found by Frederick at Bertinoro in Romagna (*Lib. Pont.*, ii, p. 444). For the other view see Lenel, *HZ*, cxxviiii, p. 227, n. 1, where the references are not clearly given.

shortly after the peace of Venice, emphasised his determination to stand up for imperial rights there. On the other hand both Ferrara and Bologna remained, as they had been before the peace, outside any meaningful imperial obedience. Ferrara closed the Po to the imperialist Cremona; Bologna remained recalcitrant, and was before long in spite of the truce to renew the war in the Imolese.[1]

The confusion of these years, and the inability of either imperial or papal officials to impose any real order, appeared clearly enough when the imperial chancellor, the warlike Christian of Mainz (one has some difficulty in remembering that he was a bishop), escorted the pope back to Rome.[2] The anti-Pope Calixtus III fled from Viterbo, and with the help of the prefect took refuge in a fort near Albano. Calixtus was the least of the problems of Christian and Alexander. When the popular party of Viterbo received Christian within the walls, the nobles got the help against Christian of a so-called imperial official, Conrad of Montferrat. Conrad had quarrelled with Christian over the custody of the forts which he held for the empire; since he had very close family connections with the Byzantine Empire (he ended his days as King of Jerusalem), it was an easy matter for him to get Greek money to finance a rebellion in the Tuscan patrimony and the duchy. The Romans were also glad for an excuse to attack Viterbo, and took it. So the 'restoration' of papal rights degenerated into a civil war which involved the whole northern patrimony. In September 1179 Conrad allied with the Tuscan towns, and their joint forces kidnapped Christian of Mainz near Camerino. The chancellor of the empire spent two years in prison in the north of the patrimony[3] in the custody of Conrad or his brother Boniface, and was released on payment of a thumping ransom only after Conrad had left for Constantinople.

John the Prefect did homage to Alexander III after the pope's return to Rome in 1177; the pope was admitted to the city with all the customary ceremonies. The senators also did homage to the pope, and 'restored' the Church of St Peter (which may refer either to fortifications or to

---

[1] Cf. F. Güterbock, 'Kaiser, Papst, Lombardenbund nach dem Frieden von Venedig', *Quellen*, xxv (1933–4), pp. 158–91, esp. pp. 167 ff.; Vehse, ibid., xxvii (1936–7), pp. 12–13. See also below.

[2] For what follows see especially Rom. Sal., p. 295; Benedict of Peterborough, *Gesta Regis Henrici*, i (1867), pp. 243–4; *Chron. Rogeri de Hoveden*, ii (1869), pp. 194–5; *I.P.*, ii, p. 177, no. 4. Both the English chronicles quoted were probably written by Roger Howden; see Lady Stenton's 'Roger of Howden and Benedict', *EHR*, lxviii (1953), pp. 574–82.

[3] Cf. Güterbock's article, *Quellen*, xxv, p. 165; D. Hägermann, ibid., xlix (1969), pp. 218–37.

Roman enjoyment of the church revenues) and the other church lands
and tax revenues (*regalia*). Until the end of the great Lateran Council
of 1179 (which was no doubt a source of fat profits for the Romans)
Alexander stayed in Rome. But his reconciliation with Rome was only
superficial; her murderous enmities with the surrounding cities, particularly with Tuscolo, remained a stumbling block. In the summer of 1179
Alexander again left the city for Tuscolo and the Campagna, where his
court stayed until after the release of Christian of Mainz from captivity
in 1181; it then transferred to the northern patrimony, principally to
Viterbo. After his long struggles as pope – and his pontificate was one of
the longest – Alexander was perhaps grateful when death overtook him
at Città Castellana (30 August 1181).

In the area between Rome and the Norman border Alexander had
ruled, after a fashion, from the German withdrawal in 1167 until his
death. Papal deputies in temporal government were not very successful.
Hadrian IV's rector in Campagna was Cardinal Simon, the Abbot of
Subiaco, who was ignominiously chased out of his own abbey. Alexander
appointed Cardinal Vitellius, about whose rectorate (or possibly, legation)
in Campagna nothing is known; the career of a papal rector, a papal
sub-deacon, is equally obscure.[1] Nevertheless, there are signs of activity
by papal administration in the Campagna from 1173 onwards. The pope
and his cardinals or judges intervened in the quarrels of Alatri and
Frosinone, of citizens of Anagni with the neighbouring monastery of
Villamagna, of Sermoneta with the barons of Aquapuzza (who had
been made to submit to Hadrian IV) and of Terracina with Piperno.[2]
In the summer of 1176 Alexander invested the unruly Filippo di Marano
with Genne, and thus ended an extremely turbulent passage in the
history of the abbey of Subiaco.[3]

After the peace of Venice in 1177 there are some signs of papal
assertion in areas which had slipped out of obedience during the schism,

---

[1] *I.P.*, ii, p. 159, no. 23. The possible dates are 1167–70. Galloco the subdeacon, ibid. p. 163,
no. 4.

[2] Alatri: *I.P.*, ii, p. 150, nos. 2, 3 (6 February 1174); Anagni, ibid. p. 14, no. 4 (7 January,
1174), also in De Magistris, *Storia di Anagni*, ii, p. 117, no. 71; Sermoneta, *I.P.*, ii, p. 129,
no. 1 (11 August 1175); Terracina, ibid. p. 119, no. 9 (14 March 1175). The pope sent his
hostiarius, a member of his feudal household, to settle the quarrel of Sermoneta.

[3] Filippo de Marano had ejected Cardinal Simon from the abbey and installed his own brother
Rainaldo as abbot. Simon was not able to re-enter the abbey until Rainaldo's death in 1167.
The chronology is extremely unclear. The bull of 11 July 1176 is in *Gött. Nachr.*, 1908, pp.
258-60. Other references in Ganzer, *Entwicklung des auswärtigen Kardinalats*, pp. 102–3. There
is doubt about the date of Filippo's ejection of Simon, which may have been a early as 1158 or
1159.

such as Città di Castello and Montefeltro, in the Apennines.[1] In Campagna the pope strengthened his possession in the Alban hills by acquiring by exchange the important fort commanding the pass of Lariano; there is also some suggestion that other nobles in the Alban hills such as the Gandulph who gave his name to Castel Gandolfo, lost their fortresses to church claimants in the wars of Alexander III.[2] The position of church property in Rome and the Campagna was by no means desperate; the bishops, the Roman churches, and the curial bureaucracy were powerful still.[3] Particularly interesting is a lawsuit in Veroli which seems to show the papal chamberlain, Franco, using his great influence to frustrate the drawing up of papal letters, and behaving in a despotic way.[4] The Bishop of Veroli was tightly connected with the directing elements of the commune, employing his money and power to purchase land and feudal influence in Monte San Giovanni and the surrounding villages; the pope meanwhile tried to protect the city from the seditious activity of the exiles, and of the nobles of Alatri.[5] At Anagni the bishop was buying landed property, and the pope conceded to the town rights in the castle of Sgurgola, which Hadrian IV had earlier granted to a feudatory.[6] In the upper valley of the Aniene, Pope Alexander was attempting to keep order by inciting one feudal baron to make war on another.[7] Further south, he enfeoffed other minor barons for the promise of feudal service, as Hadrian IV had done.[8] No doubt the pope kept order only with the help of the much-favoured Frangipani, and with that of other feudal barons; but there were few if any feudal states

---

[1] *I.P.*, iv, p. 105, no. 3 (14 January 1178), which is a re-issue of Lucius II's privilege of 1144. A census of one den. Lucen. was to be paid for each hearth (Pflugk-Hartung reads *locos*, for *focos*). The restoration to the pope of a quarter of the castrum of Maiolo, near Montefeltro, ibid. p. 229 (*Liber censuum*, i, p. 406), 7 April 1181.

[2] See the bull of 2 April 1183 recording a judgement of Alexander III, in N. Ratti, *Storia di Genzano con note e documenti* (Rome, 1797), p. 10; cf. *I.P.* i, p. 175, no. 15; ibid. ii, p. 33, no. 1, and the later indemnity, *Lib. cens.*, i, p. 255. The Church of S. Maria in Aquiro fortified Genzano.

[3] The material for Roman churches for this period published by Egidi, Ferri, Schiaparelli and others does not reveal any startling losses of church property. See below, p. 225.

[4] Scaccia-Scarafoni, *Le carte*, no. 182, pp. 231–4 (not recorded in Kehr, *I.P.*), 18 May 1181. This is a valuable document for the early history of the papal chamberlain.

[5] *I.P.*, ii, p. 163, nos. 3–5; cf. Falco, *ASR*, xlii (1919), pp. 592–5.

[6] Above, p. 195. Cf. Falco, loc. cit.; *ASR*, vii (1884), p. 268; De Magistris, *Storia di Anagni*, ii, no. 77, p. 128.

[7] The Lord of Cave, against Raone of Roiata (*I.P.*, ii, pp. 50–1). A document entirely misunderstood by C. Pacaut, *Alexandre III* (Paris, 1956), p. 214, no. 3. Pacaut makes the document refer to Rieti.

[8] Enfeoffment of Falvaterra near Ceprano, 11 January 1178, *I.P.* ii, p. 173, no. 1. They paid 300 *lib. prov.*, and promised the usual *servitium*.

where the central power did not depend at least to some extent on such alliances.

Even while Alexander was at the conference of Venice in 1777 he was extremely active in settling the affairs of the churches of Romagna.[1] The rest of the pontificate saw the continuation of papal competition with the emperor's officials in Romagna; Ferrara and Bologna in particular remained firmly anti-imperialist, and in 1180 Alexander protested to Bologna and other Romagnols because they were breaking the truce signed with the empire.[2] Frederick's protest to Alexander in 1178 over Ferrara's barring of the Po to the Cremonese suggests that the emperor recognised the papal position of direct government in Ferrara.

IV

The successor to Pope Alexander, Lucius III (elected 1 September 1181) refused to pay the Romans the bribes which were customary after a papal election. He refused also to let them vent their spite against Tuscolo, whose inhabitants had begun to rebuild the town after the demolition of 1173. So the papal war with Rome was resumed, and the Romans devastated the Alban hills once more, until Christian of Mainz returned to take the offensive against them and their lands. The Roman attack on Christian in Tuscolo was thrown back, but in the summer of 1183 the soldier archbishop died (of poison, it was claimed, though more likely of fever). Another German official, Berthold of Künsberg, came to take Christian's place. The Romans wasted Campagna, and took the hil fort of Rocca 'di Papa' (which is probably a corruption of *Cavum*). Lucius sought money from far-off England and from other princes to pay mercenaries or make peace, and according to the English chronicler Roger Howden he did make peace with Rome. The war, and German domination of the patrimony north of Rome, made Lucius's political position difficult; but his administration nevertheless functioned in Campagna,[3] and he probably exacted an oath of fealty from Orvieto.[4]

---

[1] e.g. *I.P.*, v, p. 81, no. 6; ibid. p. 65, nos. 230–2; ibid. p. 258, no. 12. Ibid. p. 66, no. 233 is the concession to the Archbishop of Ravenna of the newly acquired rights of the Roman See in Bertinoro by the will of Cavalcaconte, but this failed to take effect. See above.

[2] *I.P.*, v, p. 67, no. 235; p. 273, no. 10. See also above, and cf. Hessel, *Bologna*, pp. 128 ff.

[3] Waley, *P.S.*, p. 20, is of another opinion. Cf. *I.P.*, ii, pp. 55 (Farfa), ibid. p. 129: and *Annales Ceccan.* (*MGH*, xix), p. 287. (Landulph of Ceccano, Ceccano and Sermoneta). Also *I.P.*, ii, p. 163, no. 5 (Veroli and the nobles of Alatri); ibid, p. 169, no. 10 (Lucius's agreement with the lords of Monte San Giovanni; cf. p. 161, no. 30); ibid. p. 98, no. 62 (the citation of

Lucius shared and indeed accentuated the aggressive attitude which his predecessor had adopted towards heresy, and he sharpened the penalties and prohibitions which had been issued at the Lateran Council of 1179. The heresies which were spreading over Europe in the late twelfth century were in part a protest against the immense wealth of the Church. That heresy should have flourished in the papal patrimony, which was the most conspicuous of all the great clerical landholdings, was certainly no accident; this had been proved already by the success in Rome of Arnold of Brescia. In Romagna some of the communes had been compelled to impose on their incoming elected officers an annual oath not to offend against church property, besides an oath not to receive or abet heretics. Both these oaths had been abandoned in Rimini, which was an ancient papal demesne. In Faenza there was a general attack on church property.[1]

But the great unfinished political game, which transcended all local affairs, was the still open question whether there could be 'perpetual peace' between the popes and the empire. The peace of Constance, which settled the main questions of imperial relations with the Italian communes, was signed in June 1183. As Frederick wrote in a remarkably frank letter to Lucius III shortly after the Constance agreement, the 1177 peace of Venice between Empire and Church was as far as the territorial questions were concerned likely to give rise to further disputes. The imperial ambassadors had already put to Lucius the first of a remarkable series of imaginative and far-reaching proposals, made by the empire in the search of 'perpetual peace' with the Church. The first proposal was that from the sum total of the cash revenues enjoyed by the empire in Italy, a tenth share should be paid in future to the pope, and a ninth to the cardinals. Such a handsome offer would only have been made on the understanding that the Church gave up all or most of its territorial claims.[2] The alternative offer (made in spite of the doubts which Frederick professed about the practicability of settling the

---

Riccardo of Arsoli to judgement over Arsoli and Roviano; cf. also Allodi and Levi, p. 206, no. 158, Mirzio, pp. 273–4; *I.P.*, ii, p. 120, no. 13 (the grievances of Terracina against the Frangipani). The presence or absence of an official calling himself papal rector of Campagna seems to me irrelevant to the question of whether or not papal rule was respected there.
[4] *MGH, Const. et Acta publica*, i, no. 322, p. 461, lines 4–5.

[1] Tolosanus (*RRIISS*, xxviii, pt. 1), pp. 92–3; *I.P.*, iv, p. 163, no. 22. It is significant that, though involving an oath to be sworn by the incoming consuls, the bull to Rimini is addressed to the bishop and not to the commune.
[2] The text in *MGH, Const. et acta publica*, i, no. 296, p. 420. I agree here with Waley (pp. 22–3) that the two offers were alternative and not complementary. The reference to the cardinals is an important indication of the strength of their corporate financial privileges at this time.

territorial question) was that local arbitrators should be appointed to look into the whole complex question of the ownership of imperial and papal lands in Italy. Where it seemed desirable, imperial and papal lands might be exchanged. The Church would then hold the lands attributed to it freely, except for the payment of *fodrum* (the hospitality duty which was, after all, the main imperial exaction).

That a pope even in a disastrously weak political position would accept such terms was extremely unlikely. The offer, indeed, in its sweeping impracticality recalls the offer made by Henry V to Paschal II in 1111. To give up all church lands in favour of a rent whose payment depended entirely on imperial goodwill would make the Roman bishop into the emperor's serving man. And equally, to expose all church lands in Italy to an enquiry likely to be more severe than Edward I's 'Quo Warranto' enquiries in England a century later, would be extremely disadvantageous for the Church. As for the idea of exchanging lands, the hard bargains of this sort which Henry VIII enforced on the English bishoprics in the Reformation period are probably the sort of transaction which Frederick had in mind. Certainly the papal position was in some ways not very strong.[1] But though the active power of the popes was small, their passive strength was immense. Through law and custom, landed power, financial resources, control of intellectual expression and communication, the *sacerdotium* was able in the last resort to maintain its hold on European society against old-fashioned aggression such as that of Frederick I and Henry II of England, and against new challenges such as those of the merchant-usurers and the heretics.

The ground covered in the negotiations between emperor and pope was far wider than the Italian territorial issue alone. The pope was anxious for imperial help with the crusade, and against the heretical sects. The strongest card in the papal hand was the German dynastic question; it would be impossible to crown the young Henry emperor in his father's lifetime, as Frederick wanted, without papal consent. But the projected marriage between Constance, the heiress to the Sicilian kingdom, and Frederick's heir Henry, which was being discussed in early 1184, threatened to revolutionise Italian politics. That the pope knew of these negotiations before the agreement was published in October 1184 is quite possible; that he was actually a party to them, and gave his

[1] Cf. K. Wenck, 'Die römischen Päpste zwischen Alexander III. und Innocenz III.', *Papsttum und Kaisertum* (Munich, 1926), pp. 415–74.

encouragement to the match has never been proved.[1] Few historians are willing to attribute such disinterested motives to the popes.

Lucius and Frederick met at Verona in the autumn of 1184. All outstanding questions between the empire and the Holy See were discussed, including that of the Matildine lands. But no result was reached. Ferrara, where a papal count had been ruling earlier in Lucius's pontificate, and where Lucius seems to have been contemplating a prolonged stay, was also discussed at Verona; quite possibly Frederick asked for its transfer to him along with the other Matildine lands.[2]

Lucius died (25 November 1185), and the brief era of good feelings ended. His successor, Urban III (the former Archbishop of Milan), was not very well disposed towards Frederick, whose promise to co-operate with the new pope was soon broken. The hostile line taken by Urban about north Italy, and also about the disputed see of Trier, led to the dispatch of a German army under Frederick's son Henry. By June 1186 Narni, Viterbo and Perugia had been occupied, while the imperialist Duke of Spoleto captured and ransomed clergymen in the duchy. The town of Orvieto, which had fought imperialist nobles during the schism, resisted Henry, and was made to submit after a siege. Imperialist partisans were easily found among the Roman nobility, and one of them (possibly Leo de Monumento) was invested by Henry with the clearly papal town of Sutri; the king referred to rights exercised there by the empire for the preceding thirty years. The young king marched south of Rome wasting the land and besieging towns; only the papal fortress of Fumone and one or two other castles like Lariano held out against him. He found Roman nobles to collaborate with him; the Frangipani took his side and treated Terracina as an enemy town, torturing its inhabitants on the rack 'in the German manner'.[3] The pope remained shut up in Verona, powerless to influence events in the Tuscan patrimony, though his numerous interventions in the affairs of the churches of Ravenna and elsewhere in Romagna suggest that he was not without influence in eastern Italy. When he had to leave Verona, Urban fled to the still faithful city of Ferrara, where he died (20 October 1187). In Ferrara his successor Gregory VIII was elected and consecrated.

Gregory VIII reigned only for three months. His negotiations with

---

[1] Cf. J. Haller, 'Heinrich VI. und die römische Kirche', *MIöG*, xxxv (1914), pp. 384–454, 545–669. Haller's thesis has not been generally accepted.

[2] Cf. P. Zerbi, 'Un inedito dell' Archivio Vaticano e il convegno di Verona', *Aevum*, xxviii (1954), pp. 470–83; Vehse, *Quellen*, xxvii (1936–7), pp. 15–16. Vehse's use of the document later printed by Zerbi is rather inadequate.

[3] Contatore, *De historia Terracinensi*, p. 56.

King Henry did not have time to lead to anything. He was of a notably more idealistic stamp than his predecessor or successor: the Roman annalist says that he wanted to recognise imperial rights, and attributes to him the remark: 'Popes and cardinals may not safely take up arms and wage war: they should only give to the poor, and praise the Lord day and night.' This certainly meant a conciliatory, appeasing policy with the empire, though how far Gregory would have gone in this direction had he lived cannot be known. In the administration of canon law, which was the foundation of the whole papal position, Gregory was a vigorous innovator.[1] The difference between popes like Gregory and other popes could only be a distinction between more pious and less pious bureaucrats, and Gregory's policies could not differ in kind from those of any other holder of his office.

V

On 19 December 1187 the cardinals elected a pope of a very different stamp and origin. The Roman Paolo Scolari had built a palace for himself beside the basilica of S. Maria Maggiore (where he had been brought up) even while he was Bishop of Palestrina. Though his unscrupulousness may have been exaggerated by some,[2] he was certainly a realistic man of business. The first Roman to occupy the papal throne for thirty-five years, Clement III took on himself to solve the quarrel with the Roman people which had remained open during practically the whole of that period.

In February 1188 Clement III entered Rome. On 31 May his pact with the Roman people was drawn up. It was by no means a complete victory for the papacy, and its most important political clauses were modelled on the treaty which had been drafted, but perhaps never executed, in 1149.[3] In other respects it reflected the shortlived agreements with Alexander III. In agreeing to restore the 'senate and city'

---

[1] Cf. W. Holtzmann, 'Die Dekretalen Gregors VIII.', *MIöG*, lviii (1950), pp. 113–23.

[2] Wenck, *Papsttum und Kaisertum*, p. 429, 'der haltlose Finanzkünstler'. The opinions of the Canterbury monks, on which Wenck relies, are much influenced by the ups and downs of their lawsuit. Cf. the favourable opinion they pronounced on Clement a few weeks after his election, when they thought he was going to decide in their favour: *Epistolae Cantuarienses* (*R.S.*, 1865), p. 178. Clement III was not popular in England: Richard I was said to have identified him with anti-Christ (*Gesta Regis Ricardi*, ii, p. 154).

[3] Cf. the conveniently collected texts in Bartoloni, *Codice Diplomatico del Senato Romano*, pp. 9–10, 31, 57–8, 68–74. Bartoloni's edition of the 1188 treaty is better than earlier ones (e.g. his *usure* for *mensure*).

to the pope, the Romans were not therefore offering more than they had been prepared to give soon after the original revolution; the oath to be sworn by the senators, though modified, was the 'customary' oath, and the guarantee by which five men from each sub-district (*contrada*) were to swear fealty to the pope was like a similar guarantee in the 1149 document. The most novel part of the political content was that the mint of Rome was restored to the pope, with reservations. The most important concession by the pope was over Tuscolo, which Alexander and his successors had tried to defend from Roman aggression for at least twenty years. Clement III as a Roman was less prepared to take a hard line over Tuscolo. He promised if the town failed to submit to Rome by January of 1189 to excommunicate the Tusculans and mobilise papal Campagna against them. When they submitted, the walls and defensive ditches (*carbonaria*) of the town, fortress, and 'suburbs' (i.e. Frascati) would be demolished, and never rebuilt during Clement's lifetime. He also promised not to defend Tivoli if the Romans decided to attack it.

The heart of the 1188 agreement was its financial clauses, which committed the papacy to heavy payments, some recurring and others not. The Romans agreed to return St Peter's and the other Roman churches, and those suburbicarian bishoprics which they had seized. This seizure of church revenues had been ruthless, and must have meant a serious financial loss to the Church. Roman citizens had been compensated by their government for ransom of their persons, horses and goods in the war against Alexander III and the Germans by payments made from the offerings on the altars of St Peter's.[1] Small wonder that Christians from less sophisticated parts of Europe denounced Roman avarice! In order to indemnify Romans who claimed damages or war losses the most elaborate arrangements were made. Those who had previously been allocated church revenues were to receive money from the third share which was allotted to the senate from the profits of the papal mint, until both principal and interest had been repaid (the open reference to usury is interesting, nine years after its prohibition at the Lateran Council). Others received payment of compensation from the chamberlain of the Roman Church, according to terms determined by an arbitration committee of cardinals. This committee went right

---

[1] G. Falco, 'Documenti Guerreschi di Roma medievale', *BISI*, no. 40 (1921), pp. 1–6.

through the claims, dealing with the regions of Rome in turn; the investigation took from August 1188 until February 1189.[1]

The Romans returned the *regalia* to the pope, except Ponte Lucano, which they probably retained because of its economic and strategic importance in a future war against Tivoli. The customary gifts or *beneficia* were to be paid by the pope to the senators and other Romans – presumably he had already paid the *beneficium* of 500 pounds which was usual on his first entry, and the treaty was made with Pope Clement only, without mention of his successors. The lesser donatives, including the present-called *presbyterium,* which the pope gave at various points of the liturgical year to senators and many other Roman officials, were to continue.[2] Finally the pope was to pay 100 pounds of Provins a year for the upkeep of the walls of Rome. The treaty represented a certain financial load for the papacy, as far as settling the war damage claims was concerned. It is not evident that the annual payments would have been an intolerable burden, but they were not negligible. The *presbyterium* of one *malachinus* for each of fifty-six senators meant eight ounces of gold, which was perhaps at a very rough guess three-quarters of the annual oblations at St Peter's. The 100 pounds for the walls is a twentieth of the 2,000 pounds which the German historian Pfaff has reckoned as the approximate annual cash income from ascertained sources of the papacy.[3] This income was itself not very large – perhaps a tenth of the contemporary income of the English kingdom. The impecuniosity of the Roman court at this time may have been exaggerated by some modern historians,[4] as its avarice was perhaps exaggerated by contemporaries. But the importunacy of the Romans was certainly an embarrassment. They might have claimed that they had made appreciable financial concessions in the 1188 agreement: the renunciation of the mint, the return of the income of the churches and the rest of the *regalia,* and finally the clause renouncing transit taxes on petitioners to the *curia.*[5]

---

[1] Documents listed in *I.P.*, i, pp. 199–200. The total payments approach 400 *lib. prov.*, but most of the payments settle only half the claims, leaving a further sum still owing.

[2] *Ordo Romanus xii*, in the *Liber censuum*, i, pp. 291, 299. Cf. also Bartoloni, *Codice diplomatico del Senato Romano*, no. 44, p. 78.

[3] Cf. V. Pfaff, 'Die Einnahmen der römischen Kurie am Ende des 12. Jahrhunderts', *VSWG*, xl (1953), pp. 97–188; Ordo Romanus, xii. Pfaff's figures do not include the income of the Roman churches, or the income from taxes on bulls or on justice, or the dues in kind from the papal estates, or the profits of the mint. Cf. Brühl, *Fodrum, Gistum, Servitium Regis*, i, p. 751.

[4] e.g., by Wenck, in the article quoted above.

[5] The English envoys at the papal court in 1170 only secured their transit through Rome by giving the senators 20 pounds: *Materials for the history of Thomas Becket*, R.S., vii, p. 485.

Early in 1189 the negotiations with the empire resulted in new agreements. The pope agreed to crown the young King Henry as emperor. The empire agreed to restore the places in the Papal State which it had seized in the preceding period, though this restoration was only possessory, and was made without prejudice to imperial claims to ownership of at least some of the rights which were given up. King Henry released both the unnamed barons of Campagna and 'Romania' (i.e. the area round Rome) from oaths taken to his father or himself, and the men of certain named towns of which the most northerly was Orvieto, the most southerly Terracina.[1] The king sent envoys to order these places to swear obedience to the pope to obey him 'as lord'. But the caution with which the document is worded shows the empire guarding its rights, ready to hold the pope to ransom for his possessions once again if this should be politically convenient. 'Perpetual peace' with the Church was far from King Henry's mind.

When Clement III died (late March 1191) the Romans had still not succeeded in getting the better of Tuscolo; the mutilation of Tusculan prisoners only stiffened resistance. Nor had papal help against Tuscolo been effective.[2] Clement's successor was the very aged Cardinal Hyacinth Bobo, of a well-known Roman family, who had when he came to the papal throne already been an active political cardinal for half a century. Although some historians have accused him of weakness there is no real sign that Celestine III was anything less than a firm upholder of the rights of his office, in spite of his eighty-five or so years.[3] Frederick Barbarossa had died on crusade in Anatolia in the summer of 1190. A few weeks after Celestine's election, by 12 April 1191, Henry had reached the lake of Anguillara north of Rome; three days later the imperial coronation took place. Prior to the coronation the Romans approached Celestine and asked him to obtain from Henry the possession of Tuscolo, which they claimed Celestine's predecessor had promised the Romans under the 1188 agreement.[4] According to the English chronicler

---

[1] *MGH, Const. et acta publica*, i, p. 460, no. 322. Others were Viterbo, Tivoli, Corneto, Vetralla, Orte, Narni, Amelia, Tuscolo. Petronianum and Cincellam (? Petrignano and Centocelle, near Civitavecchia) were to be restored to Cardinal Hyacinth Bobo, the future Celestine III. Another clause concerned Massa Marittima, in Tuscany.

[2] *I.P.*, ii, p. 45, no. 16 (23 July 1188), to the Abbot of Grottaferrata, looks like an attempt to wage economic warfare against Tuscolo; the abbot is not only forbidden to enfeoff laymen with the possessions of the monastery, but also told not to sell them grain.

[3] Cf. V. Pfaff, 'Papst Coelestin III.', *ZSSRG, Kan. Abt.*, lxxvii (1961), pp. 109–28; Zerbi, *Papato, Impero e Republica Christiana*, pp. 175–6.

[4] *Chron. Rogerii de Hoveden (R.S.)*, iii), pp. 101–5. P. Zerbi, 'Ebbe parte Celestino III nella consegna di Tuscolo ai Romani?', *Aevum*, xxviii (1954), pp. 445–69, points out that on a

Howden, Celestine agreed to represent to Henry that the king ought to help the pope fulfil the 1188 treaty.[1] In spite of having acepted an oath of fealty from Tuscolo at some time before 1189, Henry in his anxiety to be crowned agreed to do what was asked. It was a dubious decision, since the Tusculans were clearly guilty of nothing but resistance to Roman greed, and the memory of the Battle of Monte Porzio in 1167, in which the Tusculans had been the allies of the Germans against the Romans, was by no means forgotten. German troops had subsequently assisted Tuscolo under Lucius III, only a few years earlier. Neither the pope (in spite of being a Roman) nor the emperor can have been entirely happy about the business; it is noticeable that Celestine asked for the handing over of Tuscolo not on grounds of justice but of 'necessity', which in the Middle Ages often meant what was later understood as *raison d'état*.[2] But though the decision was criticised, Henry made it. The day after his coronation (according to Howden) he handed over Tuscolo to Celestine; on the day after that, the pope handed the city over to the Romans. They destroyed it stone by stone and massacred a good many of the population; one might be doubtful about this statement in the chronicles, if it was not that modern excavation of Tuscolo has revealed nothing but classical remains. When it is remembered that most of the town had been destroyed twenty years earlier, and that it had never been more than a biggish village, the destruction is less remarkable. The Romans immediately carried out their part of the treaty by transferring the Tusculan lands to the Church; Celestine then re-granted the lands to various Roman churches. Thus the Church profited in a transaction which it is hard to describe except as one of betrayal and murder. But it might in fairness to Celestine be said that the temptation to allow Rome to wreak its will on Tuscolo dated as far back in papal policy as Alexander III's concession to allow the Romans to destroy the walls of Tuscolo, in 1172.

VI

William of Sicily had died in 1189, and his death faced the popes with the most serious threat to their political system since the days of Henry

---

strict interpretation, the 1188 treaty did not require the pope to hand over Tuscolo to the Romans.

[1] Howden's information about Rome at this time probably came from someone accompanying Archbishop Walter of Rouen and Queen Eleanor. Cf. *EHR*, lxviii (1953), pp. 574 ff. E. Jamison, *Proceedings of the British Academy*, xxiv (1938), pp. 25–9.

[2] Roger Howden, loc. cit.

IV and Gregory VII. The Normans had not always been kind to the popes, but the disappearance of independent Norman Sicily would knock out the linch pin of the papal cartwheel. Who would then supply the popes with money, troops and refuge, as Alexander III had been supplied in the darkest days of the schism? Not unnaturally, Clement and Celestine supported the claim to the throne of Tancred, the bastard nephew of the dead King William, against Henry VI's claim in right of his wife Constance. The failure of Henry VI's military expedition to the kingdom of Sicily, after the imperial coronation of 1191, was received by Pope Celestine with hardly-disguised glee. In 1192 Tancred swore homage to Celestine for the kingdom of Sicily. But it was only a respite, and the last days of Norman Sicily had indeed come. Tancred's death early in 1194 made things easy for Henry, who now had only the infant William III to contend with. In a short campaign which did not increase his reputation for mercifulness or chivalry, the emperor in 1194 took his Sicilian inheritance.

Financial administration had been one of the main concerns of the popes who followed Alexander III. Exceptionally the chamberlain, the official in charge of the finances in general, was retained from the pontificate of Clement III to that of Celestine III. This was the Cardinal Cencius, the best known of all the medieval papal chamberlains, later himself to become pope as Honorius III. Collections of documents illustrating the rights of the Roman See were made from the earliest times. These collections frequently included extracts from early rent books; the eleventh-century work of Cardinal Deusdedit included many such. A later rental may have been consulted in the mid-twelfth century in the case of the Bishop of Rimini. In the 1180s Cardinal Albinus made an important collection of titles and canons. But the most systematic of the investigations into financial rights was the *Liber censuum* which Cardinal Cencius began to compile in 1192. V. Pfaff has made a thorough examination of these titles, and has concluded that of 682 *census* payments which his research has discovered to have been due to the Holy See in 1192, only 154 were not noted by Cencius. Medieval accounting methods were a good deal less systematic than the methods of some modern historical research, but when the limitations are allowed for, the *Liber censuum* seems an honest and substantial attempt to reduce the complex and various evidence of the papal titles to some sort of order.

I do not think that anyone who has toiled through the labyrinth of the *Liber censuum* would cite it as one of the great achievements of human reason; it is only a particularly complicated cartulary, of a sort which was proliferating among clerics all over Europe at that time. The autocratic simplicity which lies behind the English Domesday Book, of a century earlier, is foreign to it. The *Liber censuum* is a magpie sort of book, which records things from the forged Donation of Constantine to the purchases of mills by Hadrian IV. It belongs to a concept of life which, while we call it 'bureaucratic', was by our standards domestic. For all the learning which we have lavished on the orderly workings of the papal bureaucracy, one has to remember that Pope Clement III admitted that he often could not remember to whom he had committed the hearing of a lawsuit,[1] and that the papal liturgical manual is careful to record that on Christmas Eve the Bishop of Albano was wont to offer 'an excellent meal' to the papal *curia,* and to send them 'two fine boxes of pork'.[2] No one knows how important the farmlands of the Roman churches continued to be at this time in the economy of the Roman court, but it is probable that the bishop's pigs, scrabbling in the woods above the Alban Lake, were resources of a kind more important for the Roman clerks than the tribute money from distant transalpine monasteries. The patrimonies which were the concern of individual Roman churches, and not of the papal chamber, are naturally not recorded in the *Liber censuum,* but they would have to be considered in any attempt to work out the material resources of the Roman Church as a whole.

There are signs that neither the papal chamber nor the individual Roman churches were struck by absolute poverty during the last decade of the twelfth century. In 1193 Cencius the chamberlain received back from Pietro Latro and his family some villages and strongpoints which had been pledged with Civitavecchia to the father of Pietro Latro by Innocent II. Although Civitavecchia was meant to have been handed back to Alexander III by the Latri, the sum paid for redemption in 1193 was close enough to the original total sum pledged (200 ounces of gold, which was according to Pfaff's tables close in value to the original payment of 200 pounds of pence of Pavia).[3] Since they concern the same area, and since the families of the Latri and of John of Vico were closely connected, it is likely that a transaction two years later was bound up with that of 1193; it is also possible that

---

[1] See the document printed by Holtzmann, in *MIöG*, lviii (1950), pp. 113–23.
[2] *Ordo Romanus*, xi (p. 125 of Mabillon's edition, *Museum Italicum*, vol. ii).
[3] *I.P.*, i, pp. 190–1. Cf. C. Calisse, *Storia di Civitavecchia* (Florence, 1898), pp. 130–4, 139–40.

Pope Celestine himself had a personal interest in the area.[1] In 1195 Cencius received back for the Roman Church the town and county of Città Castellana and the town of Montalto, both in the northern patrimony, which had been pledged by Hadrian IV to the then Prefect of Rome (John of Vico) and his family for the very large sum of 1,000 marks. This sum had been repaid, and physical possession of the places given back to the papal representative.[2]

There is some doubt whether Celestine's position *vis-à-vis* the Romans was strong enough in 1192–3 for him to exercise more than a rather feeble control over the patrimonies.[3] The Romans had at some time between June 1191 and October 1192 overturned the rule of the fifty-six or more senators, and against papal wishes substituted a single senator, Benedict Carushomo, who according to the unreliable testimony of the *Gesta Innocentii III* governed Sabina and the Maritime province and sent his judges there. This Roman revolution was probably a popular reaction against the gradual infusion of magnates and 'captains' from the Campagna into the senate. Carushomo had by 22 May 1194 been succeeded by John Capoccio, with whom the pope's relations were good,[4] but who in 1196 is found with the prefect in attendance on the emperor.

Henry VI's use of physical force to place pressure on the pope was entirely ruthless. In 1194 he carried out a second savage devastation of the Campagna south of Rome. His brother Philip, his representative in Tuscany, carried out aggression north of Rome as far away as Vetralla, though the restoration of Città Castellana to the pope by the provincial nobility in 1195 suggests that German control was not continuous or complete. If the chronicler Howden is right in suggesting that Henry guaranteed to restore papal patrimonies before his coronation in 1191, then he broke his word, doubtless because of Celestine's partisanship for Tancred. But even if a promise was not made at the coronation, Henry was bound by the agreement of 1189.

In the summer of 1196 Henry rather grudgingly agreed to the restoration of the village of Vetralla, north of Rome, which the pope claimed that the emperor's brother Philip had taken. Radicofani and the border

---

[1] See above, p. 222. See also *I.P.*, i, p. 60, no. 3, for a lawsuit in course in 1195 about Oliario in the territory of Albano.

[2] *I.P.*, ii, pp. 186–7, nos. 3–8.

[3] The *census* payments listed in *Liber censuum*, i, pp. 377–8, suggest that the *curia* was getting normal taxes in Sabina, Narni and Amelia, Cf. also Celestine's citation of the lords of Civitella, *Chron. Subl.* (*RRIISS*), p. 277 (wrong date): *I.P.*, ii, p. 98, no. 64.

[4] *I.P.*, v, p. 470, no. 55; cf. *Gött. Nachr.*, (1900), p. 70.

forts were occupied by Germans. At the end of the year negotiations were still dragging on slowly, and Henry accused Celestine of protracting them deliberately. An important part of Henry's objectives was in eastern Italy.[1] The nomination of the imperial official Markward of Anweiler as Duke of Ravenna and Romagna, and Marquis of Ancona, marked an important step in the attempt to impose imperial rule on the area which secured communications between the kingdom of Sicily, north Italy and Germany. Clement III and Celestine III both attempted to meet the imperial challenge by close supervision of the churches of Umbria and Romagna,[2] sending legates and deciding lawsuits which involved the relations of communes with church lands. In the duchy of Spoleto Henry appointed as duke the magnate Conrad of Urslingen (who had earlier been granted the same duchy by Barbarossa, and who was made vicar of the kingdom of Sicily). The important town of Perugia, which was clearly papal, had earlier submitted to the empire. On 4 September 1196 Celestine encouraged the Bishop of Fermo not to flee the country in face of the persecution of churches which Markward of Anweiler was carrying out all over the march of Ancona.[3]

The political importance of the papacy, and the strategic importance of the papal patrimony, were such that Henry VI was prepared to mix very substantial blandishments with the bullying he also employed. At the end of 1196 he referred to offers he had made to Pope Celestine 'for the profit and honour of the pope's person and the Church' which went much further than the offers made by his father or any of his predecessors in the empire. What these offers were we do not know, and the only available indications of their nature either come from that unreliable gossip, Gerald of Wales, or have to be deduced from the very dubious evidence of the document which purports to be the will of Henry VI.[4] If the 'will' is accepted as evidence of the emperor's intentions (which it probably cannot be, though it may reflect negotiations between the pope and Markward of Anweiler), then the empire

---

[1] Cf. Hessel, *Bologna*, pp. 130 ff.; Vehse, *Quellen*, xxvii, p. 16; Ficker, *Forschungen*, ii, pp. 221 ff.
[2] e.g., *I.P.*, iv, p. 10, nos. 5–9, p. 12, no. 5, p. 48, nos. 4–6, p. 64, nos. 4–9, p. 73, no. 3, p. 97, no. 17 (Celestine III's legate, August 1197), p. 181, no. 6, p. 210, no. 2; ibid., v, pp. 72–3, nos. 267–73, pp. 99–100, nos. 15–19, p. 126, no. 9, p. 13, no. 3, p. 148, no. 5, pp. 186–7, nos. 35–6, p. 196, no. 7, p. 219, nos. 52–5, pp. 225–6, nos. 19–24, pp. 253–4, nos. 40–5, pp. 274–5, nos. 1–4, pp. 282–3, nos. 26–30, p. 287, nos. 9–12 etc.
[3] *I.P.*, iv. p. 138, no. 17.
[4] Waley, *P.S.*, pp. 27–9; Pfaff, 'Die Gesta Innocenz III. und das Testament Heinrichs VI.', *ZSSRG, Kan. Abt.,* l (1964), pp. 78–126. For the feudal nature of the concessions made to Markward by the Emperor in Romagna, see T. C. Van Cleve, *Markward of Anweiler and the Sicilian Regency* (Princeton, 1937), pp. 48–9.

was perhaps willing to concede the pope the Matildine lands, with certain named exceptions. It is clear that in spite of the great physical weakness of the papacy in face of imperial power at this time, the emperor was aware of the intrinsic strength of Celestine's position, and was prepared to make big concessions in the pursuit of the 'perpetual peace' which had eluded popes and emperors ever since the end of the Alexandrine schism in 1177.

But the wheel of fortune, that favourite device of the medieval moralist to symbolise the discomforture of kings and princes, was about to take a fatal turn for the house of Hohenstaufen. On 28 September 1197 the thirty-one-year-old emperor died of dysentery in Sicily; the ninety-year-old pope outlived him by four months, and had time before his death to set in motion the policies which were in time to lead to the utter defeat of the empire on most of the great issues which were at that moment in debate.

Chapter 7

The foundation of the Papal State

I

Innocent III, of the family of the counts of Segni, was elected pope on 8 January 1198. In zeal, energy and political ability this young pope (he was born in 1160–1 and was a child by comparison with his predecessor) was the equal of any other Roman pontiff of the Middle Ages. As a nobleman of the Roman Campagna he renewed the tradition of his patron, the Roman Clement III. His political knowledge of the Papal State and his family with their troops and local alliances made it especially easy for him to effect, in the new political conditions brought about by the death of the Emperor Henry VI, the territorial 'recuperations' of the Roman See. If the Papal State has a founder, it is Innocent III, not only for his actions in claiming lands as papal property, but for the organisation and the institutions which he gave to the papal territories.

Few of the policies of Innocent III were innovatory, and that of the recuperation of papal lands was no exception. In the autumn of 1197, after the death of Henry VI but before that of Celestine III, papal representatives toured the duchy of Spoleto and the march of Ancona taking oaths of fealty to the pope, and inciting the provincials to throw off German tyranny for ever, and to accept papal protection.[1] At the same time papal legates gave their patronage to a league directed against the empire by the communes of Tuscany and of the northern part of the papal Tuscan patrimony. It is significant that at this moment of the birth of the Papal State, the papal provincials combined in a league with the Tuscan communes which were outside papal

---

[1] For all that follows see D. P. Waley, *The Papal State in the Thirteenth Century* (1961) (hereafter Waley, *P.S.*) which is fundamental. For Innocent see H. Tillmann, *Papst Innocenz III.* (Bonn, 1954), and Miss Tillmann's articles quoted there; F. Kempf, *Papsttum und Kaisertum bei Innocenz III.* (Rome, 1954), especially pp. 1–27. For Celestine's actions after Henry VI's death see Waley, p. 31; Tillmann, p. 84; Kempf, p. 10; Pfaff, 'Die Gesta Innocenz III.', pp. 84 ff.

jurisdiction. Innocent III saw both the political and the juristic dangers of this alliance, and after his accession he attempted to deal with both, by alleging that the duchy of Tuscany was assigned to the Church in the ancient privileges (an untrue statement), and by complaining that the league was paying insufficient respect to papal rights and authority.[1]

The legal basis of the recuperations of the Church was that of the Carolingian donations. In some areas such as the duchy of Spoleto these donations had never taken political effect; in others such as the march of Ancona the papal claims had only partially and at very remote periods been acknowledged by the empire. Only spasmodically and at long intervals had the popes made even indirect references to these claims during the twelfth century, and although it has been maintained that they flowed beneath papal policy 'like an underground river',[2] the course of this stream was unplotted and unheard.

The political reality had been for some forty years the sharp and aggressive domination of central Italy by the Hohenstaufen. Several parts of the Papal State had been ruled directly by the empire during the reign of Henry VI. From the time of Christian of Mainz in the 1170s onwards Viterbo had been an imperial town containing an imperial palace. Philip of Swabia had during his brother Henry's lifetime called himself 'Duke of Tuscany and Campagna', and claimed to rule as far south as the gates of Rome, and even within the city in Trastevere. The prefect of the city had sworn allegiance to the emperor. Imperial taxes had been collected throughout the Papal State.

Why the popes should have reacted so sharply after Henry VI's death, claiming not only what was theirs by custom and usage, but also what was theirs only on a literal interpretation of archaic and almost forgotten documents, needs some explanation. The aggressive personality of Innocent III is no sufficient answer. In the *Liber censuum* of the Papal Chamberlain Cencius, drawn up five years before Henry VI's death, the papal officials copied the imperial donations of the early period, and remarked that certain marches and duchies belonged to the papal patrimony by right.[3] Resentment against the 'tyranny of the Germans' was widespread in Italy. The popes were themselves Italians, and were skilful enough also to realise the political capital they might

---

[1] A. Luchaire, 'Innocent III et les ligues de Toscane et de Lombardie', *Séances et Travaux de l'Académie des Sciences morales et politiques, Compte Rendu*, n.s., lxi (1904), pp. 490–514: O. Hageneder, 'Das Sonne-Mond-Gleichnis bei Innocenz III.', *MIöG*, lxv (1957), pp. 340–68. The question of recognition of Philip of Swabia was also involved.

[2] Kempf, p. 3.

[3] Ibid. p. 9; *Liber censuum*, i, p. 346.

make by playing on it. The rising against German rule in Tuscany and the Papal State in 1197 corresponded with the rising in Sicily at the same time. Only by pressing home their legal claims to the full could the popes make a proper political use of the opportunities afforded by Henry VI's death, and avert the danger of a return of the imperial oppression for the past forty years. That the danger to church liberty was great could be read from the relations of the Church with Henry VI, and the treatment of church property in central Italy by his agents.

Politics after 1198 were dominated by the double election of the Guelph Otto IV and the Hohenstaufen Philip of Swabia to the German kingship. In this great conflict, the *negotium imperii,* the pope was willy-nilly involved. But the status of Henry VI's infant son Frederick was of great importance to the papacy. The Sicilian regime of the Empress Constance accepted the claim of Innocent III to exercise the regency as feudal lord of the kingdom. With Philip of Swabia's encouragement the imperial official who had ruled Romagna and the march of Ancona for Henry VI, Markward of Anweiler, contested the papal claim to exercise the regency. Markward was the one powerful military leader of the former German regime to challenge the papal position in central and south Italy. The German Duke of Spoleto put up little resistance to Innocent III, and soon left Italy. But the struggle with Markward, though in the Romagna it did not last long, led to a protracted and expensive war in the kingdom of Sicily, in which the pope was committed to supplying men and money.[1] A realistic assessment of papal policy has to take account of the civil war in the kingdom, which was more important for the Papal State than the minor campaigns which Innocent waged in the Tuscan patrimony.[2]

An account of temporal power policy at the time the Papal State

---

[1] The amounts cannot be calculated exactly. Innocent's first legates in the Sicilian business brought 1,500 gold ounces to enlist mercenaries, and shortly afterwards the pope's cousins Lando of Montelongo and James the marshal were despatched with mercenary troops (*Gesta*, ch. xxiii–xxiv, apud *P.L.*, 214,cols. xli , xlvi). The pope naturally drew on the revenues of Sicily for the war; see O. Hageneder and A. Haidacher (ed.), *Die Register Innocenz III., Publikationen der Abteilung für historische Studien des österreichischen Kulturinstituts in Rom, Quellen, 1 Reihe*, Bd.1, (1964), no. 554 (557), p. 802. For another loan of 3,000 gold ounces see *P.L.*, 214, col. 1072. Cf. F. Baethgen, *Die Regentschaft Papst Innocenz III. im Königreich Sizilien* (Heidelberg, 1914), pp. 24, 41–3, 71–2 et passim. T. C. Van Cleve, *Markward of Anweiler and the Sicilian Regency*, pp. 77 ff.

[2] Waley's treatment of Sicily as irrelevant to the Papal State seems to me slightly to misrepresent the issue (cf. *P.S.*, p. 40). Cf. my comments on his book in *EHR*, lxxviii (1963), pp. 324–6. Professor Dupré-Theseider's balanced comments in *Studi Medievali,* 3rd ser., iv (1963), pp. 669–77, are relevant.

was established falls into three phases: the vital eleven years from 1198 to 1209 when Italy was without an emperor; Otto IV's stay in Italy until the autumn of 1211; and finally the long period which then elapsed before the Hohenstaufen Frederick II began to assert his power in areas claimed by the popes, in the early 1220s. Thus for over twenty years, with a single short break, imperial power was quiescent in central Italy, and the kingdom of Sicily was ruled by a government friendly to the popes if not actually under their control. This might be described as a 'power vacuum' in Italy, but not strictly accurately, since the continuance of Hohenstaufen power in Sicily was an important part of the papal system. The beneficiaries of German decline were not the popes alone, but also the central Italian communes, for whom this period was just as important for the establishment of local government as it was for the popes for the establishment of central government. Moreover, by absorbing the Matildine lands the communes invaded the rights of both pope and emperor; Bologna had occupied Medicina, Argelata and Monteveglio, all Matildine lands, within a short time of Henry VI's death.

The attempt of Innocent III to reclaim the lands of the Church stretched over a very wide area; so wide that one can only wonder at the ability and energy which brought him such solid gains. Conditions in Italy after Henry VI's death were chaotic; Markward of Anweiler was a formidable opponent in the march of Ancona both before and after Innocent's accession, and the towns were reluctant to come down on one side or the other. In Romagna, where Innocent sent legates claiming, as they did in the march, that the area was the full property of the Holy See, the political conditions were very unsettled; a five-years war between Ravenna and Ferrara ended only in 1200 after the Ferrarese had destroyed the important archiepiscopal castle of Argenta.[1] Bologna, Faenza and Imola were locked in almost permanent conflict; in 1201 both Romagna and the march of Ancona were in turmoil, and Innocent sadly remarked that things were far worse in the march now that the communes were 'free' than when they were in servitude to the empire.[2]

[1] A. Torre, 'Relazioni di Ravenna con Ferrara e Mantova alla fine del sec. XII', *Stud. Romagn.*, iii (1952), pp. 227–34. Cf. Hageneder and Haidacher (ed.), *Die Register*, no. 27, p. 40; Theiner, *C.D.*, i, no. 41. It is unclear whether the statement in the *Gesta* that Innocent withdrew his claims in the Romagna in favour of the Archbishop of Ravenna is accurate (ch. xii, *P.L.*, 214, col. xxvii).

[2] *P.L.*, 214, col. 937. Cf. Waley, *P.S.*, p. 41; Tillmann, p. 99. For Romagna, Hessel, *Bologna*, pp. 165 ff.; Tolosanus, *Chronicon Faventinum* (*RRIISS*, xxviii, pt. 1), pp. 116 ff.

Opposite: 10 Portrait of Boniface VIII in the Lateran Basilica

11 The pope judging heretics, *c.* 14th century, showing troops with the papal insignia

12 Relief inscription on Porta San Sebastiano, Rome, referring to the occupation of the city by Louis of Bavaria

Innocent III was born a noble of the Roman Campagna, and his mother was of the Roman family of Scotti. Because he knew and understood this part of Italy best, and because it was geographically more accessible to him, he scored his main political success between the Neapolitan border and the Umbrian Appenine. Most of this zone was the ancient patrimony of St Peter, but Innocent also very effectively extended papal rule in Umbria, both to Perugia and towns hitherto only nominally papal in allegiance, and to the Valtopino, the duchy of Spoleto proper. All the hill towns from this zone to the border town of Rieti were brought into allegiance. Rome itself was bullied by Innocent, and deprived to some extent of the proud semi-independence it had enjoyed under Celestine, when its senator had been said to 'rule' Campagna and the Maritime province.

The methods employed by Innocent to achieve these ends were those which had been reinstated in the tradition of the Roman See by the Roman Clement III, ten years before him. They included the use of the aristocratic clan, the pope's own family, whose feudal power again became the instrument of papal policy as it had been during the eleventh century in the period before the Reform. It was in some ways a regressive step; it could be viewed as a continuance of the methods of Anaclete during the schism of 1130. But the bureaucratisation of the Roman See, and the extending scale of its administration, made nepotism less dangerous or at least less immediately fatal than it had been. The cardinals, with their growing collegiate organisation, had become a powerful defence against nepotistic corruption.

Innocent's most powerful feudatory from his own family was his brother Richard, Count of Sora. Richard, however, was not invested with Sora, in the Neapolitan kingdom, until 1208; this was the keystone of an edifice of feudal holdings in the southern Papal State held by the Conti (Innocent's own family), by Innocent's brother-in-law Pietro Annibaldi, and by their ally Richard of Ceccano, the Lord of Sezze. Ceccano and many other strongpoints, some of which he held from the Roman churches. The lavish feast at Ceccano in June 1208 at which in his brother's presence Richard of Segni was made Count of Sora, amid the rejoicing of all papal Campagna, marks the triumph of the house of Segni and its allies.[1] Papal officials and generals were drawn liberally from the pope's family and their connections. James the papal marshal,

---

[1] Cf. Tillmann, ad indicem, p. 306; Waley, *P.S.*, pp. 54–5. Richard of Ceccano, Pressutti, *Regesta Honorii III*, i, pp. LXXXV–LXXXVI; Theiner, *C.D.*, i, no. 144. For the creation of Richard as Count of Sora, *Annales Ceccan.* (*MGH, Scriptores*, xix), pp. 296–7.

I

feudatory of Ninfa (which Innocent redeemed from the Frangipani), leader of the Sicilian army, Count of Andria, and at one time rector of the Tuscan patrimony, was one of the most important. The office of papal chamberlain, a key one in financial and temporal power policy, was given in succession to two cousins of Innocent: it was held by Octavian in 1204, and then until the end of the pontificate by Stephen of Fossanova, from 1212 a cardinal.[1] Other minor noblemen of Innocent's family were given more or less important jobs in papal government.[2] In many of these affairs, but particularly in those directed by the pope's brother Richard, the money of the Conti family played an important part.[3] Perhaps the most spectacular intrusion of Innocent's family into papal politics was the plan to marry the daughter of Philip of Swabia to Richard's son, Innocent's nephew, and to grant the son the duchy of Tuscany; but this project came to nothing.

Such nepotistic methods had been characteristic of papal temporal rule from its origins. What was new under Innocent III was the scale and style of his temporal policy. Reading his letter to the bishops of the Sicilian kingdom in 1198,[4] with its vigorous recital of the war against Markward, its references to the very large sums of money already provided and yet to be raised for mercenaries, its boast of the Markward fortresses in the march reduced to cinders and ashes, its promise of forces numbered in thousands to be sent to the Sicilian kingdom from Tuscany and Campagna – the reader is made aware that Innocent was a great feudal prince. Nowhere in the letters of Alexander III in his struggle with the empire is this note of grandiose bellicosity struck. The political foundation of this new style was in the first place the regency of Innocent in the kingdom of Sicily for Frederick II, which in theory

---

[1] Octavian, *Lib. cens.*, i, p. 256. This was almost certainly the Cardinal Deacon of SS. Sergius and Bacchus (cf. Tillmann, p. 290). For Stephen, who became chamberlain in May, 1206, see *Annales Ceccan.*, *MGH*, xix, p. 296. There are numerous references to Stephen's activity in the temporal power, particularly concerning Perugia from 1210 onwards. Interesting for his powers as chamberlain is the important political concession made by him to Viterbo to buy and sell in Corneto, *P.L.* 216, col. 894 (21 August 1213). Cf. also *JEccH*, viii, p. 144.

[2] e.g., Carzolo, the pope's relation, to whom the rectorate of the patrimony of St Peter in Tuscany was conceded in 1203, 'tamquam fideli et vassalio nostro'. *P.L.*, 215, col. 112. Cf. Waley, *P.S.*, p. 309. Another rector, of the Campagna in 1199, Innocent's cousin (not nephew), Lando of Montelungo. Cf. Waley, pp. 51, 309.

[3] Tillmann and Waley, passim. For the Poli lands see below. Conti money played a part in the redemption of Ninfa and its grant to James the marshal (*Lib. cens.* i, p. 256; other refs in Waley, pp. 43, 55n., 67 and cf. also *I.P.*, i, p. 192, ii, p. 109); for Richard of Sora's redemption of various lands of the bishopric of Ostia, the Lateran chapter, etc., see Potthast, no. 7557. *P.L.*, 216, col. 13; and also cf. *Lib. cens.*, i, p. 13.

[4] Hageneder and Haidacher (ed.), *Die Register*, i, no. 554 (557).

united the whole south of the Italian peninsula under the pope.[1] The
papal regency was temporary. But when Frederick assumed control of
his own kingdom, and even when at a later date he opposed the Papal
State and threatened its very existence, the new political scale of papal
temporal power did not change. Never again in the Middle Ages did the
pope revert to the status of an unusually powerful Italian bishop.

II

The legal titles of the papal patrimony underwent important changes
during Innocent III's pontificate, and assumed substantially the form
which they were to retain for the rest of the Middle Ages. From an
early date in the pontificate the candidates for the German throne
showed themselves willing to make important concessions – concessions
possibly which Henry VI might also have considered, if the evidence of
the 'will' is correct. Philip of Swabia was by the end of 1198 willing
to offer 'lands, castles, possessions and money' to make a settlement
with Innocent.[2] In June 1201 at Neuss, Otto of Saxony made a guarantee to Innocent which in effect abandoned the position taken up by the
Hohenstaufen in the papal patrimony, and recognised all the most
important of the 'recuperations' of territory which the Holy See had
made since the death of Henry VI. 'All the land from Radicofani to
Ceprano, the exarchate of Ravenna, Pentapolis, the march, the duchy of
Spoleto, the land of the Countess Matilda and the county of Bertinoro'
and the other lands mentioned in imperial privileges from that of Louis
the Pious onwards.[3] This promise has not unfittingly been called the
'birth certificate of the Papal State'. It was confirmed (with the addition of the small Apennine area of Massa Trabaria) by Otto at Speyer
in 1209; at Eger in 1213 and again at Hagenau in 1219 Frederick
of Hohenstaufen was to make substantially identical promises.

The nature of the obligations imposed by Innocent III on the
newly-submitted towns was in part derived from canon law and in part
from the feudal and pre-feudal customary law. The obligation to pay

---

[1] I dissent from Waley's opinion that 'Until 1207 Innocent III had been dependent for his
central Italian achievements on skilful improvisation and the support of his family.' (*P.S*,
p. 50.) Nor do I entirely accept the implication that after 1207 Innocent's success is accounted
for by the increased tidiness of his administration.
[2] Kempf, *Regestum Innocentii III papae super negotio Romani imperii* (Rome, 1947), no. 13, at p. 32.
[3] Ibid. no. 77; cf. Kempf, *Papsttum und Kaisertum*, pp. 32–3; Waley, *P.S.*, pp. 43–4 ('the birth
certificate of the Papal State').

census in token of papal supremacy had existed for some towns in
Romagna and the march in the twelfth century; its origin was the
canon law. Canonical also was the principle that appeals must always
lie to the pope or to his representative. But the obligations of military
service, carriage service, attendance at parliaments, of keeping the roads
free from brigands, were feudal or customary.[1] Oaths of fealty and
allegiance were made to the pope by barons who held fiefs from the
regalia or temporal possessions of St Peter; such oaths were taken by
the Aldobrandeschi, who held Montalto of the pope though their main
holdings were in imperial Tuscany.[2] Feudal law penetrated deeply into
that of the Papal State; not only did the prefect of the city swear
feudal homage to the pope, but Innocent in committing a papal castle
to the papal rector of the patrimony in Tuscany entrusted it to him
'as our liegeman and vassal'.[3]

It is not easy to assess Innocent's material power with any degree of
accuracy. His biographer lays a lot of stress on his wealth, and recounts
his charity during the Roman famine, his rebuilding of the Lateran
and Vatican palaces, his gifts to the Roman churches, and his supplying
vestments to the Archbishop of Ravenna when the occupant of the one-
time rival see to Rome was too poor to own them. Certainly the
temporal income of the Holy See must have risen very steeply from
the bargains made by Innocent's agents with the communes of the
march of Ancona, apparently on the basis of a standard payment to the
church of fifty pounds a year; this is a great deal more than the payments of two or three pounds of silver a year which had been paid
to the papacy by places in the march owing *census* in the twelfth
century.[4] The income accruing to the Church after it had taken the
place of the empire in the duchy of Spoleto must also have been far
from negligible; both here and in the Tuscan patrimony the Church
from Innocent's time onwards collected the imperial *fodrum* payment
of twenty-six pence from each assessed hearth; in only a part of the

[1] Cf. Hagemann's comments in *Quellen*, xxxvi (1956), pp. 147–8.

[2] Cf. F. Kempf, 'Zu den Originalregistern Innocenz III.', ibid., pp 86–135, at pp. 125 ff. By
1207 Aldobrandeschi also held the county of Rosellae, which was not strictly inside the borders of the Papal State. Cf. *I.P.*, iv, p. 262.

[3] The prefect's oath in Hageneder and Haidacher (ed.) *Die Register*, i, no. 23. The concession
of the fortress (*munitio*) of Montefiascone to Carzolo, who was a relative of the pope, in *P.L.*,
215, col. 112. For Carzolo cf. Waley, pp. 51, 309.

[4] Cf. *P.L.* 214, cols. 933–40; for the earlier twelfth-century payments of *census* see Pfaff's articles
in *VSWG* (1953 and 1957), quoted above. Waley, *P.S.*, p. 258, is sceptical that these payments
were enough to alter the pope's finances materially, but see immediately below.

duchy the total payment due annually was 825 pounds of silver.[1] The military service of the towns was also an important access of power; that owed by a town of the size of Perugia must have been substantial.

The death of Markward of Anweiler in 1202 meant the end of any serious German-led resistance to Innocent's plans of temporal rule in Italy, until Otto IV entered Italy for coronation as emperor in 1209. Philip of Swabia sent a representative, Bishop Liupold of Worms, to Italy in 1204, but he never succeeded in establishing any serious control of imperial lands, far less papal lands. Yet even in the absence of German opposition, Innocent found that he lacked the material power to impose papal direct rule outside Latium and Umbria. In the march of Ancona the local communities made leagues in complete disregard of papal interests, and resisted their bishops with impunity.[2] In Romagna the pope exercised no direct government at all, and the Archbishop of Ravenna was hard-put to defend his castles against Faenza and other communes.[3] The most northerly of the possessions claimed by the pope, Ferrara, was entirely outside church control. Politically Ferrara was disputed by the two magnate families of Este and Guidoguerra. Innocent III was unable to recover from the local inhabitants the papal estates of Ficarolo and Fiscaglia.[4] The situation of church property in the Romagna was deteriorating; lay tenants of church lands could alienate them by a simple notification to the clerical owner.[5] There is no sign that the temporal power of Innocent III exercised much influence on this situation. While the achievement of Innocent III in the Papal State is undisputed, the territorial and practical limits of his power there are equally striking.

[1] Cf. *Liber censuum*, i, pp. 534–7; C. Brühl, *Fodrum, Gistum, Servitium Regis*, i, p. 728; Waley, *P.S.*, p. 256. The cash sum mentioned in the submission of Rieti in 1198 is not impressive, however: 13 shillings and 30 den., and a half share in the profits of tolls and justice. *Liber censuum*, i, p. 8*.

[2] Cf. W. Hagemann, 'Studien und Dokumente zur Geschichte der Marken im Zeitalter der Staufer', i, 'Corridonia (Montolmo)' *Quellen*, xxxvii (1957), pp. 103–35; iii, 'Sant' Elpidio a Mare', ibid. xliv (1964), pp. 72–151.

[3] G. Rossini, 'Un' antica controversia per il possesso di Lugo e di S. Potito', *Stud. Romagn.*, iv (1953), pp. 103–17.

[4] Theiner, *C.D.*, i, no. 47; cf. C. Levi (ed.), *Registri dei Cardinali Ugolino d'Ostia e Ottaviano degli Ubaldini*, (Rome, 1890), no. 3, p. 6; *P.L.* 216, cols. 899, 934. For the general process of the break-up of the ancient church estates see C. M. Cipolla, 'Il tramonto della organizzazione economica curtense', reprinted in *Storia dell'economia italiana* (Turin, 1959), pp. 61–80, from *BISI*, no. 62 (1950); E. Conti, *La formazione della struttura agraria moderna nel contado fiorentino*, i (Rome, 1965), pp. 8–79.

[5] F. Crosara, 'La "concordia inter clericos et laycos de Ravenna" negli statuti di Ostasio da Polenta', *Stud. Romagn.* iii (1952), pp. 31–62. Cf. *P.L.* 215, col. 27, which seems to refer to this archiepiscopal constitution of 1193.

Rome was as aggressive, as greedy, as intent on exploiting church lands and getting submissions and economic privileges from her less powerful neighbours, as any other of the central Italian communes of her size and power. But while the temporal power of other bishops had been largely broken, that of the Roman bishop was to an unprecedented degree increasing. The Romans aspired to a sort of condomium with the pope, for which the only possible comparison was the situation obtaining at the time between the Archbishop and commune of Ravenna. This was quite unacceptable to Innocent, who interpreted the 1188 settlement between the Romans and Clement III in a new way; in particular he insisted on appointing a single senator of the city through an intermediary official, a *medianus,* thus pressing the papal claim to appoint the *podestà* rather further in Rome than in most other towns of the Papal State. In other matters he went more cautiously. It is unclear whether he merely deferred payment of the customary gifts to the Romans on his election, or whether he avoided their payment altogether. Concerning the other traditional Roman method of soaking their bishop, the pressure put on him to contribute to the communal war chest, he was perhaps firmer in appearance than in reality. When war broke out between Rome and Viterbo Innocent himself refused to conform to this 'deplorable custom', but his brother Richard contributed a thousand pounds to the war, which comes close to the same thing.[1]

Provided that they were obedient, the pope was willing to support the Roman policy of aggrandisement to a certain extent and to give the Romans a place in his system of government. In the Roman war with Viterbo (between 1199 and 1201) Innocent and his brother Richard gave the Romans full support. From 1199 until 1203, and again in 1207 after the papal quarrel with Rome had ended, Innocent made Roman magnates into the 'legates and rectors' of the papal patrimony in Tuscany, besides giving the prefect of the city an important judicial function in the same province.[2] But this was not what many of the Romans wanted. The partisans of the faction which had ruled Rome under Innocent's predecessor represented the new pope as plucking Rome's feathers until the city was naked. Anti-clericalism and envy of clerical possessions were endemic in Rome, though they less often took in

---

[1] This is how I interpret (rather differently from Waley) paras. 8 and 133–4 of the *Gesta.* The evidence of Roger Howden (*Chronica,* R.S., iv, p. 45) is not conclusive.

[2] *P.L.* 214, col. 755; *ASR,* xxii (1899), no. 57, p. 520, (14 April 1202), 'd. Guntblacca. . . legato Tuscie'; ibid. p. 523 (3 March 1207), 'ante. . . Octavianum Thedaldi urbis Rome senatorem et ante Petrum eius filium legatum et rectorem de tota Tuscia'. Waley missed Peter in his lists (*P.S.,* p. 309, and cf. also ibid. p. 51).

Rome the heretical form they assumed in the surrounding cities. The radical-minded teacher of rhetoric, Boncompagno of Signa, was in Rome at this time, and his comments on the military and political ambitions of Innocent, though veiled, are hostile. It was 'shameful' for soldiers to serve under a clerical banner, and such soldiers were not knights but thieves. The priestly office concerned prayer and psalms, and these were the only way in which a priest ought to support the wars of laymen.[1]

When the direct clash came in 1202–4, it concerned the role of Innocent's own family. The murder of one of the Orsini (the family of Celestine III) by one of the Conti began the quarrel. Its next stage involved one of the many acquisitions of property which Richard was making under protection of his brother the pope, in this case by settling and taking over the debt-laden estates of the lords of Poli in the southern Campagna. The heir to the Poli lands challenged the redemption of the estates, and offered to hold them for the senate. The Roman government itself split, and the opposition took the chance to challenge Innocent's appointing a single papal senator through a mediator (*medianus*). There were two disputed senatorial elections, and the nobles in Rome closed themselves in their towers; the traditional form of warfare followed in central Rome, and the leader of the opposition, Giovanni Capoccio, was attacked in his tower from a wooden structure built on top of an ancient monument by the papal party. Hohenstaufen money was distributed to the anti-papal opposition, papal money to the loyalists. Innocent in the summer of 1204 proposed to accept arbitration, accepted for a time a renewal of the rule of fifty-six senators, and finally wore the opposition down. The eventual result was the re-establishment of papal rule in Rome, the restoration of Innocent's method of nominating a single senator, and the confirmation of Richard of Segni in the Poli lands. From the end of 1204 Innocent experienced no more serious trouble with the Roman dissidents.

Viterbo was a city with a tradition of imperialist sympathies and heretical tendencies, and a healthy dislike for Rome and the Romans. For these reasons Innocent chose to show his power by holding at Viterbo in 1207 a parliament which was attended by bishops, abbots, barons and communal representatives from most of the Papal State with the exception of Romagna.[2] Oaths of fealty and peace observance

[1] *Liber de obsidione Ancone* (*RRIISS*, vi, pt. 3), p. 41; Nathan (ed.), *Amicitia di maestro Boncompagno da Signa* (1909), p. 65. The speech in the *liber de obsidione* is supposed to refer to Archbishop Christian of Mainz, but it is clearly meant to apply to Boncompagno's own day. For Boncompagno in Rome, see Zimolo's introduction.

[2] Good discussions in Waley, pp. 52–3, 110–11.

were taken from those who attended, and lawsuits heard by the pope.
The rectors of the papal provinces were made responsible for keeping
the peace under the oath taken at Viterbo, and for hearing cases which
came to them in appeal, or cases involving reprisals claimed by one
commune against another. The communes were forbidden to pass laws
prejudicial to church liberties – Innocent made this prohibition by virtue
of his 'temporal as well as his spiritual authority'. They were also
required to make their officials swear annually to keep the statute
promulgated in this parliament against heresy.

That the parliament of Viterbo set up a scheme of government for
the Papal State is to be doubted. For a good many years after the
parliament the only provinces to which resident clerical rectors were
appointed continued to be those of the Tuscan patrimony and of the
Campagna-Maritime.[1] The growth of a system of papal provinces was
slow, and not complete until the second half of the thirteenth century.

The parliament of Viterbo is most remarkable for the performance
of the feudal duty of *parlamentum* by the representatives of this wide
area, and for the vigorous assertion of church rights against laymen
which is so typical of Innocent III. It is also interesting for the rules
made there for cases referred to papal courts in appeal from lower
courts. Most but not all the communes were obliged to refer appeals
immediately to a papal court; a notable exception was Perugia.[2]
The appeals could be heard by rectors or cardinal-legates, or by the
pope himself or auditors appointed by him in the papal court.[3] The
question of appeals was one of the thorniest to concern the relation
of the papal government with the communes, and the determined papal
attempt to control such appeals begins with Innocent III.

III

If the great European struggle between Guelph and Hohenstaufen was
to turn out, eventually, to Innocent's disadvantage, his work in the
temporal power would prove to have been built on sand. At no time
did this appear more probable than during Otto IV's stay in Italy in
1209–10. Less than two years before, Innocent had practically concluded negotiations to recognise as emperor Otto's rival, Philip of

---

[1] See the lists of officials in Waley, *P.S.*, pp. 407 ff.

[2] Hageneder and Haidacher (ed.), *Die Register*, i, no. 375.

[3] For hearing of an appeal first by the papal judge of appeals (in this case the prefect of the
city) and then by a cardinal legate, see *P.L.* 215, col. 1219, and cf. Tillmann, in *Historisches
Jahrbuch*, xlv (1931), p. 357.

Hohenstaufen. This arrangement had only been frustrated by Philip's murder in 1208. Now in the summer of 1209 Otto came to Italy as emperor-elect, for coronation by Innocent at Rome. Though Otto had renewed at Speyer in March 1209 the promises he had made under very different circumstances to Innocent at Neuss in 1201, the likelihood of discord was great from the beginning. Otto's instructions to his agents in provinces claimed by the pope were from the start scarcely compatible with papal temporal claims.[1] The coronation took place, amid the usual Roman riots, on 4 October 1209. Otto's army left the city and camped outside Rome in the natural fortress of Isola Farnese, near the ancient city of Veii. From here Otto summoned Innocent to a conference to which the pope never came; the break between the two powers had virtually coincided with the imperial coronation. German troops occupied the same keypoints in the Tuscan patrimony as during Henry VI's reign: Vetralla, Radicofani, Montefiascone. Innocent's fortification of these places made no difference to their fate. In the summer of 1210 Viterbo was besieged; by this time Otto had turned to seek the support of the powerful Italian feudatories, and had invested Azzo VI d'Este with the march of Ancona and the duty of opening this important route to the south. The German royal officer (*ministerialis*) Dipold of Schweinspeunt, who had an important career in the kingdom before defecting to the Guelph, was invested by Otto with the papal duchy of Spoleto. Otto in November 1210 invaded the south Italian kingdom. Innocent waited for over a year before deciding that the best policy was to excommunicate Otto (31 March 1211), as he had earlier and for different reasons excommunicated Otto's English uncle, John of England. It cannot have been a decision lightly taken, since it involved approval of the Capetian-Hohenstaufen alliance of Philip Augustus and Frederick II, and meant supporting Frederick's claim to the empire. But its result was the one desired in the short term. In October 1211 Otto left the kingdom of Sicily and returned to Germany to fight the renewed civil war which three years later led to his utter defeat. The pressure was removed from Frederick's Sicilian kingdom and from Innocent III's temporal power.

Otto IV fielded a powerful army, but like all the medieval emperors he could not terrorise more than one area of Italy at a time. Surprisingly few of the major cities in the Papal State submitted to him, and he also quickly lost the support of Azzo d'Este. The motive of Azzo's

[1] Ibid. pp. 56 ff.; Tillmann, pp. 133 ff. For what follows see Tillmann, 'Azzo von Este, Markgraf von Ancona und Graf von Loreto', *Hist. Jahrb.*, lxxxv (1965), pp. 28–49.

desertion seems to have been his jealousy of another imperial partisan, Peter of Celano. Having, therefore, accepted the march of Ancona in fee from Otto in 1210, in the spring or early summer of 1211 he accepted it in fee from Innocent III. If the march was the bribe to detach Azzo d'Este from Otto, it was a very substantial one, and costly for the papacy. Although Azzo d'Este died in November 1212 the march of Ancona was re-infeudated by Innocent to his son, Aldobrandino. The feudal grant of this province shows how impossible it was for the pope to rule directly the whole of the territories he claimed.

That Perugia, Orvieto and most of the towns in Umbria refused to submit to Otto may have been comforting to Innocent. He would have known however that submission of most towns to the papacy was made because they confidently expected papal rule to leave them little short of independent. 'My yoke is easy and my burden light' was quoted by Innocent to the towns with a strictly political significance. The treaties of the Roman Church with Perugia[1] give some idea of the motives which actuated the communes. One of these was certainly the internal strife in the towns, which led to their welcoming papal agents as mediators between the 'knights' and the 'footmen', and in the case of Perugia caused them to accept a papal decision about the apportionment of taxes between the two parties. The Perugians distinguished between the taxes imposed in the countryside on the subject population (which were normally farmed out to the highest bidder) and the *collecta* which was imposed in the city in order to finance warfare. The *collecta* for military expenses was in 1214 said to be liable to be exacted for service for the Roman Church, for the Roman people, for the emperor or his representative, and in cases when the Perugians made war on a neighbour by common consent. That the pope shared with the emperor and the Roman commune the right to call on the Perugians for military aid is in itself interesting. But perhaps it is more interesting that the papal representative should (in spite of the order to keep the peace given to papal subjects at the Viterbo parliament) officially sanction arrangements for private war. Later Perugia appealed to Honorius III to decide whether the *collecta* should be imposed for their recent war against Gubbio. In 1223 there was a further civil war between the

---

[1] Ficker, *Forschungen*, iv, no. 225, p. 276 (1210); Theiner, *C.D.*, i, nos. 58 (1214), 127 (1218, 1223, 1224), 145, 146 (1227, not 1228 as dated by Theiner); *Reg. Greg. IX*, no. 34. Cf. G. de Vergottini, 'Il papato e la comitatinanza nello stato della chiesa (sec. XIII–XIV); *AMDR*, n.s., iii (1951–5), pp. 75–162, at pp. 105–13; D. Segoloni, 'La civitas Perusina nel pensiero di Bartolo', *Atti del Congresso Internazionale per il VI Centenario della morte di Bartolo di Sassoferrato*, ii (Milan, 1962), pp. 513–671, at pp. 580 ff., 609 ff.

knights and footmen, in which neighbouring communes took part, and a curial cardinal arbitrated between the factions. There was similar papal mediation between the factions in Todi and Assisi. The severe limits of papal power in Umbria appear from the history of Innocent's relations with the second-rank commune of Narni, straddling the Via Flaminia at the outlet of the valley of the river Nera. Narni's punishment for disobedience was decided on by Innocent in 1213, but never effected; the main result appears to have been the destruction (for the second time) of the papal castles at Otricoli and Stroncone. Only in the small towns of the duchy and the Tuscan patrimony – particularly where they contained a papal castle – was Innocent able to appoint the town's office holders and exercise effective control.[1]

In Campagna and the Maritime province the problems of papal government were as much feudal as communal. On the whole the alliances led by the pope's kinsfolk and the family of Ceccano were successful in dominating the province; the most notable victory was the expulsion of the German castellan Conrad of Marlei from Sora and other fortresses just over the Neapolitan border – which were then bestowed on the pope's brother. But the concessions which had to be made to the feudal lords are clearest in the case of Terracina. When the Terracinese destroyed the Frangipani fortress of Traversa, which dominates the town, in 1202, the pope and his brother Richard treated them as rebels against the Church. The pope took into his own hands the fortress of Monte Circeo (earlier enfeoffed by him to the Frangipani), which he handed over to his kinsman Pietro Annibaldi. Terracina, after the alliance of the Frangipani with Richard of Segni in 1206, had to submit once more to Frangipani domination; a judgement in which the town had recognised the rights of the Church did not alter the practical effect of this settlement.[2] But the Church continued to be strong in the south of the Papal State and the north of the Sicilian kingdom. When the Count of Fondi (in the kingdom) willed his possessions to the Roman Church, Frederick II issued orders that Innocent should be free to enter the count's lands anywhere between the river Garigliano and the frontier.[3]

---

[1] e.g., Città Castellana, Radicofani, Città di Castello, Sutri, Acquapendente. Cf. Waley, *P.S.*, p. 70 (for Narni, ibid. p. 65).
[2] Cf. G. Falco, 'I comuni della Campagna e della Marittima', *ASR*, xlviii (1925), pp. 44–53. My interpretation differs from Falco's.
[3] Huillard-Bréholles, *Historia diplomatica Frederici Secundi*, i, pt. 2, pp. 201–2. Cf. Tillmann, p. 149.

IV

When Innocent III died on 16 July 1216, he left the temporal power radically transformed. Not without meaning had he spoken of the Papal State, in a famous decretal, as a field in which the pope exercised supreme princely power.[1] But if Innocent made the Papal State, he had not guaranteed its future continuance. To enable his young son Henry to be crowned, Frederick of Hohenstaufen shortly before Innocent's death promised that Henry as king of Sicily should owe fealty only to Innocent, and that the regent in Sicily during Henry's minority should be a person acceptable to the pope. This, and Frederick's taking the cross, were together with Frederick's promise at Eger the most binding obligations which an emperor or an emperor-elect could reasonably be expected to give. But what could stop a powerful government which ruled both north and south Italy, and had good legal claims for dominant rights in the Papal State, from exercising these? It was particularly tempting for Frederick that the two provinces in which papal rule was weakest, Romagna and the march of Ancona, were the provinces which constituted a 'corridor' between Lombardy and the Sicilian kingdom, and which were therefore of the greatest strategic importance.

Innocent's successor Honorius III (Cencius Savelli) was like him in coming from the nobility of the Roman Campagna; under him the clergy of the little towns of the Sacco valley and the Alban hills continued to find important missions to perform and lucrative posts to fill, all over Europe. Even more than his predecessor Honorius was a curial bureaucrat; in 1192 he had as papal chamberlain overseen the compilation of the *Liber censuum,* the great index of the rights and revenues of the Roman Church. His policy was pacific, unimaginative and much concerned with detail. So far as the temporal power was concerned he was in some ways an ideal successor to the sweeping political *coups* of Innocent, which he had neither the desire nor the opportunity to repeat. Fortunately for Honorius, Frederick II was too much concerned with Germany and with his own coronation as emperor (Rome, 1220), to be for most of the pontificate a serious worry for the pope. At the coronation he enacted a severe law against heresy which was quite in line with papal views, and which the popes subsequently required to be enforced in papal lands such as the march of Ancona

[1] *P.L.* 214, col. 1130; *Per venerabilem,* X, 4, 17, 13. Cf. Hageneder and Haidacher (ed.), *Die Register Innocenz III.,* no. 27.

and Romagna; he also extended protection to church liberties of property and legal immunity. Honorius said that no previous pope had felt such affection for an emperor as he felt for Frederick, but it was an affection which had begun to wane before Honorius's death.

The most important way in which Honorius took advantage of the lull in papal-imperial hostility was his recuperation of a substantial part of the Matildine lands.[1] The aim that lay behind this was not to assume direct papal control of the lands but to obtain recognition of papal supremacy from the holders. The magnate Salinguerra had been invested with a substantial number of Matildine lands before Innocent III's death. The recovery of church lands was, with the preparation and financing of the crusade, one of the main aims of the legation in Lombardy and Emilia of the able Cardinal Bishop Ugolino of Ostia in 1221. At the same time the pope had been trying to get the support of the emperor for the recovery of the Matildine lands, on the whole with considerable success. By the end of 1221 a considerable proportion of these lands, together with other papal lands usurped by the communes, such as Massa Fiscaglia, had been recovered: that is to say that papal supremacy had been acknowledged. With the help of imperial officials Ugolino also tackled to some extent the disorders of Romagna, made Faenza compensate the clergy of Imola and Ravenna, and caused Bologna to disgorge a couple of her illegally held villages. But when the larger political issues were considered, all this was of little moment. The power of papal agents in Romagna was purely nominal; real power there and in the march was shared between imperial officials and the communes, with the papal ally Azzo VII d'Este exerting a certain amount of influence as a territorial lord and also in his capacity as papal feudatory of the march of Ancona.

The importance attached by Honorius to some kind of formal supremacy in the lands of the Church was shown in a curious manifesto which he issued in February 1221, a sort of white paper on the action he had taken in the Papal State to assert papal rights, and how successful it had been. He referred to imperial co-operation and also to the species of parliament which his representative had held for the towns of the duchy of Spoleto, at Bevagna (within a few miles of which St Francis had recently held a parliament of a rather different kind, when

---

[1] Overmann, *Gräfin Mathilde von Tuscien*, pp. 105–19; R. Manselli, 'Onorio III, Frederico II e la questione dei beni matildini', *Dep. di Storia Patria per le antiche provincie Modenesi, Atti e Mem.*, 9th ser., iii (1963), pp. 244–51; Levi (ed.), *Registri dei Cardinali Ugolino d'Ostia e Ottaviano degli Ubaldini*, nos. 3, 42, 54, 55, 79, 80, 82; Theiner, *C.D.*, i, nos. 7, 79, 85, 111; *Statuta Urbis Ferrariae nuper reformata* (Ferrara, 1567), lib. ii, c. 137, folios 112–15.

he preached to the birds, but to this the pope did not refer). And as late as 1222 Frederick was willing to disown the actions of those of his vassals who had challenged papal authority in the march and in the duchy of Spoleto.[1]

The treaty between Frederick II and the Church signed at S. Germano in 1225 was intended to bind Frederick to the crusade and to ensure peace in Italy. Neither of these aims was reached. In 1226 the Lombard League was renewed against Frederick; its members included two cities of the Papal State, Bologna and Faenza. Honorius averted the imminent conflict, with its threat to re-open the great wars of Frederick I and Alexander III, and obtained a truce and the cancellation of Frederick's acts against the rebels. By the time of the death of Honorius (18 March 1227) his policy of peace and appeasement was practically in ruins. He was replaced by yet another cardinal of the Campagna nobility, the distinguished Bishop Ugolino of Ostia, a relation of Innocent III, an able canonist, the patron of St Francis and his order, who as Gregory IX provided the political leadership which the Roman Church badly needed if it was to survive the challenge of renewed imperial power. Gregory was a man of far higher ability and moral quality than Clement III. Gregory IX was a pope of underlying idealism and outstanding intellectual gifts, a very able administrator and a ruthless politician. To these talents, whose use survived into old age, he added a taste for theatrical oratory and for the plaudits of the crowd. This was a man capable of defending the liberties of the Church against Frederick II's renewal of his father's policies.

V

Gregory IX did not take long to seize the initiative against Frederick. He excommunicated the emperor in the autumn of 1227, after refusing to accept the outbreak of sickness at Brindisi as an excuse for Frederick's postponement of his crusade. After the excommunicated emperor had set off for the crusade in June 1228 his lieutenants in Italy (it is unclear whether they were obeying his instructions or not) launched attacks on the Papal State. Rainald of Urslingen advanced into the march of Ancona, while his brother Bertold intensified his activities in the duchy of Spoleto, to which his family had a feudal claim which it had acquired from the Emperor Henry VI. Azzo VII d'Este, the papal feudatory in the march of Ancona, took up a neutral stance. John of Brienne,

[1] Theiner *C.D.*, i, no. 104; cf. Waley, *P.S.*, pp. 125–34.

Frederick II's elderly and disillusioned father-in-law, had been entrusted by the pope with the rectorship of the Tuscan patrimony, but as a soldier he did not prove to be a great catch for the papacy. The war bulletin which Gregory IX issued to his legates and commanders on 1 December 1228 spoke enthusiastically of the troops which were being raised, and the campaigns planned.[1] In the event the subsequent papal invasion of the Sicilian kingdom proved to be a successful operation, which relieved the military pressure on the Papal State. The most significant remark in Gregory's letter on 1 December 1228 was however its reference to the need to raise a papal subsidy for the financing of the war. For the first time in church history, the clergy and laity of England and other countries were asked to contribute to a papal war against Christians. The doctrine of the crusade, and the more recent doctrine of crusading tenths, had produced consequences which were in some ways logically justifiable, but in others morally disastrous.

The treaty signed in July 1230 at S. Germano, some months after Frederick's return from Syria, shows clearly how strong Gregory's position was, in spite of his mediocre military power.[2] The treaty could be taken as an example of the way in which the strength or weakness of papal temporal government was on some occasions hardly relevant to the strength or weakness of the papacy. Not only was the independence of the Papal State again recognised, but the pope was given rights over Gaeta and Sant'Agata deep in the Sicilian kingdom, while other Sicilian castles were held by the pope to guarantee execution of the treaty. The reminiscence of Innocent III's rights over the area north of the Garigliano is clear; Frederick had still not exorcised the spirit of the papal regency of his boyhood.

But material power continued profoundly to matter. Although the sources of its financial history at this time are obscure, and not very thoroughly worked over by modern historians, there are signs that financially the Roman bishopric had been moving into a different class among the European states since 1198; there are signs also that in the third and fourth decades of the thirteenth century it was passing through a financial crisis. The 1,000 marks alone, which from 1213 were due

---

[1] Hagemann, 'Tolentino', *Quellen*, xliv (1964), pp. 197–9, 247–9. Cf. also Waley, *P.S.*, pp. 135–8; Hagemann, 'Corridonia', *Quellen*, xxxvii (1957), pp. 113–14; idem, 'Herzog Rainald von Spoleto und die Marken in den Jahren 1228–9', *Adel und Kirche* (Tellenbach Festschrift, Freiburg-Basle-Vienna, 1968), pp. 436–57. For papal subsidies in England (below) see W. E. Lunt, *Financial Relations of the Papacy with England to 1327* (Cambridge, Mass., 1939), pp. 178–96.

[2] Cf. K. Hampe, *Die Aktenstücke zum Frieden von S. Germano 1230 (MGH, Epist. sel.* (1926)).

annually from England as feudal tribute (and under Henry III were usually paid), were a huge sum when compared with the total recorded papal income before Innocent III, which was barely equal to this. Very frequently in the judicial proceedings with towns in the Papal State sums of two or three thousand pounds are mentioned by way of pledge or penalty; we have no means of knowing how often these sums were forfeited or collected, but it is at least possible the popes on some occasions actually took and kept them. The popes are also known to have spent very large sums. Even by 1230, the wars of Innocent III and Gregory IX in south Italy had been very expensive, so much so that Gregory had in 1228 called on the English clergy for a tenth of their estimated income of £80,000; Honorius had earlier called on them to guarantee him benefices in England which would ease the strain on papal resources, and make the charging of high legal fees to litigants in Rome less necessary. But quite the biggest of all the financial transactions in which the popes were involved at this time was the financing of the crusade.

Very often, papal expenses were, as they had always been, for the benefit of the Romans. Innocent III had not been so successful as it appeared in stopping this. Transactions which seemed to be acts of papal power, such as the redemption of the port of Civitavecchia in 1224 from its servitude to Viterbo (which had in turn bought the mortgage from Corneto), or the purchase by the pope of the customs rights from the port of Ostia to Rome, were carried out for the profit of Rome.[1] There were also large bribes paid to the Romans at times of political crisis in the old-fashioned way; Gregory IX paid as much as 10,000 pounds to end his quarrel with Rome in 1237, and this was not the first of such payments by him. Gregory made similar large payments to keep Perugia quiet.

The redemption of papal castles from the feudatories into whose hands they constantly fell, or from the avaricious grasp of the communes, was also an expensive business, even if again a traditional one for the popes.. Honorius III paid large sums to recover the fort of Ariccia, controlling the viaduct of the Via Appia near Albano. Gregory IX paid many thousands of pounds for the recovery of papal rights in other castles: Stroncone (constantly disputed throughout the period with Narni) and other castles in Umbria such as Miranda (which cost 8,000

---

[1] Cf. Calisse, *Storia di Civitavecchia*, 2nd ed., pp. 128–32; Levi (ed.), *Registri dei Cardinali Ugolino d'Ostia e Ottaviano degli Ubaldini*, pp. 142–7; P. Pressutti, *Regesta Honorii Papae III*, ii (Rome, 1895), no. 5886 (Potthast, no. 7557).

pounds) and Gualdo Tadino; in Latium forts such as Fumone, Paliano and Serrone.[1]

Gregory made a determined attempt to list the castles of the Holy See which were from henceforth inalienable, not to be granted or sold by him or future popes.[2] Such attempts by the sovereign to recover and control castles were common in thirteenth-century monarchies. In Gregory's case the prohibition of alienation was connected with a draft decree from the beginning of 1234, which said that cardinals always were to be consulted about the government of the temporal power, that papal castles were to be governed henceforth by clerks, and that the cardinals were henceforth to have a third share in the revenues of the papal patrimonies.[3] Thus the growing oligarchic power of the College of Cardinals had its part in Gregory's temporal power policy. Like so many things which happened in the papal monarchy of the thirteenth century, this was an institutionalised and formalised version of what had happened in the twelfth. Whereas in the treaty with Genoa in 1120[4] cardinals had participated as members of the *curia* which included clerks and laymen of varying ranks, now they assisted in the running of the Papal State and shared in its profits as members of an organised college, which by now had its own financial administration.

Neither Honorius nor Gregory had smooth relations with Rome, but Gregory's were notoriously bad. He came from a family connected with that of Innocent III, but he seems to have had no feudal magnates in his immediate family, and he was not able to use his relations in the same way as Innocent III. Since the beginning of the century Romans had often been appointed by communes in Umbria and the Tuscan patrimony as their *podestà*, and cities as distant and important as Perugia

---

[1] *Liber censuum*, i, pp. 455, 456, 470, 483–516, 520–34, 537–41. The *Vita Gregorii* describe the lords of Miranda as supporters of heresy, highwaymen, forgers, coiners; their crimes did not relieve him of the necessity to buy them out!

[2] *Reg. Greg. IX*, nos. 1715, 2056; Theiner, *C.D.*, i, no. 174 (misnumbered no. 124). For this list see Waley, *P.S.*, p. 69n. It is not clear to me that these places constituted papal domain in central Italy (ibid.) in any exclusive sense. Some important papal forts such as Castro dei Volsci are not named in the list. But in any case I question whether the term 'domain' will bear the sense put on it here. Cf. G. Ermini, 'Caratteri della sovranità temporale dei papi nei secoli XIII e XIV', *ZSSRG, Kan. Abt.* xxvii (1938), pp. 315–47, at pp. 317 ff., 341–2. And Theiner, *C.D.*, i, p. 89 'in demanio sicut Anagniam et alias civitates Campanie'; also E. Jordan, *Les origines de la domination angevine en Italie* (Paris, 1909), pp. cxxx–cxxxi.

[3] Cf. Waley, pp. 122–3, 139–40; Partner, Papal State pp. 138–9. The draft decree was published by K. Hampe, 'Eine unbekannte Konstitution Gregors IX.', *Zeitschrift f. Kirchengesch.*, xlv, n.s. 8 (1926), pp. 190–7. It is unlikely that this constitution took effect. Cf. *Liber censuum*, i, p. 27.

[4] P. 160 above.

had recognised some form of Roman supremacy. The increase of papal
temporal power was indeed from one point of view an increase in
Roman temporal power. In the third and fourth decades of the century
Roman aggression and ambition increased to an unheard-of degree.
Boundary stones were placed to mark the limits of Roman jurisdiction –
a sort of antiquarian approach to politics which often marked Roman
communal policy. Having resisted Gregory and flirted with the emperor
during Gregory's first war with Frederick in 1228, Rome returned to
obedience and issued a very detailed and oppressive statute against
heresy, which could have been a fearsome political weapon in the hands
of a papalist senator.

Essentially, although Roman expansion led the city into conflict in
the southern Campagna also, the struggle was over Rome's drive to the
north-west, against the powerful city of Viterbo, and the less powerful
maritime towns to whose subordination Viterbo was the key. This was
the thirteenth-century equivalent of the struggles for Tivoli and Tuscolo
in the preceding century, though the economic basis was rather different.
Tivoli and Tuscolo meant control of the sheep-runs in the Aniene
valley, the Alban hills, and the Abruzzi; Viterbo meant control of the
wine and grain producing areas north of Lake Bracciano, and of the
ports of the Maremma. How desirable these places were can still be seen,
not only in the rich medieval buildings of Viterbo, but in the extraordinary group of beautiful medieval churches in Tuscania.

In 1233 Gregory allowed the Romans (after many wars) to impose
oaths of fealty on Viterbo. He swiftly regretted this; not only were the
terms imposed harder than he had stipulated, but the Romans rapidly
overran the whole Roman District, taking feudal oaths from all Sabina,
and occupying strongpoints on the Tyrrhenian coast as far north as
Corneto and the important fortress of Montalto. South of the city, Rome
was resisted by Gregory's old diocese of Velletri, by places controlled
or influenced by his relations like Segni and Anagni, and by papal fortresses like Aquapuzza. Against him fought the family of his predecessor Honorius III, the Savelli. War was general in the entire Roman
area. In Rome some of the churches and the dwellings of cardinals were
demolished by 'diggers' (*fossatores*) who weakened the walls until
they collapsed; church lands were seized and their revenues assigned
against war expenses; the Lateran was looted. This was the most severe
clash between Rome and its bishop since the wars of the Alexandrine
schism in the 1160s. It was also an important point in the process by
which very many of the estates of the great Roman churches fell out of

clerical control, some of them then enjoying a short period of freedom as rural communes, but most of them falling in the end into the hands of the Roman nobility. By 1238 the lands of the great monastery of S. Paolo fuori le Mura, most of which lay in the area of severe Roman pressure in southern Etruria, were said to be all heavily indebted, and their incomes consumed by usury.[1] The old denominations and divisions of the ancient papal estates or *massae* were being forgotten by the intruding laymen who held and worked the lands, in the Roman District just as much as in the Romagna; this at least is suggested by the defence offered against the claim of the Bishop of Porto to his lands in the *massa Cesana* east of Lake Bracciano.[2]

For subsidies to fight the Romans Gregory appealed to France and Germany, and for troops to Frederick II and to the communes in Umbria and the march, besides to the 'loyal' communes in the Roman District on whom the brunt of the fighting fell. His allies in the Tuscan patrimony captured many Roman prisoners. But other factors probably also persuaded the Romans to come to terms. The Roman merchants doing profitable business in France collecting the monies for the crusade suddenly had their activities stopped.[3] In May 1235 a compromise was struck; the oppression of Roman clerks and churches was abandoned and the oaths taken by the towns in the District to Rome released; the Roman claims against the pope for war indemnities were waived.[4] But the Romans were far from capitulating to Gregory; the attempt to stop them from summoning the subject towns to the Capitoline court was abandoned, and they also subsequently went back on their engagement to restore the important fort of Montalto, which had been the original cause of the dispute.[5]

In the rest of the Papal State, Gregory's success in the period between the peace of San Germano and the excommunication of the emperor

---

[1] *Reg. Greg. IX*, nos. 3207–8, license to sell S. Severa on the Tyrrhenian coast, and land South of Rome in Cave and Anagni. For the fate of the lands of the monastery on the Via Cassia and the Via Flaminia, see Tomassetti, *C.R.*, iii, pp. 113–4, 284–5, 289–90, 298 et passim; S. Severa ibid. ii, p. 542. On the free communes see *Statuti della Provincia Romana* (Rome, 1930).

[2] *Reg. Greg. IX*, nos. 3955–62 (5 November 1237). The Bishop of Porto got judgement, but it is clear from the defence offered that the landholdings no longer bore any relation to the ancient titles.

[3] Ibid. no. 1991 (1 July 1234).

[4] Some authors take 5,000 pounds 'recepta mutuo super Rocca de Papa' to refer to a loan by the Romans to the pope, but it seems much more likely to refer to a loan raised by Rome on the security of Rocca di Papa. Ibid. no. 3032; Bartoloni, *Codice Diplomatico del Senato Romano*, no. 81.

[5] *Reg. Greg. IX*, no. 2021; Rodenberg (ed.), *Epistolae Saeculi XIII e Regestis Pontificum Romanorum selectae, MGH* (1883), i, no. 591, p. 479. Cf. Waley, *P.S.*, p. 143

in 1239 can only be described as modest.[1] In the march of Ancona, where the feudal tenure of the Marquis of Este had lapsed, the expedient of entrusting the area to a French warrior-bishop, Milo of Beauvais, was unsuccessful, and ended in the revolt of several towns. Milo was withdrawn, but his successor was hardly more successful; and although papal rule in the march was perceptible, it was not strikingly effective. In Umbria even Perugia, where Gregory spent much of his time when excluded from Rome, was often engaged in alliances which were forbidden by the pope, and Orvieto in defiance of papal absolute prohibition went on occupying the north-east shore of the Lake of Bolsena (Val di Lago) as she was to continue to do for most of the rest of the century.[2] In Romagna, where the position of papal temporal power remained very ambiguous, there was hardly a trace of its exercise. Frederick II called parliaments in the papal cities of Ravenna (1232) and Ferrara (1238), and appointed his counts of Romagna. Papal intervention in the struggle to control the important salt-pans of Cervia, which the other towns sought to wrest from Ravenna, got no further than judgements which were never enforced. The realities were shown painfully in a bull of 1238 which admits that the cathedral seat of the Bishop of Cervia (which lay outside the town) was deserted and ruined after three years of war, flood, fire, and plunder: the description is detailed enough to show that this was not a rhetorical flourish.[3]

Tension between Pope Gregory and the Emperor Frederick continued to rise, but its main source was Frederick's action against the Lombard communes; his interference in the Papal State was by comparison a minor irritant. In Rome the Frangipani, anxious to prop up their declining territorial power in the Maritime province, sought money and influence as the agents of Frederick II. This brought them little luck; in a brief outbreak of war in 1236–7 the main Frangipani fortress in Rome, the *turris cartularia* on the Palatine above the Arch of Titus, was utterly destroyed. Frederick II's appetite for grandiose propagandist gestures led him in 1237, after his great victory over the Lombard League at Cortenuova, to make the Roman commune a present of the captured Milanese *carroccio*, the palladium of the defeated city; a suitably

---

[1] Ibid. pp. 136–45.

[2] Ibid. See also for Perugia *Reg. Greg. IX*, no. 959 (Rodenberg, no. 493) and Potthast, nos. 9842, 9843, referring to Perugian participation in the wars of Gubbio and Cagli (1235). For Orvieto see also Waley, *Orvieto*, pp. 27 ff.

[3] *Reg. Greg. IX*, no. 4183. Cf. ibid. no. 1320 (Potthast, no. 9199) and Hessel, *Bologna*, pp. 206–10. There was a papal attempt to mediate in the wars of Romagna in 1235, *Reg. Greg. IX*, no. 2436; Rodenberg, no. 628, p. 513.

sonorous inscription was erected in Rome at the same time. But if one seeks significant symbolism, one might find it equally in the collapse in 1239 of the rebuilt *turris cartularia,* which by Frederick's orders had been restored, but so badly that it fell into ruins when his soldiers climbed onto it.

VI

If any one action can be taken as decisive for the fate of the late medieval papacy, it is probably Gregory IX's second excommunication of Frederick II, on 20 March 1239. In the citation of papal grievances against Frederick the Papal State plays only a minor part: Gregory instances the emperor's occupation of Ferrara and of several Matildine lands such as Bondeno, and Frederick's claims to Città di Castello, Massa Carrara (in Tuscany) and Sardinia.[1]

The great war in which the papacy now engaged created a demand for money which the papal bureaucratic machine was in a better position than ever before to provide, though it still could not provide enough. Within a few months demands for subsidies went out to England and many other parts of the Catholic world. Not only subsidies but prebends conferred on Roman clerks were a part of the growing fiscal apparatus. In the midst lay the College of Cardinals, its interests sprawling octopus-like through the *curia* itself and out into the world of lay princes, some-times opposed to certain types of exercise of papal power, but always stimulating the growth of the main fiscal and administrative machine. This was not a very efficient machine; on the contrary it was full of gaps, delays and anomalies. But for its time it was impressive enough.

The wars of the 1240s showed that the unquestioned military superiority of German arms in Italy had gone for ever. Both the pope and the emperor were the leaders of Italian political parties, not their masters; each was seeking to outbid the other in grants and concessions to the communes and *signori.* If Frederick's vicar Enzo made a concession to Iesi, the papal rector of the march, Cardinal Ranier of Viterbo, was ready to do the same; if the papal rector made a concession to Fabriano, it was repeated by Frederick; if Tolentino

---

[1] Rodenberg (ed.), *Epistolae saec. XIII,* i, nos. 741, 749. There was some action in the march by Frederick in 1238; cf. Waley, *P.S.,* p. 145n. and *Reg. Greg. IX* no. 4115 (Rodenberg, no. 722).

received a row of imperial privileges, they were counter-balanced by papal concessions when the commune had changed sides.[1] Of the great 'Guelph' communes in the lands to which the papacy laid claim, Bologna probably profited most from the eleven years of anarchy in eastern Italy which elapsed between Frederick's excommunication in 1239 and his death in 1250. At the end of his period Bologna virtually shared the government of Romagna with the papal legate Ottaviano degli Ubaldini.[2] A much earlier example is the joint attack by the Guelphs on the imperial-held city of Ferrara in 1240. After its capitulation the terms showed clearly the extent to which this was a trade war; Bologna and Venice both secured the free passage of their goods across the Po, and the free access to the salt of Romagna, for which they had been struggling for most of a century.[3] Comparable transactions went on elsewhere; the concessions made by Cardinal Ranier to Spoleto in 1247 came close to a sale of the town to the papacy as highest bidder.[4] Naturally the popes sought to compensate their friends at the expense of their enemies, but the scramble to change sides when the balance of power shifted was so fast that this policy often led to difficulties: papal attempts to settle the clamorous demands of three communes of the march for the village of Pitino may stand as an example,[5] and so also may the rather clumsy papal move of transferring the episcopal see of imperialist Osimo to the papalist city of Recanati.

The watershed of the war was the long vacancy in the papal see which followed the death of Gregory IX on 22 August 1241. Up to this point there had been periods when it seemed that victory in central Italy was within Frederick's reach, particularly in 1240 when the march of Ancona had much of it capitulated to Frederick's son Enzo, and when Frederick had overrun most of Umbria and Latium. Rome seemed imminently threatened, and like the popes of the early Middle Ages Gregory made a solemn procession across Rome with the holy relics (22 February 1240). But perhaps the danger was more apparent than real; Frederick never attacked Rome, and the city did not see the brutal onrush of German troops into the churches which it had known in

---

[1] Hagemann's important articles quoted above, and also his: 'Fabriano im Kampf zwischen Kaisertum und Papsttum', *Quellen*, xxx (1940), pp. 88–136 and ibid. xxxii (1942), pp. 51–109; idem, 'Iesi im Zeitalter Friedrichs II.', ibid., xxxvi (1956), pp. 138–87. Ranier of Viterbo's privilege was not confirmed by Innocent IV

[2] Hessel, *Bologna*, pp. 248 ff.

[3] Ibid. p. 219; cf. Theiner, *C.D.*, i, no. 191.

[4] Waley, *P.S.*, p. 151, and cf. Jordan, *Origines*, p. cxxxiv.

[5] *Quellen*, xliv (1964), pp. 225–6. The communes were Tolentino, Camerino, and Treia.

1167.[1] The thirteenth-century method was to play on the Italian spirit of party, rather than rely on the German knights alone; and on this occasion the Roman parties gave Frederick no satisfaction. Fresh imperial victories in the following year, including the capture of the bishops coming to Gregory's council at Rome, still did not move the Romans; two months before the sea battle of Meloria in which the clerks fell into Frederick's hands, the Roman senators had renewed their fidelity to the pope and to the terms of the Roman agreement with the pope made in 1235.[2]

By this point the Italian factions in the communes had come to consider themselves either as imperialist or papalist, 'Ghibelline' or 'Guelph'. But the politics of Rome in these years make nonsense of such classifications; what counted was the egotisms of the factions and the larger, yet more ferocious egotism of the commune. The guarantee of church liberties was signed in March 1241 by Annibaldo Annibaldi and Oddo Colonna as senators, and also by the war-like Cardinal Giovanni Colonna, who a few months earlier had been in rebellion against the pope and assisting Frederick II in his devastation of the Roman countryside. Colonna had been one of the most important administrators of the temporal power under Gregory, and his rebellion was not the irresponsible action of a factional leader, but an act of despair on the part of the leader of the peace party in the *curia*. A few months later the tyrannical Matteo Rossi Orsini was appointed sole senator, and immediately after Gregory IX's death (following the instructions of the dead pope) he compelled the cardinals to come to the Septizonium 'palace' for the conclave, dragging at least one or two of them there in chains through the streets.[3] The regime of Matteo Rossi Orsini was opposed to the emperor and to the Colonna, whose forts and houses he destroyed, and whose cardinal, Giovanni of Santa Prassede, he kept in prison from the end of the conclave until 1243.

When the pope elected by the Septizonium conclave died after a few days in office (Celestine IV, 25 October–10 November 1241), the cardinals fled from Rome to escape a repetition of their noisome imprisonment; they re-assembled gradually at Anagni, but did not finally elect a new pope until 25 June 1243. When this new pontiff, Sinibaldo Fieschi of Genoa, took office as Innocent IV, he proved to be a tough and

---

[1] Cf. Waley, p. 148.

[2] Bartoloni, *Codice Diplomatico del Senato Romano*, no. 98, p. 161 (4 March 1241).

[3] Cf. K. Wenck, 'Das erste Konklave der Papstgeschichte', *Quellen*, xviii (1926), pp. 101–70 especially pp. 120 ff; B. Sütterlin, *Die Politik Kaiser Friedrichs II. und die römischen Kardinäle in den Jahren 1239–50* (Heidelberg, 1929), pp. 46–66.

worldly politician, a bureaucrat inexorable in squeezing every penny which papal fiscality could extort, and absolutely intransigent in his dealings with Frederick. His pontificate is seen by good judges as marking a sinister date in the history of the late medieval papacy, even though he sought in good faith to defend church 'liberties' against lay power.[1]

Innocent IV went into exile to Genoa and Lyon in 1244, and papal temporal power continued to be in eclipse. At the Council of Lyon in 1245, when Frederick was 'deprived' of the empire, Innocent in the deposition sentence mentioned his occupation of the march of Ancona, the duchy of Spoleto, and Benevento, besides other church lands (presumably the Matildine lands) in Tuscany and Lombardy.[2] But in 1248 the resistance of north and central Italy to the emperor began to harden after the battle of Vittoria, and the communes of the march of Ancona and the duchy of Spoleto began to drift back to the papal side. By the summer of 1249 a determined attempt to threaten and cajole imperialist 'rebels' was being made in the march of Ancona, at a parliament called by Cardinal Peter Capocci, which is also the earliest parliament of the sort known to have been held in the Papal State.[3] Similar regulations were issued in Romagna shortly afterwards by Cardinal Ottaviano degli Ubaldini and Bologna, after the capitulation of Modena on 22 October 1249.[4]

The revolt of Ravenna against the pope and the defeat of Cardinal Capocci in August 1250 at Cingoli in the march left the issue still in question. The papal generals failed to raise the army with which they planned to invade the kingdom. If one looks back to the fiasco of Gregory IX's attempt to do the same thing in 1228, this is hardly surprising. If Frederick had lived, it is not inconceivable that sheer war-weariness would have driven the combatants to seek a compromise, in the end. But the end did not come in this way. On 13 December 1250 Frederick II died at Fiorentino. The struggle between the popes and the Hohenstaufen for the control of Italy was not over, but the priesthood had gained advantages which it later proved impossible to reverse. On

---

[1] Cf. Jordan, *Origines*, pp. 35–40, 78–9; G. Barraclough, *The Medieval Papacy* (1968), pp. 118–20.

[2] *MGH, Const. et acta publica*, ii, no. 200.

[3] Waley, 'Constitutions of the Cardinal-Legate Peter Capocci, July 1249', *EHR*, lxxv (1960), pp. 660–4; idem, *P.S.*, pp. 149–50. See also Hagemann's articles, for conditions in the march at this time.

[4] Hessel, *Bologna*, pp. 250–1. For conditions in the Romagna cf. also O. Canz, *Philipp Fontana Erzbischof von Ravenna. Ein Staatsmann des XIII. Jahrhunderts* (Leipzig, 1910), pp. 39 ff.

the other hand, the Church had failed to secure all its objectives. The war had shown how strong the papacy was in defence; the next fifteen years were to show how weak it was in attack. With Frederick's death the Church was rid of the great aggressor, but it had not yet found the champion who could give it temporal security.

VII

One of the most striking things about the disappearance of the authority of Frederick II is the relatively small difference this made to political realities in Tuscany, Romagna and the Papal State. The proscription of former Imperialist 'rebels' was far from pitiless; quite small communes in the march such as Sant'Elpido which had returned to imperialist obedience as late as the summer of 1250 were within three or four years forgiven and re-instated in their privileges by the papal government. Particularly in Tuscany the Ghibelline party sympathies of Cardinal Ottaviano degli Ubaldini produced what might seem remarkable anomalies, if the Guelph was to be regarded as the 'papal' party. The main political development in Romagna was the acceleration of the growth of the hegemony of Bologna, which was the price which the Archbishop of Ravenna had to pay for the restoration of the Guelph in Bologna, and the pacification of the province. With double the population (probably) of any city in the Papal State, Bologna was immensely formidable. How far Innocent IV helped the situation in Romagna by getting his nephew appointed imperial vicar in Romagna by William of Holland, and then making him the heir to the Traversari lordship in Ravenna, is doubtful.[1] This was an expedient which looked back to the nepotism of Innocent III in the Papal State, and which was to be adopted by many other later thirteenth-century popes, most strikingly by Boniface VIII.

In the rest of the Papal State the rule inexorably followed in the 1250s was the oppression of the smaller communes by the greater, either with the explicit consent of the papacy or at the worst at the price of ineffective papal protest. Innocent IV returned to Italy from Lyons in 1251; he is sometimes reckoned to have been more successful than his Conti successor Alexander IV (12 December 1254–25 May 1261) in the control of the temporal power, but if the difference exists it is a fine one. Orvieto immediately after Frederick's death made a bargain with

---

[1] Jordan, *Origines*, pp. 35–7. For Romagna see also the works of Hessel and Canz, quoted above.

the imperial vicar and the Aldobrandeschi counts, which gave the city virtual control of the area between Monte Amiata, the lake of Bolsena and the sea. Thus the commune kept its former illegal hegemony over Acquapendente and Val di Lago, and added to it. Condoned by Innocent IV, Perugia pursued a ruthless war with Foligno, and eventually succeeded in persuading Alexander IV to give it the lease of the *contado* of Gubbio. Innocent's allowing the Perugians to tax their clergy is significant of his weakness.[1] Viterbo continued to pursue an aggressive career the limits of which were dictated by the interests of the feudal prefects of Vico and of the Roman commune, not by the popes. Spoleto was given papal privileges which allowed the town to claim supremacy over the area of papal domain known as the *terra Arnulphorum* (near Cesi), and also over the lands of the once rich but now ruined abbey of Ferentillo.[2]

Rome was, as always, not the least aggressive of the great communes. In August 1252 the city took the unorthodox step of appointing a 'foreign' senator, the Bolognese noble Brancaleone degli Andalò. The intention was evidently to achieve a brusque change in the control both of Rome and of the District. In the preceding decade the family of Annibaldi had been important both as senators and (through Cardinal Richard Annibaldi the papal rector of the Campagna and the Maritime province and later papal vicar of Rome) as papal officials; this had assisted the family in the control of Terracina, where they had supplanted the Frangipani. Neither the Annibaldi nor the Colonna were acceptable to the new Roman regime, which stiffened Roman demands against Viterbo, Tivoli, and Terracina.

The place of the pope in these developments shows his political weakness. Innocent IV returned rather hesitantly to Rome in October 1254, and stayed only a few months, annoyed by the importunity of the Roman bankers to whom he owed money, and by that of other Romans who demanded bribes. When he had passed briefly through Rome in the early summer of 1254 the pope went on, significantly, to the Annibaldi fortress of la Molara, in the Alban hills. His notary Arlotus acted as intermediary between the Romans and Tivoli, to which Brancaleone was laying siege.[3]

[1] Rodenberg (ed.), *Epistolae saec. XIII*, iii, no. 29, p. 22.
[2] Cf. Jordan, p. 254. For the reform of the monastery of Ferentillo see R. Brentano, *Two Churches: England and Italy in the Thirteenth Century* (Princeton, 1968), pp. 262–73.
[3] Nicholas de Carbio's life of Innocent IV, in *ASR*, xxi (1898), para. 40. For the Annibaldi see A. di Pietro, A. di Trasmondo, Cardinal Richard A., in *Dizionario biografico degli Italiani;* cf.

The election of Alexander IV, of the Conti family, and the uncle of Annibaldo Annibaldi whom he later made papal rector of the march, entailed evidently a sharp hostility with Brancaleone's regime in Rome.[1] Brancaleone had achieved the subjection of Tivoli and the quadrupling of its annual tribute, and had also been invested with dictatorial powers to deal with the rebellion of the Colonna, but this did not save him from expulsion from Rome in November 1255. The noble and pro-papal regime set up after Brancaleone's fall lasted only for about eighteen months. In the spring of 1257 Brancaleone returned as senator, more terrible than ever against the papalist nobles, whose towers and palaces he destroyed. The social conflict of nobles and people (present in many other cities in Latium) was an element in Brancaleone's return to the senate. The pope had his party in the Campagna against Brancaleone, and he also played Viterbo off against Rome in the traditional way; but altogether Alexander's family policy in Rome was a complete failure, and only the death of Brancaleone when besieging Corneto (summer of 1258) saved the pope from further humiliation. Roman-papal relations in the period between Frederick II's death and Manfred's invasion of the Papal State in 1258 explain well enough why the popes failed to seize the 'opportunity' to create a strong Papal State in this period.

VIII

If the popes lacked the material power to rule strongly in the Papal State, they did not lack the bureaucratic machine, and their possession of this machine was not unimportant, even if its functioning was irregular.[2] Innocent III had set up the basic provincial government of the Papal State, giving to each province (after some hesitation) a clerical rector rather than a lay governor. Under the rector were one or more judges, notaries, a handful of subordinate officials and soldiers. The proposal to make all rectors members of the College of Cardinals, put forward under Gregory IX, was not executed, any more than was the proposal made at the same time that the pope should share the temporal

---

also Falco in *ASR*, xlviii (1925), pp. 58 ff.; Bartoloni, *Codice Diplomatico del Senato Romano*, pp. 177 ff.

[1] For Alexander IV's protest against Roman coercion of Rocca Antica in Sabina in August 1255 see *Gött. Nachr.*, 1903, pp. 590–1. For his family see S. Andreotta, *La famiglia di Alessandro IV e l'abbazia di Subiaco* (Rome, 1963), and *Atti e Mem. della Società Tiburtina di Storia e d'Arte*, xxv–xxvi (1962–3).

[2] By far the best account is in Waley, *P.S.*, pp. 69–80, 91–124, and see also his important chapters on the financial and military utility of the Papal State, pp. 252–96.

revenues with the college. The rector was responsible for the finances of the province, but by the middle of the century he had not yet been given a treasurer to help him. The judicial organisation of the provinces was fairly clearly defined. The most important question was whether the larger communes were to be allowed to hear lawsuits on appeal from inferior courts; although successful with the smaller communes in this the papacy was on the whole unsuccessful with the larger (Rome was a special case, but no exception). The places of the Papal State had fiscal obligations (usually defined in the march of Ancona by papal grant, but customary elsewhere), obligations of feudal military service, and obligations to give counsel, which from time to time, though very infrequently in the first half of the century, led to participation in a provincial 'parliament' at the behest of the rector. The historical origins of the obligations of the pope's subjects, which varied very widely from one province to another, were of great complexity. Wide differences lay between papal rights in Campagna and the Maritime province, and the area north of Rome now known as the 'patrimony of St Peter in Tuscany', which together made up the ancient patrimony of St Peter, and the parts of the duchy of Spoleto in which the popes viewed themselves as the successors to the imperialist government of the dukes. Different again were papal rights in the march of Ancona, most of which (though not all, for Rimini and Osimo were ancient demesnes of the Holy See) dated from agreements and concessions made in the thirteenth century. Some of these concessions (such as that to Ancona, which had the right to coin its own money) were far-reaching. Different yet again were towns in which the rights of the popes had other origins – Perugia, Orvieto, Rieti. The Papal State was no exception among European states in consisting of bundles of feudal, demesnial and regal rights of various kinds.

The fate of southern Italy, and the relations of the popes with the Hohenstaufen, were the great political issues which overshadowed the regional politics of the Papal State in the 1250s. Unable either to summon enough military force to conquer south Italy, or to get acceptable terms from Frederick's legitimate heir Conrad, Innocent from early in 1253 was fishing for a new champion of the Church on whom the fief of the southern kingdom could be conferred. In the summer of 1253 Charles of Anjou, brother of the king of France, was proposed, though the negotiation failed. From the first, huge sums of money were mentioned as necessary to finance the expedition – annual loans of 400,000 pounds of Tours by the pope to Charles were suggested in the first proposals. Conrad's death on 21 May 1254 appeared to remove obstacles from the path of papal diplomacy; by this time the idea of the candidature of Edmund, son of Henry III of England, for the throne of the southern kingdom, was being taken seriously. Innocent's attempt to come to an understanding with Frederick's illegitimate son Manfred in the summer of 1254 had a temporary success. But when the pope, having made Manfred papal vicar in the kingdom, crossed the Neapolitan border and went with his new vassal to Naples, old rancours and new friction caused a rupture and a fresh state of war. Innocent died in Naples (7 December 1254); his successor Alexander swiftly clinched the bargain with Henry of England (May 1255). There may have been great financial advantages for the papacy in this grant, but the political advantage was small. Manfred remained powerful and unreconciled.

Alexander IV died on 25 May 1261. His irresolute nature denied him any great triumph in the temporal power. But when his relative inactivity is compared with the frenetic energy displayed by his successor Urban IV, during a three years' pontificate, the contrast between the results achieved by one pope and the other is not so striking as to persuade that unaided papal power could really do very much to impose order on central Italy. After the disastrous battle of Montaperti (4 September 1260), when the blood of every Tuscan commune faithful to the pope (and the blood of the Florentines who were not) stained the river Arbia red, there was no hope of a war-like papal policy in Tuscany or in papal Umbria. Even before the battle, in the spring of 1260, Perugia had allowed Manfred's troops to pass without hindrance; once Montaperti had been fought both Perugia and the other Umbrian communes refused to enter a papal coalition against Manfred.[1]

Rome was not alone in listening to papal instructions with only half an ear. In April 1261 the Romans (probably encouraged by the Anglophile party among the cardinals) elected Richard of Cornwall, King of the Romans and brother of Henry III of England, as senator for life.[2] Roman rapacity was (as usual) an element; Richard paid for this privilege. The Romans were a creditor group; the pope owed the Roman bankers very large sums, and so did many communes, including

[1] V. Ansidei, *Regestum Reformationum Comunis Perusii*, i (Perugia, 1935), pp. 136, 318, 326-7; and cf. Waley, *P.S.*, p. 164.
[2] F. R. Lewis, 'The Election of Richard of Cornwall as Senator of Rome in 1260', *EHR*, lii (1937), pp. 657-62; E. Duprè-Theseider, *Roma dal Comune di popolo alla Signoria pontificia (1252-1377)* (Bologna, 1952), pp. 70-8. For Perugian debts to Rome (below), see Ansidei, *Regestum*, i, pp. 277-8, 320-4.

one as important as Perugia. Roman moneylenders operated in Germany and France. But their power was insufficient to change papal policy in essentials; that an English prince should be senator of Rome for life was against papal interests unless the English candidature for Sicily was revived, and it was not. Richard of Cornwall's election had no important political effect.

The election of Jacques Pantaléon of Troyes as Urban IV (29 August 1261) brought a forceful and logical mind to the control of the Holy See. The former Patriarch of Jerusalem, Urban IV was the first of the able French bureaucrats and politicians who were at intervals to occupy the papal throne for a century and a half. Like the Englishman Hadrian IV, the last northerner to be pope before him, Urban was a man of humble origins who applied great energy and skill to the central control of the Papal State. Like the great Cardinal Gil Albornoz in the fourteenth century, Urban came to the temporal power with experience from the Crusade. Urban's biographer, Thierry de Vaucouleurs, in verses which deserve a place in any anthology of bad Latin poetry, lists the dozens of strongpoints he recovered for the Church in central Italy.[1] Urban used Hospitaller and Templar knights, as he had done in the East. Certainly his firmness in government was of some importance in the history of the temporal power, after the nepotistic laxity of Alexander. But after three years as pope all Urban could boast about the Papal State was that he had not actually lost it.[2] Things subsequently got worse, and shortly before his death in the autumn of 1264 Urban claimed to be seriously considering a flight to France.

Urban IV was also remarkable for the energy of his financial policy; having paid 150,000 marks of his predecessor's debts, and spent very large sums on troops and fortifications, he turned to Christian Europe. He asked the English clergy for a gracious aid and a hundredth on property, made great churches such as Winchester pay large amounts for the relatively new impost of 'common service', and made the English king pay his tribute.[3]

The real importance of Urban IV lies not in his financial or temporal power administration, but in his diplomacy. For the first eighteen months of his pontificate he negotiated continuously with the French

---

[1] e.g. in the *Vita* (*RRIISS*, iii, pt. 2, col. 410), about the recovery of Marta on the lake of Bolsena: 'Dicto P. (the prefect of Vico) libras septingentas dedit ipse. De Perusinis dicta moneta fuit. Quingentas Jacobo (the Lord of Bisenzio): fuit illa moneta Senensis.'

[2] Quoted by K. Hampe, *Urban IV. und Manfred (1261-4)* (Heidelberg, 1905), p. 61.

[3] Lunt, *Financial Relations*, pp. 153, 227, 290, 464–5. For Winchester see also *Reg. Urban IV*, i, no. 68. Cf. also A. Gottlob, *Die Servitientaxe im 13. Jahrhundert* (Stuttgart, 1903), pp. 76–88.

court and intermittently with Manfred. The acute German pressure on the Papal State was for a time relaxed, though Manfred remained in control of much of the march. The negotiations for the future status of the kingdom were slow. The English claim was at last liquidated, and the idea of a Spanish candidature abandoned. It took much persuasion to overcome the reluctance of Louis IX of France to risk delaying the crusade in order to provoke a quarrel with Manfred which he considered avoidable. Only after papal negotiations with Manfred had broken down in 1263 did the King of France finally come round to admitting the candidature of his brother Charles of Anjou for the throne of Sicily.

The adoption of Charles of Anjou as King of Sicily, for which detailed proposals were drawn up in the papal *curia* in June, 1263, was the most important change in the political system of the papacy since the Norman connection of the eleventh century. In effect it recognised French as the successor to German power in Italy, and sought to bind it to the Holy See by engagements similar in nature to the guarantees given to the Church by Frederick II and Otto IV. But the new Angevin guarantees were not determined by the texts of the ancient donations; they reflected the political conditions of the thirteenth century and not those of the eighth. The new king of Sicily bound himself to supply 300 horses for feudal service in the named lands of the Papal State, and in the unnamed 'other lands of the Church' (an expression later taken to include Romagna).

The immediate aim of the Angevin candidature was to get rid of Manfred. But beyond this the agreements had to contemplate a new situation in which French power dominated Italy. Urban IV certainly gave thought to this, and so far as treaties could bind a new great power, those which he drafted did so. One could quote the Joachimite writing which told the Roman See that French power was a hawthorn staff which pierced the hand of him who leaned on it.[1] But Urban could look at papal impotence during the thirteen years which had elapsed since the death of Frederick II, and reflect that there was no security except in French help. The fiasco of the employment of England as a papal auxiliary in Italy and Germany had ended with the Barons' Revolt of 1258, which reduced England to a state of civil war and collapse. A compromise with German power in south Italy had been attempted by Alexander IV and (with far less determination) by Urban himself, but had failed utterly.

It is arguable – and the same argument can be used of the transfer

[1] Hampe, p. 63.

of the papacy to Avignon in the following century – that the popes
fixed their minimum security requirement too high, and so condemned
themselves to buying security at an excessive political price.[1] It was, of
course, a violation of the rights of the Holy See that Manfred occupied
most of the march of Ancona, and sent his agents to stir up trouble in
other parts of the Papal State. Yet Louis IX thought that Urban IV
ought to be able to reach a compromise with Manfred, and he was
well informed on the subject. Urban IV did not apparently want such
a compromise, and was from the start disposed to pay the price for
Angevin intervention.

The immediate result of the break with Manfred and the offer to
Charles of Anjou was an intensification of the military struggle. One
of Urban's rectors, the layman Guiscard of Pietrasanta, rector of the
Tuscan patrimony, was murdered by dissident barons near Montefiascone (February 1264). Another, the Bishop-elect of Verona, rector of
the march, was captured by Manfred's troops. In 1264 one German force
attacked Campagna and the Maritime province while another under
Percival Doria crossed the passes from the Abruzzi and struck north
towards Spoleto, with the intention of cutting off Urban and his court
in their headquarters at Orvieto. Only Doria's death by drowning while
fording the Nera near Spoleto in July 1264 saved the pope from an
urgent danger. At the same time the revolt of the magnate Peter of Vico
in the Tuscan patrimony pressed papal forces hard, and the situation
of the papal court at Orvieto continued to be unsafe.

The kind of price Urban was paying became apparent in 1263 when
the Romans elected Charles of Anjou as Senator for life. For the pope
and the cardinals the election was politically acceptable though constitutionally rather alarming; it made nonsense, before Charles even set
foot in Italy, of his solemn guarantees of non-interference in the Papal
State. Urban used of Charles and Manfred the ominous metaphor of
Scylla and Charybdis. But as his military situation worsened in Italy,
Urban's bargaining position in France deteriorated also. He was ending
the pontificate in debt as his predecessor had done; his current expenses
for the war were over 200,000 pounds of Sienese money. In May of
1264 Urban was ready to accept a compromise about the senate; and

---

[1] Cf. Haller, *Das Papsttum*, iv, p. 370, where the German historian says that the papacy had to
pay the price for its victory over the empire, if it is recognised that the domination of Italy
was an essential (*Lebensbedürfnis*) for the papacy. G. Mollat, *The Popes at Avignon*, says, English
translation from the ninth French edition (London, 1963), p. 67, 'temporal power, on which,
in the Middle Ages, spiritual power depended'.

by this time the first Angevin officials had arrived (and been accepted by the pope) in Rome. In August the conditions of the offer by the kingdom were finally agreed with Charles of Anjou. Within a few weeks of receiving the news of their acceptance, Urban IV died (2 October 1264). He had put into motion a train of events as irreversible for the papacy as for Italy.

Chapter 8

The Papacy and the Royal House of France

I

Charles of Anjou evaded the Sicilian blockading fleet, and his galleys were towed up the Tiber to S. Paolo fuori le Mura on 21 May 1265. The force he brought with him was not large, but the moral effect of his arrival was spectacular. The Prefect, Peter of Vico, who had a few weeks earlier been attacking the walls of Rome, submitted to the Angevin; the most important partisan of Manfred in the Roman area thus changed sides without a blow being struck. The slowness of Manfred to react during the six months which followed Urban IV's death in October 1264 has never been satisfactorily explained. Another French pope, Guy Foulquois (Clement IV) had been elected by the conclave in February 1265 in the expectation – fully justified by his pontificate – that he would faithfully execute the politics of his predecessor. Manfred's inactivity in the critical period before and after the arrival of Charles of Anjou may perhaps be put down partly to idleness and over-confidence ('the bird is in the cage') and partly to lack of resources. He was after all not the legal representative of the house of Hohenstaufen but in effect an Italian party leader, whose freedom of action in international affairs, though appreciable, was limited.

Manfred brought his army through the passes from the Abruzzi up the Via Valeria, and for a few weeks his army and that of Charles faced each other in the Aniene valley near Tivoli. But there was no general engagement; at the other end of the Papal State the Orvietan and Angevin troops alarmed Manfred's Sienese allies into withdrawing from the papal fort of Radicofani. Manfred remained relatively inactive through the summer and autumn of 1265, while the diplomatic preparation for the march of the main Angevin army through north Italy was being skilfully executed. The army assembled at Lyons in October, made its way through Italy in November and December, and arrived in Rome in mid-January 1266. On 20 January Charles of Anjou left Rome with the united army; on 2 February he crossed the border of the kingdom at Ceprano; on 26 February Manfred's army defiled into the plain of Benevento, to be defeated and massacred by the French and their allies. By offering pitched battle instead of avoiding it as Roger of Sicily had done with Lothar in 1137, Manfred had lost the game at one throw. Frederick II's Italian kingdom was almost at an end, though the legitimate heir, sixteen-year-old Conradin, still lived in Germany.

The alliance which had conquered at Benevento was not only that of the pope and the county of Anjou. Particularly in the financing of the expedition, which was almost certainly the biggest money transaction in which the popes had ever engaged, a whole new 'Guelph' political constellation had come into existence in Italy. Without the resources of the Tuscan and Roman merchants, and the financial power of the Holy See which induced them to lend, no Angevin army could have marched a step.[1] The financial power of the Church had been stretched to its limit; there were anxious debates at the end of which the cardinals finally agreed to mortgage some of the lands of the Roman churches.[2] Many of the bankers who lent money were given rights in Charles's new kingdom, others penetrated into the Papal State as treasurers of provinces; with his victory a new privileged class of 'Guelphs' came into existence, which almost enables us to talk of Tuscan (as well as French) colonialism in southern Italy.

The Guelph victory was not complete while Conradin, the legitimate Hohenstaufen heir, lived. In 1268 Conradin obligingly put himself in hazard by invading Italy. He was welcomed at Rome, which he entered on 24 July 1268. The support he got from the Roman nobility, and from figures such as the twice-perjured Peter of Vico, shows how unpopular Angevin power already was. It is unlikely that Conradin's party appeared a lost and desperate one, when members of such families as the Annibaldi, Normanni or Orsini accompanied him to the war. Roman nobles had not in the past shown themselves to be romantic

[1] Jordan, pp. 536–58. For some remarks on 'Guelphs' after 1266 see my article, 'Florence and the Papacy 1300–75', *Europe in the Late Middle Ages*, J. R. Hale, J. R. L. Highfield, B. Smalley (ed.), (1965), pp. 76–81, and see also A. Vasina, *I Romagnoli fra autonomie cittadine e accentramento papale nell'età di Dante* (Florence, 1965), pp. 59–61, 166–7; D. Waley, 'Il governo papale in Romagna nell'Età di Dante', *Dante – Atti della Giornata internazionale di studio per il VII centenario*, (Faenza, 1965), pp. 27–8.
[2] Potthast, nos. 19296, 19298, 19322. Only the titular churches and major basilicas were (with one or two minor exceptions) exempted. Named lands of churches which were pledged in G. del Giudice, *Codice diplomatico del Regno di Carlo I° e Carlo II° d'Angiò* (Naples, 1863), i, pp. 57–64; also in *I Registri della Cancelleria Angioina ricostruiti da Riccardo Filangieri*, i (Naples 1950), p. 10. Cf. also Potthast, no. 19500; Jordan, pp. 553–5.

supporters of lost causes. 'Charles came to Italy and made of Conradin
a victim' wrote Dante, but that was military wisdom after the event.

Having left Rome on the Via Tiburtina-Valeria to find out the enemy
in the Abruzzi, Conradin made the error of leaving the main road for
the mountains, and arrived tired and possibly disorganised at Tagliacozzo. Here Charles of Anjou found and crushed his army (22 August
1268). The Hohenstaufen state had been defeated in 1266 at Benevento;
now in 1268 Charles had defeated the last of the Hohenstaufen family.
The subsequent capture and execution of Conradin (29 October 1268)
made the victory final.

II

For the Papal State the results of the Angevin victory were undramatic
but decisive. The peace imposed on central Italy was only partial;
the old communal wars and rancours, and the assertion by the communes of local autonomy in most matters, continued. It was moreover a
pax Gallica rather than a *pax Romana*. There was no question of a
firm imposition of papal – or French – central power over the whole
Papal State, because the material and military force which would have
been needed to do this simply did not exist. But the gradual strengthening of the institutions of papal government – above all of its power to
tax and fine – was undoubted.[1]

Charles of Anjou gave important guarantees that he would not
encroach on the rights of the Church in the Papal State as the Hohenstaufen had done.[2] These engagements concerned his tenure of the
senate, his abstention from the acquisition of legal titles to property, and
his not naming to the offices of *podestà*, captain and so on int he Papal
State communes. On the whole Charles honoured these engagements,
and where he most notably broke them he probably did so because his
political commitments to the Romans made this unavoidable. The city of

---

[1] Waley, *P.S.*, p. 183, is cautious but positive on this point. He makes a distinction between
the period 1266–78, which he considers unfavourable for the popes, and that which followed
(p. 176). Hagemann, writing about Fabriano in *Quellen*, xxxii (1942), pp. 73–4, is firmer in his
assessment of the administrative results of 1266. Cf. also G. Luzzatto, *Dai Servi della Gleba agli
albori del Capitalismo* (Bari, 1966), pp. 272–6. Conclusions about the results of 1266 depend on
judgements about the period 1239–66; in this connection Waley's opinion (against Jordan)
that 'most towns won little in constitutional status by the papal Hohenstaufen struggle' is
important (*P.S.*, p. 163).

[2] Cf. Rodenberg, *Epistolae saec. XIII*, iii, pp. 515, 581–2, 660; E. Martène and O. Durand,
Thesaurus Novorum Anecdotorum (Paris, 1717), ii, cols. 38–40; F. Bock, 'Il R(egistrum) super
senatoria Urbis di papa Nicolò III', *BISI*, lxvi (1954), pp. 79–113, at pp. 105–6, 111.

Benevento, the papal enclave in the kingdom, returned to papal rule with Charles's support. As senator he was inevitably involved in the multiple claims of the Roman commune to jurisdiction in the Roman District. One of the most important aspects of the senatorship for Charles of Anjou was that it gave him control of the whole Tyrrhenian coastline from his own Neapolitan border as far as Monte Argentario (Orbetello). For a maritime power such as his, this control was critical. Clement IV had tried to oppose Charles's domination over the ports, but by 1275 Charles had an official in charge of Corneto, and was superintending all the ports of the Tyrrhenian coast of the Papal State. Civitavecchia did not fall under direct Angevin control until the early 1280s, but it was inevitably under Angevin influence.[1]

On the whole, however, though there was friction, the connection between the popes and the Angevins was imposed by political factors which the popes could modify, but not fundamentally change. For forty years after 1266 much of the political interest in the various phrases of papal policy lies in the degree to which the popes found it possible or desirable to seek independence from French power. Some accepted it willingly, particularly, and naturally enough, the popes of French extraction.[2] Others sought to minimise it, particularly the Roman popes Nicholas III and Boniface VIII. But the friction was far from being merely a regional (still less a national) matter, even though the mutual resentment of Frenchman and Italian played a certain part.

Two important non-national issues in papal policy were the linked ones of the oecumenical question and the crusade. It is significant that the north Italian Gregory X, elected in 1271, who placed these two questions at the head of his political aims, conducted a policy in Italy which had few of the anti-Angevin overtones of the policies of his successors Nicholas III and Boniface. Gregory even listened without protest to a French suggestion that the Papal State should be governed by a French prince – although it is possible that his tepid reaction was due to his knowledge of how impractical the idea was.[3]

The close administrative association of the papal and Angevin governments was to be of first-class importance for over a century. The careers of magnates and officials demonstrate it from the beginning.

---

[1] C. Calisse, *Storia di Civitavecchia*, 2nd ed. (Florence, 1936) pp. 125–7, 136–40. Cf. S. Terlizzi, *Documenti delle Relazioni tra Carlo I d'Angiò e la Toscana* (Florence, 1950), no. 707, p. 377. For, Corneto cf. also Potthast, nos. 19494, 20114, and p. 278 below.

[2] Cf. Jordan's remark about Clement IV: 'loin de redouter son inmixtion (i.e. that of Charles of Anjou) dans l'Etat pontifical, il semble à la favoriser.' (p. 531).

[3] Cf. L. Gatto, *Il pontificato di Gregorio X (1271-76)* (Rome, 1959), pp. 169–71.

Jacques de Gantelme, the first Angevin vicar of Rome, arrived there for Charles in 1264, was vicar again 1269; in 1276 he was serving as captain of the Angevin forces in the papal march of Ancona, and in October of that year was again vicar in Rome.[1] Fulk de Puyricard, papal rector of the march of Ancona under Gregory X and his successors, was an important figure in Angevin government before he went into papal service.[2] Count Taddeo of Montefeltro, one of the main Angevin officials in Tuscany, was a papal-state magnate introduced to Charles by Clement IV.[3] When Gregory X appointed a new Archbishop of Ravenna, Bonifacio Fieschi, the prelate selected was a 'close friend' of Charles of Anjou.[4]

But the papacy could not disregard Germany, nor the probable renewal of German interest in Italy. Gregory X's negotiations with Rudolph of Habsburg, after the latter's election to the empire in October 1273, were directed to including the empire in a new papal political system, which sought to exclude conflict between the empire and Angevin power, and to extend and protect the lands of the Church in Italy. These aims did not fit too easily with papal-Angevin partnership. No doubt, also, an understanding with the empire was partly intended to give the papacy rather more freedom of action than Charles of Anjou had so far been willing to allow it. There was a direct conflict between imperial and Angevin interests in Tuscany, where Clement IV and Gregory X had taken it upon themselves 'during the vacancy of the empire' to appoint Charles of Anjou as 'imperial vicar'. The legal justification for this action was dubious; once elected, Rudolph of Habsburg lost little time in appointing his own imperial vicars in Tuscany.[5]

Of more direct concern to the papacy was the temporal power. The repetition of the old imperial privileges by Rudolph of Habsburg was

---

[1] A. de Boüard, *Le Régime Politique et les Institutions de Rome au Moyen-Age 1252-1347* (Paris, 1920), pp. 237, 239, 243; *ASI*, 3rd ser., xxv (1800), p. 408; M.-H. Laurent, *Le Bienheureux Innocent V (Pierre de Tarentaise) et son Temps* (Vatican City, 1947), p. 410.

[2] Waley, *P.S.*, pp. 186, 315. He had earlier been Charles's justiciar of the principate and captain in Sicily (Filangieri, *I Registri*, ad indices); cf. also E. G. Léonard, *Les Angevins de Naples* (Paris, 1954), pp. 64, 112. Also M. Fuiano, 'Le relazioni di Carlo d'Angiò col Piceno meridionale', *ASPN*, 3rd ser., lxxxiv-lxxxv (1968), pp. 117-74, especially at pp. 147, 163 ff.

[3] Potthast, no. 20490 (30 October 1268). Cf. G. Francheschini, 'Un caduto del "sanguinoso mucchio", il conte Taddeo di Montefeltro (1230?-1284) e la sua discendenza', *Stud. Romagn.*, vii (1956), pp. 45-81; idem, *I Montefeltro* (Varese, 1970), pp. 63 ff.

[4] Vasina, *I romagnoli*, pp. 37-8.

[5] *MGH, Const. et Acta Publica*, iii, no. 93, p. 85. See F. Baethgen, 'Ein Versuch Rudolfs von Habsburg, die Reichsrechte in Toskana wahrzunehmen (Ende 1275)', *Hist. Vierteljahrschr.*, xxii (1924) pp. 70-5. For what follows see also Gatto, *Gregorio X*, pp. 235-40; Laurent, *Le Bienheureux Innocent V*, pp. 337-42.

perhaps not in itself very meaningful; his undertaking not to molest Charles of Anjou was far more important. Rudolph's renewal of the old imperial guarantees to secure (among the other papal lands) the exarchate of Ravenna and the county of Bertinoro, had quite a new meaning in the political situation of 1275–8. Gregory X and his successors intended to make good the one big omission among papal territorial claims which thirteenth-century popes had so far managed to press home – the Romagna. The Romagna was the key to effective papal control of the march of Ancona – a matter particularly in the minds of the papal court at this time, because of Venetian hostility to Ancona which in 1276–7 led to a Venetian siege of the town. Of even more immediate military urgency in the Romagna was the disastrous defeat of the Guelphs there by Guido di Montefeltro at the Battle of S. Procolo (13 June 1275), which seemed to be the preface to his political domination of the whole area. The Romagna was also important to the Angevins for the same reasons as had affected Frederick II; it was a corridor between the kingdom and Emilia-Lombardy. Gregory X and Innocent V therefore opposed Rudolph's rather feeble attempts to assert imperial rights in Romagna.

Innocent V lived in office only a few months. In November 1277 Cardinal Giangaetano Orsini was elected pope, and took the title of Nicholas III. The first Roman pope since Alexander IV, Nicholas was in a sense *the* Roman pope of the later Middle Ages. Dante placed him in hell for simony, and wrote to the nepotistic cupidity with which he enriched his 'little bears' (*orsatti*). His policies were grandiose reflections of his pride in his family and in Rome; in some ways he foreshadows the more bizarre and extravagant figure of Benedict Caetani, Boniface VIII, whose arrival in the fiery pit Dante makes Nicholas eagerly anticipate.

Nicholas carried out two great strokes of policy in the temporal power, one of them perhaps of more symbolic than practical importance, the other fundamental for the later Papal State. As one of the leaders of the Roman nobility Nicholas was unfavourable to Angevin autocracy in Rome. The ten-years' tenure of the senate which Clement IV had allowed to Charles of Anjou expired in 1278. Nicholas failed to renew it, and secured the withdrawal of Angevin administration from Rome; he then issued a constitution which excluded kings and princes from holding the Roman senate.[1]

This stately document, which appeals to the Constantine Donation to

[1] Theiner, *C.D.*, i, no. 371. Analysed by Waley, *P.S.*, pp. 190–1.

justify the 'spiritual and temporal monarchy' (*utriusque potestatis monarchiam*) of the popes in Rome, contains a rather thinly veiled denunciation of the perils which Angevin rule in Rome held for the freedom of cardinals to advise or elect the Roman pontiff. It was a piece of special pleading on behalf of the anti-Angevin faction among the cardinals. Linked with this determination to reduce Angevin influence in Rome and the patrimony of St Peter was Nicholas's refusal to renew for Charles the conferment of the 'imperial vicariate' in Tuscany. This refusal seems however not to have been unreasonable, as the vicariate in Tuscany was incompatible with the policy of co-operation with Rudolph of Habsburg which Nicholas inherited from his predecessors.

Like his predecessors, Nicholas wanted to include Charles of Anjou in his negotiations with Rudolph.[1] The pope's aim was a settlement which gave the imperial infeudation of Provence to Charles and which arranged the marriage of Clemencia of Habsburg to Charles's grandson, a match which in fact took place in 1281. The possible concession of the kingdom of Arles to the Angevin was discussed, but never concluded; the proposal remained intermittently as a factor in imperial-Angevin relations for a century.

Finally in the summer of 1278 Nicholas got Rudolph to consent to papal occupation of the Romagna in full sovereignty.[2] Through negotiations were not complete until the following year, papal occupation of the province followed Rudolph's agreement immediately. At the same time Nicholas called on Charles of Anjou to furnish troops to pacify the Romagna, under the terms of the concession of the kingdom of Sicily. There were in fact already Angevin troops in the Romagna under the command of John de Montfort, but John was unacceptable to the pope because he was cousin to the murderers of the English Prince Henry of Almine.[3] A more acceptable Angevin captain was found in William Estendart, who like Puyricard was a former vicar of Sicily. Angevin troops continued under Nicholas to be the nerve of the papal

---

[1] *MGH, Const. et acta publica*, iii, nos. 210, 217, 237. No. 235, p. 223, dated 3 June 1279, clearly shows the importance attached by Nicholas to a Habsburg-Angevin settlement. It is also printed by F. Kaltenbrunner, *Actenstücke zur Geschichte des deutschen Reiches unter den Königen Rudolf I. und Albrecht I.* (Vienna, 1889), no, 162, p. 173; *Registres de Nicholas III*, no. 765. Cf. Léonard, *Les Angevins*, pp. 126–7.

[2] Waley, *P.S.*, pp. 195 ff.; Vasina, *I Romagnoli*, pp. 62 ff.

[3] Simon and Guy de Montfort murdered Henry of Almaine in Viterbo on 13 March 1271. For the relationship see C. Bémont, *Simon de Montfort Earl of Leicester 1208–65*, E. F. Jacob, (trans.) (Oxford, 1930), pp. 268–9. For the papal call for Angevin troops, *Reg. Nich. III*, no. 710; Kaltenbrunner, *Actenstücke*, no. 129. Cf. Vasina, *I Romagnoli*, pp. 75–6.

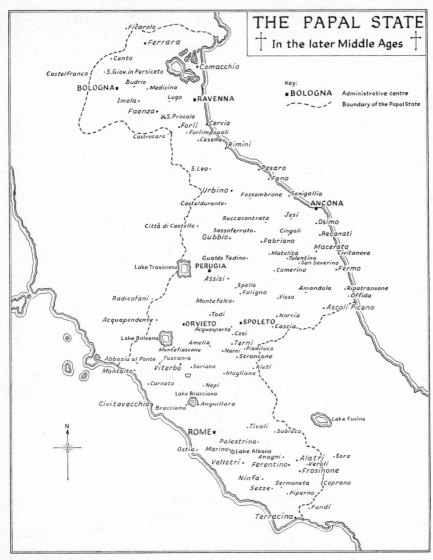

.Ficarolo
.Ferrara
.Cento
Castelfranco!   .S.Giov. in Persiceto
        Budrio
BOLOGNA■   .Medicina
    Imola.   Lugo
    Faenza.
          ※S.Procolo
.Comacchio
■RAVENNA
.Forli .Cervia
.Forlimpopoli
Castrocaro   .Cesena~Rimini

THE PAPAL STATE
† In the later Middle Ages †

Key:
■BOLOGNA   Administrative centre
‒ ‒ ‒ ‒ '   Boundary of the Papal State

. S.Leo.   .Pesaro
                .Fano
    Urbino. Fossombrone .Senigallia
Casteldurante.   ■ANCONA
      Roccacontrata   Jesi
Città di Castello.   .Osimo
        Sassoferrato. Cingoli .Recanati
        Gubbio.   .Fabriano
                    Macerata
Gualdo Tadino. .Matelica ■Civitanova
Lake Trasimeno   .Tolentino
        ■PERUGIA   .San Severino
        Assisi.   .Camerino   .Fermo
            .Spello
Radicofani. .Foligno .Visso
        Montefalco.   Amandola .Ripatransone
Acquapendente.   .Offida
        .Todi   .Norcia .Ascoli Piceno
Lake Bolsena ■ORVIETO ■SPOLETO
        Acquasparta. .Cesi .Cascia
        Amelia.   .Terni
Montefiascone .Narni .Piediluco
Abbazia al Ponte ,Tuscania .Stroncone
Montalto.   Viterbo .Soriano .Rieti
        .Magliano
    .Corneto   .Nepi
        Lake Bracciano
Civitavecchia Bracciano Anguillara
                    Lake Fucino
        .Tivoli .Subiaco
ROME■
    Palestrina.
Ostia. Marino Lake Albano
    Anagni.   .Alatri .Sora
Velletri. Ferentino. .Veroli
            .Frosinone
    Ninfa.   Sermoneta Ceprano
    Sezze.   .Piperno
                .Fondi
    Terracina.

N

recovery of Romagna, and one of Nicholas's last letters to Charles called
on him to provide more.

Nicholas III made his brother Cardinal Matteo Rosso Orsini his vicar
in the office of senator of Rome. The pope appointed his two nephews,
Cardinal Latino Malebranca and the layman Bertoldo Orsini, to carry
out together the great enterprise of the political recovery of the Romagna
and the integration of the province in the Papal State. Other members
of the Orsini family were made rectors of papal provinces or were given

K✳

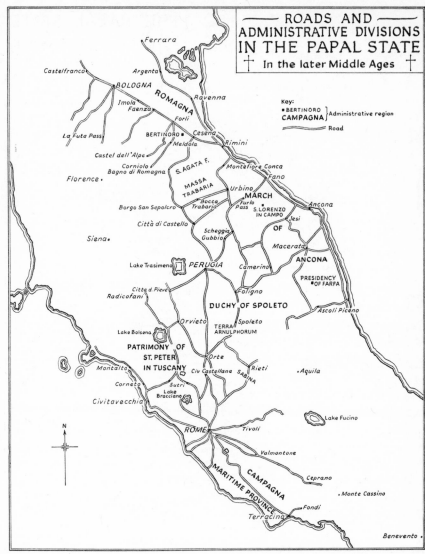

ROADS AND
ADMINISTRATIVE DIVISIONS
IN THE PAPAL STATE
† In the later Middle Ages †

Key:
■ BERTINORO ⎤
CAMPAGNA ⎦ Administrative region
━━━ Road

important offices by the Guelphs of Tuscany. With his grandiose public building projects in Rome for St Peter's, the Lateran palace and the Campidoglio, with his new castle at Soriano in the Monti Cimini, Nicholas was a great Roman prince whose state looks back to the rule of the house of Theophylact in the early Middle Ages, and forward to that of the pope-tyrants of the Renaissance. Dante's satire, and the cartoons of the little bears tugging at the pope's skirts to be fed express the bitter but also perhaps intimidated feelings of the men of his age.

But Nicholas's grandiosity and brilliance, and the friction and coldness between him and Charles of Anjou, should not conceal the continuity of his policy with that of his predecessors. Even in such a minor matter as bickering with the Angevin government over its treatment of Terracina, the record goes back to Gregory X.[1] As for Nicholas's being 'anti-Angevin', the question seems to be largely semantic. To describe the Angevin as having 'encircled' the Papal State until Nicholas III deprived him of the Tuscan vicariate seems entirely inappropriate. 'Encirclement' can only properly be used if Charles had contemplated military action against the Papal State, which he certainly did not.[2] The fact was that in 1266 the papacy and the French royal house had linked themselves in a political system of immense strength and durability. Inevitably the Angevin sought to exploit this by intimidating the College of Cardinals and seeking advantages in the Papal State; equally inevitable was the anti-Angevin reaction, both in the College of Cardinals and on the papal throne itself. But ultimately the Angevin state was the protector and the pope the protected; even Boniface VIII never forgot this. Ruin came to the papal political system at the end of the thirteenth century, when Boniface VIII – while remembering his dependence on the Angevin – issued a direct challenge to the French power which stood behind the Angevin kingdom.

Too much, possibly, has been made of Nicholas III's nepotistic 'methods'. His relations were the instruments of his policy, but the policy would in most respects have been just as effective if executed by anyone else. What particularly distinguishes Nicholas's attempt to recover Romagna from the policies of his successors, is his decision to try to reconcile the Guelph and Ghibelline factions, to secure the recall of the exiles to the cities, and to attempt to conciliate the Ghibelline lords who were led by Guido di Montefeltro.[3] This appeasing policy was in many ways realistic, and hung together with Nicholas's military weakness, and

---

[1] Cf. G. Battelli, 'Una supplica ed una minuta di Nicolò III', *Quellen*, xxxii (1942), pp 33–50. The document is photographically reproduced in his *Acta Pontificum* (Vatican City, 1965).

[2] F. Baethgen, 'Der Anspruch des Papsttums auf das Reichsvikariat', *ZSSRG, Kan. Abt.*, x (1920), pp. 168–268, at pp. 226–7. Cf. also his 'Ein Pamphlet Karls I. von Anjou zur Wahl Papst Nikolaus III.' *Sitzungsberichte der Bayerischen Akademie der Wissenschaften, Phil.-Hist. Klasse* (1960). A not very well-balanced thesis in the opposite direction was maintained by F. Savio, 'La pretesa inimicizia del papa Niccolò III contro il re Carlo d'Angiò', *Arch. Stor. Siciliano*, n.s., xxvii (1902), pp. 358–429. Cf. also R. Morghen, 'Il cardinale Matteo Rosso Orsini', *ASR*, xlvi (1922), pp. 271–372, at p. 300. I share, rather, the opinions of Waley (*P.S.*, p. 201 and note).

[3] Vasina, *I Romagnoli*, pp. 65 ff.; Waley, *P.S.*, pp. 195 ff.; J. Larner, *The Lords of Romagna. Romagnol Society and the Origins of the Signoria* (London, 1965), pp. 44–7.

his reluctance to fall into an excessive military dependence on Charles of Anjou. It was continuous with the policy of reconciling Tuscan Guelphs with Ghibellines, carried out by Gregory X. But its execution meant reversing one of the most important political events of the century in the history of the Romagna, the expulsion of the Ghibelline Lambertazzi faction from Bologna by the Geremei in 1274. This led to the embittered and expropriated exiles installing themselves with the Ghibelline faction in Faenza and Forlì, and so to the creation of a militant evicted class which made hate and political instability even more endemic in the region than before. On the other side the victorious Guelphs set up extremist organisations such as the 'Company of the Cross', which made matters yet worse.

In the late spring of 1279 Nicholas III issued a document intended to settle the internal factions of Bologna, and on 25 July the Geremei and Lambertazzi swore in front of Bertoldo Orsini to observe the peace. Cardinal Latino Malebranca went on to Tuscany to extend the peace of the factions there, and the reconciliation between Tuscan Guelphs and Ghibellines was published in January 1280. To put an end to the blood-thirsty strife of the factions was certainly a noble ambition. Latino Male-branca, son of an Orsini mother and a Frangipani father, a distinguished and austere Dominican theologian, was a man idealistic and able enough to make the attempt. But the pacification of Romagna did not last long. By the end of 1279 the factional conflict in Bologna was fully alight again, and the Lambertazzi exiles had fled to Faenza to re-open the war. In March 1280, when Nicholas III directed two long memorials to Cardinal Latino (who only then returned from Tuscany) and to Bertoldo Orsini, to try to co-ordinate and correct the policies of the two cousins, those policies had already failed. The pope wasted his time in adjuring his representatives to dissimulate; the time for fine-spun diplomacy was already over. More important was the anxiety expressed by Nicholas about money, his concern for the enrolment of mercenaries, and his hopes that Charles of Anjou would supply more troops. When Nicholas III died on 22 August 1280 the province of Romagna was still in flames.

In spite of Gregory X's recent decree on the procedure for papal elections, the conclave after the death of Nicholas III was long, tumul-tuous, and subjected to overt Angevin pressure. Charles of Anjou's wishes were fulfilled on 22 February 1281, and a French cardinal, Simon de Brie, was elected as Martin IV. The change in papal policies was dramatic. The attempts to find counterpoises to Angevin power which had been evident in papal policy since 1270 were brusquely abandoned, and the papal relation to Charles of Anjou became one of close dependence. Instead of the most Roman of popes, Rome now had a bishop who entered the city only for consecration, and spent the rest of his pontificate in Umbria. The great constitution of Nicholas III on Roman government was not applied; after the Romans (who had rebelled after Nicholas's death) had conferred the rule of the city upon Martin IV for life, the pope promptly granted the senatorship for his own lifetime to Charles of Anjou. The Angevin regime was immediately re-installed in Rome, the District and the coast. In the Romagna the policy of conciliation was reversed, the extremist Guelph factions received full papal support, and great Angevin-papal armies were assembled for an all-out attack on the cities of Guido di Montefeltro and the Ghibellines of Romagna and the march.

III

A year after the beginning of the pontificate, on 31 March 1282, the people of Palermo rose against French rule and launched the massacres known as the Sicilian Vespers.[1] Sicily was stripped from the Angevin crown for ever. Manfred's daughter Constance of Hohenstaufen had married Peter III of Aragon, and this marriage gave rise to an Aragonese claim to Sicily which turned the local revolt of 1282 into a happening of central importance for the history of the Mediterranean in the later Middle Ages. Peter accepted the invitation of the Sicilian rebels to take the crown. This acceptance of Aragonese involvement in Italy fell in with many of the long-standing maritime interests of Catalonia, and stimulated the growth of an Aragonese programme of expansion in the central and western Mediterranean. The immediate result of the Vespers was therefore the occupation of Sicily by Aragonese troops, and the outbreak of a great war between the crown of Aragon on the one part, and France and the Angevin kingdom of Naples on the other.

The role of the papacy in this great conflict, which stretched from the Pyrenees to the Greek islands of the Aegean, was dictated by the position of the pope as feudal lord of the kingdom of Naples and Sicily. But in practice the popes tended to behave as the auxiliaries of the Franco-Angevin political system. Martin IV treated the Sicilian revolt as

---

[1] The accounts of the Vespers in S. Runciman, *The Sicilian Vespers* (Cambridge, 1958) and T. S. R. Boase, *Boniface VIII* (1933) should be supplemented by that in F. Soldevila, *Història de Catalunya* (Barcelona, 1962), i, pp. 377–402; and cf. also S. Tramontana, 'La Spagna Catalana nel Mediterraneo e in Sicilia', *Nuova Rivista Storica*, l (1966), pp. 545–79.

one directed against himself; when the Sicilian delegation waited on him
at Orvieto to beg forgiveness he replied 'Hail King of the Jews! and
they smote him'. Excommunications followed; crusades were preached;
the whole diplomatic and financial apparatus of the papacy was turned
to the service of the wronged dynasty of Charles of Anjou, and against
the house of Argaon.

Angevin domination of Rome was not a ruthless process of centralisation which geared Rome to the needs of a great state; on the contrary,
the rule of Charles of Anjou in Rome was very favourable to that
subjugation of the Roman District to the city which had been engaging
Roman attention for some centuries.[1] The minor communes from
Corneto to Terracina were forced to supply troops, pay imposts, send
contributions for the Roman 'games'; there was also a fierce system to
guarantee Roman economic domination of the area, and to assure Roman
control of the grain and pasture resources of the north-west of the
Tuscan patrimony, particularly through control of the port of Corneto.
In 1274 and 1282 military expeditions were sent against Corneto to
recall the town to this duty. The great monasteries such as Subiaco and
Farfa were not spared.[2] There was resistance both anti-Roman and
anti-French; Civitavecchia did not submit any more supinely than
Corneto, and there was an anti-French riot there over the possession of
a stranded whale in 1282.[3] But Charles on the whole backed up his
Romans, and supplied them with grain from the kingdom when
they ran short.

In the Romagna Martin IV appointed French rectors and officials
and French generals, to wage a great war against the Ghibellines and
to impose papal rule not by compromise and conciliation but by force.
Along the line of cities on the Via Emilia, and in the foothills 'between
the mountain and the plain' a large papal army began a savage and
cruel war of sieges, assaults, and corrupt suborning of the internal
opposition in the Ghibelline towns. This army and the manner of its
raising set a new pattern. The time of exclusively mercenary forces had
not yet come, and the *milites* of the towns and the *fideles* of the country
districts were still genuine bodies of fighting men. The papal armies were
a mixture of Guelph levies from towns in the Romagna (from Bologna
above all) and Umbria, of Angevin regular troops, of French soldiers

---

[1] Cf. E. Dupré Theseider, *Roma dal comune di popolo alla signoria pontificia (1252–1377)* (Bologna,
1952), pp. 224–54; de Bouard, *Le régime politique*, pp. 199–224.
[2] Cf. Mirzio, p. 348.
[3] Calisse, 2nd ed., pp. 137 ff.; cf. Theiner, *C.D.*, i, no. 422.

levied in France and Italy by the Angevins (who were paid by the pope),
and of Italian mercenaries.[1] The financing of the armies was from the
main papal funds, from taxes of a scutage nature in Romagna and the
march called the *stipendia* or *tallia militum,* and from drawings on the
large funds held by the Templars in France against the possibility of a
crusade. The generals were Angevin officials, the chief of whom, Simon
d'Eppe was also papal rector of the Romagna. The ecclesiastic given
to d'Eppe as adviser and colleague ('rector in spirituals') was the
distinguished French canon lawyer, Guillaume Durand. Another of the
generals was the Guelph, Taddeo of Montefeltro, and a third, employed
later in the war, was Guy de Montfort, the murderer of Henry of
Almaine and husband of the Tuscan heiress Margaret Aldobrandeschi.

Martin IV's war in the Romagna has acquired a certain glamour
from a few references by Dante,[2] though the war in fact was typical of
the sordid hatred and terrorism, the skirmishes, sieges and massacres
which characterised all the Italian party conflicts of the time.[3] The
details of the war are not very interesting; the acquisition of the salt-
fields of Cervia by the Guelphs was one of the most important episodes.
On 1 May 1282, only a month after the Sicilian Vespers, d'Eppe's troops
forced their way into the Ghibelline stronghold of Forlì, only to be
massacred in the narrow streets and left there a 'bloody heap' (*dei
Franceschi sanguinoso mucchio*) by Guido di Montefeltro. This was a
bad time for papal reputation; the Perugians were so irritated by
papal condemnation of their war with Foligno that effigies of the pope
and the cardinals were publicly burned in the city. But the money and
effort poured into the Romagnol war by the pope gained in the end
some result; Forlì and Cesena both fell to the Guelphs, and the
threatened Montefeltro *signoria* on the Via Emilia was averted. Guido
di Montefeltro and his partisans retired to mountain fortresses where
the Guelphs were powerless to harm them much (one of them the
former papal fortress of Meldola), and the war spread into the Apennine
sector of the march, around Urbino.

The Papal State was only a minor war-front in the War of the Sicilian
Vespers, which extended from Greece to Sicily and Spain, and brought

---

[1] Waley, *P.S.*, pp. 203, 288 ff.; idem, 'Papal Armies in the Thirteenth Century', *EHR*,
lxxii (1957), pp. 1–30. The pope tried to establish the principle that mercenaries should be
paid from the *tallia militum* of the Romagnol towns, and that papal central funds should be
drawn on only exceptionally (cf. Theiner, *C.D.*, i, no. 430). But see the receipts for 76,210
florins paid by the papal rector to French mercenaries (ibid. no. 440).

[2] *Inf.*, xxvii, 43–4; xxxii, 122–3. Cf. Larner, *Lords of Romagna*, passim.

[3] Vasina, *I Romagnoli*, pp. 45–6 and note.

in the French monarchy as a participant. Its financing had important results. Martin IV had refused the 'absurd' French demand to make over the tenths from the whole of Christendom for the war, and the 'scandalous' request for the application of the annates ('first fruits') of newly bestowed benefices to be applied for the same purpose. He none the less assigned ecclesiastical tenths from the whole of France to finance the abortive 'crusade' which Philip III of France led against Aragon in 1285, and on which he died. The huge fleets and armies (10,000 horse and foot against Reggio in 1284; 17,000 horses and 100,000 foot against Aragon, the largest force yet commanded by a king of France) were largely financed by the parishes of Christendom. Nor was direct papal taxation the only means adopted to raise money. The general reservation of benefices to the nomination of the Popes, first authorised by the constitution *licet ecclesiarum* of 1265, was now pressed and extended. The availability of lucrative sinecures for papal nominees all over Europe must be counted a part of papal fiscal policy and diplomacy. If there ever had been a moment when the great papal machine of centralised and bureaucratic government could be halted, if not dismantled, it was after the victories of 1266–8. Now, after the Sicilian Vespers, it was too late.

The main event of the Sicilian war was the defeat and capture by the Aragonese of Charles of Anjou's heir, the Prince of Salerno, in the sea-battle off Naples on 5 June 1284. In January 1285 Charles of Anjou died, and the Angevin kingdom was left with its sovereign in captivity – always a delicate situation for a medieval state.

Martin IV survived Charles of Anjou by only a few weeks (the pope died supposedly of a surfeit of the eels of Bolsena, 28 March 1285). The great imperialist operation which the two men had tried to carry out together had to a large extent failed. Angevin rule in Rome had broken down in January 1284, over a popular revolt occasioned by grain shortage. The revolt was fatal to Angevin but not to papal administration; within a few months the rule of two papal senators was re-established.

The new pope was the Roman, Giacomo Savelli (Honorius IV, elected 2 April 1285), of a family with feudal holdings in and around the Alban hills. He took charge of the Church in a period of pessimism and defeat. He assumed the role of guardian and protector of the Angevin kingdom during the captivity of Charles II, whose release was a main object of papal diplomacy. Under Honorius papal policy in the Sicilian question took a shape which it retained for some ten years. His aim was to obtain peace between the house of Anjou, the papacy and Aragon by separating the Sicilian question from the other disputed issues.

In the Papal State Honorius had little success. In Romagna and Umbria papal rule was virtually disregarded, and the advantages won by the great military effort of Martin IV melted away under a fresh tide of disorder led this time by 'Guelph' magnates – Maghinardo Pagani, Malatesta of Rimini, Guido and Ostasio da Polenta of Ravenna. When a congress met in Faenza to consider the pacification of the Romagna in 1285, it was not even attended by a representative of the Holy See.[1]

Honorius IV lived only two years in office (he died 3 April 1287). He was succeeded (15 February 1288) by the Franciscan Jerome of Ascoli (Nicholas IV), the first pope to come from the provinces newly-won by the Papal State during the thirteenth century.[2] During the long papal vacancy the papal-Angevin cause had received further hard knocks. On 23 June 1287 the Aragonese captain, Roger Lauria, scored his fourth great victory in the Gulf of Naples. Forty-eight Angevin ships carrying four or five thousand troops, among them the greatest magnates of south Italy, were captured. The Angevins had to come to terms with Aragon, and at Oléron in Béarn on 25 July 1287 King Alfonso of Aragon (eldest son of Peter III) conceded provisional liberty to the captured Charles II.

The eclipse of Angevin power, and the relations he had with the Colonna family before he was pope, persuaded Nicholas IV to rely rather heavily on that family; Colonna laymen were made rectors of the main papal provinces, and the Colonna became very powerful in the government of Rome, although they had no monopoly of the senatorial office.[3] The pope was cartooned with his head stuck fast in a column, with two other columns (the Colonna cardinals) flanking him. Rome was no easier to govern than usual; during the papal vacancy it had plotted with the Aragonese Prince James of Sicily, and under Nicholas concessions had to be made to Roman expansionism. In 1290–1 Nicholas was unable to stop the Romans from effecting an aggressive war against Viterbo, and from mulcting the commune for huge sums to buy peace. The chief figure in this war was the senator John Colonna, and although the story that a Colonna senator at this time arranged a Roman 'triumph' for himself is almost certainly false, it is an indication of what was thought of Colonna pretensions.

[1] Unless the Archbishop of Ravenna is counted as such. Cf. Vasina, p. 179.
[2] Cf. Waley, *P.S.*, pp. 212 ff.
[3] De Boüard, pp. 247–8; Dupré Theseider, pp. 259 ff.

IV

The self-governing commune which had been the standard form of local government in central Italy for over a century was now in decay, and was on the way to being replaced by the *signoria,* which is sometimes rather misleadingly translated into English as 'tyranny'. Essentially the *signoria* may be described as the answer of the Italian communes to the murderous civil wars of the civic factions and the permanent instability produced by the exiles. Unstably constituted by a balance of power between the richer bourgeoisie and the lesser artisans, with the rural nobility still a far from inactive element, the Italian communes were torn by class war and family vendetta. To protect themselves and their property against ever-increasing violence, the 'intrinsic' citizens often caused a broadly-based council to elect a *signore,* who then on top of an already dyarchical administration (*popolo* and *podestà*) imposed a third and final tier of government, the *signoria.* The *signore* was therefore not the arbitrator between the factions, but the party leader who made permanent and secure the dominance of one faction over others. The opposition either remained in exile or returned to their homes to live as second-class citizens paying discriminatory taxes. However the most important and early of the *signorie* of the Papal State, that of the Este of Ferrara, corresponds only rather approximately to the definitions here offered.[1]

When Charles II of Anjou entered Italy early in 1289, still on parole and seeking peace terms which his French and papal allies could accept, he entered a country profoundly changed by the Angevin collapse. Not only were the Ghibellines everywhere resurgent after the Vespers, but the drift towards the regime of the *signoria* was everywhere accelerated. The decades following the Vespers saw the establishment or consolidation of a dozen or more famous dynasties of tyrants. In Milan the Visconti were rapidly developing the most formidable *signoria* in the peninsula; in the process they passed from the Guelph to the Ghibelline camp. In Mantua the Bonacolsi (1291), in Verona the Della Scala ruled. Obizzo d'Este added Modena and Reggio to his *signoria* of Ferrara, thus dominating all the lower reaches of the Po; his Guelph professions made him no less of a menace to Bologna and the Papal State. Arezzo

---

[1] Cf. L. Simeoni, 'L'elezione di Obizzo d'Este a signore di Ferrara', *ASI,* 1935, i, pp. 165–88. The best general discussion is that of P. J. Jones, 'Communes and Despots: the City-State in late-medieval Italy', *TRHS,* 5th ser., xv (1965), pp. 71–96. The Este lordship was unusual in that Este interests were largely external to the city.

and Pisa passed for a time (1288–93) under the rule of the most formidable of Ghibelline captains, Guido di Montefeltro. In Romagna the Malatesta and the Polentani seized power in the cities on the Adriatic coast and the southern stretch of the Via Emilia.

The Sicilian negotiations after the release of Charles II from captivity were tortuous and difficult. Nicholas IV refused to recognise the Olerón agreements, and crowned the reluctant Charles II King of Sicily on 29 May 1289. After further negotiations at Perpignan and Tarascon preliminaries of peace between Alfonso of Aragon and the papal *curia* were signed on 19 February 1291. The position assigned to Sicily in this agreement is obscure, but it is possible that if it had ever come into effect, Alfonso of Aragon would have abandoned his brother James in Sicily to the Franco-papal wolves. But Alfonso's death on 18 June 1291 rendered it abortive, and the war continued.

If Nicholas's patronage of the Colonna was based on the idea that a single Roman magnate family could be decisive for the control of the whole Papal State, he might have reflected that this had already been proved wrong several times during the century; certainly his own experience proved it wrong yet again. Such magnate influence could be useful in a single region (though the fate of the Roman area itself under the Colonna was not very reassuring), but the Papal State was too large and various for a single Roman family to dominate it. Too many regions were concerned; the Romagna for example was influenced by Tuscan politics and Tuscan bankers, by Venice and the powers of the lower Po valley, by the feudal magnates of the Umbrian-Marchigiano Apennine, and by the Umbrian communes. The appointment of Stephen Colonna as papal rector of the Romagna turned out to be disastrous; when he entered Ravenna and challenged the seigniorial power of the Polentani, Ostasio da Polenta on 10–11 November 1290 brought his forces into the city and made Colonna captive; it was the most humiliating experience any papal rector had had since the province began. His replacement by the magnate bishop Ildebrandino of Arezzo was on the whole a retrograde step, which still failed to retrieve the Romagnol situation for the papacy.[1]

Nicholas IV's work in the temporal power was more fertile in bureaucratic expedients than in political achievement. He accepted the challenge which the growth of the *signoria* offered to papal authority, and nullified all elections to office in the towns of the Papal State which

[1] Cf. Vasina, *I Romagnoli*, pp. 209 ff.

were prolonged beyond a single year.[1] Other developments formalised the arrangements for the appointment of the *podestà*'s office, which by this period was in many if not most cases sold to the highest bidder. Many towns now automatically received their *podestà* from the pope; in the case of communes which normally had free election Nicholas recognised this as a 'privilege' for which the papal court hoped to receive money.[2]

It may be that the long papal vacancy which had preceded the election of Nicholas IV had strengthened the already strong position of the cardinals in the administration of the Papal State, to a point where the pope found it difficult to refuse formal concessions to them. In the bull *Caelestis altitudo* of 18 July 1289 Nicholas, following a tendency visible in the draft decretal on the same subject prepared under Gregory IX, allocated half the temporal revenues of all sorts from the papal lands to the College of Cardinals. Nicholas also expressed the opinion that this would improve the government of the temporal power, and promised besides that rectors of papal lands would only be appointed with the consent of the cardinals.[3] The same administrative programme included a bull forbidding the alienation of lands in Campagna to any nobles save those who were also cardinals, and the concession of the main papal castles in Campagna to the custody of various cardinals, including Benedict Caetani and Latino Malabranca.[4]

The bull *Caelestis altitudo* followed a trend well established in papal administration, particularly the practice that the 'common services' paid by bishops and abbots appointed through the papal court should be shared between the cardinals and the papal chamber. The oligarchic pretensions of the college were well established, and were to remain important for the rest of the Middle Ages. How effective the bull was in practice is another matter; the most obvious impediment to its implementation was that the expenses of the various papal provinces, especially their military expenses, normally swallowed up the ordinary

---

[1] Waley, *P.S.*, p. 220, and cf. pp. 70–2, ibid.; G. Ermini, 'La libertà comunale nello stato della chiesa da Innocenzo III all'Albornoz', *ASR*, xlix (1926), pp. 1–126, at pp. 84–5. It is not certain that the constitution applied to all provinces; there is no trace of it in the Romagna where it was most needed.

[2] Waley, pp. 221–3; Ermini, pp. 25–48. Cf. Kamp, *Istituzioni comunali in Viterbo nel medioevo*, pp. 37–8, 62–5, 137.

[3] Theiner, *C.D.*, i, no. 468. Cf. Waley, *P.S.*, pp. 223–4, and p. 290 above.

[4] *Reg. Nich. IV*, nos. 6967, 7072–5, 7059–64; Potthast, no. 22823. Cf. Falco, *RSI*, n.s., vi (1928), p. 241; G. Digard, *Philippe le Bel et le Saint-Siège* (Paris, 1936), i, p. 142n. The castles were Fumone and Castro dei Volsci (B. Caetani), Paliano and Serrone (Berardo of Cagli), Segni and Ninfa (Latino Malabranca).

revenues, and often claimed more. No one could really say when the provinces showed a profit and when they did not; only for special payments like the big *census* for the kingdom of Sicily was the bull easily applicable.[1]

The institutional development of the Papal State was by this point in the thirteenth century far advanced. From the time of the establishment of papal power in the Romagna onwards the provincial parliament, which had hitherto been a rather occasional feature of the administration, became a regular and important characteristic of papal government.[2] At the parliaments held by papal rectors or legates the constitutions of popes or papal officials were promulgated; the important *tallia militum,* now the most onerous of the taxes, was voted; the feudal duty of council was proffered. The judicial organisation of the Papal State was naturally one of its most advanced aspects, since it reflected the canonical learning of the papal *curia* itself. Judges formed part of the rectoral court in each province, and jurisdiction of appeal, on which much emphasis was laid, lay with judges of appeal or occasionally with judges of appeal who heard cases from all the papal provinces.[3]

The central administration of the Papal State was carried out increasingly by the Apostolic Chamber, which assumed a more and more direct responsibility in this respect. This was connected with the appointment in Romagna and the march (and later in the other provinces) of provincial treasurers, who were normally lay bankers. The Papal State was thus inserted more directly into the relationships between the Holy See and the Tuscan banking firms which were such an important feature of the Angevin invasion of 1265–6 and its aftermath.[4]

V

Nicholas IV's death on 4 April 1292 was unfortunate for the Colonna family. Cardinal Jacob Colonna had just placed in the apse of S. Maria Maggiore in Rome the golden mosaics of Torriti, depicting the pope and the cardinal side by side before the figure of the Virgin – a cynic

---

[1] F. Baethgen, 'Quellen und Untersuchungen zur Geschichte der päpstlichen Hof- und Finanzverwaltung unter Bonifaz VIII.', *Quellen,* xx (1928–9), pp. 114–37, at pp. 161–9. The Comtat Venaissin incomes were the only appreciable ones to be divided with the cardinals besides the Sicilian *census,* whose division with the cardinals was promised in the 1265 treaty.
[2] Cf. Waley, *P.S.,* pp. 110 ff.
[3] Ibid. p. 108. Cf. for the judges in appeal B. Rusch, *Die Behörden und Hofbeamten der päpstlichen Kurie des 13. Jahrhunderts* (Königsberg–Berlin, 1936), pp. 61–2.
[4] Waley, pp. 120–1, 106–7. In the fourteenth century these lay treasurers were replaced by clerks.

might have remarked that where the Virgin once ordered snow to fall, it now rained gold. The long and bitter conclave began in the palace of Nicholas IV beside the basilica. 'There is not one so holy among the cardinals who has not offended another or been offended by another. If it is he who has committed the offence, he seeks to impede the other's election; if he himself is the injured party he wants the tiara for himself, so that he may have his revenge.[1] Fighting broke out in Rome, and the Colonna blockaded themselves in the Mausoleum of Augustus and the Baths of Constantine while they fought the Orsini. Plague followed civil war in the summer of 1293, and most of the cardinals retired to Rieti, and then to Perugia. But Umbria was no safer than Rome; the Orvietan general Orsello Orsini attacked Bolsena and Acquapendente, while Narni (as on many previous occasions) attacked the papal fortress of Stroncone. Roman and Angevin troops were called in to protect the cardinals;[2] the Romans expelled both Colonna and Orsini and threatened to call in Frederick of Aragon. 'From the length of the papal vacancy,' Boniface VIII later remarked, 'God knows what bloodshed and disorder followed.'

Intimidated by this disorder, and perhaps also by the presence of Charles of Anjou in Perugia, the cardinals elected an 'Angevin' candidate, the Neapolitan hermit Peter of Morrone (Celestine V, 5 July 1294). The unworldliness of this old man may have been exaggerated; there was no doubt of the political result of his rule. Seven French cardinals and two from the Angevin kingdom were appointed; by November 1294 it must have been evident to the Roman cardinals that heroic measures were needed if the papacy and the Papal State were not to fall into a dependence on Angevin power more complete than ever before. The Colonna cardinals were probably at one with another Campagnole cardinal, Benedict Caetani, about this; when Celestine V had been persuaded to abdicate the papacy (13 December 1294), they voted for Caetani at the subsequent conclave.[3]

Elected on Christmas Day 1294, Boniface VIII adopted traditional papal policy in the Sicilian question. As the price of an undertaking to

---

[1] H. Finke, *Aus den Tagen Bonifaz VIII.* (Münster i.W., 1922), p. XC.

[2] Waley, *P.S.*, pp. 225–6; idem, *Orvieto*, pp. 64–5; cf. also Stefaneschi, *Opus metricum*, F. X. Seppelt (ed.) (1921), p. 39.

[3] Cf. Finke, *Aus den Tagen Bonifaz VIII.*, pp. 44–54; *MGH, Scriptores*, xxiv, p. 261. For co-operation between Benedict Caetani and the Colonna during the papal vacancy, see his part in the Colonna purchase of Nepi, Caetani, *Regesta Chartarum*, i, pp. 67–76. Cf. also Digard, *Philippe le Bel et le S.S.*, i, p. 160; Falco, *ASR*, xlvii (1924), pp. 180–1, in note (co-operation with James Colonna at Alatri). See also T. S. R. Boase, *Boniface VIII* (1933).

return Sicily to the Church the pope offered to Frederick of Aragon, younger brother of King James, the hand of Catherine de Courtenay, the heiress to the Eastern Latin Empire (peace of Anagni, June 1295). The peace of Anagni was agreed to by King James of Aragon, and marks an important stage in the settlement of the War of the Vespers.[1] The Aragonese crown and the Angevins in signing this peace accepted the papal wish that the Sicilian question should be separated from the rest. Boniface aimed to reduce the scale of the conflict, converting it as far as possible from a great international issue into one which primarily concerned the lordship of the Sicilian island. But Boniface achieved less success than he had hoped; although the peace of Anagni appeared to be a renunciation of Aragonese ambitions on Sicily it did not in fact have that effect. The most important thing was to persuade Frederick of Aragon to renounce his claim on the Sicilian crown. The peace offered him an inducement to make this renunciation, in the form of marriage with Catherine de Courtenay, but unfortunately for papal plans this marriage did not take place. Catherine refused Frederick, who had himself crowned king of Sicily in December 1295. Huge sums therefore continued to flow from papal funds to Angevin political and military ends – 100,000 silver marks for the dowry of Charles's daughter Blanche and upwards of three-quarters of a million florins to Charles himself during the course of the pontificate.[2]

Boniface's nepotism was more flagrant than that of any pope of his age, because he started as a member of a middling Campagna family; to make such a family into great magnates during one pontificate the most drastic measures were necessary, which could not easily be concealed. Boniface claimed that as a cardinal he had amassed a treasure of 200,000 florins[3] (an interesting comment on the finances of the cardinals, at a time when their income from the 'college' is known to have been small). But such a sum was not enough for the grandiose programme of the new pope. In 1296 he married his great-nephew Roffred Caetani to the middle-aged and disreputable Margaret Aldobrandeschi, whose lands bordered on the Papal State in southern Tuscany. Boniface had been her guardian when he was cardinal. Margaret was the widow of the murderer Guy de Montfort, and the lover of a local Sienese baron, Nello de' Pannochieschi, reputed to have murdered his wife on her account.[4]

---

[1] Cf. Soldevila, *Història de Catalunya*, i, pp. 391 ff.; V. Salavert y Roca, *Cerdeña y la expansion mediterranea de la corona de Aragón 1297–1314* (Madrid, 1956), i, pp. 107 ff.

[2] Baethgen, *Quellen*, xx, pp. 186–9.

[3] *MGH, Scriptores*, xxiv, p. 477. He had been a cardinal since 1281.

[4] This was the Pia recorded by Dante, *Purgatorio*, v, 133.

Her next husband, the mercenary soldier Orsello Orsini, had died in 1295. But Roffred was unable to control Margaret or her lands, and the political benefits of the marriage turned out to be disappointing. In 1298 Boniface blandly remarked that he had been unaware that her 'husband' Nello de' Pannochieschi was alive at the time of her marriage to Roffred Caetani. So he granted Margaret a divorce, and re-married Roffred to the more attractively dowered Neapolitan heiress, Giovanna dell'Aquila, who brought with her the great fief of Fondi.

More offensive to the Roman magnates was the Caetani acquisition of lands in Campagna. It did not in its early stages affect a very big area; the nucleus of the new *signoria* was the Norma, Ninfa, and Sermoneta villages on the slopes and at the foot of the Monti Lepini, commanding the Via Appia between Rome and Terracina. Now a picturesque ruin with English rose walks, Ninfa then was a strong castle which controlled the fertile plain between the mountains and the sea.

The Colonna, the former lords of Ninfa, did not like this. They worked against Boniface 'first secretly and then openly'. Boniface in April 1296 is said to have 'blown into his hand' and announced that he was going to annihilate the Colonna of Palestrina and the lords of Ceccano, and that his brother Roffred (papal governor of the Campagna) would then 'have the whole countryside under his feet'.[1] Perhaps we should not believe this story which comes from a French propagandist source, nor the story that in 1297 he told the French ambassador that he was going to make terms with France, crush the Colonna, and then turn against Philip the Fair of France and drive him from the throne.

The Colonna had more specific grievances. They claimed that Boniface had impeded a reconciliation between their family and the Orsini, and had also fomented a quarrel between the heirs of Stephen Colonna and their disinherited uncles.[2] He was also supposed to have revived the even older quarrel between the Colonna of Palestrina and the branch of Genazzano. 'When you want a castle,' says a poem of Jacopone da Todi which refers to Boniface VIII, 'you throw a dagger between brother and brother.'[3]

On 3 May 1297, as Peter Caetani's mule train drew near the gates

---

[1] P. Dupuy, *Histoire du différend d'entre le Pape Boniface VIII et Philippe le Bel Roy de France* (Paris, 1655), Preuves, p. 330.

[2] Document in L. Mohler, *Die Kardinäle Jakob und Peter Colonna* (Paderborn, 1914), p. 269.

[3] Ferri (ed.), *Laude*, no. 58, p. 83. Cf. Dupuy, Preuves, pp. 334 ff. For the Colonna lands: P. A Petrini, *Memorie Prenestine disposte in forma d'Annali* (Rome, 1795), p. 418; *Reg. de Boniface VIII*, nos. 2388, 3862; *MGH, Scriptores*, xxiv, pp. 477–80; Mohler, *Die Kardinäle*, pp. 62–3; G. Presutti, 'I Colonna di Riofreddo', *ASR*, xxxiii (1910), pp. 313–32.

of Rome, bearing with it a treasure of some 200,000 florins destined for the purchase of the maritime lands from the Annibaldi, Stephen Colonna attacked and seized it. The following morning the pope sent a message to Cardinal Peter Colonna, 'wishing to know, whether he was pope or no'. The Colonna were willing to return the treasure, but would not agree to the delivery of castles or to the punishment of the guilty Stephen. Before dawn on 10 May, in their castle of Longhezza, the Colonna cardinals drew up a manifesto which denounced the 'tyranny' of Boniface, and appealed to the future council to decide on the legitimacy of his election. Before midday on the same day Boniface issued the bull *in excelso throno* which deprived and excommunicated the Colonna cardinals without time for defence or exceptions. Later that day he denounced the Colonna for their 'pride, power and malice' to the Romans – though he admitted that the Colonna cardinals were condemned for abetting in crimes and not for their commission.

Although his Colonna enemies were 'neither Saracen nor Jew',[1] Boniface preached a crusade against them, raised a crusading tenth to fight the civil war in the Tuscan patrimony, and sent Florentine and other Guelph troops against the Colonna castles. In the New Year of 1298 the crusaders were using mines and catapults against the castle of Colonna, which when it fell in the summer was destroyed, as were the Colonna palaces in Rome. Palestrina surrendered in September, probably unconditionally, although Dante suggested that Boniface offered terms which he failed to keep.[2] It was levelled 'to the ground'.

The Colonna cardinals waited on Boniface at Rieti, barefoot and in halters. In June 1299 the family broke house arrest at Tivoli and fled to 'savage and remote places'; according to Petrarch who was a friend of the family, as far as Egypt, Persia and Arabia. Their partisans were rooted out of their last strongpoint in Zagarolo, and their ally John of Ceccano was captured by a force under the papal chamberlain. The last Colonna castle in the Romagna, Montevecchio, fell in the autumn of 1299.

After the civil war the strict legality which until then had marked Caetani land transactions began to slip. Peter Caetani acquired Trevi, a hill fortress commanding the Via Tiburtina-Valeria, by questionable methods. One of the dispossessed lords was the Raynald of Supino who had lost his Neapolitan castellanships through Boniface, and whose sister Mary had been divorced by Francis Caetani so that the latter could

---

[1] Dante, *Inferno*, xxvii, 85.
[2] Ibid. 110, 'lunga promessa con l'attender corto'.

become a cardinal.[1] By even more dubious legal expedients Boniface's agents seized Sgurgola, facing the Caetani's native town of Anagni, on the southern side of the Sacco valley.[2]

Although Roffred Caetani had now taken possession of the great county of Fondi, had become dominant in Terracina, and the fortress of San Felice Circeo had been purchased for him, the attempt to create a Caetani *signoria* extending from Astura to the Garigliano failed. Boniface pressed Charles II of Anjou to grant Roffred the city of Gaeta to hold, not as a fief of the kingdom but directly of the Church: no doubt memories of papal claims to Gaeta earlier in the century played a part in this. Charles refused, which brought upon him to his face from Boniface the epithet of 'good-for-nothing' (*ribaldus*).[3] But other castles and villages continued to go into the Caetani bag, most of them designed to build up the holdings in southern Campagna.[4] The total cost of these purchases to papal funds was immense – probably between half and three-quarters of a million gold florins.[5] Boniface VIII was probably just as rich in money income as the Avignonese popes who followed him in the next century, and his treasury was well able to support his nepotism.

Boniface's sharp practice on behalf of his family should not obscure his ability as a canonist.[6] The series of constitutions issued by Boniface for the provinces of the Papal State (excluding Romagna and, apparently, the duchy) is a distinguished addition to the statutory legislation of the Papal State. Boniface's intention was not to make large new concessions to the communes, but to recognise and codify the legal situation actually in practice, and suppress some abuses which had been practised by papal rectors. The value placed on his legislation by the

---

[1] G. Falco, 'Sulla formazione e la costituzione della signoria dei Caetani 1283–1313', *RSI*, n.s., vi (1928), pp. 261 ff.; Digard, ii, pp. 148–9; Caetani, *Regesta Chartarum*, i, pp. 109–10, 115 ff., 152–5, 160, 166; Dupuy, Preuves, pp. 334, 343–4.

[2] Falco, loc. cit.; *Regesta Chartarum*, pp. 176 ff.; *Domus Caietana*, i, pp. 125 ff.

[3] Finke, *Aus den Tagen*, pp. XLV–XLVI.

[4] Pofi, Carpino and Gavignano, the first two near Ceccano, the other on the Sacco. Falco, p. 270; *Domus Caietana*, i, p. 75; Mohler, p. 221. Sgurgola and Gavignano command the road to two other Caetani holdings, Carpineto and Collemezzo. Monte Porciano and Giove were far off, near Amelia in Umbria (*Regesta Chartarum*, i, pp. 224 ff.).

[5] Baethgen, *Quellen*, xx, p. 193. Cf. Dupuy, Preuves, p. 343. 'Et quod dicta guerra contra Columnienses ultra id quod expenderat, ultra sexcenta millia florenorum habeat et plus credo decem mille millia.' And cf. my article on the 'secret' finances, *JEccH*, iv (1953), pp. 55–68. For Boniface's total income, see Baethgen, pp. 190–1.

[6] There is a lyrical appreciation of this by G. Le Bras, 'Boniface, symphoniste et modérateur', *Mélanges Louis Halphen* (Paris, 1951), pp. 383–94. For Boniface as legislator in the Papal State see Waley, *P.S.*, pp. 230–5, 240–1, and cf. Vasina, p. 249.

communes can be judged from the tenacity with which the communes of the Campagna-Maritime provinces clung to the *Bonifacianes* when later popes wanted to abrogate them.[1] On the other hand, there is no doubt that an important motive of his legislation was fiscal, in that he simply wanted to sell privileges.[2]

Boniface failed to find a solution to the great international questions of the Sicilian war and of his relations with the French monarchy. For a time James of Aragon co-operated with the Angevins against his brother, and the great Angevin-Aragonese victory off Cape Orlando on 4 July 1299 seemed to promise a solution of the Sicilian question. But on 1 November Frederick of Sicily turned the tables at Falconaria in north Sicily, and destroyed the invading Angevin army. The Sicilian stalemate was re-established, and while chests of gold florins continued to go from the papal to the Angevin treasuries, nothing was achieved.

The situation of the Guelphs in Italy had been described by Boniface in 1296 as 'full of discord, troubled by the turbulence of war, and in several places exposed to ruin'. Azzo VIII d'Este, head of a house which had for long been formally Guelph, drifted into war towards the end of 1295 with the great Guelph commune of Bologna, which could no longer tolerate the growing *signoria* of Este in Emilia. A general war developed, in which most of the Romagnol towns allied themselves with the Este and the Pagani against Bologna; the papal rector was a powerless spectator.[3] On 1 April 1296 the Bolognese were heavily defeated on the Santerno. Boniface's part was restricted to helping negotiate peace between Bologna and the Este in 1298–9.

In the march of Ancona and the duchy of Spoleto the government of the supine papal rector Peter Caetani collapsed in May 1300 before the assault of Uguccione della Faggiola on Gubbio. At the same moment papal relations with the great Guelph city of Florence reached a crisis. Boniface, having patronised a small circle of Florentine magnates and bankers to the exclusion of the faction known as the White party, found himself defied by the White government (of which Dante was a

---

[1] Falco, *ASR*, xlix (1926), pp. 251–2, idem, *ASR*, xlviii (1925), pp. 69–72 and ibid. xlvii (1924), p. 129.

[2] Waley, pp. 231–2. Waley's point about the 'draft' bull submitted for sale to the commune of Iesi does not quite convince, however. Bulls 'of grace' were normally dated when the supplication was granted (H. Bresslau, *Handbuch der Urkundenlehre für Deutschland und Italien*, 2nd ed. (Berlin, 1958), ii, p. 475. Iesi's supplication was approved, then the commune debated whether it was worth having the bull engrossed.

[3] Waley, pp. 240 ff.; Vasina, pp. 260 ff.; Boase, pp. 247 ff. Cf. also A. Goretta, *La lotta fra il domune bolognese e la signoria Estense (1293–1303)* (Bologna, 1906), pp. 40 ff.; V. Vitale, *Il cominio della parte Guelfa in Bologna (1280–1327)* (Bologna, 1901), pp. 66–74.

member) by the prosecution in 1300 of his protégé Corso Donati; the quarrel led to the excommunication of the Florentine priors in July by Boniface's agent and confidant Cardinal Mathew of Acquasparta.

VI

To solve this familiar problem of Italian disorder Boniface turned to the traditional papal expedient, the armed might of the French monarchy. In 1300 Charles of Valois, younger brother of Philip the Fair, was pledged to the much-affianced Catherine de Courtenay, and his expedition to Italy was arranged under papal auspices, with the usual machinery for financing it from papal revenues. In May 1301 Philip set out, though with a far smaller military force than the task before him required. In September he arrived in Anagni, and was invested with the title of 'pacifier' of Tuscany and papal vicar in all the lands of the Papal State. In November the French prince entered Florence: 'He comes alone and unarmed, and with the lance with which Judas jousted, and so he directs its point that it slits open the belly of Florence.'[1] The Blacks re-entered Florence with Charles, the Whites were massacred or exiled. In the spring of 1302 Charles marched south to Naples to aid his cousin Charles of Anjou, and to proceed to yet another Angevin invasion of Sicily. But the operation degenerated into the usual series of desultory sieges. The final effect of the intervention of Charles of Valois was exactly that which Boniface had chosen him in order to avoid – the solution of the Sicilian question without consulting the interests of the papacy. At Caltabellotta in August 1302 Robert of Anjou (vicar of his father Charles II) agreed that Frederick of Aragon should preserve the title of King of Sicily until his death. He was to marry Eleanor, sister of Robert of Anjou, and after his death their issue were to receive Sardinia, Cyprus and a hundred thousand ounces of gold. For the papacy, which had spent millions of florins pressed from a groaning Christendom to recover the island, there was no crumb of comfort, not a florin of compensation. Boniface had been described in the later summer of 1301 as 'nothing but eyes and tongue in a wholly putrefying body . . . a devil'.[2] Reluctantly, after further negotiation with Frederick, Boniface ratified the treaty. But when Charles of Valois was received by this grim pontifical figure on his return north, his reception was such that in the presence of the pope his hand went to his sword.

[1] Dante, *Purgatorio*, xx, 73.
[2] H. Finke, *Acta Aragonensia* (Berlin, 1908), i, p. 104.

French intervention had failed to serve papal interests. Central Italy was in as much confusion on the return of Charles of Valois as when he came. The party strife in Tuscany had only been intensified. In the Papal State disorder was unchecked. In Umbria the greater communes, Perugia and Orvieto in particular, consumed their lesser neighbours like wolves, and received papal rectors only when they wished. In the march of Ancona and Romagna, where Charles of Anjou had been named rector after the withdrawal of Charles of Valois, disorder went equally unpunished.[1]

But Italian affairs had become of small moment for the papacy beside the great quarrel unfolding in France. In December 1301, while Charles of Valois was still in Florence, Boniface had despatched the bull *Ausculta fili,* which challenged the French king on all the principal issues – taxation, bestowal of benefices, jurisdiction over clergy. In November 1302 Boniface published the great bull *Unam sanctam,* which finally summed up the papal case against the French monarchy, and placed before Europe the last great exposition of the hierocratic authority of the medieval popes. The quarrel became the main theme of European diplomacy. To prevail, Boniface accepted Albert of Habsburg, the murderer (or so he called him in 1298) of his old protégé Rudolf of Nassau, as Emperor-elect, and accepted reconciliation with Frederick of Sicily. Philip turned the screws on the French clergy. In the summer of 1303 he had a council of French bishops accept an elaborate indictment of Boniface's personal character, and of the validity of his election to the papacy. The bishops appealed to a future council of the Church to decide on the justice of the charges; the attack had passed from the issue of jurisdiction to the general one of Boniface's fitness to hold the papal office. When this became known in Rome, the bull of excommunication against Philip was drawn up, and it was decided to publish it in September.

The final stage of the conflict had now arrived, and it was settled, not by action on a grand European scale, but by the plot of a handful of Italian conspirators. Some of the Colonna exiles, particularly Sciarra, had long since found refuge at the French court. Their influence may be traced in the polemic literature of the French publicists, and in the council of French clerics called by the French government. There is

---

[1] Waley, *P.S.,* pp. 242–9; idem, *Mediaeval Orvieto,* pp. 72–3. Waley perhaps tends to minimise the extent of Boniface's failure. For Umbria, e.g., cf. Davidsohn, *Geschichte von Florenz,* iii, p. 124–6; *Reg. de Boniface VIII,* nos. 2621–2, 2624, 2900, 3130, 3727, 3897; Theiner, *C.D.,* i, no. 564, p. 385.

no doubt that their knowledge of the politics of the Papal State was drawn on by Philip the Fair. Probably with the help of the Franco-Florentine banker, Musciatto dei Francesi ('Monsieur Mouche') they drew up for the French king a plan to surprise Pope Boniface in his own countryside.[1] In the spring of 1303 the lawyer and royal councillor William of Nogaret was sent to Italy to effect the *coup* against Boniface. His first base was at Staggia near Siena, in the castle of Musciatto dei Francesi.

That Nogaret came almost alone into Italy shows how confident he was of finding support there against Boniface. The King of France did not need to send troops against the pope; the pope's own subjects would suffice. At Staggia Nogaret made contact with the Campagnole opposition. Apart from the Colonna themselves, the most important rebels were Raynald of Supino, 'knight of the king of France' as he afterwards called himself, and Gottfred of Ceccano, son of the John of Ceccano whom papal forces had captured and imprisoned in 1299.[2] Many of the rebel gentry were the clients or relations of the Caetani. Hardly credible is the treason of the Picalotti family, a minor stock from Paliano and Anagni which owed everything to Boniface's friendship.[3] Another traitorous group closely connected by marriage and interest with the Caetani was the family of Mattia 'De Papa' – other collaterals of Alexander IV. They had, it is true, sold lands to the Caetani; but Boniface referred to them as his 'nephews' and had overwhelmed the clerical members of the family with favours.[4]

Finally, although there is no evidence that he consented to the violent events which took place at Anagni, the most important political figure to desert Boniface at this point was Cardinal Napoleon Orsini. A relative by marriage of the Colonna, and at one time guardian (with Benedict

---

[1] For what follows: R. Holtzmann, *Wilhelm von Nogaret* (Freiburg i.B., 1898); P. Fedele, 'Per la storia dell'attentato di Anagni', *BISI*, xli (1921); F. Bock, 'Musciatto dei Francesi', *Deutsches Archiv*, vi (1943); W. Holtzmann, 'Zum Attentat von Anagni', in *Festschrift A. Brackmann* (1931); H. Schmidinger, 'Ein vergessener Bericht über das Attentat von Anagni', *Melanges Eugène Tisserant*, v (Vatican City, 1964), pp. 373–88. R. Fawtier, 'L'attentat d'Anagni', *Mélanges*, lx (1948) pp. 153–79, leans over as heavily on one side as Bock, 'Bonifacio VIII nella storiografia francese', *RSCI*, vi (1952), pp. 248–59, leans on the other.

[2] Mohler, *Die Kardinäle*, p. 245; for what follows, J. Rubeus, *Bonifacius VIII[a] e familia Caietanorum* (Rome, 1651), pp. 338–41.

[3] *Reg. de Boniface VIII*, nos. 328, 418, 2232, 3479, 3677, 4493, 5097, 5233, 5519–21, 5527; *Regesta Chartarum*, i, pp. 53, 58.

[4] *Domus Caietana*, i, pp. 49–50; *Regesta Chartarum*, i, pp. 100–1, 163, 202, and ii, pp. 27–8; *Reg. de Boniface VIII*, nos. 3830, 4778, 5005. They were also relatives of the Colonna, Mohler, *Die Kardinäle*, p. 248.

Caetani) of his brother's widow Margaret Aldobrandeschi, he had always stood somewhat apart from the rest of his house. At this critical moment, in spite of having held important office under Boniface, he chose to throw in his lot with the Colonna.

In September 1303 Nogaret went through the heart of the Papal State to Ferentino, having been joined at some point by Sciarra Colonna. The occult influence of the Colonna and their friends sufficed to raise an army overnight. The Campagnole rebels supplied Nogaret with a force of over a thousand men; with these he and Sciarra Colonna arrived outside Anagni, where Boniface unsuspectingly lay, before dawn on Saturday, 7 September. Treason within the walls made success certain. One of the conspirators, Adenulf Mattia De Papa, was 'captain' of the town; the assailants found the gates open. So they entered freely under the flag of the lilies of France 'which entered Anagni when Christ was seized in the person of his vicar'.[1] Within an hour the unprepared defenders were penned into the fortified palace of the pope and his nephew. The attackers offered terms, but the demand for his abdication from the papacy was too much for Boniface to swallow. So at three o'clock in the afternoon the attack was renewed, and at six o'clock Boniface was taken, in his chamber with his Templar and Hospitaller attendants. In full papal robes they found him, and holding a cross. 'Ec le col; ec le cape!' – 'My head and my neck' – he shouted, when they again demanded that he abdicate the tiara, and at this he probably bowed his head to receive the sword cut. It was a gesture of blind defiance, and not of resignation.

Strangely, this was not quite the end. On Monday the population of Anagni took up arms, released the pope, and expelled the alien forces from the town. It was a more important development than is usually recognised, as it frustrated the plan to abduct Boniface to France and have him judged by a church council – a plan which if effected would have turned the result of a casual feat of arms into an official act of the Church. Boniface remained in Anagni for a few days, his spirit broken, conversing with the poor as equals – such a disaster was needed to convert Benedict Caetani to a mood of evangelical fraternity. Then under the protection of the Orsini faction he returned to Rome. The nerve of his power was broken, Rome and all the country round it in chaos, and every man's hand against his neighbour. The Caetani *signoria* was attacked on all sides, and although in the end the support they received from the kingdom of Naples enabled the Caetani to save more than a

[1] *Purgatorio*, xx, 86.

little of it, at this moment this did not appear likely. For three weeks Boniface lived on in the Vatican palace, broken by shock and anger, his affairs at such a point that life was no longer bearable. On 12 October 1303 he died, a miserable end for a man to whom power and splendour were the breath of life.

Chapter 9

The failure of the Franco-papal plan

I

On the day of Boniface VIII's death, Charles II of Anjou and his army entered Rome.[1] The Neapolitan protectorate could not do much to stop the civil war which raged in the Campagna, directed by Nogaret and the Colonna from their headquarters at Ferentino. But it could give some security to the cardinals in conclave in Rome, who after ten days (before the excluded and contested Colonna cardinals could arrive) gave the Church a pope in the person of the mild Niccolò Boccasini.

Benedict XI in his short pontificate seems to have been feeling his way towards a compromise which would allow the re-opening of normal relations with the French monarchy, while he protected the papal dignity by refusing to withdraw the more notable acts of his predecessor.

On 7 July 1304 Benedict died of dysentery. The Bonifacian and Colonna parties again faced one another in a long, bitterly contested conclave which lasted almost a year. The cardinals accepted, on 5 June 1305, the candidature of the Gascon Bertrand de Got, Archbishop of Bordeaux,[2] a man initially biased towards the French monarchy, and in some respects unfitted to carry the great burden of his office. The unexpected and unintended result of his election was the physical transfer of the papacy to Avignon for seventy years and the capitulation of the papacy to the French monarchy on most of the issues in dispute. Clement V did not finally take up residence in Avignon until March 1309, as a result of the decision to hold a church council in Vienne, and then his installation in the city was provisional. But his political dependence on the Capetians was a powerful factor in inducing the papacy to reside not (it is true) on French soil, but in a city which was adjacent to France, and subject to the French dynasty of the Angevin kings of Naples.

[1] Fedele, *BISI*, xli (1921), pp. 219–27.
[2] G. Fornaseri, 'Il conclave perugino del 1304–1305', *RSCI*, x (1956), pp. 321–44.

L

The conditions of Italy, though not fundamentally different from those which had obtained for the past forty years, gave the sick Clement V some semblance of excuse for his reluctance to travel there. In spite of a brief and illusory peace in 1305, the Colonna-Caetani war continued. Bologna and Florence were controlled by oligarchies as hostile to one another as indifferent to the papal leadership to which they paid lip-service. The old war between Bologna and the Este of Ferrara broke out again, and sowed confusion among the Emilian Guelphs. Two papal nuncios were sent to Italy in September 1305. Having carried out a tour of the whole Papal State, besides Tuscany, they reported to the pope in the gloomiest terms. The efficacy of government in the Papal State was nil, and the Guelph cause in Italy sadly disorientated and divided.[1]

One clue to the Italian politics of these confused years is the disruption which the exaggerated policies of Boniface VIII had caused among the never-too-firmly cemented allies of the Guelph block. A pope such as Boniface VIII, who divided the Guelphs even further among themselves, and who cavilled at the French alliance on which the whole structure was based, threatened it with ruin. The reconstruction of the Guelph block was the work of many years, though whether the Avignonese popes did well to lavish the money of the universal Church on the ramshackle building of Italian Guelphism, is to be doubted.

Certainly the re-assembly of the Guelph alliance was an aim which, in his earlier years at least, Clement V expressly avoided. Napoleon Orsini, who had in effect placed the tiara on Clement's head, was bound to the Colonna party which wished revenge and destruction on all the works of Boniface. It was not that Napoleon Orsini was 'Ghibelline'; his own judgement was that 'you will never find a true Roman who is either Guelph or Ghibelline'.[2] But he was certainly a poor choice for an agent to reconcile the 'Black' and 'White' Guelphs of Tuscany, and his departure as legate for central Italy in February 1306 was the signal for increased confusion. A fortnight before Orsini's appointment the great rising against Este rule in Emilia occurred which

---

[1] A. Eitel, *Der Kirchenstaat unter Klemens V.* (Berlin-Leipzig, 1907), pp. 14 f.; Davidsohn, *Geschichte von Florenz*, iii, pp. 281–308; idem, *Forschungen zur Geschichte von Florenz*, iii, pp. 287–95; E. Göller, 'Zur Geschichte der italienischen Legation Durantis des Jungeren von Mende', *Röm. Quart.*, xix (1905), pp. 16–24; cf. Theiner, *C.D.*, i, no. 577, p. 398; Waley, 'An account book of the Patrimony of St Peter in Tuscany, 1304–6', *JEccH*, vi (1955), pp. 18–25. The judgement of the state of the papal lands made by Waley here seems to me nearer the truth than the more optimistic view in his *P.S.*, pp. 248–9.

[2] Finke, *AA*, i, no. 393, pp. 615–17 (7 February 1324).

broke the power of the Este of Ferrara for a generation. The White government of Bologna, which had kept itself in power on a programme of fighting the Este and the Florentine Blacks, collapsed as soon as its *raison d'être* was removed. There was a revolution in Bologna (February–March 1306). So Napoleon Orsini arrived in Tuscany at the moment of the complete triumph of the Florentine Black government. 'Pure' Guelphism was re-established in Tuscany and Emilia with the consequent purge and exile of all those tainted with 'White' or Ghibelline tendencies. Orsini went to Bologna, where his treatment grew colder and colder, until in May 1306 he was insulted and expelled. By now the chances of Orsini's acting as an angel of peace were remote. He joined the White army at Arezzo and laid Florence and Bologna under interdict, indeed, so debased was the spiritual currency, he preached a crusade against them. It was a crusade followed by no one but a few embittered exiles, and by the beginning of 1307 it was evident that such plans as Clement V had had for the pacification of central Italy were in ruins.[1]

On 1 May 1308 King Albert of Habsburg was murdered, and the question of the succession to the German kingdom and the empire was placed before Europe. Philip the Fair was eager to press his brother, Charles of Valois, for the imperial office. The imperial candidature of Henry of Luxemburg was far more acceptable to the pope than that of Charles of Valois, and although there is no evidence that he worked for it, there is some that he welcomed it.[2] Certainly a prince of modest resources and repute, a vassal of the French crown, of French speech and culture, whose election was the work of the west-German princes unconnected with the suspect house of Austria – all this seemed to offer a pope of Clement's peculiar position and temperament an emperor as acceptable as any emperor could be to any pope. Rapidly – too rapidly for the liking of the French court – Clement confirmed the election and approved the person of the elected in July 1309.

It is unlikely that Clement V confirmed Henry VII's election without receiving from him satisfactory guarantees about his intentions in Italy. Probably Henry, in his own right a prince of little account, would undertake an Italian expedition as the best material and psycho-

---

[1] Vitale, *Il dominio*, pp. 80, 85, 98–105; Eitel, *Kirchenstaat*, pp. 157–63; Davidsohn, *Geschichte von Florenz*, iii, pp. 313–43; A. Veronesi, 'La legazione del card. Napoleone Orsini in Bologna nel 1306', *AMDR*, 3rd ser., xxviii (1910), pp. 79–133.

[2] Cf. E. E. Stengel, *Avignon und Rhens. Forschungen zur Geschichte des Kampfes um das Recht am Reich* etc. (Weimar, 1930) pp. 31–5; C. Wenck, *Clemens V. und Heinrich VII.* (Halle, 1882), pp. 134–5; F. Kern, *Die Anfänge der französischen Ausdehnungspolitik bis zum Jahr* 1308 (Tübingen, 1910), p. 311; G. Barraclough, *The origins of modern Germany* (Oxford, 1947), p. 307.

logical way to exploit his new dignity. It was not necessary that Clement should oppose this, and he may have encouraged it. Papal policy in Italy had collapsed, and to the failure of Cardinal Orsini's mission had now to be added the danger of a seizure of the papal city of Ferrara by Venice. Neither Charles of Anjou, who died on 5 May 1309, nor his son Robert were suitable instruments for papal designs; they were too deeply involved with the Bonifacian faction in Italy and too anxious to press Angevin interests to the exclusion of papal ones. As for the King of France, it had now become one of the main objects of Clement V to fend off his smothering embraces. Clement V may have meant what he said, or something near it, when in December 1310 he told Nogaret that Henry VII was going to Italy 'for the honour and protection of the Church, and to give peace to the querelants in Italy, which is a good third of the Catholic world'.[1] The good faith of Henry VII himself was evident; he had the same touching belief in the efficacy of the papal office as in that of his own. To this he added, in the long series of guarantees and grants which he gave the pope in Lausanne in August 1310, the most comprehensive and far-reaching engagements ever under-taken by an emperor or emperor-elect on entering Italy.[2]

Henry VII accepted Clement V's injunction to proceed in Italy with no partiality 'either for right or left'; the old dispensation of a Ghibelline emperor was to be replaced by a new, by which the emperor reconciled Guelph and Ghibelline and recalled the exiles to the cities. It was evident, of course, that in political terms this meant reaching an agreement with the Guelph leader, Robert of Anjou, King of Naples. Henry accepted this in principle, and as he made ready to go to Italy agreed to the idea of a marriage alliance with Robert's house, to be negotiated through the pope. As the peace of Caltabellota was still in force and Robert of Anjou himself married to an Aragonese princess, the eventual aim of papal-imperial policy was something which for Italy came close to the millennium, with all four major powers concerned with Italy (Henry, Clement V, Robert of Anjou, Frederick of Sicily) linked in a single political system.

But the hates of the Italian factions stood between Henry VII and Robert of Anjou. So also did the interests of the King of France, who

[1] *MGH, Const. et acta publica*, iv, pt. 1, p. 469.
[2] H. Otto, 'Die Eide und Priviligien Heinrichs VI und Karls IV', *Quellen*, ix (1906), pp. 316 f.; F. Schneider, *Kaiser Heinrich VII.* (Greiz and Leipzig, 1924–8), iii, p. 234; W. M. Bowsky, *Henry VII in Italy. The conflict of Empire and City-State* 1310–13 (Lincoln, Nebraska, 1960), pp. 45–9.

saw in the Angevin-Luxemburg understanding a dangerous threat to his own ambitions on his south-eastern border. Robert of Anjou asked for the kingdom of Arles as the price of his alliance with the empire. But Clement V on 1 May 1311 issued a bull which declared that to ensure peace between France and the empire he would never permit Henry VII to confer the rights of the empire in the kingdom of Arles without papal consent. Thus the French monarchy obtained a guarantee from the pope that he would not allow Henry VII to pay the price which Robert of Anjou demanded for an Imperial-Angevin alliance.

Henry VII crossed into Italy in October 1310 with a far from overwhelming force. He did not long remain neutral between Guelph and Ghibelline. Order broke down in Lombardy in February 1311, when the Della Torre, the former ruling faction of the city, were expelled from Milan. By April, when Henry's troops plundered the rebel Guelph city of Cremona, the logic of the Italian parties had begun to operate. While Henry and his army from May to September of 1311 lay under the bitterly contested walls of Guelph Brescia, the whole of Guelph Italy north of Rome prepared for war.

But the two great Guelph powers, the papacy and the Angevin kingdom, still stood aside. At the siege of Brescia Henry was attended by the papal legate and nephew Arnaud de Faugères, and under the very walls of the town the Angevin envoys still treated with Henry for the proposed alliance. But although the Angevin-Imperial alliance was accepted in its main lines by both sides,[1] the state of Italy made its final conclusion unlikely. The old enemy of the Angevins, Frederick III of Aragon the ruler of Sicily, was by the turn of the year 1311 near to the conclusion of an alliance with Henry VII. Such an alliance meant tearing up the peace of Caltabellotta, and threatened Robert of Naples with a war on two fronts. Thus by the agency of the emperor-elect, who came with a high heart to bring peace to Italy 'which formerly was worthy of pity by the very Saracens',[2] the treaty which guaranteed the peace of southern Italy was destroyed.

As Henry's march on Rome became imminent in the early spring of 1312, the tension with Robert of Anjou grew. Far-sighted and able politician as he was, Robert could not stop the drift to war. The critical question became, whether Henry would be allowed to enter Rome unopposed for his coronation, or whether the Guelph faction in Rome

---

[1] Caggese, *Roberto d'Angiò e i suoi tempi* (Florence, 1921), i, p. 139; E. Haberkern, *Der Kampf um Sizilien in den Jahren* 1302–37 (Berlin and Leipzig, 1921), pp. 35–46.
[2] Dante, *Epistola* 5.

would try to stop him. In February 1312 the Roman Guelphs expelled the imperialist senator, and handed over the Roman Capitol to John of Gravina, the brother of Robert of Anjou. John of Gravina then ordered the Roman Ghibellines under Sciarra Colonna to lay down their arms. Sciarra, the fierce enemy of Boniface VIII and of the Caetani whom the Angevins patronised, refused. The refusal of the ultimatum released a civil war.

Still seeking to preserve peace, Clement V drew up two bulls which ordered John of Gravina to withdraw his troops from Rome and hand over the Capitol to the imperial senator. Before he could publish them there appeared simultaneously in Vienne before the pope an Angevin embassy and an extraordinary French mission, consisting of the three sons and the brother of the King of France. On 29 March (if the Aragonese report is to be believed) the princes solemnly protested against the action proposed by Clement against John of Gravina, which they said would mean the end of the Angevin kingdom of Naples. They demanded, and obtained, the withdrawal of the bulls.[1]

Only now did the main Angevin army mobilise, and then only at Gaeta to protect the northern passes of the kingdom. It was Florence, the vigorous leader of the Guelph league, which while Robert of Anjou continued to negotiate with Henry, prepared to pour troops into Rome. When on 30 April 1312 Henry's ambassadors appeared before Ponte Milvio, Rome was held against him in strength. Summoned to admit the emperor-elect, John of Gravina after some hesitation refused. The Leonine city and St Peter's were so strongly held that Henry, when he arrived with the main force on 6 May, had to enter Rome from the north-west and fight his way to the Lateran (already held for him by Louis of Savoy). Henry prepared to drive through the centre of the city, to take the Capitol and then St Peter's, in which custom demanded that the emperor be crowned. In bitter street-fighting between 23 and 30 May he smashed his way through the barricades and achieved the first of these objectives, though he lost some of the greatest men in his entourage in doing so. But he failed to clear the route from the Capitol to the Tiber and to St Peter's. Henry was crowned emperor on 29 June 1312 in St John Lateran and not in St Peter's.

The bloody weeks of street-fighting in Rome put paid for ever to

---

[1] Finke, *AA*, i, no. 201, p. 285. Finke (followed by others) has slightly mistaken the date of this consistory. References for events in Rome at this time in the biographies of Annibaldo and Giovanni Annibaldi, *Dizionario Biografico degli Italiani*, iii (1961), pp. 345–7. Further, Bowsky, *Henry VII in Italy* (Lincoln, Nebraska, 1960), pp. 155–70.

reconciliation between Henry and Robert of Anjou. War, the great war which everyone said they had not wanted, was decided upon. On 4 July the final ratifications of the alliance between the emperor and Frederick of Sicily were exchanged. The Sicilian fleet prepared for war, and Frederick agreed to pay his imperial ally a hundred thousand florins towards its cost.

In September 1312 Henry left the environs of Rome and marched north against Florence. The campaign failed; though not contemptible his army was insufficient, and Frederick of Sicily had not yet sent him much aid. Henry retired to Pisa. In April 1313 Robert of Anjou was condemned to every penalty, including death, by the imperial court. In August Henry began to move south from Pisa with an army almost double the size of that under arms in the preceding year. The German invasion of the kingdom of Naples was imminent. At the same moment Frederick of Sicily, without declaration of war, seized Reggio and opened a destructive campaign in Calabria. Before this threat of a great war on two fronts, Angevin resistance was feeble. It was already reported that Robert of Anjou was fitting out galleys for flight to Provence.

At this point, on 24 August 1313, one of the great dates in the history of the Italian Guelphs, Henry VII died at Buonconvento near Siena. 'L'alto Arrigo', who tried to govern Italy before she was ready for him, was dead.[1] The campaign against the Neapolitan kingdom collapsed. Frederick of Sicily found himself isolated and exposed to a perilous revenge. But the Ghibellines remained; no less bitter, no less rich, little less united. The war in Tuscany was renewed with increased savagery. The Guelphs already had cause to regret their haste in lighting torches and bonfires when the 'Imperial tyrant', the 'most cruel Emperor' died.[2]

II

As for Robert of Anjou, he thought at last to realise the dream of effective Angevin power throughout the Italian peninsula. In the last month of his life Clement V prepared (14 March 1314) but did not issue a bull to appoint Robert of Anjou, during the vacancy of the empire, imperial vicar in all the lands of the empire in Italy with the exception of Genoa. Though not put into effect until its re-issue by the new Pope John XXII, on 16 July 1317, this constitution marks a decisive

---

[1] Dante, *Paradiso*, xxx, 137.
[2] Cf. E. Cristiani, 'Il trattato del 27 febbraio 1314 tra Roberto d'Angiò, Pisa e la lega Guelfa oscana', *BISI*, lxviii (1956), pp. 259–80: and *Europe in the Late Middle Ages*, pp. 82 ff.

step in the Italian policies of the popes. The first important exercise of the papal claim to authority in imperial lands during the vacancy of the empire had been made in 1267, when Charles of Anjou was named 'captain' of Tuscany.[1] Now after a long period of political and legal elaboration a decision had been promulgated which was to lead to a new variety of papal imperialism, and to twenty years of costly and bloody struggle in north Italy.

Clement V died on 20 April 1314. Jacques Duèze of Cahors, who after a vacancy of over two years in the papal see was elected pope on 7 August 1316 under the name of John XXII, was the ex-chancellor of Robert of Anjou, but his character was very different from that of his predecessor. The complaisance which, as pope, he showed his ex-master, was of an entirely political order, and was exercised within the limits imposed by a passionate belief in the dignity of the papal office and an iron will. Compelled until almost the end of his pontificate to co-operate with Robert, the new pope treated him with severity and sometimes with contempt. Already only a few months after he had conferred the imperial vicariate on him, the pope bitterly complained that since then he had done nothing to exercise it, and had constantly asked for money. 'If you had exercised the vicariate in a way befitting a king, men and money would have poured in from everywhere, and you would have had no need to beg for alms.'[2] In 1324, speaking to the Pisan envoys, he was abusive. Robert was 'a wretched, miserly king', a 'miserable poltroon' who had not the courage to stop James of Aragon from conquering Sardinia – 'so much the worse for him'.[3]

The direction of John XXII's policy was shown in April 1317 by the publication of the bull *Si fratrum,* which declared that in the continued vacancy of the empire its jurisdiction devolved upon the papacy, and that anyone exercising the imperial vicariate in Italy without papal authorisation would be excommunicated and subjected to temporal sanctions. The double election of Louis of Bavaria and Frederick of Austria to the empire in 1314 was thus exploited for the papacy along the lines which had been first indicated by Innocent III, but this time with a new legal doctrine. This bull provided legal grounds on which

---

[1] See above, p. 270. The bull of 16 July 1317 in *MGH, Const. et acta publica,* v, nos. 195–6. In 1324 John XXII appealed to Clement IV's nomination of Charles of Anjou as a precedent. Ibid. v, no. 835, p. 653.

[2] W. Preger, 'Über die Anfänge des kirchenpolitischen Kampfes unter Ludwig dem Bayern', *Abhandlungen der historischen Classe der kgl. bayerischen Akademie,* xvi, pt. 2 (1882), no. 36, p. 199. Cf. Caggese, *Roberto d'Angiò,* ii, p. 23.

[3] Finke, *AA,* ii, no. 392, p. 611.

the Ghibelline tyrants who either claimed that their vicariates from Henry VII had not expired, or accepted new ones from the Bavarian, could be held guilty of a severe offence in the eyes of the Church. They thus exposed themselves to excommunication and in the case of their indefinite refusal to submit, to charges of heresy. It was a wide extension of papal temporal power in Italy.

The publicists of Robert of Anjou busied themselves with tracts which sought to exploit the imperial vacancy for their master's aggrandisement.[1] The most drastic of their demands was that no further emperor be elected, or at least that no further election be confirmed by the pope. Even Clement V could not approve this, and the draft bull conferring the imperial vicariate on Robert of Anjou specified that the grant came to an end two months after the confirmation of the election of a new king of the Romans by the Roman court. Resentment against the 'harsh and intractable race', the 'barbarous nation' of the Germans, runs conspicuously through Angevin propaganda. So also does the demand for a new kingdom – perhaps two – in Italy; the two regions in question seem to be Lombardy and Tuscany. Nor was this the only thing which the Angevins were disposed to demand from the moribund empire. It was probably at this period that the false bull *Ne praetereat* was forged in the Angevin chancery; the effect of the 'bull' was to declare Lombardy to be cut off from the empire altogether. Lombard opinion was said to be that the region 'could never have peace until it had its own hereditary king and natural lord, who ought not to be of barbarian (i.e. German) stock'.[2] But these dreams were scarcely more substantial than the propagandist fantasies of the French minister Pierre Dubois, who a few years earlier had suggested that in the interests of the crusade the French king ought to take over the government of the whole papal patrimony from the pope.[3] Dubois's tract is the first notable expression of the opinion, in the later Middle Ages, that the

---

[1] F. Bock, 'Kaisertum, Kurie und Nationalstaat im Beginn des 14. Jahrhunderts', *Röm. Quart.* xliv (1936), pp. 105–22. Effectively criticised by G. Tabacco, 'Un presunto disegno domenicano-angioino per l'unificazione politica dell'italia', *RSI*, lxi (1949), pp. 489–525.

[2] S. Riezler, *Vatikanische Akten zur deutschen Geschichte in der Zeit Ludwigs des Bayern* (Innsbruck, 1891), no. 50, at pp. 36–7.

[3] In the *Summaria brevis* and the *De recuperatione terrae sanctae*, for which see Waley, *P.S.*, pp. 301–2, and F. Bock, *Reichsidee und Nationalstaaten vom Untergang des alten Reiches bis zur Kündigung des deutsch-englischen Bundnisses im Jahre 1341* (Munich, 1943), pp. 94–7, 486–7. For the bull *Ne praetereat* see the same book (p. 174), and also Bock's article quoted above. See also P. Fournier, *Le Royaume d'Arles et de Vienne (1178–1378)* (Paris, 1891), pp. 509–14; Denys Hay, *The Italian Renaissance in its Historical Background* (Cambridge, 1961), p. 94 (he dates the forgery to 1331).

L*

pope ought to give up the Papal State to be administered by laymen. But French power in this period was in fact so far from hostile to the papal temporal power that it may be counted among the most important factors in strengthening the Papal State.

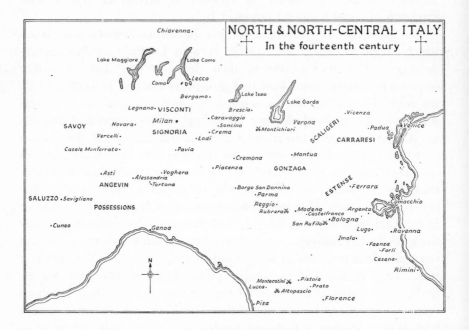

In 1316 during the papal vacancy Robert of Anjou negotiated a marriage between his son Charles of Calabria and Catherine, the widow of Henry VII and sister of Frederick the Fair of Austria, who since 1314 had been a claimant to the empire.[1] In the marriage treaty Frederick of Austria conferred the imperial vicariate in Italy (in so far as it affected the Guelph towns) on Robert of Anjou. Thus by the following year, 1317, Robert enjoyed two separate titles to the imperial vicariate in Italy, one emanating from the pope, and the other from a claimant to the empire whom the pope did not recognise. Like much of Robert's diplomacy, it was little more than clerical paperwork.

The principal weakness of Angevin imperialism was the great length of its lines of communication. Rector of Romagna and ruler of Ferrara for the popes; protector of Florence against Pisa and Lucca, of Brescia

[1] G. Tabacco, 'La politica italiana di Federico il Bello re dei Romani', *ASI*, cviii (1950), pp. 3–77; idem, in *RSI* lxi (1949), p. 513; T. E. Mommsen, *Medieval and Renaissance Studies* (N.Y., 1959), pp. 3–18 (German in *Neues Archiv*, l (1935).

and Cremona against the greatest Ghibelline *signore* after the Visconti, Can Grande della Scala; holding and extending the line of Angevin lands in Piedmont against the Visconti of Milan and the house of Savoy; maintaining the anti-Ghibelline faction in Genoa; fighting a great war for the re-conquest of Sicily – all this amounted, even for a power with respectable armies and fleets, to an impossible task. The tyrants of Lombardy and Tuscany all moved on interior lines of communication which were only slightly impeded by the string of Guelph communes which ran south from Brescia to Cremona (where it cut the Po), and thence to Parma and Bologna. Compared to these compact and well-rounded Ghibelline seigniories, which moved forces rapidly from one well-defended centre to another, the problem of communication and supply which faced the Angevin armies was of nightmare size. Small wonder that these armies were usually small, ill-equipped, and of extremely low morale. Nor were Robert's own temperament and talents those of a conqueror.

On 20 September 1313 Matteo Visconti was proclaimed lord and rector-general of Milan. The roots of the Visconti *signoria* in Milan went far back into the thirteenth century; but the advent of Matteo Visconti marks an era in the history of the *signoria* in Italy. A great city was now ruled by a great dynasty. An Angevin army reached Milan, but then dispersed, and a chance to root out one of the two greatest Ghibelline centres of Lombardy was lost.[1] A year later the performance was repeated; a large Guelph army was assembled at Parma under the local magnate Gilberto da Coreggio and the Angevin official Hugh des Baux for the attack on Milan. But instead it attacked Piacenza, where Gilberto da Coreggio had ambitions, and even here the attack failed.

The main effort of the Angevins in 1314 was made against Sicily. In Tuscany the war with the great Ghibelline leader Uguccione della Faggiola had continued without decisive action. Robert of Anjou in the early summer of 1315 sent his brother Philip of Taranto with the young Angevin princes, to seek a military decision in Tuscany. Around a nucleus of Angevin and Catalan troops were grouped large forces of the Guelphs of central Italy. The point of battle was Montecatini, the besieged stronghold in Val di Nievole which commanded the approaches to Pistoia. The battle was fought on 29 August 1315, and proved to be one of the worst military disasters ever suffered by the Guelph cause in

---

[1] Johannes de Cermenate, *Historia*, L. Ferrai (ed.) (Rome, 1889), pp. 140–3. Cf. Cognasso in *Storia di Milano*, v (Milan, 1955), pp. 93 ff.

Italy. The Guelph army was annihilated, and two of the Angevin princes fell in the field.

Robert of Anjou coveted the lordship of Genoa, a city still powerful and rich, with its great fleet and its chain of Levantine colonies. Essentially its acquisition was a move in the re-conquest of Sicily.[1] On 27 July 1318 the *signoria* of the city was conceded to Robert of Anjou and the pope jointly. There were three great battles for Genoa; in February 1319, in September 1320, and finally the great Guelph victory of 17 February 1323. The last finally broke the five years' siege, and marked an important check on Visconti expansion.

The Angevin lordship of Genoa was perhaps Robert's greatest success. On other sectors of the long, fluctuating front of the *italico regno* he did less well. His responsibilities in the Papal State were numerous and hard to fulfil. In making him papal vicar in the Romagna and Lord of Ferrara, Clement V had conferred on him the government of an area which had shown itself virtually ungovernable. It is true that Bologna, the firm rock of the Guelph cause in Emilia, co-operated with the Neapolitan government and bore the arms of Robert of Anjou on the banners of its army. But Bologna itself was torn by faction, and weakened by the intrigues of the rich and ambitious family of the Pepoli, who aspired to the *signoria*. When John of Gravina, brother of Robert of Anjou, entered Bologna in October 1315, there was a major riot.

Both geographically and politically the position of the Angevins in Ferrara was precarious. The collapse in 1308 of the well-established *signoria* of Azzo d'Este had opened the way to a bitter war between the papacy and Venice for the control of Ferrara. Ended successfully by Clement V in 1310, the war still did not enable the Church to govern Ferrara peacefully. The partisans of the Este were strong, and there was continual disorder, which the pope hoped to end by conferring the vicariate of the city on Robert of Anjou in 1312. This proved no solution; the Catalan agents of Robert of Anjou were just as unpopular, as rulers of the city, as the Gascons of Clement V. The local power of the Este, though displaced for a decade by the political failure and disputed succession of Azzo VIII, was too deeply grounded in Emilian soil for the Aragonese officers of a French ruler in Naples to be able to contain it.

---

[1] Finke, *AA*, iii, no. 131, at p. 293, and no. 374. Cf. G. Tabacco, *La casa di Francia nell'azione politica di papa Giovanni XXII* (Rome, 1953), p. 173, and doc. 2, p. 348. For what follows see Caggese, *Roberto d'Angiò*, ii, pp. 27 f.; G. M. Monti, 'Da Carlo I a Roberto d'Angiò. Ricerche e documenti'. *ASPN*, xviii (1932), pp. 146–55; Haberkern, *Kampf um Sizilien*, pp. 92–102, 107–8; and cf. Finke, *AA*, iii, nos. 190, 201, pp. 416, 440.

In March 1317 John XXII asked Robert, who had been ruling Ferrara 'without any great profit' to return it to the papacy. But too late. On 4 August 1317 a revolution in Ferrara overthrew Angevin rule. When the papal nuncios, Gui and Da la Tour, arrived in the city a fortnight later they made no apology for Angevin misgovernment, but merely asked the revolutionary government to submit to the Church. The pope was forced to accept the *coup* and to condone a situation in which the Este again became the actual if not the legal rulers of the city.[1] The Este re-occupied their own palace, garrisoned strongpoints with their troops, destroyed the remaining papal fortifications at Tedaldo, and built a bridge which gave direct access from their palace to the centre of the city. By the spring of 1320 Ferrara was lost not only to the Angevin but to the Church.

In effect the Papal State was an Angevin protectorate, however inefficiently this was exercised, for twenty years and more after Henry VII's death in 1313. The supreme government of Rome was conferred on Robert of Anjou by John XXII on 23 January 1317. Thereafter Rome and the Roman District were governed by an Angevin clientele among the Roman nobility, drawn particularly from the Orsini, Annibaldi, Farnese, and Caetani. But the efficacy of Angevin control was small, and only areas actually bordering on the kingdom (such as the coastal town of Terracina) were continuously controlled by King Robert. An important city in Umbria such as Orvieto, though it did Robert the honour of electing him *podestà* on several occasions, was more or less ruled by Poncello Orsini, who with Sciarra Colonna was a little later to emerge as the leader of the main anti-Angevin party in Rome. Neither the Angevins nor the papal rector had much control over the patrimony of St Peter in Tuscany, north and north-east of Rome, where the two local magnate families of the Prefects of Vico and the

---

[1] The *Chronicon Estense* (*RRIISS*, xv, pt. 3), pp. 88–9, claims that the Este actually obtained the *signoria* from the commune on 15 August, but this seems in conflict with the documents, and also with Mussato, *Sette libri del De gestis italicorum post Henricum VII*, L. Padrin (ed.) (*Monumenti storici publicati dalla R. Deputazione Veneta di Storia Partia*, 3rd ser., iii (1903), pp. 9–14. The text of Mussato as given by Padrin is corrupt. See also Riezler, *Vatikanische Akten*, nos. 50, 51, 72, 79, 109, 111–12, 114, 124–5, 139, 140, 144; C. Cipolla, *Documenti per la storia delle relazioni diplomatiche fra Verona e Mantova nel secolo XIV* (*Miscellanea di storia veneta edita per cura della R. Dep. Veneta di Storia Patria*, 2nd ser., xii, pt. 1 (1907), pp. 233–63; Theiner, *C.D.*, i, nos, 651, 660, 710, pp. 491, 660, 531; and cf. F. Bock, 'Studien zum Inquisitionsprozess Johanns XXII.', *Quellen*, xxvi (1935–6), pp. 21–142 and ibid., xxvii (1936–7), pp. 109–34; idem, 'Der Este Prozess von 1321', *Arch. Frat. Praed.*, vii (1937), pp. 41–111. For Angevin rule in Ferrara see M. T. Ferrer i Mallol, 'Mercenaris Catalans a Ferrara (1307–17)', *Anuario de estudios medievales*, ii (1965), pp. 155–227, pp. 196 ff.

Gatti of Viterbo did pretty well as they pleased. There was a serious local war in the Tuscan patrimony in 1318–20, in which the Roman government, though under Angevin control, intervened against Viterbo and other towns. In 1320 the papal rector of the Tuscan patrimony reported despairingly to Avignon that he was obeyed by no one save by a few miserable communes too poor to resist him. The revenues of his province were cut by a half – a fact perhaps not unconnected also with the embezzlements of his predecessor.[1] A year later a similarly despondent report was made by the papal rector of Romagna, where direct Angevin control had effected nothing, and had been terminated in 1320.

The sporadic interventions of Angevin troops in the Papal State could never be of more than minor importance. Naples was too distant; its armies already quite inadequate for their immense tasks. Papal rectors, with a few dozen men at arms in some centre in the hills such as Montefiascone in the Tuscan patrimony or Montefalco in the duchy of Spoleto could do little more than petty police work, unless they asked the communes and *signori* to fight for them. The rector of the central mountain zone, the duchy of Spoleto, had no adequate control of the mountain passes. He was unable to prevent, in September 1319, the plunder of the historic treasure of the Roman Church, in its deposit at Assisi, by the Ghibelline Muzio di Francesco.[2] That part of the costly symbols of the wealth and dignity of Rome which Boniface VIII had saved from the spoilers at Anagni was again looted. Rebellion spread rapidly to Spoleto, and papal rule in the duchy of Spoleto, then in the neighbouring march of Ancona, collapsed. The two leaders of this

---

[1] M. Antonelli, 'Vicende della dominazione pontificia nel Patrimonio di San Pietro in Tuscia dalla traslazione della Sede alla restaurazione dell'Albornoz', *ASR*, xxv (1902), pp. 367–95; idem, 'Una relazione del vicario del Patrimonio a Giovanni XXII in Avignone', ibid., xviii (1895), pp. 447–67; F. Bock, 'Roma al tempo di Roberto d'Angiò, ibid, lxv (1942), pp. 163–208; G. Falco, 'I comuni della Campagna a della Marittima nel medio evo', ibid. xlix (1926), pp. 153 f., especially at pp. 166, 180. For the finances of the Tuscan patrimony, Waley, *JEccH*, vi (1955), pp. 18–25; Antonelli, 'Estratti dai registri del Patrimonio del secolo xiv', *ASR*, xli (1918), pp. 59–85; Vatican Archives, Introitus et Exitus, vol. 21, folios 21v–22r refers to dishonesty of Guillaume Coste, canon of Toul.

[2] F. Ehrle, *Historia Bibliothecae Romanorum pontificum* (Rome, 1890), pp. 16–17; L. Fumi, 'Eretici e ribelli nell'Umbria dal 1320 al 1330 studiati su documenti inediti dall'Archivio Segreto Vaticano', *BSU*, iii (1895), pp. 257–85, 429–89; ibid. iv, pp. 221–301, 437–86; ibid. v, pp. 1–46, 205–425; F. Bock, 'I processi di Giovanni XXII contro i Ghibellini delle Marche', *BISI*, lvii (1941) pp. 19–70; Davidsohn, *Geschichte von Florenz*, iii, 663–9; V. Ansidei, 'Su alcuni rapporti fra Perugia e Spoleto nel secolo xiv', *BSU*, iii (1895), pp. 549–66; M. P. Fop, 'Il comune di Perugia e la Chiesa durante il periodo avignonese con particolare referimento all'Albornoz', *BSU*, lxv, fasc. 2 (1968), pp. 1–102; ibid. lxvi, fasc.1 (1969), pp. 67–150.

movement, who between them co-ordinated the action of the Ghibellines in the Papal State, were Guido Tarlati the Bishop of Arezzo, who became *signore* of the town in 1321, and Frederico II di Montefeltro.

Appeals to Charles of Calabria having gone unanswered, the only way to fight this sedition, was to unleash the Guelph towns and *signori* – Perugia in Umbria, the Malatesta of Rimini in Romagna and the march – against the Ghibellines. Perugia, whose last war against Spoleto had ended under papal mediation in 1314, was very happy to oblige; no less so the Malatesta. In 1322 a formidable Guelph army of 'crusaders', led by the fierce Fulcieri da Calboli who had in 1303 'slaughtered the Florentines like a wild beast'[1] descended on the march, and had success in a short campaign which saw Frederico di Montefeltro taken in his own town of Urbino and beheaded. Parts of the march submitted, and in the following year Spoleto fell to the Perugian army under Poncello Orsini. But little benefit came to the papacy even from these victories which were supposed to be its own; Perugia proceeded to enserf Spoleto in a manner which the Holy See found most unpalatable. The economic results of such warfare were enfeebling; in 1327, 340 landholdings belonging to the Ghibelline rebels of Spoleto were said to be desolate and uncultivated; in 1339 the condition of Spoleto was still said to be 'wretched'.[2] Local interests were the only ones served. In the march of Ancona the Malatesta were defeated in 1324, and the local confusion went on until the descent of Louis of Bavaria three years later.

III

It was not in the territory of the Papal State that the future of the papal temporal power could be decided. The real struggle was with the Ghibelline tyrants of north Italy, and above all with the Visconti. When John XXII was elected to the papal throne on 7 August 1316 Visconti power extended over the Lombard plain from the line of the Oglio on the east to the line of the Sesia on the west.

The new pope possessed a legal instrument of peculiar power against the Lombard tyrants. As long as the imperial vacancy lasted, the Ghibelline tyrants had no means of legitimising the *signoria* by turning it into an imperial vicariate. The bull *Si fratrum* of 1317 now claimed to make the papal veto on the exercise of the imperial vicariate in Italy

---

[1] Dante, *Purgatorio*, xiv, 61.
[2] *BSU*, iv (1896), pp. 281–2; Theiner, *C.D.*, ii, no. 72, p. 56.

a peculiarly binding one, which the pope was prepared to enforce with the direst sanctions of the Church.

The resulting political trials of the Ghibelline tyrants may appear to a modern mind eccentric and somewhat perverse. These extremely complex legal proceedings[1] began in October 1317, after the return of the papal nuncios from their fruitless Italian journey to reconcile the Lombard Ghibellines. The first stage was a peremptory order or requisitory to free the political prisoners and obey the papal truces; what in May had been a diplomatic request, in October was turned into a court order. Soon afterwards the charges were extended to those of implementing the imperial vicariate in spite of the bull *Si fratrum*. Between January and April 1318 the first stage of the lawsuit against the Ghibellines Matteo Visconti, Can Grande della Scala, and Raynaldo Bonacolsi was brought to a close; they were excommunicated and their lands placed under interdict.

By the summer of 1318 it had become impossible for John XXII to isolate from one another the various issues which confronted him in Italy – Ghibellinism and anti-clericalism in Lombardy and the Papal State; the Angevin *signoria* in Genoa; Sicily; the possible intervention of Frederick of Austria – all these were so interlocked that they could only be dealt with by a single Italian policy. Fragmented though the Italian peninsula was, its problems were eventually one.

The arrival of Robert of Anjou in southern France in April or May of 1319 thus coincided with a period in which the pope began to take the initiative in the prosecution of the great war against the Ghibellines. He continued to support and subsidise the Angevin; by December 1319 he was lending Robert, who already owed the pope huge sums for the unpaid feudal *census* of the kingdom, large amounts of money for the waging of war.[2] But in July 1319 the pope appointed his own agent Cardinal Bertrand du Poujet, as papal legate in north Italy. Du Poujet was to be the generalissimo of papal armies and policies in north Italy,

---

[1] Bock, articles quoted in *Quellen*, xxvi–xxvii (1935–7) and *Arch. Frat. Praed.*, vii (1937); C. Cipolla, 'Il processo ecclesiastico contro Rinaldo Bonacolsi dal 1323 al 1326', *Scritti vari di erudizione e di critica in onore di Rodolfo Renier* (Turin, 1912), pp. 391–9; R. André-Michel, 'Le procès de Matteo et de Galeazzo Visconti', *Mélanges*, xxix (1909), pp. 269–327; K. Eubel, 'Von Zaubereiunwesen anfangs des 14 Jahrhunderts', *Hist. Jahrb.*, xviii (1897), pp. 608–31; G. Biscaro, 'Dante Alighieri e i sortilegi di Matteo e Galeazzo Visconti contro papa Giovanni XXII', *ASL*, 5th ser., xlvii (1920), pp. 446–81; H. Otto, 'Zur italienischen Politik Johanns XXII', *Quellen*, xiv (1911), pp. 140–265.

[2] K. H. Schäfer, *Die Ausgaben der apostolischen Kammer unter Johann XXII. Vatikanische Quellen zur Geschichte der päpstlichen Hof- und Finanzverwaltung*, ii (1911), pp. 816–17.

and so he remained until his failure and recall in 1334. For such an important figure, little is known of his personality. He was popularly, but wrongly, supposed to be the pope's son. Certainly a ruthless man – he is often described as 'cruel', 'ferocious' – he seems to emerge as a clever political technician, adept at exploiting the Italian parties and factions, an able if rigid administrator.

Having at first discouraged Robert of Anjou's project for a combined operation in Italy with the aid of France, the pope changed tack and persuaded King Philip the Long to agree to an expedition to north Italy led by his cousin Charles de Valois. Charles de Valois did not cover himself with glory. Having failed to relieve the besieged Angevin city of Vercelli, he came ignominiously to an understanding with Galeazzo Visconti, and dismissed his army. The French monarchy was too much weakened by dynastic and internal problems to intervene on a decisive scale in Italy.

One form of foreign intervention having failed, the pope and the Angevin king turned to another, this time to Frederick of Austria.[1] In 1320 Frederick concluded a military alliance with Robert of Anjou, and the pope asked him to act against Frederick of Sicily and Can Grande della Scala. But when Henry of Austria marched to Brescia in April of 1322 he found that the pope had cast him in a role for which he had neither mind nor stomach. The Patriarch of Aquileja, Pagano della Torre, leader of the 'crusade' against the Ghibelline 'heretics', was waiting for him at Brescia with the Guelph army. Henry had come to vindicate imperial prestige and perhaps to gain some sort of territorial advantage. But to stay meant fighting a great war against the Visconti and the Lombard Ghibellines, which had never been the Austrian intention. He had come 'to uphold and not to put down the loyal subjects of the Empire'.[2] The Austrian army retired from Italy. A few months later Austrian effectiveness was ended by Frederick's decisive defeat at the hands of Louis of Bavaria, the other claimant to the empire, at Mühldorf on 28 September 1322.

The Angevin-papal forces in Piedmont under Cardinal Bertrand du Poujet thus remained the only reliable instrument of papal power in north Italy. They were backed by the papal fiscal machine and by the ruthless employment of the spiritual power, and were not negligible.

---

[1] Tabacco, 'La politica italiana di Federico il Bello re dei Romani', *ASI*, cviii (1950), pp. 34–77.

[2] Jacopo Malvezzi, *Chronicon* (*RRIISS*, xiv), col. 997. Cf. *MGH, Const. et acta publica*, v, pt. 1, nos. 647, 655–7, pp. 511, 520.

From the autumn of 1319 onwards, Spanish, French and German
mercenaries began to congregate in Provence at the stipend of the
Church; in May 1321 they were placed under the command of Raymond
of Cardona, an Aragonese captain in Angevin service.

The legal processes against the Ghibellines in the end implicated all
the leaders, from the Visconti and Della Scala down to small fry like the
Rusca of Como and the opposition in the Papal State. The pattern was
in most cases the same. The fundamental charges were the imprisonment
of Guelph leaders, attacks on Guelph towns, misuse of the title of imperial
vicar, and the maltreatment and illegal taxation of clerks. After the first
excommunication and interdict had been pronounced, other charges
were added to the file: violation of the interdict, association with heretics,
interference with the papal agents who served the summonses, expres-
sions of anti-clerical sentiments of an heretical nature. Matteo Visconti
was accused of trying to work the death of Pope John XXII by causing
a magic image of the pope to be made.

Heresy: this was the eventual gravamen in which all other charges
culminated. Canon law in matters of heresy was so unfavourable to the
defendant that once a person was *suspectus de haeresi* his condemnation could be made practically inevitable. Contumacy, or failure to appear
in person to reply to the heresy charges after a year, automatically
entailed condemnation for heresy.[1] By this means plausible reports of
anti-clerical remarks current in any court in Europe became the grounds
of a condemnation for heresy, with all the extremely serious civil and
religious consequences which this carried in medieval society. The inter-
rogation of Opizzo and Raynaldo d'Este, who, exceptionally, appeared
in court to meet their clerical accusers, makes it clear that political
remarks, such as the denial that Ferrara was a part of the Papal State,
were thought an adequate basis for heresy prosecution.[2] It is noticeable
also that some of the charges had been used with suspicious similarity
against others; for example, Boniface VIII, the Templars and in this
series of trials Galeazzo Visconti, were all accused of saying that fornica-
tion was no sin.

There had been some negotiations between Bertrand du Poujet and
Matteo Visconti, but these broke down. By January 1322 the final stages

---

[1] *Sext.*, lib. v, tit. ii, c.vii, *Cum contumacia.*
[2] F. Bock, *Arch. Frat. Praed.*, vii (1937), pp. 68–74, and the same author in *Quellen*, xxvii
(1936–7), pp. 119 ff. and ibid. xxvi (1935–6), pp. 49–52. Raynaldo and Obizzo d'Este could
appear before the inquisitors because they were cited to appear in their own territory.
Matteo Visconti was cited to Avignon, a citation which it was politically impossible to obey.

of the heresy affair were in the hands of the inquisitors of Piedmont. The Visconti were described as 'beyond doubt' heretics and a crusade proclaimed against them; crusading subsidies were levied for its prosecution. On 14 March 1322 the final verdict was pronounced: Matteo Visconti was condemned as a heretic, his goods and honours forfeited, and the Milanese citizens implicated as supporters of heretics. A fortnight later Venice was instructed to imprison Milanese subjects in Venetian territory as heretics and to seize their goods.[1]

Over 800 of the 1,400 or so persons cited before the Inquisition in the Ghibelline heresy cases were Milanese. At Easter 1322 the economic and religious sanctions against Milan began to tell, and in May the personal power of Matteo Visconti suddenly collapsed. Twelve representative Milanese magnates came to the legate in Valenza to make terms with the Inquisition. Matteo Visconti abdicated his powers to his son Galeazzo and on 24 June died, a sick and gouty old man who proclaimed his religious orthodoxy to the last.[2]

The Visconti heirs fought desperately. But on 9 October an exiled noble of Piacenza was bribed to breach the wall of that city and to admit papal troops. Piacenza operated a stranglehold on Milanese commerce to and from Venice (a bridge was built across the river for this specific purpose),[3] and offered a base for the invasion of Milan. On 8 November the German troops in Milan mutinied, and went over to the government of the twelve notables. Milan was in chaos, and Galeazzo Visconti fled; though he returned after Bertrand du Poujet refused to accept the Milanese invitation to enter the city.

At Genoa the Ghibellines were finally defeated, and the five years' siege of the city came to an end. The three Guelph armies, commanded by Raymond of Cardona (in Piedmont), by the legate du Poujet (in Piacenza) and by the Patriarch of Aquileja (in Brescia) effected a junction at Monza, thus concentrating a huge force against Milan. German troops again mutinied. Galeazzo Visconti was 'everywhere deserted'.

At this crisis the empire lifted a feeble but nevertheless providential hand on behalf of its faithful subjects. On 5 May 1323, while the great Can Grande della Scala and Raynaldo Passerino Bonacolsi were actually in conference in the bishop's palace in Mantua with the papal diplomats, the three German commissioners of Louis of Bavaria entered the room.

---

[1] Cf. H. Otto, 'Zur italienischen Politik Johanns XXII.', *Quellen*, xiv (1911), pp. 140–265, at pp. 214 ff.; Bock, ibid. xxvi (1935–6), pp. 41–9.
[2] Cf. *Storia di Milano*, v (Milan, 1955), pp. 154–79.
[3] Cf. H. Spangenberg, *Can Grande della Scala* (Berlin, 1895), ii, pp. 32–3.

Peremptorily they charged Can Grande and Bonacolsi, on the oath they had sworn to the Emperor Henry VII, to send armed help to the imperial city of Milan besieged by the legate. Only a few hundred armed men came with the German commissioners, but the mere sound of the imperial name rallied the Ghibellines. Negotiations with the papal envoys were broken off on the spot; the Ghibelline league (adhered to also by the Este of Ferrara) reformed; and a force assembled for the relief of Milan. On 23 June the Imperial Vicar Berthold of Neiffen entered the city with a small force, and received Galeazzo Visconti's oath of obedience as 'protector and defender' of Milan for the empire.[1]

Large as it was, the Guelph army at the siege of Milan was too mixed in race, region and interest to be effective. German, Aragonese and French mercenaries, Lombard exiles, Tuscan Guelphs, quarrelled and bickered. On the arrival of Von Neiffen the Germans mutinied and went over to the Visconti. The sight of two prelates of the Church regulating the train of whores and campfollowers damped what religious ardour there was among the crusaders. It was mid-summer, and plague broke out in the besieging army; the legate's nephew was one of the first victims. The Florentine contingent on 4 June impudently ran the *palio* under the walls of Milan but this bravado availed them nothing. In late July the Guelph army broke up, leaving a garrison in Monza; the siege was over and the Visconti *signoria* was safe.

By August 1323 John XXII recognised that the Guelph effort had failed.[2] On 8 October 1323 Louis of Bavaria was accused by the pope of exercising imperial rights in contempt of the bull *Si fratrum,* and of supporting the hertical Visconti. In the papal consistory, four days before the bull against Louis had been published, there had been an angry scene. Cardinals Napoleon Orsini and Peter Colonna, who saw in the pope's actions the final triumph of the extremist policy which they had fought for over twenty-five years, protested. The pope, who said that he did not recognise the right of conquest over his opponent which the cardinals claimed the Battle of Mühldorf had conferred on Louis, said he would issue a decretal (that of 8 October) to the contrary. When Cardinal Jacopo Stefaneschi, the former confidant of Boniface VIII, told the pope to 'beware of German ferocity', the reply was: 'By God!

---

[1] *MGH, Const. et acta publica,* v, no. 752, p. 586, and ibid. no. 897, p. 711n. Cf. Otto, *Quellen,* xiv (1911), pp. 222–30.

[2] *MGH, Const. et acta publica,* v, no. 780, p. 607. Tabacco, *La casa di Francia nell' azione politica di papa Giovanni XXII,* pp. 212 ff. is fundamental for the understanding of this period.

We will teach the Germans what ferocity is!'[1] Thus spake Christ's vicar.

After the failure before Milan, the Guelph military position collapsed. Raymond of Cardona was defeated and captured (though later released in order to lose other battles) at Vaprio on 16 February 1324. Monza capitulated to the Visconti; on 16 March 1325 Azzo Visconti seized the fortress of Borgo San Donnino, lying astride the Via Emilia between Parma and Piacenza. In May of the same year the Angevin expedition against Sicily fizzled out in a couple of futile skirmishes. Then on 23 September the Florentines and the Guelph league under Raymond of Cardona met at Altopascio near Lucca with a serious defeat. Bologna became the hinge of the Guelph position. But at Zapolino north of the city, Bologna was on 15 November utterly defeated by Raynaldo Passerino Bonacolsi and his allies. Two thousand Bolognese fell, and another six hundred of the best of the Guelph nobility in Bologna went to the prisons of Modena.

After Zapolino the Florentines decided that they could no longer postpone submission to their only possible protector, the Angevin kingdom. With the enemy besieging San Miniato and Fiesole, Florence on 23 December 1325 conferred the *signoria* of the city for ten years on Charles of Calabria, the heir of Robert of Anjou. In the return for the annual subsidy of 200,000 florins, he was to provide a thousand French men-at-arms for the defence of the city.

The drift to the *signoria* of the Church was accentuated in Emilia. Reggio had received its *podestà* from the Church since 1322, and in a moment of enthusiasm in 1323 had proposed to have a bull of John XXII engraved in gold letters on the wall of the Palazzo Comunale.[2] In Parma nearby the internal faction of the Rossi had been happy to collaborate for their own purposes with the legate (who made Ugolino Rossi bishop of the city) while covertly aiding the Visconti. On 30 September 1326 the legate obtained the *signoria* of Parma, alleging papal authority over the city in the vacancy of the empire – that is, relying on the bull *Si fratrum* of 1317. The smaller and weaker commune of Reggio gave the *signoria* to the legate five days after the submission of Parma. Finally on 8 February 1327 the great city of Bologna submitted, and gave itself to the legate without conditions. The greatest city – apart from

---

[1] 'Per deum! Et furiam invenient et iterum furiam invenient.' Finke, *AA*, i, no. 262, at p. 395. For the expression see E. Dümmler, 'Über den furor Teutonicus', *Sitzungsberichte der königlich-preussischen Akademie der Wissenschaften zu Berlin* (1897), pp. 112–26.

[2] L. Giommi, 'Come Reggio venne in podestà di Bertrando del Poggetto (1306–26)', *AMP Mod*, 5th ser., xiii (1920), at p. 107.

Rome – in the Papal State, whose submission to the papacy had always been formal rather than actual, now foɪ the first time in its history accepted direct papal rule.

The *signoria* of Bologna was Bertrand du Poujet's most notable achievement, recognised as such by John XXII when in 1332 he proposed to transfer the seat of the papacy from Avignon to Bologna. Du Poujet's implementation of his rule in Bologna was among the most thorough, radical and authoritarian of any of the *signori* of his day, and among the least careful to preserve the forms of communal government.[1] The Church enjoyed the full disposition of the offices and revenues of Bologna, abolished the *consiglio del popolo,* and imposed a quite new administration on the city. Like the other *signori,* du Poujet built a fortress to house the mercenaries with which he over-awed the population.

Politically the papal *signoria* in Bologna was supported and rounded off by the subjection of other parts of Emilia and Romagna. In the course of a new papal offensive Cesena and Imola were taken under the direct rule of the Church. A notable success was the seizure by Bertrand du Poujet of Modena on 5 June 1327.

Far less impressive were the operations of Angevin-papal power in Tuscany. Cardinal Giovanni Caetani Orsini, named legate in April 1326 in Tuscany and the papal lands south of Romagna, arrived in Florence in June 1326 almost at the same moment as Charles of Calabria. But in spite of Charles's *signoria* in Florence, and of the huge sums paid him by the Florentines, neither he nor the new legate achieved anything of note. In the march of Ancona and the patrimony of St Peter in Tuscany the fighting went on, perhaps rather more to the advantage of the Church than earlier but without achieving any decisive results, and with the clerical forces led usually by *signori* or barons (Tano of Iesi, the Malatesta, the Farnese) whose local power would be the chief beneficiary of victory.

IV

In the New Year of 1327 the pretender to the empire, Louis of Bavaria, at last entered Italy. The fate of his intervention was to show how disastrously German power in Italy had declined, even since 1313. Louis arrested Galeazzo Visconti and his family in Milan on 6 July 1327

---

[1] L. Ciaccio, 'Il Cardinale Legato Bertrando del Poggetto in Bologna (1327–34)', *AMDR*, 3rd ser., xxiii (1905), p. 126.

– probably because Marco Visconti revealed to Louis how far Visconti negotiations with the papacy had already gone.[1] Crowned with the iron crown in Milan, on 13 August Louis took the route of Henry VII, passing through Tuscany to Pisa. His passage of the Apennines was uncontested, and this unopposed march set the pattern for the two years of military activity which followed – a small, determined, German force marching freely through open country, too much feared by the Guelphs to risk a general action, but too weak, usually, to take any sizeable town which would not open its gates.

Unopposed, therefore, Louis marched in December 1327 south through the Maremma to Rome. In Rome, the way had been prepared nine months earlier by a *coup d'état* against the Angevin government by Sciarra Colonna and Jacopo Savelli in April 1327. The Angevin-papal senator, Annibaldo Annibaldi, had to leave Rome, and an Angevin army which arrived under John of Gravina was unable to enter the city. Reinforcements were landed by Genoese ships in the mouth of the Tiber, and in September John of Gravina and the papal legate tried to carry Rome by assault, but were bloodily repulsed. Louis entered the city by the invitation of the Romans: his own coronation took place on 17 January 1328.

On 12 May 1328 the ideological war between Louis of Bavaria and the papacy reached its natural term with the election in Rome of an anti-pope, Peter of Corbara (Nicholas V). Peter of Corbara had a mixed following, ranging from learned theologians to ignorant enthusiasts. But the acceptance of Peter of Corbara in Italy, so far as it went, was mainly political, and coincided with a political Ghibellinism which had little to do with religion. The papal heresy charges pursued both the political Ghibellines and the religious objectors proper, but it seems probable that the majority of those charged with heresy belonged to the former and not to the latter category.

Louis was poorer than Henry VII, and large numbers of troops deserted his standard because he could not pay them; he left Rome in August 1328 with a force half the size of that which entered the city eight months earlier. Frederick of Sicily, who promised support, could not give it in time, and a German attack on the Angevin kingdom was impossible. Louis could only sack the fortress of La Molara on the Via Latina and a few other villages in the Roman Campagna, and then retire north through a half-hostile Umbria. All that the imperial march had achieved was a coronation whose validity few people believed in, and

[1] Cognasso, in *Storia di Milano*, v. p, 198; cf. Biscaro, *ASL*, xlvi (1919), p. 104.

a feeble anti-pope who scarcely believed in himself. Louis retired through
Pisa to northern Italy, where on 15 January 1329 he was forced to
concede the imperial vicariate of Milan to Azzo Visconti, Giovanni's
son.[1]

The pope continued to assert the community of interest of the papacy
and the French and Angevin monarchies. He repeatedly instructed that
the armies of the legate in Romagna and of Charles of Calabria in
Florence should help one another, and these orders were carried out,
even to the extent of sending papal troops south into the kingdom of
Naples. When Charles of Calabria protested early in 1327 that the
papacy had taken Parma and Reggio for itself, and not handed them
over to the Angevins, John XXII coolly replied that he would sooner
the Angevins held such gains than himself, were they only strong enough
to defend them, but 'if the papal command had not reinforced Robert
of Anjou in Lombardy, he would not have advanced a foot there'.[2]
But this was an evasive answer, which made no reference to the
undoubted aim of papal policy to annexe to the Papal State the newly-
conquered towns in the Po valley.

Where papal policy erred was in continuing to believe, after the great
consolidation of the north-Italian Ghibelline *signorie* between 1325 and
1328, that Bertrand du Poujet could create and maintain a defensible
block of Guelph territory in the area between Piacenza and Bologna.
If the papal army garrisoned the cities, it had no striking power. If not,
they would fall away.[3] It is true that Guelph Brescia still held out in
north Lombardy, and that a string of papal forts now skirted the north-
east of the Visconti possessions (to their great annoyance) from Lecco
down the Adda to Caravaggio and Crema. But this tenuous line of
possessions, though it provided a safer line of communications with
Brescia in the north, did nothing to protect the exposed line of the Via
Emilia.

The peak of Bertrand du Poujet's success had come with the occupation of Modena in June 1327, just before the invasion of Louis of
Bavaria. But on 1 August 1328 the Fogliani and Rossi seized Reggio

---

[1] *MGH, Const. et acta publica*, vi, pt. 1, no. 579, p. 482. For the Visconti, ibid. no 587, p. 488,
and cf. nos. 647–8a, infra, p. 544.

[2] Tabacco, *La casa di Francia*, doc. v, at pp. 354–5. Cf. Tabacco's text at pp. 251, 284–7; and
see also A. Mercati, 'Dagli *Instrumenta Miscellanea* dell'Archivio Segreto Vaticano', *Quellen*,
xxvii (1936–7), pp. 135–77, especially docs. vii (p. 148) and xi (p. 156).

[3] See John XXII's discussion of the tactical problem, in the document published in Mercati's
article cited above, doc. ix, p. 151 (24 August 1326). The letter cited above in Tabacco,
La casa di Francia, p. 354, is on the same lines.

from the Church, and on the following day Parma followed, returning to the *signoria* of the Rossi.[1] The rule of the Church in Emilia had insecure foundations. The Este of Ferrara in September 1328 returned to the allegiance of the Church,[2] but all that occurred was the movement of the Este to a position of neutrality.

On 6 May 1329 the interdict on Milan was suspended, and in the following month a Visconti embassy arrived in Avignon. In September the Visconti were absolved. Like the Este, they became neutrals, careful to keep an escape route to the empire open. Like the Este, however, they were somewhat attracted to the Church by the bait, always tempting to the *signori*, of legitimisation of their rule. John XXII offered Azzo Visconti the imperial vicariate of Milan, and by the early summer of 1330 this bargain had been struck.

In the New Year of 1330 Louis of Bavaria returned to Germany. His Italian ambitions had collapsed, and his anti-pope, deserted by all, was in August ignominiously handed over to Avignon by the Pisans. The pope was reassured by fulsome submissions which arrived at Avignon throughout the year from the ex-partisans of 'Nicholas V' all over Ghibelline Italy. But politically the papal position in Italy was far from triumphant. John XXII was still playing with the idea, in late 1330 and early 1331, of making over Lombardy to France as a papal fief.[3]

V

King John of Bohemia was heir (in a sense) to that policy of reconciliation between Guelph and Ghibelline with which his father Henry VII had entered Italy. But his political position was a very different one. Educated in the French court, and brother-in-law of Charles IV of France, John as King of Bohemia had acted as a French satellite in German politics. The stalemate which obtained between the Austrian and the Bavarian in the struggle for the empire gave him a peculiar importance, and offered him chances of aggrandisement. A subtle – an over-subtle – politician, John was also a feudal romantic; a volunteer to lead the abortive crusade against the Moors in Granada in 1329–30;

---

[1] Cf. Spangenberg, *Can Grande*, ii, pp. 73–5; *Chronicon Parmense* (*RRIISS*, ix, pt. 9), pp. 187–90.
[2] L. Muratori, *Delle Antichità Estensi*, ii, pp. 178, 190, 194–5; Tiraboschi, *Memorie storiches modenesi*, ii, p. 239; T. Mommsen, *Italienische Analekten zur Reichsgeschichte des 14. Jahrhunderts* (Stuttgart, 1952), nos. 177, 178, 194; cf. also de Vergottini, 'Ricerche sulle origini del vicariato apostolico', *Studi in onore di E. Besta* (Milan, 1938), ii, pp. 301–50.
[3] H. Otto, 'Die Eide und Privilegien Heinrich VII. und Karls IV.', *Quellen*, ix (1906), pp. 316–78, at p. 342; idem, *Quellen*, xiv (1911), pp. 192–3; Tabacco, *La casa di Francia*, pp. 297–311.

destined to die as a blind and brave old man on the battlefield of Crécy.

The position of John of Bohemia as a prince who entertained friendly relations both with the French and the imperial courts was a worrying one for John XXII. The fear became uppermost in the pope's mind in 1330 that the Bohemian, going to Italy as Louis of Bavaria's agent would undo the reconciliation of the Church with the Lombard tyrants which was just being so painfully brought to a conclusion. The clash of interests came to the surface in July 1330, when John of Bohemia offered to meet Azzo Visconti.[1]

It was thus as an ambiguous if not a double-dealing figure that John of Bohemia came to Italy. In the last few days of 1330 he arrived at Brescia, which was still hard pressed by the Della Scala, and immediately had the *signoria* of the city. In the following few months, with no large army employed and no threats made, the cities of north Italy seemed to fall into John's hands like ripe fruit. Mantua, Cremona, Parma, Reggio, Modena, Lucca and Milan submitted to him in one form or another.[2] The rumour current in Italy was that the Bohemian came with papal approval, but in fact the papal reaction was one of impotent horror. John of Bohemia met the Legate Bertrand du Poujet at Castel Franco near Bologna on 17 April 1331; nothing is known of what occurred at this interview, but papal letters of a few weeks later suggest that the pope's fear and hostility remained.[3]

John of Bohemia's expedition was a diplomatic juggling trick. It was known in Italy that behind the Bohemian king might lie the power of Louis of Bavaria, or else of the French monarchy – or even that of both! The prudent course was submission, a course the more acceptable in that it entailed no real sacrifice of power. Nowhere, save perhaps at Lucca, did the *signoria* of the Bohemian substantially change the status quo. Not only the great tyrants, the Visconti and Della Scala, but even the pettiest – the Rossi of Parma, Fogliani of Reggio, Pii of Modena – all stayed in power, their rule often confirmed by the grant of an imperial

---

[1] *MGH, Const. et acta publica*, vi, pt. 1, no. 799, p. 678; better text in E. Stengel, *Nova Alemanniae* (Berlin, 1921–30), i, no. 223, p. 128. The papal reaction, *MGH, Const. et acta publica*, vi, pt. 1, no. 868, p. 721.

[2] Cf. C. Cipolla, *Doc. per la storia delle relazioni diplomatiche fra Verona e Mantova*, pp. 269–71. Not all these cities recognised John as *signore*.

[3] Otto, *Quellen*, xiv (1911), pp. 241–4. For the correct dating of Riezler's *Vatikanische Akten*, no. 1457 (mistaken by Mollat, *The Popes at Avignon*, p. 106), see A. Lehleiter, *Die Politik König Johanns von Böhmen 1330–4* (Berlin, 1908), pp. 2–3, and references given there. This document must be dated to the visit of John of Bohemia to Avignon in November 1332, or soon after; it is not 'the pact of 17 April 1331' (Mollat). Cf. also Tabacco, *La casa di Francia*, pp. 316, 320.

vicariate. As a tract written in the Angevin court bitterly comments, tyrants such as the Rossi of Parma stayed in power under pope, Bavarian, and Bohemian, merely changing their allegiance as necessary.[1] The great losers by the Bohemian expedition were the Angevin monarchy and the papacy. The divergencies of policy between Paris, Avignon and Naples, which for the past fifteen years had been kept to a prudent minimum, now became so great as to wreck the whole political system on which the Avignonese papacy depended.

By January 1332 John of Bohemia was in Paris, and the whole year was consumed in negotiations with the French and papal courts, in the course of which the pope showed himself reluctant in the extreme to endorse the support which Philip VI wanted to give the Bohemian. To Philip VI John offered Lucca, and in the event of the acquisition of the empire by his son Charles, the kingdom of Arles. To the papacy John represented himself as one who would extirpate the 'tyrants' of Italy by setting up the French-dominated 'Lombard kingdom' which had been in the pope's mind since 1317.[2] Such was John XXII's impotence to unravel the diplomatic knot before him that early in 1332 he was seriously proposing to quit Avignon for Bologna – surely not out of fear of France, as some contemporaries suggested, but perhaps because he thought that his presence in Italy could stop the collapse of the Guelph alliance. Transfer of the papal court to Bologna seemed politically feasible at this moment when the Este of Ferrara had submitted and other tyrants had been expelled from the Romangol towns.[3] There was a parliament at Faenza in March 1332 which marked the highest point of papal power in Romagna at this period.[4] But the hub of the negotiations, which concerned not only Italy but the Anglo-French difficulties and the proposal for a French crusade, was in France, and the pope could not leave Avignon until they had been satisfactorily concluded. Petrarch's prediction that the pope would soon return to the nest, to Bologna· and Rome (a prophecy already qualified by the sceptical '*s'altro accidente nol distorna*'), was never fulfilled.

By September 1332 all Italy, whether Guelph or Ghibelline, had turned against the Bohemian. At the end of April 1332 the Visconti and their clients were negotiating to join a league which was sub-

---

[1] C. Müller, *Der Kampf Ludwigs des Bayern mit der römischen Kurie* (Tübingen, 1879–80), i, p. 402.
[2] Cf. A. Mercati, 'Dall'Archivio Vaticano', etc., *Mélanges*, lxi (1949), pp. 195–209.
[3] Vasina, *I Romagnoli*, pp. 328 ff.
[4] Ibid.; cf. also Matteo Griffoni, *Memoriale historicum* (*RRIISS*, xviii, pt. 2), p. 40; *Annales Caesenates* (ibid. xiv), col. 1152.

stantially a repetition of the Ghibelline–Este alliance of the 1320s. In the summer of 1332 the diplomatic revolution took place which astonished Italy and announced a new era in Italian politics. On 16 September the league of Ferrara was concluded, aligning Florence with the existing alliance of the Este and the Lombard Ghibellines and leaving room for entry into the alliance by Robert of Anjou and the remaining Guelph communes of Tuscany. Robert of Anjou certainly took part in these negotiations, even if he was not a contracting party. Unlike the leagues which immediately preceded it, the league of Ferrara was specifically directed against John of Bohemia.[1]

The league of Ferrara surprises somewhat less when it is considered that long before the Guelphs thought of entering an alliance against the Bohemian (who was not yet, after all, the declared protégé of the pope), the Ghibellines had deserted the cause of Louis of Bavaria. Nevertheless, when Florentine troops bore the arms of Robert of Anjou into battle beside those of the Visconti viper in the campaign of 1333, they showed that the system of alliances which had grown from Charles of Anjou's invasion in 1266 had finally cracked.

That John XXII, no less than Bertrand du Poujet, failed to understand what the league of Ferrara meant, is not surprising. When John of Bohemia made his long-delayed visit to Avignon in November 1332, the pope decided to sacrifice the Angevin alliance to the French, and to come to terms with the Bohemian. The pope agreed to cede him Parma, Reggio and Modena (still by virtue of the bull *Si fratrum* of 1317), and undertook to mediate on John's behalf with Azzo Visconti and Robert of Anjou, whom the Bohemian promised not to attack. At the same time John of Bohemia accepted over 100,000 gold florins from Philip of France, with which he proceeded to enlist a largely French army for his descent into Italy in the following year. It is unlikely that the French monarchy would have gone so far, if the suggestion of the French-dominated 'kingdom of Lombardy' was not still in the air.

But the Bohemian cause in Italy was already lost before the talks in Avignon began. Brescia and Bergamo were lost by September 1332; in November Pavia fell to Azzo Visconti. The defeat inflicted by the Bohemian's forces on the Este at San Felice in the territory of Modena on 25 November 1332 may have created the illusion in papal circles that

---

[1] Ficker, *Urkunden zur Geschichte des Römerzuges Ludwig des Bayern*, no. 316, p. 152. Cf. T. Mommsen, *Italienische Analekten zur Reichsgeschichte des 14. Jahrhunderts* (Stuttgart, 1952), nos. 212, 217, 220; Müller, *Kampf Ludwigs des Bayern*, i, pp. 401–2. For the earlier leagues, Cipolla, *Documenti*, nos. 99–105, pp. 271–83; Muratori, *Piena esposizione*, doc. ix, p. 366.

the league of Ferrara could be split, and the war restricted to one against its weakest member, the Este. Early in the New Year of 1333 (presumably as soon as news of the Avignon agreements reached him) Bertrand du Poujet launched a savage and unprovoked attack on Ferrara – which he had personally and solemnly recognised as an Este vicariate exactly a year earlier. In February John of Bohemia arrived in Italy with his French reinforcements, and on 14 April 1333 the whole papal-Bohemian force, led by John of Armagnac, but incorporating large numbers of Italians from Emilia and Romagna, met the forces of the league outside Ferrara. The result was the utter rout of the army and fleet of the legate and the Bohemian. Thousands of the papal army were slaughtered: hundreds more drowned in the bloody waters of the Po di Volvano. Practically all the leading tyrants of Romagna – Malatesta, Polenta, Alidosi, Manfredi, Ordelaffi – were captured, as was John of Armagnac. No clearer indication could be needed that, unsatisfactory as the Angevin army was, the papal army could not survive without it. By early June the Bohemian was negotiating for a truce, which he obtained on 19 July.[1] For the papal forces besieged at Argenta in the district of Comacchio the war dragged on. But the great game, as John XXII had conceived and played it for the past seventeen years, was over. On 18 October King John left Parma for Germany, never to return, and leaving not even a noble idea to relieve the destruction and disillusion which he left behind him.

As the captured tyrants of Romagna ransomed themselves after the Battle of Ferrara they hastened into mutiny – Rimini, Forlì, Cesena, Ravenna, Cervia and even Bertinoro, the main papal strongpoint of Romagna, one after another rebelled, so that by the autumn of 1333 the authority of the Church in Romagna had virtually disappeared. The pope now had to negotiate with the league of Ferrara; this was the task of a new papal legate, Bertrand de Déaulx, Archbishop of Embrun, whom John XXII appointed in October 1333. In early March 1334 Bertrand de Déaulx met the leaders of the league at Peschiera near Brescia. While he negotiated, on 8 March the strongpoint of Argenta, which du Poujet had in spite of vigorous efforts been unable to relieve, capitulated. Bertrand de Déaulx then returned to Bologna to confer with du Poujet. Du Poujet wanted to fight on. But it was in any case too late. On 17 March 1334 Bologna rebelled against the legate with the aid of the Este. The French mercenaries were massacred; the castle of Galliera

[1] Ficker, *Urkunden*, nos. 322–8; cf. Cipolla, *La storia scaligera*, doc. 12, p. 49; idem, *Documenti*, doc. 106, p. 288.

which du Poujet had built to house them was destroyed. After ten days of siege in his palace, du Poujet was extracted on terms from the city by the Guelph mediators, the Florentines. The cardinal's recall to Avignon was already on the way.

John XXII's plan to exploit the disputed title to the empire by creating a Franco-papal dominion in north Italy had utterly failed. It had never been a very good plan, because it had never been clear whether this dominion was to be ruled by France, by the Angevin kingdom of Naples, or by the papacy. The whole policy which lay behind the bull *Si fratrum* of 1317 was one of ambiguity and opportunism, and the advent of John of Bohemia had brought into the open all the latent contradictions which hindered its execution and made it ultimately impossible. The Bohemian revealed also, what was to be made plain more than once in the century, that the dependence of the Avignon papacy on the French monarchy, though usually kept within limits which were politically manageable, could sometimes, even under a strong and able pope, lead to situations which were quite intolerable.

For the Western Church as a whole the effects of John XXII's Italian policies were unhappy. The war of Lombardy cost the pope over three million gold florins, about two-thirds of the total income of the papacy during his pontificate.[1] To raise these huge sums the pope devoted his brilliant administrative gifts, and the result was a further expansion and elaboration of the whole machinery of taxation and centralised government in the Western Church. It can of course be argued that the administrative tendency in this direction was already too strong to stop, and it can also be argued that papal centralisation was in many ways only effected in response to widespread clerical demands and needs. Nevertheless, many of the more objectionable features of papal fiscality, and so some of the weakness of the late medieval Church, can be blamed onto John XXII's Italian wars.

---

[1] E. Göller, *Die Einnahmen der apostolischen Kammer unter Benedikt XII.* (Paderborn, 1920), p. 10*.

Chapter 10

Popes, legates and tyrants

I

The rebellion of Bologna and the final failure of Bertrand du Poujet in 1334 enforced a pause of twenty years upon the grandiose papal plans to dominate Italy which had characterised the previous twenty. The split between papal and Angevin policies in Italy was wider than ever before; the Guelph connection in Italy persisted, but it was now linked with Robert of Anjou rather than with the pope.[1] As a result of the alienation of the two powers, Angevin influence declined in Rome. When John XXII had been granted the *signoria* of Rome for life, he had conferred it on Robert of Anjou. John XXII died at the end of 1334, and was succeeded by the Cistercian, Benedict XII (elected 20 December 1334). Benedict XII reversed the temporal power policies of his predecessor in most respects. There was no question of a return to the expensive imperialism of du Poujet. In Rome Benedict objected to the disorders which the Angevin senators failed to control; in 1336 a papal envoy took over the government of the city, and the series of Angevin senators ended.[2] It was a bad time for the Roman area. In late 1336 the poet Petrarch was at Capranica in the Tuscan patrimony, as the guest of Orso Count of Anguillara. He wrote: 'Peace is the one thing I have not found. The shepherd goes armed to the woods, the armoured labourer uses a lance instead of a goad...at night-time there are dreadful cries without the walls; in the day, cries of "To arms, to arms!" '

[1] For a defence of Angevin policy against papal criticism see the document printed in C. Müller, *Der Kampf Ludwigs des Bayern mit der römischen Kurie* (Tübingen, 1879–80), i, pp. 393–405, especially at pp. 400–3, which is a defence of the League of Ferrara. Cf. also G. Tabacco, 'La tradizione guelfa in Italia durante il pontificato di Benedetto XII', *Studi di Storia medievale e moderna in onore di Ettore Rota* (Rome, 1958), pp. 97–148, and *Europe in the Late Middle Ages*, pp. 76 ff.

[2] Cf. my article 'Annibaldi, Annibaldo' in *Dizionario biografico degli Italiani*, and also the article of L. Gatto, 'Annibaldi, Paolo' (ibid.). The feuds of the Roman magnates became uncontrollable after the murder of Bertoldo Orsini by Stefanuccio di Sciarra Colonna (6 May 1333).

Benedict XII took the view, as a politician later in the century wrote, that money spent on recovering the Italian lands of the popes was as good as thrown in the Rhône; the financial records of his pontificate confirm this statement.[1] Provincial rectors in the Papal State, far from being able to draw on large sums from the pope to pay their troops, were reproached by him for failure to pay their way. But to represent Benedict's pacifism as merely parsimony is perhaps unfair. He had promised that in his time the Roman Church would not wield the material sword, or fight wars even to recover the patrimony.[2] He tried to conciliate the Visconti, and renounced the policy of great wars in the peninsula.

Benedict XII's envoy Bertrand de Déaulx (originally the choice of John XXII) was in May 1335 appointed 'visitor and reformer' of all the papal lands in Italy. Bertrand's main achievement in the Papal State was the partial codification of public law in the various provinces through the issue of 'constitutions' which he promulgated at various parliaments in 1335–6. The pope himself supervised this legislation, intervening occasionally even on points of detail. The 'corruption' of officials, even of French ones, in the Papal State was probably no greater than the corruption of officials elsewhere in Europe at that time, and its control was not the main aim of Bertrand's laws, though it was a subsidiary one. Their principal objects were to regulate papal relations with the communes, and to reform the administration of the provincial courts and finances.

But when Bertrand de Déaulx came to dealing with the tyrants who were in charge of very many papal towns, the results were less tidy. With those in the march of Ancona and the Romagna – such as Gentile da Camerino, Mercenario di Monteverde, the Polentani, Manfredi, Alidosi, Malatesta, Ordelaffi – the 'reformer' was quite powerless. A small Florentine force helped the Church against Francesco Ordelaffi for

---

[1] G. Romano, *Niccolò Spinelli da Giovinazzo Diplomatico del sec. XIV.* (Naples, 1902), p. 617. Cf. K. H. Schäfer, *Die Ausgaben der apostolischen Kammer unter Johann XXII. (Vatikanische Quellen zur Geschichte der päpstlichen Hof- und Finanzverwaltung,* ii (Paderborn, 1911), p. 15*.

[2] In his first consistory. Quoted by J. Haller, *Papsttum und Kirchenreform* (Berlin, 1903), p. 122. Cf. also J.-M. Vidal and G. Mollat, *Benoît XII (1334–42): Lettres closes et patentes intéressant les pays autre que la France,* nos. 1109, 2459; *ASR,* xxvi (1903), pp. 307–8. The general survey of Benedict XII's Italian policy in Mollat's introduction to the work just quoted is misleading, because based on the registers alone; his survey in *The Popes at Avignon,* pp. 110 ff. is better, though still not entirely satisfactory. Cf. also H. Otto, 'Benedikt XII. als Reformator des Kirchenstaates', *Röm. Quart.,* xxxvi (1928), pp. 59–110. Literature is quoted in the tenth French editon of Mollat, *Les Papes d'Avignon* (1965), and also in my article 'Bertrando di Deux (Déaulx)', in the *Dizionario biografico degli Italiani.*

13 Antonio da Rido, the castellan of Sant'Angelo, with Eugenius IV and the Greek Emperor – on the doors of St Peter's, Rome (see p. 413)

a time, but the result was derisory; even a small commune such as Recanati in the march could defy the papal authorities. Umbria was in no better state, and Spoleto was described as in a 'miserable condition'. The treasure of the Church, and many precious books and records, were precariously stored at Assisi; much of this was subsequently transferred to Avignon. Greater and lesser tyrants, *signori* and *signorotti*, pullulated here as elsewhere. The Baglioni of Perugia, though not dominant in their native city, were already in conflict with the papal officials. In 1334 the important city of Orvieto fell for the first time to a local tyrant, Ermanno Monaldeschi. Nor did Bertrand's mission get worthwhile results in the Tuscan patrimony; his reforms and changes of rector left things just as they were.[1]

The presence of Bertrand de Déaulx in Italy had no effect on the factions in Rome: in September 1335 there was a bloody conflict for the control of the bridges over the Tiber, and the 'tower' which the Orsini had shipped from Naples in view of the future siege of the Colonna castle of Castelnuovo di Porto in the Tuscan patrimony, was burned in the Roman port.[2] The election of Benedict XII as senator for life of Rome in 1337 is usually counted as marking an important stage in the decline of Roman communal liberty, but it failed to improve the state of public order in the city. The truces which Bertrand had managed to arrange were prolonged, but in 1338 the situation was again so difficult that the papal representatives had to agree to the baronial families resuming control of the Tiber bridges. A second papal 'reformer' Jean Amiel (the former treasurer of the duchy of Spoleto), was sent from Avignon to Italy in 1339, with if anything even less impressive results than those achieved by his predecessors.

In Campagna and the Maritime province papal authority hardly made itself heard above the clash of swords. The area was convulsed by warfare between two branches of the Caetani family, and the attempts of Robert of Anjou to intervene only annoyed the papal officials (whom he expelled from Ferentino) still further.[3] Anagni 'gave itself' to the pope for a few months, but was taken by storm by Benedetto Caetani in 1340. In the Tuscan patrimony things went from bad to worse: the

---

[1] M. Antonelli, 'Vicende della dominazione pontificia nel Patrimonio di S. Pietro in Tuscia', *ASR*, xxvi (1903), pp. 306–7.; Fop, *BSU*, lxv (1968), pp. 23 ff.

[2] Cf. A. Mercati, *Nell'Urbe dalla fine di settembre 1337 al 31 gennaio 1338* (Rome, 1945), pp. 1–84, especially p. 15, Duprè-Theseider, *Roma dal comune di popolo*, pp. 496 ff.

[3] Falco, 'I comuni', *ASR*, xlix (1926), pp. 175–90. Cf. *Domus Caietana*, i, pp. 244–9. Numerous documents not used by Falco in G. Caetani, *Regesta Chartarum*, ii, pp. 96–125. Mollat (Introduction to Vidal-Mollat, p. xix) is rather misleading about these events.

Opposite: 14 Ponte Milvio

constantly rebellious John of Vico, the Prefect, became *signore* of Viterbo in 1341.[1] To oppose him the papal rector could only lean on the Orsini family, and consent (while saving appearances by accepting the captaincy of the people there himself) in the continued effective *signoria* of Matteo Orsini in Orvieto.

Benedict XII's policy was to send officials rather than satraps to Italy: the most important matters were kept in his own hands. Negotiations with the major Italian powers – Visconti, Este, Florence, Bologna – were conducted from Avignon. The papal vicariate for Ferrara was conferred on Obizzo d'Este in 1339, and he retained the much disputed fortress of Argenta, which he had given up to John XXII and then recovered (massacring the papal garrison in the process) after the defeat of du Poujet. No doubt the *census* of 30,000 florins a year promised for the vicariate of Ferrara was thought by the pope and the cardinals (who shared in this income) as sufficient amends for Obizzo's sins.[2]

With the great commune of Bologna, whose rebellion had precipitated the rout of clerical power in 1334, Benedict was as firm as his position allowed. In August 1337 the *signoria* of Bologna was seized by Taddeo Pepoli, who was related by marriage to the Este family, closely connected with the Florentines, and one of the richest men in Italy. In the long negotiations which followed Benedict took a hard line with Bologna – but only on paper! The first pacts agreed to by Pepoli were too onerous for the commune, and the *maggior consiglio* rejected them. An interdict was proclaimed against Bologna in March 1339, though no papal army was assembled. The Florentines pleaded for Pepoli with the pope, and finally in June 1340 a settlement was reached. Benedict was careful to avoid making Taddeo Pepoli a papal vicar, and his stipulations about the election and powers of a *conservatore* and *gonfaloniere* (in the earlier proposals) excluded the legal institution of the *signoria* as it was then understood. But Taddeo did eventually secure (for a three-year term) the title of 'administrator' for the church in Bologna, which seems half-way to the powers he wanted.[3]

---

[1] References in my article, 'Bernardo del Lago', in the *Dizionario biografico degli Italiani*.

[2] Theiner, *C.D.*, ii, no. 78 (Vidal-Mollat, no. 2419); and cf. G. de Vergottini, 'Note per la storia del vicariato apostolico', *Studi in onore di C. Calisse* (Milan, 1940), iii, pp. 341–65. The statement in the sixth life of Benedict XII that he conceded the Este the vicariate in Modena, Comacchio and Argenta is, like some other statements in this life, erroneous (G. Mollat, ed.) *Vitae Paparum Avenionensium*, i, 1914, p. 231).

[3] The main bulls in Theiner, *C.D.*, ii, nos. 63, 99. N. Rodolico, *Dal comune alla signoria, saggio sul governo di Taddeo Pepoli in Bologna* (Bologna, 1898), p. 138, is wrong in calling Pepoli 'vicario per la chiesa'.

The account of the state of the march of Ancona given by its rector and other witnesses in 1341 is a classic description of the superficiality of papal power in the provinces.[1] It would be wrong to call the papal rector powerless. The two large communes of Ancona and Ascoli Piceno gave him what support they could, and communes of the second rank were obedient, or occasionally so. The revenues of the march were not enormous, but they were collected and were not negligible, and the same was true of other papal provinces at the same period.[2] Fermo in the march had returned to papal obedience after the death of the hated Mercenario di Monteverde. But half of the most important places in the march, from Senigallia to Camerino, were held by tyrants or less formally dominated by magnates. Such *signori* as the Malatesta or the Montefeltro did not always refuse to fit in with papal policy, but the practical result was that papal officials played only a minor part, while the tyrants disputed for the spoils. The same was true of the Romagna, where the lawsuits (typical resorts of the legalistic papal *curia*) begun by the papal officials against the tyrants had no practical effect whatsoever. Far more important was Benedict XII's concession of the papal vicariate of Imola to the Alidosi, the first Romagnol tyrants to win this important form of legal recognition from the Church.[3]

Papal isolation in Italy increased in the early 1340s. The Guelph league proposed by Robert of Anjou to the Florentines in 1341 was unacceptable to the pope. The league actually organised by Florence in June 1341 included papal-state communes such as Bologna, Ferrara and Perugia, and was little more acceptable to him. In October 1341 Benedict XII ended the profitable monopoly of papal banking which the Florentine firms had so long enjoyed.[4] In January 1343 the Guelphs in Italy were badly shaken by the death of Robert of Anjou. His heiress was the feeble and frivolous Joanna, the murder of whose husband Andrew of Hungary in 1345 weakened the Guelph block even further. How far it was realised in Avignon that the worms were getting at the foundations of the papal temporal power in Italy, is not clear.

---

[1] Theiner, *C.D.*, ii, no. 128.

[2] K. H. Schäfer, *Deutsche Ritter und Edelknechte in Italien während des 14. Jahrhunderts*, i (Paderborn, 1911), pp. 16–42. The biggest source of income, the *tallia militum*, usually brought in 16,000–18,000 florins.

[3] G. de Vergottini, 'Ricerche sulle origini del vicariato apostolico', *Studi in onore di E. Besta*, ii (Milan, 1938), pp. 301–50, at p. 345. Cf. Larner, *Lords of Romagna*, p. 88. The *processus* of 1340, Vidal-Mollat, no. 2805; for the Alidosi cf. Theiner, *C.D.*, ii, no. 119.

[4] *Europe in the Late Middle Ages*, pp. 87–8; and cf. also G. Biscaro, 'Le relazioni dei Visconti con la Chiesa. Azzone, Giovanni e Luchino e Benedetto XII', *ASL*, xlvii (1920), pp. 197–271, at p. 228.

The austere Benedict XII died in 1342 (25 April), and was succeeded by the worldly and elegant Clement VI (elected 7 May 1342). But Clement VI's Italian policies were essentially a continuation of those of Benedict, especially in his wish to conciliate the Visconti. Clement sent legates to Lombardy to impose truces on the Lombard and Piedmontese lords, a thankless and Herculean task at which they worked for years, without much result. Emilia also was in turmoil: the struggle for Parma between Este, Pepoli and Della Scala on one side, and the Visconti on the other, went on until it ended in a Visconti victory in 1346. The huge military and territorial power of the Visconti was no longer checked by an effective political counter-weight: it sought new markets and new trade routes, and so thrust south into Emilia towards Bologna, and south-west over the Apennines to Tuscany. The Tuscan Guelphs were in no good position; in 1342 the Florentine constitution collapsed under the strain of economic depression and of a disastrous foreign policy, and Walter of Brienne became for a time *signore* of Florence. He was overthrown, and popular government was re-established, but it was weak.

Faced with these pressing problems, Clement VI returned in one respect to the policies of John XXII. The political situation in Italy was too complex and too serious to be controlled satisfactorily from Avignon. French rectors of papal provinces, attempting to rule with local resources and soldiers, got nowhere.[1] The alternative was the appointment of a papal delegate in Italy with the sort of quasi-monarchical powers which had once been enjoyed by Bertrand du Poujet. So in August 1346 the former envoy – now cardinal – Bertrand de Déaulx was sent to Italy with powers which have been called those of a 'vice-pope'. His main object was to deal with the situation created in the kingdom of Naples by the murder of Andrew of Hungary, Joanna's former husband. He proved rather unequal to the hard task set him, but the example of a satrap-legate was important for the future policies of Avignon popes in Italy. The next such legate was the great Cardinal Albornoz, in the next pontificates, and similar legates were appointed until Gregory XI's return from Avignon to Italy in 1376.

In Rome Bertrand came into conflict – if conflict it can be called – with one of the great symbolic figures of the later Middle Ages. Niccola di Lorenzo (called Cola di Rienzo) was the son of a tavern keeper and a laundry-woman, the Roman equivalent of a London Cockney. By

[1] See my article on Bernard du Lac (del Lago), 'captain' of the Tuscan patrimony from 1340 until his death in 1347, in *Dizionario Biografico degli Italiani*.

profession he made himself a notary, and by 1343 had hoisted himself into the ranks of the urban middle class.[1] Going with the Roman delegation to Avignon at Clement VI's accession, he secured papal favour and also met Petrarch. Petrarch, besides being a great poet and scholar, was a considerable publicist, the most brilliant exponent of opposition to French control of the Roman See. Petrarch's view of the temporal power policy of the Avignon popes was that it was a French conspiracy; his story was that when the cardinals discussed whether Rome and Italy ought to be in peace and unity, their unanimous decision was that they should not.[2]

There is no other example of a tyrant who seized the *signoria* of an Italian city, not by mercenaries and menace but by his tongue. It is probable, though not proven, that the famine which gripped central Italy from the beginning of this year made a radical regime more acceptable. In May 1347 the Roman people voted Cola da Rienzo their *signore*, 'but along with the papal vicar'. The idea of a popular dictatorship which would curb the Roman nobility was not repugnant to Avignon, and the rule of Cola as 'rector' of Rome was confirmed by the pope, though with the qualification that he should rule jointly with the papal 'vicar in spirituals'. But the actions of the 'tribune', as he liked to call himself, were against papal interest and custom. Like all strong rulers of Rome, Cola imposed tyrannical government on the communes of the Roman District taken in its widest geographical sense from Corneto in the north to Terracina in the south. Details of his financial reforms are obscure, but he seems to have imposed a hearth tax in Rome and to have abolished some of the customs taxes or *gabelle*, though not that of salt. Any financial deficiencies seem to have been made up by his impositions on the communes of the District.

Cola, in his grandiloquent way, arranged alliances with the Guelph communes of Umbria. He took military action against the dissident Roman nobles, notably against John the prefect of Vico, the Lord of Viterbo and old enemy of the popes. This action was popular with his supporters among the Roman people, but would have been impossible without the help of the great family of Orsini. On 2 August the 'knight

---

[1] There is a good passage on the social importance of notaries in Larner, *Lords of Romagna*, pp. 147–53. A. de Boüard, 'Les notaires de Rome au moyen-âge', *Mélanges*, xxxi (1911), pp. 291 ff. is legal in treatment. Cf. also J. Grisar, 'Notare und Notariatsarchive im Kirchenstaat des 16. Jahrhunderts', *Mélanges Eugène Tisserant*, iv (1964), pp. 251–300; C. Guttinger, 'Le collège des notaires de Spolète au XIVème siècle', *Mélanges*, lxxix (1967), pp. 679–97.

[2] P. Piur, *Petrarchas Buch ohne Namen und die päpstliche Kurie* (Halle, 1925), p. 172 (Epist. sine titulo, no. 3).

of the Holy Spirit', as Cola had had himself dubbed, received embassies from twenty Italian 'cities and provinces'. Most of these, with the exception of the Tuscan city of Arezzo, were Rome's usual Guelph allies. But all was done in the name of universal 'Roman' power, and was to be the prelude to an Italian parliament.

The tribunate of Cola di Rienzo, one of the most discussed episodes in Italian history, lasted for just over six months. The humiliations which he imposed on some of the Roman magnates, and the challenge which he offered to papal sovereignty, were too blatant for such great men to allow a fat little lawyer to lord it over them with speeches. By the early autumn the papal legate Bertrand de Déaulx had been ordered to proceed against Cola. His confrontation with the tribune in Rome was rather farcical; the demagogue declaimed and the cardinal was mute. But the Roman nobles were harder to deal with than papal clerks. Cola di Rienzo achieved a last victory over the baronial forces on 20 November, when he butchered Stefanuccio Colonna. Before the battle, according to Cola, he had been encouraged to overcome the 'tyrants' in a vision by the 'holy' Boniface VIII. The tribune announced himself, ironically enough, as the avenger of the outrage of Anagni. Modern historians might certainly have taken more notice than they have done of this declaration of sympathy by the supposedly modern tribune for the last great 'theocratic' pope. But it would perhaps be more realistic to see the whole affair in the context of the strife of Roman families and parties; Cola was not only the avenger of the Caetani pope, but the avenger of the murder of Bertoldo Orsini in 1333.

The star of the tribune set only two or three weeks after the battle. A Neapolitan soldier with a handful of troops stirred up a riot to which Cola's Roman militia opposed no resistance. Cola's nerve broke at once; he fled to Castel Sant'Angelo, where his Orsini friends and patrons protected him. The tribunate was over. Bertrand de Déaulx had also had enough. He did something to pacify the Tuscan patrimony, but gout and politics troubled the legate, who was glad to return to Avignon in the autumn of 1348.

Though Cola was to make one more brief appearance in Roman politics the time of his glory was over. In the history of the Papal State he cannot be assigned the important place which can be claimed for him in the history of Italian culture. The weakness of his Roman regime was that in so far as contemporaries could understand it, it stood for the traditional liberties of the Roman commune. These liberties had a good juridical basis, but as he himself admitted they had to be accommodated with the rights of the Roman Church; if sovereignty itself was brought in question, then the historic rights of the Church were bound to prevail.[1]

II

The fate both of the Papal State and of the Neapolitan kingdom was in those years in doubt. It had been the Hungarian threat to Naples rather than the only too familiar disorders of the Papal State which had induced Clement VI to send Bertrand de Déaulx to Italy. There was a connection between the disorder in one state and the other which was neatly shown by the wars of Niccolò Caetani, Count of Fondi, in 1345. Although Niccolò was a feudatory of the kingdom and not of the Papal State he disturbed the peace of papal Campagna, and conducted operations against Terracina which led to the seizure of the port by a Genoese fleet in 1346. In September 1346 he completely destroyed, at Itri, the army which Queen Joanna sent against him.[2]

At the end of 1347 Clement VI appointed Astorge de Durfort to govern the Romagna as papal rector. Astorge was a connection of the pope by marriage, and a relation of the Bertrand de Durfort who had been a papal castellan in the Romagna.[3] A year later Astorge was followed to Italy by the Cardinal-Legate Annibaldo di Ceccano, who had the same very extensive powers as Bertrand de Déaulx, and proved equally reluctant to use them. The main duties of Annibaldo were to try to settle the civil war in the Neapolitan kingdom, and then in 1350 to organise the administration and finances of the Roman Jubilee. He was unpopular both in Rome and in the Campagna. Someone engaged

---

[1] 'quod nec Romane Ecclesie neque Romano populo fiant in iuribus uiolentie hinc inde nec alique lesiones.' K. Burdach and P. Piur, *Briefwechsel des Cola di Rienzo* (Berlin, 1912), *Vom Mittelalter zur Reformation*, ii, pt. 4, no. 48, p. 186; also in A. Gabrielli (ed.), *Epistolario di Cola di Rienzo* (Rome, 1890), no. 29, p. 91. For Cola see especially E. Dupré Theseider, *I papi di Avignone e la questione romana* (Florence, 1939), pp. 87 ff.; idem, *Roma dal comune di popolo*, pp. 517–611. Cf. also K. Burdach, *Rienzo und die geistige Wandlung seiner Zeit* (Berlin, 1913), *Vom Mittelalter zur Reformation*, ii, pt. 1, especially at pp. 140 ff. (though Burdach's discussion does not deal with the political factors to any significant extent).

[2] E. G. Léonard, *Histoire de Jeanne I reine de Naples* (Monaco and Paris, 1932), i, pp. 549–54; *Domus Caietana*, i, pp. 252–61; Falco, *ASR*, xlix (1926), pp. 197–202.

[3] Déprez, Glénisson and Mollat, *Clément VI: Lettres closes patentes et curiales se rapportant à la France*, nos. 3657–60, 3662–3, 3665–8. The relationship of Astorge with Clement VI, *Clément VI: Lettres closes patentes et curiales intéressant les pays autre que la France*, no. 2011. For his relation Bertrand de Durfort, papal castellan of Meldola under Benedict XII, T. G. Leporace, *Le suppliche di Clemente VI* (Rome 1948,), i, no. 303; Déprez, *Clément VI: Lettres closes patentes et curiales analysées d'après les registres du Vatican*, no. 164.

an archer to shoot him, and when this failed he was killed by poison.[1]

The policy of the Church in Romagna continued to be one of conciliation and concession to the great *signori,* and also of recognition of the ambitions which other powers of the Po valley entertained in the province. The Este of Ferrara had received in 1344 a new grant of the 'apostolic vicariate', which included the disputed castle of Argenta, and which set the legal pattern for the concession of the vicariate to legalise tyrannical rule for the rest of the medieval period. In 1345 Clement VI had extended his recognition of the dominant position of Taddeo Pepoli in Bologna by a further four years.[2] Astorge de Durfort sought to utilise the friendship of the Pepoli and of the Della Scala of Verona, in order to counter-balance the lesser tyrants of Romagna.

This system collapsed almost before it began. When Giovanni di Ricciardo de' Manfredi seized Faenza in February 1350, Astorge de Durfort got little help against him from either the Pepoli or the Florentines, though he asked both.[3] The Malatesta rebelled, and there was a great falling away from the Church in both the march of Ancona and the Romagna. Possibly out of exasperation, but much more probably from design, Astorge arrested and imprisoned his supposed ally Giovanni Pepoli (6 July 1350), and in alliance with the Este and the Della Scala began a campaign designed to reduce Bologna and the rest of Romagna to obedience.

The alliance of Astorge de Durfort with the tyrants of the Po valley was a dangerous policy, liable to turn against the user. But his other military expedient set the pattern for papal campaigns for the rest of the century. The 'Great Company' of German mercenary troops had been in service under Werner of Urslingen in Italy for some ten years. The dangers which these mercenaries could present for the church lands

---

[1] His appointment, Déprez and Mollat, nos. 1758–1838, and cf. Baluze, *Vitae,* i, pp. 254, 548. For his unpopularity see Duprè-Theseider, pp. 619–21, and also the protest of the Countess of Fondi, 16 July 1350, Caetani, *Regesta Chartarum,* ii, pp. 147–8. Annibaldo belonged to the comital family of Ceccano (ibid.); he was related to the Caetani through his mother, Perna Caetani Stefaneschi.

[2] The kind of concession which was bought from the *signori* by this policy can be seen in A. Torre, 'Le contese per Lugo nel secolo XIV', *Stud. Romagn.,* iv (1953), pp. 131–41, at pp. 135–6. The disputed castle of Lugo was recognised by the Pepoli as the property of the Archbishop of Ravenna, and an annual *census* of 500 florins promised for it. The document quoted here by Torre (A. Tarlazzi, *Appendice ai Monumenti Ravennati de' secoli di mezzo del conte M. Fantuzzi* (Ravenna, 1884), ii, pp. 238–43) was executed at Avignon in the presence of Cardinal Bertrand de Déaulx, not in that of Cardinal Bertrand du Poujet as stated by Tarlazzi, and followed by Torre.

[3] References in *Europe in the Late Middle Ages,* p. 94n., and cf. *Storia di Milano* (Milan, 1955), v, pp. 332 ff.

were shown in 1348 by the massacre which the Great Company carried out at Anagni. But the advantages seemed to be shown in 1350 by the engagement of Werner of Urslingen with 1,150 horse and 400 foot in the service of the Church in Romagna.[1]

The appearance of the Companies on the Italian scene changed it a great deal, especially in the Papal State, where armies of the size and efficiency common among the Lombard tyrants had been relatively rare. The Companies opened rather alarmingly the military possibilities available to the papacy, and enabled the popes to transform their financial power into military power with more facility than before. It was still necessary for the popes to conduct 'Guelph' diplomacy among the communes, and to use communal levies on many occasions; it remained true also that the kingdom was the primary object of temporal power diplomacy, on which success or failure in the Papal State ultimately depended.

Effective use of the Companies required a return at Avignon to the bellicose Italian policies of the period of John XXII. It required also the subordination of the crusade in the eastern Mediterranean to Italian political considerations, and the restriction of the political and financial help which the popes had been giving to the French monarchy. The huge sums supplied to Philip VI of France by Clement VI (even if much of the money was raised from the French Church), lessened the capacity of the pope to supply money to raise troops in Italy.[2] It is untrue that Clement VI spent all his money in France, and refused to finance the campaigns of Astorge de Durfort. In the year beginning March 1350 he is known to have transferred over 163,000 florins to Italy for this purpose, and to have raised a loan from the College of Cardinals.[3] But

---

[1] Schäfer, *Deutsche Ritter und Edelknechte*, i, pp. 82–6; ii, pp. 138–9, 191–200. Though he brought only 1,150 horse to the service of the Church, his earlier *condotta* with the Pepoli had been for 2,375 horse and 125 sergeants (ibid.).

[2] Clement VI's financial relations with the French crown are interesting, but they have never been clearly analysed by scholars. H. Hoberg, *Die Inventare des päpstlichen Schatzes in Avignon 1314–76*, (Vatican City, 1944), p. xix, has an interesting note, and on the crusading question and the finances of this period A. Luttrell, 'The Crusade in the Fourteenth Century', *Europe in the Late Middle Ages*, pp. 134, 143, has some remarks. It seems clear that Philip VI had a 'loan' of at least 2,800,000 florins which was in some way connected with the tenths for the crusade: M. Faucon, 'Prêts faits au rois de France par Clément VI, Innocent VI et le comte de Beaufort', *BEC*, xi (1879), pp. 570–8. But there were other 'loans' of over half a million florins unconnected with the crusade (ibid. and see also E. Goeller, 'Inventarium instrumentorum camerae apostolicae', etc., *Röm. Quart.*, xxiii (1909), pp. 65–109, and J. Viard, in *Revue des Questions historiques*, xliv (1888), pp. 213–14). There were also very large loans to French magnates by the pope, e.g. a loan of 333,000 florins to Robert de Lorris in 1347.

[3] Y. Renouard, *Les relations des papes d'Avignon et des Compagnies commerciales et bancaires de 1316* à

the effort put into the war of Romagna by Clement VI, though considerable, was not enough to get military results, and the same can be said for his subventions to the crusade. Clement was neither a consistent pacifist like his predecessor, nor a consistent war-maker like his successor. The percentage of papal income recorded in the ordinary account books as spent on war was 63.7 per cent for John XXII, 5.6 per cent for Benedict XII (who had a low total income), about 21 per cent for Clement VI, and at least 40 per cent (possibly even 66 per cent) for Clement's successor, Innocent VI.[1]

When Giovanni Pepoli had been ransomed he no doubt realised that he was involved in a quarrel among the great powers which was too large for his capacities. He therefore gave the Visconti the opening which they had long sought, and 'sold' Bologna to Archbishop Giovanni Visconti, the Lord of Milan (16 October 1350). It was the final shipwreck of Astorge de Durfort's efforts in Romagna; instead of recovering the province he had lost its most important city to an enemy infinitely more powerful than the Pepoli.

It was not a moment in which a great war could be undertaken by the Church in Italy. The Tuscan communes did not want war, and fought Milan in the following year only because of the unprovoked attack made by the Milanese general Giovanni di Oleggio. Charles IV of Bohemia, though in principle willing to assist the papacy, was a broken reed; the Neapolitan kingdom had not yet settled its civil war; the change of king in France did not favour a bold policy. Astorge de Durfort's attack on Bologna after the Milanese entry there failed, and his mercenaries deserted to the enemy. A Guelph congress met in the spring of 1351, and decided nothing. There was no real alternative to appeasement of the Visconti, especially as this was also the policy of the French crown. A Visconti embassy was despatched to Avignon to treat for the grant of Bologna in the autumn of 1351. The negotiations took

---

1378 (Paris, 1941), pp. 250–7; the addition is mine. Mollat, *The Popes of Avignon*, p. 120 is mistaken on this point. For the loan of 16,000 florins by the College of Cardinals, Déprez and Mollat, no. 4836. Cf. Spinelli's judgement on Astorge (Romano, p. 617), 'expendit inaniter multas pecunias'.

[1] Schäfer, *Die Ausgaben unter Benedikt XII.*, p.182, 519. The 40 per cent for Innocent VI excludes 6.2 per cent spent on the defence of Avignon and 8.8 per cent on 'wax and extraordinary', and 12 per cent transferred to the pope's private treasury (cf. *JEccH*, iv (1953), p. 60). Money from the private funds may well have gone to military purposes. The percentage for Clement VI includes 'wax and extraordinary' (12 per cent). Cf. also the tables in Renouard, *Relations des papes d'Avignon et des Compagnies*, pp. 32–3. The figure of 67.3 per cent for John XXII's war expenditure given by E. F. Jacob, *Essays in the Conciliar Epoch*, 2nd ed. (Manchester, 1952), p. 242, is a slip.

some months, but in April 1352 the Visconti were granted Bologna for a term of twelve years, at the price of a war indemnity of 100,000 florins and an annual *census* of 12,000 florins.

It was a period of weak papal policy. Clement VI was sick and, according to the Florentines, under the influence of his aristocratic relative by marriage, Aliénor de Comminges. Clement had inherited a papal treasury of approaching one and a half million florins from his predecessor; his resources were now exhausted, and only 35,000 florins remained there at his death in 1352.[1] The Florentines, whose policy had for some time diverged widely from that of the popes, were left by Clement to find their own way out of the war with the Visconti; when they made peace at Sarzana in 1353 the Church took no part in the negotiations.[2]

There is little doubt that Clement VI thought of the defence and not of the 'restoration' of the Papal State.[3] Even this provoked much harder than he thought, and his attempt to recover Bologna from the Pepoli had ended by making matters much worse. Orvieto fell to the Visconti for a short period, at this time. Whether Clement would have been right to make the seizure of Bologna and the attack on the Tuscan Guelphs into an occasion for a great new war against Milan by a great Guelph coalition, is doubtful. It is unlikely that such a coalition would have been very effective. Probably Clement VI's biggest mistake had been to try to enlist Visconti and Della Scala support for his proposed war against the Pepoli, in the first place. To try to use the great warlords of Lombardy in such a way was little short of frivolous, and Clement's failure was well-deserved.

III

On 6 December 1352 Clement VI died. His successor Stephen Aubert (Innocent VI) intended from the beginning a much firmer policy in Italy. In order to execute it, he hit on one of the most remarkable men in the history of the temporal power, the former Archbishop of Toledo, Gil Albornoz.[4] Albornoz was a distinguished servant of the crown of

[1] Hoberg, *Die Inventare des päpstlichen Schatzes*, p. xviii; cf. Déprez and Mollat, no. 2359.
[2] Cf. *Europe in the Late Middle Ages*, p. 96n. For reservation of the rights of the Church in the treaty, see Fop, *BSU*, lxvi (1969), p. 89.
[3] Cf. F. Baldasseroni, 'La guerra fra Firenze e Giovanni Visconti', *Studi Storici*, xii (1903), pp. 41–94, at pp. 73–5. Mollat, *The Popes at Avignon*, pp. 119–25 is not at all satisfactory.
[4] The most recent surveys are those of J. Beneyto Perez, *El Cardenal Albornoz Canciller de Castilla y Caudillo de Italia* (Madrid, 1950), and of E. Duprè Theseider in the *Dizionario Biografico degli Italiani*. I am grateful to Dr Anthony Luttrell for advice about Albornoz.

Castile, concerned as royal chancellor in administration and finance, and Archbishop of Toledo from 1338. He played an important part as papal legate or royal official in the wars against the Muslims, at the Battle of the river Salado in 1340, probably in the conquest of Algeciras in 1344, and at the siege of Gibraltar in 1349–50. In 1350 Albornoz left Castile for Avignon, where he was made a cardinal. He became estranged to some extent from Pedro the Cruel, who had recently succeeded to the throne, though the stages of this estrangement are unclear; but the end of it was his failure to return to Castile, his resignation of his archbishopric, and the gradual withdrawal of his family from Castilian service.[1]

Albornoz applied to the Papal State the mentality and the skills which he had acquired in the direction of the Castilian *Reconquista*; at least twice during his career in Italy he was to proclaim crusades against recalcitrant Christians. In a sense the idea of appointing such men as Albornoz in the Papal State was not new; during the thirteenth century Templars and Hospitallers had often been used as castellans in the papal patrimony, and more recently Hospitallers had been employed as rectors of papal provinces.[2] Albornoz brought a passionate temperament and the highest political and military ability to the task of pacifying central Italy – if 'pacifying' is the right word to use of a man who drenched the Italian countryside with blood from the Po to the Garigliano. It was not altogether odd that the new legate was Castilian; the Papal State was ruled by French officials and bishops and served largely by German mercenaries, and something of the same cosmopolitan sort was true of the Neapolitan kingdom, where a Franco-Italian aristocracy was attempting to stem a Hungarian invasion. In Sicily an Aragonese dynasty ruled. On the other hand, there were relatively few Castilians in the Avignonese *curia*.

The powers delegated to Albornoz for his legation were wide both in

---

[1] His brother Álvaro García Albornoz was Pedro's ambassador to France in September 1351 (Déprez and Mollat, nos. 5068, 5071). The estrangement of the family from Pedro the Cruel was less brusque, than it is sometimes represented.

[2] Hospitaller rectors of papal provinces: Napoleone de Tibertis in the Campagna-Maritime (Vidal, *Benoit XII*, no. 2317); Giovanni de Riparia in the march of Ancona and Raymbaldus de Montebrione in the duchy of Spoleto (ibid. nos. 2883, 2229; Schäfer, *Deutsche Ritter u. Edelknechte*, i, pp. 18, 30 in notes; J. Delaville le Roux, *Les Hospitalliers de Rhodes* (Paris, 1913), pp. 76–8). For the Hospitaller Juan Fernández de Heredia in the temporal power see Luttrell, *EHR*, lxxvi (1961) lpp. 13–19. Cf. also G. Silvestrelli, 'Le chiese e i feudi dell'ordine dei Templari e dell'ordine di S. Giovanni di Gerusalemme nella regione romana', *Rendiconti R. Acc. Lincei, Classe di Scienze Morali, Storiche e Filologiche*, 5th ser., xxvi (1917), pp. 490–539; ibid. xxvii (1918), pp. 174–6.

legal force and geographical extent. As an 'angel of peace' (an epithet whose unsuitability was yet to be demonstrated) he was given full powers not only in the Papal State but in all north Italy and on both sides of the Adriatic coast. The only part of Italy excepted from his legation was the kingdom of Naples. In mid-September of 1353 Albornoz was in Milan, where Archbishop Giovanni Visconti promised him money to raise troops, under the terms of the concession of Bologna to the Visconti by the Church. On 2 October the legate was in Florence, where his brusque behaviour offended the Tuscan Guelphs. On 23 October he was in Perugia, and a month later he arrived at the papal fortress of Montefiascone in the Tuscan patrimony. He later said that when he came to Italy he found only one fortress held for the Church, and only one loyal subject, Giordano Orsini[1] (who was papal rector of the Tuscan patrimony).

In Montefiascone the legate passed a miserable winter, unable to recruit enough troops to act effectively against the rebel Giovanni di Vico, the tyrant of Viterbo and Orvieto, and the virtual ruler of the Tuscan patrimony. The almost despairing letters Albornoz wrote from Montefiascone are among the most human that have survived from him, and they bring out the powerful conviction of moral outrage which was typical of a man trained to fight in the Castilian *Reconquista*: 'Pity, my lords, the patrimony of the Crucified One!'[2]

Albornoz was confident that he could reduce the Papal State to order, provided that he had enough money to engage troops. It did not take him long to re-conquer the Tuscan patrimony once spring came and he was able to enroll German mercenaries; by the early summer Viterbo was reduced, and the submission of Giovanni di Vico provisionally received; the papal army then besieged Orvieto, setting up two great earthworks (*bastie*) against the town. It submitted in early July of 1354. By the end of the year the duchy of Spoleto had sub-

---

[1] Romano, *Niccolò Spinelli*, p. 618. Cf. also Fop, *BSU*, lxv (1968), pp. 40–4.

[2] *Studi Storici*, v (1896), doc. 5, pp. 102–3, 'compatiamini igitur vos, domini mei, Patrimonio crucifixi: compatiamini michi licet inutiliter'. F. Filippini, *Il Cardinale Egidio Albornoz* (Bologna, 1938), p. 32, mistranslates this: 'Egli pregava i Cardinali che compatissero lui "crocifisso nel Patrimonio" ' (followed by Mollat, *Popes at Avignon*, p. 132). There is a reference to the 'patrimonium crucifixi' in Mathew Paris, *Cronica Majora (R.S.)*, iii, p. 390. The Albornoz document is numbered 25 in the collection: *L'Administration des Etats de l'Eglise au XIVe siècle. Correspondance des Légats et Vicaires-Généraux. Gil Albornoz et Androin de la Roche (1353–67)* (Paris, 1964), ed. Glénnison and Mollat. Although the methods of calendaring adopted in this work have been criticised by E. Petrucci in *Studi Medievali*, 3rd ser., viii (1967), pp. 239–49, it remains a useful instrument for Albornoz studies. The editors unfortunately omitted some important archives, e.g. the Archivio di Stato at Bologna.

mitted, and the legate was moving on to the march. Behind him he left
agents planning the construction of some of the strongest fortresses in
central Italy: one in Viterbo, and another built in an immensely strong
position at Spoleto by Matteo Gattaponi. Like Bertrand du Poujet, whose
policy he followed much more closely than is usually admitted, Albornoz
copied very closely the governmental methods of the tyrants.

The possibility of intervention in Italy by Charles IV, son of John of
Bohemia, had for some years pre-occupied both the pope and the Tuscan
Guelphs. Like his father and grandfather, Charles wished to come to
Italy with the blessing of the Church – but like his grandfather he
wanted imperial coronation. He was willing to give assurances to the
pope, which included guarantees for the Papal State. Both the alarm
felt by the Tuscan Guelphs and the hopes at one time cherished by the
papal *curia* were dispelled when Charles in the early spring of 1355
marched south to Rome. He made neither troops nor money available
to the Church, and the hope that he would act against the Great
Company or the disobedient Malatesta was equally frustrated. The
coronation of the emperor in Rome (5 April 1355) was an isolated
incident. The small German army marched rapidly back across the Alps
with the emperor, having had little practical effect on Italian politics.
Though neither the Lombard lords nor the Tuscan Guelphs, nor the
papal city of Perugia, could shake off a certain legitimist respect for
the titles the emperor could confer or deny,[1] his expedition seems
a poor thing even beside that of the schismatic Louis of Bavaria, twenty-
eight years earlier.

In the march and Romagna Albornoz had to face a diplomatic
situation much less favourable than that of the Tuscan patrimony. The
tyrants of this area were many of them powerfully placed to influence
the papal court at Avignon. Galeotto Malatesta had acted ruthlessly

---

[1] D. Segoloni, 'La civitas Perusina nel pensiero di Bartolo', *Atti del Congresso Internazionale per
il VI Centenario della morte di Bartolo di Sassoferrato* (Milan, 1962), ii, at pp. 659, 661–2, launched
the hypothesis that on the occasion of the visit of Charles IV to Perugia in 1355 there took
place some kind of 'passagio di Perugia dalla Chiesa all 'Impero', a sort of transfer from papal
to imperial sovereignty. This theory was taken further by M. P. Fop, *BSU*, lxv, fasc.2 (1968),
p. 48, where it is asserted that Perugia was transferred by Albornoz from papal to imperial
sovereignty as a form of punishment. Neither of these assertions seems to me to have any
foundation in fact. The relevant documents which are printed by Signora Fop in *BSU*, lxvi,
fasc.1 (1969), pp. 99–103, refer to the annulment of sentences emanated against Perugia by
Henry VII, and to the confirmation of imperial privileges issued by former emperors. The
reference is too vague to be a derogation from papal sovereignty. The territorial privileges
conceded to Perugia by Charles IV at this time relate to places outside the Papal State in
Tuscany (Böhmer, *Regesta Imperii*, viii, no. 2127).

against church lands and authority, imprisoned the Bishop of Ascoli, and drawn on himself from Avignon the epithet 'a scourge of God worse than Totila'. But Galeotto and Malatesta were important in Guelph politics; as the ally of Florence and also as the vicar of Apulia for the Neapolitan government, Galeotto Malatesta had powerful friends at the papal court.[1] While the canon law process against the Malatesta dragged on in 1354 their allies and connections did not cease to work for them at Avignon. In the spring of 1355 Albornoz mounted a military operation against Malatesta and defeated him at the Battle of Paderno (29 April 1355). But this seems almost an incident in the negotiations; Niccolò Acciaiuoli the steward of the kingdom was mediating between the legate and the Malatesta very shortly before the battle, and was important in the peace between the Malatesta and the Church which followed (June–July 1355). The terms of the peace pointed to the method which Albornoz was to use with most of the tyrants: the concession of the 'apostolic vicariate', by which the Malatesta became the vicars of Rimini and three other towns for a ten-years' period on the model of the concession of Bologna to the Visconti, in return for a *census* payment of 6,000 gold florins annually, and the military service of 100 horsemen every year in Romagna and the march.

In many ways these were attractive terms for the papacy (ninety years earlier Charles of Anjou had agreed to give the Roman Church the service of only 300 knights for the whole Neapolitan kingdom). The large *census* payment and the big military contingent due as service made it possible for the papal authorities to maintain a large force, and no doubt this fitted in with the policy consistently followed by Albornoz, of maintaining the largest possible armies. The large *census* also probably made the policy of granting vicariates more acceptable to the cardinals at Avignon, since the College of Cardinals sometimes drew a half share in such big *census* payments from the papal chamber, whereas it did not normally share the ordinary provincial temporal revenues.[2] This was especially important for Albornoz, who met with a lot of opposition

---

[1] *Europe in the Late Middle Ages*, p. 102, but see especially Léonard, *Histoire de la reine Jeanne*, iii, pp. 503 ff. Correct my reference to Gerola's article, 'Fra Moriale in Toscana', to *ASI* 5th ser., 1906, xxxvii, pp. 261–300. Cf. also P. J. Jones, 'The Vicariate of the Malatesta of Rimini', *EHR*, lxvii (1952), pp. 321–51.

[2] See p. 284 above. Although the papal chamber is shown as sometimes dividing the *census* of Ferrara and Bologna with the College of Cardinals under Innocent VI, it is not shown as similarly dividing that of the Malatesta. Cf. H. Hoberg, *Die Einnahmen der apostolischen Kammer unter Innocenz VI.* (Paderborn, 1955), pp. 41, 82, 86, 166–8. The *census* was rather less than the old *tallia militum*, which the Malatesta ceased to pay: cf. Larner, *Lords of Romagna*, p. 224.

in the college. It is also arguable that the institution of the *signoria* was in any case so imbedded in the social and political structure of the Papal State by this time that the only possible policy the popes could follow was to legalise it, while exacting the maximum price for doing so. It was after all only a variant on earlier forms of local autonomy.

But it is also possible to argue that the apostolic vicariate gave a legitimate title to the formerly abusive domination of certain families in the Papal State, and that partly as a result of this it became impossible to eradicate the dominion of these families for the rest of the Middle Ages. Albornoz is usually represented as the great innovator in the imposition of papal sovereignty in the Papal State, but viewed in this light his actions seem very different; he was in another way the man who began a policy of explicitly granting away a lot of important papal government rights. Perhaps if the terms of concession of vicariate had been faithfully kept by the holders this would have been less serious, but from the start he can scarcely have expected such men to be scrupulous. He was, of course, not the first papal official to urge the grant of vicariates, just as he was not the first papal official to promulgate 'constitutions' of a centralising nature, but these reservations about the vicariate policies of Albornoz were felt in the papal court at the time; in 1362, at the end of seven years of this policy, Urban V wrote to Albornoz telling him to discourage nobles from sending embassies to Avignon to ask for the concession of church lands in vicariate, 'which we will on no account concede them, nor will you proffer any further advice for such concessions'.[1] Probably all that can be said in conclusion is that in allowing laymen to retain the use of church lands, while exacting from them the recognition of church title, Albornoz was only following a policy which in the Roman Church went back to the early Middle Ages!

Within a year of the peace with the legate, Galeotto Malatesta was the captain of 2,000 mercenaries in the service of the Church, and within a few years after that he moved on to even further grandeur in the kingdom as 'captain-general'. He was, after all, a Guelph. The Polentani of Ravenna submitted, and received Ravenna in vicariate: the Manfredi of Faenza also submitted, but without being given the vicariate.

The Ghibellines of the march were less accommodating, because in this political system they had less to gain. The lords of Fermo and Urbino submitted rapidly, so did Ancona and the communes except for Ascoli, but Francesco Ordelaffi, the tyrant of Forlì and Cesena, opposed a

[1] Theiner, *C.D.*, ii, no. 371.

desperate resistance, and his wife Cià degli Ubaldini an equally desperate one. Against him Innocent VI had a crusade preached, but the campaign dragged on into 1357. In the Tuscan patrimony Corneto still resisted.

The cost of these operations was substantial. Between August 1353 and August 1357 at least 560,000 florins of papal funds (in round figures) were transferred to Albornoz, and at the end of this period expenses were running at over 40,000 florins a month.[1] In the summer of 1354 Albornoz was employing thirty banners with 600 horsemen, in 1355 fifty banners with over 1,000 horse, in 1356–7 about 100 banners with over 2,000 German horse. On the other hand, the war was not yet a great war, and these expenses may be contrasted with the debt of £300,000 sterling (rather over two million florins) which Edward III of England contracted for the campaign in the Low Countries in 1338–9.[2] The expenses were increased by the need to buy off the Great Company when it threatened to devastate papal lands. There was a certain amount of trouble with the mercenaries commanded by the Provençal Hospitaller 'Fra Moriale', who was in the pay of the Church before Albornoz arrived in Italy, and was in the summer of 1354 betrayed and executed by Cola di Rienzo (who had himself been released from Avignon and had briefly returned to Rome as papal senator). But the first big crisis in the relations of the legate with the Company came in 1357, when even after defeat by a papal-Florentine force (26–7 July) it was still strong enough to have to be bought off by the two powers.[3]

Until 1360 the temporal policy of Innocent VI in Italy was distinct from papal policy in the 1320s in one essential: it was pacific and appeasing towards the tyrants of the Po valley, and especially towards the Visconti. In this way it was continuous with papal policy since Benedict XII. This policy of appeasement could be justified on two grounds: first because after the disastrous failure of du Poujet a peaceful policy in Emilia and Lombardy seemed to be in accordance with papal ideas and interests, second because important factions both in the kingdom of Naples and the Roman court at Avignon were in one way or another connected with the Visconti. In particular, the Neapolitan

---

[1] Calculated from the figures in Renouard, pp. 258–70. Cf. also the document drawn up by Albornoz's successor, Androin de la Roche, printed by Glénisson and Mollat, *Albornoz et de la Roche*, no. 427. Expenses were naturally at their height during the summer. For mercenary pay see Partner, *Papal State under Martin V*, p. 155.

[2] Cf. M. McKisack, *The Fourteenth Century* (Oxford, 1959), pp. 155 ff. and especially p. 161n.

[3] *Europe in the Late Middle Ages*, pp. 103 ff.

Prince Robert of Durazzo and his powerful uncle Talleyrand the Cardinal of Périgord were thought pro-Visconti,[1] and Robert married a Visconti niece in 1354. It is on this second aspect that historians have mostly seized, and the 'corruption' of cardinals by Visconti bribes has been much emphasised. But the idea of a peaceful policy towards the Visconti was not merely that of a corrupt clique; it had a solid basis in preceding papal policy, and it was justifiable also on the moral grounds that the popes ought not again to plunge northern Italy into a bloody war. The Florentines were extremely anxious to observe the peace of Sarzana of 1353, and not to give the Visconti grounds for the renewal of a great war.[2]

What tempted – one might say, fatally tempted – Albornoz to urge the abandonment of a conciliatory policy was the death of Archbishop Giovanni Visconti (3 October 1354), and the consequent weakening of the Visconti *signoria* through the division among his heirs. On 17 April 1355 the Visconti captain in Bologna, Giovanni di Oleggio, rebelled against his masters with the support of the Marquis of Este, one of the leaders of the old league against the Visconti. The immediate reaction of the pope was to reprimand Oleggio for his rebellion and to require him to restore the city to its legitimate vicar, Matteo Visconti.[3] When Oleggio's rebellion was prolonged, and he established himself as the *signore* of Bologna, two schools of thought began to appear in papal counsels: one wanted to support the Visconti as the legitimate holders of a papal vicariate, the other wanted to exploit Oleggio's rebellion as a possible stepping stone to the recovery of Bologna under direct papal rule. To this second opinion, perilous for the peace of Italy, Albornoz perhaps began to veer.

In September 1356 Bernabò Visconti asked the pope for military help to recover Bologna, and Innocent deferred a decision, referring Bernabò to Albornoz.[4] By the end of February 1357 the peace treaty at Avignon obtained the decision to send a new envoy to Italy, Androin de la Roche, the Abbot of Cluny. On 6 May 1357, a month after the arrival of the Abbot of Cluny in the Papal State, he was named legate in succession to Albornoz. It is evident that one of his duties was to effect

---

[1] This should not be assumed dogmatically of Talleyrand, for whom Albornoz wept 'as for a father' at his death. Glénisson and Mollat, no. 998.

[2] *Europe in the Late M.A.*, pp. 105–6.

[3] Vatican Archives, Reg. Vat. 237, fo. 84 (30 April 1355). Cf. Biscaro, *ASL*, n.s., ii (1937), p. 120.

[4] Ibid. p. 123, from Reg. Vat. 238, fo. 176 v, but not quite accurately. It is interesting that the minute for this bull in Reg. Vat. 244F, fo. 50 had first civitatis Bononien, in qua vicarius noster *es. es* was cancelled, and *eras* substituted. Cf. also Theiner, *C.D.*, ii, no. 322.

a drastic reduction of military expenses.[1] The complement to this was the negotiations with the Visconti which were now going on at Avignon about Bologna. A committee of four cardinals, including the influential Guy of Boulogne and Francesco degli Atti, the Bishop of Florence, agreed in July–August 1357 that the pope would support the forcible recovery of Bologna by Bernabò Visconti, recognising him as papal vicar there.[2]

At the end of April 1357, in the parliament of Fano, Albornoz had issued the celebrated 'Constitutions' which re-arranged the public law of the papal provinces and which remained the basic law of the Papal State until Napoleon. Though issued initially for the march of Ancona, these 'Constitutions' were applied to all the papal provinces, and they constitute a notable advance in the centralised administration of the Papal State. Albornoz had also made a remarkable series of arrangements for the government of the major towns in the Papal State, where it had not proved necessary to concede these to *signori* as vicariates, or to recognise seigniorial power as with the da Varano of Camerino or the Montefeltro of Urbino. In coming to terms with the towns Albornoz showed great flexibility. Clearly his aim was to impose direct rule modelled on the rule of the tyrants; he achieved this in Orvieto and Viterbo, where he left 'vicars' with complete powers. Ancona (where he built a fortress) and Fermo also made complete submissions, granting personal seigniorial powers to Albornoz and the pope, but at Ascoli (which had resisted for some time) the legate had to promise not to build a fortress in the city, nor to impose a rector. At Spoleto, where a great fortress and aqueduct were later built, the main problem was to combat the influence of Perugia, which retained more or less full independence.[3]

Probably the most important single factor in the reconquest of Albornoz was the weakness of the Visconti *signoria* after the death of the archbishop in October 1354. This was the equivalent for the Ghibellines of the weakness which had overtaken the Guelphs after the death of Robert of Anjou in 1343. It may also be that the Great Company, stalking

---

[1] For Guy of Boulogne and his connection with the Visconti see G. Pirchan, *Italien und Kaiser Karl IV. in der Zeit seiner zweiten Romfahrt* (Prague, 1930), ii, pp. 96*–7*.

[2] Many of the documents dealing with these towns are in Theiner, *C.D.*, ii, nos. 271, 328, 334, 319, 321, 310; cf. also Glénisson and Mollat, no. 174 (Spoleto). For the difficulties with Perugia, Theiner, ii. nos, 313, 316. Innocent VI withdrew the claim made by the rector of the duchy of Spoleto to intervene in the appointment of a rector of Perugia, Reg. Vat. 237, fo. 15v (21 January 1355).

[3] Cf. Glénisson and Mollat, no. 427 (quoted above).

over Italy with its 20,000 effectives like a locust plague, was also an advantage for Albornoz, since he possessed the financial power to buy it off, and it harassed his enemies. It has been suggested that the aftermath of the Great Plague created 'psychological conditions' which favoured the victory of Albornoz over communal liberties at Orvieto and elsewhere, but in truth these liberties had collapsed in favour of one form or another of the *signoria,* ever since the early 1330s at the latest.[1] The same was true of Viterbo, where the *podestà* had been appointed either by the pope or a *signore* since the time of Boniface VIII, and of Fermo. It is quite possible that the depopulation of the Italian countryside by plague did make it more difficult to organise resistance to the German mercenaries of Albornoz; there is a suggestion of this in the submission of the Malatesta, which refers to the economic exhaustion of their lands.[2]

The legislation of Albornoz was essentially recapitulatory; it could not be called a work of codification, since in most instances the 'Constitutions' consists of documents which had emanated from earlier popes or provincial rectors. In very many respects the work of Albornoz in this field closely resembles that of his far less well-known predecessor, Cardinal Bertrand de Déaulx, whose constitutions, published in the parliaments held by him in the Papal State in 1335–6, are a notable anticipation of the work of Albornoz in 1357.[3] And behind the work both of de Déaulx and of Albornoz lay a very long series of ordinances published by the rectors of papal provinces in their parliaments, beginning substantially in the period following the Angevin descent into Italy in the preceding century.[4] To these rectoral ordinances various popes had added their own constitutions, notably those of Boniface VIII. The fourteenth-century legates followed the tendencies of the canon law

---

[1] Cf. E. Carpentier, *Une ville devant la peste. Orvieto et la Peste Noire de 1348* (Paris, 1962), p. 200. Waley's opinion that 'the tyranny of Ermanno Monaldeschi (1334) marks the close of the history of the free commune' (*Mediaeval Orvieto*, p. 138), seems preferable. Cf. also G. Mollat, 'L'administration d'Orvieto durant la légation d'Albornoz (1354–67)', *Mélanges*, lxx (1958), pp. 395–406.

[2] Theiner, *C.D.*, ii, no. 303, p. 293. It also refers to the devastations of the Company. Cesena and Faenza were in the same state for the same reasons; cf. Glénisson and Mollat, no. 427, at p.150.

[3] The *Costituzioni Egidiane* were edited by P. Sella (Rome, 1912). For references to the legislative work of Bertrand de Déaulx see the article in *Dizionario Biografico degli Italiani*.

[4] Cf. P. Sella, 'Costituzioni dello stato della chiesa anteriori alla riforma Albornoziana', *ASI*, 7th ser., viii (1927), pp. 1–36; U. Aloisi, 'Sulla formazione storica del liber constitutionum S. Matris Ecclesie', *AMSM*, n.s., i (1904), pp. 317–68; ibid. ii (1905), pp. 369–422; ibid. iv (1907), pp. 129–67; ibid. v (1908), pp. 260–310. See also Waley, *P.S.*, pp. 116 ff.; Esch, *Bonifaz IX. u.d. Kirchenstaat*, pp. 453 ff.; Partner, *Papal State*, pp. 101 ff.

of their own time in re-arranging and sorting this legal heritage. They were anxious to some extent to rationalise, but anxious also to preserve ancient titles and customary rights of the papal government; and the documents collected by Albornoz for the rectoral *curia* of the patrimony of St Peter in Tuscany make this plain.[1]

IV

Albornoz was active in Italy until September 1357, and his absence in Avignon was in the event brief. Androin de la Roche attempted to execute the policies of Albornoz, using the subordinates bequeathed by him, but his understanding of the basic principles was defective, and he had been sent to reverse the anti-Visconti trend which was the most important of the policies of the previous legate.[2] Not surprisingly he failed, and Albornoz was again appointed legate on 18 September 1358. He arrived in Florence in November, and unsuccessfully tried to persuade the Florentines to enter a new 'Guelph' league. Forlì was still holding out against the Church under Francesco Ordelaffi, who had employed the Great Company against the besieging forces, and against Ravenna and Cervia. The problem was to buy off the Great Company, which Florence was unwilling to do; the Florentine preference was for military action against the Great Company in combination with the legate and the Visconti.[3] Eventually Florence was dragged into an expensive agreement (which she did not ratify) to buy the Company off. As a result, Forlì fell and the hegemony of the Church in Romagna was re-affirmed.

Bologna remained the most important problem. The Church had in 1357 agreed to allow the Visconti to make a military effort to recover the city from Oleggio. Albornoz was determined to tear up this agreement. Playing partly on the cupidity of the *curia*, Albornoz persuaded the pope to accept payment of *census* from Oleggio. The Visconti army was now besieging Bologna, and a decision on the attitude of the Church became daily more urgent; Oleggio on his side began to lose hope of holding Bologna alone, just as Giovanni Pepoli had done in 1350. Albornoz waited 'as the kite waits for his prey'. Pavia had fallen to the Visconti in the north, and Visconti armies were freed to turn against Bologna. Early in 1360 a bargain was struck between Albornoz

---

[1] Cf. P. Fabre, 'Un registre caméral du Cardinal Albornoz', *Mélanges*, vii (1887), pp. 129–95.
[2] For his patronage of the idea of a league with the Visconti see *Europe in the Late Middle Ages*, p. 103.
[3] Ibid.

and Oleggio, who in return for the vicariate of Fermo and other offices agreed to hand back Bologna to the Church.

The great question was, whether Albornoz could persuade Innocent VI to agree to this arrangement, which was sure to provoke a great war with the Visconti, and which directly contradicted the agreements made by the Church with the Visconti only two years earlier. The frantic indecision of the papal *curia* is shown by the three bulls drawn up by the pope on the same day, 1 February 1360: one stated that the Visconti vicariate remained in force; one left action concerning Bologna to the discretion of Albornoz; and the third instructed him to accept Bologna.[1] If these three bulls were all forwarded to Albornoz to use as he saw fit (as seems probable) then the fate of Bologna was sealed by them. Albornoz's nephew, Gómez Garcia, entered Bologna and accepted it for the pope as rector on 17 March 1360. The immediate Visconti protest that the engagements of the Church had been broken was overruled by the pope, who at last came down firmly on the side of war. The great struggle of the Church with the Visconti was renewed.

The war of Bologna followed the usual destructive and indecisive course of such wars. In the summer of 1361 there was a papal victory at San Ruffilo as a result of a ruse by Albornoz; the nearby *bastia* of Canonica di Reno was abandoned and for a short time the Milanese troops withdrew. They returned, but the pace of peace negotiations quickened, and by the end of the year it seemed that a compromise was within sight, guaranteed by the European powers – the emperor, and the kings of France and Naples.[2] But Bernabò Visconti, the fiercest and most acquisitive tyrant in Italy, could not be satisfied; the negotiations broke down and the war was renewed. The death of Innocent VI and the accession of a new pope, Urban V (28 September 1362) did not affect papal determination. New Visconti embassies went to Avignon, but without result, and in March 1363 the old device of proclaiming the Visconti heretics was adopted.

The Della Scala of Verona and the Este of Ferrara had joined the Church in the war, whose bitterness increased (though the Florentines still refused to take part). Armies marched and counter-marched in Romagna and Emilia, adding their horrors to those of the plague which broke out with terrible severity in 1361–3. In repressing rebellion at

---

[1] Ibid., p. 106, Mollat's statement that Albornoz failed to consult Innocent VI (*The Popes at Avignon*, p. 140) is wrong.

[2] Glénisson and Mollat, nos. 710, 711. These are annexes to a treaty whose text is lost; they are signed, but Albornoz did not ratify them. See also Werunsky, *Kaiser Karl IV.*, iii, p. 258; Martène and Durand, ii, nos. 247–50, cols. 1068–72 (but read 'anno X' for 'anno nono').

this critical period of the war Albornoz showed a ferocity hard to reconcile with his priest's orders. After Galeotto Malatesta had suppressed the revolt of the little township of Corinaldo in the march (17 August 1360), among 170 prisoners the men and their wives were massacred; by a Christian disposition widows and children were spared. Forlimpopoli infuriated the legate to such an extent by its loyalty to the exiled Ordelaffi that on 30 May 1362 the town was destroyed in the presence of the surviving inhabitants, and its bishopric transferred to Bertinoro.[1]

The war was general; its fiercest manifestations were now in the Modenese, but it was being fought as far away as Brescia. The many enemies of the great Visconti *signoria* pressed it hard, and defeated its army in the Modenese *bastia* of Solaria on 9 April 1363. But the withdrawal of the Della Scala from the clerical league, and the Venetian attack on another clerical ally, Francesco da Carrara the Lord of Padua, cancelled the advantage. The pope's will to continue the war was also weakened by a new factor, the appearance in Avignon of the chancellor of King Peter of Cyprus, Philippe de Mézières, and the fanatical Pierre Thomas, to demand papal support for a new crusade.[2] In June–July 1363 negotiations with Bernabò once more began, this time through Albornoz at Bologna.[3] In September a truce was finally agreed, and embassies went to Avignon to work out the main details of the peace settlement.

Neither Albornoz nor his allies the Lombard lords were anxious for peace, but under papal pressure a treaty was gradually hammered out, and its main lines were agreed by February 1364; the main grounds of dispute were the forts in Emilia. Androin de la Roche, the instrument of the peace party in the papal *curia,* was appointed legate in December 1363, and in January 1364 was in Milan.[4] By the summer the peace

---

[1] Corinaldo, Filippini, *Albornoz*, p. 228. He quotes documents in the Arch. di Stato in Bologna, which Glénisson and Mollat did not catalogue for their calendar. Forlimpopoli, Filippini, pp. 294–7; Duprè-Theseider, 'L'Albornoz, Forlimpopoli e Bertinoro', *Stud. Romagn.*, xv (1964), pp. 3–14. The 'destruction' of Forlimpopoli, as in the case of most 'destroyed' medieval towns, consisted of the demolition of the town walls (ibid.).

[2] Werunsky, iii, pp. 279 ff.; N. Jorga, *Philippe de Mézières, 1327–1405, et la Croisade au XIVe siècle* (Paris, 1896), pp. 202–44, and docs. xxix–xxxi; Luttrel, in *Europe in the Late M.A.*, pp. 135 ff.

[3] Cf. *Studi Storici*, xiii (1904), p. 31. doc. 45. Mollat, *Popes at Avignon*, pp. 144–5, gives what I feel to be a misleading account of the negotiations.

[4] On 16 February 1364 the pope was still unsure whether Bernabò had accepted the latest papal amendments to the draft treaty. Theiner, *C.D.*, ii, no. 386. Cf. also *The Life of Saint Peter Thomas by Philippe de Mézières* (ed. J. Smet, Rome, 1954), pp. 110–14, 213–15.

was finally concluded. A huge war indemnity of half a million florins was to be paid to the Visconti by the Church, though a fifth of this was later remitted by Bernabò in return for papal help to have him re-instated as imperial vicar in Milan. No doubt Albornoz found the treaty humiliating, though it might be argued that a priest should be prepared to lose face in the cause of peace among Christians, and of the prosecution of the crusade against Muslims. The quibbling of his principals at Avignon, and the carving up of his legation in favour of de la Roche, angered him. On 14 January 1364 he expressed himself to his faithful agent Niccolò Spinelli as 'disgusted and fed up'.[1] The Church kept the possession of Bologna *de facto,* but an important concession of legal form was made to Bernarbò Visconti; Bernabò was allowed to retain the title of papal vicar in Bologna until over an eight-year period the whole war indemnity due from the papacy to Milan had been liquidated.

From personal economic necessity (since the pope 'inhumanly' refused to allow him to return to Avignon) Albornoz was compelled to ask for the legation to Naples, which he received in April 1364.[2] But it was a long time before he left on this mission, since the problem of the Visconti had been succeeded by that of the mercenary companies. To the existing German companies had been added the English companies, formed of soldiers disbanded after the Treaty of Brétigny in 1360. The genie which Albornoz and the Italian cities had conjured out of the bottle was now too powerful to control. The conclusion of peace in Lombardy and the end of the Florentine war with Pisa released the unemployed marauding mercenaries on a scale which made the problem intolerable, and threatened to make the pacification of the Papal State into a mockery. The control of the companies was also connected with two new questions: the approaching second descent of Charles IV into Italy, and the plans for the return of the papacy from Avignon to Italy, which were now more seriously entertained than at any time since the beginning of the Avignonese 'captivity'.[3]

The fact was, although historians usually ignore it, that the ten years of bloody warfare conducted by Albornoz had done very little to secure that pacification of Italy which was deemed a necessary prerequisite for the return of the Roman bishop to his own see. Four mercenary

---

[1] 'tamquam attediati et stomacati.' Glénisson and Mollat, no. 986.
[2] Ibid. no. 1012; cf. Theiner, *C.D.,* ii, no. 389, Lecacheux-Mollat, *Lettres secrètes et curiales du pape Urbain V,* no. 3274.
[3] Cf. *Europe in the Late M.A.,* pp. 108 ff.

companies roved through Italy, one of them commanded by the Englishman Hawkwood. In January 1365 Albornoz and the Neapolitan kingdom (represented by its captain-general, Albornoz's nephew) promised 160,000 florins and a hundred English bows, to buy off the White Company for a six-month period.[1] The peace of the Visconti with the Church continued to be fragile, and there were constant quarrels over Lugo and the other disputed border forts. The idea of persuading the English mercenaries to join the crusade, seriously entertained by the pope, was a chimera. Charles IV promised aid against the companies, but as a military force in Italy he had always been negligible, and he was to continue to prove so. The Papal State was itself far from completely pacified; a savage and devastating war went on from 1361 to 1367 between Rome and Velletri, which the papal officials were too busy elsewhere to quell, and in 1366–7 there was a general rebellion in Campagna.[2]

Albornoz finally left the Papal State to take up his legation in the Neapolitan kingdom in the autumn of 1365. He had instructions to carry out fairly drastic reforms in the kingdom, and he tried to execute these with habitual brusqueness. Shortly before 3 February 1366 he called the Neapolitan nobles to the inn of the Golden Pear in Naples, and made a speech in which he demanded that the 'heretics' (*paterini*) who were holding royal demesne lands in the kingdom should be made to disgorge them. The usage was typical of a man who had come to view political disobedience as synonymous with heresy. But on this occasion he was disappointed; the nobility refused to swear to effect anything of the sort, and the cardinal threw down his cap and his books in anger.[3]

The attempt to form a league against the mercenary companies ended after long negotiations in failure. On the side of Albornoz there was understanding that this league was basically a means of providing the finance to enlist enough mercenaries to overawe the other companies; on the side of Florence there was reluctance on the ground that enough money had been paid to companies (like that of Hawkwood) which might not be in the pay of the league. There was also the fear that if the peace between the Church and the Visconti broke down (as already seemed probable) the league would be used as a lever to drag

[1] Theiner, *C.D.*, ii, no. 399.

[2] Falco, *ASR*, xlix (1926), pp. 213–38.

[3] Florence, Arch. di Stato, Carte del Bene, 52. Letter from Borgognone del Bene in Naples to Francesco di Jacopo del Bene in Florence, dated 3 February 1366. I owe this reference and part of the transcription to the great kindness of Dr Gene Brucker. For the demesne lands see also Lecacheux-Mollat, nos. 1554, 1705–6, 1910, 1915, 2222, 2223, 2247.

Florence into a new war against the Lombard lords.[1] Eventually in September 1366 a league against the companies was made, but against future and not present companies, and consequently without real political value. The companies were useful if not essential to papal policy. In 1367 the English Company imposed a serious defeat on Perugia, and as a result the duchy of Spoleto passed from Perugian to papal control.[2]

In June 1367 the long-awaited return of Urban V to Italy took place. Before the papal court assembled in Viterbo Albornoz left his headquarters in Ancona and travelled across Italy to the Tuscan patrimony. The great cardinal died on 22 August 1367. In one sense his re-organisation of the Papal State had been decisive, in that he had taught the clerks how to use the administrative methods of the tyrants, and had made plain that the Papal State need not be an exception in the process by which most Italian governmental units were becoming larger, and more centrally controlled. But in another sense his work was far from decisive. In accepting a duel between the Visconti and the Church he had placed on the shoulders of the Papal State and the Neapolitan kingdom a burden which they were unable to support. The duel was still unfinished at his death, and its further prosecution had disastrous consequences for the Church and the kingdom. The companies, which had some of them been kept in existence by the money of Albornoz, remained as a threat to the peace of Italy. Albornoz had not made the Papal State into a peaceful and flourishing land; he represents a period of depopulation and economic decline,[3] where once-free communes were bullied and taxed by a papal government which at the same time supported and legitimised the rule of many tyrants.[4] Petrarch (who by this time was better disposed to the Visconti than to the

---

[1] 'Tenendosi tal modo che contra la pace fatta co' Melanes inon si venisse.' Florence, Arch. di Stato, Signori Missive 14, fo. 65a (instructions to embassy in Viterbo, 27 July 1367). Cf. *Europe in the Late M.A.*, pp. 108–9; Pirchan, ii, 6*–8*.

[2] Fop, *BSU*, lxv (1968), pp. 68–71; Glénisson-Mollat, nos. 1290–2.

[3] This is how the Papal State is referred to in a papal letter of 4 February 1368: 'cum propter mortalitatum pestes et bellorum excidia terrae istae vacuatae existant'. Lecacheux-Mollat no. 2685.

[4] To the other well-known tyrants whose state was in some sense confirmed by Albornoz the counts of Montefeltro should be added. Nicholas of Montefeltro was engaged as captain-general of the forces of the Church, 19 April 1367 and used for the reduction of Todi. Vat. Arch. Arm. 60, t. 21, fo. 12 v. He had earlier been given the 'custody' of Urbino (ibid. fo. 16v, 30 October 1364). Cf. G. Franceschini, *Saggi di storia Montefeltresca e Umbra* (Selci Umbro, 1957); L. M. Tocci, 'I due manoscritti urbinati dei privilegi dei Montefeltro', *Studi e ricerche nella biblioteca e negli Archivi Vaticani in memoria del Cardinale Giovanni Mercati*, L. Donati (ed.) (Florence, 1959), pp. 206–57, at p. 245.

popes) described Bologna in 1364 as 'defaced by war, slavery and famine, and recognisable only by its great churches and towers; singing had given way to sighing, and dancing troops of girls to bands of robbers and murderers'.

V

The pope did not disclaim the policies of Albornoz after the death of the great statesman. On the contrary, at the end of 1367 the pope's own brother Cardinal Anglic Grimoard was sent as legate to Italy to replace the pacific Androin de la Roche (who was for the last time withdrawn) and to sponsor a renewal of the war with the Visconti.[1] The need to balance Albornoz by a less bellicose official was over. The *signori* of Romagna and the march were assembled in preparation for a new war, and the Este of Ferrara and Gonzaga of Mantua and the rest of the Lombard lords opposed to the Visconti were also ready. As often before, Bernabò swiftly took the initiative, by attacking Mantua and seizing the important passage of the Po at Borgoforte. The weary lands of the Church supplied fresh troops, but not without a grumbling that in Umbria was soon to break into rebellion. There was another papal card to play; Charles IV began in April to take his army over the Alps to Italy, to carry out a policy closely aligned to that of the pope.

The renewal of the war did not favour the papal cause, nor did the first intervention of the emperor. In the summer of 1368 a truce was made with Bernabò by the allies, to Urban's discomfort. In papal Umbria the important city of Perugia was ripe for rebellion. This proud town, which had never submitted to Albornoz in the form in which other cities had done, had also a long tradition of free alliance and association with the Tuscan Guelph towns. The war of Albornoz against the neighbouring town of Todi had frightened the Perugians, and one of his last acts, the assumption of direct papal rule in Assisi, had directly threatened them. Fear of plots sponsored by papal agents made Perugia nervous; there were executions and banishments. The throwing-off of Perugian supremacy by Città di Castello, though discouraged by the pope, increased the tension. Like Florence and Siena, Perugia feared

---

[1] The detailed and distinguished book of G. Pirchan, *Italien und Kaiser Karl IV.*, has a full account of this period. There are other good accounts in Romano, *Niccolò Spinelli* (which was issued, without the documents, in a series of articles in the *ASPN*, 1899–1901) and in the new *Storia di Milano*. Some other references are to be found in *Europe in the Late M.A.*, pp. 110 ff.

imperial interference; she also resented the papal co-operation with rival cities such as Arezzo.[1]

On 21 October 1368 the emperor entered Rome with the pope, for the coronation of the empress and to work out joint policy by pope and emperor to pacify Italy. The papal palaces in Rome had been partly repaired, trees and shrubs planted in the Vatican gardens, and much money already spent on the fabric of the Roman churches – though the great Lateran basilica was still half in ruins. For a short time both the Holy Roman Emperor Charles IV and John Palaeologus the Greek emperor were guests of Pope Urban V in the Vatican – a meeting of powers which two centuries earlier would have been of critical importance for all Christendom, but was now of only passing interest.

Negotiations with the Visconti were continuous, and they signed a treaty with the pope and his allies, in Bologna on 11 February 1369. Visconti interest in Tuscany and Umbria was too keen for any real peace to last. The end of the war in Lombardy freed the Visconti mercenaries; they were sent south through the Romagna and over the Apennines to harass papal allies in Tuscany and give support to the Perugians, who were in revolt against Urban and in correspondence with Bernabò.[2] Bernabò's troops, under the Englishman Hawkwood, met with a reverse near Arezzo on 15 June and had to retreat. The pope was ready to show grace to the Perugians; but Visconti money was supplied to the city, more troops levied, and the revolt continued. The Neapolitan troops sent to Umbria to join the papal forces achieved little, and though the emperor supplied the troops to defeat Hawkwood, by early July he was on his way home. Florence, though unhappy about papal treatment of Perugia, was alarmed enough by the Visconti threat to Tuscany to be willing to ally with the Church and fight (November 1369); the new league was re-formed in April 1370.

The renewed war was again half-hearted. Hawkwood ravaged Tuscany, and the papal allies again fought in the Modenese. War-weariness and doubt hampered the papal alliance; negotiations with the enemy were hardly interrupted by hostilities. The main papal aim

---

[1] Pirchan, i, pp. 422–7; ii, pp. 196*–7*, 229*–31*; P. Balan, 'La ribellione di Perugia ne 1368 e la sua sottomissione nel 1370', *SDSD*, i–ii (1880–1). Belan did not publish the final acts of submission as he promised. Cf. E. Duprè Theseider, 'La rivolta di Perugia nel 1375 contro l'abate di Monmaggiore e i suoi precedenti politici', *BSU*, xxxv (1938), pp. 69–166; and also G. Franceschini, 'Il cardinale Anglico Grimoard e la sua opera di legato nella regione Umbro-Marchigiana', ibid. li (1954), pp. 45–72.

[2] Probably the revolt was in April: *ASI*, 1st ser., xvi, pt. 1, pp. 203–17. Duprè Theseider places it later, but see Bernabò's letter of 16 May in Pirchan, ii, p. 205*.

was to secure Perugia, and this was achieved (through Florentine mediation) by the late summer of 1370. In November the final submission of the Perugians was sealed, and a new peace made with Bernabò. But the papacy had in September suffered a serious moral defeat; on 5 September Urban V had embarked from Corneto for Avignon, leaving Bernabò to boast that he 'chased out the pope as he had chased out the emperor'.

The much-praised work of Albornoz seemed to promise the popes that with one more effort they might quiet Italy and return from Avignon to a secure and peaceful Roman See. But was this promise not a political will-o'-the-wisp, which led them deeper into the bogs of war and bankruptcy? After fifteen years of war, eight of them with the greatest power in Italy, the position of the Papal State was still insecure, and its own allies were some of them distrustful and hostile. Both politically and financially, the balance of profit and loss is hard to establish. It is true that for the first time since the Avignonese exile the Papal State was beginning to yield profits which seemed to suggest that the pope might one day 'live of his own', or support himself (as most late medieval men thought the sovereign should support himself) from his demesne lands.[1] But the reality was very different. For most of this period the papal chamber had continued to send huge sums to Italy for the prosecution of war. Papal agents in Italy, though on the whole conscientious, did not possess the political ability to press the policies of Albornoz to final success; and even Albornoz himself died with many of his biggest problems unsolved.

That the authoritarian rule imposed by Albornoz on formerly free communes and formerly unfettered *signori* should arouse resentment and, eventually, rebellion, was hardly surprising. War and pestilence filled the whole decade of the 1360s, and conditions before then had been far from favourable. Bologna, the prize for which the great wars had been fought, was heavily taxed and firmly governed. Both here

---

[1] Cf. Partner, 'The "budget" of the Roman Church in the Renaissance period', *Italian Renaissance Studies*, E. F. Jacob (ed.) (London, 1960), pp. 256–78, esp. at p. 259. The *peacetime* surplus in the Papal State was reckoned at 86,000 florins annually in 1367 (ibid.). The even more optimistic surplus of over 200,000 florins was thought possible in the future by Pierre d'Estaing the 'Cardinal of Bourges', in the first year of his legation, 1371. *ASR*, xxxi (1908), pp. 324–5. But it is most unlikely that this was more than wishful thinking, and in any case it supposed peacetime conditions which were never achieved. The average annual gross income of Romagna between 1358–64 before expenses were met was 29,651 florins, and that of the march of Ancona between 1353 and 1364 was 35,331 florins (Vat. Arch., Coll. 203, folios 21, 105). When expenses had been deducted there was virtually no surplus at all (ibid.).

and elsewhere papal officials were resented and complained of.[1] The aims of papal legates were largely fiscal – like those of most medieval governments – and where their rule was efficient it was with taxes in mind.[2] And the attempt to drive the *signori* from their privileged positions in the towns, impoverishing them and reducing them either to mere mercenaries or pensioners of the Holy See, was bound to arouse fierce resistance; both the Montefeltro and Gubbio and the Chiavelli at Fabriano found themselves in this position, but managed to emerge from it and to regain their old predominance.[3]

The peace of Bologna lasted only just long enough for the Church to re-occupy Perugia.[4] In the early spring of 1371 the hostility between the Este and the Visconti re-opened the war in Emilia. Sassuolo in the Modenese Apennine revolted against Niccolò d'Este, and then the important city of Reggio (attempted first by the Este) was seized by Bernabò. The smouldering war at once caught fire. Papal envoys, including the well-known nephew of Albornoz, Gomez, went to Italy to revive yet again the alliances against the Visconti.

But papal policy was no longer as hesitant as in recent years. The Holy See had since the end of 1370 been occupied by Gregory XI, one of the most active and purposeful of the Avignon popes. Like his predecessors Gregory sought to promote peace between England and France, to revive the crusade against the Turks, and to pacify Italy. The last of these entailed war, as it had done throughout the century. Once again tedious clerical lawsuits 'condemned' the Visconti. New legates, and energetic papal agents were appointed. At the time of the renewal of the war in May 1371 Cardinal Pierre d'Estaing succeeded Anglic Grimoard as legate in Romagna and most of the eastern part of

---

[1] Cf. O. Vancini, 'Bologna della Chiesa (1360–76)', *AMDR*, 3rd ser., xxiv–xxv (1906–7). Between 1365 and 1371 the customs dues (*dazi*) were raised from 190,000 lib. (round figures) to 246,000 lib. (ibid., xxv, pp. 22–3; pp. 134–5 of the offprint). Cf. Theiner, ii, no. 526, at pp. 522–3, and Orlandelli, *AMDR*, 1950–1, pp. 204 ff. For papal promises to reduce taxation and to restrain the excesses of papal officials in the provinces, Lecacheux-Mollat, nos. 2522, 2555–6; Mirot-Jassemin, *Lettres secrètes et curiales de Grégoire XI*, nos. 2468, 3035, 3044, 3196.

[2] An example is the great description of Bologna and Romagna by Cardinal Anglic Grimoard, Theiner, *C.D.*, ii, nos. 525–6. Its accuracy is discussed, and its limitations pointed out largely from a demographic point of view, by Larner, *Lords of Romagna*, pp. 208–28. Larner's statement that 'we need not doubt Anglic's assertion that the province yielded 100,000 florins after expenses had been deducted' (p. 223) seems to me mistaken, because irreconcilable with the figures in V. A., Collectorie 203. See note 1 above, p. 358.

[3] Franceschini in *BSU* (1954), quoted above, and R. Sassi, 'L'anno della morte di Alberghetto II Chiavelli', *AMSM*, 6th ser., iii (1943), pp. 1–30.

[4] Cf. J. Glénisson, 'La politique de Louis de Gonzague pendant la guerre entre Gregoire XI et Bernabò Visconti, *BEC*, cix (1951).

the Papal State, with full financial and political powers.[1] In the rest of the Papal State Cardinal Philippe de Cabassole was appointed as legate. The able, but ruthless and unpopular Gerald du Puy Abbot of Marmoutier was made the main papal fiscal agent in Italy.[2] These were the men who were to anger the pope's Italian subjects more than any earlier papal agents in the century by their bureaucratic zeal. Fortresses were built at Perugia and other important towns, tax lists were revised, even the Constitutions of Albornoz were carefully examined,[3] and the war in Emilia vigorously pressed forward.

For the time being the revived structure of Guelph alliances held firm. Even the reluctant Florentines were held for a time in the framework of the papal alliance, and were persuaded to join the papacy in engaging German troops.[4] But from the time of the papal recovery of Perugia in 1370 the Florentine distrust of papal-imperial manoeuvres which had been so apparent during Charles IV's activities in Tuscany became extended to papal intentions in the north of the Papal State.[5] Florence feared the Visconti, but she also feared both external and internal threats to her liberties. The unrest of the Tuscan towns – San Miniato, and still more Pistoia – made her nervous.

The combined effort of the Angevin monarchy of Naples and the Church to dominate Italy, which had been going on in one form or another since 1266, now entered its final spasm. Bernabò was unwilling to accept the clerical challenge, and repeatedly (though falsely) assured the legates that it was not his intention to break the peace with the Church.[6] But the war against the Visconti in Lombardy was ruthlessly pressed by the Este and their associates – ruthlessly but unsuccessfully, as the Visconti heavily defeated the papal coalition at Rubiera, between Modena and Reggio, on 2 June 1372. This only sharpened the pace of the war. Though the Florentines dropped out of the papal alliance, their place was taken, in a treaty made 7 July 1372, by the Green Count, Amedeo of Savoy (and adhered to also by Monferrat, Joanna

[1] He had earlier been the pacifier of Perugia. Cf. Mirot-Jassemin, nos. 2153, 2199, 2201, 2257, 3163. Instructions to Anglic Grimoard to return to the Roman court and to hand over the area of his vicariate to d'Estaing, ibid. no. 2242 (25 June 1371).
[2] Ibid. nos. 2231–40 (June 1371). For him see E. Duprè Theseider's article in *BSU* (1938), quoted above.
[3] Mirot-Jassemin, no. 2505 (Theiner, *C.D.* ii, no. 539).
[4] Mirot-Jassemin, nos. 2167, 2371, 2390; cf. Schäfer, *Deutsche Ritter*, iv, pp. 291–5.
[5] *Europe in the Late M.A.*, pp. 113–14. Cf. Theiner, *C.D.*, ii, no. 519.
[6] *Repertorio Diplomatico Visconteo*, i (Milan, 1911), nos. 1738, 1796. 1804, 1807, 1809. These letters are of 1371, not 1372, as dated.

of Naples and others). The fighting ceased to be confined to Emilia, and became extended to a very wide front, which included Piedmont, Liguria, Lombardy, Lunigiana, and the Valtelline (which Amedeo of Savoy sought to control in order to block the passes to German Visconti mercenaries).[1] Great subsidies were required from the clergy in France and England for the war (though those in England were recalcitrant).

Perhaps more than any of the campaigns of Albornoz, this one recalled the great combined military operations of John XXII.[2] Acting with the support of the French government, Gregory appointed a series of French aristocratic captains to fight the Visconti, notably Enguerrand de Coucy and Raymond Viscount of Turenne, but many German mercenary captains fought under Otto of Brunswick, and Angevin troops fought under the command of Albornoz's pupil Niccolò Spinelli, and of Spinelli's brother-in-law Giovanni Orsini. Local bishops – those of Vercelli and Luni – and other clerical officials such as Bérenger the Abbot of Lézat and the Bishop of Arezzo, took part in the conduct of the war. The defection of Hawkwood and the English Company from the Visconti to the Church was an important gain.

The military results were satisfying, and the great Visconti lordship was almost exhausted by the effort to repel the attack. On 8 May 1373 the papal alliance won a victory at Montechiari south of Brescia, which was followed in October by the fall of the town of Vercelli, in Piedmont. This was the peak of papal success. From this time the gains had to be defended and provisioned against Visconti attack, while the English and German mercenaries, in arrears of pay, recouped themselves from the countryside. The Visconti were hard-pressed, but so was the Church. Though the first Visconti overtures of peace were repulsed, the cooling off of the Count of Savoy from the war meant that the papal effort was seriously hampered. Otto of Brunswick again defeated the Visconti outside Vercelli, but in the summer of 1374 matters were swiftly moving towards peace.[3]

---

[1] Chiavenna was also disputed. Reg. Vat. 244 F, fo. 78 refers to Chiavenna and not to Cilavegna, as conjectured by Romano in *Bol. Soc. Pav.*, iii (1903), p. 430n.; cf. G. Mollat, *Lettres secrètes et curiales du pape Grégoire XI (1370–1378) intéressant les pays autre que la France* (Paris, 1962–5), nos. 2861–4, 2950, 3440–2. Cf. also E. L. Cox, *The Green Count of Savoy* (Princeton, 1967), pp. 267 ff.

[2] Probably because its eventual political result was so negative, it gets short shrift in Mollat's book. L. Mirot, *La politique pontificale et le retour du Saint-Siège à Rome en 1376* (Paris, 1899) is hardly more satisfactory (pp. 21–5), and rather inaccurate in detail.

[3] Glénisson, *BEC*, cix (1951), pp. 273–4; A. Segre, 'I dispacci di Cristoforo da Piacenza procuratore mantovano alla corte pontifica (1371–1383)', *ASI*, 5th ser., xliii–xliv (1909).

15   St John Lateran in the early sixteenth century

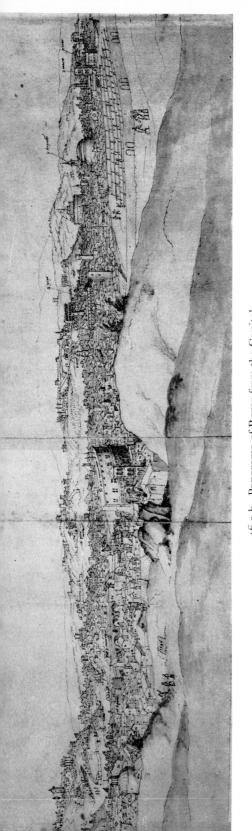

16 a b Panorama of Rome from the Capitol

VI

In the autumn of 1374 Gregory's relations with the French crown were poor, and he wished also to be in Italy to deal with the Visconti, and to combat the rather menacing plans which the Hungarian and French governments were drawing up to the prejudice of the pope's Neapolitan vassal, Joanna.[1] But at the same time his relations with Florence, 'the faithful people of holy mother Church', were deteriorating rapidly. Papal-Savoyard intervention in Lunigiana and Lucca seemed to confirm earlier suspicions that the pope was machinating in Tuscany to the disadvantage of Florence. The political unpopularity in Florence of some of the oligarch families connected with the Church tended to exacerbate matters, and so did both a quarrel over clerical jurisdiction, and the refusal of the papal governors to permit export of grain to Florence in an autumn of dearth.[2]

In these years the Italian laity seem to have come near to disgust or discontent with the papal temporal power as such. Only a few years earlier the Bolognese canonist Giovanni da Legnano had defended the right of the Church to make war; not surprisingly he wrote this soon after the fall of Bologna to Albornoz, whose partisan he was.[3] But in the 1370s much was said of the 'bad shepherds', the worldly clerical officials in Italy of whom St Catherine of Siena complained. Their denunciation became a commonplace.[4] The most powerful voice was St Catherine's plea – '*Pace, pace, pace, babbo mio dolce, e non più guerra!*'.[5] Complaints of a more worldly kind were also heard. The running of the Papal State by a French clerical élite, who occupied not only most of the governmental positions but also very many of the bishoprics, was fiercely resented. While papal government tightened its grip, so did communal and seigniorial government; there was less room for a mixed regime, now that the loosely organised and relatively

---

pp. 27–95, 253–326; cf. Mirot-Jassemin, nos. 3456, 3461, 3468, 3556–8, etc.; and see also Cox, *The Green Count*, pp. 279–81.

[1] *ASI*, 5th ser., xliii (1909), p. 57. Cf. Léonard, *Les Angevins de Naples*, pp. 445–6.

[2] *Europe in the Late M.A.*, pp. 114–17.

[3] F. Bosdari, 'Giovanni da Legnano canonista e uomo politico del '300', *AMDR*, 3rd ser., xix (1901), pp. 1–37; cf. Filippini, *Albornoz*, pp. 249–51; J. P. McCall, 'The writings of John of Legnano with a list of manuscripts', *Traditio*, xxiii (1967), pp. 415–37; G. da Legnano, *Tractatus de Bello, de Represaliis et de Duello*, T. E. Holland (ed.) (Oxford, 1917), pp. 209 ff.

[4] The long passage in the *Chronicon Placentinum* (*RRIISS*, xvi), cols. 522–36, is often quoted about this period. It was however written in 1400 or thereabouts (see col. 530), when the schism was far advanced.

[5] Tommaseo (ed.), Lett. 218.

N

easy-going administration of the earlier communes was overtaken by sterner forms of rule.[1]

Once Florence turned against Gregory XI, her way was easy. By January 1375 Gregory was complaining that she was inciting the cities of the Church to revolt with the 'damnable sophistry' of 'popular liberty'. Nor were the communes of the Papal State her only targets. What tends to be neglected in assessing Florentine policy at this time is her acute interest in the petty tyrants of the Papal Sate, who for her were mercenaries, allies, and pensioners.[2]

The position of the Church, eighteen months earlier imposing, was now fragile. Money had run out; the pope had borrowed from emperor, cardinals, and French nobles, and raised what he could from the European clergy. The unpaid troops in Lombardy mutinied, took the Bishop of Arezzo and threatened to hand him over to the enemy.[3] The haughty stance taken by the pope with the Milanese envoys was no longer credible; the balance of power in Italy had tipped against him. But at the same time the negotiations between England and France were going forward towards a truce, and the preparations for the return of the pope to Italy were at last almost definite. It had seemed that the pacification of Italy, on which the popes had spent twenty years of war and millions of money, was almost complete, so that the Roman bishop could go back in peace to his people. The facts were otherwise. The whole position of the temporal power in Italy, so painfully constructed, was about to collapse.

On 4 June truces were signed between the Church and its allies and the Visconti, in Bologna; far off in Bruges another truce was arranged in the same month between France and England. The departure of the pope for Italy was announced for September. But the end of the contracts of the English mercenaries in papal service had the effect of threatening Tuscany. Hawkwood left his camp near Imola and prepared to march over the Apennines towards Florence; the Florentines met him on the river Idice near Bologna and promised him 130,000 florins to give them immunity (26 June 1375). Other fears and suspicions – that the cardinal legate in Bologna had been privy to an

---

[1] Some of the remarks in M. V. Becker, 'The Florentine Territorial State and Civic Humanism in the early Renaissance', *Florentine Studies, Politics and Society in Renaissance Florence*, N. Rubinstein (ed.) (1968), pp. 109–39, may be relevant here.

[2] Cf. Becker, p. 113n.; Partner, 'Florence and the Papacy in the earlier fifteenth century', ibid. pp. 381–402, at pp. 385–6.

[3] Cf. K. H. Schäfer, 'Ergänzende Urkunden zur Geschichte des deutschen Adels im päpstlichen Dienste', *Röm. Quart.*, xxvii (1913), pp. 146*–58*; Mirot–Jassemin, no. 3686.

attempted rebellion in Prato against Florence, that the papal agent in Perugia had acted against her in Castiglione Aretino – grated on the nerves of the Florentines. Perhaps the unpopularity of some families with papal connections such as the Albizzi and Ricasoli was the most potent factor of all. In July Florence signed a public alliance with Bernabò Visconti; the queen of Guelph cities allied with the enemies of the Church.

The political programme which Florence put to the towns of the Papal State was destructive but attractive. It was simply to revolt against the 'rapacity and avarice' of the priests. Its success was startling. The first towns to revolt were those of the Tuscan patrimony – Orte and Narni rebelled in October, Montefiascone on 1 November, and finally Francesco di Vico entered Viterbo and recovered the *signoria* of the city on 18 November; shortly afterwards the towns from Corneto on the coast to Terni in the hills acclaimed him as lord.[1] The early participation of the prefect of Vico is significant; it marks the importance of the petty tyrants in the rebellion.[2]

On 3 December the next stage of the rebellion occurred on the edge of the Florentine dominions, in the little town of Città di Castello. The papal garrison and officials were either thrown from the windows of the palazzo comunale into the square, beheaded in it beneath, hung from the battlements, killed while resisting, or driven into the sewers. The communal officials described the rebellion with affectionate detail.[3] On 7 December Perugia rebelled. The papal troops and the important papal official, the Abbot of Marmoutier, remained in the fortress and bombarded the city. Frightened by the threat of the English Company, the Perugians gave the garrison free exit on 22 December. The wave of rebellion engulfed most of the Papal State, except Rome and Campagna. Forlì, Faenza, Fermo – most of the important cities of Romagna and the march, with a few exceptions – rebelled. Ascoli fell, and Gomez Albornoz was besieged in the citadel. On the night of 19 March 1376 Bologna, the great prize for which so much blood and

---

[1] Cf. M. Antonelli, 'La dominazione pontifica nel Patrimonio', *ASR*, xxxi (1908), at pp. 141–50. To eject these tyrants the Church could only rely on others, as in the ejection of the prefect from Corneto by the Vitelleschi.

[2] Typical were the Montefeltro of Urbino, for whom see Franceschini, in *BSU*, xlii (1945), pp. 179–99, at pp. 181 ff., and also the text published by G. Sommi Picenardi, 'Trattato fra Barnabò Visconti, Antonio di Montefeltro e la Repubblica di Firenze etc. 1 febb. 1375', *Miscellanea di Storia Italiana ed. per cura della Reg. Dep. di Storia Patria*, xxiii (1884), pp. 169–82. The treaty is dated 1376, not 1375.

[3] The document is published by Franceschini in *BSU* (1945), p. 182n.

treasure had been spent, followed the rest.[1] There was little clerical resistance; the garrisons were far too small to offer any. Many of the seventy-two fortresses in the Papal State on which the treasure and ingenuity of Albornoz had been spent were demolished. The only policy was the traditional one of waiting until enemies could be played off against one another, and until more money was available to raise large mercenary forces. The importunate Hawkwood had to be allowed to seize the Romagnol town of Bagnacavallo; he was able to show his loyalty by sacking Faenza. The inability of the Church to pay its mercenaries properly was to lead to frequent 'atrocities'.

The 'Eight of War' whom the Florentines elected to conduct the war received the by-name of the 'Eight Saints', a name which came to be applied to the war itself. The Florentine position was difficult and vulnerable. Since the main offence of Florence was to call out into rebellion cities which she subsequently had no means of recalling to obedience, the way in which she could atone for her sins was unclear. But as one of the greatest European trading and banking powers she could be despoiled easily at the word of the Church, by any prince with the energy and interest to do so. Even at sea, Florentine ships were taken as prizes. Finally, and for the future this was the gravest result, Florence by destroying the temporal power of the Church and disorganising the Guelphs, renewed Visconti power and made the Visconti menace to Tuscany once more into a serious threat.[2] For the moment the Visconti remained neutral, promising Florence support but failing to give it. In June 1376 Breton mercenaries entered Italy for the Church, to force the Papal State into submission. They were led by their commanders Budes and Malestroit, under the orders of Cardinal Robert of Geneva. They were used together with the English mercenaries of Hawkwood; the forces were neither well-co-ordinated nor powerful, and there was a war of attrition in Romagna and the march of Ancona, characterised by extreme brutality and destruction. The pope was paying out large sums to finance his own return to Italy, and he found it hard to find adequate and regular payments for his armies. The pattern of mercenary dominance which was to become standard in the Papal State for the following half-century and more, was already taking shape.

---

[1] O. Vancini, *La rivolta dei Bolognesi al governo dei vicari della Chiesa (1376–7)* (Bologna, 1906).

[2] That the Florentines made a grave error in launching the war of the Eight Saints was later recognised by the Florentine Chancellor, Coluccio Salutati: 'quo bello quantum potentie temporalis ecclesie amiserit, ad quantamque nos impotentiam ducti sumus'. F. Novati (ed.), *Epistolario* (Rome, 1893), ii, p. 122.

The worst of the mercenary atrocities was committed not against a rebel city, but against one of the few which had remained faithful to the Church, Cesena. As a result of one of the riots inevitable where such troops were in occupation, some Bretons were killed, and the legate forced to take refuge in the citadel. The reprisal, which appears to have been executed with the consent or approval of the papal legate, was a horrifying one. On 3 February 1377 the Breton and English mercenaries combined to enter the town by stealth, and to massacre practically the entire population. Though possibly little worse than other acts of the time, the massacre of Cesena struck the imagination of contemporaries, and was used by Florentine propaganda to very good effect. The 'de casu Cesenae' of a Romagnol (or Marchigiano) notary is one of the first literary protests in European history against an 'atrocity'.[1] It could perhaps be argued that this was one of the first occasions in Europe when a lay public was willing to entertain the idea that massacre by the soldiery was anything but legitimate.

Three weeks before the massacre of Cesena, Gregory XI had entered Rome. He came with a force of mercenaries under Raymond of Turenne, landing first at Corneto and then at the ruined village of Ostia. The thirteenth-century papacy had ended with warfare and political confusion in the Papal State; the exile at Avignon was not ending very differently.

[1] Cf. R. Sassi, 'Il vero nome del notaio Fabrianese autore del *de casu Caesenae*', *AMSM*, 6th ser., ii (1942), pp. 149–55. Cf. also P. Herde, 'Politik und Rhetorik in Florenz am Vorabend der Renaissance. Die ideologische Rechtfertigung der Florentiner Aussenpolitik durch Coluccio Salutati', *Archiv für Kulturgeschichte*, xlvii (1965), pp. 141–220.

Chapter 11

The crisis of the medieval papacy

I

The rebellion of the Papal State in 1375 would under normal circumstances have petered out in the usual way, with grants of papal privileges and acts of forgiveness. The great city of Bologna, to the disgust of the Florentines, made peace with Gregory XI in July 1377. Francesco di Vico, the main rebel in the Tuscan patrimony, made peace in October of the same year. In Campagna only Terracina had given serious trouble to the papal government, and the commune had submitted in February of 1377. Ascoli and Fermo and other places remained in rebellion in the march, Perugia remained the centre of the Florentine league in Umbria. Breton, English, German and Italian mercenaries roamed central Italy in the service of one league or the other, sparing no one. To some extent political initiative was falling into the hands of these men – John Hawkwood, Luz von Landau, Alberigo da Barbiano, Silvestre Budes and many others. To buy support the papal government had had to make concessions which bit deeply into the centralised regime set up by Albornoz – particularly at Bologna, where a revived independent communal regime was recognised by the popes. Concessions were made elsewhere – Orvieto was granted her ancient claims in Val di Lago, Ancona was given important privileges, innumerable nobles and *signorotti* were made grants which began or confirmed little tyrannies.[1]

The Florentine attack on the popes had been in many ways bizarre. The war, though terrible, was also rather absurd. In 1377 the two commanders-in-chief on the opposing sides exchanged places: the papal feudatory Ridolfo da Varano of Camerino returned to his papal allegiance, and Hawkwood was bought by the Florentines and Bernabò Visconti to lead the anti-papal forces. But so long as the popes still had

---

[1] Many examples in Antonelli, 'La dominazione pontificia nel Patrimonio', *ASR*, xxxi (1908), pp. 151 ff. The Vitelleschi and the Farnese are typical families; less known are the Baglioni of Castel di Piero.

the money to pay their troops and the political authority to command their lands, the possibility – even the probability – remained that in the end papal power would be restored. Gregory XI still had the political support of the French and the Neapolitan monarchies; the old associate of Albornoz, Niccolò Spinelli, now chancellor of the kingdom, was the agent of the reconciliation of Bologna. Albornoz's nephew, Gomez, became Senator of Rome. Opposition to papal rule was much too fragmented to have any hope of overthrowing it altogether; this was apparent by the autumn of 1377, though the Florentines did not begin to treat for peace until the following spring.

On 27 March 1378, while the Florentine ambassadors were negotiating for peace, Gregory XI died at Rome. The political world of the *curia* had already been gravely shaken. Gregory XI had talked of returning to Avignon; a French pope elected after him would probably do so, but the Romans would not allow the conclave to elect such a man. The election of an Italian would imperil the position of the French clerical élite which had controlled the *curia* for seventy years. Reluctantly, in fear of the Roman mob, the conclave elected the Neapolitan Archbishop of Bari, Bartolomeo Prignano.[1] It was one of the fateful elections of papal history. Prignano (Urban VI) turned out to have a dirty temper; but it was politically more important that he did not intend to go back to Avignon, nor did he try to convince the great holders of curial patronage that he intended to protect their interests. Even Joanna of Naples and her great magnates such as Spinelli, though at first willing to accept Prignano as a Neapolitan, decided that the Franco-Angevin political world could not deal with a pope so resistant to its main principles.

Avignon, and France beyond Avignon, were far. But French officials, French troops, French nobles, were to be found in considerable numbers in the Papal State. And in the Neapolitan kingdom, where Joanna had recently been willy-nilly married to the papal *condottiere* Otto of Brunswick, French political interests continued to dominate. The nobility of the kingdom and the Papal State were inextricably mingled; such families as the Caetani and the Orsini were equally important on either side of the papal-Neapolitan border. Typical of such nobles was Onorato Caetani, the Count of Fondi, who took his title from the kingdom, but was equally powerful in Campagna and the Maritime province. Since

---

[1] The literature on the schism is vast, and little of it is directly relevant to the Papal State. See however R. C. Trexler, 'Rome on the eve of the Great Schism', *Speculum*, xlii (1967), pp. 489–509.

1358 he had claimed the *signoria* of Anagni,[1] and although for a long time the Church had resisted the claim, papal weakness at the time of the War of the Eight Saints had induced Gregory XI to make this turbulent feudatory the papal governor of the province, and to accept large sums from him as loans.

Though he accepted Onorato Caetani as papal Count of Campagna for a short time, Urban VI shortly after the beginning of his pontificate deprived Onorato of the office, intending (it is said) to replace him by another baron from the kingdom, Tomaso di Sanseverino.[2] It was therefore to Anagni, the centre of Caetani power in Campagna, that the ultramontane cardinals went in late May; from then and throughout the summer, as the anti-Urbanist opposition developed in the Sacred College, the movement against Urban's election took place under the protection of the disgruntled Onorato Caetani. From early August the movement had the official support of Joanna of Naples; both her husband Otto of Brunswick and her chief minister Niccolò Spinelli were intimately concerned in the negotiations. The ultramontane cardinals eventually retired to the main seat of Onorato's power, at Fondi in the kingdom, where they were joined by the Italian cardinals. Here on 20 September 1378 a 'conclave' effected the election of Robert of Geneva as pope (Clement VII). The new pope was accepted by the Neapolitan and French courts, and the schism began which was in many ways to obliterate the medieval papacy.

The Breton mercenaries had been practically out of the control of the Holy See since before the death of Gregory XI.[3] They passed even before the election of Robert de Geneva into hostility to Urban VI, and after the election they began a desultory civil war with the Urbanists in the Tuscan patrimony and Campagna, whose military aim was the relief of the French garrison of Castel Sant'Angelo in Urbanist Rome – though its practical aim was the usual one of plunder and loot. Urban engaged to defend him the *condottiere* Alberigo da Barbiano, who was also a papal vassal from the Romagna. At the end of April military control of Rome and its area passed into the hands of the Urbanists; Castel Sant'Angelo surrendered, and the Bretons were decisively defeated

---

[1] Cf. Falco, *ASR*, xlix (1926), pp. 227–9, 258 ff.

[2] It is noticeable that from Clement VII Onorato held the office not of papal rector but of 'count' of Campagna, thus reverting to the traditions of the twelfth century. Cf. *Documenti dall'Archivio Caetani. Regesta Chartarum*, iii, p. 51. If he became rector under Gregory it was late in the pontificate; Daniele del Caretto was rector still on 23 July 1377 (ibid. p. 48).

[3] Cf. L. Mirot, 'Silvestre Budes et les Bretons en Italie', *BEC*, lix (1898), pp. 292–4, 296 ff.

at the foot of the Alban hills below Marino,[1] by Alberigo da Barbiano. How little Urban's government was in control was shown by the attempt of the Romans to destroy Castel Sant'Angelo after its surrender. It was a gesture which ended as mere vandalism, with the destruction of the marble reliefs round the drum of the castle; but its aim was clearly the same as that of the Papal State rebels of 1375, the destruction of the main papal fortress.

Alberigo da Barbiano is said to have been given a banner inscribed '*Italia liberata da' barbari*' by Urban VI, and there is a strong temptation (which few historians have resisted until recently), to treat the outbreak of the Great Schism in more or less national terms. Such a tendency should certainly be opposed.[2] The most important political support for the revolt of the cardinals came from the Italo-French ambience of the kingdom of Naples, where Fench policy was by no means completely in control, since the French court was still considering giving its support to the Hungarian opposition to Joanna. Two of the most important laymen were Italian – Onorato Caetani and Niccolò Spinelli. In Italian terms, the schism can perhaps be considered as an extension of the break-up of the 'Guelph' world, which had already been strikingly manifested in the War of the Eight Saints. Now the southern part of the Guelph political connection showed the same incoherence and confusion which had three years earlier been shown by Tuscany and the Papal State.

The news of the battle of Marino sent Clement VII from Fondi to the little port of Sperlonga, thence to Gaeta, Naples and in June 1379, to Avignon. The future of papal power in Italy was bleak. All over the Papal State a civil war between so-called Urbanists and Clementists developed, in which the positions assumed by the participants were dictated (as they were in the combat of the two allegiances all over the Latin world) by political convenience. The more important rectors of papal provinces were lay magnates who were offered the office as an inducement. Rinaldo Orsini of Tagliacozzo[3] became the Urbanist rector

---

[1] Marino belonged to the important Clementine magnate, Giordano Orsini. Cf. N. Ratti, *Storia di Genzano con note e documenti* (Rome, 1797), p. 104; Caetani, *Regesta Chartarum*, iii, pp. 60-92 et passim.

[2] There is a good discussion in Léonard, *Les Angevins de Naples*, pp. 453 ff. The device on Alberigo's banner was probably to exploit the fear and dislike of the Breton and Gascon mercenaries.

[3] Cf. E.-R. Labande, *Rinaldo Orsini Comte de Tagliacozzo* (+ 1390) *et les premières guerres suscitées – Italie centrale par le Grand Schisme* (Monaco-Paris, 1939). The appointment of Orsini as rector in the Tuscan patrimony and the adjoining areas on 21 May 1378 was a normal one, and did not include any special 'military' areas (*pace* Labande, pp. 38-9).

N*

of the Tuscan patrimony; Pandolfo Malatesta became the Urbanist rector of Romagna. These laymen calculated their advantage closely; when Rinaldo Orsini was required to hand over the citadel of Orvieto to a cardinal, he defected to the Clementine cause. He thus achieved his object; by June 1380 he was *signore* of Orvieto, and with the Bretons a serious threat to Urbanist control of the rest of the province. By the summer of 1381 Urban had to make another layman into papal rector, Simonetto di Cecco Baglioni of Castel di Piero.

The foundation of Urban's position was the obedience of Florence, Perugia, Bologna and Rome. This remnant of the 'Guelph' alliance stood firm for him in central Italy. Clement's hopes in Italy were dimmed by the tragic confusion which developed in the Neapolitan kingdom. Both Clement VII and Joanna of Naples placed their hopes in the royal house of France, and particularly in the house of Anjou. On 17 April 1379, without the assent of the cardinals and at a time of disarray and panic, Clement VII at Sperlonga had made over the whole Papal State (less the Tuscan patrimony, Campagna-Maritime, Sabina and Rome) to the Duke of Anjou. The name chosen for the new state was the 'kingdom of Adria'.[1] This donation (which Clement himself later decided was probably illegal) came to nothing, but it showed the way for the later adoption of Louis of Anjou by Joanna of Naples as her 'son' and heir (June 1380).

Two major foreign interventions in Italy followed, one Hungarian and one French. In July 1380 another claimant to the Neapolitan throne, Charles of Durazzo the grandson of Robert of Anjou, brought a Hungarian army to Italy with the blessing of Urban VI. Long before French or Provençal aid could reach the Neapolitan kingdom, Charles (who bore the inappropriate soubriquet of *'della Pace'*) was in central Italy. On 1 June 1381 Urban VI invested him at Rome with the kingdom of the Two Sicilies. By the end of the month he had crossed the Neapolitan border, and in mid-July he besieged Joanna in Naples in Castel Nuovo. Having defeated the Queen's husband, Otto of Brunswick, Charles sent Joanna into captivity and assumed absolute power in the kingdom (though he could not take the crown while Joanna lived).

The death of Charles V of France (16 September 1380) paralysed French policy for a year. But in the New Year of 1382 the Great Council

---

[1] Cf. P. Durrieu, 'Le Royaume d'Adria', *Revue des Questions Historiques*, xxviii (1880), pp. 43–78; N. Valois, 'L'expédition et mort de Louis d'Anjou en Italie (1382–4)', ibid. n.s., xi (1894), pp. 84–153; Léonard, pp. 460 ff.; M. de Boüard, *La France et l'Italie au temps du grand schisme d'occident* (Paris, 1936), pp. 38 ff.

of Charles VI approved the Italian expedition of Louis of Anjou, to rescue his adoptive 'mother' Joanna. Clement VII's duty was to give the assent of the feudal sovereign of the kingdom to his arrangement, and to raise the money. The theoretical abandonment of all papal revenues of the Avignonese obedience to Louis of Anjou which was made at this time was not strictly executed, but the sums transferred by Clement VII to finance the Angevin expedition (particularly the naval side) were large.[1]

The Angevin expedition of 1382 was thus the supreme effort of the Avignonese papacy to regain southern and central Italy. But though he had the support of the French, Milanese and Savoyard governments, and disposed of a huge number of men, Louis when he actually took his army to Italy in the summer of 1382 achieved pitifully little. He disappointed Clement VII by making no attempt to recover the Papal State; he marched south past Bologna and Ancona without even ravaging the countryside, and did not attempt to cross the Apennines towards Rome. But his approach was fatal for the poor captive queen; on 27 July 1382 Joanna was suffocated by her jailers in the castle of Muro in the Abruzzi.

Louis's arrival in the region of Naples in the autumn of 1382 thus came too late to save the queen. The incompetence and inaction of Louis then frittered away the resources of the great French army. Before he could bring Charles of Durazzo to battle Louis ran out of money, and for over a year the Angevin did little. The money sent by Clement VII and the Visconti stuck to the fingers of the corrupt emissaries (one of whom was Rinaldo Orsini). The relief expedition of Enguerrand de Coucy got no farther than Tuscany. In September 1384 a fever caught while attempting to restrain his troops from pillage cost Louis his life. He was too idealistic a character to compete with success in the iron

---

[1] Just how large is unclear. Noel Valois estimated that by the spring of 1384 they amounted to at least 130,000 florins (*Revue des Questions historiques*, n.s., xi, p. 134). M. Jean Favier, *Les Finances Pontificales à l'époque du Grand Schisme d'Occident 1378–1409* (Paris, 1966), p. 624, seems to suggest that *all* the sums received by Nicholas de Mauregart in the name of Louis of Anjou from the pope were used for Italian affairs. But as Valois pointed out in the article quoted (not quoted by M. Favier) and as M. Favier himself implies later in his important work (p. 688), the money received by Nicholas de Mauregart was applied for many other purposes besides those of Louis of Anjou, and the sums received by Nicholas de Mauregart may be considered as the total income of the Avignonese pope. It is therefore unlikely that 'La papauté avait fourni (to Louis of Anjou) une moyenne de 240,000 francs par an'; the total was much more modest. The franc was valued at 30 shillings of Avignon, the papal florin at 28 shillings (Favier, p. 36).

politics of Italy. His army fell to pieces, and de Coucy returned to France. The great French effort had achieved nothing.

Both Charles of Durazzo in 1380 and Enguerrand de Coucy in 1384 had established short-lived zones of influence in the upper valley of the Tiber, in both cases to the detriment of Arezzo, which was twice sacked, and finally sold by de Coucy to the Florentines. But these expeditions, and the march of Louis of Anjou, were brief episodes in the struggle for power in central Italy, in which the forces in play were almost entirely regional and local.[1] The situation of Urban VI's government cannot be described except as miserable. Francesco di Vico and Rinaldo Orsini, together with the Breton and other Clementine mercenary troops, terrorised those areas of the Tuscan patrimony which they did not actually control. In 1383 the Manenti of Spoleto had revolted against the Church, and brought the town to the obedience of Clement and the *signoria* of Rinaldo Orsini. The fortress held out for a time, but the petty English mercenaries like Richard Romsey who were sent to relieve it were simply bought off by Orsini, who cut the bridge and captured the fort in the following year.

The lords and petty lords of the Papal State were changing, under these troubled conditions, from vassals who frequently changed their allegiance to mercenaries who openly sold their swords. Alberigo da Barbiano, from the counts of Cunio in Romagna, was the prototype of the feudatory turned mercenary after the pattern of the English or German 'Companies' in Italy.[2] The scale of seigniorial domination in the Papal State ranged from that of the Malatesta, who were now the lords of several cities in the Romagna, and by their purchase of Borgo San Sepolcro from Gregory XI were extending their influence into the valley of the Upper Tiber, to their connections by marriage, the Pietra-

---

[1] The learned articles of Dr Gino Franceschini give some idea of the political forces at work in the Apennine areas of Umbria and the march: 'Soldati inglesi nell'Alta Valle del Tevere seicent' anni fa', *BSU*, xlii (1945), pp. 179–208; 'Boldrino da Panicale (1331?–91)', ibid. xlvi (1949), pp. 118–39; 'Il gran conestabile Alberico da Barbiano ed i Conti d'Urbino', *Stud. Romagn.*, iv (1953), pp. 19–36; 'La signoria di Antonio di Montefeltro Sesto Conte d'Urbino dagli inizi all'annessione di Gubbio', *AMSM*, 6th ser., i (1943), pp. 81–149; 'Gian Galeazzo Visconti arbitro di pace fra Montefeltro e Malatesti (1384–8)', *ASL*, n.s., iii (1938), pp. 291–325; 'Alcune lettere inedite del cardinale Galeotto da Pietramala', *Italia medioevale e umanistica*, vii (1964), pp. 375–404. G. Cecchini, 'Boldrino da Panicale', *BSU*, lix (1962), pp. 43–95, and V. Ansidei, 'La tregua del 21 marzo 1380 fra Galeotto Malatesta signore di Rimini e Antonio di Montefeltro conte d'Urbino', ibid. xxii (1916), pp. 19–40, may also be consulted.

[2] The article by P. Pieri in the *Dizionario Biografico degli Italiani* is the best commentary on his career. See also D. M. Bueno de Mesquita, 'Some Condottieri of the Trecento', *Proceedings of the British Academy*, xxxii (1946), pp. 224–5.

mala lords of the minuscule *signoria* of Citerna, in the Umbro-Tuscan Apennine.[1] The *signori* who had been expelled by Albornoz or his immediate successors had now returned; the Montefeltro were back in Urbino, and had the *signoria* of Gubbio in 1384; the Chiavelli of Fabriano, the Manfredi of Faenza, were again the acknowledged lords of their cities.

The lowest point reached by Urban VI was in the early spring of 1385 when his protégé Charles of Durazzo had turned against him and had sent Alberigo da Barbiano to besiege him at Nocera in the Abruzzi. The pope held 'neither consistory, nor audience, nor office of graces, nor chancery, nor penitentiary, nor issued any papal act'.[2] The papal bureaucracy had stopped. Not surprisingly, this was also the lowest moment of the Urbanist cause in the Roman area; Montefiascone and Civitavecchia fell to Clementine lords, and Simonetto Baglioni the papal rector of the Tuscan patrimony was captured and imprisoned at Marta on the lake of Bolsena.[3] In June 1385 two the of great Clementine magnates (Onorato Caetani and Giacomo Orsini) made a treaty in Marino, a few miles from Rome, one of whose objects was to guarantee Caetani the free use of the port of Astura. The condition of the Campagna-Maritime province was chaotic.[4]

Even without these political disasters the administration of Urban VI would have been weak, partly because of its lack of experienced personnel.[5] When Urban VI returned to the Roman area from Genoa after the murder of his enemy Francesco di Vico in 1387, the situation began to improve for the Urbanists, though slowly. Slight advantages gained for the Urbanists in the Tuscan patrimony by the Orsini Cardinal, Napoleone di Manopello, were nullified by Urban's squalid quarrel with him. Far more serious for Urban was the growing authority of Gian Galeazzo Visconti in Tuscany and the Papal State, which began to force Florence and her ally Bologna to swing towards Avignon, as a preliminary to a possible last appeal to France against Visconti aggression. In the summer of 1387 Florence concluded an understanding with the

---

[1] Cf. G. Franceschini, 'Alcuni documenti su la signoria di Galeotto Malatesta a Borgo San Sepolcro', *Stud. Romagn.*, ii (1951), pp. 39–56.

[2] Sienese letter quoted in Franceschini, *Italia medioevale e umanistica*, vii (1964), pp. 391–2.

[3] The vicar-general in temporals and spirituals was Cardinal Pileo da Prata; cf. P. Stacul, *Il Cardinale Pileo da Prata* (Rome, 1957), pp. 170 ff. Labande's book on Rinaldo Orsini is the best authority for the Tuscan patrimony at this period.

[4] Falco, *ASR*, xlix (1926), pp. 264 ff.; Caetani, *Regesta Chartarum*, iii, p. 106.

[5] Favier, *Finances Pontificales*, pp. 141 ff.; see also the qualifications made by A. Esch in his review of Favier's book, *Göttingische Gelehrte Anzeige*, 221 Jahrg. (1969), pp. 133–59.

Clementine leader Rinaldo Orsini.[1] In 1388 Bologna went even further by tentatively and secretly offering to submit to Clement VII.

Urban VI was irascible, bullying and incompetent; though no matter what his personality had been, the Roman obedience would have been hard put to weather the political storm, once the fact of the schism was accomplished. In Italian political terms, things began to look rather better for the Roman obedience after 1386. The murder of Charles of Durazzo in Hungary in February 1386 meant that the Neapolitan kingdom was no longer controlled by a prince ungrateful to Rome. With typical wilfulness, Urban VI after Charles's death refused to support the young Ladislas of Durazzo or the regency of Margherita, and persisted in a fantastic dream of military intervention on his own account in the papal vassal kingdom.[2] The pope rode out of Perugia with an army which was supposed to march south to the kingdom in August 1388, but the troops never even left Umbria. Urban's military strength rested on such petty *condottieri* that it was built on sand; he had been reduced to naming the Englishman John Beltoft, the leader of 200 lances, as 'Rector of the duchy of Spoleto'.[3] The projected attack on the kingdom was absurd not only in terms of Italian politics, but because it disregarded the continued threat of French intervention in southern Italy.

Urban summoned a 'parliament' of all the lands of the Papal State, to meet at Rome on 1 November 1388;[4] what came of the initiative is unclear. Urban's quelling a revolt of the communal officials, the *banderesi*, of Rome, in 1389, shows that he was not entirely powerless.[5] The Urbanists north of Rome turned to the offensive, and besieged the (now Clementine) Cardinal Pileo da Prata in Rinaldo Orsini's city of Orvieto, while Rinaldo himself was besieged in Spoleto.[6] In the march of Ancona the Urbanist rector (Cardinal Andrea Bontempi, a Perugian)

---

[1] Labande, *Rinaldo Orsini*, pp. 207–22. Labande refers to this as an alliance against the pope which on paper it was. But Florence never took part in hostilities against Urban. Cf. Mancarella, *ASPN*, n.s., v (1919), p. 139; and also *Florentine Studies*, pp. 382–5.

[2] For what follows see A. Cutolo, *Re Ladislao d'Angiò-Durazzo* (Milan, 1936). For Milanese policy D. N. Bueno de Mesquita, *Giangaleazzo Visconti Duke of Milan (1351–1402)* (Cambridge, 1941) is definitive.

[3] Labande, p. 206; cf. *Calendar of Entries in the Papal Registers relating to Great Britain and Ireland. Papal Letters*, iv (1902), pp. 265–9. Beltoft was the only mercenary leader to remain with Urban during the fiasco of the 'Neapolitan' expedition of 1388.

[4] P. Compagnoni, *La reggia Picena* (Macerata, 1661), pp. 253–4.

[5] Cf. A. Natale, 'La Felice Società dei Balestieri e dei Pavesati a Roma e il governo dei Banderesi dal 1358 al 1408', *ASR*, xlii (1939), pp. 1–176, at p. 95. This study is unsatisfactory because documented only from the archives of Rieti, apart from the obvious printed sources.

[6] Labande, pp. 245–6; Stacul, *Pileo da Prata*, p. 211.

headed a modest coalition of Urbanist communes, and Gentile da Varano the Lord of Camerino offered his submission.[1] The continued allegiance of Perugia and of the Malatesta, and the engagement of Ugolino Trinci, the Lord of Foligno, as an Urbanist *condottiere,* meant that in military terms the Papal State could continue to exist.

II

In the last two years of Urban VI the rivalry of Florence with Gian Galeazzo Visconti began to dominate the politics of central Italy. In the struggle the cities and *signori* of the Papal State were deeply involved. Perugia, though beginning under Florentine influence, began at this time to swing towards the Visconti. Bologna like Perugia was at this time finding genuine independence impossible; her resources were too small, and her tradition of communal independence was too inter-rupted. The Bolognese turned in despair to France, raising the fleur-de-lys and offering to pay *census* to the French crown in return for protection.[2] Menaced by the Este of Ferrara, threatened by Visconti subversion, opposed by the feudatories of the Bolognese Apennine and the Romagnol *signori* like the Manfredi, the Bolognese were not enjoying their inde-pendence. Visconti influence penetrated far south in the Papal State, as it had done for much of the century. Carlo Malatesta, the most loyal Urbanist of all the Romagnol lords, was involved with the Montefeltro in the Visconti system of alliances.

On 15 October 1389 Urban VI died in Rome. He was succeeded (for there was no question of the Roman cardinals abandoning their claims to legitimacy against Avignon) by another Neapolitan subject, Piero Tomacelli, who took the name of Boniface IX. The Roman obedience was now in the hands of a man who, while no genius, knew better how to make sense of Italian politics than his choleric and blundering predecessor. The Florentine-Visconti war was about to break out; the final attempt at a negotiated settlement reached a lame and ineffective conclusion only a fortnight before Urban's death.[3] In

---

[1] Cf. G. Cecchini, in *BSU*, lix (1962), pp. 62–5; Theiner, *C.D.*, ii, no. 648; Compagnoni, loc. cit.

[2] Cf. L. Mirot, *La politique française en Italie de 1380 à 1422. I. Les préliminaires de l'alliance Florentine* (Paris, 1934), p. 19; de Boüard, *Les origines,* pp. 96 ff.; for Bologna and Clement VII, see Stacul, *Pileo de Prata,* pp. 203–4. Cf. also F. Bosdari, 'Il comune di Bologna alla fine del secolo XIV', *AMDR*, 4th ser., iv (1914), pp. 123–88, though with little satisfactory reference to these events.

[3] Cf. de Mesquita, pp. 107–11, 332–3.

the spring of 1390 war was declared, involving Bologna and a large number of papal feudatories. What probably to Urban would have been merely the occasion for further confusion, was to the new pope the opportunity to assert himself, and to make modest political gains at the expense of the combatants. It was the more important that he should do this, in that once more in France there was serious talk of a big Italian expedition.

Three firm temporal power policies characterised the pontificate of Boniface IX: the support of Ladislas of Durazzo in the kingdom, the clever use of the favourable position given to the Roman pope by the Visconti-Florentine rivalry, and the ruthless exploitation of the temporal rights and revenues of the Holy See.[1] Boniface's brother Andrea Tomacelli was made rector of the march of Ancona, where he proceeded with vigour and ability. Liberal use was made of the legal device of the 'apostolic vicariate', which was conceded to communes such as Ascoli Piceno or Fermo, and to the petty tyrants: Trinci of Foligno, Varano at Tolentino, Chiavelli of Fabriano, Montefeltro of Urbino and Gubbio, and so on. Particularly important were the Malatesta of Rimini, who were conceded the vicariate there and elsewhere for two generations, instead of for the usual term of years.[2] Separate concessions were made to the Malatesta of Pesaro. Such were the rewards of the long fidelity of the Malatesta to the Roman obedience; Boniface also made it his business to reconcile them with the Montefeltro, thus supplanting Gian Galeazzo Visconti in the function which the Lord of Milan had formerly fulfilled. In dealing with inconvenient mercenaries, Andrea Tomacelli showed the same resourcefulness demonstrated by Cesare Borgia a century later. The mercenary commander, Boldrino da Panicale, was bidden by Tomacelli to a feast in Macerata in 1391, and murdered.

The pacification of Umbria and the Tuscan patrimony was a long and hard business, as might have been expected. The Roman commune was still so strong that it had to be treated as an ally rather than a sub-

---

[1] Arnold Esch, *Bonifaz IX. und der Kirchenstaat* (Tübingen, 1969). M. Jansen, *Papst Bonifatius IX. und seine Beziehungen zur deutschen Kirche* (1904) is now out of date. For Boniface's finances in the Papal State see Favier, *Les finances pontificales*, pp. 181–94, 399–404, 432–50, and Esch's remarks in *Göttingische G.A.*, quoted above.

[2] Cf. Jones, *EHR*, 1952, p. 330. Esch, *Bonifaz IX. u.d. Kirchenstaat*, pp. 594–5. For the Malatesta and Montefeltro see Theiner, *C.D.*, iii, no. 17, and L. Tonini, *Rimini nella signoria de' Malatesti, Appendice di Documenti al vol. iv.* pp. 397–406.

ordinate.[1] The main gains were incidental. On 14 April 1390 Rinaldo Orsini was murdered in Aquila, and Spoleto and Orvieto returned, as a result, to the Roman obedience. The Bretons and the prefect's nephew, Giovanni Sciarri, continued to hold Viterbo; Cardinal Pileo da Prata changed sides for the third time, and became the papal legate in Umbria. Perugia was disillusioned and alarmed at the perils she had undergone during the Florentine-Visconti war, especially from the Raspanti exiles. So in May of 1392 Pileo da Prata entered Perugia, and shortly afterwards Assisi. Perugia agreed to submit to the pope and to give him complete control of communal revenues, on the understanding that he would transfer the papal *curia* to the city. On 17 October 1392 Boniface entered Perugia. The exiled Raspanti, or many of them, were recalled, and an even more complete submission made by the city in November.[2] But the strains involved in the reconciliation between the Baglioni and the exiles were too great, in spite of the benevolent mediation of Florence. Though a further sentence of arbitration between the Perugian parties was given in May 1393, a Raspanti rising occasioned the flight of Boniface from Perugia on 30 July 1393. Shortly afterwards the city fell under the *signoria* of the most powerful of the exiles, the mercenary soldier Biordo dei Michelotti.

The recovery of papal power was not, in fact, so easy. The seizure of Todi by Malatesta dei Malatesti was only settled by its concession to him in vicariate in August 1392; the extension of the Malatesta dominions into Umbria was thus consolidated. The 'submission' of Giovanni Sciarra in Viterbo in 1393 was only feigned, though some other places in the Tuscan patrimony were recovered from him and from the Bretons. In the march there was a widespread rising under Gentile da Varano of Camerino, Guido Chiavelli of Fabriano and many others, which led to the capture of the pope's brother, Andrea Tomacelli, by the rebels. To ransom him, concessions had to be made to Biordo dei Michelotti and other *signorotti* (April 1394). Only by capitulation, it seemed, could the pope win.

The danger from the French court was far from over. At the end of 1392 the old pupil of Albornoz, Niccolò Spinelli, now an adviser at the Visconti court, was in Paris as agent for Gian Galeazzo to propose a new French invasion of Italy under Gian Galeazzo's son-in-law, Louis of Orleans. The project of a 'kingdom of Adria', in effect the partition of

[1] Stacul, *Pileo da Prata*, pp. 222 ff.
[2] Theiner, *C.D.*, iii, nos. 20, 23; Stacul, loc. cit.; H. M. Goldbrunner, 'Die Übergabe Perugias an Giangaleazzo Visconti (1400)', *Quellen*, xlii–xliii (1963), pp. 285–369.

the Papal State, giving most of it to Louis of Orleans, was revived. It was an idea with a long history, going back to the projects of Pierre Dubois at the end of the thirteenth century. Spinelli in its defence wrote a long, bitter and eloquent memorial, which is in effect a polemic history of the papal temporal power in the fourteenth century, composed by the disillusioned disciple of Albornoz. As a man who had made his career in the temporal power, the papal administration,[1] and the Angevin kingdom, and had seen all three of these slide into ruin, Spinelli had become a prophet of doom for the temporal power. The drift of his argument is best summed up in the popular proverb which he quotes: *'la glesia de Roma voli botti e denari* (the Church of Rome wants kicks and pence).[2] Clerical taxes were misused.

Spinelli was pleading for Gian Galeazzo; the Visconti demand in these negotiations was for an unspecified papal city after the French conquest was complete – the city was clearly to be Bologna.[3] Spinelli had also to show that the Papal State would be easy to conquer. To do this he wrote a brief description of the Papal State[4] which shows clearly how powerful Gian Galeazzo was among the *signori* of the Papal State, even after the relatively unsuccessful conclusion of his war with Florence.

The problem of finance was at the heart of the difficulties of the Roman obedience. It may, in the end, have sharpened papal fiscality in the Papal State that the Avignonese obedience commanded more of the 'spiritual' revenues, while the Roman sphere commanded more of the temporalities. It was certainly a time of financial improvisation and expedients for the Roman papacy.[5] The Roman churches were subjected to heavy and extraordinary *collectae* under all three of the Roman popes, and were also frequently compelled to alienate their lands.[6] To

---

[1] Durrieu, 'Le royaume d'Adria', *Revue des Questions historiques*, xxviii (1880), cited above. Spinelli's memorial was printed by Durrieu with the offprint of his article (but not in the *Revue*) and re-edited by G. Romano in his book, *Niccolò Spinelli*, pp. 611–20 (but not in his articles in *ASPN* on which the book was based.) I give these details to spare others the tedium I have experienced with this document.

[2] For his activity as *advocatus fisci* in the papal *curia* in 1366–7 see Opitz, *Quellen*, xxxiii (1944), pp. 185–6, 190n.

[3] Mirot, *La politique française*, pp. 23, 49–54. The demand was made in March 1391.

[4] Spinelli's description (which is to be distinguished from the memorial referred to above) has been re-edited by Esch, *Bonifaz IX. u.d. Kirchenstaat*, pp. 639–44.

[5] Cf. Favier, pp. 432, 637 ff.; Esch, 'Bankiers der Kirche im grossen Schisma', *Quellen*, xlv (1966), pp. 277–398.

[6] Cf. P. Fidele, 'S. Maria in Monastero', *ASR*, xxix (1906), pp. 221, 224; L. Cavazzi, *La Diaconia di S. Maria in Via Lata e il monastero di S. Ciriaco* (Rome, 1908), pp. 359–60; J. Guiraud, *L'Etat Pontifical après le Grand Schisme* (Paris, 1896), pp. 40–44, (for 'Civita Vecchia' on p. 44,

meet the pressing needs of *condottieri* many if not most of the proceeds of the *tallia* and also of the *census* from apostolic vicariates were assigned to particular mercenaries. Very often the mercenaries were allowed to collect the assignment themselves from the town concerned, which gave rise to obvious abuses.[1]

The war in the kingdom and the Papal State was closely influenced by the ecclesiastical politics of the schism. The expedition of the Duke of Orleans to Italy was put off as a result of the death of Clement VII (16 September 1394). Then in the summer of the following year French opinion began to turn towards the way of the withdrawal of obedience from the Avignonese pope (Benedict XIII). The assumption of French sovereignty over Genoa took place, but the project of the 'kingdom of Adria' was quietly dropped. Other imperialist ambitions were now replacing this in the minds of the French princes, who were now ready to turn against their relative-by-marriage, Gian Galeazzo Visconti, and to contemplate the partition of his states. In September 1396 the Franco-Florentine alliance was signed in Paris. French support for the struggling armies of Louis of Anjou in the kingdom of Naples was sharply reduced, and the eventual victory of Ladislas of Durazzo in the kingdom assured.

All this was gain for Boniface IX. For the first time the prospect of a military victory in the kingdom and in papal Campagna became dimly visible. Boniface's part was that of mediator rather than conqueror. He had already mediated in the first Visconti-Florentine settlement of 1392. Bologna had returned to his obedience, though the terms gave the papacy no more than an annual *census,* and Bologna was more under Florentine control than papal. Boniface made grants of the apostolic vicariate to the Polentani of Ravenna and the Alidosi of Imola,[2] but his influence in Romagna was small; he was willing to grant the Florentines, for a loan of 18,000 florins, the strongpoint of Castrocaro near Forli.[3] A similar pledge of the ancient papal fortress of Bertinoro was made to Carlo Malatesta in return for a loan.

Civitella di San Paolo should be understood). Cf. Esch, *Bonifaz IX u.d. Kirchenstaat*, pp. 81, 226–7.

[1] e.g. Boldrino da Panicale collecting the *tallia* from Macerata in 1391, Compagnoni, *La Reggia Picena*, p. 256. For the practice, Favier loc. cit. and also Partner, *Papal State*, pp. 22–3; Esch, pp. 309–10.

[2] The town of Imola was granted to the Alidosi, but the *comitatus,* the country district, to Bologna. Theiner, *C.D.*, iii, nos. 22, 25.

[3] Castrocaro is not itself a port, as I seem, unfortunately, to imply in *Florentine Studies*, p. 385. Cf. also de Mesquita, pp. 194–5, who points out the quarrel this grant occasioned between Florence and Bologna.

The position of Boniface in Rome had been rather firmer since he had returned there from Perugia in 1393.[1] Though tension with the Roman commune continued, and there were Clementine plots in the City and the Tuscan patrimony, these failed. By 1396 Onorato Caetani, the arch-enemy of the Roman obedience, was held in check, and Boniface began to re-conquer the papal castles of Campagna.[2] The Colonna family, whose political importance had not been great for many years, rebelled, together with the Savelli, in 1394, but in 1397 they made truces. In the summer of 1398 there was a final attempt by Onorato Caetani and the Colonna to unite the opposition to Boniface inside and outside Rome. The attempt failed, and it marked the final collapse of the communal *banderesi* and the autonomous communal government in Rome, as well as the failure of Onorato. In 1399 Boniface and Ladislas opened a campaign against the Caetani and the Colonna which at last met with military success. Anagni, Veroli, Sezze, Piperno fell to the papal troops under Andrea Tomacelli, as did the Orsini strongholds in the Alban hills. Giovanni Sciarra of Viterbo also at last found himself compelled, after fighting and making and breaking truces for many years, to edge towards a genuine submission. The Gascon and Breton mercenaries no longer dominated the Tuscan patrimony as they had done. In 1401, with the death of Onorato Caetani and the submission of the Colonna, the travailed Tuscan patrimony and Campagna found themselves, for the first time since the beginning of the schism, in a condition which resembled peace.

Though contemporaries were impressed by the success of Boniface IX in the government of the temporal power,[3] they were making comparisons with the chaotic conditions which obtained earlier in the schism, and not with papal rule in the late Avignonese period. Papal direct government in the Romagna collapsed, after 1378, for a century and more. Papal taxation in the Romagna had fallen almost to zero, if the financial bargains with the Romagnol tyrants are discounted. In the revolutions of the great city of Bologna the pope was virtually powerless. In May 1398 the *coup* of the Zambeccari faction against the Gozzadini showed how delicate was the factional balance in Bologna. The gradual break-up of the communal regime was leading imperceptibly not towards

---

[1] Theiner, *C.D.*, iii, no. 30; see the important chapter in Esch, pp. 209–76.

[2] Falco, *ASR*, xlix (1926), pp. 278 ff.

[3] Cf. Partner, *Papal State*, p. 16; Stacul, *Pileo da Prata*, p. 255n. My interpretation of Boniface IX's order that all officials in the temporal power should be appointed by him is wrong (ibid.). Boniface was merely trying, in the face of communal and seigniorial opposition, to preserve traditional papal rights. His main interest was probably in the sale of offices.

papal or even Florentine dominance in Bologna, but to the victory of Gian Galeazzo Visconti.[1]

The same impotence was shown by the Church in Umbria. After the Perugian revolution of 1393 Biordo Michelotti became the virtual *signore* of the city.[2] Michelotti had already terrorised the march; he now became ruler of a substantial part of Umbria. Giovanni Tomacelli (the pope's brother) and the Orsini Cardinal of Manopello having failed to pacify the factions in Orvieto, these now called on Michelotti. Malatesta power was no longer able to maintain itself in its advanced bastions in Todi and Orte, and the Malatesta withdrew in the summer of 1395. Biordo Michelotti in consequence became *signore* of Todi and Orvieto, then of Assisi, Nocera, Spello and other strongpoints in the Umbrian Apennine. Though the ruler of these places, he continued to think of himself as primarily a *condottiere* offering his sword to the Italian powers. He set the pattern for a new variety of *signoria* in central Italy, not so securely based on feudal power and influence as that of the Romagnol tyrants, and tied in much more closely with the conventions of mercenary warfare. His power was formidable; the Trinci of Foligno and the other mercenaries of the papal government (which he called 'the Neapolitan pastors') were unable to cope with him. In the spring of 1396 Boniface IX recognised Michelotti as 'vicar in temporals' in Todi, Orvieto and other places, for the price of an annual *census* which was no doubt wiped out by the money due from the pope for a *condotta* of 500 lances which he purported to hold from Boniface.

In 1397–8 a great effort was made to finish with the Breton troops in the Tuscan patrimony. To raise money from England, Boniface's principal source of income, John Holland, Earl of Huntingdon, was given faculties to collect a tenth, which he was supposed to use in order to lead a crusade against the Bretons. Military operations against them did meet with some success.

Michelotti made an error in deserting the Milanese *condotta* for a Florentine one in 1397, and by the summer he was diplomatically isolated. In September Boniface IX launched Pandolfo Malatesta and the rest of the papal *condottieri* against him. The war was the usual one of investments of hillside castles round Orvieto and Todi; no doubt

---

[1] De Mesquita, p. 243; cf. F. Bosdari, 'Giovanni I Bentivoglio signore di Bologna (1401–2)', *AMDR*, 4th ser., v (1915), pp. 199–307.

[2] Cf. G. Franceschini, 'Biordo Michelotti e la dedizione di Perugia al duca di Milano', *BSU*, xlv (1948), pp. 92–133. Franceschini does not deal with Michelotti's legal position in Perugia, nor does Goldbrunner in *Quellen*, xlii–xliii, 1963. In May 1394 Michelotti referred to the priors as 'li miei signori di Perogia' (Franceschini, p. 117).

Michelotti would have survived, had he not become the victim of a treacherous murder engineered (10 March 1398) by the Abbot of S. Pietro of Perugia – that the head of one of the most venerated monasteries in Italy should have been responsible for the crime shows where church discipline was tending.

The collapse of the *signoria* of Biordo Michelotti should have given Boniface IX direct control of all papal Umbria, but it failed to do so because Boniface was so weak. The revived communal government of Perugia was too feeble to survive.[1] The far from disinterested mediation of Florence led to a settlement of a sort with Boniface IX, which was sketched out in the summer of 1398, but not completed until the spring of 1399. The inability of the papal *curia* to control its own *condottieri* meant that the commune had to to try make separate bargains with Broglia di Trino and the mercenaries who went on devastating the Perugian countryside, paying no attention to the negotiations of Rome.

It seemed in the end to the Perugians – as it seemed to many other Italians at this time – that security and stability could be best purchased by submission to the great Milanese *signoria* of Gian Galeazzo Visconti. His influence reached deep into the Papal State; Antonio di Montefeltro was his pensioner and councillor, and Carlo Malatesta and many others of the Romagnol *signori,* after the end of the Mantuan war in 1398, were looking to Milan rather than to Florence. Divided and financially exhausted, still harassed in the countryside by the exiles and the papal mercenaries, Perugia was by late 1399 at the end of its tether. The neighbouring state of Siena had for some time been a virtual Milanese protectorate, and had just formally submitted to Gian Galeazzo. The Florentines were working feverishly for a great league of north and south Italy against Milan, but their diplomats were still talking. On 20 January 1400 Perugia gave itself formerly to the Duke of Milan. Florentine humanists shortly before the final submission had written a fine exhortation to the Perugians to resist the Milanese tyrant; in their reply the Perugians did not fail to mention the 'tyranny' of Boniface IX, who had subdued Assisi and Todi and the surrounding places. The issue was as much a defeat for Boniface IX as for Florence, although the payment of an annual *census* of 5,000 florins by Perugia to the pope was reserved by the Milanese in the treaty.

Though Boniface IX did not concede Gian Galeazzo Visconti the vicariate of Perugia, he tacitly allowed him to hold the city. The Floren-

[1] Goldbrunner, article cited above.

tine project of a league with Boniface and Ladislas came to nothing. And Bologna, the second great city of the Papal State, began to go the way of Perugia. The Florentines thought that the state of Boniface IX was 'not worth a chestnut', and it looked as though they were right. The Zambeccari *coup* against the other Milanese faction, the Gozzadini, in May of 1398, left the factions still at one another's throats. The murder of Giovanni da Barbiano by the Bolognese in September 1399 brought his brother Alberigo, who was both constable of the kingdom and the mercenary of Gian Galeazzo, to Bologna to avenge it. After a further change of regime in Bologna, Alberigo and his Milanese troops stayed in the Bolognese countryside to help the commune fight Astorre Manfredi.[1]

The factional strife in Bologna showed no sign of stopping, and Milanese interests in the city grew. In March 1401 Giovanni Bentivoglio, leader of one of the Bolognese groups, recalled the Zambeccari and made himself *signore* of Bologna. Bentivoglio after some hesitation plumped for the Florentine alliance against Milan; the choice turned out to be mistaken. A formidable group of Milanese *condottieri* – da Barbiano, Gonzaga, Malatesta – began to operate against Bologna, while the Milanese engineers tried to divert the waters of the Brenta from the Bolognese. On 26 June 1402 Bentivoglio and his Florentine allies fought a pitched battle at Casalecchio outside Bologna, the allied commander being the Gascon Bernadon de Serres. The Milanese troops won a complete victory, which was treated as a victory of Italian over non-Italian commanders. The Bentivoglio regime in Bologna immediately collapsed, and the city offered itself to the Duke of Milan. The situation of the early 1350s was now renewed in an even more unfavourable form; Bologna was in the hands of the Visconti again, and so also was the second great papal city, Perugia. It might be argued that Bologna was in any case already lost to Boniface, and it can certainly be argued that Boniface, unlike Clement VI, refused to concede Bologna in vicariate to the Visconti.[2] But both Florence and the papacy were saved from worse at Gian Galeazzo's hands by his death on 3 September 1402. The Papal State and the cities of the Guelph alliance were reprieved.

---

[1] Bueno de Mesquita, pp. 242–3; Franceschini, in *Stud. Romagn.*, iv (1953).
[2] Bueno de Mesquita, pp. 282–3.

III

The peripheral conquests of Gian Galeazzo Visconti all broke away from Milanese rule after his death. From this disintegration Boniface IX was a main beneficiary. The initial papal attack on Perugia in 1402 by Giovanni Tomacelli was a failure. But the able papal legate in Romagna, Baldassare Cossa, by skilful manipulation of the Bolognese factions introduced the direct rule of the Church into Bologna once more. Perugia (20 November 1403) and Assisi returned to papal rule. Ladislas of Naples was busy in preparing an expedition against Hungary; the rest of Italy was lapping up what fragments it could of the Milanese pickings. It was at this point, at the very end of his pontificate, that Boniface IX was most powerful.

The balance of Boniface's pontificate can in political terms be called favourable, and the confusion of the time has been by some exaggerated.[1] What remained as acute at Boniface's death as at any time earlier in the schism was the alarming political dependence of the Holy See on the *condottieri* it employed. The financial results of this dependence were onerous both for the papacy and for its subjects. It was perhaps less serious that the *census* of many holders of apostolic vicariates was after 1401 assigned to the *condottiere* Paolo Orsini,[2] since these *signori* were themselves most of them Paolo's own kind, and the pope would be lucky in any case to see their money. More painful for the pope's subjects were the widespread assignments of *tallia* and other dues from the provincials to the mercenaries.[3] The pope found it difficult to keep satisfactory mercenaries in his service, since he could only pay a sum amounting to three florins a lance less than that paid by the Florentines and the Visconti.[4] The consequences of this weakness, in terms of bad discipline, military ineffectiveness, and domination by mercenaries over areas where the *tallia* were assigned to them, are easy to imagine.

Church property suffered severely during the schism, both in alienations to laymen and in the method by which it was administered. The

---

[1] Notably by Guiraud, *L'Etat Pontifical*. His distinguished and pioneering book suffers from that which its geographical approach makes inevitable; the lack of a coherent political narrative. For example, he refers (pp. 35–6) to the *signoria* of the mercenary Broglia di Trino in Assisi in 1398, but does not mention that Milanese rule followed there in 1400, and direct papal rule again in 1403, nor the concession to Montefeltro in 1408. Cf. Esch, p. 432.

[2] Favier, *Finances Pontificales*, pp. 436–7. Cf. Esch, *Göttingische Gelehrte Anzeigen* (1969), p. 136.

[3] Favier, loc. cit. and also pp. 638–9; cf. Cutolo, *Ladislao*, ii, p. 138.

[4] Esch, *Gött. Gelehr. Anz.*, p. 155.

great Roman monasteries and churches – S. Paolo fuori le Mura, S. Lorenzo fuori le Mura, S. Spirito, S. Anastasio alle Tre Fontane – alienated numerous lands to Roman nobles.[1] The monasteries of the Papal State were being gradually stripped of their possessions, very often by the local seigniorial families, and sometimes with papal assistance through the expedient of placing them *in commendam,* i.e. to be administered by an ecclesiastic who was not abbot of the community. Great monasteries such as S. Vittore delle Chiuse sul Sentino, in the march, were in ruins and were being suppressed; S. Maria di Pomposa was absorbed by the Este.[2] In the Roman area, Farfa and Subiaco were in decline;[3] the abbey of Sassovivo in Umbria was governed by a Trinci abbot.[4]

The most interesting of Boniface IX's concessions to laymen was a bull which allowed the free alienation of the lands of the Church of Ferrara held by laymen, whether the leases were made out in emphyteusis or *per libellum,* and deprived the clerical owners of their right to exact the return of their lands if the pact of investiture expired.[5] The value attached to this grant can be guessed from its being inscribed in gold letters on the tomb of Alberto d'Este. If this was held such an important concession, the rights of clerical landowners cannot by any means have fallen into utter disuse. The erosion of church property in central Italy was a continuous process which went far back in the history of the later Middle Ages – one thinks for example of the complete disintegration of the great episcopal exempt area of Fermo in the marches, which had been one of the main landowning phenomena of the early thirteenth century in the area, and by the mid-fourteenth had broken up into a

---

[1] Guiraud, pp. 40–6. Cf. the accusations brought by Cardinal Orsini against John XXIII, Finke, *Acta Concilii Constanciensis,* iv, pp. 789 ff.

[2] S. Vittore had been in the possession of the Chiavelli family; it was ruined by war and in 1406 was incorporated in the Olivetan monastery of S. Caterina di Fabriano. Sassi, *AMSM,* 5th ser., v (1942), pp. 176, 186; cf. also Sassi's introduction to *Le carte del monastero di S. Vittore delle Chiuse sul Sentino* (Milan, 1962); G. Colucci, *Antichità Picene* (Fermo, 1786–96), ii, pp. 249–52. In the Roman area the great monastery of S. Paolo fuori le Mura was near bankruptcy at this period (I. Schuster, *La Basilica e il Monastero di S. Paolo fuori le Mura,* pp. 173–82). For the absorption of S. Maria di Pomposa into the Este *signoria* at this time, see A. Ostoja, 'Vicende della commenda pomposiana in relazione al piano di assorbimento della signoria estense', *Analecta Pomposiana* (1965), pp. 195–215.

[3] Cf. I. Schuster, *L'imperiale abbazia di Farfa,* pp. 347 ff.; Egidi and Frederici, *I monasteri di Subiaco,* i, pp. 141 ff.

[4] Cf. M. V. Prospero Valente, 'Corrado Trinci', *BSU,* lv (1958), pp. 104n., 110.

[5] Usually dated 13 February 1392, *Statuta Urbis Ferrariae nuper reformata* (Ferrara, 1567), lib. ii, c. 127, folios 102–4. The date is corrected by Esch (p. 560n.) to 4 March 1391. Cf. also A. Lazzari, 'Il signor di Ferrara ai tempi del concilio del 1438–9', *Rinascita,* ii (1939), p. 676.

tissue of small communes and *signorie*.[1] Similar piecemeal, but no means complete encroachment, had been taking place for the benefit of the seigniorial families of the Roman area. It is doubtful if the schism played a decisive part in this long process, but it cannot have been without effect.

The nepotism shown by Boniface IX as the instrument of his temporal power policy was typical of his time, and is difficult to blame.[2] It can be paralleled at almost any point in medieval papal history by similar expedients of other popes, and the choice before Boniface was not between making such grants or refraining, but between making them to other *signori* or mercenaries, or to members of his own family. Being a minor family extraneous to the Papal State, it never succeeded in establishing itself there, and the Tomacelli were not added to the long list of Papal State families which owed their origin to a papal relative. Only Marino Tomacelli had a modest career before him as a papal governor, after Boniface's death.

Boniface died on 1 October 1404. He was succeeded by another Neapolitan, Cosimo Migliorati (Innocent VII).[3] The impatience of Latin Christian Europe with the failure of the rival popes to solve the schism was now increasingly to weaken their political effectiveness. Ladislas of Naples had now overcome all serious Angevin resistance in the kingdom, and was beginning to look north of its borders to an area where his military power could make itself felt. The Roman papacy was now to be made to feel far more dependent on its Neapolitan protectors; it was a situation in some ways comparable with the protectorate of Charles of Anjou over the popes after 1266, but with the added disadvantage for the popes that their legitimacy was challenged by the Avignonese obedience. Ladislas clearly could not accept a French solution of the schism, since this would mean the resurrection of the Angevin claim to his kingdom. In his smothering embraces the Roman papacy was to come near to death.

From Innocent VII's accession there was a noticeable difference between the firm temporal power policy carried out for the Church by Baldassare Cossa the legate in Bologna, and the weakness of the Neapolitan-dominated regime in Rome. Cossa was the ally of the Florentine

---

[1] Cf. Waley, *P.S.*, p. 69n.; D. Pacini, *Il codice 1030 dell' Archivio Diplomatico di Fermo* (Milan, 1963).
[2] Cf. Esch, *Bonifaz IX. u.d. Kirchenstaat*, pp. 12 ff., 575–81.
[3] A narrative of the political history from this point is to be found in Partner, *Papal State*, pp. 17 ff.

bankers[1] and of the Este of Ferrara, implicated in the struggle against the Terzi of Parma and the constable of the kingdom, Alberigo da Barbiano, in Romagna. He recovered Faenza and Forlì for the Church, and thereafter added the profits of their rule to those he drew from Bologna.[2] It was a modest beginning of a recovery of papal power in Romagna.

In the rest of the Papal State the short pontificate of Innocent VII saw a rapid deterioration of papal power. Innocent was elected under the protection of Ladislas's army; thereafter he found himself only able to react against the bullying of the Neapolitan king by relying more and more heavily on the Roman lords, and especially on the formidable Paolo Orsini, who had already in the last few months of Boniface IX became the most lavishly subsidised of all the papal *condottieri*. Like the Angevins and the Normans before them Ladislas wanted an effective protectorate over the papal provinces of Campagna and Marittima. Innocent's attempts to resist this pressure and to stand out against Roman claims for autonomy culminated in a bloody *coup d'état* carried out by his nephew, Ludovico Migliorati, against the Neapolitan-influenced popular government of Rome (6 August 1405).[3] At this point the number of papal troops under arms reached their maximum: about three or four thousand horse and a thousand foot, among which the most important contingents were those of Paolo Orsini.[4] With this force Innocent was able to re-enter Rome, and to negotiate peace with Ladislas in the following summer. It was a humiliating peace, by which the rebellious Roman nobles in Neapolitan service went unpunished, and Ladislas was given the right to appoint papal officials in the Campagna-Maritime. In return he promised a loan of 20,000 florins.[5]

Innocent VII died on 6 November 1406. His successor, the Venetian Angelo Correr (Gregory XII), was in an even weaker position from an ecclesiastical point of view. From the time of his decision in 1407 to go to Savona to meet Benedict XIII, Gregory seems to have made up his mind that the temporal power was not worth defending. Rome was as insecure as ever, menaced by the Colonna and the party of Roman

---

[1] Cf. G. Holmes, 'How the Medici became the Pope's bankers', *Florentine Studies*, pp. 357–80, at 362–3.

[2] Cf. G. Orlandelli, 'Le finanze della comunità di Forlì sotto il vicariato di Baldassare Cossa', *Stud. Romagn.*, viii (1956), pp. 183–92.

[3] Cf. P. Brand, 'Innocenzo VII e il delitto di suo nipote Ludovico Migliorati', *SDSD*, xxi (1900), pp. 179–215.

[4] Cf. Favier, *Finances Pontificales*, pp. 641–2.

[5] See below.

nobles which had given so much trouble under Innocent. Innocent's nephew, the former rector of the march, Ludovico Migliorati, had made himself *signore* of Fermo, and tyrannised over much of the march. The French government had made an understanding with the Orsini. Gregory's first reaction was to prepare to grant very large parts of the Papal State to his own brother and nephews in fee. Though in 1407 Gregory was still strong enough to protest against the encroachments of Ladislas in the Papal State, by the following year he was no longer in a position to do so.

In the spring of 1408, while Gregory XII was still in Tuscany, Ladislas proceeded to occupy Rome and a very large part of the Papal State. In June he accepted the *signoria* of Perugia, to the great alarm of Florence. Most of the Papal State, with the exception of Romagna, was now occupied by Neapolitan troops or by nobles who were dependents (*raccomandati*) of Ladislas. That this was done with Gregory's consent seems hardly disputable.[1] Guidantonio di Montefeltro, the key *signore* among the Umbrian lords who adhered to Ladislas, was granted Assisi by the pope in August 1408. Gregory in the autumn sent his nephew to Naples, and probably made a formal concession of most of the Papal State to Ladislas, in return for the pathetically small consideration of 20,000 florins.[2]

But while Gregory XII was willing to grant away the patrimony of the Church – as the Avignonese popes had been to the French princes – the dour Baldassare Cossa, the legate in Bologna, was made of sterner stuff. Gregory's cardinals had deserted him in May of 1408 and fled to Pisa, where in the summer they announced the holding of a council in the following year to end the schism. Cossa immediately adhered to the council, whose pro-Florentine policy was closely aligned with his own. The spring campaigning season of 1409 saw a fierce war in Umbria, southern Tuscany and the Romagna, between the Neapolitan and Florentine-conciliar forces. In the march of Ancona Ludovico Migliorati adhered to the council, which had the curious effect that when Gregory XII fled for protection to Carlo Malatesta of Rimini at the same time (end of 1408), he found himself geographically isolated, with hostile forces in control of most of Romagna to the north and most of the march to the south.

---

[1] Cf. Partner, *Papal State*, pp. 40–1; Franceschini, *BSU*, xlix (1952), pp. 115 ff. is also relevant.
[2] For the payment of this sum, which is mentioned in most of the literary sources, see Favier, *Finances pontificales*, pp. 433, 639 (December, 1408). It may be that this was the payment of the loan which Ladislas had promised to Innocent VII on 16 August 1406 (Partner, p. 18n.). If this is so, it cannot really be considered a bribe (cf. Partner, pp. 40–1).

The Council of Pisa, in which the legists of Bologna took a prominent part, 'deposed' Gregory XII and the pope of the Avignonese line, Benedict XIII, on 5 June 1409, and elected a new pope, the Cretan Alexander V, three weeks later. The election of this third pope opened the way to renewed Angevin intervention in Italy. At the same time that Alexander was elected, the Florentines signed agreements for the expedition of Louis II of Anjou to Italy, in combination with the papal legate Baldassare Cossa. Within a few weeks Louis was in Tuscany. In September he met Baldassare Cossa, and the allied armies assembled for the campaign against Ladislas.[1] One of the most prominent *condottieri* in the Florentine-Angevin army was the Perugian exile, Braccio da Montone, who was destined to make a great career at the expense of the temporal power. But more important at this time was the treason of Paolo Orsini, who abandoned Ladislas for the enemy.

What followed showed how fragile was the power of Ladislas, which rested on the shifting sands of Neapolitan feudalism, and lacked the immensely firm social and economic basis of the Visconti *signoria*.[2] Perugia and a few Roman magnates held out for Ladislas, but many towns in Umbria and the Roman District were cleared of his troops. Rome itself fell to the Angevin league in the New Year of 1410. But Angevin power was no more soundly based than that of the house of Durazzo. Louis II returned to France in the New Year of 1410 to raise more troops, and a large relief army embarked from Marseilles in May. On 16 May the Genoese galleys intercepted the convoy and destroyed it. It would have been hard to forecast that when these ships went to the bottom, they represented the last major army to set out from France to southern Italy for over three-quarters of a century.

On 3 May 1410 Alexander V died. On 17 May the Pisan cardinals made the obvious choice of Baldassare Cossa, the legate of Bologna, who had been the main promoter of the temporal security of the Pisan obedience since its beginning. As John XXIII he was eventually covered, at the Council of Constance, by an obloquy for which there seems to be little basis in fact. Able, energetic, worldly, he was a typical pope of his time, hardly to be distinguished from those who went before or those who followed. The charges of moral depravity brought against him in 1415 at the Council of Constance were circumstantial, but may still have been fabricated.

The hesitant hither-and-thither of Italian politics at this time

---

[1] Partner, *Papal State*, pp. 20–2; de Boüard, *Origines des guerres d'Italie*, pp. 366 ff.
[2] Cf. the remarks of Franceschini, *BSU*, xlix (1952), pp. 123–4, 144–5.

represents the policies of regimes which were war-weary and lacking direction. Florence was uncertain of the degree to which she wanted to oppose Ladislas; Ladislas was uncertain how far his own military imperialism could get in central Italy. Louis II was clearly most unsure of his ground; after the important victory won by his forces at Rocca-secca on 19 May 1411 his reaction was not to thrust his army deep into the kingdom, but to retreat to Rome and from there to embark for Provence. No doubt he saw that like the other principals in the conflict he was hardly more than the tool of the mercenary bosses.

This shifting terrain was the kind of ground on which John XXIII could move with some hope of survival. He was dealt a hard blow when at the same time as the battle of Roccasecca was won, Bologna with the encouragement of Carlo Malatesta and Guidantonio di Montefeltro rebelled against the Church (11 May 1411). 'Trembling like a leaf in the wind,' the papal governor was expelled; the papal castle was destroyed, just as Bertrand du Poujet's fortress of Galera had been destroyed in 1334. The Florentines had by now withdrawn from the war, but their bankers continued to finance John XXIII on a large scale, confident in the expectation of profits.[1] There was now a sub-stantial hope that Sigismund of Hungary would intervene in Italy on behalf of the Pisan pope. Rome was ruled by John XXIII even if Bologna was not, and the indirect taxes of Rome were pledged to finance his loans. Wherever John ruled, the taxes were pledged to pay his mercenaries.

The main military conflict was, and was to remain for the next thirteen years, the struggle for the Apennine zones of Umbria, the march, and the Abruzzi. In these remote, infertile passes from the upper Tiber to the Tronto, in the valleys of the Marecchia, the Metauro, the strategic key to the control of central Italy was to be found.[2] The allegiance of the military leaders who controlled these areas was worth having. No doubt Cardinal Oddo Colonna, who had been appointed vicar in the Umbrian area in February 1411, was a useful man to help persuade the important Guidantonio di Montefeltro to change his allegiance, since the cardinal had been appointed Bishop of Urbino in 1380, at the age of twelve.[3] The Cardinal de Challant and Sigismund

---

[1] Holmes, in *Florentine Studies*, pp. 366–9.

[2] See the remarks of Franceschini on the importance of Urbino in *Studi di Storia Montefeltresca*, p. 27; and also p. 431 below.

[3] He is mentioned as a referee in the eventual treaty, Theiner, *C.D.*, iii, p. 194. Cf. also Frances-chini, in *BSU*, xlix (1952); Partner, *Papal State*, p. 24. The papal concession of the vicariate of Urbino, Cagli, Gubbio and Assisi to Guidantonio is in Reg. Vat. 341, fo. 186 (25 July 1412).

of Hungary also put pressure on Guidantonio, who in the spring of 1412 deserted his former employer Ladislas and accepted a papal *condotta*.

On 17 June 1412 Ladislas recognised John XXIII as pope, and signed peace with him on the Tyrrhenian coast, in papal territory, at San Felice Circeo. Considering the grants made by previous popes, the concessions to him of papal territory in the peace were modest; Perugia, Terracina, San Felice Circeo itself, Benevento, Ascoli Piceno. Probably the most important clauses in the treaty were financial.[1] The great problem for everyone was how to pay the *condottieri* without reducing their own lands to utter indigence and breakdown. One of the most important clauses in the treaty was certainly that obliging John XXIII to undertake responsibility for the enormous payments due to the oft-perjured Muzio Attendolo Sforza, who was now emerging, with Braccio da Montone, as one of the most effective and feared of the new generation of *condottieri*. How these great sums were to be paid, when already huge sums were due to Paolo Orsini, Braccio da Montone, Guidantonio di Montefeltro – to name only the most important and exigent of the papal *condottieri* – is unclear. It has been shown that John's bankers had great difficulty in finding the money even to pay the initial sums due to Ladislas under the treaty. For the pope the only answer was in the end to grant papal lands to the mercenaries in vicariate, and to hope – presumably – that the fortunes of war would one day bring them back to him. By this means Paolo Orsini, Braccio da Montone and Ludovico Migliorati had been retained in the papal camp,[2] and Guidantonio di Montefeltro bribed to enter it. But the logical end of this policy was likely to be the disintegration of the Papal State.

The return of Bologna to papal direct rule on 14 August 1412 was an apparent justification for John XXIII's policy. But soon there was a fresh quarrel with Ladislas. Paolo Orsini moved his main force to the march of Ancona, but allowed himself to be trapped by Muzio Attendolo Sforza in Braccio's fortress of Rocca Contrata (Arcevia), in the Apennine near Staffolo.[3] On this obscure strongpoint half the *condottieri* of Italy concentrated their forces. Eventually Braccio managed to get to Rocca Contrata to relieve Orsini (6 August 1413). In the interim, Rome had

---

[1] Cf. Holmes, *Florentine Studies*, pp. 371–2; Partner, *Papal State*, pp. 24–5.

[2] For Orsini's vicariate in Narni and elsewhere, Reg. Vat. 342, fo. 137. Ludovico Migliorati was 'rector' of the march besides, with Gentile Migliorati having the vicariate of Fermo, Ascoli, S. Elpidio sul Mare and many other places. Reg. Vat. 341, folios 27v–54v (May 1411). The long list of castles held by Braccio in the Perugian *contado* is in Cod. Vat. Barb. lat. 2668, folios 43, 142, together with his (evidently unfulfilled) promises to restore them. Cf. *BSU*, xxv (1922), pp. 117, 119n.

[3] Its population in 1390 was about 2,500 (600 hearths) Esch, pp. 534–7.

fallen to Ladislas (8 June 1413). John XXIII fled ignominiously to Florentine territory. The adherence (after some hesitation) of Guidantonio di Montefeltro to his cause was not enough to save the papal possessions. Only Bologna remained in papal hands, and the Florentines claimed when they made peace with Ladislas in June 1414, that to save Bologna they had had to agree to make disagreeable concessions.

It was at this time of utter bankruptcy of the papal temporal power that John XXIII began to discuss seriously with Sigismund, the emperor-elect, the calling of a great church council to settle the schism. This was the theme of the meetings between the pope and Sigismund in Lodi in November 1413. Then on 6 August 1414 the Italian political scene was drastically changed by the death of Ladislas, whose *signoria* outside the kingdom immediately collapsed. It immediately appeared how overwhelmingly political John XXIII's motives had been in agreeing to the calling of a church council. Delivered unexpectedly on the quarter from which he had most to fear, he immediately sought about for excuses to postpone the council and to remain in Italy: the most convincing of these was that he wished to return to Rome and to recover the lands of the Church. But it had been agreed that the council should assemble at Constance in the autumn of 1414, and John was not politically strong enough to back out of his engagements now. Unwillingly, but swept along by a current which was now too strong for him, John reversed the political habits which had guided his whole career, and sacrificed the temporal power to the search for church unity through the council.

IV

John XXIII left Bologna for Constance on 1 October 1414. The situation he left behind in Italy was a peculiar one not only because of the weakness of the Papal State, but because of the almost equal weakness of the new Neapolitan government under the sister of Ladislas, the widowed Joanna II. It was a situation which fifty years earlier would almost certainly have attracted a great French invasion. But France was politically decadent, unable to control the feuding of the royal princes or to resist effectively the aggression of Henry V of England. Sigismund, equally, was politically too weak to intervene in southern Italy; his chosen field of activity was the diplomacy of the council. When a husband was sought for Joanna, the best that France could provide was the feeble and incompetent Jacques de Bourbon, Count of Marche, who

17 Fantastical drawing of Rome by a fifteenth-century antiquary

18 Siege of Perugia by Totila

when he came to Italy to marry Joanna in the summer of 1415 brought with him neither troops nor political ability nor money.[1] The bleak political future of both the kingdom and the Papal State was as the field of the struggle for power and dominion of the great *condottieri*. In practice this was gradually to emerge as the struggle between Braccio da Montone and Muzio Attendolo Sforza. Both the feudal nobility and *condottieri* of the kingdom and the Papal State were closely linked, and the traditional feudal relationship of the two powers made the connection even closer. It is for a long period difficult to consider their history apart from one another – as had often been true in the past.[2]

John XXIII appointed clerical rectors in the Papal State before he left it; the most important was the Bolognese lawyer, now a cardinal, Jacopo Isolani. But essentially he had to confide in the loyalty of the mercenaries; it was rumoured that the pope thought of having Braccio da Montone murdered when he called him to Bologna before he left for Constance, but in the event he entrusted him with the guard of Bologna. 'He left the sheep in the care of the wolf', as a contemporary put it.[3] Isolani was able to enter Rome (19 October 1414), and in a formal sort of way to receive the submission of some of the papal towns; the new Neapolitan regime was on the whole friendly to him, and truces were made in November 1414 with Joanna.[4]

All real power rested with the *condottieri*. Tartaglia di Lavello in Tuscania and the north of the Tuscan patrimony, Sforza in the Sienese *contado,* Paolo and Francesco Orsini in Narni and Todi, Braccio da Montone in the Perugian and Bolognese *contado* – these were the real rulers. Rome itself was plundered by Paolo Orsini in November 1415. The deposition of John XXIII from the papacy (29 May 1415) and the abdication of Gregory XII (4 July 1415) made little difference to Italian politics. The Council of Constance was prevailed on to send commissioners to the Papal State in the autumn of 1415; their effect was almost purely formal, though where they had any discretion they continued the policies of John XXIII.

On 5 January 1416 Bologna rebelled against the papal governor and revived its communal autonomy. In the general confusion Braccio da

---

[1] See my article on this personage in *Dizionario Biografico degli Italiani.*
[2] This is emphasised by G. Beltrani, 'Gli Orsini di Lecce e di Taranto durante il regno di Giovanna II', *ASPN,* n.s., xxxvi (1956), pp. 94–125, at pp. 110 ff.
[3] A. Minuti, 'Vita di Muzio Attendolo Sforza', in *Miscellanea di storia italiana,* vii (1869), p. 190. For Braccio's position see Partner, *Papal State,* p. 31.
[4] G. M. Monti, 'La tregua di novembre 1414 fra Giovanna II e Giovanni XXIII' in *Nuovi Studi Angoini* (Trani, 1937), pp. 385–96.

o

Montone was emerging as the strongest leader in the Papal State. Muzio Attendolo Sforza was imprisoned by his enemies in the kingdom; Paolo Orsini was murdered. Carlo Malatesta of Rimini, the protector of Gregory XII and an important figure in papal politics, was defeated and captured by Braccio (12 July 1416). Orvieto and his native city of Perugia submitted to Braccio, who now organised the strongest *signoria* in Umbria since that of Biordo Michelotti twenty years earlier. The kingdom was immersed in the struggle for power between Jacques de la Marche and the Sforzeschi. In June 1417 Braccio occupied Rome, against the will of the legate. Isolani shut himself up in Castel Sant'Angelo, and Braccio after the custom of the time used siege engines to bombard him with filth. But Sforza had now been released from prison; he marched north to Rome and compelled Braccio to withdraw from the city.

In the general examination of conscience of the Western Church which the fathers conducted at Constance between 1414 and 1418, the papal patrimony had to be discussed. On the whole the discussion was technical and administrative rather than moral, though there was some condemnation of papal nepotism, and some complaint about the weight of papal taxation in the Papal State.[1] Only one tract was so idealistic as to ask that the pope should not enrol men-at-arms to shed blood, but should use only the spiritual sword, and if that failed then call on the emperor and Christian princes to use the secular arm on his behalf.[2] This was the authentic voice of Bernard of Clairvaux, but it was seldom heard. The more usual assumption was that the pope and the cardinals ought to 'live of their own', and to manage their own patrimony properly so that they would not need to tax other churches.[3] The pope was also to spend less money on warfare, though how he was to cut war expenses and also to govern more effectively was not made clear.

The unstated assumption behind most of what was said about the papal patrimony at Constance was that it was a church estate like any other, and that the methods the popes had used to run it were wrong only in detail. Both the distinguished Bolognese canonist, Cardinal

---

[1] For nepotism see especially the *Avisamenta* of Dietrich of Niem, cited by E. F. Jacob, *Essays in the Conciliar Epoch* (Manchester, 1953), p. 39. For secular papal taxation see the accusations against John XXIII in H. Finke, *Acta Concilii Constanciencis* (Münster, 1896–1928), iii, pp. 184–93. Cf. Partner, *Papal State*, p. 30.

[2] Finke, *Acta*, ii, pp. 672–3, and cf. p. 561. Cf. also the *capitula agendorum*, ibid. iv, p. 582: the treasure of the Church should not all be spent on mercenaries so that nothing remains for the poor.

[3] Mansi, *Concilia*, xxviii, col. 205. I owe this reference to the kindness of Mr A. V. Antonovics.

Zabarella, and the radical curialist, Dietrich of Niem, felt that John XXIII had on the whole acted for the benefit of the Church in his temporal power policies.[1] And in the 'Articles of the German Nation', the opinion is advanced that the cardinals ought to continue to draw their share of the common services and annates for the next five years (i.e. until the next council) 'unless the patrimony of the Roman Church has been recovered'.[2] The implication that it ought to be recovered is clear.

Only the heretics, in fact, made radical criticisms of the temporal power. Orthodox reforming opinion accepted it more or less as it was.

---

[1] The passages are quoted in Partner, *Papal State*, p. 30n.
[2] Von der Hardt, *Rerum concilii oecumenici Constanciencis*, i, p. 1000.

Chapter 12

The beginnings of the Renaissance principate

I

On 11 November 1417 Cardinal Oddo Colonna was elected pope at Constance; he took the title of Martin V. The fathers had not made a very revolutionary choice. As a member of one of the great Roman families, relative of many others, and the friend of other great *signori* of the Papal State such as Guidantonio di Montefeltro, he was a Roman magnate pope of a familiar kind. His administrative experience had been very largely in the service of the temporal power under John XXIII. He was prudent, affable, and the master of all the arts of deceit which were so necessary for survival in Italian politics.

Not only was the temporal power in ruins, but the situation in the kingdom gave cause for much concern. Since the end of 1416 Jacques de la Marche had been virtually a prisoner in Castel dell'Ovo in Naples. From October 1418 Muzio Attendolo Sforza was pressing his own interests in the kingdom as much as in the Papal State.[1] Florence feared Sforza, and was quite happy to use Braccio against him and to support the great *signoria* in Umbria which Braccio had carved out at papal expense.[2] Most disturbing of all was the threat of the revival of Spanish imperialism in Italy by Alfonso of Aragon; the Spanish reluctance entirely to abandon the anti-pope Benedict XIII made this particularly dangerous to the conciliar pope.

Martin entered Italy in the autumn of 1418. His temporal power policy took shape slowly and cautiously; it was essentially a continuation of that of John XXIII, with the difference that Martin did not have to deal with a hostile Ladislas. Martin also had to contend with an occupation of papal rights by mercenaries and *signori* quite as widespread and deep-rooted as that which John XXIII had known. The

[1] For what follows see E. Pontieri, 'Muzio e Francesco Sforza nei conflitti dinastico-civili nel regno di Napoli al tempo di Giovanna II d'Angiò-Durazzo', *Studi Storici in onore di Gioacchino Volpe* (Florence, 1958), pp. 787–883.
[2] Cf. Partner, in *Florentine Studies*, pp. 389–90.

new pope's task was, nevertheless, far from impossible. So long as he could retain effective influence over Joanna in the kingdom, he had cards in his hand which had not been played by the popes for a very long time. Martin also enjoyed the advantage that the recovery of Visconti power under Filippo Maria had by the time of his election reached a point where the Duke of Milan was an effective counterbalance to Florence, yet not strong enough directly to menace papal rule in Romagna. Venetian expansion on the terra firma, later to be such a menace to the popes, had not yet seriously begun.

It would be tedious to record here the submissions of the *signori* of the Papal State during Martin's first two years, and the grants of vicariate and confirmation of privileges which the pope made.[1] What is interesting is the anxiety which the *signori* showed to have the pope legitimise their rule, even at the price of substantial payments of *census*. That papal confirmation of their rule was not regarded as an empty formality is clear from their behaviour.

The weakness of Martin's position while he stayed in Florence (26 February 1419 – 9 September 1420) is well known. Having risen from 'sleepless nights' of worrying how he was to deal with Braccio, he heard the Florentine urchins singing that he was 'not worth a farthing', while 'our friend Braccio takes all'. The traditional alliances of Florence with the papal state *signori* who were her actual or potential mercenaries made Florence at the best an unfriendly neutral for the pope. Yet the Florentine curial bankers continued to manage papal monies.

The promotion of Colonna influence in the kingdom was an important part of Martin's policy. Martin V's brothers Lorenzo and Giordano, and Lorenzo's sons Antonio and Odoardo, all were given the highest feudal grants in the kingdom – Lorenzo became Grand Chamberlain and Giordano Prince of Salerno. This was in a long tradition of papal-Neapolitan relations; as recently as Boniface IX the obscure Tomacelli had become Grand Chancellor of the kingdom. After the flight of Queen Joanna's husband, Jacques de la Marche, from Naples in May 1419 the question of the kingdom itself was re-opened. An heir to the childless Joanna had to be found. Sforza also had to be secured to fight against Braccio in the papal cause.

Sforza marched north against Braccio in the spring of 1419. Braccio had already sharply chastised the papal ally Guidantonio di Montefeltro; when he finally encountered Sforza's army near Viterbo the papal champion was defeated, and subsequently penned up in Viterbo. This

[1] See *Papal State*, pp. 47–59.

reverse was accepted by the papal *curia* as excluding an early military solution, and at the end of 1419 Martin and his allies were willing to come to terms with Braccio. The great *signoria* in Umbria and the march was recognised by the grant of papal vicariates; of his important conquests only Orvieto was returned to the pope. Guidantonio di Montefeltro had to give up Assisi to Braccio. With his allies the Trinci of Foligno and the da Varano of Camerino, Braccio controlled most of the Apennine passes from the Savio to the Esino.

The peace with Braccio (26 February 1420) was the necessary preliminary to the formal re-establishment of papal power, and also to Martin's return to Rome, which from a prestige point of view was essential. Church unity was not symbolically restored until the Roman bishop had returned to his see. Before this could take, the rebellion of Bologna (26 January 1420) had to be crushed. The compromise grant of autonomy to the commune made by the pope in 1419 had broken down. The rebellion, in which Antonio Bentivoglio was closely concerned, was settled by the striking success of Martin and the cardinals in raising money, and in calling on most of the tyrants of Romagna to act against Bologna – besides Braccio, who came not for the first time to spoil the Bolognese countryside. In July the rebellion collapsed, and Martin was able to impose more or less direct papal government on Bologna.[1]

On 28 September he arrived in Rome. The misery of the city at the time of his arrival has often been dwelt on by historians. Certainly Rome was not a very populous city (upwards of 25,000 persons at this time), and as it lacked any substantial industries it depended a great deal on the administrative, pilgrim, and diplomatic activity which only the papal presence could give it. Not unnaturally, since the pope was the main reason for their proper occupation and use, the churches and papal palaces were in a state of ruin. We know something, from the papal accounts, of the way in which they were put in order. But of the economic state of the population of Rome at this period we know little, nor have we much idea of what difference Martin's return made to them The indirect taxes of Rome were being assigned to repay considerable sums as late as 1411; they were again being so used under Martin V.[2] The state of the Roman countryside is even more obscure. Certainly many of the villages had been hard hit by constant warfare, and some were abandoned at this time without ever again being inhabited. But other

---

[1] Ibid. pp. 67, 177–9.
[2] Ibid. pp. 166–8; cf. Holmes, *Florentine Studies*, p. 370, and below, p. 420.

villages described as 'derelict' or 'abandoned' in the tax lists of the period later were re-occupied.[1] Much more historical work has to be done before we can speak with any certainty about the fate of the economy and population at this period.

On 4 November 1419 Martin V had returned to the traditional policy of the Holy See, the Angevin candidature for the throne of the kingdom. On that date Martin announced that he would invest Louis of Anjou with the kingdom in the event of Joanna's death. This decision was not accepted by the Neapolitan court, and it had the unwished-for result of pushing Joanna to the acceptance of Alfonso of Aragon as her adoptive son and heir (September 1420). A civil war in the kingdom between Sforza (as the Angevin *condottiere*) and Braccio (who fought for Alfonso) followed. The cost of the war to the papal chamber was over 170,000 florins a year, which is at least equal to the sums expended by John XXIII at the height of the war with Ladislas, and amounted to the whole of the average papal revenue at that time, without deduction of other expenses.[2] The war was from the papal point of view a failure, since it ended in a compromise by which the two kings withdrew from the kingdom, and thus left Braccio free to re-enter the Papal State to exact fresh tribute under the agreements of *condotta*. It is not sufficiently emphasised in the history books that much of the money paid to *condottieri* was in effect not by way of salary but by way of blackmail, or protection money. It was at this time that to keep him quiet Braccio had to be granted Città di Castello.

It was not in the papal interest to oppose Milanese policy. From the beginning of the pontificate Martin and his vassal Niccolò d'Este had co-operated with Filippo Maria Visconti, especially in the return of Parma to the Visconti in 1419. So long as Florence supported Braccio in Umbria and the Abruzzi, Martin would be willing to support the Visconti in Romagna. In 1422 Giorgio Ordelaffi the tyrant of Forlì died, leaving a minor as heir. A rebellion against Ordelaffi's widow (14 May 1423) was made the excuse for Milanese troops in the name of Niccolò d'Este to occupy the city. For Florence, anticipating a Milanese occupation of the Romagnol Apennine, this was a *casus belli*; for Martin it was a good opportunity to get Milanese financial help against Braccio in the civil war in the kingdom. Braccio had laid siege

[1] Cf. Mallett in *PBSR*, xxxv (1967), p. 115n. It is hard to believe that the list of *terrae destructae et inhabitatae* in the 1416 tax list had more than a temporary application, since it includes many of the best known places of the area. Cf. Pardi, *ASR*, xlix (1926), pp. 345–6, 349–54.

[2] Cf. Partner, *Papal State*, pp. 69, 193–4; *Italian Renaissance Studies*, p. 259.

to the royal city of Aquila, acting now as a rebel against the queen. It was here that the vital interests of the papacy lay, in the Abruzzi, and not in the Romagna, where a temporary Milanese occupation cost the pope nothing, provided he did not lose Bologna. War began between Florence and the Milanese mercenaries in the Romagna, but Martin remained neutral.

On 3 January 1424 Muzio Attendolo Sforza was drowned at the crossing of the Pescara. The one great hope of the pope and the Angevin was dead, and Braccio remained at the siege of Aquila. It was decided to try to re-victual the city with an army led by Giacomo Caldora and Ludovico Colonna. They were brought to battle by Braccio on the plain outside the city (2 June 1424) and in a savage battle Braccio was defeated and killed. Martin was scarcely able to believe his luck, that one of the greatest captains of the age should be destroyed by a couple of undistinguished mercenaries. *Virtù* had succumbed to mediocrity.

While Martin triumphed, Florence suffered. On 28 July 1424 the Florentine army, led by Carlo and Pandolfo Malatesta, was routed at Zagonara (near Lugo, in the neighbourhood of Ravenna). Martin was now sought after by all sides in the Italian struggle. This power was however enough to enforce the most complete recovery of papal temporal authority since the early years of Gregory XI in the preceding century. With very modest forces of troops,[1] papal officials cleared Braccio's supporters out of almost every part of the Papal State. Well-established tyrants such as the Migliorati of Fermo and the Carrara of Ascoli were driven from their cities, besides lesser fry such as the Smeducci of San Severino and the Alfani of Rieti; other considerable *signori* such as Corrado Trinci of Foligno were disciplined.[2] Perhaps more important, the city of Perugia accepted papal direct rule. In all these operations in Umbria and the march, the papal *condottiere* and relative (he had married Caterina Colonna in 1424) Guidantonio di Montefeltro was probably the advising voice. His share of the loot was Castel Durante, ancient seat of the Brancaleoni family.[3] Braccio's widow, Nicola da Varano, was allowed to hold Città di Castello for her infant son Carlo until 1428, but she was then driven out.

---

[1] This is the impression given by the two registers of *condotte*, Arm. XXIX, vols. 14 and 15; it is doubtful if there were other registers, as these two were the only ones listed in 1440 (see *Papal State*, p. 202).

[2] Cf. M. V. Prosperi Valenti, 'Corrado Trinci ultimo signore di Foligno', *BSU*, lv (1958), pp. 1–185.

[3] Cf. G. Franceschini, *I Montefeltro* (Varese, 1970), pp. 387 ff. He did not however receive an apostolic vicariate for it. Cf. Guiraud, pp. 193–7.

In 1426 Venice reversed the policies of two decades and joined the Florentine alliance against Milan. The long-term consequences of Venetian policy veering towards an active policy on the terra firma were serious for the papacy. When the powers met to discuss peace at Ferrara in 1427 under the mediation of Niccolò d'Este and the papal legate, it swiftly became clear that while Florence was merely interested in getting Milanese guarantees of non-interference in Tuscany and Romagna, Venice wanted much more from the Visconti.[1] Martin took a more or less pro-Visconti line in these negotiations, but this did not save him from the consequences of Filippo Maria's thinking more and more in terms of getting help from outside Italy, from Sigismund or Alfonso of Aragon. Either of these alternatives could have been dangerous to Martin, from both a political and an ecclesiastical point of view.

The limitations of Martin V's power were shown by the rebellion of Bologna in the summer of 1428. The Canetoli faction eventually proved too powerful for the legate (Louis Aleman) to control, and they seized him and took command of the city. Niccolò Albergati, the holy and popular Bishop of Bologna, was unable to resist the revolution, and had to escape from the city disguised as a monk. 'Reformers' were appointed and independence from the papacy proclaimed. It proved impossible to use the faction of the papal *condottiere* Antonio Bentivoglio to oppose the revolutionaries, as he had been kept out of the city since 1420.

Martin V had one striking success, in that he managed to keep the rebels of Bologna completely isolated; they received no help from any other power in Italy. But the military problem of subduing the city still proved to be too difficult. The papal general Jacopo Caldora was incompetent and idle, and the war, at least as expensive as the war in the kingdom in 1421, languished. Eventually in September 1429 a peace had to be signed with the rebellious commune which failed to re-impose the direct rule of the Church in Bologna, did not punish the instigators of the rebellion, and even made Martin responsible for the war debts and ransoms of the rebels. Constitutionally it was little more than a return of the *status quo* before the revolution. Within a few months of the peace Martin's new legate in Bologna was driven from the city by fresh rioting (April 1430), and the papal siege of the city recommended. This was the condition in which Martin left the most important city of the Papal State on his death; it is a reflection on the power of the

---

[1] Cf. Cessi, 'Venezia alla pace di Ferrara del 1428', in *Nuovo Archivio Veneto*, n.s., xxxi, pt. 1 (1916), pp. 361–2, and also *Florentine Studies*, p. 391.

O*

great restorer of the papal dominion, the 'happiness of his times' (*suorum temporum felicitas*), which is not always considered.

II

Perhaps one of the lessons of Martin's pontificate was that the smaller *signorie* in Romagna and the march, which rested on the whole on alliances of magnate interests which had come into existence in the fourteenth century, could not all of them expect to continue in a world which was swept by larger armies and dominated by larger and more tightly organised political units. Their budgets were modest,[1] and they were not all able to survive long periods of political and military strain. The *census* which they paid for the apostolic vicariate was a heavy charge on income. Much depended on whether they chose the right side on which to fight. Carlo Malatesta was not helped by his defeat and capture in 1416 by Braccio and again by the Milanese army in 1424 at Zagonara. After his death in 1429 the pope was able to intervene as feudal lord and to recover for the Holy See some of the most important Malatesta holdings, notably Borgo San Sepolcro which stood near the recently recovered Città di Castello. With the ruin of the Malatesta rule in the Upper Tiber, other smaller *signorie* such as those of the Brancaleoni and the lords of Petramala were involved.[2] So thick was the undergrowth of alliances among the seigniorial families that to strike one branch was to break another, like the dogs in the wood of the suicides (*Inferno*, XIII).

The financial power of a great free commune such as Bologna was far greater than that of the average Romagnol *signore;* provided the political will and consent existed among the Bolognese, they were quite rich enough to assert and defend their independence.[3] The Umbrian commune of Perugia, rich but less rich, was another story. The political factions of Perugia had become accustomed to the *signoria*, which they

---

[1] Forlì, see Orlandelli in *Stud. Romagn.*, vii (1956), pp. 183–92; the profit in 1407–9 was about 11,000 pounds of Bologna annually. For the whole question see P. J. Jones, 'The end of Malatesta Rule in Rimini', *Italian Renaissance Studies*, pp. 217–55, especially at pp. 232–5. Ferrara recorded only the modest credit balance of 25,000 pounds, on a gross income of something over 120,000 pounds, in the 1440s. P. Sitta, 'Saggio sulle istituzioni finanziarie del ducato Estense nei secoli XV e XVI', *Atti della Deput. Ferrarese di S.P.*, iii (1891), p. 136n.

[2] *Papal State*, pp. 93–4; Franceschini, in *Stud. Romagn.*, ii (1951), and in *AMSM*, 7th ser. iv (1949). If Eugenius had been able to retain the salt-pans of Cervia, which Martin V took into his hands in 1430 but which were recovered by the Malatesta in 1433, the blow to Malatesta interests would have been far more important.

[3] Cf. G. Orlandelli, 'La revisione del bilancio nel comune di Bologna dal XII al XV secolo', *AMDR*, n.s., ii (1950–1), pp. 157–218.

had experienced under one ruler or another since the early 1390s. When the papacy accepted control of Perugia in 1424, it established a balance of power with the commune and the factions which was to prove extremely durable. The rule of the papal governor had to humour the factions, and had been made to consent to the continued banishment of the Michelotti. But though compromises had to be made with the Baglioni, their follower who compared the papal governor with 'the flies of January' saw the inside of a prison. The papacy asserted for itself, and kept, the essential control of the finances of the commune.[1]

Other middle-sized communes such as Orvieto, Ancona, Ascoli Piceno, now remained firmly inside the framework of papal government. The revenue from such places had for a long time – in the case of the important port of Ancona, since the reconquest of Albornoz – been among the most important props of temporal power income.[2] For such places the weight of papal fiscality was heavy: Ancona paid over half the communal income as tribute to the Church. That the Church in return normally recognised the rule of the city over its surrounding countryside (*comitatus*) was no hardship to the papal government, which was perfectly happy to accept the tyranny of the town over the countryside which was so typical of Italian society in the late medieval and Renaissance period. It is true that population decline and war losses had impoverished the cities to a considerable extent.[3] It is true also that practically everywhere the Church either favoured a particular faction, or was unable to prevent the political predominance of another. The Gatti of Viterbo, Monaldeschi of Orvieti, Ferretti of Ancona, Baglioni of Perugia were the local bosses without whom nothing could be done at the level of communal government. But we are not dealing with an ideal model of 'absolute' government as it might have been,[4] but with Italian fifteenth-century government as it actually was. If it can be admitted that the importance of local and feudal magnates in the Papal

---

[1] The papal governor was the humanist Domenico Capranica, who replied that the difference between a cardinal and a January fly was more than a jest ('differentiam cauda leporis maiorem'). Partner, *Papal State*, pp. 79–80, 169–76, 227–9. The continued effective political and financial control by the papacy of Perugia, even at the time of the supposed Baglioni *signoria* at the end of the fifteenth century, has been shown by Mr Christopher Black in his unpublished Oxford University thesis, *Politics and Society in Perugia*, 1488–1540 (1966); cf. now his 'The Baglioni as Tyrants of Perugia, 1488–1540', *EHR*, lxxxv (1970), pp. 245–81.

[2] Cf. *Papal State*, 179–80, 183–4. Esch (*Quellen* (1966), p. 308) notes the economic importance of Perugia and Ancona under Boniface IX.

[3] For the economic exhaustion of Orvieto at the end of the schism, see R. Valentini, 'Braccio da Montone e il comune di Orvieto', *BSU*, xxvi (1923), at pp. 92–6.

[4] This seems to be the comparison implied by Guiraud in *L'Etat Pontifical*.

State was not exceptional among Italian 'despotisms' at that time,[1] the reality of papal government can perhaps be recognised.

Of the importance of papal state government to papal finance there is little doubt. The 'spiritual' income of the popes had been sharply reduced by the schism and the council, and the temporal revenues now represented a much more important proportion of total papal income than they formerly had done.[2] Of a total papal income roughly estimated at 170,000 florins in 1426–7, about 80,000 florins came from the Papal State. It may well be that attempts at estimating 'surplus' income in this way are not very logical,[3] and in any case the income did not have to be 'surplus' in order to serve as a gage for the Florentine bankers who kept the *curia* supplied with ready money. Financially the pope lived from hand to mouth, like most other rulers. The revenues of Rome alone were at a minimum 120,000 florins a year gross, and papal credit was very dependent on them for the whole Renaissance period.[4] The gradual increase in population and economic activity which Rome experienced during the fifteenth century was of the utmost importance to the papacy. Politically, Rome had been firmly under papal control since the pontificate of Boniface IX. Martin V only re-imposed and tightened an absolute rule on the city which had been in existence under his former master, John XXIII.

Martin V was the first Roman magnate pope since Boniface VIII. His policies are a direct reminiscence of those of his predecessor of over a century earlier. The Colonna of Paliano were endowed, partly by the grant of papal lands and partly by the use of papal money, with a thick group of strongpoints strategically placed in Campagna and the Maritime province, and another (rather less numerous) in the Tuscan patrimony.[5] Like the Caetani before them, they were equally lavishly treated by royal grant in the kingdom. Martin intervened frequently in the kingdom on behalf of his family, and even exempted the county of

---

[1] See, for example, D. M. Bueno de Mesquita, 'Ludovico Sforza and his vassals', in *Italian Renaissance Studies*, pp. 184–216, and Jones, 'The end of Malatesta rule' in the same work. The question of papal officials and local oligarchic interests is discussed by I. Robertson, 'The return of Cesena to the direct dominion of the Church after the death of Malatesta Novello', *Stud. Romagn.*, xvi (1965), pp. 123–61.

[2] Partner, in *Italian Renaissance Studies*, pp. 256–78 and see p. 357 above.

[3] 'Un revenu n'a de signification qu'au regard des charges qu'il supporte', Favier, *Finances pontificales*, p.690.

[4] A. Gottlob, *Aus der Camera apostolica des 15. Jahrhunderts* (Innsbruck, 1889), pp.239–40 reckoned the profit on the Roman indirect taxes in the first half of the fifteenth century at about 25,000 florins annually.

[5] *Papal State*, pp. 197–8.

Celano, which his nephew Odoardo held in dower from his wife, from Joanna's jurisdiction.[1] When Martin died the whole Campagna and Maritime provinces, from Castro on the Neapolitan border and Astura on the coast to Frascati in the Alban hills, were effectively controlled by his relatives. It was almost a revival of the lordship of the distant eleventh-century forebear of the Colonna, Ptolemy of Tuscolo.

III

Martin V died on 20 February 1431.[2] The conclave which followed was an anxious one: the Colonna princes were already assembling their forces outside the city. The question of whether a pope could be found who would be 'Guelph', that is, friendly to Florence as Martin had not been, and not a 'tyrant' to the cardinals as Martin had been, was decided in the affirmative. Gabriele Condulmer was one of three candidates who had been posted as acceptable to Florence: he was elected on 3 March and took the title of Eugenius IV. The electoral capitulations which the cardinals had agreed to during the conclave contained stipulations that the new pope should share the government of the temporal power more equally than before with the cardinals, and also that he should divide the temporal revenues with them.[3] There is no evidence that the second demand was fulfilled, and Eugenius never had the power to fulfil the first!

In 1297 the Colonna had stolen the treasure of Boniface VIII; in 1431 they refused to part with the treasure of Martin V. Oddo Poccia of Genazzano, the Regent of the Apostolic Chamberlain and the secret agent of Martin V for financial business, was on 15 April seized by Stefano Colonna on the orders of the pope, 'to find out where the money and goods of holy church were'.[4] A week later Antonio Colonna, Prince of Salerno, attacked Rome through Porta San Sebastiano. He was repulsed, but he had unleashed a state of war and insecurity which Eugenius was unable to end for some fourteen years. The defection of the Colonna in Rome led to a revolution in Naples, where the queen's

---

[1] This may be a reminiscence of ancient papal claims in the Abruzzi, but it seems unlikely. Ibid. pp. 100–1. Odoardo and Jacobella of Celano were subsequently divorced (Reg. Vat. 365, fo. 16, 1435).

[2] See the remarkable article by W. Brandmüller, 'Der Übergang vom Pontifikat Martins V. zu Eugen IV.', *Quellen*, xlvii (1967), pp. 596–629.

[3] Criticism of Martin V's failure to share the temporal power with the cardinals had been made by reform commissions in his pontificate (quoted by me in *Papal State*, pp. 139–40).

[4] Cf. Partner, *Journal of Ecclesiastical History*, iv (1953), pp. 66–7; idem, *Papal State*, p. 194. The treasure was in Castel Sant'Angelo after Martin's death, Brandmüller, p. 612n.

favourite, Giovanni Caraccolo, was pleased to assist in their disgrace. In the Tuscan patrimony the Prefect of Vico rebelled in Civitavecchia and Vetralla. In Umbria Niccolò della Stella called Fortebraccio (son of Braccio's sister, Stella) attacked Città di Castello. Guidantonio di Monte-feltro, anxious to profit from the revolt of his Colonna relations, seized the town for himself.[1] The Neapolitan general Jacopo Caldora, the victor of Aquila, had been engaged in April to operate against the Colonna, but by the time he arrived in the Roman District he had changed his mind, and he took the side of the Colonna instead of that of the pope. There was a fresh plot to introduce the Colonna into Rome and Castel Sant'Angelo – troops were going to be introduced into the latter in 'wooden chests'. Though in the course of the summer the revolt simmered down, and though the Colonna were in the end persuaded to repay large sums from Martin's treasure to the papal chamber, it was a poor start for the new pontificate.[2]

The essential weakness of Eugenius IV was that from the start he leaned heavily on two Italian powers, Florence and Venice, whose motives in their dealings with the Papal State were far from dis-interested. Perhaps it was natural that a Venetian who had had a reputation for being a pro-Florentine cardinal – Martin had dismissed him from the legation of Bologna for this reason – should take this stance, but the temporal power certainly suffered from it. As legate in Bologna during the war of Romagna in 1423 Eugenius had wanted to support Florence against Milan. When in 1431 he found Florence at war with Siena, with the Sienese enjoying Milanese support, Eugenius was as disingenuously friendly to Florence as his predecessor would probably have been covertly friendly to the Visconti.

The misfortunes of Eugenius stemmed above all from his inability to deal with the *condottieri,* and from the renewed political weakness of the papacy caused by the opening of the Council of Basle (July 1431). This, and the negotiations for the journey of the Emperor Sigismund to Italy, enfeebled every papal act. The *condottieri* engaged jointly by Eugenius and Florence, notably Niccolò Fortebraccio, were expensive both in money and in grants of papal lands,[3] and their effectiveness

---

[1] Cf. *Florentine Studies*, p. 393n.

[2] The Colonna transferred 100,000 florins from their account in the Florentine *Monte Comune* to the pope (ibid. p. 397, no. 2) and Antonio, Prince of Salerno, paid 32,000 florins into the papal chamber between October 1431 and January 1432 (V. A., Introitus et Exitus vol. 390). For the July revolt see Pastor, *Ungedruckte Akten*, i, pp. 20–1.

[3] He was granted Borgo San Sepolcro, Scalvanti, *BSU*, xii (1906), pp. 302–7. Cf. *Florentine Studies*, p. 394n.

was small. Guidantonio di Montefeltro returned to papal obedience, but his real political role at this time was as a Venetian *condottiere*. The situation was tolerable for Eugenius until with the approach of the peace of Ferrara in 1433 the unemployed Milanese *condottieri* were launched by Filippo Maria Visconti on the Papal State. Francesco Sforza plundered papal lands in the march from one end to another, without resistance being offered by papal mercenaries. Niccolò Forte-braccio turned against his papal employer and plundered the Roman District mercilessly. The Prince of Salerno and others of the Colonna rebelled again, and added their mite to the troubles of the Roman District.

Sigismund's long-delayed voyage to Italy took place at last in 1431. It quickly appeared that he was no more powerful than Eugenius against the Italian powers and their mercenaries, and for nine months, from July 1432, he remained blockaded within the walls of Siena. He emerged in the spring of 1433 to march south to Rome for his imperial corona-tion (31 May 1433). The conversion of Sigismund from the blandish-ments of the Council of Basle was an advantage for Eugenius, but so far as the security of the Papal State was concerned the friendship of the emperor was worthless.

One advantage at least which Eugenius drew from the Venetian-Florentine alliance, was that his allies were for the time in a good position to assure for him his possession of Perugia and Bologna, which from a financial and strategic point of view were both essential. He succeeded in negotiating fresh settlements with both these communes early in the pontificate, and so almost from the beginning was able to draw on their revenues.[1] But this did not help Eugenius to survive the military pressure in Umbria and the march from Francesco Sforza, which at the end of 1433 and in the New Year of 1434 was becoming intolerable. The appeal to Florence for help brought no effective aid; Niccolò da Tolentino, the Florentine *condottiere,* was like the rest of his kind more interested in easy loot than in fighting pitched battles against leaders of the calibre of Sforza. By mid-February Francesco Sforza was thought to be marching on Rome, and Eugenius was in despair.

---

[1] The agreement with Perugia is in Div. Cam. 22, folios 25–34, dated 20 June 1431. Cf. P. Paschini, 'Da Medico a Patriarca d'Aquileia Camerlengo e Cardinale di S. Romana Chiesa', *Memorie Storiche Forogiuliesi*, xxii (1927), pp. 1–56, at p. 4. The agreement with Bologna is in Theiner, *C.D.*, iii, no. 266, dated 22 August 1431. Extracts from the Perugian accounts were printed by Fumi, *Inventario e Spoglio dei registri della Tesoreria Apostolica di Perugia e Umbria* (Perugia, 1901). The accounts of the papal treasurer in Bologna for 1432 show a gross income of just under 140,000 florins, Rome, Arch. di Stato, Arch. Cam. pt. i, Tesorerie Provinciali, Bologna, Busta 1.

At this low moment of his fortunes Eugenius took a grave step, the wisdom of which it is now hardly possible to assess. Francesco Sforza was the adherent of the Duke of Milan, to whom Eugenius and his allies continued to be hostile even after the peace of the preceding year. His descent into the march in December 1433 on the pretext of transit to his lands in Apulia had been marked by atrocities, particularly at Montolmo, and he had already received a grovelling act of subjection from the da Varano brothers of Camerino.[1] Eugenius accused him of claiming to come in the name of the Council of Basle. In January 1434 he had passed into Umbria, taken Todi and a number of other towns, and reached the coast, or almost so, at Tuscania, which fell to him at the same time as the main castles of Sabina.

In March Eugenius sent two envoys to find Sforza at the little village of Calcarella, near Tuscania; one of them was the well-known secretary and humanist historian, Biondo Flavio of Forli. There the papal negotiators signed a treaty (21 March 1434) which virtually settled the fate of the Papal State for most of the rest of the pontificate of Eugenius.[2] The pope agreed to make Sforza standard-bearer of the Church and Marquis of the march of Ancona for Sforza's lifetime, with a full concession of all the temporal rights of the Holy See in the province. This was the granting away of the richest provinces of the temporal power, with no guarantee that the papacy would ever recover it. There were other promises to grant vicariates in the march and Tuscan patrimony, but these are of less fundamental interest.[3] Eugenius was to put pressure on Joanna II to make Sforza great constable of the kingdom. The full brutality of the agreement is most apparent in the military service which Sforza offered for the march (though as a *condotta* and not as feudal service). Neither Francesco nor Lorenzo Sforza would command these troops except in the most exceptional circumstances. The pope was made to bow low to the soldier.

This agreement was said by Biondo Flavio, one of the papal negotiators, to have marked the beginning of the greatness of Francesco Sforza. Its significance would have been less, if Florence and Venice had been

---

[1] Published in the notes to P.C. Decembrio, *Opuscola Historica* (RRIISS, xx, pt. 1), p. 640. Cf. also *AMSM*, n.s., v (1908) pp. 434–7.

[2] I found this treaty in the Vatican Library, MS Chigi F 4, 103. Cf. *Florentine Studies*, p. 394n. I hope soon to publish it.

[3] They were of: Fermo, Acquapendente, Proceno and San Lorenzo, Todi, Toscanella, Gualdo Cattaneo, Rispampano; the pope was also to grant Offida to Ardizzone da Carrara, and (when they were recovered) Imola to Michele Attendolo Sforza, and Nocera to the da Varano of Camerino. Sforza was also to be allowed to exact all the money he had asked from the inhabitants of Magliano, and the agreement he had 'extorted' from the da Varano was confirmed.

unwilling to accept Sforza, or if he had proved unwilling to desert Filippo Maria Visconti – there was a clause in the agreement in which the papal envoy guaranteed the pope's benevolence and good faith in the negotiations which were going on with the Milanese representative in the papal court. But six months after the Treaty of Calcarella was signed there was a revolution in Florence (26–9 September) which led to the fall of the Albizzi regime and return of Cosimo de' Medici from exile. Whether or not the Albizzi regime would have welcomed Sforza as a recruit (and the probability is that they would have done so) Cosimo was only too willing to do so. Practically the day on which Cosimo's banishment was revoked, the Florentine treaty with Sforza was signed. From a Florentine point of view Sforza was a most valuable gift in the power struggle, at a time when the Florentine prestige and military force were low. True, they and the Venetians had to contribute a lot of money towards his *condotta;* but the essential political price was being paid by the pope, in the form of the cession of the march of Ancona. It was as though, seventeen years earlier, Martin V had welcomed the *signoria* of Braccio in papal Umbria and hastened to confirm it.

The Treaty of Calcarella was of no value to Eugenius in Rome, and the refusal of Sforza to lead the pope's troops in the existing emergency[1] had the consequences in Rome which could have been predicted. Niccolò Fortebraccio continued to hammer on the gates of Rome, and though Sforza's troops managed to defeat him at Tivoli on 17 May, the Romans were war-weary, and sympathetic with the Colonna opposition outside the city. When it was announced that Niccolò Piccinino was hurrying south on behalf of the Visconti, to support Fortebraccio against the traitorous Sforza, Rome rose against the pope (29 May 1434), and Eugenius was faced with the prospect of captivity under the control of the council and the Duke of Milan.[2] To escape from the Romans he embarked on the Tiber, disguised as a monk, in a skiff in which he crouched to dodge the missiles the Romans flung as the boat went down the tide. No pope had escaped in this way since poor Gelasius had been shot at by German archers as he went down the Tiber in 1118. On

---

[1] There was to be a *condotta* for 200 lances only and 200 foot, which came into force on 1 April 1434. But Sforza himself refused to lead the troops. 'Sed de impresia presenti comes uult omnimode (sic) personam suam liberam esse.' MS. quoted above, fo. 14. The Sforzesco captain assigned to command the troops in papal service was Michelotto Attendolo (appointed captain-general, 29 February 1434: *condotta* dated 10 April. Reg. Vat. 370, fo. 137: Diversa Cameralia 22, fo. 65).

[2] Cf. M. Creighton, *A History of the Papacy from the Great Schism to the Sack of Rome*, ii (London 1897), p. 233.

23 June Eugenius reached Florence, and the political dependence which had been evident since the beginning of the pontificate became even closer. Whether he had any hand in the *coup d'état* in Florence which brought back Cosimo de' Medici has never been proved. The Medici were the curial bankers, and had been so for a long period; but it seems rather unlikely that a pope as politically naked as Eugenius was at this time would have risked involvement in such a chancy business, wherever his sympathies lay.

IV

For the following six years the chief figure in the temporal power was the fierce and bizarre figure of Giovanni Vitelleschi, a member of a magnate family of Corneto which had originated in Foligno. Vitelleschi had served Tartaglia di Lavello, the mercenary Lord of Tuscania, but he entered papal service as a notary, and was castellan of Bologna in 1420.[1] Early in the pontificate of Eugenius he was made Rector of the march of Ancona and Bishop of Recanati. He was not an unfamiliar type; the Abbot of Rosazzo had been employed by Martin V in the same office of rector, and Eugenius used the abbots of Subiaco and Monte Cassino as soldiers and papal governors; the second was responsible for an unpleasant massacre at Spoleto. But Vitelleschi beat all other clerics at the game of war, besides being an able administrator in the intimate confidence of the pope. Appointed governor of Bologna and Romagna in 1434, he was unable to enter the city because of the recent rising against papal rule.[2] He was made Patriarch of Alexandria, and was papal commissioner in Rome and the western papal provinces.[3] He entered Rome in October 1434 and in collusion with certain favoured families, especially the counts of Anguillara, terrorised the city and the surrounding areas. Alessandro Sforza had defeated and killed Niccolò Fortebraccio; and the other dissident mercenary, Antonio da Pisa, withdrew to the kingdom.[4] Vitelleschi subdued Rome, and executed or provoked the murder of two important magnate families in the Apennine of Umbria and the march, the da Varano of Camerino and the Trinci of Foligno. He defeated and executed the head of the house which tradi-

---

[1] Partner, *Papal State*, p. 67n.
[2] The appointment was dated 9 July 1434, Reg. Vat. 373, fo. 13 v. Cf. *Corpus Chronicorum Bononiensium* (*RRIISS*, xviii, pt. 1), iv, pp. 72–3. The identification of the Bishop of Recanati in the note is mistaken.
[3] 5 March 1435, Reg. Vat. 373, fo. 143 (not 5 May 1434, as in *ASR* viii (1908), p. 357).
[4] See the biography by A. Petrucci in *Dizionario biografico degli Italiani*.

tionally had dominated his own town of Corneto, the prefect Jacopo di Vico. The traditional strongholds of the Colonna and the Savelli in the Alban hills were stormed, and many of them destroyed. When Antonio da Pisa returned from the kingdom he was defeated and hanged. The Colonna villages of Palestrina and Zagarolo were demolished.

These peacekeeping operations were spectacular, although in practice the depredations of Vitelleschi were not unlike those of the *condottieri* he was supposed to suppress. While he savagely attacked one group of feudal magnates, he thrust land and concessions into the hands of others; the Orsini of various branches, the Anguillara, the Farnese, the Baglioni all knew a period of power and influence under Eugenius.[1] On the other hand Vitelleschi was a less unusual and irregular figure in papal government than has sometimes been made out; his role was not unlike that of some of the henchmen of the Colonna pope in the preceding pontificate.[2] Even the devastation of lands of opponents was a sort of barbarism which was common practice.

The Roman area was only one of those subject to papal government. In the march of Ancona Sforza ruled without any reference to the pope, and paying little attention to his subjects except for the money he could squeeze out of them.[3] Sforza perhaps did not intend to use the march for more than a reserve of men, money and victuals, though it is doubtful if his depredations were different in kind from those of papal governors, if the emergencies of war are taken into account. As for Bologna, Eugenius was gradually learning that he had little alternative between a Venetian or a Milanese protectorate over the city. The increase of Venetian influence in the Bolognese, especially in control of the castles, was bitterly resented, and was one of the main causes of the rebellion of 1434. Eugenius only managed to recover Bologna by leaning over to the other side in the following year, and asking for Milanese help to recover Bologna. The Bolognese accepted a papal governor – not one

[1] Cf. Guiraud, *L'Etat Pontifical*, pp. 104–36; C. Pinzi, 'Lettere del legato Vitelleschi', *ASR*, xxxi (1908), pp. 357–407.

[2] Especially in financial matters. Between 7 March 1436 and 30 April 1449 he spent 318,086 florins and received 238,167 florins (Reg. Vat. 366, folios 321v–323v, 357; the addition of totals is faulty).

[3] Cf. A. Gianandrea, 'Della signoria di Francesco Sforza nella Marca', *ASL*, viii (1881), pp. 68–108, 315–47, ibid. 2nd ser., ii (1885), pp. 33–64, 281–329, 475–513; idem, 'Nuovi documenti sforzeschi fabrianesi', *ASI*, 5th ser., xvi (1895), pp. 225–43; G. Valeri, 'Della signoria di Francesco Sforza nella Marca', *ASL*, 2nd ser., i (1884), pp. 35–78, 252–304; T. Valenti, 'Francesco Sforza e il comune di Monte dell 'Olmo', *AMSM*, 4th ser., ii (1925), pp. 117–66; M. Rosi, *Della Signoria di Francesco Sforza nella Marca* (Recanati, 1895). Benadduci's book of the same title (Tolentino, 1892); B. Feliciangeli, 'Delle relazioni di Francesco Sforza coi Camerti', *AMSM*, n.s., v (1908), pp. 311–462.

of Eugenius's hated Venetian relations – one of whose pacifying measures was to effect the murder of the returned exile, Giangaleazzo Bentivoglio. The Ordelaffi had returned to Forlì, and the Malatesta family had recovered most of the lands taken away from them by Pope Martin in 1430. Though there was still papal rule in Umbria as well as in Rome,[1] it was a lame and halting state which Eugenius tried to rule from without its borders, leaning heavily on outside powers. The savagery of Eugenius's agents in Bologna and Rome, the attempt of the papal *condottiere* Baldassare da Offida to murder Francesco Sforza, reflected the position of a power with its back to the wall. All central Italy, including the bellicose *signori,* was straitened by the fiscal pressure of the wars. The Malatesta of Pesaro referred to themselves in 1435 as 'beggars rather than paupers'.[2]

The key to the Papal State – as always – lay in the kingdom. Joanna's death in 1435 meant that the war between the Aragonese and the Angevins in the kingdom had to be fought to a finish. There was little choice for Eugenius, who in spite of the captivity of René of Anjou by the Burgundians had to plump for the French candidate. The need for French support at Basle, and the urgency of reaching an Anglo-French peace settlement, made it almost impossible for the papal court to abandon the Angevins. In 1437 Eugenius decided to send Vitelleschi with an army into the kingdom, to support the Angevin cause and perhaps also to help free the pope of his humiliating dependence on Francesco Sforza. Sforza fought the Aragonese claim for control of the kingdom, largely because he could see that Aragonese rule would be stronger than Angevin. But although in a sense Sforza was an Angevin supporter, his campaigns against the Aragonese faction were virtually independent of those of the other Angevin partisans or those of Vitelleschi.

Like many earlier papal invasions of the kingdom, that of Vitelleschi in 1437–8 had a disastrous ending, though it began well enough. Having quarrelled with the all-important Orsini faction, Vitelleschi in the early spring of 1438 abandoned his disintegrating army in Apulia, and embarked alone in a small boat from Bisceglie for Venice and Ferrara. It was a crushing defeat, and papal prestige felt its effects as far as the Romagna.[3]

The Council of Ferrara-Florence in 1438–9, the last great oecumenical

[1] L. Fumi, 'Il governo di Stefano Porcari in Orvieto', *SDSD*, iv (1883), pp. 33–93.
[2] Theiner, *C.D.*, iii, no. 280. Cf. Jones, *Italian Renaissance Studies*, p. 232; idem, in *EHR* (1952), pp. 348–9. For the preliminaries see Guiraud, *L'Etat Pontifical*, pp. 216–19.
[3] Cf. *I diurnali del Duca di Monteleone* (*RRIISS*, xxi, pt. 5), p. 146.

achievement of the Medieval Church, thus took place, as had the Council of Constance, at a time of prostration of the temporal power.[1] A degree of security was necessary for the council, and also a degree of financial security, since its expenses were heavy. Both these were found by Eugenius from the Veneto-Florentine alliance and from the Florentine banks. The problem of protection for the council became acute early in its sittings at Ferrara, when Niccolò Piccinino with the help of the Bentivoglio occupied Bologna (18 May 1438), and Milanese influence invaded all Emilia and Romagna. Niccolò d'Este, the great moderator and peace-maker of the Po valley, managed to protect the council, but both the Greeks and Eugenius became increasingly nervous, and Piccinino was the main reason for the transfer of the council to Florence (January–March 1439).

The last year of Vitelleschi (who had now also become Archbishop of Florence) is an unsolved puzzle. In May 1439 his legation in Rome was confirmed, and he was also appointed commissioner to reduce Bologna and the Romagna to obedience – it was the last which really interested Florence, who wanted to remove him from his operations in the Apennine of the march, detrimental to their ally Sforza.[2] In the spring of 1440 the machinations of Vitelleschi's many enemies were successful. The patriarch was arrested as he entered Castel Sant'Angelo by its castellan, Antonio da Rido, wounded and probably a few days later murdered. Whether Eugenius ordered his arrest (as da Rido claimed), or merely consented to it, is unknown; certainly if the deed took place against his will Eugenius must have been too frightened of its perpetrators to speak out. If the bait was the supposed riches of Vitelleschi the pope at least got little of them; the reported hoard of 300,000 ducats reduced itself in the end to a modest 911 florins 16 shillings.[3] Antonio da Rido became one of the right-hand men of the new chief papal courtier and master of *condottieri*, Ludovico 'Scarampo', and achieved a sort of eternal fame in the relief portrait which shows him marching before his castle of Sant'Angelo, on the bronze doors of St Peter's executed for Eugenius IV by Filarete.

[1] The definitive history of the council is that of Father Joseph Gill, *The Council of Florence* (Cambridge, 1959).
[2] The re-appointment of Vitelleschi in Reg. Vat. 366, folios 323v–4 (19 May 1439). Vitelleschi's legation was extended to the duchy of Spoleto on 1 June 1439, presumably to give legal cover for his operations against the Trinci of Foligno (ibid. fo. 344 v). Cf. *Florentine Studies*, p. 397.
[3] Introitus et Exitus 406, fo. 58. Cf. P. Paschini, 'Ludovico Cardinale Camerlengo e i suoi maneggi sino alla morte di Eugenio IV (1447)', *Memorie Storiche Forogiuliesi*, xxiv (1928), pp. 39–72. The second part is in the same periodical, xxvi (1930), pp. 27–74.

V

The last great days of the papal-Florentine alliance had come with the victory of the Florentines over Piccinino's troops at Anghiari near Borgo San Sepolcro, on the border of Florence with the Papal State (29 June 1440). After the battle Florentine supremacy on the northern frontiers of the Papal State was assured by the cession to Florence of the papal town of Borgo San Sepolcro, and by Florentine occupation of the adjacent Città di Castello. At the same time the other papal ally, Venice, occupied Ravenna, the historic heart of papal Romagna. Eugenius felt that his allies were treating him badly. All the major powers in Italy were for the moment reconciled at the peace of Cavriana in November 1441. But Eugenius was probably the most discontented of the signatories of this peace. Sforza remained in control of the march of Ancona, and had papal legal titles to justify his rule there.[1] Bologna remained under the rule of Piccinino, even though the published text of the Treaty of Cavriana contained promises to restore the city to the pope.[2] The north of the Papal State was thus split up into spheres of influence under the control of Venice, Florence and Milan respectively. The east of the Papal State (the march of Ancona) was ruled by Sforza, whose possession also stretched west into Umbria as far as Todi and Assisi.

The last *condotta* of Sforza from the Church was issued in April 1442. Two months later Naples fell to Alfonso of Aragon, and the kingdom was finally lost by the beaten René of Anjou. The time was ripe for diplomatic revolutions in Italian politics. Both Eugenius IV and Filippo Maria Visconti were discontented (to say the least) with Sforza. Together they patched up their old feuds, and united to employ Piccinino to attack the lands of Sforza in Umbria and the march of Ancona. Consequently in the summer of 1442, for the first time since he had acquired them in 1434, Sforza was violently attacked in his possessions in central Italy. Todi, Assisi, Gualdo in Umbria fell from his grasp, and the towns in the march of Ancona began to fall away. Eugenius was not the only instigator of the war, but he had much to hope from it. In the spring of 1443 Eugenius took the next logical step, and accepted Alfonso of Aragon as the legal ruler of the kingdom, securing from him formal

---

[1] As he had been before the treaty; cf. Reg. Vat. 366, fo. 402, addressed to rebels against Sforza in the march (13 March 1440).
[2] Cf. *Florentine Studies*, p. 398, and n.4. The formal *signoria* of Bologna was taken by Piccinino in March, 1442: cf. C. M. Ady, *The Bentivoglio of Bologna* (Oxford, 1937), p. 22.

recognition of papal rights over the fief.[1] Eugenius had to cede Alfonso the cities of Terracina and Benevento, but the sacrifice was worthwhile. The negotiations which the pope was conducting with Francesco Sforza and the Duke of Milan in Siena broke down.[2] It was the end of the Florentine alliance, and the end also of the Angevin policy which the papal *curia* had followed since 1419. Eugenius now at last found the freedom of diplomatic movement which Martin had always enjoyed, and which the unhappy circumstances of the 1430s had denied him. Sforza was placed on the defensive in the kingdom and in the Papal State. Alfonso's army marched north into Umbria to make a junction with Piccinino, and to operate in concert with the papal forces under Scarampo. The alliance with the kingdom which curial diplomatists had come to think of as in some way a natural one, had again – for the moment – come into being.

The first round of Eugenius's new war was not decisive. The Papal State, north and south of Rome, suffered badly from the attentions of Sforza's *condottiere*, Ciarpellone. The younger Piccinino lost Bologna to a revolution of the Bentivoglio faction (June 1443) and the elder was defeated in November in the march by Sforza at Monte Loro. Every turn in the war had its effect on the small and insecure *signorie* of the Papal State. After Sforza's victories the young Oddantonio di Monte-feltro, created first duke of Urbino by Eugenius IV, was murdered (22–23 July 1444).[3] The margins, political and economic, of these little states were precarious.

The northern powers – Venice, Milan, Florence and their satellite Bologna – united to support Sforza. Negotiations with Sforza were difficult,[4] but after the victory of Monte Loro peace had to be made. In May 1444 a bargain was struck with Sforza at Perugia, and a general peace was signed in October in the same city. While excepting certain places which had defected from Sforza in the recent war, Eugenius

[1] For Alfonso's oath see Pontieri in *Studi Filangieri*, i. p. 566n.; G. Fasoli, in *RSI*, lxv (1953), p. 323.

[2] Cod. Vat. lat, Chigi F. IV, 103, fo. 19. 'Capitula pacis et conuentiones inita et conclusa inter s.d.n. Eugenium papam 4 et illustrm dominum comitem franciscum sfortiam etc. Et tandem non acceptata per prefatum s.d.n., persuasionibus et ad instantiam regis Aragon. et N. Piccinini.' Cf. L. Osio, *Documenti Diplomatici tratti dagli Archivi Milanesi*, iii (Milan, 1872), pp. 285–8.

[3] Cf. Franceschini, *Saggi di Storia Montefeltresca e Urbinate*, pp. 212–33; idem, in *AMSM*, 7th ser., xi (1956).

[4] MS cited above, fo. 21v. '1444 die 17 martii indictione 7a pontificatus... anno 14. Copia capitulorum exhibitorum per R.d.C. Comen. et L. Aquilegien. cardinales legatos apostolicos, Senis dictis anno et die, et non acceptatorum.'

again – for the last time – recognised him as legal ruler of the march of Ancona.[1] But Eugenius had little intention of accepting a verdict which was imposed on him by force, and by his late, now resentful allies. A year earlier he had returned to Rome at last (September 1443). The Council of Basle was diplomatically beaten, and was dragging out its last sad days under the anti-pope Felix. The crusade of Varna, while shedding no great glory on Hungarian or Venetian arms, showed Europe that the pope possessed the power and leadership to take a major part in the struggle with the Ottoman Turks. It also showed that the financial resources of the Holy See were exhausted, but the irritation of the Venetians and Florentines on learning this only formed part of their more general disillusionment with Eugenius.[2]

The renewal of the struggle against Sforza was made possible by Filippo Maria Visconti, who again turned against his son-in-law in the spring of 1445, angered by Sforza's execution of Ciarpellone. In May 1445 new alliances were formed against Sforza by Eugenius and Visconti and Sforza's other old enemies. Sigismondo Malatesta showed the rest of the *signorotti* in the march the way things were going, when he abandoned Sforza, and at the end of the year took from him the important point of Rocca Contrata (Arcevia); at the same time he became Standard-Bearer of the Church – a title which while it carried traditional honour and dignity, was at one time or another held by all the most greedy and ferocious enemies of the Holy See. Sforza was badly pressed in the march, and in the spring of 1446 he allowed Cosimo de' Medici and the ruined leaders of the Angevin faction in the *curia*, Cardinal Niccolò Acciapaccia,[3] to persuade him to attempt the dangerous expedient of marching through Umbria to attack Rome. The campaign was an utter failure, and Sforza only lost prestige by it.

But the march of Ancona was only one of Sforza's spheres of interest in Italy, and not even the first in time, since he had had great lands and claims in the kingdom before he ever came to the march. What was to change the pattern of politics in central Italy from this point was the increased importance placed by Sforza and Venice on the issues at stake in the Po valley. Venetian ambition was now thoroughly engaged there; Sforza had to think not only of his present interests but of his hopes in the event of Filippo Maria's death, as heir through his daughter. Sforza was not going to commit his main forces in the march, especially since

---

[1] Cf. Theiner, *C.D.*, iii, nos. 303–4; Raynaldus, ad a. 1444; Reg. Vat. 382, fo. 238v.

[2] D. Caccamo, 'Eugenio IV e la Crociata di Varna', *ASR*, lxxix (1956), pp. 35–87.

[3] For whom see the article by Manfredi in *Dizionario Biografico degli Italiani*.

Piccinino was now dead, and his son in captivity. The erosion of Sforza's position in the march at this time is probably as much due to declining political interest as to any other factor. By July 1446 Ancona had returned to papal allegiance, and the only remaining Sforza stronghold was the little town of Iesi. Alessandro Sforza had been made lord of the former Malatesta possession of Pesaro by his brother; the pope was willing to condone this if Alessandro promised obedience.

VI

As Eugenius neared death in the New Year of 1447 the clouds began to lift from the temporal power at last. The Papal State was not secure, nor was it to be so in that century. Ravenna had passed under Venetian rule. Sforza remained the ruler of one city in the march – Iesi – for a short time, and continued to dominate the port of Ancona until after the death of Eugenius's successor. Under the *signoria* of the Bentivoglio Bologna was in the 1450s effectively a zone of Florentine influence, though the Church retained enough political and financial control to conserve its juridical position there.[1] The relationship of the Papal State with the Neapolitan kingdom was by no means satisfactory for papal interests. Terracina and Benevento had been ceded by Eugenius to Alfonso of Aragon in 1443 as part of the price of his political turn-about. Alfonso's campaign in Tuscany in 1447 brought Spanish power into the heart of central Italy for the first time. Spanish influence was shortly to gain intimate access to the papal *curia;* in 1455 the first Spanish pope was elected.

The anguished years of the wars and diplomacy of Eugenius IV had not ended in failure. The efforts of Cardinal Giovanni Vitelleschi and the successes which Eugenius himself had achieved against Sforza in the last four years of the pontificate had led to a papal restoration of a sort. It was a restoration which reflected the change in the style of papal temporal governments which had taken place under Martin and Eugenius. The re-imposition of strong papal government in Rome was permanent; the revolutions of 1435 and 1453 did nothing to modify it. The decay of the independent institutions of the communes of the Papal State meant that where the communes were not ruled despotically by *signori* they tended to be ruled despotically by papal governors; only Perugia, among the larger cities, was perhaps an exception to this rule. When

---

[1] Cf. Miss Ady's *Bentivoglio of Bologna*. She gives a synopsis of the 1447 agreement between the commune and the Church, on pp. 39–40 – an agreement made by Nicholas V, not by Eugenius.

papal officials assumed power in the papal restoration they often stepped
into the shoes of dead or expelled tyrants. They had, naturally, to make
endless compromises with the oligarch families, some of whom like the
Vitelli of Città di Castello or the Baglioni of Perugia remained politically
important to the end of the fifteenth century and beyond. Other
seigniorial families such as the Chiavelli of Fabriano or the da Varano
of Camerino had been eliminated through internal feuding. In such
cases the Church took the towns under direct rule, and Fabriano (for
example) became the favourite residence of Pope Nicholas V.

It remained true that the Papal State was divided into war-like little
signorie to an extent unknown in any other region of Italy.[1] The
economic basis of the *signorie* was fragile. But the extraordinary resilience and expansion of a little lordship such as that of the Montefeltro,
based on the willingness and ability of the tenantry of an arid Apennine
region to serve as mercenary soldiers, shows that there was nothing pre-
determined about the decline of the petty tyrants. The Church could
attack and subdue a single disobedient *signore,* as Pius II subdued the
Malatesta of Rimini in 1462. But the tyrants remained embedded in
papal state politics until the intervention of French and Spanish power
in Italy in the sixteenth century.

On 27 February 1447 Eugenius IV died. He was succeeded by Tommaso
Parentucelli of Sarzana (Nicholas V, elected 6 March 1447). Nicholas
came at an opportune moment in papal temporal policy. Born on the
edge of the Florentine dominions, he was willing to renounce the political
heritage of the last years of Eugenius, and to return to the papal-
Florentine *entente*. Sforza also was willing to abandon his old claims
in the Papal State in order to clear the way for his new and far more
grandios ambitions in Milan. Within a few days of the election of
Nicholas V Sforza was negotiating with the new pope in Tivoli. Sforza
was unwilling to abandon Iesi, his last dominion in the march, but was
unable to contemplate waging a major war to recover his lost position
in central Italy. On 13 August 1447 Filippo Maria Visconti died, and
the face of Italian politics changed in every way. A new understanding
between the papacy and Florence came into being, tolerant of Sforza's
ambitions, hostile to Venice, distrustful of Alfonso. In 1454–5 this new
policy of balance which Nicholas V and Cosimo had worked out between
them expressed itself in the peace of Lodi and the Italian League.

One of the dominating factors, after 1443, was the return of the
popes to Rome, where they were to stay without serious hindrance until

---

[1] Cf. C. Cipolla, *Storia delle Signorie* (Milan, 1881), pp. 397–8.

the city was sacked by the troops of Charles V and the Duke of Bourbon in 1527. A period was beginning when the Roman bishops were to renew the intimate link with their own see which had been broken in 1305, and only intermittently re-established since then. The population, the cultural and economic resources of the city were gradually to grow, until in the sixteenth century it became a great Renaissance capital, dignified and rich. All this was far in the future. When Biondo Flavio looked down on the distant city from Marino in the Alban hills, where he found himself with Cardinal Prospero Colonna on a hunting expedition, a year after the return of Eugenius to the city in 1443, he saw all Latium at his feet in the evening light, and Rome with its monuments and fortresses, 'like a wood of castles and towers'.[1] Rome was still a medieval city, and the first major building in Rome which might be called 'Renaissance', the Palazzo Venezia of Paul II, was still unbuilt. The Papal State had survived the turbulence and the perils of the Conciliar epoch, and in the following century it was destined to survive the dangers of the period of the Reformation.

[1] B. Nogara, *Scritti inediti e rari di Biondo Flavio* (Rome, 1927), p. 156. There is a longer romantic description of Rome from Monte Mario by Aeneas Sylvius Piccolomini, made apropos of his accompanying Frederick III to his coronation in 1452. *Historia Frederici III*, p. 275, quoted by Pastor, *History of the Popes*, ii, pp. 149–50, and Miss C. N. Ady, *Pope Pius II* (1913), p. 116.

Rome at the end of the Middle Ages; St. Peter's and the Vatican.

Chapter 13

The Papal State at the end of the Middle Ages

I

The population of Rome at the end of the fourteenth century is unlikely to have exceeded 25,000 inhabitants; by the mid-fifteenth century it may have risen to 35,000.[1] This modest collection of people lived mostly in the quarters between the Capitol and St Peter's; much of the rest of the city was waste, or given over to vineyards or pasture. The most important Roman occupation was stock-farming; every winter thousands of cattle, sheep, goats were brought down from the hills to pasture within the city. During the wars of Eugenius IV the sheep and cattle of the Romans wandered as far as the shops in the precincts of St Peter's.[2]

But the economic importance of Rome was not small. The stockfarmers, the *bovattieri*, were the basis of a variety of other important activities of 'merchants', money-changers, textile-workers, whose activities in the late fourteenth century were extending.[3] In times of peace and security Rome also had the hotel business of pilgrims and travellers, and the other economic benefits of the residence of the papal court.[4] The last amounted to far more than the residence of a number of ecclesiastics. It is not clear that the households kept by cardinals in Rome were as numerous or important earlier in the fifteenth century as they

[1] K. J. Beloch, *Bevölkerungsgeschichte Italiens*, ii (Berlin-Leipzig, 1939), pp. 1–5. These figures are problematical. For what follows see Partner, *Papal State*, pp. 119 ff., 161 ff.; Esch, *Bonifaz IX. u.d. Kirchenstaat*, pp. 209 ff.

[2] Vespasiano da Bisticci, *Vite di Uomini Illustri del secolo XV*, P. d'Ancona and E. Aeschlimann (ed.) (Milan, 1951), p. 20. 'si tenevano le pecore e la vacche in sino dove sono oggi i banchi de' mercatanti.' Cf. P. Pecchiai, 'Banchi e botteghe dinanzi alla Basilica Vaticana nei secoli XIV, XV e XVI', *Archivi*, 2nd ser. xviii (1951), pp. 81–123. The entry he quotes for 1437 (p. 105) suggests that in the wars of Eugenius the shops were poorer, but still in existence.

[3] C. Gennaro, 'Mercatanti e bovattieri nella Roma della seconda metà del Trecento', *BISI*, lxxviii (1967), pp. 155–203.

[4] M. Romani, *Pellegrini e viaggiatori nell'economia di Roma dal xiv al xvii secolo* (Milan, 1948) unfortunately says little about the earlier period.

were later,[1] but they were certainly not negligible. The national hospices such as those of the English and the Germans were only single instances of the great clerical influx to the administrative centre of Christendom. Though much of the curial financial business was in the hands of Florentine bankers, Roman banking families such as the Astalli had a share.

The direct economic importance of Rome to the papal government was considerable. More than a hundred thousand florins a year passed through the hands of the treasurer of the city, and the net profit on this sum after the expenses of government had been paid was substantial.[2] More important to the Papal Chamber than the net profit was the use of these assured incomes as security for loans. The salt monopoly of Rome and its District, using salt from the pans at Ostia, was also important and profitable for the Chamber. All these were revenues which the victory of Boniface IX over the Roman commune had assured for the papacy.

The drastic fall in the population of the Roman District in the later Middle Ages is undisputed. Such figures are no more than guesses, but the population in the early fifteenth century of the whole area bounded by Montalto di Castro on the north-west coast, Terni in the Tiber valley, and Terracina in the south, has been reckoned to be about 150,000 inhabitants.[3] The District claimed as subject by the Roman commune contained 366 towns, castles and villages which are listed in the Roman salt-tax lists. If we adopt the figure of 150,000, and exclude Rome, the average population of each of these places was 420 persons approximately. The rise in population believed to have taken place by the seventeenth century amounted to about 25 per cent of this total figure, which seems for the fifteenth century to represent a population density of ten persons to the square kilometre. This is a tenth of the

---

[1] Cf. D. S. Chambers, 'The Economic Predicament of Renaissance Cardinals', *Studies in Medieval and Renaissance History*, iii (Univ. of Nebraska, 1966), pp. 289–313.

[2] Cf. Partner, *Papal State*, pp. 168–9, 194; idem, 'The Budget of the Roman Church in the Renaissance Period', *Italian Renaissance Studies*, pp. 266–7.

[3] Beloch, ii, pp. 37 ff.; G. Pardi, 'La popolazione del distretto di Roma sui primordi del Quattrocento', *ASR*, xlix (1926), pp. 331–54; G. Tomassetti, 'Del sale e focatico del comune di Roma nel medio evo', ibid. xx (1897), pp. 313–68. Tomassetti's figures were corrected by Pardi and Beloch, but the totals remain very uncertain. J. Delumeau, *Vie économique et sociale de Rome dans la seconde moitié du XVI siècle*, ii (Paris, 1959), p. 528, continues to accept Tomassetti's figure of 500,000 persons. He quotes Pardi's article in the note, but very mysteriously assigns the salt tax document to 1300; Pardi showed it to be of 1422–4. There are also some hearth tax figures for the Campagna-Maritime for this period, but they are useless for population statistics. Cf. Beloch, ii, p. 37, and below, p. 439.

average density of population in the same area in the 1951 census.[1]

The littoral zone of the Roman District is relieved by the volcanic hills which occur round the lake of Bolsena in the north, and round the other volcanic lakes (the Monti Cimini and Sabbatini round the lakes of Vico and Bracciano, and the Colli Albani round those of Albano and Nemi). Outside these volcanic crater areas, the hills and plateaux of southern Etruria are to be distinguished from the flat littoral which begins in the north with the Maremma Maccarese, and on the southern side of the Tiber widens into the Pontine plain, continuing as far as Monte Circeo and Terracina.

Further east are the limestone hills of the Anti-Apennine of Latium running from the middle Tiber valley in the north, and curving round to form the Sabini, Carseolani and Ernici ranges of hills. The main breaks in the Apennine chain are those of the rivers Corese, Nera, and Aniene, and through these river valleys run the main routes of the Via Salaria, the Via Flaminia, and the Via Tiburtina-Valeria. On the north side of the River Nera and the Via Amerina (which left the Cassia at Baccano) provided an alternative route into the Apennines, passing through Todi and Perugia, and rejoining the Flaminia at Scheggia.[2] The Prenestini hills follow the curve of the River Aniene on its western side; the Lepini hills follow the Sacco basin, and then curve round to meet the sea at Terracina.[3]

The most important road to Tuscany and the north was the Via Cassia, known in the Middle Ages as the Via Francigena or Via Francisca – the Frankish road. Though diverging at some places from the ancient Cassia,[4] its main route was closely similar. Skirting the lakes of Bracciano, Vico and Bolsena, and passing or skirting the Sabatini, Cimini and Volsi

---

[1] Cf. F. Milone, *L'Italia nell'economia delle sue regioni* (Turin, 1955), p. 603. Rome is excluded in both cases. I have taken the area of the Roman District to have measured about 15,000 square kilometres, less than the modern region of Lazio (which includes the province of Rieti).

[2] Cf. D. A. Bullough, 'La Via Flaminia nella storia dell'Umbria (600–1100)', *Aspetti dell'Umbria dall'inizio del secolo VIII, Atti del terzo convegno di Studi Umbri* (Perugia, 1966), pp. 211–33.

[3] For the geography Milone's book is very useful. I have also consulted J. M. Houston, *The Western Mediterranean World: An introduction to its regional landscapes* (1964), and the T.C.I. *Conosci l'Italia*, vii, by A. Sestini, *Il Paessaggio* (Milan, 1963).

[4] J. B. Ward Perkins, 'Notes on Southern Etruria and the Ager Veientanus', *PBSR*, xxiii (n.s. x, 1955), pp. 44 ff.; idem with M. W. Fredericksen, 'The Ancient Road System of the Central and Northern Ager Faliscus', ibid. xxv (n.s. xii, 1957), pp. 67–208; Ward Perkins, Kahane and Threipland, 'The Ager Veientanus, North and East of Rome', ibid. xxxvi (n.s. xxiii, (1968), especially pp. 161 ff. For the Via Francigena in the Papal State, see J. Jung, 'Das Itinerar des Erzbischofs Sigeric von Canterbury und die Strasse von Rom über Siena nach Lucca', *MIöG*, xxv (1904), pp. 1–90, at pp. 1–46. For what follows the works of Tomassetti and Guiraud are essential.

hills, the Cassia runs through Sutri, Viterbo, Montefiascone and Acqua-pendente. Each of the last three towns was at times the seat of the provincial rector of the patrimony of St Peter in Tuscany. The Via Clodia takes a route on the west of Lake Bracciano. The ancient road eventually joined the Via Aurelia, but it is uncertain if it was used beyond Bracciano in the Middle Ages.[1] The Clodia passed through an area which by the early fifteenth century was certainly in decline (e.g. Galeria, Manziana). To the north west of Lake Bracciano were the metalliferous Tolfa hills, which in the second half of the fifteenth century were found to contain important alum deposits.[2]

Far more definitely in decline was the tract of the Via Aurelia from the city to Civitavecchia. The saline marshes of Maccarese, and the rather higher area between the Aurelia and the Clodia (Boccea, Santa Rufina) as far as Santa Severa on the coast – most of the diocese of Porto, in fact – were sown with abandoned or depopulated settlements. Civitavecchia and Corneto were, however, relatively flourishing places, both with port facilities, although Corneto's harbour at the foot of the river Marta could not really be called a port. Corneto (in the present century called Tarquinia) knew a brief moment of prosperity at the time of the hegemony of its distinguished citizen, Cardinal Vitelleschi. But in general the importance of the Via Aurelia was much diminished by bad security, depopulation and fever.

The road system south of Rome presented other difficulties. The road to Ostia was of no great practical importance, since Rome was now its own port (the *Ripa* and *Ripetta*), and the ancient harbours at the mouth of the Tiber had silted up. Nor was the Via Laurentina of any note. The basic political trouble since the early Middle Ages had been and remained the control of the Via Appia and of the Via Latina by noble families, especially at Capo di Bove on the Appia and at Borghetto (Grottaferrata) on the Latina. Martin V had tried to deal with this in his own way by granting strongpoints to his own family to control the routes from the Alban Hills to Ardea and to the small but important harbours at Anzio and Nettuno.[3] The Alban Hills were covered in fortresses embedded in the *macchia* and the beechwoods; the most important was the papal castle of Lariano, but there were others such as the Colonna fort at Malafitto, on the road which skirted the east side

[1] E Wetter, 'Studies and strolls in Southern Etruria', *Etruscan Culture Lands and People* (Malmö and N.Y., 1962), pp. 165–96, at p. 180, has little to say on the medieval fate of the road.
[2] J. Delumeau, *L'Alun de Rome XV–XIXe siècle* (Paris, 1962).
[3] Partner, *Papal State*, pp. 197–8.

of Alban lake to lead to the pass at Lariano.[1] The aim of many of these defensive systems, and of further forts on and round the Via Palestrina, was the control of the Via Labicana, which followed the Sacco valley from its upper course at Valmontone[2] to the Neapolitan border at Ceprano. In effect the basic problems of papal defence and control of these communications had changed hardly at all since the time of Innocent III.[3] It was a poor indicator for the effectiveness of papal government that the Colonna family politics of Martin V at the end of the Middle Ages only echoed the Conti family politics of Innocent III, or the Caetani family politics of Boniface VIII.

II

For most of recorded history the littoral plain of Latium has remained predominantly woods, scrub, undergrowth and marsh. It is country whose main agricultural use has been as transhumance pasture for sheep, and as wild grazing for cattle, horses, pigs and other beasts. Interspersed with this type of stock farming there have always been in the Roman Campagna extensive areas of grain cultivation, and, especially on the volcanic hillsides, olives and vines. The last are in the modern period frequently in *coltura promiscua,* i.e. scattered in the fields in inter-culture with other crops; in the Middle Ages this system was less common because of the difficulty of protecting the vines against pasturing animals.[4]

How far the deforestation of the great woods of Latium had gone by the later Middle Ages seems a question at present impossible to answer.[5] The economic value of the woods was partly for building purposes, but more for pannage for swine, and pasture for other beasts.

The system of cereal cultivation was that of the *maggese* and *ristoppio,* that is to say of leaving the land fallow for two, three or four years,

---

[1] Ibid. For Lariano see Esch, pp. 480–2, 490–1. All these forts, including that of La Molara on the Via Latina, were subsequently deserted, but there is no reason for thinking them so in the early fifteenth century.

[2] Valmontone was at the junction of the Via Casilina and the Via Labicana. From Torre Nuova to Valmontone the ancient Via Labicana was disused in the Middle Ages (cf. Ashby, *PBSR*, i(1902), p. 132).

[3] Waley, *P.S.*, pp. 81 ff.

[4] Cf. E. Sereni, *Storia del Paesaggio Agrario Italiano* (Bari, 1961), pp. 62 ff.

[5] Some guidance for the situation in the sixteenth century can be obtained from D. Boccamazzo, *Della caccia della trasteverina* (Rome 1548), and from T. Ashby, *La Campagna Romana al tempo di Paolo III. Mappa della Campagna Romana del 1547 di Eufrosino della Volpaia* (Rome, 1914). C. Fries, 'Forest and soil in Etruria', *Etruscan Culture Land and People*, pp. 233–52, is disappointing, though the photographs are interesting.

Opposite: 19 Bologna in 1505

20 The north-west of the Papal State showing forestation in the late
seventeenth century (see p. 424)

the fallow being open to communal pasture. The stubble was burned high to enrich the soil, after the harvest. The primitive methods of ploughing and winnowing, which went on until the nineteenth century, seem to mark the Roman area as especially conservative.[1] The yields were low, and Rome could seldom get enough cereals from its hinterland even to feed its own modest urban population, for whom Roman officials had to import from the march of Ancona, or to buy in southern Italy and elsewhere.

The problem of determining how far drainage systems and their deterioration affected agriculture at any given period in the Roman area seems as hard to answer as that of deforestation. No doubt even where ancient drainage systems like those of the underground *cuniculi* had earlier served, changes in water courses had rendered them less useful. The general problem of the Roman littoral was the absence of fall in the land level. But there is a penury of good historical work on this subject, as there is also of the history of malaria.[2]

In so far as we can assess the evidence, it does not seem to point to the wholesale abandonment of agricultural centres in the Roman District in the later Middle Ages; though there was widespread depopulation and the temporary abandonment of some places.[3] There are wide geographical differences in the Roman District which must mean that the agriculture in differing areas had different histories. The saline and marshy flat lands behind dunes on the coast (in places like the abandoned 'Statua' near Cervetri); the deeply scooped channels of the river beds of northern Etruria, picturesque and dramatic, carved from volcanic rock and its underlying clay; the wooded volcanic heights in the Alban hills; the terraced and smiling slopes of Monte San Giovanni on the Monti Lepini above the river Liri; all these are too diverse to bring into a single formula.

The patrimony of St Peter in Tuscany stretched from Radicofani on

---

[1] Cf. Renzo de Felice, *Aspetti e momenti della vita economica di Roma e del Lazio nei secoli XVIII e XIX* (Rome, 1965), pp. 33 ff.

[2] A. Celli, 'La malaria nella storia di Roma', *ASR*, xlvii (1924), pp. 1–44, is far from satisfactory. The German version of Celli's work, *Die Malaria in ihrer Bedeutung für die Geschichte Roms und der römischen Campagna* (Leipzig, 1929) is rather better.

[3] Cf. M. Mallett and D. Whitehouse, 'Castel Porciano: an abandoned medieval village of the Roman Campagna', *PBSR*, xxxv (n.s. xxii, 1967), pp. 113–46. Castel Porciano was taxed at 80 florins in two tax lists of Martin V, Arm. XXXIII, vol. 11, fo. 9v, and Arm. XXIX, vol. 13, fo. 20v. B. Thordeman, 'The Medieval Castle of San Giovenale', *Skrifter utgivna av Svenska Institutet i Rom*, xxvi, vi, fasc. 4–5 (Lund 1967) and H. Stiesdal, 'Three Deserted Medieval Villages in the Roman Campagna', *Analecta Romana Instituti Danici*, ii (1962), pp. 63–100, may also be consulted.

P

the Sienese border to the north, to the sea at Montalto di Castro, and south to the mouth of the Tiber. On the east it was bounded by the county of Orvieto. South of Orvieto, on the west bank of the Tiber the hill areas of Narni, Terni and Amelia, and the little hill province of Sabina, and the *terra Arnulphorum* were distinct from the patrimony although sometimes administratively attached to it.[1]

The Campagna-Maritime province was dominated by the Roman baronial nobility; its communes were in decadence, and its littoral was largely occupied by scrub, forest, sand-dunes, or marsh. Its southern boundary with the kingdom was at Ceprano; the papal border fortress was Castro dei Volsci; the boundary reached the sea at Terracina. Inland the border climbed with the river Liri above its junction with the Sacco at Ceprano, until on the other side of the watershed the frontier descended with the river Turano on a course roughly parallel with the more westerly Aniene, and it joined the province of Sabina.

If the records of papal taxation are a guide, the patrimony of St Peter in Tuscany was a far richer area than the Campagna-Maritime province. The annual income of the Treasurer of the Tuscan patrimony after the Great Schism was in the region of ten thousand florins annually, of which about 36 per cent was in 1429–31 surplus to expenses.[2] The customs taxes on the salt-pans of Corneto, and the revenue from licences to export grain from Corneto and its hinterland were additional to this, and very substantial.[3] To this must be added the important profits of the taxation and pasture of sheep, for which the main centre was in the extreme north-west of the Papal State, the Abbazia *ad pontem* near Musignano in the diocese of Castro. The Abbazia *ad pontem* had in the thirteenth and early fourteenth centuries been an important papal castle, but by the time of Boniface IX it was in the hands of the Orsini; from them it passed in the following century to the Conti family,[4] to whom the Apostolic Chamber paid rent.

[1] Details in Partner, *Papal State*, pp. 96–7, and cf. Guiraud, *L'Etat Pontifical*, pp. 85–8; Esch, pp. 491–500; Waley, *P.S.*, pp. 81–4. For Radicofani, which was granted to Siena, by Eugenius, see Guiraud, pp. 85–6.

[2] Rome, Archivio di Stato, Arch. Camerale, pt. i, Tes. Prov., Patrimonio, Busta 1, vol. 3, folios 74, 88v. Cf. A. Anzilotti, 'Cenni sulle finanze del Patrimonio di S. Pietro in Tuscia nel secolo XV', *ASR*, xlii (1919), pp. 360–5.

[3] Partner, *Papal State*, pp. 122–3, 143–4. The sums from this source were substantial, e.g. 1,000 florins paid to the Apostolic Chamber in one payment in 1426 (Introitus et Exitus, vol. 385, fo. 42 v).

[4] The revenues of the *dogana* of the Tuscan patrimony in 1424–5 were 5,620 florins 3 *bon.* (*Papal State*, p. 119n.). For the Abbazia *ad pontem* see E. Serafini, *Musignano e la rocca al ponte* (Rome, 1920); for its revenues see *Papal State*, p. 121n. and cf. *Quellen*, xx (1928–9), pp. 136, 142; Esch, p. 608; Guiraud, p. 124.

Compared with these sums drawn from the Tuscan patrimony, the papal income from the Campagna-Maritime was negligible, and hardly sufficed to pay the salaries of the officers.[1] This official penury was partly due to the inability of provincial governors to control the Roman baronial nobles, but it must also reflect the penury of the countryside. Both north and south of Rome had suffered from plague and war during the schism. Viterbo and Corneto were richer cities than any south of Rome in the Papal State, but they also were less populous and rich than they had been in the early fourteenth century.[2]

III

Geographically continuous with the volcanic hills of Latium, but exercising its political influence also over the mountain area between the Tiber and Chiana valleys, Orvieto had greatly fallen off from its earlier splendour.[3] The population of Orvieto subsided, from approximately 15,000 in 1292 to something perhaps like four-fifths of that number by the beginning of the fifteenth century, and yet lower by 1449.[4] The economy of Orvieto, based primarily on cereals and viticulture, but including also a share in inter-regional trade, and on artisan manufactures, was evidently also in decadence. There is a certain contrast here with Perugia, whose political history was not dissimilar, but whose success in retaining its economic position and its control over its *contado* was far greater. Orvieto was normally ruled by its own papal governor.

An important group of towns commanding the Via Amerina and the Via Flaminia was usually united in a single jurisdiction, though often also under the rule of the rector of the Tuscan patrimony. Amelia (on

[1] Rome, Arch. di Stato, Arch. Cam., pt. i, Tes. Prov., Campagna, vol. i (accounts for 1427). In this year the treasurer of the province paid the modest sum of 56 florins into the Apostolic Chamber (Introitus et Exitus, vol. 385, fo. 41). Cf. *Papal State*, p. 186; Guiraud, pp. 47–83, Esch, pp. 480–91; Falco, 'I comuni della Campagna e della Marittima nel medio evo', *ASR*; xlix (1926), pp. 282–4. Some revenues from this province went to the communal administration of Rome, e.g. those of the *doganerius salis* (*Papal State*, p. 120).

[2] Guiraud, pp. 146–8. Cf. Calisse, *Storia di Civitavecchia*, 2nd ed., pp. 196–7. Beloch estimated 3,000 inhabitants for Corneto and 6,000 for Viterbo in 1449 (ii, pp. 56–7); but it is remarkable that in 1400 the plague was said to have caused 6,663 *deaths* in Viterbo (Esch, p. 340).

[3] The fourteenth-century *contado* of Orvieto is indicated in the maps of Waley, *Mediaeval Orvieto* and in E. Charpentier, *Une Ville devant la Peste*. The *contado* of Orvieto in 1432 is defined in the list of *castra* in Guiraud, p. 154. For the Monaldeschi see Guiraud, pp. 156–9; and cf. also Esch, pp. 504–10; Partner, *Papal State*, pp. 183–4.

[4] Charpentier, pp. 30–3, 214–21; Beloch, ii, pp. 45–8; G. Pardi, 'Il catasto d'Orvieto dell'anno 1292', *BSU*, ii (1896), pp. 225–320, at pp. 269, 313, 317. The hearth co-efficient used by Pardi and Beloch was five.

the Via Amerina, now less important than earlier in the Middle Ages), Narni commanding the crossing of the river Nera, and Terni, commanding the junction of the roads to Spoleto and to the kingdom through Rieti, were the main centres.[1] Narni, not surprisingly, was the site for the construction of one of Albornoz's fortresses; the bridges over the Nera at Narni and Terni were both fortified. Cesi, the centre of the little jurisdiction known as the *terra Arnulphorum,* commanded the road from Terni back to the Flaminia on the eastern side of the Nera, and was equally a fortress.

Adjacent to these areas were the very ancient papal county of Sabina, and the city of Rieti. Through Sabina ran the Via Salaria to Rieti and thence through the passes into the kingdom. Both Rieti and Sabina tended to be united to the jurisdiction of the rector of the Tuscan patrimony in the fifteenth century. The Abbey of Farfa, once the dominating political influence in Sabina, was now fully in decline.[2] Rieti resisted successfully the attempt of the Roman commune to control the city, and quarrelled interminably with Terni about the control of the waters of the Velino – a quarrel which went back, eventually, to the period of the Roman Republic. Politically, Sabina was a continuation of the Roman District in that it was dominated by the same Roman baronial families.

In the low hills of the Anti-Apennine areas just described, the agriculture was of vines, olives, and a certain amount of cereal especially where the land was terraced. Further east and further into the Apennines, the most important natural phenomena are the great Pliocene basins through which the rivers run.[3] Of these basins the most important is that of the Tiber, which becomes better defined when it reaches the Upper Tiber. The valley of the Nera runs through the basin of Terni, and the Velino descends through the basin of Rieti. The Valle Spoletana follows a gradually widening valley from Spoleto in the south-west until it becomes the wide and fertile Val Topino, and then joins the Chiascio and the Upper Tiber. In the mid-Apennines are other important basins – that of Lake Trasimene, so important (with the northern Val

[1] Esch, pp. 510 ff.; Guiraud, pp. 165 ff.; Partner, pp. 63n., 96–7. Guiraud is mistaken in thinking this grouping to have been a creation of Eugenius IV.

[2] Esch, pp. 496 ff. Guiraud, pp. 88–98, 167–8; Partner, loc. cit. Cf. also E. Duprè Theseider, *Il lago Velino Saggio Storico-geografico* (Rieti, 1939), pp. 67 ff. A lawsuit about the watercourses was in progress between Rieti and Terni in 1426; cf. Div. Cam. 9, fo. 298.

[3] Sestini, *Il Paesaggio*, pp. 105 ff.; Houston, *Western Mediterranean World*, p. 507. Milone, *L'Italia nell'economia delle sue regioni*, pp. 533 ff.

Topino) for the economy of Perugia, those of Gualdo Tadino, Norcia and Gubbio.

It was these basins, with their relatively rich alluvial soils, which were the scene in Umbria of that 'economy of the plain' (*economia di pianura*) which was such an important factor in central Italian agriculture in the later Middle Ages.[1] But while agriculture was sufficiently advanced at least to begin to drain and exploit the plain, with the exception of the road junction of Foligno, the cities and in general the more populous areas continued to be sited in the overlooking foothills. In the lower Tiber valley a powerful and typical example was Todi, on the Via Amerina from Orte to Perugia, described by Niccolò Spinelli in 1392 as an important city with over 300 villages in its district.[2]

A considerable part of the Umbrian Apennine was covered by forests, or by low brushwood and coppice (*ceduo*). Both these gave pannage for pigs, which were an important part of the Umbrian economy. There was also in the high plateaux of Umbria an economy of transhumance sheep pasturage. The biggest centre of transhumance pasture was the Piano Grande of Castelluccio (1,300 m.) on the eastern side of the Monti Sibillini, and on the watershed which divides the rivers draining into the Tiber system from those draining through the march of Ancona into the Adriatic. Sheep pastured in this plateau in the summer, and wintered in the basin of Norcia, or as far away as the pastures of Corneto and Tuscania;[3] Norcia, in consequence, was rich enough to be the object of seigniorial covetousness, and independent enough to resist it.[4] Transhumance was important also in the mountains of Massa Martana, Subasio, Trevi, Campello.

One of the provinces acquired under Innocent III, the duchy of

---

[1] Cf. D. Herlihy, *Medieval and Renaissance Pistoia* (New Haven and London, 1967), pp. 48–54; C. Tabarelli, *Liber Contractuum* (1331–2) *dell'Abbazia Benedettina di San Pietro in Perugia* (Perugia, 1967), p. IX (Professor Mira's introduction); F. Bonasera, *La casa rurale nell'Umbria* (Florence, 1955), pp. 47, 163.

[2] Esch, p. 642. Todi was taxed for the subsidy at 1,200 florins, while Viterbo was taxed at 1,100. Partner, *Papal State*, p. 214; Arm. 33, vol. 11, fo. 9. For Todi see also Esch, pp. 516–18. Esch remarks that '300 *castra*' is an exaggeration, but that the list of eighty-one dependent places in the communal archives shows the city to have been important enough.

[3] In the winter of 1442–3 the mercenary soldier Ciarpellone seized in the pastures of the Tolfa area some 20,000 sheep belonging to the men of Norcia and elsewhere. Niccola della Tuccia, in I. Ciampi, *Cronache e Statuti della città di Viterbo* (Florence, 1872), p. 187.

[4] Sestini, *Il Paesaggio*, p. 109; G. Schmiedt, 'Contributo della fotointerpretazione alla conoscenz della reta stradale dell'Umbria nell'alto medioevo', *Aspetti dell'Umbria dall'inizio del secolo VIII*, pp. 177–210, at pp. 203–4. Guiraud, pp. 188–90, failed to see that the war of Norcia with Spoleto in 1436 was an incident in the struggle of Francesco Sforza to dominate Umbria. This is shown in the documents in Reg. Vat. 366, folios 121, 185v.

Spoleto, was by the late fourteenth century very reduced from its ancient boundaries, and by the time of Martin V and Eugenius IV amounted to little more than the territories of Spoleto and Norcia.[1] Administratively the powers of the Governor of Perugia after the submission of 1424 swallowed up the former duchy.[2] He ruled Perugia and its district, the duchy of Spoleto, Todi, Assisi, Nocera, Spello, Montefalco and Gualdo Cattaneo. But his practical power was naturally circumscribed by political necessity; the vicariate of Francesco Sforza in Todi, or the rule of Piccinino in Assisi, naturally nullified the papal governor's powers in these places and in the surrounding areas for the time being. The suppression of the Trinci *signoria* of Foligno by Cardinal Vitelleschi was of considerable importance for the future of papal power in Umbria.

The commune of Perugia remained, with Rome and Bologna, one of the principal places of the Papal State. Its population in the early fifteenth century is conservatively reckoned for the city and *contado* together something between 40,000 and 50,000.[3] The gross value of the revenues of the city to the Apostolic See was about 28,000–35,000 florins annually, and the net profit or subsidy not inferior to a sum which varied between minimum figures of 12,000 florins annually under Martin V, and 8,000 florins under later popes.[4]

The *contado* controlled by Perugia was large and rich. It corresponded approximately with the diocese of Perugia, except for the small group of villages which reached out along the Chiascio towards Gualdo Tadino, and for the grain-growing area of Chiusi on the western side of Lake Trasimene. There was also a number of places held as fiefs or apostolic vicariates by the Baglioni of Perugia, of which the most important were in Val Topino (Bettona, Spello, Cannara, Bevagna). The most productive farming area was Perugian Chiusi (which satisfied at least a third of the city's grain requirements); Lake Trasimene's fish were sold on both shores for the Umbrian and Tuscan markets; and Montemalbe

---

[1] Esch, pp. 520–1, says that the boundaries under Boniface IX were those of the dioceses of Gubbio, Nocera, Assisi, Foligno, and Spoleto. For later developments see *Papal State*, p. 97; Guiraud, pp. 186–90.

[2] Ibid. pp. 175–85; *Papal State*, pp. 97, 213–14.

[3] G. Mira, 'Il fabbisogno di cereali in Perugia e nel suo contado nei secoli XIII–XIV', *Studi in onore di A. Sapori*, i (Milan, 1957), pp. 505–17, gives 5,529 hearths to the city and 8,979 to the *contado* in the late thirteenth century; using a five co-efficient this would give a population of 28,000 for the city and 45,000 for the *contado*. A much lower figure seems likely for the early fifteenth century: see S. Majarelli and U. Nicolini, *Il Monte dei Poveri di Perugia: Periodo degli Origini (1462–74)* (Perugia, 1962), pp. 54–5.

[4] *Papal State*, pp. 171–3.

was used for pasture and timber.[1] The mercantile activity of Perugia was extremely important, and the forty-four *arti* or merchant guilds traced in the fifteenth century show how sustained this economic activity was, even in a period of lower productivity and population. The university assured Perugia of a certain international cultural importance; and learned Perugian clerks such as those of the Guidalotti family often held important posts in papal administration.

To the north-east of Perugia, in the upper Tiber valley, the only fertile area was the valley running from Città di Castello to Borgo San Sepolcro. The rest of this zone was mountainous and poor, important to Florence, to the Papal State and to the numerous *condottieri* whose armies marched through it, for the control of the passes between Tuscany, Romagna and the marches. It was with these military considerations in mind that Eugenius IV pledged Borgo San Sepolcro to Florence. The papal governor of Città di Castello ruled a frontier area which was hard to defend (as Eugenius found in the early 1430s) and poor in revenue.[2]

The seigniorial family which exploited most effectively its control of strategic points in the Apennine of Umbria and the marches was that of the Montefeltro. The Montefeltro state was like a grid thrown across the Apennine passes, from the Savio and the Marecchia in the north to those of the Sentino in the south. The pass of Viamaggio in the Marecchia valley, that of Bocca Trabaria in the upper Metauro valley, were in the hands of this family. By their possession of Gubbio both the Via Flaminia proper and its divergent branch running from Perugia to Scheggia through Gubbio were in Montefeltro control, so was the pass of Scheggia itself, the lowest and most practicable of the Apennine passes east of Florence.[3] Their possession of Cagli and (after 1447) Fossombrone gave them complete control of the Passo del Furlo, whose importance the engineers and soldiers of antiquity had so well understood.[4] On the other hand, the economic basis of the Montefeltro state was weak; its possessions were, with the exception of the Gubbio basin, mountainous and arid, and by the mid-fifteenth century weakened by long wars.[5] The Montefeltro counts were sometimes rectors of the small papal

[1] There is a good description of the Perugian economy in the unpublished B. Litt. thesis of Mr C. F. Black, *Politics and Society in Perugia, 1488–1540* (Bodleian Library). For the fishing see G. Mira, *La pesca nel Medioevo nelle acque interne italiane* (Milan, 1937).

[2] Guiraud, pp. 171–4; *Papal State*, p. 99; L. Fumi, *Inventario e Spoglio dei Registri della Tesoreria Apostolica di Città del Castello* (Perugia, 1900).

[3] Cf. T. Ashby, 'The Via Flaminia', *The Journal of Roman Studies*, xi (1922), pp. 125–90, at p. 182.

[4] For Fossombrone see G. Franceschini, *Federico da Montefeltro dalla concessione del vicariato apostolico alla pace di Lodi 1447–54* (Sansepolcro, 1961), pp. 20–9.

[5] See the petition of the clergy of Urbino in 1447 cited ibid. p. 23.

jurisdiction of Massa Trabaria, which was included in the northern part of their dominions.[1] By this period deforestation had already removed a great part of the timber from which Massa Trabaria took its name, though the supply had not ceased. Other parts of the Montefeltro *signoria* fell in the provinces of the march of Ancona, of Romagna, and of the duchy of Spoleto.

IV

As an area of human settlement the march of Ancona is one of the foothills which follow the deeply dissected river valleys from the Apennines to the sea. This *collinare* zone of west-east contours has since the early Middle Ages been worked with immense industry for cereals, stock-farming, vines, and to a less extent olives. To the west of the hills, the great Apennine reliefs of hard limestone, from the Catria range in the north to the San Vicino and Sibillini ranges in the south, stand high above the soft Miocene and Pliocene sediments of the hilly area. Only at Monte Conero south of Ancona, and in the Cingoli hills, were the limestone reliefs at all thickly populated. The vegetation of the Apennine areas is sparse; the march is not, like Umbria, a land of woods, coppice, or forest.[2] The *collinare* area extends farthest west in the central marches, where the upper valleys of the Esino, and Potenza (on either side of the Cingoli hills) reach almost as far as the boundaries of the duchy of Spoleto; at the latitude of the Metauro in the north the mountains come far closer to the sea.

The most prominent feature of human settlement in the march is the multiplicity of small agricultural centres, of which a very large number were in the Middle Ages free communes.[3] Fano, at the terminus of the Via Flaminia, Iesi, and Ancona both as a road terminal and port, owe their importance to communications factors, but the same cannot be said of the rich and formerly powerful city of Fermo. The only genuine port in the march was Ancona, a rich and populous place with communications as far afield as Alexandria and Constantinople, in close trade relations with Venice and the other trading cities of the Adriatic. The other coastal towns had harbours rather than port facilities. In general the impressive thing about the march is the resilience of the

---

[1] *Papal State*, p. 98; cf. Guiraud, pp. 193–7.

[2] For the physical geography see Milone, pp. 570 ff.; Houston, pp. 394–5; Sestini, *Il Paesaggio*, p. 107 ff., 116 ff. See also *Atti del Convegno sui Centri Storici delle Marche (Ministero della Pubblica Istruzione. Direzione Generale delle Antichità e Belle Arti. Studie Documentazioni*, ii (Rome, 1968).

[3] Cf. Waley, *P.S.*, pp. 87–90; Esch, pp. 530–53; Guiraud, pp. 191–211.

small and middle-sized communes. Politically this spread-out character of Marchigiano settlement favoured the papal authority; except under very exceptional circumstances such as those of the *signoria* of Francesco Sforza, it was usually possible for papal rectors to rule and tax the communes in a fairly direct way. The total of the subsidies or *talliae* demanded from communes and *signori* in the march came in 1426 to an annual total of something like 40,000 florins, as compared with the total of 13,500 florins which the rector of the Tuscan patrimony tried to collect from his subjects.[1] The areas of the two provinces are comparable, which can only suggest a far higher level of wealth and population in the march.

Though hit by falling population and productivity as were other parts of the late medieval Papal State, the march of Ancona counted two or three towns (Ancona, Ascoli Piceno, and probably Fermo) with a population in excess of 10,000 persons, and at least a dozen others of substantial importance.[2] The importance of Ancona, and its ability to negotiate independently with its trading partners and competitors outside the Papal State, is evident – but its political and fiscal subordination to the papacy was nonetheless an accomplished fact by the end of the schism.[3] Grain was perhaps the most important single economic asset of the march, and its export, coming under the control of the papal officials, was a valuable fiscal asset to the Papal State, as was also the salt monopoly of the march.[4] But the economic activity of the march was very varied, and besides the vines and olives grown in all the *collinare* zone[5] included the paper industry of Fabriano and the fustians and woollen cloths of Ascoli Piceno and Recanati.[6] The fairs of the march were well-known from the early Middle Ages, and Marchigiano trade dealt both with Venetians and the kingdom. Anyone who has

---

[1] Arm. 33, vol. 11, folios 6–10. For this list see Guiraud, loc. cit. and *Papal State*, pp. 115, 118n. I have added in the list of 'exempt' places. There are other tallage lists of the period for the Tuscan patrimony in Arm. 29, vol. 13, fo. 20, and Rome, Arch. di Stato, Arch. Cam. pt. i, Patrimonio, busta 1, no. 3 (for 1429). Esch deals with the earlier lists of this kind (pp. 533 ff.). The modern march of Ancona measures 9,700 sq. km., the modern Lazio (which includes Rieti and the medieval Campagna-Maritime) 17,200 sq. km.

[2] Esch, pp. 530 ff. The Ascoli *catasto* of 1381 has not yet been studied in detail. Cf. P. Varese and G. A. Rota, 'Il catasto ascolano del 1381', *AMSM*, 8th ser., ii (1942), pp. 43–147.

[3] It is a pity that this is not recognised in the excellent article of P. Earle, 'The commercial development of Ancona, 1479–1551', *Economic History Review*, xxii (1969), pp. 28–44.

[4] Cf. *Papal State*, pp. 122–3 and notes pp. 143–6.

[5] Market gardening was an obligation in most Marchigiano communes: cf. D. Cecchi, *Statuta Castri Campirotundi* (Milan, 1966), pp. 113–17.

[6] G. Fabriani, *Ascoli nel Quattrocento*, i (Ascoli, 1950), pp. 300–26; Fuiano, in *ASPN*, 3rd ser., lxxxiv–lxxxv (1968), pp. 142 ff.

The Lands of St Peter

looked out from one walled city of the march – Macerata or Fermo, perhaps – to other walled cities visible across the intensely cultivated hills, can understand that its local patriotisms were too small to favour the development of a regional consciousness which could offer some resistance to the government of a pope or of a Sforza.

The papal rector of the march ruled a well-defined area; the only sub-divisions were the small jurisdictions of S. Agata Feltre and Massa Trabaria in the northern Apennine area, which were ruled by *signori,* and the presidency of Farfa, the lands of the abbey of Farfa in the area of Montalto delle Marche, which was a distinct but unimportant sub-jurisdiction, with a papally appointed 'President'.[1] The *signori* of the march were on the whole too local in influence for any one of them to present a serious political challenge to papal authority. It was in the march rather than in Romagna that Martin V and Cardinal Vitelleschi were successful in suppressing the *signori* – Carrara of Ascoli, Chiavelli of Fabriano, da Varano of Camerino, Smeducci of San Severino, Brancaleoni of Castel Durante. By the end of the pontificate of Nicholas V there were no *signori* of any political importance in the march except for the Montefeltro of Urbino and Francesco Sforza of Pesaro.

V

The discussion of Romagna is complicated by an uncertainty about the geographical limits of the province which has lasted from the Middle Ages to the present day.[2] 'Romania' was in origin an ethnic or linguistic area, which was not directly related either to the Byzantine boundaries of the exarchate or to the boundaries of the dioceses. It is tempting to adopt the thirteenth-century imperial definition of 'from the river Foglia to the river Reno, from the sea to the Apennine',[3] but this clearly does not do justice to the issues involved. Although Bologna and Ferrara were included with the exarchate in the early imperial donations, later administrative practice tended to treat them separately from the province of Romagna. The negotiations with Rudolph of Habsburg in 1277–8 for the restoration of Romagna to the popes spoke

[1] *Papal State*, pp. 98–9; Esch, loc. cit. S. Agata Feltre was ruled by the Malatesta of Rimini, and Massa Trabaria by the Montefeltro, at the time of Martin V.

[2] Esch, pp. 553 ff.; Larner, *Lords of Romagna*, pp. 205–8; Milone, *L'Italia nell'economia delle sue regioni*, pp. 382–5.

[3] *MGH, Const. et acta publica*, ii, no. 97, p. 121, lines 5–6. The reference is to the creation of a 'count' of Romagna. The phrases used are borrowed from eleventh-century imperial diplomas directed to the archbishops of Ravenna.

not of 'Romagna' but of the exarchate and Pentapolis, listing the cities (including Bologna and Ferrara) they were listed in the ninth- and tenth-century donations.[1] Thirteenth- and fourteenth-century administrative practice was to distinguish between Bologna, Ferrara, Romagna and the county of Bertinoro, each of which was separately named in papal bulls of appointment of provincial officials.

Geographically the present constitutional region of Emilia-Romagna, which includes the whole area south of the Po as far as Piacenza, makes far better sense than the papal province did. Angevin and papal statesmen after 1266 also tended to treat the region between the rivers Trebbio and Foglia as a unity. Down to the time of the wars of Gregory XI in the 1370s, the papal *curia* very often thought not in the narrow terms of its own provinces, but in the wider context of the fate of the whole Po valley as far west at least as Piacenza. Only by looking at Italian politics in this broad way can we make sense of the policies of the Avignonese popes. Papal officials were frequently from the time of Gregory of Montelungo in the thirteenth century onwards appointed with powers over the whole geographical area.[2]

The region of Emilia-Romagna is to be distinguished as areas of mountain, foothill, and plain. The high Apennine tract, beginning in the south-east on the upper Savio, and ending in the north-west on the upper Trebbio in the Apennine of Parma and Piacenza, has very little vegetation, and is on the whole useful only for transhumance pasture. In the medieval period the forest cover of the lower Apennine area was thick, especially in the Romagnol Apennine, though by the end of the Middle Ages already very much reduced. On the clay scales of the lower slopes there was chestnut, beech and mountain oak coverage, which gave charcoal and some pannage for pigs. The middle hills are a much more fertile zone, and a large proportion of the *collinare* area is arable, and was sown with cereals in the Middle Ages. Vines were grown – as they still are – on a large scale in the hills, and the wines of Dozza and Sangiovese were already known. Olives were more widely planted in the hills than they are today. But the garden of Emilia-Romagna was and is the plain. Especially in Romagna proper, the grain crops were among the most important in Italy. The luxury food, wheat, predominated, but millet, spelt, oats and barley followed close behind. Pietro de' Crescenzi of Bologna at the beginning of the fourteenth

Theiner, *C.D.*, i, nos. 361, 362; cf. A. Vasina, *I romagnoli fra autonomie cittadine e accentramento apale*, pp. 62 ff.

Vasina, pp. 2–3 and note.

century wrote a treatise, in effect a description of Romagnol agriculture, which portrays a farm economy still recognisable. The flax of Romagna and its varied uses are carefully described; the accounts of the modes of pruning the vines in various parts of the province show an advanced and careful husbandry. The mulberry was grown for the silk industry. Romagnol fruit was already well-known, but difficulties of transport and marketing meant that there could be nothing comparable to the scale of modern market-gardening in the area.

The coastal zone provided other ecological conditions. From Cervia to the north of Ravenna the pinewoods provided a great area of pannage for pigs, of pasture for cattle, of deerleaps.[1] Rimini had a harbour of modest importance, but its wealth came also from its position as a communications centre, the junction of the Via Emilia with the Via Flaminia, and also with the Apennine route from the Flaminia at Acqualagna through Urbino and Montefiore, and with the coast road to Ravenna. Wheat also made Rimini populous and rich, though by the mid-fifteenth century both Rimini and Fano were economically in decline; the silting up of the harbours was a symptom of their decadence.[2] The salt of the Cervia salt-pans was economically of prime importance, and the failure of the papal *curia* to keep Cervia after it had been wrested from the Malatesta in 1430 assisted the survival of the Malatesta house. Cervia was one of the many points where Venetian economic imperialism pressed heavily on Romagna; in the fourteenth century Cervia was pressed into a series of agreements with the Venetians about the disposal of its salt production, and later in the fifteenth century its cession to Venice by the papacy marked a notable point of weakness in the papal hold on Romagna.[3]

The splendours of early medieval Ravenna had by the early Renaissance period gone for ever. The once great church of S. Maria in Porto stood in 1391 a frequently robbed and sacked shell.[4] The political

---

[1] F. Ginanni, *Storia civile e naturale delle Pinete Ravennati* (Rome, 1774); cf. Larner, *Lords of Romagna*, pp. 123–4. Half the income of S. Maria di Pomposa came in 1338 from the products of the abbey's woods. G. Gurrieri, 'Notizie e problemi della storia economica di pomposa nei sec. X–XIV', *Analecta Pomposiana*, A. Samaritani (ed.) (Giari-Codigoro, 1965), pp. 144–63, at p. 161.

[2] Jones, 'End of Malatesta rule in Rimini', *Italian Renaissance Studies*, pp. 234–6.

[3] A. Torre, 'I patti fra Venezia e Cervia', *Stud. Romagn.*, xi (1960), pp. 21–62; idem, 'L'oggetto delle relazioni fra Ravenna e Venezia nel medio evo', *Miscellanea in onore di Roberto Cessi*, i (Rome, 1958), pp. 121–41; G. Soranzo, 'La cessione di Cervia e delle sue saline a Venezia', *La Romagna*, a. iv (1909), fasc. 5–6.

[4] 'Memorie Portuensi', in Fantuzzi, *Monumenti Ravennati*, ii, pp. 125–6. Cf. G. Zattoni, 'Le memorie portuensi', *Felix Ravenna*, fasc. i (1919), pp. 1–37.

power of the Archbishop of Ravenna was long since at an end. The possessions of the church of Ravenna had in many instances been conceded by the Holy See to *signori* in vicariate.[1] Ravenna itself was from the late fourteenth century conceded to the da Polenta in vicariate; in 1441 it fell under a Venetian protectorate. Ravenna had its port, but this had been in effect controlled by Venice for most of the later medieval period.[2]

The history of the coastline of the Po delta and the area south of it is by no means clear to modern scholarship, and it is not certain whether periods of emergence from the submergence into the sea may have followed one another in the Middle Ages, or whether there was a steady process of retreat by the sea from the coastal lagoons; the former is perhaps the more likely.[3] The earlier deltas of the Po were almost all south of the present one. The most important identifiable point in this process is the breaking of the banks of the Po at Ficarolo in 1152, a disaster which caused the river to deviate far to the north and to mix with the waters of the Adige to form a new delta. In the lagoon of Comacchio to the north of the Po di Primaro, the sea was gaining on the land, and settlements round the ancient bishopric were being lost to the sea. The whole zone from the Po di Primaro to the north of the main delta was one of marshes and lagoons. The great land reclamations and the construction of drainage canals did not seriously begin until the *bonifiche* of the dukes of Ferrara in the late fifteenth century. Disastrous floodings and inundations of the countryside were common. Fishing was naturally an important natural resource of the area, and the fishing guild of Ravenna was not only an ancient association dating back to the early Middle Ages, but also a rich one possessing its own landed estates.[4]

It was frequent for the papal governor of Romagna to be also governor of Bologna. But the situation of papal government worsened greatly in Romagna during the early years of the schism, during which the laymen Pandolfo and Carlo Malatesta were successively papal rectors of Romagna,[5] and Bologna was only barely in the control of the Holy See. Baldassare Cossa did much to restore papal powers in Romagna, both as legate and pope, but by the end of the schism the *signori* of the

[1] Esch, pp. 560–1.

[2] Larner, pp. 10–11; A. Torre, 'Il porto di Ravenna', *Felix Ravenna*, n.s., anno iv (1934), pp. 186–206.

[3] Milone, pp. 425–7; Sestini, *Il Paesaggio*, pp. 71–2; cf. Houston, p. 385; Larner, p. 7.

[4] Mira, *La pesca nel medio evo*, pp. 36 ff.

[5] Esch, p. 588.

province had established their position as papal vicars so firmly that only a few could be dislodged; the turbulent pontificate of Eugenius IV did nothing to improve this situation. Although the popes of the mid-fifteenth century were not entirely powerless in Romagna,[1] and Pius II was able to act successfully against the Malatesta there, the fourteenth-century situation was not re-established, and the Romagna was no longer an important area of direct papal rule.

The key road of Romagna was the Via Emilia, like the Via Cassia called the 'Via Francigena' in the Middle Ages. The various roads leading to Tuscany through the Alpine passes were of some strategic importance, especially the upper reaches of the Savio, the Bidente, and the Montone. Bagno di Romagna, Valbona, Corniolo, Castel dell'Alpe were among the important frontier posts. Important also were the roads into Umbria through the pass of Bocca Trabaria, and the route via Urbino to the Via Flaminia.[2] But on the Via Emilia were strung most of the principal towns of Romagna: Rimini, Cesena, Forlì, Faenza, Imola. All these towns were granted in apostolic vicariate to *signori*. They were essentially agricultural in character; most trade was in the hands of Venetians or Florentines, and there was little but local industry.[3] All politics centred round the *signori* and the groups of oligarchic families who formed their favoured supporters, and whose power was based on a mixture of land and office.[4] The main towns on the Via Emilia each had an extensive *contado* which stretched into the hills or even into the Apennines. Cesena also had its own small port, and the vicariate of Cesena usually included the ancient county of Bertinoro. In the high Apennine areas political power usually lay with the feudal families of the mountains such as the Ubaldini, who effectively closed to the Church the passes of the Santerno, the Senio, the Lamone.[5]

VI

The great city of Bologna was, apart from Rome, the most important in the Papal State. Its district went from the northernmost point of the

---

[1] Cf. I. Robertson, 'The return of Cesena to the direct dominion of the Church after the death of Malatesta Novello', *Stud. Romagn.*, xvi (1965), pp. 123–61, at pp. 126–8.

[2] For the last-mentioned road see Ashby, *Journal of Roman Studies*, xi (1921), p. 185; P. Montecchini, *La Strada Flaminia detta del Furlo* (Pesaro, 1879), pp. 58 ff.; Larner, *Lords of Romagna*, pp. 114–15. Cf. also J. Delumeau, *Vie économique et sociale de Rome*, i, p. 43.

[3] Larner, pp. 130 ff.

[4] Jones, in *Italian Renaissance Studies*, pp. 242 ff.; Robertson, *Stud. Romagn.*, xvi (1965), pp. 136 ff.

[5] Theiner, *C.D.*, ii, p. 515. The Lamone was from 1376 onwards controlled by the Manfredi of Faenza. Cf. G. Cavina, *Antichi Fortilizi di Romagna* (Faenza, 1964).

course of the Reno river almost to the source of the Reno in the district of Pistoia in the south. In population and area it was perhaps half the size of the zone administered by the papal government as 'Romagna'.[1] Rough and none-too-reliable estimates of the population of the city are between 32,000 and 50,000 for the late fourteenth century, and 45,000–50,000 for the late fifteenth.[2] Reliable estimates for the population of the *contado* are not available, but there is no doubt of the political and economic importance of the whole area. The gross income of Bologna from its customs' dues varied between 150,000 *lib. bon.* and 300,000 *lib bon.* annually, in cameral florins between something over 90,000 and over 180,000.[3] The subsidy payable by Bologna to the popes was at first agreed as 5,000 florins annually under Martin V, but so long as papal control was effective the agents of the Apostolic Chamber disposed freely of the city's revenues.

The great economic power of Bologna, not only as an agricultural centre for the east Emilian plain, but as a commercial and to some extent (through its silk production) an industrial city, needs no emphasis. The University of Bologna was of European importance. The foothill area of the Bolognese *contado* was quite densely populated, and both here and in the Apennines the commune had an apparatus of local government controlled by Bolognese vicars. The passes to Tuscany were among the important responsibilities of the Bolognese;[4] these passes had not only military but great commercial importance. The strongpoints of the northern *contado* of Bologna such as Budrio, Cento, San Giovanni in Persiceto, were important for the defence of the Papal State as a whole. The control of the rivers of the Emilian plain was often disputed;

---

[1] The numbers of 'hearths' in the description of Romagna and Bologna in 1371 are unreliable for population figures; cf. Larner, pp. 209–19. But they perhaps give a sort of ratio for comparison. 10,893 hearths are listed for the county of Bologna, and 8,000 for the city. The hearths of Romagna are calculated to total 34,644. Theiner, *C.D.*, ii, pp. 516, 517, 522.

[2] The same doubt applies to these figures, which are based on the document just quoted. Cf. G. Salvioni, 'La popolazione di Bologna nel secolo XVII', *AMDR*, 3rd ser., viii (1890), pp. 19–120, at pp. 31 ff.; Beloch, *Bevölkerungsgeschichte Italiens*, ii, pp. 91–2; A. Bellettini, *La popolazione di Bologna dal secolo XV all'unificazione italiana* (Bologna, 1961), pp. 21–5; P. Montanari, *Documenti sulla popolazione di Bologna alla fine del Trecento* (Imola, 1966). The last is the only population study of Bologna for this period which is based on modern demographic methods.

[3] *Papal State*, p. 179n.; Favier, *Finances Pontificales*, pp. 177–8; G. Orlandelli, 'La revisione del bilancio nel comune di Bologna', *AMDR*, n.s., ii (1950–51), pp. 157–218, at pp. 204 ff. Cf. Esch, p. 557n.; G. Zaoli, *Libertas Bononie e Martino V* (Bologna, 1916), pp. 25–30.

[4] A. Palmieri, 'Le strade medievali fra Bologna e la Toscana', *AMDR*, 4th ser., viii (1918), pp. 17–47; G. Barbieri, 'Lo sviluppo storico delle vie di communicazione tra Firenze e Bologna', *Rivista Geografica Italiana*, lii (1947), pp. 103–16. For the vicariates, *Papal State*, pp. 177–8.

and the quarrel of Bologna with Modena about the control of the Panaro, which was deviated during the wars with Bernabò Visconti, is a typical example.[1]

VII

It may be asked whether the Papal State was in the fifteenth century well or badly governed, and whether the origins of the reputation for misgovernment which it had acquired by the end of the sixteenth century can be traced back to this period.

There is no sign that the early fifteenth-century Papal State had an especially bad name for misgovernment among contemporaries, how- ever severe the judgements passed on it by modern historians. Much of what passes for bad administration among men of the modern period was welcomed by medieval men as an indication of respect accorded to legitimate privilege. There is a certain amount of evidence to suggest that the rule of the *signori* was more onerous than the direct rule of the Church, because of the heavy burden of military, building and court expenses. Dynasties such as the Malatesta of Rimini or the Bentivoglio of Bologna were in many ways wasteful and oppressive. Perhaps the only tyrants of the Papal State to carry out major public works to improve drainage and agriculture were the Este of Ferrara.

The origins of the agricultural decline of the Roman countryside can perhaps be traced back to the earlier period, though there does not seem to be much governmental complaint about the abandonment of land- holdings before the time of Pope Pius II in the 1460s. And the time of the great expansion of Renaissance Rome was still far off.

Loosely governed, disorderly, unruly, the fifteenth-century Papal State may have been. But its real enemies were the exterior mercenary marauders – Sforza, Piccinino, Ciarpellone and their kind. These men were the scourge of fifteenth-century society. The clerical government did what it could, and this was no worse than what was done by plenty of contemporary Italian governments.

---

[1] Cf. Theiner, *C.D.*, ii, p. 530; for earlier quarrels see F. T. di Valminuta, *L'antica navigazione bolognese* (Città di Castello, 1905).

Conclusion

The Papal State shared in the general crisis of papal power which occurred as a result of the Great Schism and of the Conciliar Movement. Martin V re-established the temporal power after the Council of Constance, but the Colonna settlement of the Papal State broke down under his successor Eugenius. The breakdown occurred partly because of Italian political factors but also because of the renewal of the conciliar challenge to papal authority at the Council of Basle. When Eugenius IV solved the conciliar problem he was able to solve the problem of the Papal State. There was no further great collapse of papal authority in the lands of St Peter until the next great crisis of papal power in general, that of the sixteenth-century Reformation. The sack of Rome by imperialist troops in 1527 marked a far wider and deeper distress in the body of the Church.

This was the nature of the Papal State from the beginning. It was an appendage to universal papal power as this had developed in the Western Church from the early Middle Ages. The Papal State has its own history, but it is a history dependent on that of the great institution of which it formed, in one sense, a part. It seems reasonable to bring this account of the Papal State to a close at the end of the pontificate of Eugenius IV, which was also the end of the last great crisis of the medieval papacy. In the sphere of the history of government there is also some reason for ending the book here. There is no magic in the word 'Renaissance' which transmutes the history of the late fifteenth century into a new and different metal; historians are now only too disillusioned on this point. But it could be argued that the government and the society of the Papal State in the second half of the fifteenth century can be better understood by looking forward than back, and it could be maintained that a treatment of the history of the Papal State which goes beyond 1447 ought to go to 1527.

Judgement on the medieval Papal State has to take account of its double nature. In one way the Papal State was merely an example of the temporal domains held by bishops and abbots all over the Latin Christian world. If St Edmund of Bury St Edmunds had his 'hundreds', why should not St Peter have his patrimony?[1] But medieval men were conscious also of the wider hierocratic claims which lay behind the lands of St Peter, and which they often connected (not entirely wrongly) with the Donation of Constantine. So Dante wrote: 'What ills Constantine fathered when he made the first rich clerk!',[2] and in the *Piers Plowman* of William Langland:

'Whenne Constantyn of hus cortesye holy kirke dowede
'With londes and leedes (i.e. teniments). lordshepes and rentes,
'An angel men hurde, an hih at Rome crye –
'*Dos ecclesie* this day. hath ydronke venym,
'And tho that han Petres power. aren pysoned alle.'[3]

The point was capable of a more general extension which has a more modern ring, though its origin is to be found in St Bernard. The Roman Church as Dante saw it wielded both the temporal sword and the pastoral crook; by combining the temporal with spiritual rule the Church 'fell in the mud' and dirtied both herself and the burden of Christendom which she carried.[4] Such protests continued and became even sharper throughout the fourteenth century. At the end of the Avignonese period resentment against French clerics was combined with feeling against the wars waged by the Church. The chronicler of Piacenza protested bitterly against the loss of life in the papal war against the Visconti in 1372–4, and against the clerical conduct of the War of the Eight Saints.[5]

The immense expenditure of the Church in maintaining or recovering its temporal power, the bloodshed, and the scant success of the clerical government in retaining what it recovered, were none of them unnoticed by its critics. Fifty years' income from the church lands, the chronicler of Piacenza commented, was spent in subduing their rebellion. The same was said by the distinguished politician Niccolò Spinelli, whose experience in the government of the papal state power was equal to that of any other statesman of the late Middle Ages.[6] The Piacenza chronicler suggested that the pope should content himself with granting

[1] Waley, *P.S.*, p. 299
[2] *Inf.*, xix, 115.
[3] Skeat (ed.), *The Vision of William concerning Piers the Plowman* (Oxford, 1886), i, p. 471.
[4] *Purg.*, xvi, 108–10, 127–9.
[5] *Chronicon Placentinum* (*RRIISS* xvi), cols. 522 ff., 528 ff.
[6] Cf. p. 378 above.

the papal lands in vicariate to the magnates, communes or nobles who already ruled them: the Este of Ferrara, the Bolognese, the Perugians, the tyrants of the march and of Romagna. The category of papal lands 'immediately subject to the Holy See' would disappear. Such a solution did not appeal to Spinelli, who had spent his life in fighting the fragmentation of political authority in the Papal State. Spinelli would have returned to the solution of Pierre Dubois at the beginning of the fourteenth century: the Papal State should be infeudated to a French prince.[1]

And yet, unless reformers were committed to the idea of a poor church in which no bishop possessed temporalities, it was hard to see why the pope in particular should be despoiled of his. Most conciliar reformers wanted more efficient exploitation of the Papal State, and not its confiscation. And under the new and stronger regime imposed by Martin V in the Papal State, some justification seemed to begin to appear for this conservative point of view. Particularly because the total of the 'spiritual' papal revenues had been much reduced after the Council of Constance, the proportion of 'temporal' to 'spiritual' revenues in the papal budget became substantially more important. Under Martin V when the papal restoration had been completed more than half papal income was draw from the Papal State.[2] Clearly the temporal revenues fell drastically again during the wars of Eugenius IV, and indeed during his pontificate the sad paradox of the Avignonese period, when popes were spending more money to regain temporal lands than the lands could provide in income, seemed to have returned. But the restoration of papal power under Eugenius in his last years and under his successor Nicholas V did in fact lead to a more stable situation, in which the temporal revenues again became as important, if not more important, than the spiritual ones. Additional taxation for the benefit of the crusade was made in the Papal State in the second half of the fifteenth century, and this again appeared to confirm the stability of the restored temporal power.

With withering sarcasm and some violence the humanist Lorenzo Valla in 1440 denounced the forged Donation of Constantine, and called on the pope to renounce the whole temporal power, no longer employing armed force against Christians, but 'holy father, father of all'.[3] Valla's moral authority was certainly, to say the least, less than his authority as a textual critic. But the distinguished philosopher, Cardinal Nicholas of

---

[1] Romano, *Niccolò Spinelli*, pp. 611 ff.

[2] Partner, *Italian Renaissance Studies*, pp. 259 ff.

[3] Schwahn (ed.), *L. Vallae de falso credita et ementita Constantini donatione* (Leipzig, 1928), p. 82. Cf. G. Laehr, *Quellen*, xxiii (1931–2), pp. 151–63.

Cusa, was at once with Valla in thinking the Donation of Constantine a forgery.[1]

This criticism seemed more radical than it was. There was no way in which the popes could repudiate the temporal power, or dissociate themselves from it, which did not mean the repudiation of doctrines and social assumptions which in the late Middle Ages almost all orthodox Catholics regarded as fundamental. Only the heretics held the doctrinal key to a poor church – and indeed, even when the Reformation came, in some Protestant countries the destruction of the medieval social basis of the Church was still far from complete. The doctrines of Valla and Nicholas of Cusa did not gain acceptance in the Catholic world, even though in the sixteenth century they were taken up by the great authority of Erasmus. Very many of the orthodox would have accepted the conservatism of the Guelph legist Giovanni da Legnano, the most distinguished of the Bolognese papalist lawyers at the end of the fourteenth century. He replied to the question: 'Is it lawful to defend the possessions of the Church by corporeal war, and for this purpose to assemble troops? – Obviously it is.'[2] Unless one rejected papal authority altogether, it was hard to deny the popes the possession of their lands. And if they possessed them, wars followed. The humanist historian Biondo Flavio, who himself had much experience of papal politics, took up towards the papal temporal authority and its history an attitude of rather unreflective acceptance.[3] He was more typical of his times than Lorenzo Valla.

If papal rule in the temporal power in the early Middle Ages is compared with its exercise when they ended, perhaps the most striking change is the strengthening of the papal will to rule a political entity. A great Austrian historian has commented on the feebleness of political purpose in the temporal power on the part of the popes of the ninth and tenth centuries; they were elected 'for the needs of the church', and so far as the State was concerned their political consciousness was inferior to that of contemporary rulers elsewhere.[4] It might be thought that this does them some moral credit; their role was that of the high priests of the Roman holy places and of guardians of the faith, and the powers of an Alberic of Rome were not offensive to their views of their priestly office. The Church of the later Middle Ages had an institu-

---

[1] N. de Cusa, *Opera Omnia*, G. Kallen (ed.), xiv, pt. 3 (Hamburg, 1959), pp. 328–44.

[2] Giovanni da Legnano, *Tractatus De Bello De Represaliis et De Duello*, T. E. Holland (ed.), pp. 127, 273.

[3] Cf. Denys Hay, 'Flavio Biondo and the Middle Ages', *Proceedings of the British Academy*, xlv (1959) at p. 121 especially.

[4] W. Sickel, 'Alberich II. und der Kirchenstaat', *MIöG*, xxiii (1902), pp. 50–1.

tional strength and a developed hierocratic doctrine, both of which were in the early Middle Ages lacking. Though the popes met with grave political and military difficulties, in the later Middle Ages they employed a governmental administration which was run on the same lines as that of most other contemporary governments. The 'Gregorianism' of the eleventh and twelfth centuries had meant that the primary duties of the Roman bishop had ceased to be those of the custodian of the holy places of the martyrs, and had come to be those of the head of an administrative machine.

In the end almost all discussion of the Papal State becomes discussion of the papacy. The political conditions which governed other Italian states did not apply to the Papal State. Machiavelli with his terrible radicalism saw this clearly: 'Only these princes (the popes) have dominions and do not defend them, have subjects and do not govern them; and although their dominions are undefended they are not taken from them, and their subjects, although they are not governed, pay no attention to the fact, nor do they nor can they quit the papal dominion.'[1] There are few more devastating examples of the Machiavellian irony.

What kind of judgements can modern men pass on the Papal State? Machiavelli was concerned with the political system of the Italian peninsula in his own time, and this can hardly concern us now. The criticisms of Dante and of Langland on the other hand seem to be of a sort which relates to the institution of Christianity itself: it seems to go against the nature of the Christian gospel that bishops should be 'successors not to Peter but to Constantine'. But such judgements are for theologians rather than historians, and the formulation of the question to be asked must also be left to theologians. Historians might gloss the matter by remarking (as is remarked above) that the Papal State was only a special case of the normal structure of medieval society in the Latin West, which made the clerical ruling class into landowners who habitually employed soldiers, even if they were not soldiers themselves.

The question a historian feels that he can legitimately ask is narrower. Did the Papal State in any way discredit the papal office? Clearly it provided occasions for nepotism and 'carnality', for warfare supervised by priests, for bloodshed such as that of the massacre of Cesena. Perhaps these were elements in the loss of confidence in the papacy which gradually made itself felt in the later Middle Ages. But we might also remember that accusations of spending the treasure of the Church on warfare were made against Gregory VII, without discrediting in any

[1] Burd (ed.), *Il Principe* (Oxford, 1891), p. 248.

way we can ascertain the policies which he represented. In spite of the papal wars of the thirteenth and fourteenth centuries, the popes of that period thought of themselves as peacemakers, and very frequently mediated between Christian powers. There is no evidence that they did not believe their own claims in this matter, nor that they were very widely disbelieved by others. John XXII's terrible threats of war against the Germans, and Petrarch's savage allegations that the French clerks of the papal court wanted Italy to be kept in a permanent state of war, are evidence on one side of the matter, but the peace-making policies of Benedict XII are evidence of the contrary. Morally speaking the war-like policies of Albornoz may perhaps be put to the debit account of the Holy See, but the peace policies of Cardinal Androin de la Roche and his allies in the papal *curia* may be placed in that case to credit. It is interesting that on the whole modern historians have approved of Albornoz, and represented de la Roche as a feeble and rather contemptible figure.

A distinction must be made between the attitude of medieval Italians to the Papal State and that of Christians in other parts of Europe. It might almost be said that Italians were the only Christians who did have an attitude to the Papal State, which was a part of their political system but not of that of any other region. The popes of the thirteenth and fourteenth centuries taxed Christian Europe in various ways in order to pay for the wars in the Papal State. This taxation was resented and opposed, but the main object of indignation was the taxation and not the wars.[1] There is no sign that the recovery of the Papal State by Martin V aroused indignation in Christian Europe; he was on the contrary putting the papacy into a situation which subjects of late medieval monarchies thought desirable, in that *vis-à-vis* countries outside Italy he could exist on the revenues of the papal patrimonies and 'live of his own'.

Such judgements on the Papal State as that passed half a century ago by A. L. Smith: 'a veritable body of death to the true spiritual life of the greatest institution in human history'[2] – must be rejected. The Papal State may have become a scandal to some Christians, Catholic or Protestant, in the modern period, but these are not grounds for condemning the Papal State of the Middle Ages. In the end our judgement must be made on the moral and social order of the Medieval Church as a whole, and not on the rule of the successors of St Peter over the lands which they legitimately possessed.

[1] Waley, loc. cit.; cf. also J. Haller, *Papsttum und Kirchenreform*, i (Berlin, 1903), p. 143 ff.
[2] *Church and State in the Middle Ages* (Oxford, 1913), p. 210.

Table of Events

817	Treaty between Louis the Pious and Pope Paschal	898	Pope John IX recognises Lambert of Spoleto as Emperor
824	Paschal's *coup* against Theodore the *primicerius*	904	Theophylact, *magister militum et vestararius*, later senator
	The *constitutio Romana* defines relations between the Holy See and the Frankish Empire	915	Muslim defeat on river Garigliano (Minturnae) by Pope John X and the Byzantines
827	Muslim invasion of Sicily		
835	Muslim attacks on Italian mainland		Power of Alberic of Spoleto in Rome. Marozia *senatrix*
844	Invasion of Roman territory by the Emperor's son, Louis II	916	Berengar of Friuli crowned Emperor
846	Sack of St Peter's, Rome by the Muslims	932	Hugh of Provence expelled from Rome by Alberic
850	Renewal of treaties between pope and emperor		Fall of Marozia
855	Cardinal Anastasius fails to upset the election of Pope Benedict III	932–54	Alberic of Rome, prince and senator
		935	Odo of Cluny in Rome
	Death of Emperor Lothar	951	Otto of Saxony in north Italy
	Rule of the Emperor Louis II in Italy	955	Otto defeats Hungarians on river Lech
861	Archbishop John of Ravenna made to submit to the Roman See by Pope Nicholas	962	Otto crowned Emperor by Pope John XII. Otto re-issues the treaty of the empire with the Roman Church ('Ottonianum')
864	Louis II in Rome fails to coerce Pope Nicholas over the divorce of Lothar II	963	Deposition of John XII
871	Frankish reconquest of Bari from Muslims	965–6	Anti-Ottonian revolt in Rome
		967	Otto II crowned Emperor
875	Coronation of Charles the Bald as Emperor	988	Power of Crescentius de Nomentana in Rome
876	Flight of Bishop Formosus from Rome	996	Otto III crowned Emperor by Pope Gregory V
	Treaty of Charles the Bald with Roman Church at Ponthion	997–8	Rebellion of Crescentius and of anti-pope John XVI
877	Synod of Ravenna	1001	Donation of eight counties in Pentapolis to Pope Silvester by Otto III
	Lambert of Spoleto occupies Rome		Anti-Ottonian rebellion in Rome and Italy
881	Charles the Fat crowned Emperor	1009	Revolt led by Melo against Byzantine rule in South Italy
891	Guy of Spoleto crowned Emperor	1012	Benedict VIII, first of 'Tusculan' popes
897	'Trial' of the corpse of Pope Formosus	1014	Henry II crowned Emperor
	Murder of his judge, Pope Stephen VI	1015	Resignation and death of Arduin King of Italy

1155	Frederick I (Barbarossa) crowned Emperor	1209	Otto IV crowned Emperor
1156	Treaty of Benevento between Pope Hadrian IV and William I of Sicily	1210	Excommunication of Otto IV
		1211	Infeudation of papal march of Ancona to Azzo VI of Este
1158	Second Italian expedition of Frederick I	1213	Promise of Eger by Frederick II to Innocent III
1159	Schism of Alexander III and Victor IV (Octavian of Monticelli)	1220	Frederick II crowned Emperor Recovery of some Matildine lands by Pope Honorius III
1165	Return of Alexander III to Rome	1227	First excommunication of Frederick II
1166	Fourth Italian expedition of Frederick I	1230	Treaty of San Germano between Frederick II and Pope Gregory IX
1167	Battle of Monte Porzio: Frederick I in Rome	1237	Frederick II defeats Lombard cities at b. of Cortenuova
1176	Defeat of Frederick I by Lombard cities at Legnano	1239	Second excommunication of Frederick II
	Treaty of Anagni between Frederick I and Alexander III	1241	Matteo Rossi Orsini, senator of Rome
1177	Peace of Venice between Frederick I and Alexander III	1245	First Council of Lyon deposes Frederick II
1179	Captivity of Archbishop Christian of Mainz	1248	Defeat of Frederick II at Vittoria
1188	Treaty of Clement III with the Romans	1250–73	Great Interregnum in Germany
1191	Coronation of Emperor Henry VI	1252	Brancaleone degli Andalo, senator of Rome
	Destruction of Tuscolo	1258	Manfred King of Sicily invades the Papal State
1192	Compilation of *Liber Censuum* of Roman See by Chamberlain Cencius	1261	Defeat of Tuscan Guelphs by Ghibellines at Montaperti
1194	Henry VI crowned King of Sicily: end of the Norman kingdom	1264	Adoption of Charles of Anjou by the papacy as King of Sicily
		1265	Charles of Anjou in Rome
1197	First assertion of papal temporal power in the march of Ancona		The constitution *licet ecclesiarum* allows general reservations of benefices by popes
	Markward of Anweiler, Marquis of Ancona and imperial proctor of Sicily	1266	Manfred defeated and killed at Benevento
			Charles I of Anjou, King of Sicily
1201	Promise of Neuss by Otto of Saxony to Innocent III	1268	Conradin defeated at Tagliacozzo and executed in Naples
1207	Innocent III's parliament of Viterbo	1274	Promise by Rudolph of Habsburg to Gregory X
1208	Murder of Philip of Swabia		
1209	Promise of Speyer by Otto IV to Innocent III	1275	Victory of Romagnol Ghibellines at b. of S. Procolo

1278	Pope Nicholas III's Roman constitution	1318	First excommunication of the Lombard tyrants
	Rudolph of Habsburg consents to papal occupation of Romagna	1320	Bertrand du Poujet opens campaign against Visconti in Piedmont
1282	The Sicilian Vespers	1322	Frederick of Austria loses b. of Mühldorf to Louis of Bavaria
	Peter III of Aragon becomes King of Sicily (Trinacria)	1323	Siege of Milan by Guelph army
1284	Capture of Charles the Lame, Prince of Salerno, by Aragonese	1325	Florentine defeat at b. of Altopascio
		1326–8	*Signoria* of Charles of Calabria in Florence
1287	Death of Peter III of Aragon		
	Freeing of Charles II of Anjou	1327	Louis of Bavaria enters Italy
1289	Pope Nicholas IV assigns half the temporal revenues to the cardinals in *Caelestis altitudo*	1328	Coronation of Louis in Rome
		1330	Louis of Bavaria returns to Germany
1294	Abdication of Pope Celestine V		John of Bohemia enters Italy
		1332	Guelph-Ghibelline league of Ferrara against John of Bohemia
1297	Pope Boniface VIII's quarrel with the Colonna		
1301	Charles of Valois enters Florence	1333	Defeat of John of Bohemia and Bertrand du Poujet by forces of league at Ferrara
1302	Peace of Caltabellotta between Angevins and Frederick of Aragon	1334	Rebellion of Bologna against papal rule and recall of Bertrand du Poujet
	Unam sanctam published		
1303	Boniface VIII taken at Anagni	1337	Taddeo Pepoli, lord of Bologna
1309	Clement V confirms election of Henry VII	1341	Peace between Church and Visconti
1310	Henry VII enters Italy	1342	*Signoria* of Walter of Brienne Duke of Athens in Florence
1311	Clement V cancels acts of Boniface VIII in *Rex gloriae*	1343	Death of Robert of Anjou
1312	Alliance of Frederick of Sicily with Henry VII		Expulsion of Duke of Athens
		1345	Murder of Andrew of Hungary
	Henry VII's battle for Rome	1347	Rule of Cola di Rienzo in Rome
1313	Death of Henry VII		
	Matteo Visconti Lord of Milan		First ravages of Great Company of Werner of Urslingen
1314	Double election of Frederick of Austria and Louis of Bavaria to empire	1350	Astorge de Durfort's campaign to re-impose papal rule in Romagna
1317	Bull *Si fratum* proclaims devolution of imperial rights to papacy during vacancy of empire		Sale of Bologna by Pepoli to Archbishop Giovanni Visconti
		1351	War of Florence with Visconti
	War between Angevin and Visconti for Genoa	1352	Final reconciliation of Church with Visconti and cession of Bologna by Church to the Archbishop
	Renewal of Este *Signoria* in Ferrara		

1353	Peace of Sarzana between Florence, Tuscan communes and Visconti	1370	Peace between Church, Florence and Visconti
	Arrival of Albornoz in Italy as legate in lands of Church	1371	Renewal of war between Visconti and allies of Church
1353–4	Re-conquest of Tuscan patrimony by Albornoz	1372	Visconti victory at b. of Rubiera
1354	Charles IV enters Italy	1373	Fall of Vercelli to papal-Angevin forces
	Death of Archbishop Giovanni Visconti	1375	Peace of Church with Visconti
1355	Coronation of Charles IV in Rome		Rebellion of Perugia and other cities in Papal State
	Giovanni di Oleggio Lord of Bologna. Malatesta subdued by Albornoz	1376	Rebellion of Bologna
			Florence under interdict
			Arrival of Gregory XI in Italy
1357	General league against Visconti and war of Modena		War of Eight Saints
		1377	Massacre of Cesena
	Legate and Florence buy off Great Company	1378	Beginning of the Great Schism with double election of Urban VI and Clement VII (Robert of Geneva)
	Replacement of Albornoz by Androin de la Roche		
1358	Peace made by league with Visconti	1379	Defeat of Clementine forces at b. of Marino
	Albornoz in Italy for second legation in place of de la Roche		Flight of Clement VII to Avignon
		1382	Angevin expedition to south Italy
1360	Bologna transferred by Oleggio to the Church		Murder of Joanna of Naples
		1385	Urban VI besieged in Nocera
	Outbreak of war between Church and Visconti	1393	*Signoria* of Biordo Michelotti in Perugia
1361	Papal victory over Visconti at San Ruffilo	1398	Murder of Michelotti
			End of *banderesi* government in Rome and the subjection of the city to Boniface IX
1363	End of second legation of Albornoz		
1364	Peace between Church and Visconti	1400	Perugia gives itself to Gian Visconti
1365	Charles IV in Avignon	1402	Victory of Milanese over Florentines at b. of Casalecchio
1366	Papal league against future Companies		
			Bologna gives itself to Gian Galeazzo Visconti
1367	Arrival of Urban V in Italy		
1368	Outbreak of hostilities between Visconti of Milan and the league		Death of Gian Galeazzo Visconti
		1403	Cardinal Baldassare Cossa, papal legate in Bologna
	Arrival of Charles IV in Italy		
	Rebellion of Perugia against Church	1405	*Coup* of papal nephew Ludovico Migliorati against communal government of Rome
1369	Charles IV leaves Italy		
1370	Urban V returns to Avignon	1408	Ladislas of Naples-Durazzo

List of Popes

(The anti-popes are given in brackets)

Gregory I	590–604	Eugenius II	824–827
Sabinianus	604–606	Valentine	827
Boniface III	607	Gregory IV	827–844
Boniface IV	608–615	(John, 844)	
Deusdedit I	615–618	Sergius II	844–847
Boniface V	619–625	Leo IV	847–855
Honorius I	625–638	Benedict III	855–858
Severinus	640	(Anastasius, 855; died *c.* 880)	
John IV	640–642	Nicholas I	858–867
Theodore I	642–649	Hadrian II	867–872
Martin I	649–655	John VIII	872–882
Eugenius I	654–657	Marinus I	882–884
Vitalian	657–672	Hadrian III	884–885
Deusdedit II	672–676	Stephen V (VI)	885–891
Donus	676–678	Formosus	891–896
Agatho	678–681	Boniface VI	896
Leo II	682–683	Stephen VI (VII)	896–897
Benedict II	684–685	Romanus	897
John V	685–686	Theodore II	897
Cono	686–687	John IX	898–900
(Theodore, 687;		Benedict IV	900–903
Paschal, 687)		Leo V (Christopher, 903–904)	903
Sergius I	687–701	Sergius III	904–911
John VI	701–705	Anastasius III	911–913
John VII	705–707	Lando	913–914
Sisinnius	708	John X	914–928
Constantine	708–715	Leo VI	928
Gregory II	715–731	Stephen VII (VIII)	928–931
Gregory III	731–741	John XI	931–935
Zacharias	741–752	Leo VII	936–939
Stephen II (III)	752–757	Stephen VIII (IX)	939–942
Paul I	757–767	Marinus II	942–946
(Constantine, 767–769;		Agapitus II	946–955
Philip, 768)		John XII	955–964
Stephen III (IV)	768–772	Leo VIII	963–965
Hadrian I	772–795	Benedict V	964–966
Leo III	795–816	John XIII	965–972
Stephen IV (V)	816–817	Benedict VI	973–974
Paschal I	817–824	(Boniface VII, 974; 984–985)	

Benedict VII	974–983
John XIV	983–984
John XV	985–996
Gregory V	996–999
(John XVI, 997–998)	
Silvester II	999–1003
John XVII	1003
John XVIII	1004–1009
Sergius IV	1009–1012
Benedict VIII	1012–1024
John XIX	1024–1032
Benedict IX	1032–1044
Silvester III	1044–1045
Benedict IX	1045; 1047–1048
Gregory VI	1045–1046
Clement II	1046–1047
Damasus II	1048
Leo IX	1049–1054
Victor II	1054–1057
Stephen IX (X)	1057–1058
(Benedict X, 1058–1059)	
Nicholas II	1059–1061
Alexander II	1061–1073
(Honorius II, 1061–1072)	
Gregory VII	1073–1085
(Clement III, 1080–1100)	
Victor III	1086–1087
Urban II	1088–1099
Paschal II	1099–1118
(Theodoric, 1100;	
Albert, 1102;	
Silvester IV, 1105–1111)	
Gelasius II	1118–1119
(Gregory VIII, 1118–1121)	
Calixtus II	1119–1124
Honorius II	1124–1130
(Celestine II, 1124)	
Innocent II	1130–1143
(Anaclete II, 1130–1138;	
Victor IV, 1138)	
Celestine II	1143–1144
Lucius II	1144–1145
Eugenius III	1145–1153
Anastasius IV	1153–1154
Hadrian IV	1154–1159
Alexander III	1159–1181
(Victor IV, 1159–1164;	
Paschal III, 1164–1168;	
Calixtus III, 1168–1178;	
Innocent III, 1179–1180)	
Lucius III	1181–1185
Urban III	1185–1187
Gregory VIII	1187
Clement III	1187–1191
Celestine III	1191–1198
Innocent III	1198–1216
Honorius III	1216–1227
Gregory IX	1227–1241
Celestine IV	1241
Innocent IV	1243–1254
Alexander IV	1254–1261
Urban IV	1261–1264
Clement IV	1265–1268
Gregory X	1271–1276
Innocent V	1276
Hadrian V	1276
John XXI	1276–1277
Nicholas III	1277–1280
Martin IV	1281–1285
Honorius IV	1285–1287
Nicholas IV	1288–1292
Celestine V	1294
Boniface VIII	1294–1303
Benedict XI	1303–1304
Clement V	1305–1314
John XXII	1316–1334
(Nicholas V, 1328–1330)	
Benedict XII	1334–1342
Clement VI	1342–1352
Innocent VI	1352–1362
Urban V	1362–1370
Gregory XI	1370–1378
Urban VI	1378–1389
Boniface IX	1389–1404
Innocent VII	1404–1406
Gregory XII	1406–1415
(Clement VII, 1378–1394	
Benedict XIII, 1394–1422	
Clement VIII, 1423–1429	
Alexander V, 1409–1410	
John XXIII, 1410–1415)	
Martin V	1417–1431
Eugenius IV	1431–1447
(Felix, 1439–1449)	
Nicholas V	1447–1455

Frankish and German Kings and Emperors

Pippin	King 751; d. 768
Carloman	d. 771
Charles (Charlemagne)	King 768; King of Lombards 774; Emperor 800: d. 814
Louis the Pious	Emperor 814; d. 840
Lothar I	Co-Emperor 817; d. 855
Louis II	Emperor (in Italy) 850; d. 875
Lothar II	King 855; d. 869
Louis the German	King 833; d. 876
Carloman	King (in Italy) 877; d. 880
Louis III	King 876; d. 880
Charles III the Fat	King (Francia 876; Italy 879); Emperor 881; d. 888
Arnulph	King 887; Emperor 896; d. 899
Louis the Child	King 900; d. 911
Conrad I	King 911; d. 918
Henry I	King 919; d. 936
Otto I	King 936; Emperor 962; d. 973
Otto II	King 961; Emperor 967; d. 983
Otto III	King 983; Emperor 996; d. 1002
Henry II	King 1002; Emperor 1014; d. 1024
Conrad II	King 1024; Emperor 1027; d. 1039
Henry III	King 1039; Emperor 1046; d. 1056
Henry IV	King 1056; Emperor 1084; deposed 1105; d. 1106
Henry V	King 1106; Emperor 1111; d. 1125
Lothar	King 1125; Emperor 1133; d. 1137
Conrad III	King 1138; d. 1152
Frederick I	King 1152; Emperor 1155; d. 1190
Henry VI	King 1169; Emperor 1191; King of Sicily 1194; d. 1197
Philip of Swabia	King 1198; d. 1208
Otto of Saxony, IV	King 1198; Emperor 1209; d. 1218
Frederick II	King 1212; King of Sicily 1198; Emperor 1220; d. 1250
Henry Raspe	King 1246; d. 1247

Conrad IV	King 1250 (Sicily and Germany); d. 1254
William of Holland	King 1248; d. 1256
Richard of Cornwall	King 1257; d. 1272 (Senator of Rome 1261)
Alfonso of Castille	King 1257; d. 1284
Rudolph of Habsburg	King 1273; d. 1291
Adolph of Nassau	King 1292; d. 1298
Albert I	King 1298; d. 1308
Henry VII	King 1308; Emperor 1312; d. 1313
Frederick the Fair	King 1314; d. 1330
Louis of Bavaria	King 1314; Emperor 1328; d. 1347
Charles IV	King 1346; Emperor 1355; d. 1378
Wenceslas	King 1376; deposed 1400; d. 1419
Rupert of Palatinate	King 1400; d. 1410
Jobst	King 1410; d. 1411
Sigismund	King 1410; Emperor 1433; d. 1437
Albert II	King 1438; d. 1439
Frederick III	King 1440; Emperor 1452; d. 1493

Rulers of the Kingdom of Sicily

Roger II	1130–1154	Robert	1309–1343
William I	1154–1166	Joanna I	1343–1382
William II	1166–1189	(Louis of Taranto, 1352–1362)	
(Tancred, 1189–1194		Charles of Durazzo	1382–1386
William III, 1194)		(Louis of Anjou, 1383–1384)	
Henry VI	1194–1197	Ladislas of Durazzo	1390–1414
Frederick II	1198–1250	(Louis of Anjou, 1384–1417;	
Conrad IV	1250–1254	Joanna II	1414–1435
Manfred	1258–1266	(Jacques de la Marche, 1415–1419;	
(Edmund of England, 1254)		Louis III of Anjou, 1417–1434;	
Charles of Anjou	1266–1285	René of Anjou, 1434–1443)	
Charles II	1289–1309	Alfonso of Aragon	1443–1458

Index